Heidegger's Roots

*

ALSO BY CHARLES BAMBACH
Heidegger, Dilthey, and the Crisis of Historicism

Heidegger's Roots

Nietzsche, National Socialism, and the Greeks

CHARLES BAMBACH

*

CORNELL UNIVERSITY PRESS

Ithaca and London

Copyright © 2003 by Cornell University

All rights reserved. Except for brief quotations in a review, this
book, or parts thereof, must not be reproduced in any form without permission in writing from the publisher. For information,
address Cornell University Press, Sage House, 512 East State Street,
Ithaca, New York 14850.

First published 2003 by Cornell University Press
First printing, Cornell Paperbacks, 2005

Printed in the United States of America

Bambach, Charles
   Heidegger's roots : Nietzsche, national socialism, and the Greeks /
Charles Bambach.
        p. cm.
Includes bibliographical references and index.
   ISBN 0-8014-4072-6 (cloth : alk. paper)
   ISBN 0-8014-7266-0 (pbks. : alk. paper)
   1. Heidegger, Martin, 1889–1976. 2. Nietzsche, Friedrich Wilhelm,
1844–1900. 3. Philosophy, German—19th century. 4. Philosophy,
German—20th century. I. Title.
   B3279.H49 B265 2003
   193—dc21
                                                        2002015978

Cornell University Press strives to use environmentally responsible
suppliers and materials to the fullest extent possible in the publishing of its books. Such materials include vegetable-based, low-VOC
inks and acid-free papers that are recycled, totally chlorine-free, or
partly composed of nonwood fibers. For further information, visit
our website at www.cornellpress.cornell.edu.

Cloth printing   10 9 8 7 6 5 4 3 2 1
Paperback printing   10 9 8 7 6 5 4 3 2 1

For Lucy

I am convinced that there is no essential
work of the spirit that does not have its
root in originary autochthony.

—MARTIN HEIDEGGER
GA 16: 551

Contents

Contents

Abbreviations

KNS Kriegsnotsemester (War Emergency Semester, 1919)

  SS Summer Semester.

 WS Winter Semester.

  NS National Socialism

HEIDEGGER

All references to GA below are to Heidegger's *Gesamtausgabe*, Frankfurt: Klostermann, 1976ff. Unless otherwise indicated, all translations are my own. At times I modify existing translations to provide a terminology consistent in this book.

    A *Aufenthalte*. Frankfurt: Klostermann, 1989.

AHB *Hannah Arendt/Martin Heidegger, Briefe 1925 bis 1975*. Edited by Ursula Ludz. Frankfurt: Klostermann, 1998.

ANT *Antwort: Martin Heidegger im Gespräch*. Edited by Günther Neske and Emil Kettering. Pfullingen: Neske, 1988.

  BC *Basic Concepts*. Translated by Gary Aylesworth. Bloomington: Indiana University Press, 1993.

BdW "Die Bedrohung der Wissenschaft." In *Zur Philosophischen Aktualität Heideggers*. Vol. 1. Edited by Dietrich Papenfuss and Otto Pöggeler. Frankfurt: Klostermann, 1990.

BQP *Basic Questions of Philosophy: Selected "Problems" of "Logic."* Translated by Richard Rojcewicz and Andre Schuwer. Bloomington: Indiana University Press, 1994.

  BT *Being and Time*. Translated by Joan Stambaugh. Albany: State University of New York Press, 1996.

 BW *Basic Writings*. Edited by David F. Krell. 1st ed. New York: Harper & Row, 1977.

DDP "Documents from the De-Nazification Proceedings Concerning Martin Heidegger." Translated by Jason Wirth. In *Graduate Faculty Philosophy Journal*, vol. 14, no. 2, and vol. 15, no. 1, 1991, 528–556.

DE   *Denkerfahrungen, 1910–1976.* Edited by Hermann Heidegger. Frankfurt: Klostermann, 1983.

DT   *Discourse on Thinking.* Translated by John Anderson and Hans Freund. New York: Harper & Row, 1966.

EB   *Existence and Being.* Edited by Werner Brock. Washington, D.C.: Regnery Gateway, 1988.

EdP   "Europa und die deutsche Philosophie." In *Europa und die Philosophie.* Edited by Hans-Helmuth Gander. Frankfurt: Klostermann, 1993.

EGT   *Early Greek Thinking.* Translated by David F. Krell and Frank Capuzzi. New York: Harper & Row, 1975.

EHD   *Erläuterungen zu Hölderlins Dichtung.* 5th ed. Frankfurt: Klostermann, 1981.

EM   *Einführung in die Metaphysik.* Tübingen: Niemeyer, 1976.

EP   *The End of Philosophy.* Translated by Joan Stambaugh. New York: Harper & Row, 1973.

Far   Hitherto unpublished Heidegger sources in Victor Farías, *Heidegger and Nazism.* Edited by Joseph Margolis and Tom Rockmore. Philadelphia: Temple University Press, 1989.

FarG   Victor Farías, *Heidegger und der Nationalsozialismus.* Frankfurt: S. Fischer, 1989.

FCM   *The Fundamental Concepts of Metaphysics: World, Finitude, Solitude.* Translated by Will McNeill and Nicholas Walker. Bloomington: Indiana University Press, 1995.

G   *Gelassenheit.* Pfullingen: Neske, 1988.

GA 12   *Unterwegs zur Sprache.* 1950–1959. Edited by Friedrich-Wilhelm von Herrmann. 1985.

GA 13   *Aus der Erfahrung des Denkens.* Edited by Hermann Heidegger. 1983.

GA 16   *Reden und andere Zeugnisse eines Lebensweges: 1910–1976.* Edited by Hermann Heidegger. 2000.

GA 17   *Einführung in die phänomenologische Forschung.* WS 1923/24. Edited by Friedrich-Wilhelm von Herrmann. 1994.

GA 19   *Platon: Sophistes.* WS 1924/25. Edited by Ingeborg Schüssler. 1992.

GA 22   *Die Grundbegriffe der antiken Philosophie.* SS 1926. Edited by Franz-Karl Blust. 1993.

GA 27   *Einleitung in die Philosophie.* WS 1928/29. Edited by Otto Saame and Ina Saame-Speidel. 1996.

GA 28   *Der Deutsche Idealismus.* SS 1929. Edited by Claudius Strube. 1997.

GA 29/30   *Die Grundbegriffe der Metaphysik: Welt-Endlichkeit-Einsamkeit.* WS 1929/30. Edited by Friedrich-Wilhelm von Herrmann. 1992.

GA 31   *Vom Wesen der menschlichen Freiheit: Einleitung in die Philosophie.* SS 1930. Edited by Hartmut Tietjen. 1982.

GA 33   *Aristoteles, Metaphysik Theta 1–3: Vom Wesen und Wirklichkeit der Kraft.* SS 1931. Edited by Heinrich Hüni. 1990.

GA 34   *Vom Wesen der Wahrheit: Zu Platons Höhlengleichnis und Theätet.* WS 1931/32. Edited by Hermann Mörchen. 1989.

GA 38   *Über Logik als die Frage nach dem Wesen der Sprache.* SS 1934. Edited by Günter Seubold. 1998.

GA 39   *Hölderlins Hymnen "Germanien" und "Der Rhein."* WS 1934/35. Edited by Susanne Ziegler. 1989.

GA 40   *Einführung in die Metaphysik.* SS 1935. Edited by Petra Jaeger. 1983.

GA 43   *Nietzsche: Der Wille zur Macht als Kunst.* WS 1936/37. Edited by Bernd Heimbüchel. 1985.

GA 44   *Nietzsches metaphysische Grundstellung im abendländischen Denken: Die ewige Wiederkehr des Gleichen.* SS 1937. Edited by Marion Heinz. 1986.

GA 45   *Grundfragen der Philosophie: Ausgewählte "Probleme" der "Logik."* WS 1937/38. Edited by Friedrich-Wilhelm von Herrmann. 1984.

GA 47   *Nietzsches Lehre vom Willen zur Macht als Erkenntnis.* SS 1939. Edited by Eberhard Hanser. 1989.

GA 48   *Nietzsche: Der europäische Nihilismus.* Trimester 2, 1940. Edited by Petra Jaeger. 1986.

GA 50   *Nietzsches Metaphysik.* WS 1941/42. *Einleitung in die Philosophie-Denken and Dichten.* WS 1944/45. Edited by Petra Jaeger. 1990.

GA 51   *Grundbegriffe.* SS 1941. Edited by Petra Jaeger. 1991.

GA 52   *Hölderlins Hymne "Andenken."* WS 1941/42. Edited by Curd Ochwaldt. 1982.

GA 53   *Hölderlins Hymne "Der Ister."* SS 1942. Edited by Walter Biemel. 1984.

GA 54   *Parmenides.* WS 1942/43. Edited by Manfred Frings. 1992.

GA 55   *Heraklit: Der Anfang des abendländischen Denkens.* SS 1943. *Logik: Heraklits Lehre vom Logos.* SS 1944. Edited by Manfred Frings. 1987.

GA 56/57   *Zur Bestimmung der Philosophie: Die Idee der Philosophie und das Weltanschauungsproblem. KNS 1919. Phänomenologie und transzendentale Wertphilosophie. SS 1919.* Edited by Bernd Heimbüchel. 1987.

GA 61   *Phänomenologische Interpretationen zu Aristoteles: Einführung in die phänomenologische Forschung. WS 1921/22.* Edited by Walter Bröcker and Käte Bröcker-Oltmanns. 1985.

GA 63   *Ontologie: Hermeneutik der Faktizität. SS 1923.* Edited by Käte Bröcker-Oltmanns. 1988.

GA 65   *Beiträge zur Philosophie (Vom Ereignis). 1936–1938.* Edited by Friedrich-Wilhelm von Herrmann. 1989.

GA 66   *Besinnung. 1938–1939.* Edited by Friedrich-Wilhelm von Herrmann. 1999.

GA 67   *Metaphysik und Nihilismus. 1938–1939 and 1946–1948.* Edited by Hans-Joachim Friedrich. 1999.

GA 69   *Die Geschichte des Seyns. 1938–1940.* Edited by Peter Trawny. 1998.

GA 77   *Feldweg-Gespräche. 1944–1945.* Edited by Ingrid Schüssler. 1995.

GA 79   *Bremer und Freiburger Vorträge. 1949 und 1957.* Edited by Petra Jaeger. 1994.

H   *Holzwege.* Frankfurt: Klostermann, 1972.

HBB   *Martin Heidegger-Elisabeth Blochmann Briefwechsel, 1918–1969.* Edited by Joachim Storck. Marbach: Deutsche Schillergesellschaft, 1990.

HCW   *The Heidegger Controversy.* Edited by Richard Wolin. 1st ed. New York: Columbia University Press. 1991.

HHI   *Hölderlin's Hymn "The Ister".* Translated by Will McNeill and Julia Davis. Bloomington: Indiana University Press, 1996.

HJB   *Martin Heidegger–Karl Jaspers Briefwechsel, 1920–1963.* Edited by Walter Biemel and Hans Saner. Frankfurt: Klostermann, 1990.

HMT   *Heidegger: The Man and the Thinker.* Edited by Thomas Sheehan. Chicago: Precedent, 1981.

IM   *Introduction to Metaphysics.* Translated by Ralph Manheim. New Haven: Yale University Press, 1959.

L   *Lógica: Lecciones de M. Heidegger (semestre verano 1934) en el legado de Helene Weiss.* Bilingual German-Spanish edition. Edited by Victor Farías. Barcelona: Anthropos, 1991.

Martin   *Martin Heidegger und das "Dritte Reich": Ein Kompendium.* Edited by Bernd Martin. Darmstadt: Wissenschaftliche Buchgesellschaft, 1989.

Ni   *Nietzsche, Volume i: The Will to Power as Art.* Edited by David F. Krell. New York: Harper & Row, 1979.

Nii   *Nietzsche, Volume ii: The Eternal Recurrence of the Same.* Edited by David F. Krell. New York: Harper & Row, 1984.

Niii   *Nietzsche, Volume iii: The Will to Power as Knowledge and as Metaphysics.* Edited by David F. Krell. New York: Harper & Row, 1987.

Niv   *Nietzsche, Volume iv: Nihilism.* Edited by David F. Krell. New York: Harper & Row, 1982.

NI   *Nietzsche, Volume One.* Pfullingen: Neske, 1989.

NII   *Nietzsche, Volume Two.* Pfullingen: Neske, 1989.

NH   *Nachlese Heideggers: Dokumente zu seinem Leben und Denken.* Edited by Guido Schneeberger. Bern, 1962.

OWL   *On the Way to Language.* Translated by Peter Hertz. New York: Harper & Row, 1982.

P   *Parmenides.* Translated by Andre Schuwer and Richard Rojcewicz. Bloomington: Indiana University Press, 1992.

PLT   *Poetry, Language, Thought.* Translated by Albert Hofstader. New York: Harper & Row, 1971.

PM   *Pathmarks.* Edited by Will McNeill. Cambridge: Cambridge University Press, 1998.

QCT   *The Question Concerning Technology.* Translated by William Lovitt. New York: Harper & Row, 1977.

RA   The Rectorial Address. "The Self-Assertion of the German University." In *The Heidegger Controversy.* Edited by Richard Wolin. Translated by William Lewis. New York: Columbia University Press, 1991.

RFT   "The Rectorate 1933/34: Facts and Thoughts." In *Martin Heidegger and National Socialism.* Edited by Günther Neske and Emil Kettering. New York: Paragon House, 1990.

SdU   *Die Selbstbehauptung der deutschen Universität. Das Rektorat 1933/34.* Edited by Hermann Heidegger. Frankfurt: Klostermann, 1983.

SI   *Der Spiegel* Interview. "Only a God Can Save Us." In *Martin Heidegger and National Socialism.* Edited by Günther Neske and Emil Kettering. New York: Paragon House, 1990.

SL   "Selected Letters from the Heidegger-Blochmann Correspondence." Translated by Frank Edler. In *Graduate Faculty Philosophy Journal* vol. 14, no. 2, and vol. 15, no. 1, 1991: 557–577.

SZ   *Sein und Zeit.* Tübingen: Niemeyer, 1976.

VA   *Vorträge und Aufsätze.* Pfullingen: Neske, 1954.

WCT   *What Is Called Thinking?* Translated by J. Glenn Gray. New York: Harper & Row, 1968.

WHD   *Was heisst Denken?* Tübingen: Niemeyer, 1976.

WM   *Wegmarken.* Edited by Friedrich-Wilhelm von Herrmann. Frankfurt: Klostermann, 1967.

NIETZSCHE

BGE   *Beyond Good and Evil.* Translated by Walter Kaufmann. New York: Random House, 1966.

BT   *The Birth of Tragedy.* Translated by Walter Kaufmann. New York: Random House, 1967.

EH   *Ecce Homo.* Translated by R. J. Hollingdale. London: Penguin, 1992.

GM   *On the Genealogy of Morals.* Translated by Walter Kaufmann and R. J. Hollingdale. New York: Random House, 1967.

GS   *The Gay Science.* Translated by Walter Kaufmann. New York: Random House, 1974.

HAH   *Human, All Too Human.* Translated by R. J. Hollingdale. Cambridge: Cambridge University Press, 1986.

KSA   *Friedrich Nietzsche: Sämtliche Werke: Kritische Studienausgabe.* 15 vols. Edited by Giorgio Colli and Mazzino Montinari. Munich: dtv, 1993.

PTAG   *Philosophy in the Tragic Age of the Greeks.* Translated by Marianne Cowan. Chicago: Regnery, 1962.

TI   *Twilight of the Idols.* Translated by R. J. Hollingdale. London: Penguin, 1990.

UO   *Unmodern Observations.* Edited by William Arrowsmith. New Haven: Yale University Press, 1990.

WM   *Der Wille zur Macht: Versuch einer Umwertung aller Werte.* Edited by Alfred Baeumler. Leipzig: Kröner, 1930.

WP   *The Will to Power.* Translated by Walter Kaufmann and R. J. Hollingdale. New York: Random House, 1967.

Z   *Thus Spoke Zarathustra.* Translated by R. J. Hollingdale. London: Penguin, 1969.

Acknowledgments

During the four years I have been writing this book, I have benefited from the help of several institutions whose assistance came at an opportune time. I am grateful to the Earhart Foundation for their generous financial support during my sabbatical year and to Dean Dennis Kratz of the University of Texas–Dallas for providing me with an SFDA leave in 1998–1999. I also thank Dr. Bernhard Tönnies of the Herbert Marcuse Archive at the Stadt- und Universitätsbibliothek, Frankfurt am Main, for providing me with copies of Heidegger course manuscripts, lectures, and other unpublished documents.

I thank John Ackerman, director of Cornell University Press, whose faith in this project made it possible and whose helpful suggestions and timely advice have been greatly appreciated. I also thank Teresa Jesionowski for her scrupulous manuscript editing, Kevin Millham for his careful indexing, Herman Rapaport for his many thoughtful criticisms, and the anonymous readers whose comments prodded me to rethink some of my arguments.

In Dallas, I owe a great debt to my colleagues in the DASEIN seminar, especially Rod Coltman, Jamey Findling, Frederick Hotz, Sigrid Koepke, Robyn Lee, John Loscerbo, Farshad Sadri, Dale Wilkerson, and Robert Wood, for listening to early versions of my work and commenting on drafts. I also extend thanks to Richard Owsley and Keith Brown for their generous invitations to participate in the yearly Heidegger conferences at the University of North Texas, where I benefited from conversations with other Heidegger scholars, especially Stuard Elden, Michael Eldred, and Theodore Kisiel, who helped me track down Heidegger manuscripts and graciously sent me copies of his work in progress. In matters of securing foreign books I thank Vickie Bullock. And for overcoming computer problems and bringing this book to completion, I want to extend special thanks to Peggy Eckelkamp for her technical expertise and moral support.

Friendship has mattered a great deal to me during the composition of this book, the bulk of which was written in Somerville and Cambridge, Massachusetts, over a sabbatical leave and two summers. It has buoyed me and sustained me in ways that I cannot properly acknowledge. Special thanks to Stephen Tonsor for generously sending me hundreds of books from his library on Greek civilization and on German thought and culture. John van Buren has been generous too in offering advice and encouragement over the years, even if he might differ on how to approach Heidegger. My friends in Massachusetts—Alan Andres, Bill Ellet, Albert Hobesh, Tony Lee, Tehila Lieberman, Robert Mazzetta, Elizabeth McCauley, Richard Murphy, Paul Panadero, John Scanlan, Agnes Bundy Scanlan, and Jane Winsor—have been remarkable in so many ways, listening to my arguments, helping me to settle in during times of transition, sustaining me with wisdom and laughter.

I am grateful for the good cheer of my German friends Karin Bukenberger and Gerhard Behnke, who endured trips to sleepy Messkirch and Todtnauberg. To Rolf Maier a special thanks for restoring things lost and making them live again. Most of all, I thank my friends and family in New York City—Joe Odermatt, Joe McClain, Pat Diffley, Linda and Mario Ascrizzi, my dear aunt Catherine, and my brother, John—for teaching me lessons about the meaning of "roots." Finally, I thank my wife, Lucy McCauley, whose own work as a writer has been a source of genuine inspiration. I owe much of the energy for writing this book to her love and support.

C.B.

Situating Heidegger

What is thinking? How does thinking call us to that simple, abiding near-ness to being that releases us from the cabinet of our Cartesian conscious-ness and lets us dwell poetically upon the earth? And what would it mean to think in such a way that thinking would serve as a singular, ineradicable summons calling us to our proper home in being? These are some of the questions that have helped make Martin Heidegger one of the preemi-nent philosophers of the last century, if not of the entire Western tradi-tion. But other questions plague the reception of Heidegger's work and have raised grave doubts about the viability of Heideggerian thinking in the postmetaphysical epoch. These go back to the political scandal, *l'af-faire Heidegger*, that emerged following the publication of works by Victor Farias, Jacques Derrida, and Hugo Ott on Heidegger's political involve-ment in National Socialism.[1] In the wake of this scandal we can no longer read Heidegger in the same way. By now it has become clear that Heideg-ger was a Nazi.[2] Despite this near consensus about Heidegger's political af-filiation, however, the debates continue, focused in good Heideggerian fashion on the precise meaning of the third person indicative preterite form of the verb 'to be': In what sense "was" Heidegger a Nazi? There is the "Official Story" spelled out by Heidegger: his letter of November 4, 1945, to the Freiburg University De-Nazification Committee, his retro-spective essay "The Rectorate 1933/34: Facts and Thoughts" (written just after the end of the Second World War), his interview with *Der Spiegel* mag-azine in 1966 (published in 1976), and his various letters to Herbert Mar-cuse, Hans-Peter Hempel, Karl Jaspers, and others.[3] There are the various accounts offered by Heidegger's contemporaries, including Karl Löwith,

1. Victor Farias, *Heidegger and National Socialism*, trans. P. Burrell and G. Ricci (Philadel-phia: Temple University Press, 1989); Jacques Derrida, *Of Spirit*, trans. G. Bennington (Chi-cago: University of Chicago Press, 1989); Hugo Ott, *Martin Heidegger: Unterwegs zu seiner Bi-ographie* (Frankfurt: Campus Verlag, 1988).

2. One of the first important articles to appear in the United States after the fallout was Thomas Sheehan's "Heidegger and the Nazis," *New York Review of Books* 25, no. 10 (June 16, 1988): 38–47. See also Heidegger's letter to Stefan Zemach in GA 40: 233.

3. RFT: 15–32/SdU: 21–43; SI: 41–66/ANT: 81–111; HCW: 160–164/ Herbert Marcuse Archive, Stadtsbibliothek, Frankfurt am Main and published in *Pflasterstrand* 209 (May 17, 1985): 43–44; the Hempel letter is published in Rüdiger Safranski, *Ein Meister aus Deutsch-land: Heidegger und seine Zeit* (Munich: Hanser, 1994), 269–270, 274; HJB: 171–204; HBB: 92–103.

Hermann Mörchen, Karl Jaspers, and Heinrich W. Petzet.[4] And, of course, there is the by now vast secondary literature.[5] Given this outpouring of material, only the most inveterate of Heideggerians would seriously maintain that the master had no ties to National Socialism. But did these ties persist after the failure of the rectorate in April of 1934? Did Heidegger see the light after the violence of *Kristallnacht* in 1938? Was there ever a break with the party or with official Nazi ideology? Did Heidegger ever condone the Nazi atrocities in the camps and the ghettos?

These are complicated and difficult questions whose ultimate answers will probably be left to future archivists and biographers, if they are ever adequately addressed. I frame them in this way, however, because it seems to me that they point to issues that preoccupy those readers who turn their attention to the problem of Heidegger and politics. But I would maintain that this entire approach needs to be rethought. Rather than pose the question—was Heidegger a Nazi?—I think we need to ask, what kind of National Socialism did Heidegger aspire to establish? How did Heidegger's own inimitable brand of National Socialism affect the questions he raised about Germany and its place in the history of the West? Moreover, how does this way of questioning affect Heidegger's own writing and help to shape his reading of specific philosophical texts and their place in the Western tradition?

My aim in what follows is to offer a reading of Heidegger's work that sees it as deeply embedded in the historical context of German right-wing/National Socialist thinking in the postwar generation. Instead of focusing on the question of politics as such or on the narrow relation between Heidegger and National Socialism, I want to explore the meaning of Heidegger's language and thematics of roots and rootedness for understanding his philosophical work in the period between 1933 and 1945. In particular I want to look at two crucial terms in his early political work—*Bodenständigkeit* (which I will translate as "autochthony" or "rootedness," depending on the context) and *Selbstbehauptung* ("self-assertion"). I will try to situate these two terms *historically* within the context of the right-wing conservative revolutionary lexicon of his generation. But I will also attend to the *rhetorical* context of Heidegger's various works—his political speeches, his academic orations, his university lectures, his conference papers, and his formal published writings. In this sense I am guided by at least two methodological concerns. First of all, I seek to read Heidegger's

4. Karl Löwith, *My Life in Germany Before and After 1933*, trans. E. King (Urbana: University of Illinois Press, 1994); Hermann Mörchen, *Adorno und Heidegger* (Stuttgart: Klett-Cotta, 1981); Karl Jaspers, *Notizen zu Martin Heidegger* (Munich: Hanser, 1978); Heinrich W. Petzet, *Encounters and Dialogues with Martin Heidegger*, trans. P. Emad and K. Maly (Chicago: University of Chicago Press, 1993); and Heinrich Berl, *Gespräche mit berühmten Zeitgenossen* (Baden-Baden: Bühler, 1946).

5. See chapter 5, note 4, for a list of some of these works.

texts historically, since it is my view that it matters very much when they were written. As I will argue, a text written in 1933 needs to be read differently from one written in 1938, 1942, or even 1955. As part of my approach, I emphasize how historical context shapes Heidegger's way of approaching his topic. An interpretation of Parmenides from 1942 (where Heidegger writes in defense of the German struggle at Stalingrad) will need to be weighed against one from 1954 (that reflects Heidegger's vision of a postwar European world). To rip Heidegger's texts from their historical context and to organize them around a thematics of our own choosing runs the risk of laying them upon a Procrustean bed of hermeneutic violence. Such readings—especially when they concern the question of the "political" in Heidegger—often tell us more about the politics of the interpreter than about Heidegger's own work.

Hence, I will try to read texts both in terms of their immediate context and in terms of Heidegger's overall corpus when that seems necessary to me. Second, I will read Heidegger's texts with the assumption that it mattered what Heidegger read and who his interlocutors were. As Heidegger himself attests, his dialogue partners extend from the ancient Greek philosophers and tragedians to Augustine, Eckhart, Descartes, Kant, Hölderlin, Hegel, Nietzsche, and other thinkers and poets from the Western tradition. However, there are other silent partners whose significance Heidegger will underplay or, as in the case of his postwar De-Nazification defense, from whom he will attempt to distance himself. I will try to recontextualize some of these dialogues and confrontations by reading Heidegger in terms of other German philosophers, philologists, social theorists, and scholars of the Weimar and National Socialist eras.

In what follows I will set forth the argument that Heidegger's writings from 1933 to 1945 constitute a philosophical attempt at geo-politics, a grand metaphysical vision of German destiny based on the notion of a singularly German form of autochthony or rootedness in the earth: *Bodenständigkeit*.[6] As we will see, this vision of autochthonous supremacy will

---

6. *Bodenständigkeit* is a term that will be employed by the *völkisch* right after the Great War to signify a deep spiritual bond between the *Volksgemeinschaft* and the soil, landscape, homeland, and native earth; see George Mosse, *The Crisis of German Ideology* (New York: Grosset & Dunlap, 1964), 15–17, 88–89. In Christopher Hutton, *Linguistics and the Third Reich: Mother-Tongue Fascism, Race, and the Science of Language* (London: Routledge, 1999), 308, it is defined as "rootedness in the soil, an organic bond involving territorial and cultural continuity." Nazi ideologues like R. Walther Darré, "Landstand und Staat," *Völkischer Beobachter*, April 19–21, 1931; Ernst Krieck, "Völkische Erziehung aus Blut und Boden," *Internationale Zeitschrift für Erziehung* 3 (1933–34), 308, and E. Günther Gründel, *Die Sendung der jungen Generation* (Munich: Beck, 1932), 287–288 will draw on the association between rootedness and the purity of the *Volk*. Gründel will claim further that "Marxism is the declared mortal enemy of all rooted peasant communities and wants to brutally uproot and eradicate them," 259. Alfred Baeumler, *Politik und Erziehung* (Berlin: Junker & Dünnhaupt, 1937), 129, and Kurt Hildebrandt, *Staat und Rasse* (Breslau: Hirt, 1928), 9, will also employ

not be strictly limited to a people's steadfast or long-established (*ständig*) rootedness in the soil (*Boden*) or native earth; it will also come to include the relation of a *Volk* to its indigenous landscape, its native tongue or dialect, and its rootedness in history.[7] Heidegger's notion of autochthony will serve as a way of reading German history in terms of a *völkisch* bond to the homeland and to the native earth, a *völkisch* myth of destiny that offers a way of preserving and transforming the German *Volk* against the forces of industrialization, urbanization, and the threat of foreign influence. It will also function as a way for Heidegger to structure his philosophical account of the history of the West as a narrative about ontological nihilism and the oblivion of being. Rootedness in the earth will come to signify one of the essential conditions for thinking in an originary way. Only if a *Volk* is rooted in its own earth can it summon the historical energy necessary for embracing and transforming its own destiny. As one of Heidegger's National Socialist contemporaries put it, "Soil is destiny. . . . A *Volk* can not endure whose people are not firmly rooted in the soil."[8] In Heideggerian terms this *völkisch* commitment to rootedness will be transformed, following the tradition of Fichte and Hölderlin, into a myth of autochthony that claims a privileged, originary relation between the ancient Greeks and the German *Volk*.[9] Based on this autochthonic bond of originary *Völker*, whose identity will be forged linguistically, historically, and culturally rather than through the political model of a territorial nation-state, Heidegger will frame his own account of the history of being.

---

the term; Hildebrandt will see *Bodenständigkeit* as a defense against what he calls "unrestrained racial mixing or cross-breeding." In his book, *Deutschland: Gestern und Heute* (Leipzig: Braumüller, 1934), 73–91, the NS ideologue Johannes Schmidt-Wodder, in his chapter, "Germany's Struggle for Space and a New Rootedness," will write about Germany's "spiritual uprooting" caused by the war and the Treaty of Versailles and, like Heidegger, will thematize the need to "save the German Volk" from liberalism, Marxism, and the Western model of politics.

7. See, for example, the discussion of linguistic autochthony in the National Socialist reception of the Alemannic poet, Johann Peter Hebel, in *Alemannenland: Ein Buch von Volkstum und Sendung*, ed. Franz Kerber (Stuttgart: Engelhorns, 1937), 10–13, 28–36. Heidegger will turn to these themes in his Hebel lectures from 1955–1960 (GA 16: 491–548; 565–567; and DE: 87–112).

8. Johannes Schmidt-Wodder, *Deutschland: Gestern und Heute*, 102.

9. For works on the Greek-German connection, see Suzanne Marchand, *Down from Olympus* (Princeton: Princeton University Press, 1996); Hellmut Sichtermann, *Kulturgeschichte der klassischen Archäologie* (Munich: Beck, 1996); Philippe Lacoue-Labarthe, *Heidegger, Art and Politics*, trans. Chris Turner (Oxford: Blackwell, 1990); Walter Leifer, *Hellas im deutschen Geistesleben* (Herrenalb: Erdmann, 1963); Walther Rehm, *Griechentum und Goethezeit* (Bern: Francke, 1952). Especially helpful to my work here have been three articles by Frank Edler, "Heidegger and Werner Jaeger on the Eve of 1933: A Possible Rapprochement?" *Research in Phenomenology* 27 (1998): 122–149; "Heidegger's Interpretation of the German 'Revolution'," *Research in Phenomenology* 23 (1993): 153–171; and "Philosophy, Language, and Politics: Heidegger's Attempt to Steal the Language of Revolution, 1933–34," *Social Research* 57 (1990): 197–238; and Vassilis Lambropoulos, *The Rise of Eurocentrism* (Princeton: Princeton University Press, 1993). For a fuller discussion, see my chapter 4.

In its simplest form, the story proceeds as follows: at the very beginning of the tradition, the early Greek philosophers and poets set forth their poetic-philosophical work from out of a primordial relation to earth as *chthonos*. Drawing on this rootedness these early Greeks gave voice to the power of the earth as the hidden, chthonic source for human destiny. As Heidegger put it in his 1935 essay, "The Origin of the Work of Art":

> The Greeks early called this emerging and rising in itself and in all things *physis*. It clears and illuminates at the same time that upon and in which the human being grounds its dwelling. We call this ground the earth. What this word says is not to be associated with the idea of a mass of matter deposited somewhere or with the merely astronomical idea of a planet. Earth is that whence the arising brings back and shelters everything that arises as such. In the things that arise, earth holds sway essentially as that which shelters. (PLT: 42/H: 31)

Earth, for Heidegger, is less an objectively present, thingly entity than the hidden source for all that emerges in the human world. Out of the conflict or strife between the chthonic, subterranean earth and the revealed, humanly constructed world there emerges what Heidegger will deem "truth" as *aletheia*: the Heraclitean play and conflict of all that is. As Heraclitus expressed it in fragment #123: "*Physis* loves to hide." Or, as Heidegger translated it: "Being (emerging appearing) intrinsically inclines toward self-concealment" (IM: 114/EM: 87). In this Greek confrontation between hiddenness and unhiddenness, concealment and revelation, Heidegger will rethink the originary Greek myth of struggle between the chthonic and Olympian gods as ontological strife between *physis* and *techne*.

In Heidegger's terms this narrative will be played out as the triumph of ratiocinative-technological *logos* over the Heraclitean-Sophoclean *logos* of oracular speech and poetic thought. This philosophical narrative will follow closely the fundamental outline of Walter F. Otto's story about the decline of Greek religion and the loss of myth as a primordial force in Greek existence. In *The Gods of Greece* (1929), Otto will argue that the enlightened Olympian religion of Homeric Greece covers over and occludes the elemental subterranean dimension of Greek chthonic deities, ushering in a rational-metaphysical epoch of Olympian enlightenment.[10] In this turn away from the primordial *arche* or origin of Greek culture, Olympian religion will lose touch with the very sources of divine revelation—what the Greeks called "theophany" or "the manifestation of the god(s)." For Otto, the loss of this chthonic depth-dimension of culture will mark the history of the West as a descendant of the Olympian culture of rational enlightenment, a culture out of touch with the originary mythic sources of divine

10. Walter F. Otto, *Die Götter Griechenlands* (Frankfurt: Klostermann, 1987).

[xxi]

revelation. Heidegger reads Otto's book in 1931 and finds a structural outline in it that accords with his own ontological narrative of Western history.

Like Otto, Heidegger will understand Germany's own desperate situation of economic collapse, social upheaval, and political chaos in late Weimar in terms of the same rootless forces of enlightened rationality that destroyed archaic Greece. The only way out of this situation, Heidegger will claim, is to reconnect the German *Volk* with the archaic, chthonic sources of its own tradition in language, landscape, and community. Theophany must become a fundamental happening for the *Volk;* the task at hand is to prepare the way for the return of the gods who have fled. Otto's mythic formulation of "the German Problem," nurtured on the Philhellenism of Hölderlin and Nietzsche, will be reframed by Heidegger in terms of an ontological narrative about the history of the West and of Germany's singular role in retrieving the lost chthonic elements of archaic Greek existence.[11] In the forces unleashed by the National Socialist revolution of 1933, Heidegger will find not only the awakening of a new political will to German self-assertion. He will also detect the energies for a reawakening of the *Volk* and its "fundamental attunement" to Germany's historical decision: "whether and how the *Volk* grounds its historical being in an originary, unified experience of binding itself back to the gods so that it can first grasp and preserve its vocation [*Bestimmung*]" (GA 39: 147).[12] This ontological revolution can only occur, however, if the German *Volk* wins back a sense of its originary bond to "the earth of the homeland" out of its "poetic struggle [*dichterischen Kampf*]" with the rootless forces of modernity and comes to embrace the "Greek-German mission" of saving the West (GA 39: 150–151). This conjoining of the ontological and the poetic in the service of National Socialist revolution will constitute the focus of this study.

By situating Heidegger's work in the generational context of post-WWI German right-wing thinking and its reception of Nietzsche, Hölderlin, and the Greeks, I hope to show how politically charged it was. Part of my task in what follows will be to look at how Heidegger's myth of originary German rootedness articulated in his political speeches of 1933–1934 will also get played out in the decisive philosophical texts of the 1930s and '40s—especially the lectures on Hölderlin, *Introduction to Metaphysics,* "The Origin of the Work of Art," the lectures on Nietzsche, and *Parmenides.* My

11. On Otto's background, see Hubert Cancik, "Dionysus 1933: W. F. Otto, ein Religionswissenschaftler und Theologe am Ende der Weimarer Republik," in *Die Restauration der Götter: Antike Religion und Neo-Paganismus,* ed. Richard Faber and Renate Schlesier (Würzburg: Königshausen & Neumann, 1986), 105–123.

12. The term that Heidegger uses here to describe the "originary unified experience of *binding* itself *back* to the gods" is *Rückbindung,* which derives from the Latin *re + ligare,* "to bind back," from whence we derive "religion."

argument is that if we but read these texts within the political-historical context of National Socialist ideology, we will find that Heidegger's discourses on the "first" Greek beginning, the essence of *aletheia*, the flight of the gods, the originary power of poetic speech, and the ontological character of art are themselves philosophical themes that emerge in dialogue with Heidegger's own politics of the earth and of a German homeland.[13] This does not mean, however, that I want to reduce Heidegger's elaborate critique of Western metaphysics and modern nihilism to political ideology. Whatever else we might think of him, Heidegger was more than a third-rate ideologue parroting the homologies of a political regime. He was a brilliant reader of texts and a genuinely original thinker whose philosophical insights have transformed the very practice of doing philosophy in the late modern epoch.

Despite these achievements, I think we still need to work through the political element within Heidegger's writings in a more meaningful way than we have. The work of Victor Farias, Hugo Ott, Thomas Sheehan, Tom Rockmore, and others has clearly demonstrated the persistent and deep-rooted connections between Heidegger and National Socialism. But all too often the discussion about Heidegger's politics rests on an *a*historical conception of Nazism as a moral evil rather than on the concrete ideological concepts, themes, language, and presuppositions that generated the NS movement in Germany during the 1920s and '30s.[14] National Socialism was not a monolith; it was, especially in its early form, a movement characterized by diverse aims and aspirations of political and social revolution. It neither emerged from out of a philosophical confrontation with German history nor did it ever attain the coherence of a philosophical system. Yet, as a philosopher, Heidegger sought to rethink its fundamental meaning in relation to the concrete practices of university life, as well as to the sweeping panorama of Western history. Whether he engages the thought of Heraclitus, the essence of *techne*, the language of Eckhart, or the aims of the university, Heidegger will set forth his ideas in a conversation with National Socialism that both appropriates and contests its cen-

13. *Seyn* is an archaic spelling of *Sein* ("being") that goes back to the language of German idealism; see, for example, Johann G. Fichte, *Grundlage des Naturrechts* (Jena: Gabler, 1796), 3. Heidegger will employ this spelling to indicate a dismantling of the traditional metaphysical understanding of *Sein* as "standing presence" and to point toward a postmetaphysical experience of being as a Heraclitean play of concealment and revelation, GA 65: 255–261, 264.

14. Some of the notable exceptions include Michael Zimmerman, *Heidegger's Confrontation with Modernity* (Bloomington: Indiana University Press, 1990); Hans Sluga, *Heidegger's Crisis* (Cambridge: Harvard University Press, 1993); Domenico Losurdo, *Die Gemeinschaft, der Tod, das Abendland: Heidegger und die Kriegsideologie* (Stuttgart: Metzler, 1995) and, of course, the articles of Frank Edler referenced in note 9. I read Johannes Fritsche's book, *Historical Destiny and National Socialism in Heidegger's "Being and Time"* (Berkeley: University of California Press, 1999), only after the bulk of this study was completed. See my review in *American Catholic Philosophical Quarterly* 74, no. 3 (2001).

tral tenets. This questioning confrontation will sometimes take the form of a genial disagreement; at other times it will express itself as internecine strife. In the chapters that follow I will take up this curious and fateful *Auseinandersetzung* with National Socialist thinkers such as Alfred Baeumler, Ernst Krieck, Hans Heyse, Kurt Hildebrandt, Franz Böhm, Heinrich Haertle, Richard Oehler, and others. What Heidegger will share with these party apologists is a set of cultural and political assumptions about the position of Germany in the postwar period that strongly influence the kinds of philosophical questions that he raises. Before I take up these issues in more detail, however, I want to indicate in a provisional way some of the essential points of agreement and contention that I see marking Heidegger's relation to National Socialism.

In outline these are:

- A reading of modernity as an age of crisis, one that threatens to destroy the German *Volk* if it is not committed to its own roots.

- A shared sense that the immediate roots of this crisis go back to the Great War—a war waged by the Germans against the "ideas of 1789" (belief in the rights of man, democratic equality, the liberty of the individual, social contract theory, a liberal Enlightenment faith in reason, and the ideal of a modern centralized nation-state) and in support of the "ideas of 1914" (the militaristic affirmation of Germany's cultural mission to save the West; the commitment to a view of the German *Volk* as a *Gemeinschaft* forged by the front soldiers in the trenches; the radical affirmation of the *Volk* over the individual; the sense that Germany's spiritual rebirth depends on waging a fateful battle [*Kampf*] against the Anglo-French model of nationalism and the whole Western Enlightenment definition of freedom, equality, individuality).

- A shared lexicon of *völkisch* militancy that emerges out of the language of the Great War: fate, destiny, decision, struggle, will, self-assertion, hardness, severity, danger, rescue, sacrifice; and a commitment to the ideal of the soldierly "hero" (the German dead at Langemarck; the martyrdom of Albert Leo Schlageter).

- A common rejection of the Treaty of Versailles (1919) as a Cartesian document whose own definition of political space as "territory" works against the idea of a Greater Germany (defined not by political boundaries but by language, landscape, and roots).

- A common commitment to the *völkisch* principles of soil, land, earth, landscape, and roots as essential to the life of a *Volk* and a rejection of asphalt urbanism as rootless.

- A shared antipathy toward humanism, cosmopolitanism, and the Roman-Latin tradition of ecumenical, universal culture.

- A common appeal to Plato, the Pre-Socratics, Sophocles, Meister Eckhart, Fichte, Hölderlin, and Nietzsche for a way of interpreting the German political revolution of 1933, one that is marked by both Graecophilia and German nationalism—or rather, Graecophilia as German nationalism.

- A shared anti-Bolshevism and anti-Communism.
- Commitment to the principle of leadership and the leader (*Führer*).

But Heidegger also had serious disagreements with "official" Nazi ideology:

- Heidegger never accepts any of the standard worldviews put forward by Nazi philosophers, nor does he attempt to define his own singular form of "Freiburg National Socialism" as a worldview (RFT: 23/SdU: 30).
- Heidegger explicitly rejects the National Socialist emphasis on biological racism in all its forms as Aryan supremacy, phrenological typology, or folkloric science (*Volkskunde*) as alternate forms of a metaphysics of standing presence.
- Heidegger renounces the National Socialist ideal of "political" science (i.e., *Wissenschaft* motivated and directed by purely political goals) (BdW: 10, 22).
- Heidegger will resent the officious meddling of NS party bureaucracy in German academic life, especially the role played by the *Amt Rosenberg* and its attempt at totalitarian *Gleichschaltung*.
- Heidegger will have fallouts with major NS figures—Erich Jaensch, Ernst Krieck, Alfred Rosenberg, Alfred Baeumler, and others.
- Heidegger will shun the crude *völkisch* nationalism of Teutonic Knights, Nordic gods, links to the occult, and other forms of NS propaganda.

By the end of the 1930s Heidegger will begin to see the historical form of National Socialism as an instantiation of nihilism that—in its vision of *techne* as a form of "machination" (*Machenschaft*)—expresses the Cartesian longing to gain "dominion over the earth" (*Erdherrschaft*) (GA 69: 66–73, 223).

By setting his ideas into the form of an *Auseinandersetzung* with National Socialism, Heidegger will expose them (*aussetzen*) to their limits, even as he risks separating them out from the ideas of other party ideologues.[15] In any event, what I think cannot be denied is that whether in support of or in opposition to its diverse and inchoate principles, Heidegger's writings

---

15. For a discussion of *Auseinandersetzung* in Heidegger's work, see the helpful article by Gregory Fried, "Heidegger's *Polemos*," *Journal of Philosophical Research* 16 (1990): 159–195. *Auseinandersetzung* "carries a range of meanings, from a discussion or a dispute, to a fight, to a settling of accounts. . . . A purely literal translation . . . would render it as a separating-out-and-setting-apart-from-one-another. The best English translation . . . is usually 'confrontation'—though this word captures neither the sense of mutual extrication, the *auseinander*, nor the placement and establishing, the *Setzung*, evident in the German word," 165.

of the 1930s and '40s will be shaped by his deep and abiding confrontation with National Socialist thinking.

As I will argue throughout this study, Heidegger's philosophy cannot be conveniently separated from his politics. In this sense, I strongly disagree with Richard Rorty's claim that Heidegger's work is like a toolbox from which we can pick and choose what we like, ignoring the pernicious elements of National Socialist thinking at our leisure.[16] Finding fault with Heidegger's politics, justified as it might be, does not, however, give us carte blanche to offer moral broadsides or to retreat into a liberal academic politics of self-congratulation. The challenge, it seems to me, is to engage Heidegger's work in such a way that we are forced to confront our own political assumptions even as we come to terms with his. By confronting Heidegger's politics in the works and not merely as a biographical detail, I hope to lend my voice to a debate that can hardly be settled by one book or by one scholar.

CHARLES BAMBACH

Somerville, Massachusetts

16. Richard Rorty, *Philosophy and Social Hope* (New York: Penguin, 1999), 192.

Heidegger's Roots

*

Introduction

Where is my home? I ask and seek and have sought for it. I have not found it.

—FRIEDRICH NIETZSCHE
Z: 266/KSA 4: 341

Every myth is a myth of origin.

—PAUL TILLICH
Die sozialistische Entscheidung

I. THE HUT

The hut is still there. It still stands unobtrusively at the top of a long sloping hill some 3000 feet in elevation, nestled just below a densely clustered patch of dark and towering fir trees. The small ski hut, built for Heidegger in 1922 when he was a young professor, still bears witness to the lost world of a rural peasant farm community of the nineteenth century. No number marks its front doorway; no telephone, gas, or electric lines obstruct its view of the valley below. High above the small village of Todtnauberg in the southern Black Forest, the cabin still proclaims its proud independence from the interlocking structures of modern existence with its urban-industrial vision of implacable progress and irremediable consumerism. In the early days, Heidegger would retreat to Todtnauberg during semester breaks and prepare for the rigorous regime of thinking and writing by chopping wood for the fireplace. When he was still at Marburg, students in Youth Movement circles would come out to ski, hike, camp, play guitar, sing, and philosophize. The list of visitors to the cabin—Hans-Georg Gadamer, Karl Löwith, Hannah Arendt, Alfred Baeumler, Ernst Tugendhat, Günther Anders, Jean Beaufret, Paul Celan, Carl Friedrich von Weizsäcker, and others—reads like a veritable catalog of twentieth-century European intellectual history. But what marked the life-world of the hut more than its social interactions or philosophical tête-à-têtes was its isolation and solitude. And it was this sense of solitude that marked Heidegger's work world at the cabin. As Heidegger himself expressed it:

People in the city often wonder whether one gets lonely up in the mountains among the peasants for such long and monotonous periods of time. But it is not loneliness, it is solitude. In large cities one can easily be as lonely as almost nowhere else. But one can never be in solitude there. Solitude has the peculiar and originary power not of isolating us but of projecting our whole existence out into the vast nearness of the presence [*Wesen*] of all things. (HMT: 28/DE: 11)

To the outside observer, the hut presented itself as a small three-room cabin with a low-hanging roof that stood against the outline of a scenic mountain landscape: a charming cottage with kitchen, bedroom, and study for summer vacationing and winter sports. For Heidegger, however, it stood as an entryway into the nearness and abiding simplicity of authentic existence—a site for dwelling and thinking that safeguarded the old world of the peasant community against the incursions of modernity. This "cabin-Dasein," as Heidegger called it, did not merely constitute a pleasant background for his work but became for him an essential element in the experience of thinking.[1] In "Creative Landscape: Why Do We Remain in the Provinces," a radio address of 1934 that explained his reasons for rejecting a call to the University of Berlin and for remaining in Freiburg and the Black Forest, Heidegger said:

> The gravity of the mountains and the hardness of their primeval rock, the slow and deliberate growth of the fir trees, the brilliant, simple splendor of the meadows in bloom, the rush of the mountain brook in the long autumn night, the stern simplicity of the flatlands covered with snow—all of this moves and flows through and penetrates daily existence up there, and not in forced moments of "aesthetic" immersion or artificial empathy, but only when one's own existence stands in its work. It is the work alone that opens up space for the reality that is these mountains. The course of the work remains embedded in what happens in the landscape.
>
> On a deep winter's night when a wild, pounding snowstorm rages around the cabin and veils and covers everything, that is the perfect time for philosophy. Then its questions must become simple and essential. Working through each thought can only be tough and rigorous. The struggle to mold something into language is like the resistance of the towering firs against the storm.
>
> And this philosophical work does not take its course like the aloof studies of some eccentric. It belongs right in the midst of the peasants' work. When the young farm boy drags his heavy sled up the slope and guides it, piled high with beech logs, down the dangerous descent to his house, when the herdsman, lost in thought and slow of step, drives his cattle up the slope, when the farmer in his shed gets the countless shingles ready for his roof, my work is of the same sort. It is intimately rooted in and related to the life of the peasants. . . . The inner relationship of my own work to the Black Forest and its people comes from a centuries-long and irreplaceable rootedness [*Bodenständigkeit*] in the Alemannian-Swabian soil.

1. Heidegger coins the term "Hüttendasein" in DE: 11 and NH: 217.

At most, a city dweller gets "stimulated" by a so-called stay in the country. But my whole work is sustained and guided by the world of these mountains and their people. Lately from time to time my work up there is interrupted for long stretches by conferences, lecture trips, committee meetings, and my teaching work down here in Freiburg. But as soon as I go back up there, even in the first few hours of being at the cabin [*Hüttendasein*], the whole world of previous questions forces itself upon me in the very form in which I left it. I simply am transported into the work's own rhythm and in a fundamental sense I am not at all in command of its hidden law. (HMT: 27–29/DE: 9–11)

Heidegger's paean to the elemental verities of the rural life has become a familiar staple of the Heidegger legend in the last half-century. This fundamental bond between thinking and "rootedness in the Alemannic-Swabian soil" was something that Heidegger clung to long after the carefully crafted radio address of 1934. It became part of his own fundamental strategy of self-presentation. Within his work there emerges a singularly effusive discourse about the relation of language and rootedness. In his "On the Origin of the Work of Art" (1935), he speaks about the equipmental nature of beings and a pair of peasant shoes. In other works he rhapsodizes about the "landscape," "the earth," and the "soil of the field," the "native ground," a "craftsman," a "village cabinetmaker," a "jug," a "field path," a "woodcutter," a "harvest wagon," and countless other references to the life-world of the peasant and the work patterns of agriculture, handicraft, and artisanal skill.[2] This deep, abiding connection to the earth and to a form of existence rooted in the native soil of the homeland comes to influence the very contours and direction of Heidegger's own thought path. And nowhere was this connection more enduring than at the hut in Todtnauberg. Heidegger's quasi-official biographer, Heinrich Wiegand Petzet, writes about the "hut," "Among students of Heidegger, this word had a special meaning. For the mountain hut that Heidegger built in the innermost recess of the valley on the slope above the place called the 'Rütte,' with its few old farmhouses—this hut can as little be separated from his life as the course of his thinking."[3]

Petzet's own hagiographical tendencies aside, this focus on Heidegger's hut and its relation to the master's lifelong work of thinking offers evidence that the "official" Heidegger myth—begun in the 1934 radio address—was cultivated in and through a vision of philosophy's authentic

2. See, for example, Martin Heidegger, BW: 158, 168/H: 22, 32; QCT: 15/ VA: 22; WCT: 23/WHD: 53; PLT: 152, 167/VA: 153, 163.

3. Heinrich W. Petzet, *Encounters and Dialogues with Martin Heidegger, 1929–1976*, trans. Parvis Emad and Kenneth Maly (Chicago: University of Chicago Press, 1993). Petzet's book was commissioned by Frau Heidegger and follows the family pattern of mythologizing the rustic side of Heidegger's life and work. Despite its heavy bias, this work provides some helpful biographical detail, although it needs to be read critically.

life emerging out of a creative landscape and a rootedness in the native earth. But there is another side to this pastoral, bucolic vision of philosophical solitude and creative thinking that Heidegger carefully orchestrated in his role as a *dramatis persona* on the world stage, namely, the *political* function that this discourse about rootedness played in Heidegger's work. Part of my effort in this book will be to explore the pastoral language of rootedness, homeland, and native soil in Heidegger's works from 1933–1945 and to show how deeply implicated it is in his own vision of a National Socialist Germany. By looking at Heidegger's texts and situating them within their own historical contexts, I hope to show the deep and abiding connection between the pastoral language of *Heimat* (homeland) and the militantly geo-political vision of German nationalism that come together to form what one contemporary called Heidegger's "Freiburg National Socialism."[4]

II. PASTORALE MILITANS

In his sketches, essays, portraits, and reflections gathered under the title *Heritage of Our Times* (1935), Ernst Bloch put forward a caustic and penetrating account of the rise of National Socialism in Germany. In the folkish constellation of themes around the notion of "rootedness" or *Bodenständigkeit*—themes connected to "the earth," "the soil," "the homeland," "the landscape," "the peasantry," and "the chthonic persistence" of an "archaic element" that he associates with the myth of a "secret Germany"—Bloch finds a dangerously political ideology of oppression, exclusion, violence, and terror that he identifies as belonging to the essence of an Alemannic-Swabian-Bavarian form of National Socialism.[5] In a prescient essay written in 1929, Bloch employs the openly oxymoronic term "*pastorale militans*" to capture the jarring effect of this violent conjoining of pastoral and militant themes. For Bloch, the language of the homeland and of an Alemannic rootedness in the soil betrays a political longing for "a myth that has its fantasy not in the distance but embedded beneath the soil as it were."[6] This mythic attraction of German fascism for "blood and soil" rhetoric "constitutes the chloroform practice of Hitlerism." As early as 1933 Bloch will lament that "the eternally same, ignorant arias that

4. As Carl von Weizsäcker put it in one of his later reflections, "In the circle around Heidegger they have devised Freiburg National Socialism. Under their breath they say that the true Third Reich has not yet begun at all, that it is yet to come," from "Begegnungen in vier Jahrzehnten," in *Erinnerungen an Martin Heidegger*, ed. Günther Neske (Pfullingen: Neske, 1977), 245–249.

5. Ernst Bloch, *Heritage of Our Times*, trans. Neville and Stephen Plaice (Berkeley: University of California Press, 1991), 48–51; *Erbschaft dieser Zeit* (Frankfurt: Suhrkamp, 1985), 53–56.

6. Bloch, *Heritage of Our Times*, 54, 68; *Erbschaft dieser Zeit*, 59, 74.

Hitler sings to his petit-bourgeois followers do not become any better when the university whore who he found (just as Wilhelm II found her in 1914) latinizes the kitsch and improves the deception with refinements à la Schmitt or Freyer or Heidegger."

This whole preoccupation with rootedness, Bloch will argue, cannot be accepted as an innocently bucolic affinity for hearth, field, and homeland. It needs, rather, to be understood as an encoded discourse about political exclusion, repression, and racial intolerance that serves to gird a regime ultimately bent on terror and extinction. In what follows, I want to take Bloch's guiding trope of the *pastorale militans* of National Socialism as a reference point for reading the works of Martin Heidegger between the years 1933 and 1945. From within the organizing matrix of Bloch's presentation, Heidegger's pastoral language of field paths, native soil, pathmarks, fertile ground, and folkish rootedness—what I will summarily term "Heidegger's roots"—betrays a fundamental unity with the language and axiomatics of his "other" paramilitary discourse about heroism, sacrifice, courage, will, struggle, hardness, violence, and self-assertion that marks his political works of the '30s and beyond.

Far from being a pastoral roundelay about the rural landscape, Heidegger's song of the earth in praise of rootedness and autochthony (*Bodenständigkeit*) is part of a martial-political ideology of the chthonic that was deployed in the 1930s in the name of German metaphysical-racial autochthony. In Heidegger's work this autochthonic metaphysics of exclusion aims to supplant the crude biological racism of Nazi ideologues, such as Alfred Rosenberg and R. Walther Darré, by defining the essence of a *Volk* in terms of roots and belonging. Hence, Heidegger will consistently oppose the Nazi discourse of biological racism on philosophical grounds, since Nazi scientific-ethnological categories of blood and genetic inheritance are wholly at odds with the existential categories of *Being and Time* and the early Freiburg lectures. More simply, Heidegger saw that the Nazi metaphysics of blood denied the essential historicity of a *Volk* by maintaining a positivist metaphysics of scientism and anthropologism in its place. Heidegger's critique is counter-racial, yet racial nonetheless, because it is still a version of German rootedness as a form of political metaphysics, which, of course, was not original with Heidegger. As we will see, it developed both in and against the *Kriegsideologie* of the Great War that shaped right-wing thinking during the years of the Weimar Republic.

III. THE CULTURAL METAPHYSICS OF THE GREAT WAR

In his autobiography, *My Life in Germany Before and After 1933*, Karl Löwith puts forth the argument that "the German revolution of 1933 began with the outbreak of the [First] World War. The events in Germany since 1933 have been an attempt to win the war that was lost."[7] Löwith's analysis of the German Revolution provides a helpful framework for situating Heidegger's own work of the 1930s. Like many other National Socialist thinkers of his generation, Heidegger will attempt to re-assert the force of German nationalism in a revolutionary lexicon of fate, destiny, decision, struggle, and community. As part of this revolutionary design he will recuperate from the cultural philosophy of the Great War the idea of a "special path" of German destiny, a metaphysical *Sonderweg* that grants to the Germans alone a spiritual mission to save the West. To this shared vision of Germany's historical-metaphysical singularity Heidegger will bring his own singular affinity for two other long-standing German traditions: the Hellenomania of Hölderlin and Nietzsche *and* the *Heimat*-metaphysics of the rural right. What will mark Germany's metaphysical *Sonderweg* for Heidegger is both its autochthonic bond to the ancient Greeks and its "irreplaceable rootedness" in the native soil. In both of these inseparable bonds of rootedness/autochthony, Heidegger will find a justification for Germany's revolution against Western nihilism and the forces of rootless cosmopolitanism that he sees threatening "the *völkisch* tradition of origin from the soil and blood" (GA 16: 132). Re-interpreting the German experience of World War I within a new metaphysical register, Heidegger is able to justify the German defeat by placing it against the overall design of *völkisch* destiny—and of the National Socialist revolution. As Heidegger puts it in a speech from August of 1934: "The genuine preparation for the National Socialist revolution began at first in an unconscious way during the World War—or rather, through it. A wholly new experience emerged at the front out of which was formed a wholly new idea of community. This new spirit at the front bore within itself the strong will to make war the determinative power in the *Dasein* of the *Volk*. . . . This awakening of the spirit of the front in the war and its consolidation after the war is nothing other than the creative transformation of this event into a formative power of futural *Dasein*" (GA 16: 298–300). Against "the growing rootlessness and aimlessness of the state," Heidegger will affirm "a new ground [*Boden*] for the whole historical-spiritual *Dasein* of the *Volk*."

National Socialist philosophers like Alfred Baeumler, Franz Böhm, Kurt Hildebrandt, and others shared Heidegger's vision of the Great War as an important catalyst for the National Socialist revolution. In the camaraderie at the front and in the ethos of self-sacrifice and loyalty of the heroes of Langemarck, these philosophers found a model for the *Schicksalsgemeinschaft* ("community of fate") that they believed was transforming

---

7. Karl Löwith, *My Life in Germany Before and After 1933*, trans. Elizabeth King (Urbana: University of Illinois Press, 1994), 1.

Germany from a mere national state to a vital and organic national *Volk*.[8] For Baeumler the war signifies the formation of a new *völkisch* ethos of self-sacrifice and political community at odds with the traditions of statism and national consensus that define the Western democracies. As he sees it, the whole postwar European order set out by the Treaty of Versailles (1919) appears as an Anglo-French plot to impose the alien concept of the "nation-state" on the German *Volk*. What Versailles yields, claims Baeumler, is a social-political order marked by the inevitable problems of modern Western democracy: urbanization, industrialization, political instability, and economic chaos. The Weimar Republic stands as an all too visible example of the modern democratic state out of touch with its own historic traditions. But Baeumler will go back to the history of philosophy for the sources of this problem and will find in Descartes' seventeenth-century ideal of universal mathematical principles the metaphysical ground for modern political nihilism. As he sees it, the political calculus of the Versailles Treaty merely reconfirms the abstract mathematical vision of political space that animated the seventeenth-century Peace of Westphalia (1648).[9] As the first European-wide affirmation of statism, the Peace of Westphalia represents political space as something mappable, controllable, and subject to arbitrary change—a view of political figuration that is instrumental and calculative.[10] As the symbol of the political decline of the West, Versailles attempts to shore up this collapsing tradition of statism that defines a nation as a "territory" whose boundaries can be altered and re-drawn. For Baeumler, the failures of Versailles merely reflect the rootless abstractions of both modernist metaphysics and politics.

Heidegger would share with Baeumler this antipathy for the political metaphysics of Versailles. And like Böhm, he would find in the Cartesian notion of an abstract *ego cogito* the philosophical precursor for the isolated bourgeois subject cut off from all community. Rootless and deracinated, this "free-floating" *ego cogito* comes to be understood politically as a monadic liberal-democratic subject invested with political "rights" but without any genuine connection to the earth. As Böhm will argue, with Descartes there emerges a new type—"the European man"—who sup-

8. Alfred Baeumler, *Männerbund und Wissenschaft* (Berlin: Junker & Dünnhaupt, 1934), 5. See also Ernst Gundolf and Kurt Hildebrandt, *Nietzsche als Richter unsrer Zeit* (Breslau: Ferdinand Hirt, 1923); Ernst Krieck, *Die deutsche Staatsidee* (Leipzig: Armanen, 1934). For Heidegger's reflections on the heroes of Langemarck, see GA 16: 211.

9. In his "Geleitwort" to Friedrich Kopp and Eduard Schulte, *Der Westfälische Frieden* (Munich: Hoheneichen, 1940), vii–x, Baeumler interprets the Nazi Revolution as a reaction to the legacy of the Great War and the dictatorial Treaty of Versailles. Like Heidegger, who in IM: 38/EM: 29 sees Germany "caught in a pincers. Situated in the middle . . . ," Baeumler focuses on Germany's "dominance over the middle" and its attempt to destroy the European idea of the "West."

10. For an instructive view of political space, see Stuart Elden, *Mapping the Present: Heidegger, Foucault and the Project of a Spatial History* (London: Athlone Press, 2001).

plants the man "rooted in what is of the *Volk.*"[11] Against this "victory of Cartesianism," Böhm's *Anti-Cartesianism: the Resistance of German Philosophy* will present a vision of a new German community marked by its commitment to *Kampf,* self-sacrifice, and "the destiny of the *Volk.*" From this perspective, the National Socialist revolution appears as a historical counterforce to the centuries-long legacy of French Cartesianism that has shaped the modern Western world. As this anti-Cartesian force of "self-assertion" (*Selbstbehauptung*) by the *Volk,* National Socialism wills the Germans to overcome the burdens of Versailles and reconstitute themselves as a political community of fate against the statism of the West.[12] In both its political and philosophical form, Böhm's anti-Cartesianism will be instantiated by Heidegger as an organizing structure for understanding the history of modern philosophy as a form of political conflict.

As Heidegger viewed it, Cartesianism lay at the heart of the cosmopolitan, enlightened, and liberal-democratic vision of modernity that dominated Europe. The very notion of "free-floating" consciousness—what Heidegger associated with the rootless elements in German society— came to be seen as a threat to originary autochthony (HCT: 87/GA 20: 119; BT: 32/SZ: 36; GA 16: 132; FCM: 174, 176/GA 29/30: 258, 261; GA 34: 91). Given his background as a lower middle-class sexton's son from the provinces, it is hardly surprising that he harbors animosity toward the values of modern urban culture—or that he rhapsodizes about a landed peasantry with roots in the native soil. As the historian Alon Confino argues, the image of the *Heimat* (homeland) will emerge in Germany as a means of offsetting the perceived "offensive characteristics of modernity." This powerful myth of national community will offer lower-middle and middle-class Germans an image of "a second Germany, impervious to social and political conflicts . . . to compensate for the deficiencies of the first, and real, Germany."[13] In the years just after the Great War, the National Socialist German Workers' Party (NSDAP) will seize upon this *völkisch* myth of the homeland and adapt it to fit its own political ends. And while Heidegger will not embrace all of these ends, his own version of *völkisch* autochthony will be intimately linked with the language and political vision of the NSDAP—even where, as in the disagreement over biological racism, it seeks to challenge it. This vision of political community, marked by a profound faith in the revolutionary possibilities offered by

11. Franz Böhm, *Anti-Cartesianismus: Deutsche Philosophie im Widerstand* (Leipzig: Meiner, 1938), 55, 53.

12. On *Selbstbehauptung* in Baeumler's work, see *Politik und Erziehung* (Berlin: Junker & Dünnhaupt, 1937), 27, 48, 53; *Alfred Rosenberg und der Mythus des 20. Jahrhunderts* (Munich: Hoheneichen, 1943), 12, 19–20. See also Franz Böhm, *Anti-Cartesianismus,* 218, and Heidegger, GA 16: 301.

13. Alon Confino, *The Nation as a Local Metaphor* (Chapel Hill: University of North Carolina Press, 1997), 184–186.

the NS *Aufbruch* of 1933, will come to influence Heidegger's work. As an ex-weatherman without any real combat experience at the front, Heidegger will come to glorify the martial virtues of sacrifice, strength, and valor. These masculine qualities of the war generation—what Heidegger in lapidary fashion termed "hardness" (*Härte*)—will help to form a heroic conception of the philosopher's role that will find expression in his National Socialist readings of Nietzsche and Plato.[14] At the same time, Heidegger will also develop a rustic philosophy of the homeland and of rootedness in the soil that will pervade all his work, even a biographical entry he wrote in 1934 for *Das Deutsche Führerlexikon*. In this short revelatory piece, Heidegger opens with a description of his own family roots. The Messkirch philosopher proudly states that he "is descended from Alemannic-Swabian peasant stock which, on the maternal side (*Kempf*), has been settled (*ansässig*) at the same farm without interruption since 1510, a fact that has been established" (GA 16: 247).[15] He then goes on to outline two other themes near to his heart: his military service record and his philosophical writings. This constellation of themes—the racially pure autochthonous stock of the homeland, the idealization of the military world of the Great War, and their connection to philosophical writing—will profoundly shape Heidegger's work in the years 1933–1945.

For contemporary readers weaned on the eco-poetic writings of Aldo Leopold and John Muir, Heidegger's profound commitment to both martial self-assertion *and* rootedness in the native soil will seem wildly at odds with one another. But, as Luc Ferry and others have shown, the bond between fascist ideology and ecological thinking is both deep and abiding.[16] (In this context we need to remember that Heidegger's ecological meditation on the philosophical power of native roots, "Creative Landscape," was first published in *Der Alemanne. Kampfblatt der Nationalsozialisten Oberbadens* [NH: 216–218].) I would argue that Heidegger's rustic philosophy of the homeland and his martial ideology of struggle, sacrifice, and heroic valor are not at odds. They come together to form a political metaphysics of the earth in the form of a National Socialist *pastorale militans*. In the curious and fateful conjoining of Nietzschean *Kampf* and Hölderlinian

14. Heidegger employs the term "Härte" often in the early 1930s with both Nietzschean and National Socialist resonances; for example, GA 16: 94, 96–97, 107, 131, 192, 207, 238–239, 300, 759–760, 772.

15. By comparing this NS-tailored CV to earlier versions from 1913–1915, we can see how politically motivated it was. Heidegger's use of the term *ansässig* here plays off the autochthonic implications of an earlier use of the term "*uransässig*" by Jacob Burckhardt, *Griechische Kulturgeschichte* (Leipzig: Kröner, 1930), 1: 25, where he employs it as a way of translating the Greek term *autochthon*.

16. Luc Ferry, *The New Ecological Order*, trans. Carol Volk (Chicago: University of Chicago Press, 1995), 91–107, and Anna Bramwell, *Ecology in the Twentieth Century: A History* (New Haven: Yale University Press, 1989), 195–208.

Heimat, of Heraclitean *polemos* and Eckhartian *Gelassenheit,* there emerges a Heideggerian philosophy of roots that both brings together and sets asunder the counterposed realms of the martial and the pastoral. In this *Auseinandersetzung* between the two, I try to situate Heidegger's inner relation to a Messkirchian form of National Socialism in the period 1933–1945.

In what follows I will reconstruct how Heidegger's writings from 1933–1945 constitute a philosophical attempt at geo-politics, a grand metaphysical vision of German destiny that develops both within and against the vision of political hegemony forged by the National Socialist movement. One of the most decisive forms of this philosophical geo-politics in Heidegger's work is the development of a singular metaphysics of the earth marked by autochthony—the *völkisch* belief in the rootedness of the homeland and in ancestral kinship—that presents itself as an ontological account of German national supremacy. This Germanocentric metaphysics of history emerges in dialogue with the right-wing ideologues of the Great War (Troeltsch, Scheler, Sombart) and their NS-successors (Baeumler, Krieck, Hildebrandt, Böhm) more than it does with the great thinkers of the tradition like Plato, Nietzsche, or Descartes. As part of this political reading, I want to show that Heidegger's own dialogues with the "great" philosophers of the tradition were hardly the unmediated engagements of one thinker with another. Rather, Heidegger read thinkers and poets like Plato, Heraclitus, Nietzsche, Hölderlin, Descartes, and Eckhart within the political context of his own generation. For him they became living texts as part of a deep-rooted *Auseinandersetzung* with the tradition as it comes out of the desperate German situation of the 1920s and '30s. In this sense I will try to read Heidegger's work within its own historical context with an eye toward emphasizing *when* a particular text was written. I begin by looking at Heidegger's Rectorial Address, "The Self-Assertion of the German University" (1933), a decisive philosophical document that lays out in brief the scaffolding for Heidegger's National Socialist hopes of revolution.[17] Here in an interpretation of the German special path or *Sonderweg* framed in and through his confrontation with Nietzsche and the early Greeks, Heidegger lays out his autochthonic philosophy of roots essential for the future of Germany. It is a position from which he never strays. Because the Rectorial Address is an essential text that holds the key to much of Heidegger's later work, I try to situate it carefully within the discourse of the *pastorale militans* that forms Heidegger's world. Chapters 1 and 2 analyze and situate the Rectorial Address. In chapter 3 I analyze

---

17. Although many Heidegger scholars use the adjective "rectoral" to refer to the speech, the standard English form for this term is "rectorial"; hence my reference to the "Rectorial Address."

Heidegger's geo-philosophy of European politics in terms of *Introduction to Metaphysics* (1935) and "Europa und die deutsche Philosophie" of 1936. Chapter 4 considers Heidegger's interpretation of the Pre-Socratics, and chapter 5 turns to Heidegger's understanding of Nietzsche from 1936/37 to 1944/45. Throughout, I pay particular attention to the political significance of these topics in the formation of Heidegger's philosophy of roots.

CHAPTER ONE

The Myth of the Homeland

The true is the bacchanalian revel in which no member is not drunk.

— G. W. F. HEGEL
Preface to *The Phenomenology of Spirit*

I know that everything essential and great originated from the fact that the human being had a homeland and was rooted in tradition.

— MARTIN HEIDEGGER
GA 16: 670

I. PHILOSOPHY AND POLITICS

In September of 1966 just days before his seventy-seventh birthday, Heidegger granted a three-hour interview to the German news-magazine *Der Spiegel* that has long since become a familiar part of Heidegger lore. From the documentary record we know that Heidegger had grave doubts about allowing himself to be questioned by popular journalists about any aspects of his philosophical writings or political commitments.[1] Nonetheless, he did eventually relent and decided to offer his own version of what might be called a philosophical "Apology."

The text that was produced from the interview occupies a strange and uncertain place in Heidegger's corpus, a document that was never written by Heidegger himself but rather was transcribed by a stenographer and later revised for publication.[2] Despite its status as a murky text of questionable "philosophical" significance, the "*Spiegel* Interview" remains a crucial document in the history of interpreting Heidegger, since it offers one of the most sustained discussions of Heidegger's political engagement in the *Gesamtausgabe* (or *Collected Edition*) from the author of "the Last Hand."[3] To an unusually self-conscious degree, Heidegger attempted

1. For a detailed account of the interview and the background see Heinrich W. Petzet, *Encounters and Dialogues with Martin Heidegger,* trans. Parvis Emad and Kenneth Maly (Chicago: University of Chicago Press, 1993), 90–98; Ernst Nolte, *Martin Heidegger* (Frankfurt: Propyläen, 1992), 254–268; and *Martin Heidegger/Erhart Kästner Briefwechsel,* ed. Heinrich W. Petzet (Frankfurt: Insel, 1986), 79–93, 146–148.

2. This "oral" text in written form offers a technological variation on the Platonic problem of writing in *Phaedrus* 277b–277c. See also Petzet, *Encounters and Dialogues,* xxx.

3. For a critical account of the textual practices of Heidegger's "Collected Edition," see Theodore Kisiel, "Heidegger's *Gesamtausgabe:* An International Scandal of Scholarship," *Phi-*

here to direct the way his work would be taken up and appropriated, especially in its relation to his political past. As part of his autoexegetical excursus on his involvement with National Socialism, Heidegger will offer the by now long refuted defense that his involvement was brief, of a defensive nature, and grew out of a fundamental conviction that "at the time I saw no other alternative" (SI: 44/ANT: 84). According to Heidegger's guarded formulation, the political events of 1933 were hardly unknown to him; yet he maintained that at the time he was more of an observer than a participant, someone whose genuine interest was directed away from the political realm to the realm of philosophical reflection. As he told Rudolf Augstein (one of his interviewers): "I certainly followed the course of political events between January and March of 1933 and occasionally talked about it with younger colleagues as well. However, my work itself was concerned with a more extensive interpretation of Pre-Socratic thinking" (SI: 42/ANT: 82).

Heidegger's defense of his own position in 1933 will be carried out here as a way of separating and placing into different spheres the character of his political involvement and the intensity of his philosophical commitments. According to him in the interview conducted by *Der Spiegel*, the political issues of the day appear as historically contingent occurrences that are extrinsic and peripheral to the genuinely philosophical engagement with Pre-Socratic philosophy. This strategy of separating the political and the philosophical elements would be reinforced in two other documents that Heidegger wrote on the question of his political involvement: a "Letter to the Rector of Freiburg University" from November 4, 1945, and a document written to the De-Nazification Committee, "The Rectorate 1933/34: Facts and Thoughts," from late 1945.[4] Taken together, these three documents constitute what one might call "The Official Story" of Heidegger's political engagement, a story that would be retold with ever greater force by the Heidegger family and by the loyal Heidegger following in the years after his death right on through the "Heidegger Affair," which was spurred on by the publication of works by Victor Farias and Hugo Ott.[5] Those of us who write about Heidegger in the wake of Farias, Ott, Sheehan, Derrida, and Lacoue-Labarthe can no longer separate "philosophy" and "politics" in our interpretation of the work.[6] But neither can we proceed to an interpretation of that work without ques-

---

losophy Today 39, no. 1 (Spring 1995): 3–15. GA 16: 639 and 652–683.

The GA published by Kostermann is not a historical-critical edition, but one that was revised by Heidegger himself without noting the differences between the original text and the later revisions—hence, an edition of the "Last Hand."

4. RFT: 15–32/SdU: 21–43; HCW: 61–66/GA 16: 397–404.

5. See the references in the notes to the preface, n. 1.

6. See the preface, n. 2.

tioning what we mean by these terms; we cannot take them to be self-evident givens, the contours and possibilities of which we know before we begin our inquiries. Rather, we need to consider what we mean by "philosophy" and "politics" and whether there is not indeed a more fundamental and originary relation between these two areas than that acknowledged by the later Heidegger.

As I will show, Heidegger himself was convinced that originary philosophy could only be done in dialogue with politics, something that has to be understood here not as the institutional, legal, military, or socio-economic aspects of statecraft or legislative-executive decision-making, but as the historical-ontological site within which *Dasein* struggles to find its place and its own sense of being rooted—in a community, a *Volk*, a tradition, and a history. On his reading, politics is a politics of the earth, a geopolitics whose ultimate meaning is ontological in the sense that earth becomes the site for the unfolding of basic human possibilities, the matrix or "da" ("there") within and against which *Dasein* instantiates itself as a particular, determinate, political being. As human beings dwell upon the earth, they come to form spaces whose outlines are not merely territorial in the etymological sense of the Latin *terra,* the earth as a blank graph upon which humans place boundaries. Rather, "earth" becomes what the ancient Greeks called "*chthon,*" the place where humans dwell and form a homeland. It is as this fateful account of a people (*Volk*) and its relationship to its homeland that Heidegger will conceive of "'politics' in the highest and authentic sense" (GA 39: 214).

Politics for Heidegger is not something that takes place apart from philosophy; on the contrary, philosophy itself "is" political if we understand politics as "the site of history" and as "the open site of that fitting destining [*Schickung*] from out of which all human relations towards beings . . . determine themselves" (IM: 152/EM: 117; HHI: 82/GA 53: 102). Politics, then, can never be confused with mere theory or with a general account of human nature. It is always bound up with the historicity of the moment. Toiling in the shadow of the Weimar Republic and its democratic politics imposed from without by the Versailles Treaty and enforced from within by an occupied French army in the Ruhr, Heidegger's philosophical work becomes intimately bound up with the concrete situation of German life in the 1920s. Only within the *kairos* of the present can the history of the philosophical tradition be made vital; only when the present is read through the *arche* of the tradition does it offer itself as a *kairos*-moment of revolutionary possibility. The time of politics is shot through with kairotic time, the time of "opportunity" and "decision," the time that offers "the right moment" for change and revolution. But politics alone can never transform this moment of revolutionary insight and upheaval into an enduring historical truth. For that, philosophy is needed, a philosophy in touch with the roots of its tradition.

As he came to present an account of his own political affiliations during the NS years, Heidegger sought to cover over this deep and essential relationship between philosophy and politics that he uncovered in his work of the early 1930s. In the postwar epoch he will present his work as something that takes place outside the sphere of politics, a purely thinkerly dialogue with the Western philosophical tradition that emerges in conversation with Plato, Aristotle, Descartes, Hegel, Nietzsche, and the Pre-Socratics and cannot be properly grasped in terms of its historical and cultural conditions. My claim will be that politics can never be severed from philosophy in Heidegger's sense, since philosophy for him is always a meditation on the sense of being at home amidst beings and of being rooted temporally (in an epochal history of being) and spatially (in a homeland that provides the possibilities of historical destiny).

To read Heidegger without this historical-political background is to miss the historicity of his own work and to risk reading it as if it came to us in a hermeneutic vacuum. Heidegger always sought to isolate his work from any contemporary influences, believing that reading it in this way might reduce it to the level of a worldview or an ideology. Even in the early period before *Being and Time*, he will try to insulate his work from the rostrum-style, academic *Kathederphilosophie* of his generation, which he sees as bringing about the death of original philosophy. But there are other, more philosophically decisive grounds for his efforts to keep his work free from the influence of contemporary ideology, and these are bound up with his philosophy of rootedness that develops in the early 1920s. In a decisive way this meditation on rootedness will become part of Heidegger's attempt to rethink politics in a philosophical way against the quotidian definition of politics that shaped the age.

II. THE ROOTS OF REVOLUTION

Amidst the turbulence of the Weimar years with its economic instability, social dislocation, and political upheaval, Heidegger will fight to keep philosophy free from the dominance of worldview thinking and rootless theorizing. In an informal piece from 1925, he laments that "the rootlessness of contemporary life is the root of a growing decline" (GA 16: 53).[7] In

7. Part of my argument here will be that Heidegger's work needs to be read against the social, economic, and political upheaval of late Weimar and the national mood of mourning and regeneration that extends from 1918 to 1933. After suffering two million casualties in the Great War, the German people needed to find some measure of national renewal, and Heidegger, like many of his contemporaries, would find that in National Socialism. For a typ-

Being and Time, Heidegger will offer an analysis of everyday life—idle talk, curiosity, ambiguity—that sees it as "existentially uprooted" and "entangled in a tradition . . . that uproots the historicity of *Dasein* . . . and tries to veil its own rootlessness" (BT: 159, 18–19/SZ: 170, 21). He will press the point that because *Dasein* is entangled in the rootlessness of conventional structures that comprise its tradition it cannot gain access to its own primordial roots. Given this entanglement in the structures of everyday life, "the tradition even makes us forget such a provenance altogether." By falling prey to the traditional worldview of its age and its pregiven ideological choices, *Dasein* loses its footing and becomes unsteady. What emerges from such a situation is the predominance of a "free-floating" intelligence attached to the "illusory culture [*Scheinkultur*] of the urban metropolis" whose asphalt surfaces cover over the roots of a genuine culture that is marked by its "loyalty to the soil" (GA 16: 53).[8] As part of his preparatory interpretation of *Dasein's* fundamental structures in *Being and Time,* Heidegger will point to this whole problem of an illusory culture marked by semblance and free-floating speculation, tracing it back to *Dasein's* tendency to cover over what is primordial with the cloak of oblivion, what he will term *Seinsvergessenheit* ("the forgetting of being"). In this context he will contrast the primordial thinking of phenomenology with the rootless, free-floating thinking of everyday life: "It is possible for every phenomenological concept and proposition drawn from genuine origins to degenerate when communicated as a statement. It gets circulated in a vacuous fashion, loses its autochthony [*Bodenständigkeit*] and becomes a free-floating thesis" (BT: 32/SZ: 36). In the context of the Weimar years, Heidegger would link this free-floating speculation to the various worldviews associated with liberalism, cosmopolitanism, relativism, and sociological theory.[9] *Being and Time* will self-consciously challenge the philosophical pretensions of worldview thinking as a viable answer to the crisis of Weimar German culture and in its stead will seek to retrieve the philosophical necessity of questioning that had marked the ancient Greek

---

ical account of the right-wing nationalism that Heidegger embraced, see the small book by Johannes Schmidt-Wodder, *Deutschland: Gestern und Heute* (Leipzig: Braumüller, 1934). Schmidt-Wodder will, like Heidegger, draw on the same right-wing lexicon of rootedness, deracination, self-assertion, hardness, destiny, community, and heroism that defines his generation.

8. For Heidegger's frequent references to "free-floating" intelligence in the period 1927–1935 cf. BT: 7, 17, 24, 32, 116, 135, 146, 251, 255, 258, 274, 285, 299, 312, 355, 388/SZ: 9, 19, 28, 36, 123, 144, 156, 271, 276, 279, 298, 309, 325, 339, 388, 424; FCM: 174, 176/GA 29/30: 258, 261; GA 16: 132, 221; GA 34: 91.

9. Dirk Hoeges, *Kontroverse am Abgrund: Ernst Robert Curtius und Karl Mannheim (Intellektuelle und "freischwebende Intelligenz" in der Weimarer Republik)* (Frankfurt: Fischer, 1994) offers a helpful account of the "Kampfkultur" of German intellectual life during the Weimar era. See also Klaus Lichtblau, *Kulturkrise und Soziologie um die Jahrhundertwende* (Frankfurt: Suhrkamp, 1996), especially chapter 5.

philosophical tradition. To combat the rootlessness of Weimar culture, Heidegger sets out to regain access to the very roots of the Western tradition in Heraclitus, Parmenides, Plato, and Aristotle.

Three years earlier in his course given in the summer semester of 1924, "Fundamental Concepts of Aristotelian Philosophy," Heidegger had announced to his students that "we need to win back rootedness and autochthony as it was alive in Greek science."[10] By "autochthony" (*Bodenständigkeit*) he meant the rootedness in the ground or soil (*Boden*) of a concept that would provide constancy or steadfastness (*Ständigkeit*) against the turbulence of contemporary academic "-isms." As he saw it, these modish academic forms of conceptuality (*Begrifflichkeit*) had covered over and occluded the genuine ground and soil of Aristotelian thinking. His specific focus in the 1924 summer semester course was to free Aristotle's *Rhetoric* from the sclerotic interpretations of the Neo-Kantians that had been inherited from the medieval school philosophers and to introduce, instead, a hermeneutic of *Dasein* that roots conceptuality in everyday life in its "da" (or "there"). What the Weimar worldview philosophers had succeeded in accomplishing was to dislodge and uproot conceptuality from its hermeneutic soil and to present it in the second-hand formulations of derived academic learning. But the aim of genuine philosophy, Heidegger claimed, is to question the currency of our concepts by returning back to their original ground and to constantly interrogate this ground in ways that keep it alive as something questionable, concealed, and primordial. Only in this way could the rootlessness of contemporary German life be challenged in an authentic and autochthonous way.

During the same period that Heidegger was delivering his lectures on Aristotle, he was also reading the newly released *Correspondence between Wilhelm Dilthey and Count Paul Yorck von Wartenburg* that had appeared the year before in 1923.[11] In Yorck's letters to Dilthey, which would play such an important role in helping him to work out his interpretation of historicity in *Being and Time*, Heidegger would find another important source for his concept of autochthony. In these letters, Yorck lays out a critique of the intellectual and spiritual rootlessness of the modern European tradition that he sees threatening genuine philosophical thinking. For Yorck, contemporary science with its demand for "presuppositionless" research has lost its grounding. As citizens of the sprawling urban metropolis who

10. The text of Heidegger's SS 1924 lecture course is still unpublished. I have cited the manuscript of this course, *Grundbegriffe der Aristotelischen Philosophie*, from the copy in the Herbert Marcuse Archiv #0005.01, 6, 5, 109, 41–42. Heidegger will find in Aristotle's usage of *to autochthonas* (those inhabitants who are sprung from the soil; *Rhetoric* 1360b), the Greek source for his own German understanding of those who are *bodenständig* (rooted in the earth).

11. Hans-Georg Gadamer, *Hermeneutik im Rückblick* (Tübingen: Mohr-Siebeck, 1985), 8–9.

have adopted the cosmopolitan values of modernity, we have lost our roots and have become deracinated beings. Yorck laments the spread of asphalt intellectualism and writes to Dilthey that "with the alienation from the soil the sustaining force has been lost. This rootless status yields an unsteady balance in the human being and in his life-forms that gives way to every convulsion."[12] Throughout these letters Yorck will keep returning to the thematic of rootlessness and will present himself as an advocate for a life rooted in the soil, the earth, the homeland, and in history. "The rootlessness of thinking and the belief in such thinking," he will claim, "is a historical product." As part of this bond to one's historical ground, Yorck lays strong emphasis on the ownership of land which he sees not as "a legal or economic category but [as] a pre-legal, pre-economic one" that determines the steadfastness of both the individual and the group. Those who have abandoned the permanence of the soil for the fluidity of capital have severed their ties to their own historical identity. As examples of this economic shift, Yorck will point to the Jews, "that whole tribe who lacks the feeling for a psychical and physical ground or soil." In an essay on Aristotle and Sophocles titled "Katharsis," Yorck will contend that modern humanity has become so displaced from the roots of its historical soil that it can no longer properly grasp the great pain of banishment "which the Greeks, who knew no supraterrestrial home, experienced when they were separated from their fatherland."[13] Wholly incomprehensible to the modern individual in this sense is the fate of Oedipus in his exile at Colonus where "he is homeless like a plant ripped from its native soil. Our cosmopolitan age has no feeling for the pain of this ancient Greek's homelessness. Once a being who never moved, the human being has become a mobile creature."

Yorck's paean to the homeland and to a life nurtured in the native earth struck Heidegger as something essential for coming to terms with the mobile culture of Weimar. By reconfiguring Germany's identity in terms of autochthony rather than economics or social theory, Yorck had, on Heidegger's reading, pointed to an essential dimension of German *Dasein*: its rootedness in an earth whose authentic meaning was historical rather than geological or topographical. Yorck's understanding of the native earth and the local landscape as determining forces in the shaping of German historical destiny would provide Heidegger with a model for a way of thinking through a connection between autochthony and history. In sections 73–77 of *Being and Time*, Heidegger will take up the threads of Yorck's analysis and lay out a reading of *Dasein's* historicity that will offer a

12. *Briefwechsel zwischen Wilhelm Dilthey und dem Grafen Paul Yorck von Wartenburg, 1877–1897*, ed. Sigrid V. Schulenberg (Halle: Niemeyer, 1923), 19, 20, 33, 39, 250, 254.

13. Paul Yorck von Wartenburg, "Katharsis," in *Die Philosophie des Grafen Paul Yorck von Wartenburg*, ed. Karlfried Gründer (Göttingen: Vandenhoeckh & Ruprecht, 1970), 174–175.

clue as to how he will interpret the whole phenomenon of rootedness as something essential to the authentic identity of *Dasein*. As a being marked by care, *Dasein* never exists solely in the present cut off from its inherited tradition. It exists, rather, ecstatically, in the etymological sense of *ek-stasis*. *Dasein* literally "stands out" from its "there" in the present, stretching itself along between past and future as it confronts its possibilities against the finitude of its own experience of "having been" (*Gewesenheit*) and in expectation of its hopes for a "futural" existence. This sense of "being stretched-out in stretching-itself along" Heidegger terms the "happening [*Geschehen*] of *Dasein*," a happening whose existential-temporal structure offers a key to an "ontological understanding of historicity" (BT: 344/SZ: 375). *Dasein* does not, however, "stand" in history as if the past were a field that lay there present before one, an object or "*Gegen-stand*." On the contrary, the historicity of *Dasein* brings into play the movement and projection, the "stretching-itself along" and engagement that marks *Dasein* as a being who needs constantly (*ständig*) to re-position itself in the field of possibilities—historical, contemporary, futural—that emerge for it and require interpretation. This dynamic-hermeneutic character of *Dasein's* historicity seems to stand in opposition to Yorck's focus on constancy or *Ständigkeit* as the measure of historical greatness (the enduring traditions of Prussian militarism, Christian religiosity, Greek metaphysics, Junker land ownership). But what Heidegger draws from his reading of Yorck is a way of reconceptualizing the constancy (*Ständigkeit*) of tradition and the rootedness in one's native soil (*Bodenständigkeit*) as something dynamic and in need of continual revision and reinterpretation.

If, traditionally, Germans had thought of history as something that was past and that stood there before them as a museum into which they could enter, Heidegger wants to grasp it as a horizon of possibility against which one needs to measure all hopes for future emergence. What autochthony means then is not simply a rootedness in the soil, in the past, or in the tradition from out of which one 'views' the world—a conception that more properly characterizes worldview philosophy. On the contrary, it signifies something concealed, mysterious, and chthonic whose meaning lies hidden beneath the surface of the earth, or rather whose meaning needs to be worked out in a confrontation (*Aus-einander-setzung*) with this concealment in order to grant one an authentic identity. As what is most concealed, the earth in this sense becomes an origin, an origin whose power helps to shape the fate of an individual and the destiny of a *Volk*. To grasp the earth in this autochthonous way requires a different understanding of it—neither as an object or *Gegenstand* of nature or of history but in terms of historicity. Because Yorck had set for himself the task of laying out the categorial structure of history as something ontological rather than merely ontical, and because he had thought this back to the problem of autochthony, Heidegger deemed his work essential for coming to terms with the historical destiny of the German *Volk* (BT: 364/SZ: 399). More importantly, by understanding that the categorial structure of life was marked by the temporal dynamic of historicity in its ontological sense, Yorck had pointed to the need for understanding *Dasein* not as an isolated, monadic bourgeois subject but as a being whose own being was constituted by the co-historicizing of its generation. In this way the fate of the individual became wedded to the destiny of a *Volk* (BT: 352/SZ: 384). Destiny (*Geschick*), on this account, is neither something given in advance nor something that awaits one; it is, rather, the gathering together (*Ge-*) of the historical possibilities that the tradition has sent (*schicken*) to a community, possibilities that must constantly be worked out in and through a confrontation with their historical roots. Rootedness, as Heidegger understands it, is bound up with historicity. Only through the struggle to retrieve its roots (in history, language, and landscape) can *Dasein* (understood collectively as the *Volk*) become authentically what it is (viz., German).[14]

This constant struggle to win back an authentic identity for the Germans against the rootless, superficial theorizing of the Weimar epoch emerges in Heidegger's readings of Aristotle and Yorck in his work of the 1920s. There he will attempt to raise the question of being as one that has its roots both in the tradition of ancient Greek ontology and in the concealed meaning of the German homeland. During the 1920s, however, Heidegger will never explicitly think through the meaning of this question in terms of both its ontological and *völkisch* possibilities. Despite his growing sense that the spiritual-intellectual salvation of Germany lies in establishing an inner connection between a conceptual rootedness in the Greeks and an autochthonic rootedness in the native earth, Heidegger will never fully address this question in the Weimar era. It is only with the euphoric outbreak of the National Socialist revolution in 1933 that Heidegger will set the themes of ontological and *völkisch* rootedness into an explicit dialogue with the politics of "conservative revolution." The *Aufbruch* or revolutionary "eruption" of 1933 offers Heidegger what Machiavelli termed "l'occasione": the political occasion for kairological insight into the defining moment of a people and its leader. This "moment of vision"—a Pauline *kairos*, a Nietzschean *Augenblick*—offers to the prince the possibilities of radical transformation, understood in the etymological sense of "radical" (L. *radix*)—of getting to the "roots." This philosophical

14. This same logic of becoming who one is through a confrontation with the "other" will define Hölderlin's Graecophilia and his hopes for German rebirth. The logic of this struggle with "one's own" and "the foreign" will be laid out by Hölderlin in his letter to Casimir Ulrich Böhlendorff; Friedrich Hölderlin, *Sämtliche Werke*, ed. Norbert von Hellingrath (Berlin: Propyläen, 1923), 5: 318–322. See also GA 4: 87–88, 157–158; GA 39: 135–136, 290–294; GA 43: 122; GA 52: 135; GA 53: 154–155, 168–170.

prince from Messkirch, inspired by the Platonic injunction that philosophers must rule if the polis is to endure, will attempt to seize the "occasion" of political revolution to lead Germany (in the sense of *führen, Führung* by a philosophical *Führer*). But where is the philosopher prince to lead? And in what sense will the *Führung* (*leading*) depend upon an *Einführung* (intro-*duction*, from L. *ducere*, to lead) by the philosophical prince (L. *princeps*) into the *principles* (L. *principia*) of revolution?[15] What is the underlying connection between the philosophical prince and revolution? And what would it mean to embrace a "conservative" revolution?

In many ways Heidegger's work of the early 1930s will lay out in a variety of rhetorical forms—informal, "occasional" pieces, letters, academic lectures, formal essays—the philosophical justification for conservative revolution. In its common usage, the oxymoronic term "conservative revolution" refers to the political ideology of right-wing thinkers in Weimar, such as Moeller van den Bruck, Ernst Jünger, Hans Freyer, Carl Schmitt, and others, who rebelled against the traditions of Western democratic pluralism, liberal capitalism, Marxian-style socialism, and cosmopolitan enlightenment that they saw destroying the unique character of German life. These conservative revolutionaries understood the modern epoch as an age of spiritual-intellectual crisis whose roots were deeper than the quotidian economic and political crises afflicting the Weimar Republic.

Out of the existential situation of death and affliction brought on by the Great War, these thinkers find in their generation a new ethos of masculine valor and martial heroism that defines the German spirit. Against the capitalist definition of the human being as an isolated consumer and spectator, these right-wing revolutionaries seek to affirm the *political* identity of the self as a member of a *Volksgemeinschaft* with roots in a landscape and a homeland. Against the philosophical definition of the human being as an isolated Cartesian subject who, as an exemplar of the Enlightenment's universal principles of rationality, autonomy, and cosmopolitanism embraces free-floating, rootless ideas, they conceive of the individual as a member of a nation, a community, and a race.

Many of the ideas of the conservative revolution would find fertile soil in the philosophical discourse of National Socialism which was decidedly anti-Cartesian, anti-Enlightenment, and anti-liberal. Typical of this posture was the stance of Franz Böhm, National Socialist philosopher at Heidelberg, whose *Anti-Cartesianismus: Deutsche Philosophie im Widerstand* railed against "the rootlessness of rational absolutism" and "the presuppositionlessness of Cartesian science . . . that destroys the originary meaning

---

15. For a penetrating account of Heidegger's relation to the discourse of "principles," see Reiner Schürmann, *Heidegger, On Being and Acting: From Principles to Anarchy* (Bloomington: Indiana University Press, 1990).

of Greek science . . . and at the same time is characterized by the deple-
tion of the meaning of Greek *theoria*."[16] For Böhm, the National Socialist
revolution offers what he calls "anti-Cartesian German resistance . . . to
the non-originary rationality" of the Western tradition. "In the fulfillment
of a *völkisch*-political happening there emerges the *creative foundation* for
shaping everything. From out of these *positive* origins the science of autonomous rationality is called into question. Insofar as these origins are
once again accessible to us in our political existence, we know that every
science that cuts itself off from its pre-rational roots must perish. . . ." This
creative act of shaping everything out of the revolutionary possibilities of
völkish-political existence, Böhm intimates, can never merely be a present
or future concern. "All shaping [*Gestaltung*] is only the mirroring of an
originary being; the meaning of all of our science and our art, our pledges
and our beliefs is only an answer to that which we are from our origin."
For Böhm the German revolution promises the recovery of an origin that
had been covered over and concealed by the calculative-instrumental rationality of Cartesian science. From this perspective, Böhm understands
German *Dasein* not as the product of scientific-historical development but
as the expression of myth. "Where our *Dasein* no longer understands itself
in terms of the stretching-out [*Erstreckung*] of temporal succession but out
of the depth of its own immediate origin, it has become mythic. . . . Myth
expresses that life at all times can stand in its origin and that *as* life it is
never without its 'gods', which direct it and preserve its creative possibilities."[17] On Böhm's reading, "the gods have ultimately foresaken the world,
hence we need to seek them in their temporal homeland—at the beginning of the destinies of the various peoples [*Völker*]." The energy for overcoming "the loss of the mythic in our age," he claims, lies "in the straightforward certainty of the present concerning the origin, the peasant who
feels himself at one with the forces of the soil." In these forces and in the
newly-awakened German form of "labor" and "technical will," Böhm finds
what he terms "*Durchbruchstellen*" or "points of awakening" that break
through (*durchbrechen*) the encrusted traditions of Cartesian thinking that
threaten German culture. Here, he claims, "rests our belief in the rootedness of our *völkisch* powers and in their capacity for resistance."

   Heidegger too would embrace many of these same themes: the lament
about the departure of the gods, the critique of Cartesian technicity, the
myth of origin, the forces of the *Volk,* and the need for a German revolution to retrieve the originary meaning of Greek science and *theoria*. But
whereas Böhm's assault on the tradition of Enlightenment rationality ap-

16. Franz Böhm, *Anti-Cartesianismus: Deutsche Philosophie im Widerstand* (Leipzig: Meiner,
1938), 240–241, 247.
   17. Ibid., 245, 247.

propriated philosophy for the purpose of carrying out a political revolution, Heidegger sought to establish the meaning of political revolution as only the opening salvo in a more deeply rooted and less superficial philosophical revolution. Moreover, where Böhm's conservative rebellion against the forces of Cartesian modernity aimed fundamentally at the preservation of German rootedness, Heidegger conceived a more radical form of revolution. For him the vitality of a *Volk* does not reside in the uncritical veneration of ancient customs or traditions but in the radical confrontation with their originary power. Rootedness in soil, landscape, tradition, and in history is what enables a *Volk* to become great. But rootedness alone should not be equated with mere conservation or preservation. For these roots to produce new historical life, they need to be confronted in a revolutionary way.

The Greek notion of *theoria* must not be slavishly imitated, as if we already knew what it was that we sought to preserve. On the contrary, only as something questionable, something whose meaning lies concealed in the roots of its origin and that demands constant retrieval and reinterpretation, can the meaning of Greek *theoria* be preserved. The task of ontology is to restore historical rootedness to the tradition of Western thinking, to win back or recuperate from the ingrained habits of centuries-long philosophical practice the sense of original wonderment that pervaded early Greek *theoria*. In this recuperation of Greek antiquity amidst the free-floating speculation of contemporary life, Heidegger finds an originary ground in which to think. As he will put it in his lectures entitled *Introduction to Metaphysics*, "we are, through our questioning, entering a landscape; to be in this landscape is the fundamental prerequisite for restoring rootedness [*Bodenständigkeit*] to historical *Dasein*" (IM: 39/EM: 30).

I argue that we need to understand Heidegger's turn toward politics against such a background of revolutionary consciousness whose aim is to "restore rootedness to historical *Dasein*." Perhaps nowhere in Heidegger's corpus is this energy for revolutionary renewal as palpable as in his Rectorial Address of May 27, 1933, "The Self-Assertion of the German University." There Heidegger will set out to place his ontological aim of recovering "the originary essence of Greek science" in tension with his political hopes of "the most profound preservation of the forces that are rooted in the soil and blood of a *Volk*" (HCW: 33–34/SdU: 14). In this program of ontological politics, a politics that seeks its roots both in the geographical-cultural soil of the homeland and in the philosophical-mythic *arche* of the Greek dawn, Heidegger will attempt his coup as the philosophical prince of a conservative revolution.

To read the Rectorial Address without this ontological-political call for revolution is to miss its essential meaning as a *Streitschrift* or "polemic" against the forces of counter-revolution within Germany. This includes those forces within the German university, within the National Socialist party, and within that group of NS philosophers who sought to direct the fire of revolution toward their own political and institutional ends. The Rectorial Address attempts to seize the moment of revolutionary outbreak as the wakeful moment of ontological-political *kairos* where the salvation of the German *Volk* depends upon a polemical recuperation of the originary Greek experience of being. Hence, it needs to be read within its kairological-revolutionary context as a philosophical call (*Ruf*) whose invocations, affirmations, and inaugurations were directed at a specific audience at a decisive moment: the transfer of power from the moribund democratic values of the Weimar era to the new "National Revolution" personified by the leadership of the National Socialist Führer, Adolf Hitler. As Heidegger himself put it a few months later in a speech delivered in Leipzig concerning Germany's decision to withdraw from the League of Nations: "the National Socialist revolution is not merely the assumption of power as it exists presently in the State by another party . . . rather, this revolution is bringing about *the total transformation of our German existence*" (HCW: 52/NH: 150).

In order to grasp the significance of the Rectorial Address within its proper context, we need to consider it against this background of revolutionary consciousness. Heidegger was deadly serious about the necessity of deep and abiding change when he wrote to Elisabeth Blochmann in the spring of 1933. I quote this letter at some length because in it Heidegger develops a lexicon of "revolutionary" consciousness that will mark the crucial moment of his decisive entry into the realm of the political:

> For me, the present situation—precisely because much remains dark and unbridled—has an unusual gathering power. It heightens the will and the certainty to act in the service of a great task [*Auftrag*] and to participate in the building of a world grounded on the people [*volklich gegründeten Welt*]. For quite some time now, the pallor and shadow play of mere "culture" and the unreality of so-called "values" have for me been reduced to naught and caused me to seek the new basis [*Boden*] in *Da-sein*. We can discover it, as well as the vocation [*Berufung*] of the Germans, in the history of the West only if we expose [*aussetzen*] ourselves to being itself in a new manner and appropriation. In this way, I experience what is presently happening completely from the future. Only thus can a true partaking and that *perdurable abiding* [*Inständigkeit*] grow in our history, which, of course, remains a precondition for genuine action.
>
> On the other hand, what must be tolerated in all calmness is that rash, headlong jumping on the bandwagon to join the latest things which is mushrooming everywhere: that way of gluing oneself to the immediacy of the foreground which now suddenly takes each and every thing "politically" without bearing in mind that that can only remain *one* path of the first revolution [*ein Weg der ersten Revolution*]. Admittedly, it has become and can be for many one

path of first awakening [*ersten Erweckung*]—provided that we are resolved to prepare ourselves for a second, deeper one. (SL: 571/HBB: 60)

Here, and in the Rectorial Address, Heidegger invokes a rhetoric of exuberant readiness and expectation, a language attuned to the possibilities of both futural hope and present danger. And what he values most in the present is its commitment to the future—and to the possibility of an/other beginning for thinking. Part of my strategy in this chapter will be to think through Heidegger's commitment to "the other beginning" in the context of his so-called "political" speeches of 1933–34 by considering their essential connection to Heidegger's hopes for a National Socialist revolution and for university reform. I will put forth the argument that these speeches—especially the Rectorial Address—are intimately linked to Heidegger's philosophical program for revolution within the university and, by extension, to German national life as a whole. In this sense, I want to make a strong case for the inseparable connection between Heidegger's "philosophy" and his "politics."

Against those, such as Richard Rorty, who argue for a split between Heidegger's texts and Heidegger's actions, I will hold that Heidegger's texts present themselves as a call for action and that Heidegger's own actions are rooted in the philosophical commitments expressed in these texts. In this sense, to speak of Heidegger and the political is not to entertain two themes that have been set apart; rather, it is to begin questioning the essential significance of this "and" and all that it entails. But my task here will not be directed at a critique of Heidegger's personal actions.[18] Rather, my questions will be focused back at the texts themselves and at their powerfully seductive narrative about "first" and "other" beginnings, a narrative structure that has not ceased to hold continental philosophers in its thrall but has helped determine the way we have come to think about the whole history of Western philosophy beginning with the Greeks and ending with Nietzsche.

The decisive influence on Heidegger's philosophical narrative about the history of the West was, of course, Nietzsche. Nine out of 102 volumes of the *Gesamtausgabe* deal explicitly with Nietzsche's thought,[19] and concern mainly Heidegger's lecture courses after 1935. At first glance they confirm Heidegger's own claim that in the years after he left the rector-

18. For Heidegger's prevaricating style, see Thomas Sheehan, "Everyone Has to Tell the Truth: Heidegger and the Jews," *Continuum* 1 (1990): 30–44.

19. In the Klostermann prospectus of Heidegger's *Gesamtausgabe* from March 2000, extending to 102 volumes, are included: GA 6.1 and 6.2 *Nietzsche* I and II; GA 43 *Nietzsche: Der Wille zur Macht als Kunst* (WS 1936/37); GA 44 *Nietzsches metaphysische Grundstellung im abendländischen Denken: Die ewige Wiederkehr* (SS 1937); GA 46 *Nietzsches II. Unzeitgemässe Betrachtung* (WS 1938/39); GA 47 *Nietzsches Lehre vom Willen zur Macht als Erkenntnis* (SS 1939); GA 48 *Nietzsche: Der europäische Nihilismus* (II. Trimester 1940); GA 50 *Nietzsches Metaphysik* (WS 1941/42); GA 87 *Seminare: Nietzsche*. Henceforth in the notes, winter semester will be designated WS, and summer semester will be designated SS.

ship and lost faith in the movement, they constituted a genuine confrontation (*Auseinandersetzung*) with National Socialism that was marked by "spiritual resistance" (*geistiger Widerstand*).[20] I intend to look at Heidegger's reception of Nietzsche with a more critical eye, focusing attention on the works that define Heidegger's revolutionary moment of political decision making, especially the Rectorial Address. By so doing, I want to show how Heidegger's way of reading Nietzsche was decisive for his political commitment to National Socialism.

But here the congeries of influences must be carefully traced. Nietzsche's name became almost synonymous with National Socialism in the revolutionary mood of 1933. One can trace this influence in the work of the newly elected rectors, Hans Heyse at Königsberg and Ernst Krieck at Frankfurt, and in the thought of the newly appointed chair at Berlin, Alfred Baeumler. Baeumler and Krieck were "philosophical radicals" (as Hans Sluga has termed them) who set out to colonize the university for the coming revolution of the German *Volk*.[21] Unlike their conservative colleagues within the German university who sought to recover the great tradition of German idealism (Kant, Fichte, Hegel, and Schelling) for the new political order, these philosophical radicals sought renewal and revolution by appropriating the work of Nietzsche for the new beginning that awaited the German nation. Like Nietzsche, they viewed the present age as one of profound and fateful crisis, a "crisis of nihilism" afflicting the West at its foundations. The coming era would, they believed, decide the very future of Western humanity. The stakes were not small.

Just two and a half weeks preceding Heidegger's Rectorial Address, Baeumler seized on the theme of revolution, telling his students: "the political revolution (in the narrow sense) is almost complete, but the spiritual [*geistige*] and social revolution is only beginning."[22] For the completion of the social revolution, Baeumler singled out the farmers and the workers; but the spiritual revolution, he insisted, could only be carried out by German youth at the university. Turning to Bachofen's theory of the symbol as the mythic talisman for revolutionary change, Baeumler intimated that the genuine primacy of myth lay in its power to retrieve the past for a revolutionary future. This did not signify, however, that all epochs of the past were of equal stature; on the contrary, "between epochs there occurs a battle [*Kampf*]," Baeumler went on to say, "and the great phases of the intellectual battles coincide with the great phases of political revolutions. I consider it as one of my tasks to describe as rigor-

20. Martin Heidegger, "Documents from the Denazification Proceedings," *Graduate Faculty Philosophy Journal* 14, no. 2 and 15, no. 1 (1991): 540–541.
21. Hans Sluga, *Heidegger's Crisis* (Cambridge: Harvard University Press, 1993).
22. Alfred Baeumler, *Männerbund und Wissenschaft* (Berlin: Junker & Dünnhaupt, 1943), 123.

ously as possible this profound connection between philosophy and politics, which is difficult to recognize. This task does not consist of justifying the politics of the day but in recognizing the political condition in which we live by virtue of the power [*Macht*] of fate [*Schicksal*]."[23] The very lexicon of revolutionary change that Baeumler drew upon was Nietzschean to the core. His reliance upon metaphors of battle, power, fate, and revolution indicated a new determination to forge a university on the anvil of will to power and not on the tired and worn out clichés of humanistic *Bildung* that defined the older Humboldt University of Berlin.

Baeumler maintained that "the idealist-humanist philosophy of *Bildung*" was focused too one-sidedly on the bourgeois model of a discrete, autonomous individual retreating into the isolation of aesthetic and spiritual fantasy. What genuine education demanded, against this hollow academic ideal, was a political form of pedagogy that involved students in the active life of the community or *Gemeinschaft*.[24] The model for such an education, Baeumler insisted, could only be found in the Greeks—but not in the "beautiful ideal" of Winckelmann, Schiller, or Humboldt. Baeumler turned instead to the political pedagogy of Plato, author of *Der Staat* (*The Republic*), as the model for National Socialist educational philosophy.[25] By following the outlines of Plato's *Staat*, the new German *Gemeinschaft* could begin to live "a life in the state, a political life" which would bring them "close [*nahe*] to the Greeks."[26]

But Baeumler was not alone in his enthusiastic call for Graeco-Germanic communion. Ernst Krieck also endorsed Baeumler's critique of the "aesthetic-moral humanity of Humboldt" for the heroic ideal of a "soldierly-political system of education."[27] For Krieck, neo-humanist education was at an end; the new "*völkisch*-political university," committed to the

23. Baeumler, *Männerbund*, 130.

24. During the late nineteenth century, many conservative and *völkisch* thinkers became captivated by the notion of an organic and corporative *Gemeinschaft* which, following the work of Ferdinand Tönnies, they opposed to the rational, mechanistic form of social organization, the *Gesellschaft*. Tönnies' distinction between a rational, bureaucratic "society" and an organic, integrated "community" was appropriated by *völkisch* thinkers committed to the values of *Blut und Boden*, but it was also taken over by the Youth Movement and the paramilitary organizations of the right. By 1936, Nazi organizations coined the term *Frontgemeinschaft* to denote an authentic community of the *Volk* grounded in the shared experience of battle at the front during the Great War. Ferdinand Tönnies, *Gemeinschaft und Gesellschaft* (Berlin: Curtius, 1920); George Mosse, *Fallen Soldiers* (New York: Oxford University Press, 1990); and Fritz Ringer, *The Decline of the German Mandarins* (Cambridge: Harvard University Press, 1969).

25. For a consideration of NS pedagogy, see Ernst Hojer, *Nationalismus und Pädagogik: Umfeld und Entwicklung der Pädagogik Ernst Kriecks* (Würzburg: Königshausen & Neumann, 1997); and George F. Kneller, *The Educational Philosophy of National Socialism* (New Haven: Yale University Press, 1941).

26. Baeumler, *Männerbund*, 136–137.

27. Ernst Krieck, "Unser Verhältnis zu Griechen und Römern," *Volk im Werden* 1 (1933): 77.

idea of "*völkische-Bildung*," was to replace the old Humboldtian ideal by directing its energies to the self-formation of the German *Volk*. This was to be accomplished through the renewed appropriation of the ancient Greek ideal of public service and communal life. Instead of passively accepting the inherited structure of university learning which was divided into various unrelated, specialized disciplines without any inner unity, the new National Socialist university was to be practical and functional and dedicated to the order of public life and the totality of the *Volk*, ideals which were originally developed in the early Greek polis.[28] If Krieck was not as philosophically serious as Baeumler, he shared with him the belief in the revolutionary significance of their task to re-think the meaning of German university education in the national "hour of destiny."[29] Radical measures were required, and only a philosophy that would be radical in its critique of the sciences and their comfortable arrangement within the university could offer any genuine solution. As Krieck proclaimed to the German students on May 23, 1933, in his Rectorial Address: "a decisively new epoch in German history is beginning."[30]

Hans Heyse, the new rector at Königsberg, did not quite share the radical emphasis of his National Socialist colleagues, Krieck and Baeumler, but he did believe, like them, that Germany stood at "a fateful turning point of the ages."[31] In his Rectorial Address of November 1933, Heyse repeated the standard National Socialist litany about the crisis facing Western humanity, a crisis of nihilistic proportions that could only be addressed through a Nietzschean transvaluation of values. But before this transvaluation could occur, Heyse told the German *Volk*: "We are compelled to seek a new approach to Greek culture, to seize for ourselves a new way of grasping Greek antiquity."[32] Like Baeumler and Krieck, Heyse viewed the crisis of German philosophy as a life and death struggle with the decadent forces that lay in the recent German past—especially those which had led to the loss of the Great War and the formation of a decadent liberal democracy. Trying to forge a path of reconciliation between the radicals and conservatives in National Socialist circles, Heyse looked to the ideal of "Platonic philosophy as the prototype of all philosophy and science" to heal the breach caused by the fragmented, splintered exis-

---

28. Ernst Krieck, *Die Erneuerung der Universität* (Frankfurt: Bechhold, 1933) contains the text of Krieck's rectorial address of May 23, 1933. There Krieck claims that "in place of the humanistic university we now have the *völkisch*-political university which, through science and the education and *Bildung* of the chosen rank [*Ausleseschicht*] has its part in developing a new *völkisch*-political community of Germans," 3.

29. Ernst Krieck, "Die grosse Stunde Deutschlands," *Volk im Werden* 1 (1933): 1.

30. Krieck, *Erneuerung*, 8.

31. Hans Heyse, *Die Idee der Wissenschaft und die deutsche Universität* (Königsberg: Gräfe & Unzer, 1935), 3.

32. Hans Heyse, *Idee und Existenz* (Hamburg: Hanseatische Verlagsanstalt, 1935), 24.

tence of modern thought. The possibility for healing this breach between modern scientific knowledge (*theoria*) and the existence of the *Volk* (praxis), Heyse proclaimed, lay in the willingness of the German *Volk* to confront "the greatest crisis of our existence—the World War." In its heroic struggle to wrest "the originary values of our German form of life [from] all the maskings and theories" of modern, abstract intellectual life, the German nation had found its inner unity only through the "sacrifice and fate" brought on by the war.[33]

Juxtaposing military valor and philosophical resolve, Heyse insisted that "genuine existence is heroic-tragic existence . . . From the heroic life, from heroic-tragic existence salvation grows (*soteria*, Plato)."[34] But even as he invoked military metaphors and Platonic locutions, Heyse's formidable energies were focused on the role of the German university in securing the fundamental unity of philosophy and politics in the new German Reich, a unity that Heyse saw adumbrated in Plato's *Der Staat (The Republic)*. "What does the German university signify for the renewal and education of the German people?", Heyse asked. How might it help in the work of building a new German Reich? Before it could even address these questions and truly become "the university of the Reich," Heyse claimed, it would first have to free itself from "the technical and utilitarian aims" typical of the modern educational system in the West. Only by overcoming the "terrible danger" (*Gefahr*) that this system posed to the originary unity of philosophy and science would the new university have a chance of success.

> By appealing to the Greeks, and especially Plato, we once again make them come alive for us: science and the university are not organizations for the furthering of knowledge. The idea of philosophy and of science is the originary power [*Urmacht*] by virtue of which the human being, entrusted to the force of being, seeks to preserve itself in the order of being thereby saving [*retten*] itself from chaos . . . To constantly awaken and keep watch over this living metaphysical knowledge of the truth of existence, especially historical existence, and to infuse the professions with it so that in work, in battle, and in sacrifice we endure as a *Volk* through the ordeals of existence that are imposed upon us in each moment—that is the idea of science and the university.[35]

Heyse hoped that in his fevered appeal to the German people, framed in the Nietzschean language of danger (*Gefahr*), battle (*Kampf*), war (*Krieg*), power (*Macht*), fate (*Schicksal*), crisis (*Krise*), catastrophe (*Katastrophe*), the heroic (*das Heldische*), sacrifice (*Opfer*), and bravery (*Tapferkeit*), he might be able to transform the university from its present status as a ghetto of academic specialization to a vanguard institution in the form-

---

33. Ibid., 297.
34. Ibid., 342–343.
35. Ibid., 320.

ing of a new national identity.[36] Like his colleagues Baeumler and Krieck, Heyse believed that the path to such a transformation must begin by returning to the roots of *Wissenschaft* in Greek philosophy—especially the philosophy of Plato. Modern science was, as Heyse put it in his address, "the expression of a broken existence which, as an untrue existence, leads by necessity into catastrophe."[37] Genuine reform would involve a fundamental rethinking of *Wissenschaft* in terms of philosophy and a rethinking of philosophy in terms of the polis (*Staat*). What marked the rhetorical language of Heyse's address, however, was its reliance on Nietzsche, Plato, and the popular-*völkisch* concept of the hero and the heroic. "This phenomenon of metaphysics and philosophy . . . is in no sense self-evident but is rather tied to the fact that the Greeks (this thoroughly Nordic *Volk*) in the highest deeds of their heroic-tragic existence discovered, perhaps rediscovered, the idea of being as being and sought to carry out this discovery as their national fate [*nationales Schicksal*]. *From this same fundamental position the idea of metaphysics and philosophy is ever reborn in our history.*"[38] The situation was critical. Germany faced a genuine crisis that required a heroic renewal of its ancient ties to the Greeks. As a World War I veteran who had spent three years in a French prisoner-of-war camp, Heyse's understanding of this crisis was powerfully marked by a martial and militaristic emphasis on the heroic. In this sense his philosophical critique of the present drew heavily on his own experience in the Great War. As another war veteran, Alfred Baeumler, put it in *Männerbund und Wissenschaft*: "Because the world war directs our view back to past centuries rather than to past decades, it grants us a powerful meaning—hence we call it 'the Great War.' It once again gives us standards, standards which appeared to be lost but which now stretch out beyond the present and vouchsafe to us alone an identification with a greater and freer future. The Great War leads us back to the sources of our history."[39]

Baeumler's ideal of a *Männerbund* (an "alliance of men"), modeled on the hardness and severity of the manly-soldierly experience of the Great War, provided him with the archetype for organizing German students in the new "university of the Reich." This new student *Bund* would combine the best elements of Plato's erotic male bonding in the *Symposium* with the German Youth Movement's ties to the *Volk* and to the charismatic leader or *Führer*. The new university would combine these youthful, manly, and soldierly values by putting an end to the private, interiorized, bourgeois

---

36. There are numerous references to *Gefahr, Kampf, Krieg, Macht, Schicksal, Krise, Katastrophe, Helden, Opfer*, and *Tapferkeit* throughout Nietzsche's work. For a sampling, see KSA 4: 53–54; 58–60; 144–147; 375–378; KSA 6: 365–374.

37. Heyse, *Idee der Wissenschaft*, 9.

38. Heyse, *Idee und Existenz*, 342.

39. Baeumler, *Männerbund*, 27–28.

principles of the Humboldt university and affirm in their stead a *Bund* of students committed to *Wissenschaft*. But this new "German" form of *Wissenschaft* had to be fought for and won anew in a political *Kampf* against the alexandrine forms of mere academic learning. "The university of the future," Baeumler maintained, "will be political because it is grounded in the character of *Wissenschaft* which is in itself political insofar as it always sets itself against other intellectual forces."[40] And, Baeumler claimed, the roots of this German *Wissenschaft* go back to the ancient Greeks: "science, as we know it, is a creation of the independent Germanic temper. With his sureness of instinct, Nietzsche discovered anew the valiant Nordic spirit of pre-Socratic philosophy." But the independence of this Greek spirit, renewed by the seventeenth century, "soon fell into a slumber through the *securitas* of positivism which banned and suppressed the heroic spirit of *certitudo* wherever it stirred. This is the meaning of Nietzsche's fate."[41] The new university student would be a kind of heroic philosopher-soldier who, in committing himself to the *Bund* of other soldiers of *Wissenschaft*, would heed the words of Nietzsche: "But, by my love and hope I entreat you: do not reject the hero in your soul! Keep holy your highest hope!—Thus spoke *Zarathustra*" (Z: 71/KSA 4:54).

III. THE COMMITMENT TO HARDNESS AND SEVERITY

Heidegger was not immune to the ideological forces at work within German culture. Although he painstakingly denied the effect of *Weltanschauung* and the quotidian on his writings, pointing instead to ancient Greek *philosophia* as the originary source for the "fundamental attunement" of his thinking, from the vantage point of our own time we can nonetheless see how powerfully he was influenced by the mythic symbols and rhetoric of his own day (FCM: 11–23; 59–60/GA 29–30: 15–35; 89–90). Part of that influence can be traced to the popular cult of the heroic that fused themes from Nietzsche's *Thus Spoke Zarathustra* with images from the martial and military rhetoric of patriotic, *völkisch* nationalism. These popular themes—and their corresponding rhetorical expressions—can be found in the political speeches that Heidegger delivered in 1933–34 and in his Rectorial Address. But the extent of their influence on Heidegger's writing was not limited to these epideictic orations. They also affected the genuinely philosophical character of Heidegger's writing during the 1930s and hence they merit closer examination. What a more sustained reading of these texts promises is a way to connect the whole constellation of *völkisch*, heroic, martial, *bündisch*, and mythic concepts embedded in

40. Ibid., 145.
41. Ibid., 144.

Heidegger's political oratory with his philosophical critique of Western history and destiny. Like his fellow National Socialists Heyse and Baeumler, Heidegger wanted to provide a philosophical framework for German destiny configured in the language of the hero and the fatherland. But his philosophical style had been apolitical, until 1933—or so the legend maintains.[42] Nonetheless, Heidegger's turn to National Socialism in the spring of 1933 should not have been surprising to those who knew how to read his earlier philosophical texts—especially his inaugural lecture at Freiburg in summer 1929, "What is Metaphysics?" and the decisive essay, "On the Essence of Truth," which he delivered at least three times in 1930.

In these two texts, which traditionally have been read as initiating a new turn or *Kehre* within Heidegger's work—away from the subject-focused anthropocentrism of *Being and Time* toward an inaugural unfolding of truth as *aletheia* and *Gelassenheit*—Heidegger provided hints of his future political allegiances for those who had ears to hear.[43] Both texts were

42. Before the publication of Victor Farias's *Heidegger and Nazism*, trans. G. Ricci (Philadelphia: Temple University Press, 1989), which located a Nazi strain in Heidegger's first publications from 1910 on Abraham a Sancta Clara, few commentators challenged the self-styled account put forth by Heidegger of his apolitical stance before 1933. Even those who knew him well, such as Karl Löwith, Herbert Marcuse, and Karl Jaspers, were genuinely surprised by his so-called "turn" to the political. Löwith writes in his memoir, *My Life in Germany Before and After 1933*, trans. Elizabeth King (Urbana: University of Illinois Press, 1994), 34: "Heidegger's students were surprised by his decision [in 1933]. He had previously almost never expressed his opinion about political issues, and it did not seem that he had a firm opinion concerning them." More recently, Julian Young in his *Heidegger, Philosophy, Nazism* (Cambridge: Cambridge University Press, 1997), 5, argues "that neither the early philosophy of *Being and Time*, nor the later, post-war philosophy, nor even the philosophy of the mid-1930s . . . stand in any essential connection to Nazism."

43. Heidegger writes to Elisabeth Blochmann in September of 1929, "with my 'Metaphysics' lecture in winter I hope to achieve a wholly new beginning" (HBB: 33). After his lecture course on *The Fundamental Concepts of Metaphysics* (WS 1929/30), which coincided with the period of global economic crisis and uncertainty, Heidegger began thinking of the possibility of a "new" or "other" beginning. At the same time, he also began to read Nietzsche with new eyes and, in conjunction with his readings of Hölderlin and the Pre-Socratics, began a new kind of political engagement. For the details of his shift, see Otto Pöggeler's "Besinnung oder Ausflucht? Heideggers ursprünglicheres Denken," in *Zerstörung des moralischen Selbstbewusstsein: Chance oder Gefährdung?* (Frankfurt: Suhrkamp, 1988), 251–255; *Neue Wege mit Heidegger* (Frieburg: Alber, 1992), 32–35; and "Heideggers politisches Selbstverständnis" in *Heidegger und die praktische Philosophie*, ed. Annemarie Gethmann-Siefert and Otto Pöggeler (Frankfurt: Suhrkamp, 1988), 22–25. After the "Essence of Truth" lecture of 1930 (which has never been published in its original form), Heidegger becomes convinced of the necessity to retrieve the originary Greek experience of truth as *aletheia*. Even though he is aware that this task of retrieval will be difficult, in 1931 he sees that his is an age of genuine revolutionary possibility (HBB: 46; HJB: 144). In his Plato lectures of WS 1931/32, Heidegger sees the potential of philosophy for initiating this revolution but he thinks that it remains a distant possibility. At this time he is still waiting for the right moment, the moment which comes in the *Machtergreifung* of early 1933. Suddenly, the *Augenblick* comes alive for Heidegger in all its revolutionary force. As he writes to Jaspers in April of 1933: "as dark and as questionable as so many things are, still I sense ever more that we are entering into a new reality and that an epoch has become old" (HJB: 152).

a response to the crisis of Western history that Heidegger read in the signs of his own age: the world-wide economic depression that began in 1929, the collapse of the liberal democratic coalition in Weimar, the loss of European confidence in its own mission within the world. Against this background Heidegger began to read Nietzsche with a new fervor and, in combination with his reading of Ernst Jünger's "Total Mobilization" (1930) and W. F. Otto's *The Gods of Greece* (1929), he began to understand the deeply metaphysical implications hidden in the present crisis of his age.[44] This encounter with Nietzsche in 1929 was decisive for Heidegger, providing him with a framework for understanding the revolutionary forces of change being unleashed around him. Heidegger himself admitted as much in his reflections on the rectorate from 1945:

> In 1930 Ernst Jünger's essay "Total Mobilization" appeared; this essay announced the fundamental themes of Jünger's 1932 book, *The Worker.* I discussed these writings in a small circle at the time with my assistant [Werner] Brock and tried to show how they expressed an essential understanding of Nietzsche's metaphysics—insofar as it both sees and foresees the history of the West and the present. From these writings and, more essentially, from their foundations, we thought about what was coming [*das Kommende*], i.e. we attempted at the same time to encounter it in terms of a confrontation or 'a setting asunder' [*Auseinandersetzung*]. (SdU: 24)

Nietzsche's metaphysical understanding of "what was coming" would, for Heidegger, be inexorably grounded in the history of the West and its rootless relation to the past.

On the basis of this new encounter with Nietzsche and with the dominant Nietzscheanism of his generation, Heidegger began to understand that the animating force in Western destiny was nihilism. If Nietzsche understood the history of metaphysics as a narrative tale about "How the 'Real World' at Last Became a Myth" (TI: 50/KSA 6:80), culminating in the realization about the death of God, then he based his schema on an idiosyncratic reading of Plato as the inaugurator of Western metaphysics. Heidegger embraced Nietzsche's history of the West and its corresponding critique of Platonic values which, in their post-Christian, enlightened form, resulted in the vulgarization of modern life in its various political and cultural forms as liberal democracy, mass consciousness, technical progress, and the rootlessness of urban life. But where Nietzsche oriented his critique on the Platonic transvaluation of ancient values and their later Christianization, Heidegger structured his philosophical his-

---

44. Otto Pöggeler's essay, "Heidegger, Nietzsche, and Politics," in *The Heidegger Case*, ed. Tom Rockmore and Joseph Margolis (Philadelphia: Temple University Press, 1992), 128–139, offers real insight into the deep effect Nietzsche had upon Heidegger during these crucial years between 1929 and 1933.

tory of the West in terms of the epochal shifts in the essence of truth and the way Plato altered the Pre-Socratic understanding of *aletheia*. Still, what mattered most to Heidegger was "das Kommende," and during the gloomy winter months of 1929–1930 in his lecture course *The Fundamental Concepts of Metaphysics,* he reflected on the crisis afflicting "contemporary *Dasein*":

> We ask: Is *our* Dasein attuned through and through by such *emptiness as a whole?*. . . . Are we affected by a need, does any such need concern us? More than one, we will retort: everywhere there are disruptions, crises, catastrophes, needs: the contemporary social misery, political confusion, the powerlessness of science, the erosion of art, the rootlessness [*Bodenlosigkeit*] of philosophy, the impotence of religion. Certainly, there are needs everywhere . . . [yet] the need in question is not the fact that this or that need oppresses in such and such a way. Rather what oppresses us most profoundly is the very *absence of any essential oppressiveness in our Dasein as a whole.* The absence of an essential oppressiveness in *Dasein* is the *emptiness as a whole,* so that no one stands with anyone else and no community [*Gemeinschaft*] stands with any other in the rooted [*wurzelhaften*] unity of essential action. Each and every one of us are servants of slogans, adherents to a program, but none is the custodian of the inner greatness of *Dasein* and its necessities. (FCM: 162–163/GA 29–30: 243–244)

Within the contemporary situation of the collapsing Weimar Republic and the threatening conditions of economic depression, Heidegger begins to slowly understand the political-metaphysical causes of nihilism in the "rootlessness" of the modern world, a rootlessness that he sees spawned in the nihilistic effects of the First World War. Now armed with Jünger's insight into "the universal rule of the will to power within planetary history," Heidegger begins to see in Nietzsche's proposition about the death of God a guiding thread for understanding the nihilism of the modern technological worldview. "If things had been different," Heidegger asks, "would the First World War have been possible?" (RFT: 18/SdU: 25). In the total mobilization of the world war, Heidegger believed that forces had been unleashed which had shaken the comfortable, secure, and self-congratulatory style of bourgeois life and marked it with "the fundamental attunement. . . . of profound boredom" (FCM: 160/GA 29–30: 239). What oppresses *Dasein, pace* Heidegger in the winter semester of 1929/30, is the "essential oppressiveness" of lacking anything essentially oppressive such that *Dasein* is without any connective ties, without community (*Gemeinschaft*), and hence without a fate. Within the rhetorical language of catastrophe, need, danger, and upheaval, Heidegger provides a sketch of the modern city-dweller who stands rudderless in the storm of crisis, in need of a shared destiny and a bond to both the land and the community. This modern individual, ensnared by the fashionable and the modish, has let "essential" thinking "degenerate into a kind of free-floating specula-

tion that turns entirely upon itself"—a condition that is entirely in keeping with the tenor of its rootless bourgeois existence (FCM: 174/GA
29–30: 258). But Heidegger is not concerned with proffering sociological
analysis or cultural criticism. At issue, he tells his listeners, "is *the liberation
of the* Dasein *in man*. At the same time this liberation is the task laid upon
us to assume once more our very *Dasein* as an actual *burden*."
Nonetheless, Heidegger warns his audience:

> *Dasein* is not something one takes for a drive in the car as it were, but something
> that man must specifically take upon himself. Yet because we are of the opin-
> ion that we no longer need to be strong or to expect to throw ourselves open to
> danger, all of us together have also already slipped out of the danger-zone of
> *Dasein* within which, in taking our *Dasein* upon ourselves, we may perhaps over-
> reach ourselves. That any oppressiveness as a whole is absent today is perhaps
> most pointedly manifest in the fact that today presumably no one overreaches
> themselves in their *Dasein,* but that we at most manage to complain about the
> misery of life. Man must first resolutely open himself [*entschliessen*] again to
> this demand. The necessity of this disclosive resolution [*Entschlusses*] is what is
> contained in the telling refusal and simultaneous telling announcement of the
> moment of vision [*Augenblick*] of our *Dasein.* (FCM: 165/GA 29–30: 246–247)

In writing about the oppressiveness and boredom of contemporary *Dasein* in 1929, Heidegger begins to deploy a new Nietzschean lexicon of
"strength," "burden," "danger," "refusal," "power," "courage," "hardness,"
and "severity" that would reverberate throughout his later political
speeches of 1933–34. The target of his deployment was "the universal
smug contentment in not being endangered" (FCM: 164/GA 29–30: 245)
that Jünger, in *The Worker,* termed "the Utopia of bourgeois security."[45]
But Heidegger seizes upon a more fundamental Nietzschean term in the
winter semester of 1929/30 that would offer a kind of transition between
his early Pauline commitment to originary Christian wakefulness and his
later National Socialist commitment to the militant self-assertion of the
German Volk. Here, in laying out the essential structure of fundamental
attunement, Heidegger annexes Nietzsche's term "*der Augenblick*" to signal
"the moment of vision" that crystallizes in a decisive resoluteness
(*Entschlossenheit*). It is this Nietzschean moment of visionary resolve that
will mark the turn in Heidegger's appropriation of a militant-heroic rhetoric aimed at battling "the contemporary urban man and ape of civilization" who had forgotten "the homesickness" (*Heimweh*) that characterizes
all genuine philosophizing (FCM: 5/GA 29–30: 7). Throughout these crucial lectures, we can locate a Zarathustran contempt for "the contemporary man in the street and philistine," "the animal, buffoon of civilization,
guardian of culture, and yes, even personality" who wants to make life eas-

---

45. Ernst Jünger, *Der Arbeiter: Herrschaft und Gestalt* (Stuttgart: Klett, 1982), 266.

ier and more secure and who has given in to a "complacent yearning for comfortable answers" (FCM: 172, 6/GA 29–30: 255, 9; NH: 151). Heidegger was serious about ushering in a revolutionary consciousness attuned to the "danger" and "mystery" of life. He thought of himself in 1929 as a kind of herald of the dangerous life in which attention was drawn away from the satiety of answers and toward the awakening of questions. The call was announced in the winter semester:

> We must first call for someone capable of instilling terror into our *Dasein* again. For how do things stand with our *Dasein* when an event like the Great War can to all extents and purposes pass us by without leaving a trace? Is this not perhaps a sign that no event, however momentous it may be, is capable of assuming this task if man has not prepared himself for awakening [*wach zu werden*] in the first place? The fundamental attunement of a profound boredom once awakened *can* manifest to us [*offenbar machen*] the absence of such oppressiveness [*Bedrängnis*] and this moment of vision [*Augenblick*] at the same time. (FCM: 172/GA 29–30: 255–256)

Originally, Heidegger occupied himself with the themes of wakefulness (*Wachsamkeit*), revelation (*Offenbarung*), oppressiveness (*Bedrängnis*), and the moment of vision (*Augenblick*) in his 1920/21 course, "Introduction to the Phenomenology of Religion," dealing with Paul's *Letters to the Thessalonians*. There Heidegger linked these themes to the originary Christian expectation of the *parousia,* or "the Coming of the Lord," which comes toward one [*Zu-kunft*] and manifests itself only to those who are wakeful and vigilant for the *kairos* or salvific "moment of vision." In *The Fundamental Concepts of Metaphysics*, Heidegger will refashion these primal Christian themes within a new Nietzschean context to respond to the contemporary crisis of nihilism afflicting and oppressing Weimar *Dasein*. Like the Pauline soldier of faith armed with the breastplate (*Panzer*) of love and the helmet (*Helm*) of hope (I Thess. 5:8—in Luther's translation), Heidegger admonished his listeners to do battle (*Kampf*) with the forces of ease and comfort and to prepare for what is coming: the *parousia* as "the other beginning." Here, Pauline *thlipsis* will be translated into the oppressiveness (*Bedrängnis*) of *Dasein*'s lack of oppressiveness, a condition of soporific boredom which renders *Dasein* passive and inert. Against this "absence of oppressiveness," Heidegger seeks to awaken his contemporaries to a new revelation, an *Offenbarung* that could only be a leap (*Sprung*) back to the origin (*Ursprung*), an originary leap from the first beginning. In this leap that dislodges *Dasein* from its safe moorings in the everyday world of "the age of civilization," Heidegger finds the key to the moment of vision. This possibility for finding "the essential" lies in reclaiming the legacy of "hardness" and "severity" (*Härte* and *Schwere*) from the Great War.[46]

Heidegger was always possessed by a strange fascination for the martial and the heroic. Although he claimed to have had combat experience "at the Front," in reality he served as a weatherman in the meteorological service helping to prepare poison gas attacks by aligning them with favorable weather conditions. Details concerning his service record were scarce and though he was asked several times to provide details of his war record to claim a pension, his reply was not forthcoming.[47] And yet Heidegger continued to draw on the language of the "*Fronterlebnis*" (or experience at the front) that marked German intellectual life during the 1920s and '30s. His models for the life of "new courage" and "the hard breed" (*hartes Geschlecht*) that embraces "danger," "uncertainty," and "the necessity of attack" (*Einsatz*) were Jünger and Nietzsche [HCW: 45/NH: 75]. Throughout the post-war years right on through the political speeches of 1933–34, Heidegger constantly drew on this Nietzschean lexicon and on the descriptions of battle from Jünger's war diaries. Now, after the crisis of 1929, the *Kampf*-rhetoric of Pauline Christianity will harden, tempered by what Jünger termed "the reckless spirit of the warrior, whose iron will discharges in clenched, well-aimed, bursts of energy."[48] In the embers of the war's nihilism, Jünger finds a heroic will that "does not waver from the danger for an instant" but steels itself with the power of Nietzschean resolve. What war promises, Jünger claims, is only more violence, more conflict, and the certainty of death. But it also occasions an opportunity for greatness, since it confronts the human being with its hardest task: "mastering oneself in death." Heidegger will take up this theme of Jünger's in 1933 in his speech commemorating the death of Albert Leo Schlageter, but one can notice the same influence in the lectures of *The Fundamental Concepts of Metaphysics* which discuss fear, need, oppressiveness, severity, hardness, sacrifice, strength, and "inner greatness." These same themes also form the background of Heidegger's inaugural lecture "What is Metaphysics?" which characterizes *Dasein* as "the being held out into the nothing" (BW: 108/WM: 15).[49]

---

46. See GA 16: 107, 113, 184, 191–192, 238–239, 300, 759–760, 762, 773; GA 29–30: 245; GA 39: 221, for some references to *Härte* and *Schwere*. Winfried Franzen's "Die Sehnsucht nach Härte und Schwere: Über ein zum NS-Engagement disponierendes Motiv in Heideggers Vorlesung 'Die Grundbegriffe der Metaphysik' von 1929/30" in *Heidegger und die praktische Philosophie*, 78–92, offers a penetrating analysis of Heidegger's use of martial rhetoric and its political significance.

47. Rüdiger Safranski, *Ein Meister aus Deutschland: Heidegger und seine Zeit* (Munich: Hanser, 1994), 109; Hugo Ott, *Martin Heidegger: Unterwegs zu seiner Biographie* (Frankfurt: Campus, 1988), 150.

48. Ernst Jünger, *Der Kampf als inneres Erlebnis* (Berlin: Mittler, 1922), 74.

49. In his "What Is Metaphysics?" lecture of 1929, Heidegger employs the rhetoric of *Härte*, WM: 14.

In both of these texts, Heidegger will seize upon the martial rhetoric of hardness and severity to fight against what he perceives as the destructive forces of the modern world: the rootlessness (*Bodenlosigkeit*) of urban life and its loss of an essential connection to the earth, the soil, the ground (*Boden*), and the homeland (*Heimat*). Anyone who reads the lectures from the *Gesamtausgabe* will find numerous references attacking the "literati" and café intellectuals associated with the literary-artistic culture of Berlin and Munich (FCM: 175/GA 29–30: 259; GA 34: 209). But Heidegger's assault is not only directed at the cultural elite of the bourgeoisie; his genuine concern focuses on the "*Bodenlosigkeit* of philosophy" (FCM: 163/GA 29–30: 244) that has lost its fundamental connection to the originary meaning of *philosophia* as practiced by the early Greeks. In its contemporary setting, he claims, philosophy has become merely another technical discipline taught at the university, a discipline unaware of its original relation to the other disciplines and to its own proper essence. The inaugural lecture addressed this crisis of the sciences "whose rootedness (*Verwurzelung*) in their essential ground has atrophied" (BW: 96/WM: 2).

But this concern was only preliminary. What genuinely preoccupied Heidegger in this crucial period between 1929–33 was the more fundamental, originary question of the understanding of truth and its essence that had been covered over by the nihilistic incursions of Western metaphysics since Plato. The death of God, which came to symbolize for Heidegger the very rootlessness of modernity, was only the most recent appearance in a long history of nihilistic thinking. What contemporary philosophy required was another kind of Platonic *periagoge* (*Republic*: 521c5): a "*Herum- und Herausführen*," a turning-around of the essence of human being, a "leading" of the soul out of the shrouded night into the daylight of truth (GA 34: 113).

IV. "ON THE ESSENCE OF TRUTH" AND SUBTERRANEAN PHILOSOPHY

Between the fall of 1929 and the spring of 1933, Heidegger kept pressing his call for re-thinking the question of truth in terms of an "experience" rather than as a propositional expression of language or logic. What was required was "a *genuine* return into history" which, Heidegger claimed, would provide "*the* distance from the present that first creates the space necessary for the attempt to leap out of our own present." In good Nietzschean fashion, he declares that "the present is something that should be overcome," although he maintains that this could only be done by a genuine return into history. If this return were enacted in the proper way, Heidegger maintains, it has the potential to become "the decisive beginning for genuine futurity" (GA 34: 9–10). His 1930 lecture, "On the

Essence of Truth," delivered in various contexts in the early 1930s and re-formulated in two lecture courses under the same title in the winter se-mesters of 1931/32 (GA 34) and 1933/34 (GA 36/37) is offered as the cry of one in the wilderness. In these transitional years between the crisis of 1929 and the NS rise to power in 1933, Heidegger works to lay the ground-work for what he hopes will be a radical awakening of philosophy's power. He does not think that the time for revolution has yet come, although he deems it crucial to maintain "an essential view for what is possible" (GA 34: 64; WM: 74). He sees himself as a philosopher of transition, in a time of transition, heroically confronting the danger and uncertainty of a ni-hilistic age. Like the prisoner freed from the cave in Plato's *Republic,* Hei-degger sees the situation of the philosopher in terms of radical danger.

If Plato's prisoner was threatened by physical death, Heidegger's philoso-pher confronts the inevitable prospect of "becoming powerless and being destroyed in one's own being"—not by actual violence but by "the slowly creeping more poisonous toxin" of popular interest and the fame one re-ceives from publishing journal articles (GA 34: 84). "Genuine philosophiz-ing is powerless," Heidegger claims, "within the realm of reigning truisms. Only insofar as this state of affairs changes (*wandelt*) can philosophy be well received." Hence, Heidegger turns his energies to the work of preparation: of making the way straight for the coming of a great historical *Augenblick,* a future *parousia* when philosophy will have a more essential connection to the world. But in the interim, as he confronts the ceaseless prattle within the world of the cave, the philosopher must be prepared for the decisive mo-ment, ready to liberate the prisoners from the tyranny of prevailing opin-ion. This liberation will not be carried out through persuasion, clever talk, or sociological analysis; it can only occur through a heroic "act of vio-lence"—that is how Heidegger sees the philosopher's role in Plato's alle-gory. In this vision, the philosopher is not a learned man with academic competence but a man of heroic stature, a Jüngerian warrior or a Schlageter of the spirit, who faces death in an authentic way as something fated.

Even as his hopes for this future act of violence seem unattainable, Hei-degger continues to pursue strategies for "leaping out of the present." The return to the Greeks will not simply entail "taking over what has been," he tells Elisabeth Blochmann in the Fall of 1929, but will involve "a metamorphosis" (*Verwandlung*) (HBB: 32). And yet the Zarathustran fig-ure of a metamorphosis is not merely a

> change (*Wandel*) in the essence of truth but a revolutionary transformation (*Umwälzung*) of the whole of human being at whose commencement we stand. Though only a few today are able to divine or gauge the scope and the inexorability of this transformation of humanity's being and the world, this still does not prove that this change is *not* taking place. Nor does it prove that with every hour and every day we are not moving into a wholly new his-

tory of human *Dasein*. An innermost change of this type, however, is not merely a release from all that once was; it is rather the most severe and extensive confrontation (*Auseinandersetzung*) of the forces of *Dasein* and the powers of being (*Sein*). (GA 34: 324)

If we follow the shifts in the figural language of metamorphosis, change, and transformation in the Heidegger corpus from 1929 to 1933, we find that it becomes inextricably connected to the whole discussion concerning the essence of truth. The change in the meaning of *aletheia*, which occurs in the metaphysics of Plato, becomes decisive in Heidegger's narrative. By re-framing *aletheia* as *idea* and by placing it under the isonomic demand for correctness of representation, Plato's metaphysics wrested truth from the realm of hiddenness and helped turn it into a human achievement. What was forgotten in this transformation at the very beginning of metaphysics was the powerful insight into what Parmenides termed "the untrembling heart of well-rounded unconcealment."[50] Heidegger's decisive insight in this period of transition or turning (*Kehre*) was that any call for a genuine philosophy demands a return (*Rückkehr*) to this Parmenidean understanding of *aletheia*, a word that itself sprung from an originary experience of both self and world and constituted "the ground (*Grund*) and soil (*Boden*) of human *Dasein*" (GA 34: 12). But how was this to be done? How could this momentous undertaking be carried out, especially in an age when, in Heidegger's words, "the ground (*Grund*) and soil (*Boden*) that we are looking for in our striving for truth is itself reeling"? (GA 34: 323). What is required in Heidegger's estimation is a re-thinking of the essence of truth—but not as a state of affairs that we try to approximate or as an eternal *eidos* for which we seek correspondence. Rather, Heidegger seeks to grasp truth as a movement of Heraclitean oppositions mutually implicated in the resonant interplay of harmony and conflict, concord and discord, consonance and dissonance that finds expression in the originary term "*polemos*."[51] Truth has to be grasped as a kind of *Aus-einander-setzung* or "setting-asunder" which, in exposing what is hidden to unhiddenness, allows for the coming into being of what is essential. To grasp the logic of this *Kampf* between the coming to presence and the rescinding of truth requires the hardness and severity of

50. A. H. Coxon, *The Fragments of Parmenides* (Assen, The Netherlands: Van Gorcum, 1986), 50–51; and Martin Heidegger, *On Time and Being*, trans. Joan Stambaugh (New York: Harper & Row, 1972), 67; *Zur Sache des Denkens* (Tübingen: Niemeyer, 1969), 74.

51. Later, in his Heraclitus lectures of SS 1943 and SS 1944, GA 55, Heidegger will expand on the originary significance of *polemos*, but already in his *Introduction to Metaphysics* lectures of SS 1935 and his 1936 Rome lecture, "Europa und die deutsche Philosophie," Heidegger offers a reading of Heraclitus' fragment B53 from Herman Diels, ed., *Die Fragmente der Vorsokratiker* (Berlin: Weidmann, 1922); IM: 62, 144/EM: 47, 110; EdP: 41.

that kind of martial temperament that Nietzsche termed "*meine Härte*" (GS: 51/KSA 3: 358).

In this sense, Heidegger's much-discussed "turn" (*Kehre*) needs to be understood both as a re-turn (*Rückkehr*) to the ground and root (*Boden*) of Western philosophy in Pre-Socratic *aletheia* and as a reversal (*Umkehr*) of the rootlessness (*Bodenlosigkeit*) of Western philosophy bound up with the metaphysics of modernity. Because of the history of its subsequent collocations and revisions, it is easy to forget that Heidegger originally delivered the lecture, "On the Essence of Truth," in the context of a so-called *Heimattag* put on by the province of Baden in 1930 and dedicated to the theme: "Strengthening the Homeland."[52] Given the fact that the conference marked a celebration of the recent Allied withdrawal from the Rhineland, the political context of Heidegger's remarks is unmistakable. In that original version, Heidegger made a fateful connection between the essence of truth and the necessity of what he termed "rootedness" or "autochthony" (*Bodenständigkeit*). Truth, Heidegger intimated, was something essentially grounded in "the roots of the homeland" (NH: 12). The nihilism of the modern world, where "no one stands (*steht*) with anyone else and no community (*Gemeinschaft*) stands with any other in the rooted (*wurzelhaften*) unity of essential (*wesentlichen*) action," could ultimately be traced back to its condition of rootlessness (FCM: 163/GA 29–30: 244). But the origin of this rootlessness was not merely the nihilism brought on by the war or by the social and economic conditions that grew out of Weimar and the world-wide depression.[53] The genuine origin lay elsewhere. Writers like Oswald Spengler and Jünger had pointed to some of the problems, but their contributions were merely fragmentary. The more fundamental sources for understanding the rootlessness of the modern world, Heidegger believed, lay in Nietzsche and the Pre-Socratics.

What the "Essence of Truth" lectures initiated for Heidegger, following

52. While the text of the original 1930 lecture, "Vom Wesen der Wahrheit," has never been published, a report of its contents can be found in NH: 10–12 (the original text is in the possession of the Herbert Marcuse Archive of the Stadt- und Universitätsbibliothek in Frankfurt am Main; I would like to thank Dr. Bernhard Tönnies for providing me with a copy). The later editions have elided the discourse about *Bodenständigkeit, Heimat,* and other *völkisch* themes; see Martin Heidegger, *Vom Wesen der Wahrheit,* 8th ed. (Frankfurt: Klostermann, 1997).

53. Heidegger sometimes employs the term "Wurzellosigkeit" (NH: 12, 200 and GA 16:300) and other times "Bodenlosigkeit" (FCM: 163/GA 29/30: 243–244; NH: 149; GA 16: 53; BW: 117/WM: 73) to designate the condition of rootlessness or groundlessness within Western metaphysics. In the "Origin of the Work of Art" essay (1935), Heidegger claims that in the translation of Greek *hypokeimenon* into Latin as *subjectum,* the original Greek experience of being is concealed: "Roman thought takes over the Greek words without a corresponding, equally original experience of what they say, without the Greek work. The rootlessness of Western thought begins with this translation" (BW: 154/H: 13).

Nietzsche's Dionysian retrieval of antiquity, was a triple movement: *backwards* to the first beginning in Pre-Socratic *aletheia, downwards* to the hidden sources of truth rooted in the ground and soil of the *Heimat,* and *forwards* to the futural, "other" beginning and "the revolutionary upheaval of the being of humanity" (GA 34: 324). All of these movements could only be carried out through an essential confrontation with the reigning understanding of truth. In this fundamental sense, each was a response to the rootlessness of Western thinking that began with the Platonic transformation of the essence of truth. What was needed was an *Auseinandersetzung* with the whole Western tradition—understood both as a Heraclitean *polemos* for returning to the roots of Western philosophy *and* as a *Kampf* against the rootlessness of modernity and its "free-floating speculation" (FCM: 174/GA 29–30: 258). But what did Heidegger mean by the term "rootedness" (*Bodenständigkeit*) and how was it connected to his analysis of the essence of truth?

Heidegger did not coin this term; it had been used in standard literary contexts since the nineteenth century and was even included in the Grimms' dictionary.[54] The term *"Bodenständigkeit"* evoked a *völkisch* concern for what I will call "the steadiness or steadfastness that comes from being rooted." It can refer to a rootedness in the soil or earth but it can also denote a rootedness in tradition or in a community; these meanings were closely related in the *völkisch* literature that Heidegger read, such as Adalbert Stifter's novel, *Indian Summer,* or the stories of Johann Peter Hebel.[55] As a cultural shibboleth in the years before the Great War, *Bodenständigkeit* became part of the German Youth Movement's lexicon of "authenticity," a language that rejected the rootless, urban, and cosmopolitan style of their parents' bourgeois existence for a more rooted connection to the natural landscape.[56] The *Wandervögel,* or "roamers," as they were called, set off on excursions into the German countryside where they hiked, sang songs, communed with nature, and formed their own unique

54. In the Grimms' *Deutsches Wörterbuch* (Leipzig: Hirzel, 1800), 2: 217, there is an entry under "bodenständig." In Wolfgang Pfeifer, *Etymologisches Wörterbuch des Deutschen* (Berlin: Akademie, 1989), 195, there is an entry for a nineteenth-century definition of "bodenständig" as "fest in der Heimat verwurzelt" (firmly rooted in the homeland).

55. Heidegger was attached to the works of Stifter, especially his novel *Der Nachsommer* which he gave to Elisabeth Blochmann as a present in remembrance of their "Indian Summer" of 1931 (HBB: 45, 49). He made a point of telling Elisabeth that this was also a favorite of Nietzsche's and went so far as to recommend an article from *Ariadne: Jahrbuch der Nietzschegesellschaft* (1925): 7–26, by Ernst Bertram (HBB: 146). For Heidegger on Hebel, see GA 13: 150.

56. For a helpful discussion of the Youth Movement, authenticity, and the theme of rootedness (especially its relation to the paramilitary rhetoric of the postwar era), see George Mosse, *Fallen Soldiers: Reshaping the Memory of the World Wars* (New York: Oxford University Press, 1990), 58–69, and also by Mosse, *The Crisis of German Ideology: Intellectual Origins of the Third Reich* (New York: Grosset & Dunlap, 1964), 171–189.

Gemeinschaft modeled on the erotic spirit of Plato's *Symposium*. In his early years in Freiburg, Heidegger met his wife Elfriede and her friend Elisabeth Blochmann in just such a Youth Movement circle.[57] And when he was at Marburg, Heidegger joined in with an academic student group who shared these same ideals. One can see the external traces of this *Wandervogel* style in Heidegger's mode of dress, his loden coat, knickerbocker trousers, and rural walking staff, all of which aimed at what Hans-Georg Gadamer termed his "rural folk style."[58] But what genuinely affected Heidegger from the Youth Movement was its unwavering devotion to the native earth as the place to build a new German *Volksgemeinschaft*. Yet, there were other sources for Heidegger's commitment to *Bodenständigkeit*.

In his memorial tribute to Paul Natorp from the fall of 1924, Heidegger praised Natorp for having understood the spirit of the Youth Movement—especially those who gathered on Meissner Mountain in 1913 to commemorate the centenary of the battle of Leipzig. One hundred years earlier, German youth had died trying to free their native Saxony from Napoleon's domination. From the vantage point of 1924, Heidegger sees this as an extraordinary sacrifice, for he is reminded of those *Meissner Wandervögel* of 1913 ("many of the best of whom fell" in the Great War), and his memorial remarks on Natorp are juxtaposed with his reflections on these fallen heroes. Natorp, as few other German professors, grasped the struggle of German youth "to form their lives from a sense of inner truthfulness and responsibility for oneself" (GA 19: 5). Like the fallen dead, Natorp understood the meaning of a German death. A few years earlier, Heidegger had read Natorp's *Deutscher Weltberuf* with great interest. There, in his wartime discussion of "the German soul," Natorp praised "the *bodenständige* heroic-national epic" of the Germans, the *Nibelungenlied*, which preserved something of "the originary force" of the Germanic tradition. Natorp's connection between the *bodenständig* and the heroic would not be lost on Heidegger. He would pursue this deadly connection both in his Greek studies and in his political speeches. Soldiering and the soil, especially when wedded to the Greeks, would yield a strange, intoxicating power that ex-*Landsturmmann* Heidegger could not resist.

But Heidegger found something else that attracted him in Natorp's *Deutscher Weltberuf*: his passion for the Greeks and his rejection of the tired formalities of academic classicism. As Natorp warned his countrymen:

> The sole danger is to ossify a level [of culture] that was at one time attained—therein lies the error of a petty classicism . . . Therefore, let the

---

57. Safranski, *Ein Meister aus Deutschland*, 90, 109, 159. This same Youth Movement style can also be detected in Heidegger's poem of 1916, "Abendgang auf der Reichenau," GA 13: 7.

58. Hans-Georg Gadamer, *Philosophical Apprenticeships*, trans. Robert Sullivan (Cambridge: MIT Press, 1985), 49.

dead bury their dead, but let what has immortal life in it remain alive and renew its vitality. That alone is genuine Renaissance: the rebirth of life with an aim to continue its vitality, not the re-excavation and artificial attempts at reviving the corpse of antiquity.[59]

Stripped of their language of *Lebensphilosophie* (and reenvisioned through the lens of Nietzsche's Pre-Socratic heroes), Natorp's sentiments reflected Heidegger's own attitude toward antiquity, an attitude that deepened as Heidegger broke even more radically from academic philosophy after 1929 and began to read extensively in classical philology.[60]

In the fall of 1932, Heidegger received an essay sent to him by Werner Jaeger entitled "Tyrtaeus on True *Arete*." Jaeger and Heidegger first came into contact through their shared interest in pedagogical reform within the university. Clearly, Heidegger and Jaeger had their differences but what drew Heidegger to the philologist was his passionate concern for effecting a German revolution on the basis of a new appropriation and radical retrieval of the ancient Greeks. Part of Jaeger's program for a "Third Humanism" involved a rejection of this standard philological model for education. In an essay written for Krieck's journal, *Volk im Werden,* entitled "The Education of the Political Man and Antiquity" (1933), Jaeger stressed that the new kind of *Bildung* would set before the German *Volk* the task of forming the individual person as a member of a political community. Committed to a *"Kampf* against historicism . . . and the positivistic mania for mere fact collecting," Jaeger rejected the traditional, unpolitical form of German classicism bred in the age of Goethe. What Jaeger admired among the Greeks was "the heroic Spartan ideal of the citizen (*Bürger*)" which—in contrast to the economic ideal of the bourgeoisie—

---

59. Paul Natorp, *Die Weltalter des Geistes,* vol. 1 of *Deutscher Weltberuf* (Jena: Eugen Diederichs, 1918), 67.

60. Heidegger's extensive reading in classical philology and philosophy had the effect of sharpening his critique of the rootlessness of Western metaphysics by directing him to chthonic, subterranean sources for his work. These sources included works such as Alfred Baeumler's introduction to the work of Johann Jakob Bachofen, *Der Mythus von Orient und Occident* (Munich: Beck, 1926); W. F. Otto's *Die Götter Griechenlands* (Bonn: Friedrich Cohen, 1929) and *Dionysos* (Frankfurt: Klostermann, 1933); Karl Reinhardt, *Parmenides und die Geschichte der griechischen Philosophie* (Bonn: Friedrich Cohen, 1916) and *Sophocles* (Frankfurt: Klostermann, 1933); Werner Jaeger's "Tyrtaios über die wahre *Arete,"* *Sitzungsberichte der Preussischen Akademie der Wissenschaften zu Berlin* (1932): 537–568, and "Gedächtnisrede auf Ulrich von Wilamowitz-Moellendorf," *Sitzungsberichte der Preussischen Akademie der Wissenschaften zu Berlin* (1932): cxxiii–cxxviii (both of which Jaeger sent to Heidegger); and Kurt Riezler's *Parmenides* (Frankfurt: Klostermann, 1934). Heidegger recommends Baeumler's work on Bachofen to Elisabeth Blochmann (HBB: 50); he also speaks positively about Reinhardt's *Sophocles* in his *Introduction to Metaphysics* lectures (IM: 107–108/EM: 82). Heidegger and Jaeger were also on cordial terms as their exchange of letters in December of 1932 shows. For a fascinating discussion of the whole background of Heidegger's relationship to Jaeger, see Frank Edler, "Heidegger and Werner Jaeger on the Eve of 1933," *Research in Phenomenology* 27 (1998): 122–149.

he held up as a model for German youth.[61] Within this context, Tyrtaeus (a Spartan poet from the seventh century B.C.E.) became a symbol for Jaeger of the kind of manly, warriorly virtues embodied in the political citizen needed in the new German situation.

Traditional scholarship had marginalized Tyrtaeus and viewed him as an epigone of the Homeric poetic style, but Jaeger offered an interpretation that found in his work a wholly new style of *arete* which corresponded to the formation of a new political type: "the soldier-citizen."[62] Whereas the earlier Homeric form of *arete* involved an aristocratic code of personal bravery, honor, and glory, Jaeger finds in Tyrtaeus' elegies "a new concept of political solidarity" and a new *ethos* of heroic self-sacrifice for the *polis*. As Tyrtaeus put it in one of his poems: "it is a noble thing for a man to fall in battle for his native land" (fragment 6). In Tyrtaeus' call to the youth of Sparta to "stand steadfast, with both feet rooted firmly on the ground," Jaeger found the Greek sources for merging the heroic ideal of the fallen soldier and the *Wandervogel* commitment to *Bodenständigkeit* that Heidegger would bring together in his own new political undertakings.

Given this context, it is not surprising that Heidegger wrote to Jaeger in December, 1932, telling him that "your treatment of the history of *arete* also seems to me to be paradigmatic for the history of *aletheia*. . . ."[63] Although some of the details of the essay must have struck Heidegger as arcane, for his purposes Jaeger's essay seemed "to enter that stratum of subterranean (*unterirdischen*) philosophizing in antiquity which has hardly been surmised until now." What Heidegger was attempting to express by his infelicitous phrase "subterranean philosophizing" was an originary, poetic style of thinking which had not yet been forced into the rigid and unyielding categories of logic, substance, and the metaphysics of presence that would dominate Western philosophy after Plato and Aristotle. Instead, it pointed to the deep, originary, and archaic sources of Pre-Socratic thinking that Heidegger hoped would provide the rootedness necessary for grounding the coming revolution in German thought.[64] In Jaeger's essay and in the work of classical philologists like Karl Reinhardt, Kurt Riezler, and Walter F. Otto, Heidegger found hints, pointers, and

---

61. Werner Jaeger, "Die Erziehung des politischen Menschen und die Antike," *Volk im Werden* 1, no. 3 (1933): 44–46. To understand properly the political context of Jaeger's anaylsis, we need to remember that this article was published in a leading NS journal edited by Ernst Krieck.

62. Werner Jaeger, *Five Essays* (Montreal: Mario Casalini, 1966), 121.

63. Edler, "Heidegger and Jaeger," 215–216.

64. Heidegger had positioned his own reading of the German revolution as a radical retrieval of the rootedness of Pre-Socratic thought. His commitment to the Pre-Socratics in the Rectorial Address was so decisive that Jaeger wanted to publish it in his own classicist journal, *Die Antike*. See Heinrich Petzet, *Encounters and Dialogues with Martin Heidegger*, trans. P. Emad and K. Maly (Chicago: University of Chicago Press, 1993), 26–27.

signs indicating a "great transformation in thought" in the archaic world of the Greeks.[65] And in the crucial years between 1929 and 1933, Heidegger drew on this work to sustain his hopes for initiating another "great transformation"—this time on German soil. But Heidegger also understood that the hoped-for revolution would not come of its own power. Germans would need to dispense with the complacency of *Altertumswissenschaft* ("classical studies") and its scientific model of truth for a new Nietzschean style of "subterranean philosophizing" that would retrieve the originary and chthonic forces of archaic *aletheia*. In carrying out this retrieval, Heidegger would make a decisive entry into the world of myth that would be pivotal for his political engagement. Now, revolutionary upheaval would not be aimed at the history of philosophy but at the destiny of the Germans within Europe and the West.

V. THE MYTH OF *BODENSTÄNDIGKEIT* AND THE GREEK BEGINNING

During the late twenties and early thirties, Heidegger read a number of sources dealing with the chthonic power of ancient Greek religion. Besides Otto's two books on *The Gods of Greece* (1929) and *Dionysus* (1933), he also read Alfred Baeumler's long introduction to a Bachofen anthology, *The Myth of Orient and Occident* (1926).[66] It was these kind of sources, when read within his understanding of *aletheia* from "On the Essence of Truth" lectures, that propelled Heidegger in the direction of a new mythic understanding of the *polis* and its relation to the rootedness of autochthony—or *Bodenständigkeit*. From his 1931/32 course on Plato, *Vom*

---

65. W. F. Otto, *Die Götter Griechenlands* (Frankfurt: Klostermann, 1987), 179.

66. Heidegger writes to Otto on January 29, 1931: "Ever again I read your *Götter Griechenlands* and learn from it philosophically. Why is it that (as far as I can see) our youth hardly know this book at all?" Cited in Otto Pöggeler, "Heideggers Begegnung mit Hölderlin," *Man and World* 10 (1977): 24. Heidegger also alludes to Otto in his Hölderlin lectures of WS 1934/35 where, in the context of discussing "the flight of the gods" and the possibility of a *parousia*, he praises Otto's "splendid and valuable book, *Dionysos*" (GA 39: 190). Heidegger discusses the significance of the mask as a symbol of the Dionysian play between presence and absence. He even claims that this Dionysian symbol offers "decisive evidence for the truth of our interpretation of the Greek experience of being." Like Heidegger, Otto's relationship to the Greeks was decisively marked by his reading of Nietzsche. For background on Otto's work and its relation to Nietzsche, see three helpful articles from Hubert Cancik: "Der Einfluss Friedrich Nietzsches auf klassische Philologen in Deutschland bis 1945," in *Altertumswissenschaft in den 20er Jahre*, ed. Helmut Flashar (Stuttgart: F. Steiner, 1995), 381–402; "Die Götter Griechenlands 1929," in *Theologen und Theologien*, ed. Heinrich von Stietencron (Düsseldorf: Patmos, 1986), 214–238; "Dionysos 1933," in *Die Restauration der Götter*, ed. Richard Faber and Renate Schlesier (Würzburg: Königshausen & Neumann, 1986), 105–123. See also Charlotte Zwiauer, "Der antike Dionysos bei Friedrich Nietzsche und W. F. Otto," in *"Die Besten Geister der Nation": Philosophie und Nationalsozialismus*, ed. Ilse Korotin (Vienna: Picus, 1994), 221–239.

Wesen der Wahrheit, Heidegger had come to grasp the essential character of truth as something bound up with the power of *mythos*. For him, myth had the power to break through the boundaries of historical temporality and "leap out of our own present" (GA 34: 10). In this sense, it functioned as a kind of Platonic *periagoge* or "a turning of the soul away from the day whose light is darkness to the true day of being (*des Seienden*)" (Schleiermacher translation, *Republic,* 521c). In the "subterranean cave" (*unterirdischen Höhle*) of Platonic myth, the philosopher attempts to provide "a hint towards . . . the insight into the *essence* of unconcealment" (GA 34: 22–28). In the same way, Heidegger's forays into the originary sources of *aletheia* tried to provide hints or *Winke* into the way Western philosophy had occluded any originary insight into the essence of unconcealment. As he set out to effect another kind of revolutionary *periagoge*—this time involving the soul of the German *Volk*—Heidegger turned to the mythic sources of Greek autochthony for a model of political transformation.

Myth itself always turns upon a reading of what is most essential by turning toward the origin.[67] Inevitably, the mythic impulse is not dissociable from the theme of crisis; it functions in a "time of need," as Hölderlin so poetically put it, to recapture the power of the inaugural.[68] By providing an originary and radical foundation for a community (*Gemeinschaft*), myth holds open the hope for a new instauration that will revolutionize the present by setting asunder the continuities of temporal succession granted by history and normative practice. In the space opened up by this act of sundering, mythic discourse asserts the need for a new or "other" beginning which will inaugurate a singular kind of language: "the auroral presence" of poetic saying.[69] But more than anything else, myth expresses the elemental forces of power within the natural world, the subterranean, chthonic, "*unterirdischen*" forces which ground the mythic as such. As Philippe Lacoue-Labarthe and Jean-Luc Nancy explain in "The Nazi Myth": "myth is the power to bring together the fundamental forces and directions of an individual or of a people, the power of a subterranean, invisible, nonempirical identity."[70] Since the eighteenth century, within German culture the mythic impulses of Winckelmann, Schiller, Hegel,

67. Mircea Eliade, "Toward a Definition of Myth," in *Greek and Egyptian Mythgologies,* ed. Yves Bonnefoy (Chicago: University of Chicago Press, 1992), 2–5; and Jean-Luc Nancy, *The Inoperative Community,* trans. P. Connor (Minneapolis: University of Minnesota Press, 1991), 53–70.
68. Friedrich Hölderlin, "Brot und Wein," in *Hyperion and Selected Poems,* ed. Eric Santner (New York: Continuum, 1990), 184–185. The line in the original German reads: "und wozu Dichter in dürftiger Zeit?"
69. George Steiner, *Antigones* (Oxford: Clarendon Press, 1984), 132.
70. Philippe Lacoue-Labarthe and Jean-Luc Nancy, "The Nazi Myth," *Critical Inquiry* 16 (1990): 305.

Arndt, Bachofen, and Rohde, among others, betrayed a singular predilection for returning to the Greeks. As Nietzsche expressed it in a notebook entry from 1885:

> German philosophy as a whole—Leibniz, Kant, Hegel, Schopenhauer, to name the greatest—is the most fundamental form of romanticism and homesickness (*Heimweh*) there has ever been: the longing for the best that ever existed. One is no longer at home anywhere; at last one longs back for that place in which one alone can be at home, because it is the only place in which one would want to be at home: the Greek world! (WP: 225/KSA 11: 678)

The Greek world of Nietzsche's own *mythos* was not, however, identical with the ordered, rational, enlightened world of antiquity imagined by Germany's so-called "Second Humanism," that model of sober neo-classicism that defined the project of German university *Bildung*.[71] Instead, Nietzsche sought to recover a different Greece and set his sights on "the digging up of ancient philosophy, above all the philosophy of the Pre-Socratics—the most deeply buried of all Greek temples." This attempt "to reclaim the soil (*Boden*) of antiquity" marked Nietzsche's efforts at framing a new *mythos* and joining again "the bond that seemed to be broken, the bond with the Greeks" (WP: 225/KSA 11: 679).

Heidegger lent his own philosophical energies to this twofold Nietzschean project of excavation and reclamation, and, by the time of the Rectorial Address in 1933, had committed himself fully to the Nietzschean *mythos* of a Pre-Socratic *Ursprungsphilosophie*. But where Nietzsche sought "to reclaim the soil of antiquity" against the German desire for a political

---

71. Part of what was at stake in the postwar academic debates about Greek antiquity was the conviction that Germany needed a new, vital Nietzschean transvaluation of the older mandarin values. In the forefront of this politicized form of humanism was Wilamowitz's successor at Berlin, Werner Jaeger. In 1933, Jaeger writes an article, "Die Erziehung des politischen Menschen und die Antike" in a journal edited by Krieck, claiming that "the special task which history has today set before the German *Volk* is the forming of the political human being. . . . [A]t this moment, when a new political type of human being is forming and shaping itself, we will have need of antiquity as a formative force." In *Volk im Werden* 1, no. 3 (1933): 47. For a consideration of Jaeger's Third Humanism, see William Calder, "Werner Jaeger," in *Classical Scholarship: A Biographical Encyclopedia*, ed. Ward Briggs and William Calder (New York: Garland, 1990), 211–226; Donald O. White, "Werner Jaeger's 'Third Humanism' and the Crisis of Conservative Cultural Politics in Weimar Germany," in *Werner Jaeger Reconsidered*, ed. William Calder (Atlanta: Scholars Press, 1992), 267–268; and Ute Preusse, *Humanismus und Gesellschaft: Zur Geschichte des altsprachlichen Unterrichts in Deutschland von 1890 bis 1933* (Frankfurt: Peter Lang, 1988). For works on the "Second Humanism," see Walther Rehm, *Griechentum und Goethezeit* (Bern: Francke, 1952); Hellmut Sichtermann, *Kulturgeschichte der klassischen Archäologie* (Munich: Beck, 1996), which has an excellent bibliography; Ada Hentschke and Ulrich Muhlack, *Einführung in die Geschichte der klassischen Philologie* (Darmstadt: Wissenschaftliche Buchgesellschaft, 1972), and Suzanne Marchand, *Down from Olympus: Archeology and Philhellenism in Germany, 1770–1970* (Princeton: Princeton University Press, 1996).

dispensation, Heidegger's *Ursprungsphilosophie* was tinged by a chthonic longing for the soil of the homeland in its most political form.

In this respect, Heidegger's nomination of the Greeks as the archaic bearers of German destiny followed a path similar to that of two of his contemporaries—W. F. Otto and Alfred Baeumler—who sought to bring together Nietzschean and chthonic elements as part of their new relationship to the Greeks. Otto's *Gods of Greece,* marked by a Nietzschean fervor equal to Heidegger's, attempted to grasp the great transformation between the chthonic and the Olympian gods in terms of a Nietzschean understanding of myth. Myth, Otto argued, was not merely an expression of a culture but its origin. The modern rejection of myth, carried out in the spirit of enlightenment, signified for Otto nothing less than the loss of a culture's originary connection to its own sources and to the way it understood the manifestations and revelations of being. In this way, myth offered a different path for understanding what modernity held as "truth"; it dispensed with the illusion of a control over reality, instead positioning human beings in such a way that from within the space of the myth a primordial dimension of experience could be revealed to them, a space in which they could dwell. Otto argued that with the conflict between the new Homeric gods and the older chthonic deities a new epochal shift occurred, a shift that proved decisive in the formation of Western consciousness. "We must understand," he claimed, "that great myths in the proper sense were done with when the new [Greek] *Weltanschauung* came to prevail."[72] As this new *Weltanschauung* emerged—and one sees it clearly in the struggle portrayed in Aeschylus' *Eumenides*—it rejected "the old faith which was earth-bound and as much constricted by the elemental as ancient *Dasein* itself." What Heidegger found compelling in Otto's account of "the great transformation" from *mythos* to *logos* was its subtle rendering of the tension between chthonic and Olympian forces in the poetic language of *polemos*. On his reading, a similar shift in thinking took place at the Platonic origin of metaphysics which helped to initiate a parallel movement of concealment, hiddenness, and absence in its relation to archaic thinking.

But Heidegger also found chthonic influences in the writings of Alfred Baeumler, whose work on Bachofen attempted to join the chthonic power of the homeland with the heroic *mythos* of the subterranean world. In the Romantic writers of the German Counter-Enlightenment (Arndt, Görres, K. O. Müller), Baeumler locates a deeply rooted longing for the chthonic power of the homeland that expresses a political force within the German

---

72. W. F. Otto, *Götter Griechenlands,* 43 and 21; *The Homeric Gods,* trans. Moses Hadas (New York: Octagon, 1983), 17, 34.

Volk authorized by their buried connection to archaic Greek mythology.[73] During the 1930s, especially in his *Introduction to Metaphysics* (1935), Heidegger takes up a discussion of these same themes in a reconstituted form in his discussion of the heroic Oedipus and the nature of Greek tragedy. There Heidegger locates the tragedy of the modern Western world in its rejection of both chthonic rootedness and in its loss of myth—both of which express the rootlessness of American and Russian technological frenzy (IM: 37–38, 106/EM: 27–28, 81). In "the darkening of the world, the flight of the gods, the destruction of the earth," Heidegger detects forces of nihilism at work that threaten the autochthony of the German *Volk*, bound at the root-stem with archaic Greece.

If we are to understand this Heideggerian longing for rootedness, we will need to see its own roots in this new German *mythos* of the earth, the land, the *Heimat*, and the ancestral home that forms the archaic bond between Germania and Greece in the National Socialist mythology of the early thirties. To follow the trajectory of this mythic narrative is to trace the path of Otto's chthonic religion of earth and origin, a religion of the *Volk* who seek a privileged terrain upon which to dwell. Heidegger's *Ursprungsphilosophie* re-enacts this chthonic yearning for the origin through a double move: philosophically, through a retrieval of archaic thinking, and politically, through a re-territorialization of a lost homeland. The 1930 lecture "On the Essence of Truth" attempted to carry out this twofold movement by calling for a retrieval of archaic *aletheia* at precisely the moment when the French military force withdrew from the Rhineland, thereby opening up Germany for a more achaic colonization: by the Greeks. Within that space of political withdrawal, Heidegger attempts to repatriate the *Heimat* with a *Gemeinschaft* of German youth committed to the new *Volksreligion* of Hölderlin and Schlageter, of origin and autochthony, of *Ursprung* and *Bodenständigkeit*. Whether in the form of Jünger's *mythos* of "the worker who has a new relationship to the elemental, to freedom and to power" or within a proximity to Krieck's struggle against "the repression of *mythos* by *logos* [carried out by] . . . Parmenides, the original father of Descartes, Kant, Fichte, Hegel, and all ontologists until our own time," Heidegger's own new *Volksreligion* of a German-Greek homeland attempts to repatriate the German *Volk* at the origin of Western philosophy.[74]

To miss the political significance of this attempt at repatriation—whether philosophical or otherwise—is to lose the very thread that binds

73. Baeumler, introduction to *Der Mythus von Orient und Occident*, lx, xcix, cxlv, ccviii. For Heidegger's ties to Baeumler, see Sluga, *Heidegger's Crisis*, 151, Martha Zapata Galindo, *Triumph des Willens zur Macht* (Berlin: Argument, 1995), and HBB: 67, 69.

74. Jünger, *Der Arbeiter*, 48; Ernst Krieck, "Die Geburt der Philosophie," *Volk im Werden* 10/11 (1940): 231–233.

Heidegger's thought and language. Even at the very end of his thought path, in the *Spiegel* interview of 1966, Heidegger came back to his lifelong topic of "rootedness," warning that "the uprooting of human beings which is going on now is the end if thinking and poetizing do not acquire nonviolent power once again" (SI: 56; ANT: 98–99). He concluded by saying that "I know that everything essential, everything great arises from humanity's rootedness in its homeland and tradition." This originary *mythos* of rootedness, a *mythos* nurtured by that Hegelian "aspiration . . . to be at home with the Greeks" that marks German thinking from the time of Winckelmann, left its ineradicable mark on Heidegger as well.[75] The abiding force of revolutionary upheaval that animates his work springs from this mythic aspiration for a home. But we need to situate this force within its own political context, precisely there in the language of myth that Heidegger drew upon in his political speeches.

VI. ATHENS OR JERUSALEM?

It would be naïve to think that Heidegger had an uncritical attitude toward myth or that he uncritically venerated the mythic as such. My point in underscoring his preoccupation with Greek poetry and Pre-Socratic philosophy is to show how profoundly his own conception of German politics was marked by this mythic dimension. This does not mean, however, that Heidegger self-consciously sought to establish a mythic language in his own work. Most of his fundamental terms—*Ereignis, Unverborgenheit, Lichtung, Gelassenheit, Seyn,* and others—are employed in an effort to work out a rigorous lexicon for the unfolding of hidden realms of being, and are not simply the romantic expressions of a mythographer. Heidegger is extremely serious about pursuing a critical language for expressing the play of being.

Nonetheless, when he turns his attention to the ancient Greek notion of *aletheia,* what strikes him is that such a term emerges primordially as an experience rather than as the product of conceptual understanding. In the language employed by Walter F. Otto, the characteristics of that experience could be expressed in the form of a *mythos* which functioned as a site for the revelation and unconcealment of being in its play with the hidden, chthonic forces of the underworld. In an age where "the gods have fled," where the presence of the sacred no longer evoked a response in the human soul, it would be no easy task to recover the dormant power of the Greek gods hidden within the earth.[76] For Otto—and for Heidegger—

75. G. W. F. Hegel, *Lectures on the History of Philosophy,* vol. 1, trans. E. S. Haldane (Atlantic Highlands: Humanities Press, 1983), 150; *Vorlesungen über die Geschichte der Philosophie* (Frankfurt: Suhrkamp, 1971), 173–174.

76. Friedrich Hölderlin, "Germania," in *Hyperion and Selected Poems,* 210–211, where the poet speaks of the "entflohene Götter"—the resonance with Otto's *Götter Griechenlands* is pro-

the pathway back to the archaic would have to heed the direction of Hölderlin. Following the Hölderlinian law of relation between the Germans and Greeks, Heidegger found a connection in the shared Graeco-German myth of the fatherland. The original source of the myth for Hölderlin's "vaterländische Umkehr" went back to the Athenian myth of autochthony—of that indigenous relation to the land represented by their founder Erichthonius' self-generated (*autos*), motherless birth from the earth (*chthonos*) itself.[77] According to the version propagated in the *Histories* by Herodotus about "the Athenians—the most ancient of all Greek people, the only nation never to have left the soil from which it sprang," the myth proved useful. In a political world continuously plagued by invasion, folk migration, and initiatives for imperial expansion, the myth of autochthony granted a primordial authority against foreign incursions.[78] In the context of Heidegger's own philosophy of origination or *Ursprungsphilosophie,* and the geo-philosophical heritage of Hegelian metaphysics, the German retrieval of this Greek myth would become bound to autochthony in a decidedly political manner. As a wholly masculine projection onto the civic space of a territory, Athenian autochthony effectively excluded women from the daily practice of political power. By the same token, it re-affirmed the soldierly ideal of the masculine hero who risked death in war for the fatherland. In Heidegger's own simultaneous retrieval and translation of autochthony as *Bodenständigkeit,* the same law of political exclusion applies.[79] In appropriating the heroic ideal of soldierly sacrifice for the fatherland (the *autochthon*), Heidegger simultaneously excluded those who were rootless and non-autochthonic. The logic of this Heideggerian law of exclusion can be plainly read in a letter Heidegger sent to Victor Schwoerer in 1929.

Heidegger writes to Schwoerer to recommend one of his students, Eduard Baumgarten, for a grant; the form of the letter is framed within the politically charged discourse of *Bodenständigkeit.* Baumgarten's application, Heidegger contends, stands for more than the private success of a scholar:

---

nounced. For Otto on Hölderlin, see *Mythos und Welt* (Stuttgart: Klett, 1962), 96–148. See also GA 39: 97–100.

77. On Erichthonius and autochthony, see *Greek and Egyptian Mythologies,* 41; see also Friedrich Hölderlin, *Essays and Letters on Theory,* trans. Thomas Pfau (Albany: SUNY Press, 1988), 114, and *Sämtliche Werke,* vol. 5 (Berlin: Propyläen, 1923), 259.

78. Herodotus, *Histories,* trans. Aubrey de Sèlincourt (Hammondsworth: Penguin, 1972), 498; Simon Goldhill, *Reading Greek Tragedy* (Cambridge: Cambridge University Press, 1990), 66–69. See also Jacob Burckhardt, *Griechische Kulturgeschichte,* vol. 1 (Leipzig: Kröner, 1929), 22–23.

79. In *Benselers Griechisch-Deutsches Schülwörterbuch,* ed. Adolf Kaegi (Leipzig: Teubner, 1904), 133; *autochthonos* is tied to the *Vaterland.*

I would like to say more clearly here what I could only hint at indirectly in my report. At stake is nothing less than the pressing consideration that we stand before a choice: either to provide our *German* spiritual life once more with genuine forces and educators rooted in the native and indigenous [*bodenständige*] or to deliver it over ultimately (in the broader and narrower sense) to increasing Judification [*Verjudung*].[80]

Clearly, "the Germans," the ones who stand for the rootedness of autochthony, must re-affirm their indigenous legacy or suffer the fate of "increasing Judification." What will mark the Jews as a danger to German autochthony in Heidegger's logic is their rootless wandering, their urban identity, their lack of authentic attachment to the landscape, the *Heimat*, and ultimately to the *Volk*. Heidegger ends his letter to Schwoerer by situating this difference between Germans and Jews precisely in the language of the *Heimat;* he reports that "we are enjoying the most beautiful days of fall in our new house and every day I delight in growing more deeply rooted (*verwachsen*) to my home (*Heimat*) through my work." The Jews, however, as a people marked by diaspora, migration, and exodus never have recourse to the principle of autochthony that grows roots in the homeland. Accordingly, as nomads, exiles, and strangers, they are denied the privileges and rights of "native" citizens. This principle of exclusion, endemic to Athenian autochthony and political self-definition, gets repeated in Heidegger's own quest for rootedness. For him, the Jews will come to represent a threat to the *Volksgemeinschaft* by virtue of their rootless, urban identity.

Hence, it should not surprise us that in 1933 Heidegger could speak to Jaspers about "a dangerous international network of Jews" or that in the *Beiträge* he could declare that "Bolshevism is in fact Jewish."[81] But we need to be careful about deciphering the concealed meaning(s) within Heidegger's rhetorical claims. His is no typical anti-Semitic racism; indeed, many of the Heidegger faithful repeat the by now standard defense that Heidegger rejected biological racism of all sorts. We can even find textual evidence from the master that "biology as such never decides *what* is living and *that* such beings are" (Niii: 42; NI: 520). Or we can cite the word of Heidegger's friend, Heinrich Petzet, who claimed that "if Heidegger lacked a certain 'urbanity' and was estranged from everything pertaining to city life, this was particularly so in the case of the urbane spirit of the Jewish circles in the large cities of the West. But this attitude should not be

---

80. *Die Zeit*, December 22, 1989, 50. See also Heidegger's letter to Matthäus Lang (May 30, 1928) where he writes: "how strongly all my efforts are rooted in the native soil [*heimatlichen Boden*]"; cited in Ott, *Martin Heidegger: Unterwegs*, 55.

81. Karl Jaspers, *Philosophische Autobiographie* (Munich: Piper, 1984), 101; GA 65: 54.

misconstrued as anti-Semitism, although Heidegger's attitude has often been interpreted in that way."[82] And who can challenge these kind of *ad hominem* claims?

But the real question of Heidegger's relation to the Jews cannot be decided in this way. Instead, we need to consider how Heidegger's philosophical approach to the Hebraic tradition—conceived on the basis of the Athenian principle of autochthonic exclusion—becomes in its turn decisive for the way Heidegger reads the entire history of philosophy. Given this basic question-frame, I would argue that Petzet is right: it is a mistake to see Heidegger as an anti-Semite based on racial considerations. But I would also maintain that there is another kind of racism at work in Heidegger's programmatic exclusion of the Hebraic from his reading of philosophy, poetry, and myth. Implicitly, the rootedness of autochthony comes to determine the very structures of Heideggerian thinking. Part of what I want to question in my reading is the effect of this Heideggerian question-frame on the philosophical practices of the present. Given the contemporary landscape of continental philosophy, one is tempted to speak of at least two Heideggers: the eco-poetic Heidegger who attends to the language of art, the homeland, and the earth *and* the National Socialist rector who employs the paramilitary rhetoric of hardness and severity to exclude Germany's Jews. In the political speeches of 1933–34, we can find traces of both Heideggers: of the Black Forest recluse who rhapsodized about Van Gogh's peasant shoes and of the committed Nazi who followed the party faithful in deifying the fallen soldier Leo Schlageter. By reading two speeches within their own context, I want to explore this underlying tension in Heidegger's work between Alemannic rootedness and the violence of Nazi militarism, what I earlier termed *pastorale militans,* and I want to show how this exclusionary gesture gets played out and projected onto the whole landscape of the Western tradition—especially onto the history of philosophy. What we will see is how Heidegger's *Volksreligion* of Hölderlin, hearth, and *Heimat,* fortified by the principle of autochthony, comes to determine the history of the West from the position of the autochthonic land: the Fatherland. And we will see how this double law of Athenian autochthony—as myth inspiring the heroic ideal of sacrificial death for the fatherland and as myth granting power only to the native and indigenous—helps to shape the Heideggerian *mythos* of *Bodenständigkeit.* By reading Heidegger in this way, I hope to show that Petzet is right: Heidegger's "estrangement" from the urbane spirit of the Jews is not the result of a biologistic racism. It is rather the systematic consequence of a principial exclusion of the Hebraic that forms a linguistic, historical homology of thought (what Reiner Schürmann terms "the manic denial of the non-

82. Petzet, *Encounters,* 34.

generic other") that undermines genuine philosophical thinking.[83] Within this mythic landscape, where "the 'Fatherland' is being [*Seyn*] itself," the roots of the homeland occlude any possibility of difference, alterity, or heterology (GA 39: 121).

In his *Book of Questions,* the Jewish poet Edmond Jabès (expelled from his native Egypt, writing in French) speaks of exile. He tells the story of Salomon Schwall who came from Corfu, moved to Portugal, migrated to Southern France, an antique dealer who "kept searching the ground, prodding into it."[84] Schwall, Jabès tells us, was possessed by the "need for roots, need to recognize himself, to be recognized, a creature, a plant, a presence of this soil, in its whole sweep, a living element of the landscape. Need to be reborn of it." But, in Jabès' tale, Schwall finds no roots: "at the end of his life, resigned to his fate as foreigner, he had discovered the sky and felt no more attraction to the ground which rejected him." As the poet of and for exilic wandering, Jabès expressed the ancient desire of the Hebrew tribes for roots, plentitude, homeland. But in their three-thousand-year history of absence, loss, transition, the Jewish *Volk* experience only the denial and proscription of rootedness. Their only roots are language—and the Book. As Derrida put it in his essay, "Edmond Jabès and the Question of the Book," the Jews are "autochthons only of speech and writing . . . Autochthons of the Book."[85] Language and rootedness—for Heidegger they stand beside each other, not in opposition but in unity, for what grants roots to a *Volk,* what authorizes its own principial law of exclusion, is the deep and abiding connection between the land and the language: *Heimat* and *Sprache.* The community is formed in and through the poetic speech of the Swabian/Alemannic dialect. And the dialect itself finds its roots in the homeland. For Heidegger, Jabès' exilic return to the Book can never enact the genuine law of autochthony that binds a *Volk* to the land through its language.

Heidegger's position here repeats a familiar strategy in the German tradition of privileging the German language as the only originary language (*Ursprache*)—except for the Greek. Fichte's assertion in his *Addresses to the German Nation* (1808) that "other races speak a language which has movement only on the surface but is dead at the root" became a standard Heideggerian trope in his rhetorical elevation of German rootedness in an *Ursprache* ("originary language").[86] Following Fichte's claim that "the Ger-

83. Reiner Schürmann, "A Brutal Awakening to the Tragic Condition of Being," in *Martin Heidegger: Politics, Art, and Technology,* ed. Karsten Harries and Christoph Jamme (New York: Holmes & Meier, 1994), 89–105.

84. Edmond Jabès, *The Book of Questions,* vol. 1, trans. Rosemarie Waldrop (Hanover: University Press of New England, 1991), 158–159.

85. Jacques Derrida, "Edmond Jabès and the Question of the Book," in *Writing and Difference,* trans. Alan Bass (Chicago: University of Chicago Press, 1978), 66–67.

86. Johann G. Fichte, *Reden an die deutsche Nation* (Hamburg: Meiner, 1978), 72.

man language is . . . at the very least a language of equal rank and as equally originary as the Greek," Heidegger will maintain that "only our German language still corresponds to Greek in terms of its philosophical character of depth and creativity" (GA 31: 51). As "the metaphysical *Volk*," the Germans have to confront their decisive vocation: of retrieving the originary character of Greek *aletheia* to serve as the primordial root of German rootedness (IM: 38/EM: 29). In their primordial affiliation to the Greeks, an affiliation that needed to be secured through *Kampf* and *polemos* rather than through mere cultural inheritance (*Bildung*), the Germans would finally be able to realize their suppressed dream of "a secret Germany" (*ein geheimes Deutschland*) that had sustained the *Volk* since the days of Napoleonic conquest. But they would have to be attentive to the linguistic nature of their bond. For Heidegger, the meridian that connects Greeks and Germans follows the line of affinity discovered in the poetic language of Hölderlin whose translations of Pindar and Sophocles had established a hidden allegiance to a future Germany. The Hölderlinian call to this allegiance was itself transmitted to Heidegger in the work of Norbert von Hellingrath, the fallen World War I soldier who had published some essays and a critical edition of Hölderlin's works that, Heidegger claimed, "hit us students like an earthquake" (OWL: 78/GA 12: 172).

Von Hellingrath argued that it was not merely biological descent or political heritage that defined a *Volk;* on the contrary, he maintained that "the soul of a *Volk*, its boundary and inner core, is language."[87] And the innermost core of the German language in von Hellingrath's Hölderlinian account was Greek. That Heidegger was deeply affected by this fractured logic of Graeco-German affiliation is undeniable. But what deserves closer scrutiny within this purely linguistic and historico-cultural axis of affiliation is the martial connection that Heidegger will draw from von Hellingrath. Heidegger's dedication of his 1936 lecture, "Hölderlin and the Essence of Poetry," "to the memory of Norbert von Hellingrath fallen on December 14, 1916," reinforced the connections he forged in his work between Hölderlin (and by extension the *Volk*, language, the Greeks) and the war experience (EHD: 33). This same constellation of themes becomes decisive for Heidegger precisely as he begins to confront the inner meaning of his "choice" between *Bodenständigkeit* and the "Judification" of the German spirit. What in 1929 will strike Heidegger as an underlying danger will, by 1933, appear to him as an undeniable expression of rootless nihilism. By the time of the first Hölderlin lectures in the winter of 1934/35, the link between *Bodenständigkeit* and the death of the

---

87. Norbert von Hellingrath, *Hölderlin-Vermächtnis* (Munich: Bruckmann, 1936), 128. Heidegger's strong connection to von Hellingrath can be traced in his correspondence with von Hellingrath's fiancée. See *Martin Heidegger/Imma von Bodmershof, Briefwechsel, 1959–1976*, ed. Bruno Pieger (Stuttgart: Klett-Cotta, 2000).

soldier for the fatherland will be complete. German autochthony now will be expressed both in the language of the *Heimat* and in the language of the hero.

VII. DEATH FOR THE FATHERLAND

Heidegger never fully embraced the Nazi ideology of *Blut und Boden* (blood and soil) that was expressed in its crudest forms by Walther Darré, Hitler's minister of agriculture.[88] But despite Heidegger's antipathy for biological, blood-driven racism, there are clear signs that he offered his own "philosophical" reading of what the topic of *Boden* meant for a German *Volksgemeinschaft*. He expressed this clearly in two speeches delivered in 1933–34: a memorial tribute celebrating the death of Albert Leo Schlageter and a radio address explaining his decision to refuse an academic post in Berlin. Both speeches help to place the Rectorial Address in its fullest context. And both help to provide the reasons for Heidegger's enthusiastic support of the National Socialist takeover in January of 1933. Though both speeches are free of the standard NS racial appeals that define the hardened ideology of Baeumler, Heyse, or Krieck, they offer in their stead a philosophical defense of National Socialist praxis grounded in the familiar lexicon of *Heimat, Volk,* landscape, heroic courage, and *Bodenständigkeit.*

One day before the Rectorial Address, on May 26, 1933, Heidegger delivered a speech commemorating the tenth anniversary of Schlageter's death at the hands of the French forces who occupied the Ruhr area. More than one thousand students attended this memorial, which Heidegger delivered on the steps of the main entryway to the University of Freiburg. Schlageter (1894–1923) was an ex–World War I officer who had been awarded the Iron Cross for personal bravery in 1918. After the war he matriculated at the University of Freiburg but soon became disenchanted with what he perceived as the petty academic world of careerism and bourgeois security. Given his war experience and the ethos of the front, Schlageter believed that the only authentic commitment for a German was to his comrades and to the fatherland.[89] In the wake of the Communist threat and the French occupation, he joined the right-wing Freikorps and became active in fighting Bolsheviks, first in Riga, then in Silesia and the Ruhr. Following the economic crisis and the bleak outlook of war indemnity payments, Schlageter undertook acts of resistance

---

88. Anna Bramwell, *Blood and Soil: Richard Walter Darré and Hitler's Green Party* (Buckinghamshire: Kensal Press, 1985).

89. Jay W. Baird, *To Die for Germany* (Bloomington: Indiana University Press), 13–40, and J. M. Ritchie, *German Literature under National Socialism* (London: Croom Helm, 1983), 56–62.

against the French in 1923 that propelled him into the role of a national hero. A devout Catholic who, like Heidegger, had thought of becoming a priest, Schlageter became a model of soldierly resoluteness in the face of death. Following his execution by a French firing squad, there were demonstrations held all over Germany with thousands of mourners paying tribute to his corpse which was transported by train from Düsseldorf to his homeland in southern Germany. When the train stopped in Freiburg, over thirty thousand people gathered to pay tribute to the martyr. Heidegger cancelled class to attend.[90] Ten years later in his memorial speech, Heidegger would weave together the heroic qualities of the fallen soldier with the severity and hardness of the Black Forest's landscape. Heroism and *Bodenständigkeit*—for Heidegger they became inseparably interconnected in the myth of Albert Leo Schlageter.

Heidegger began his speech by placing Schlageter's death—"the most difficult and the greatest death of all"—within his own rhetorical framework: as a "moment of vision" (*Augenblick*) which intersected another decisive moment in the history of the German *Volk* (HCW: 40–41; NH: 48–49). The young freedom-fighter had taken upon himself, with the most authentic resoluteness possible, the responsibility for his own death. In a Pauline moment of vision (*kairos*), Schlageter had determined to die "with a hard will and a clear heart." In this moment, the meaning of his whole life opened before him as he willingly embraced the consequences of his imminent execution. But since he had to suffer this most despairing of deaths in isolation, he resolved "to place before his soul an image of the future awakening (*Aufbruch*) of the *Volk* to honor and greatness so that he could die believing in this future." In other words, the *kairos* moment of Schlageter's death became, within Heidegger's rhetorical schema, the *kairos* moment of a German future. Given that the *parousia* of German destiny was not at hand at his moment of death, Schlageter had to project its meaning upon the future for a coming German *Volk*. By resolutely grasping his own fate as a destiny shared with the (futural) community, Schlageter factically enacted what Heidegger, in section 74 of *Being and Time*, had called "authentic historicity." According to Heidegger, "only a being that is essentially *futural* in its being so that it can let itself be thrown back upon its factical There, free for its death and shattering itself on it . . . can hand down to itself its inherited possibility, take over its own thrownness and be *in the Moment* [*augenblicklich*] for 'its time'. Only authentic temporality that is at the same time finite makes something like fate—that is, authentic historicity—possible" (BT: 352/SZ: 385).

By throwing himself upon his own factical "there" in a heroic moment of vision at the firing squad, Schlageter became free for his own death.

90. Pöggeler, "Heidegger, Nietzsche, and Politics," 137.

But if this had been merely a personal sacrifice, his fate would have been radically different. What made Schlageter a hero—and what decreed that he die "the most difficult death"—was his readiness to confront the "futural" within the finite context of the moment and, by so doing, yoke his individual fate to the destiny of an entire *Volk*. Heidegger found in Schlageter's "hard will" and "clear heart" a model of the kind of authentic resoluteness necessary for the *Aufbruch* of the German revolution. Again, following the analysis of authentic historicity in *Being and Time*, Schlageter embodied a resoluteness which, in the *Augenblick* of 1933, allowed for "the authentic retrieval of a possibility of existence that has been—the possibility that *Dasein* may choose its heroes ... for in resoluteness the choice is first chosen that makes one free for the struggle to come [*kämpfende Nachfolge*] and the loyalty to what can be retrieved." As Heidegger spoke that day to the thousand students gathered to honor Schlageter, he wished to emphasize that the future of Germany—a future that Schlageter had caught glimpse of in his heroic *Augenblick* of death—would require the same readiness for sacrifice that alone would secure "the futural *Aufbruch* of the *Volk*." Schlageter was not within a *Gemeinschaft* when he died; he died alone. And yet by following "the call of conscience," he was able to make his choice decisively and thereby affirm the future of the *Volksgemeinschaft* (BT: 248–258; SZ: 269–280). Drawing heavily upon both Jünger's language of "heroic realism" and the generational myth of a *Frontgemeinschaft*, Heidegger offered a portrait of Schlageter framed by the mythic image of Tyrtaeus' fallen soldier. He too, like the Spartan hero, had stood "steadfast with both feet rooted firmly on the ground." And it was in that ancient Greek image of rootedness in the earth that Heidegger found the meaning of Schlageter's death for the students at Freiburg.

Heidegger posed a basic question to his audience: where did Schlageter find the hardness of will and the clarity of heart to face his own death heroically and without defense? "What allowed him to envision what was greatest and most remote?" For Heidegger, the answer was clear: it lay in "the mountains, forests, and valleys of the Black Forest, the home (*Heimat*) of this hero." The Alemannic homeland had been the root of the hero's hardness and strength. At the close of his remarks, Heidegger admonished his listeners "to let the strength of this hero's native mountains [*Heimatberge*] flow into your will! ... Let the strength of the autumn sun of this hero's native valley [*Heimattales*] shine into your heart!"(HCW:41/NH:48) Clearly, the epideictic character of Heidegger's remarks is hard to overlook. But the rhapsodic allusions to "primitive stone" (*Urgesteine*) and autumnal lucidity have their own encoded political significance. Heidegger's conjunction of *Heimat* and hero needs to be read within the context of the moment as a radical affirmation of the martial character of *Dasein* and of the war-ideology that left its indelible

mark upon Heidegger's thought. Sacrifice, comradeship, readiness to respond to the call, hardness, severity, courage in the face of death—these
virtues of the war-generation, embodied in the heroic fate of Schlageter,
became for Heidegger not mere "values" but indications of a new *Gestalt*
for the German community of the future: the "new man" of National Socialism. With a revolutionary will to overcome the petty concerns of
bourgeois existence—"the they-self" of *Being and Time*—Heidegger found
in Schlageter's death an essential connection to Jünger's mythic experience of *Kampf.* For Jünger:

> It is war which has made human beings and their age what they are.
> Never before has a race of men like ours advanced into the arena of the
> earth to decide who is to wield power over the epoch. For never before
> has a generation entered the daylight of life from a gateway so dark and
> awesome as when they emerged from this war. And this we cannot deny,
> no matter how much some would like to: War, father of all things, is also
> ours; he has hammered us, chiselled and tempered us into what we
> are. . . . [91]

Out of this war experience Heidegger would forge an image of the
"new man" of National Socialist resolve, running toward death as an authentic way of following the call of conscience. These categories, derived
from the existential analytic of *Being and Time,* would become the philosophical foundation for the Schlageter speech. But they would re-surface
in many other of the political speeches, especially Heidegger's address of
November 27, 1933, commemorating the fallen dead from the Battle of
Langemarck. There Heidegger explicitly yoked the theme of military sacrifice to the new students' matriculation at the University of Freiburg.
What the war generation had once undertaken for the fatherland would
now be asked of the new generation of students—to endure suffering and
to be ready to sacrifice themselves for their comrades (NH: 156–157).
Here again, the strategy was familiar. As in the Schlageter address, Heidegger situated the hero's (student's) decision to fight (matriculate) in
the language of resolve rooted in the indigenous mountains, forests, and
valleys of the Black Forest. In this rhetorical juxtaposition of heroism and
Heimat, the martial and the pastoral, Heidegger would take up in a reconstituted form the theme from "On the Essence of Truth." If there he
traced the essence of *aletheia* back to the language of Pre-Socratic *arche,* in
the epideictic speeches he rooted it in the originary ground of the Black
Forest and its language of the *Heimat.* In this way the Black Forest became
for Heidegger the source and ground of Alemannic *aletheia.*

Heidegger was not alone in valorizing the martial experience of war in

---

91. Jünger, *Der Kampf als inneres Erlebnis,* xiv–xv; *Fascism,* ed. Roger Griffin (New York:
Oxford University Press, 1995), 109.

his construction of the new German *Volksgemeinschaft.* In his essay, "The Meaning of the Great War," Baeumler too had spoken of "the youth who died at Langemarck" and of "the metaphysics of war which. . . . finds in the sacrifice of one's life the high point of life itself."[92] Baeumler told his students that "the Great War calls to mind the heroic song of our race; it charges us with battling against [*zum Kampfe gegen*] urbanization by heroically affirming our life through work. It does not, however, call us to struggle in bourgeois fashion for private property." Baeumler ended his essay by locating the authentically heroic form of life in the Hölderlinian bond to nature and to the origin. Another National Socialist philosopher, Kurt Hildebrandt, developed Baeumler's notion of "a metaphysics of war" even further. He argued that Hölderlin's poem, "Death for the Fatherland," had replaced "Kant's loveless concept of duty . . . [with] authentic, life-giving love of fatherland. Only through the fatherland can our death become meaningful and full of glory; only out of love for the *Volk* can our sense of duty meet with a content."[93] In his own lectures during the winter of 1934/35, "Hölderlin's Hymns 'Germania' and 'The Rhine'," Heidegger would explicitly connect Schlageter and the myth of the war-experience to the language of the poet. But he would do so in a way that would solidify the connection between the poetic word of origin and the rootedness of the homeland. Already in *Being and Time,* in his discussion of idle talk, Heidegger had provided clues as to how he would proceed. "Idle talk," he argued, "is constituted in gossiping and passing the word along, a process by which its initial lack of rootedness [*Bodenständigkeit*] escalates to complete rootlessness [*Bodenlosigkeit*]. And this is not limited to vocal gossip, but spreads to what is written." The result is that "the average understanding of the reader will never be able to decide what has been drawn from originary sources with a struggle and how much is just gossip" (BT: 158/SZ: 168–169). Much as the soldier must struggle against bourgeois complacency and self-congratulation in order to decide authentically about sacrificing his life, so too the poet, the originary herald of the future, must struggle against the artifice of everyday speech and academic cant to win back an authentic relation to the language of the homeland. Within this curious logic, Schlageter (before the firing squad) and Hölderlin (confronting his madness) become for Heidegger indications of the selfsame German will to sacrifice oneself for the *Volk.* Hence, Heidegger's Hölderlin lectures aim at awakening his Freiburg students to the call of sacrifice for the new German future.

In his discussion of "Germania," Heidegger returns to a well-known fragment from Hölderlin's poetry: "since we have been a discourse and

92. Baeumler, *Männerbund,* 16–17.
93. Kurt Hildebrandt, *Hölderlin* (Stuttgart: Kohlhammer, 1943), 228.

can hear from one another."[94] There he uncovers an essential connection between language and an originary community of the *Volk*. Being able to hear one another, Heidegger claims, is not a merely linguistic or physiological capability; it constitutes, rather, an ontological relation to the very sources of our history and, more fundamentally, to our community. "Our being [*Seyn*] happens as discourse" (GA 39: 70). But this discourse in turn constitutes an originary community (*ursprüngliche Gemeinschaft*) that binds each individual in a way that no society (*Gesellschaft*) can. As a model of this originary bond, Heidegger turns to the kind of community formed by "the comradeship of soldiers at the front." The most profound and unique reason for this bond, Heidegger claims:

> is that the nearness of death as sacrifice placed everyone before the same void so that this became the source of an unconditional belonging together of each to the other. It is precisely the death that each individual man had to die for himself . . . precisely this death and the readiness to sacrifice oneself for it that creates, above all, the communal space from which comradeship arises . . . If, as free sacrifice, we do not compel [*zwingen*] powers in our *Dasein* to bind and isolate us as unconditionally as death, (that is, to attack the roots of each individual *Dasein*) . . . then there will be no comradeship. At best, it will only yield an altered form of society [*Gesellschaft*]. (GA 39: 73)

In this *Kampfgemeinschaft* at the front, where Schlageter had fought as a young lieutenant for the *Reichswehr*, Heidegger believed he had uncovered the authentic roots of a German community to come. This heroic language of sacrifice would bind the German people to its native soil against the idle talk of "publicness" which dominated the rootless world of *Gesellschaft*. In the authentic language of Hölderlin, a new *Gemeinschaft* would emerge, since (as von Hellingrath had intimated): "language is the soul of the *Volk*."[95] For Heidegger the revolutionary moment had arrived. Schlageter's death had provided the German *Volk* with a moment of vision (*Augenblick*) that would determine its future. "The hour of history has struck," Heidegger proclaimed; the readiness for sacrifice must now be undertaken in the service of a new instauration, a political *parousia* where "the violence of being [*Seyn*] must once again truly become a question for understanding" (GA 39: 294). Within the context of the celebration on May 26, 1933, besides the thousand students in Freiburg, 80,000 Hitler Youths and 185,000 members of the SA, SS, and Stahlhelm paraded on the Golzheimer Heath where Schlageter had been shot. Hermann Göring joined others around Germany in seeing a connection between

94. Hölderlin, "Friedensfeier," in *Hyperion and Selected Poems*, 234.
95. von Hellingrath, *Hölderlin-Vermächtnis*, 128.

Schlageter's death and a German future. "As long as there are Schlageters in Germany," Göring cried, "the nation will live."[96]

VIII. HEIDEGGER'S HÖLDERLINIAN *VOLKSRELIGION*

The year 1933 marked a crucial change in Heidegger's vision of a German future. If, in 1929, Heidegger still thought of the *parousia* as something that would come in a distant future, once Hitler came to power in January of 1933 (and after his own entrance into the party in May), he now thought the moment had arrived. In December of 1932, he writes to Jaspers: "I have dedicated the last years wholly to the Greeks and even during this sabbatical semester they won't let go of me" (HJB: 149). At the end of his letter, Heidegger then raises the question "whether it will be possible in the coming decades to create a firm foundation [*Boden*] and a space for philosophy, whether human beings will come who bear within themselves a distant command?" By May of 1933, this "distant command" (*ferne Verfügung*) will be interpreted within the context of a new moment of vision and will be brought to bear on the essential task of the German university (RA: 32/SdU: 13). What had once seemed to be merely a possibility for the distant future is now grasped as a decisive moment in the revolutionary situation of the present. Five years after his return to Freiburg, a period in which he told Gadamer "everything began to get slippery," Heidegger started "to sense the power of the old ground [*Boden*]."[97] In his radio address, "Creative Landscape: Why Do I Stay in the Provinces?," this essential bond between the National Socialist revolution and "the old ground" will become clearer. What emerges from this speech (written in the Fall of 1933 and delivered in March of 1934) are the outlines of a new Hölderlinian *Volksreligion* of the homeland, a mythic vision of autochthony that binds the German *Volk* to its archaic roots in the Alemannic soil near Heidegger's cabin in the Black Forest. The text itself seems to evoke an eco-poetic sense of the pastoral, the idyllic, and the arcadian, and yet there are other, more troubling, themes as well.[98] What Heidegger brings to language in this short composition is nothing less than his own "private version of National Socialism" (RFT: 23/SdU: 30).

In his self-styled mythology, Heidegger attempted to present this radio address as a homespun account of his reasons for declining his

---

96. Baird, *To Die For Germany*, 37. Heidegger admired Göring in the early '30s and even presented a popular biography of Göring by Martin Sommerfeldt as a gift to his friend Hans Jantzen in March of 1933. Ott, *Martin Heidegger: Unterwegs*, 147.

97. Gadamer, *Philosophical Apprenticeships*, 50.

98. Martin Heidegger, "Why Do I Stay in the Provinces?" in *Heidegger: The Man and the Thinker*, ed. Thomas Sheehan (Chicago: Precedent, 1981), 27–30; GA 13: 9–13.

second call to a chair in Berlin. He begins by describing in poetic language the topography and environs of his cabin in Todtnauberg (a small rural community in the Black Forest). He then goes on to tell his listeners that from his own perspective this is not how the landscape appears to him:

> This is my work world—seen with the eye of an observer: the guest or summer vacationer. Strictly speaking I myself never observe the landscape. I experience its hourly changes, day and night, in the great comings and goings of the seasons. The gravity of the mountains and the hardness of their primeval rock, the slow and deliberate growth of the fir trees, the brilliant, simple splendor of the meadows in bloom, the rush of the mountain brook in the long autumn night, the stern simplicity of the flatlands covered with snow—all of this moves and flows through and penetrates daily existence up there, and not in forced moments of "aesthetic" immersion or artificial empathy, but only when one's own existence stands in its work. It is the work alone that opens up space for the reality that is these mountains. The course of the work remains embedded in what happens in the landscape. (HMT: 27/GA 13: 9–10)

The account itself evokes something of the beginning of Nietzsche's *Thus Spoke Zarathustra* and, when read in context, a double structure arises: the prophet–philosopher stands alone on a mountain–hillslope, away from the world of *Gesellschaft* and the city, in a cave–cabin (*Höhle–Hütte*) waiting to proclaim his message—"remain true to the earth!" (Z: 42/KSA 4:15). But where the spiritual meaning of Zarathustra's solitude focuses on the self, Heidegger's is directed at the community. The implications for Heidegger's own private version of National Socialism are far-reaching.

By the time of the "Creative Landscape" address, Heidegger had managed to confect his own version of political community as a response to the rootlessness (*Bodenlosigkeit*) of modern thinking that preoccupied him in *Being and Time* (BT: 366/SZ: 401). As we have seen, what grated upon Heidegger about the modern world was its cosmopolitan, enlightened ideal of universal principles governing the whole of humanity, as well as its vast network of inter-locking structures that leveled the curvatures of the mountain path into the flattened boulevards of the metropolis. Weimar culture was decidedly cosmopolitan; it flourished in the theaters, galleries, and coffee houses of Berlin, Munich, and Düsseldorf. But there was no chthonic power in the life of the city. Like Spengler, who located the decay of modern civilization in the contrast between the landscape and the city, Heidegger was gravely skeptical about the prospects of urban culture.[99] In a time of defeat and foreign occupation, Heidegger was firmly convinced

---

99. Oswald Spengler, *The Decline of the West*, vol. 2, trans. C.F. Atkinson (New York: Knopf, 1979), 85–110.

that the Germans needed to counteract the rootlessness of modern urban life by (re-)turning to their authentic roots in the homeland.

Clearly, Heidegger's anti-urban prejudices were not unique. As a lower middle-class "scholarship boy" from Messkirch, Heidegger expressed the standard small town reaction to the sprawling metropolis. But he was no peasant, his poetic stylizations in "Creative Landscape" notwithstanding. What lay at the source of Heidegger's rustic observations, what moved him to "stay in the provinces," was not a quaint provincialism but a decidedly political vision of inclusion and separation founded upon a revolutionary *mythos* of the soil (rather than of the blood) and of language (rather than of biology). Heidegger rejected the biologistic, racial thinking of his party colleagues precisely because it seemed to him another rootless expression of modern "ideology"—that bastard stepson of Enlightenment thought. He sought instead an indigenous, native ground for National Socialist philosophy that would re-establish a connection to "the power of the old ground" in the Greeks. Heidegger nominates *Bodenständigkeit*—in its proper sense as the rootedness in the indigenous soil of the homeland—as his authentic *mythos* of autochthony. What is properly one's own—in the sense of *autos*, from whose root autochthony derives—is the root of the earth, what the Greeks called *chthonos*.[100] This vision of autochthony, however, is no less "National Socialist" than the theory of race. It merely grounds its own vision of exclusion and separation differently. It turns to a politics of the *arche*, a politics whose origin lies in the Greeks, in the Black Forest soil, and in the *Kameradschaft* of fallen heroes to found its origin. Schlageter and Tyrtaeus, Hölderlin and Heraclitus, Athenian autochthony and Alemannic *Bodenständigkeit*—all form the political landscape of the provinces that Heidegger calls the homeland.

This new community of the German *Volk* will, in Heidegger's estimation, be formed by limits and boundaries that are both linguistic and geopolitical. The idioms of the rooted Black Forest peasant will never be coterminus with the shibboleths of a desert tribe of wanderers. (When Paul Celan came to visit Heidegger "in the provinces," he instinctively understood this.)[101] Neither will the Enlightenment dream of a universal humanity offer any hope of salvation from the nihilism of the modern world. Only a closed community of people, a *Volk* whose means of demarcation forms an original bond to the land (understood as the father-

100. Hjalmar Frisk, *Griechisches Etymologisches Wörterbuch* (Heidelberg: Carl Winter, 1973), 191, 1098.

101. Paul Celan, "Todtnauberg," in *Poems of Paul Celan*, trans. Michael Hamburger (New York: Persea, 1988), 292–293; and Otto Pöggeler, "Mystical Elements in Heidegger's Thought and Celan's Poetry," in *Word Traces*, ed. Arios Fioretos (Baltimore: Johns Hopkins University Press, 1994), 75–109.

land), can offer any constancy (*Ständigkeit*) against the "free-floating" speculation of a modern *Gesellschaft*. Even language for Heidegger derives its uncanny power from its roots. Heidegger's chosen style of composition was to deploy words for use in his argument that shared a common stem, e.g. *fragen, be-fragen, er-fragen, hin-fragen*, etc., a rhetorical practice known as *paronomasia* (SZ: 5). But where many writers appropriate the paronomasic style merely to pun or effect word-play, Heidegger embraced it as a way to show the underlying strife and conflict at work in the movement of language itself as a form of Heraclitean *polemos*. What lay hidden within a sentence could, in this way, be made manifest in the tension between a root and a prefix. This tension itself, when rendered in the poetic language of *polemos*, could help to show the play of *aletheia* that lay at the root of all manifestations of being. Politics itself merely re-enacted this same polemical strife between roots and extremities, between those guarded by autochthony and those rootless beings who would be cast out of the community.

Jean-Luc Nancy has persuasively argued that community is defined by this selfsame tension between in- and exclusion, between what he terms "immanentism" and the "caesura."[102] By immanentism, Nancy means a condition in which it is "the aim of the community of beings in essence to produce their own essence as their work (*ouevre*), and moreover to produce precisely this essence *as community*."[103] In Heideggerian terms, this aim of producing the essence of the community by taking up the question of essence becomes the dominant theme of "Creative Landscape." What remains unspoken throughout—like the unspoken hours spent by Heidegger "in silence," smoking with his peasant neighbors—is the topic or *topos* of essence.

The essence of the folk community is its rootedness in the landscape; that is where one finds the creative power of *physis* that rages through the earth. "The force that through the green fuse drives the flower" is the same force that animates Heidegger at his work-desk overlooking "the rush of the mountain brook in the long autumn night" (HMT: 27–30/GA 13: 9–13). As Heidegger explains, "the inner relationship of my own work to the Black Forest and its people comes from a centuries-long and irreplaceable rootedness [*Bodenständigkeit*] in the Alemannian-Swabian soil." But whence does the "essence" of this rootedness come? Where does the constancy (*Ständigkeit*) of rootedness (*Bodenständigkeit*) reside? How can "we"—a favorite locution of Heidegger's political speeches, the "we" of an autochthonous community who guards its privileged homeland—connect *Eigenständigkeit* (independence) (SdU: 10; NH: 149), *Offenständigkeit*

102. Nancy, *Inoperative Community*, 43–70.
103. Philippe Lacoue-Labarthe, *Heidegger, Art and Politics* (Oxford: Blackwell, 1990), 70.

(openness) (WM: 79–81; 83), *Beständigkeit* (constancy) (EM: 28; H: 73–74), and *Inständigkeit* (standing-in-being) (WM: 106; EM: 48–49) to their roots in *Bodenständigkeit* (NH: 12, 148, 217, 218; GA 34: 209–210; EdP: 32)? Could the force of this paronomasic searching ever extend to the possibility of offering *Widerstand* (resistance), even a kind of "*geistigen Widerstand*," as Heidegger himself styled it in his letter to the De-Nazification committee in November of 1945 (DDP: 540–541)?

In "Creative Landscape," Heidegger reaffirms a *mythos* of National Socialist autochthony marked by a double patrimony: the philosophic *arche* of Pre-Socratic thinking and the topographic roots of the Alemannic soil. His thematization of "the severity [*Schwere*] of the mountains and the hardness [*Härte*] of their primeval rock [*Urgesteine*]," was not simply directed at a German audience nostalgically looking to the landscape as a source of comfort and security. Rather, the language of *Härte* and *Schwere* (a language borrowed from Jünger and his apocalyptic accounts of the war-experience) was to serve as the authentic link connecting the landscape, the fallen war dead, the native *Volk*, and the German language to the Greek language and, ultimately, to the first beginning of Greek philosophy. From his writing desk, Heidegger senses a profound connection between the landscape and his own philosophical work, since "the course of the work remains embedded in what happens in the landscape." But this "cabin-*Dasein*," as Heidegger terms it, is not only "intimately rooted in an immediate belonging to the life of the peasants"; it also locates its roots in the distant origin of Western thinking among the Greeks (GA 13: 10–11). Even the fallen hero Schlageter gets brought into this circle of mythic affinity between Greeks and Germans, and between the hardness-severity of martial will and the primeval landscape of the Black Forest. Like Heidegger, Schlageter was a bright, ambitious Catholic boy whose academic abilities propelled him from the village schools near Messkirch to the gymnasium in Konstanz and later to the Bertholdsgymnasium in Freiburg—the same schools where Heidegger studied. But the parallels went even farther. Schlageter had been a favorite of the same Greek teachers as Heidegger was and also excelled in his study of Greek authors. In this sense, he comes to embody both a common connection to the homeland soil and to the Greek linguistic tradition.

This myth of affinity between the homeland and the Greeks persists in Heidegger's work, extending throughout his later career. In the 1930s, it is wedded to a political reconstruction of the history of being according to a new National Socialist *mythos* of origin and future. In his lectures of summer semester 1933, "The Fundamental Question of Philosophy," Heidegger interprets this mythic affinity as one rooted in language. The vocation (*Bestimmung*) of the German Volk, Heidegger contends, is to reclaim its authentic "spiritual-political mission [*geistig-politischer Auftrag*]": to face up to the task of "an essential questioning" (Far: 132–133/FarG:190–191). The task of the present historical *kairos* is "to awaken and to root in the heart and will of the *Volk* and of each and all that constitute it" a knowledge of this hidden vocation. "We" can be in a position to begin this task of essential questioning, Heidegger tells his students, only if we are "forced to do so out of actual need and authentic necessity." What propels this need is the originary linguistic bond between the Greeks and the Germans.

> When and where, however, was the decision made concerning the fundamental question of philosophy and its own essence? At that time when the Greek *Volk*—whose root stock [*Stammesart*] and language has precisely the same origin as our German roots—set out to create through its great poets and thinkers a uniquely new form of human-historical *Dasein*. What began there, still is. . . . This beginning of the spiritual-historical *Dasein* of Western humanity still is and it survives as a distant command [*ferne Verfügung*] which far in advance grasps our fate as a Western one. This beginning survives—as we know—as a distant command to which German destiny is bound. Now we are faced with the question . . . (the greatest affliction [*Bedrängnis*] of our *Dasein*) . . . whether we want to create a spiritual world for the development of our *Volk* and state or not. If we do not want it and if we are unable to make it happen, then some form of barbarism will sweep us away and we will have finally played out our role as a *Volk* who shapes history. . . . [But] if we want to succeed at this . . . then we must find the will to begin to create this spiritual world and to fall in line for a second great armed conflict, a spiritual confrontation [*Auseinandersetzung*] with our whole history . . . We must learn to grasp this historical moment [*Augenblick*] and to know that it is great enough and pregnant with enough forces so that we can dare to inaugurate once again the authentic beginning of our historical *Dasein*. Our sole aim here is to create a spiritual future for our *Volk* and to assure its calling among other peoples. (Far: 134–135/FarG:192–194)

In his Rectorial Address of May 1933, the whole scaffolding for this new vision of a German future is laid out in a decisive way. To read it is to engage the world of mythic autochthony that shapes Heidegger's world.

CHAPTER TWO

The Nietzschean Self-Assertion of the German University

Any philosophy founded on the belief that the problem of *Dasein* has been changed or solved by a political event is a parody of philosophy and a sham.

— FRIEDRICH NIETZSCHE
UO: 184/KSA 1: 365

Revolution, the upheaval of what is habitual, is the genuine relation to the beginning.

— MARTIN HEIDEGGER
BQP: 38/GA 45: 40–41

I. THE NIETZSCHEAN CONTEXT OF THE RECTORIAL ADDRESS

If Heidegger's Rectorial Address gets read at all, then it usually meets with one of two responses: either it gets read quickly and is dismissed with an embarrassed reaction from the Heidegger faithful or, conversely, it is eagerly mined by Heidegger critics for its National Socialist contentions and its opprobrious political ideas. Few philosophers have taken the time to read this work carefully and consider its underlying significance for Heidegger's thought path.[1] I would like to proceed differently by taking this

1. There are a few notable exceptions to this widespread neglect of the Rectorial Address as a crucial philosophical (rather than merely political) text: Charles Scott, "Heidegger's Rector's Address: A Loss of the Question of Ethics," *Graduate Faculty Philosophy Journal* 14, no. 2, and 15, no. 1 (1991): 237–264; Graeme Nicholson, "The Politics of Heidegger's Rectorial Address," *Man and World* 20 (1987): 171–187; Istvan Feher, "Fundamental Ontology and Political Interlude: Heidegger as Rector of the University of Freiburg," in *Martin Heidegger: Critical Assessments*, ed. Christopher Macann (New York: Routledge, 1992), 4: 159–197; and Christopher Fynsk, *Heidegger: Thought and Historicity* (Ithaca: Cornell University Press, 1986), 104–120. Hans Sluga's *Heidegger's Crisis* (Cambridge: Harvard University Press, 1993) offers an excellent reading of the political context of the Rectorial Address—especially its relation to other such addresses of its day—but it does not aim at a textual analysis of the address. More typical of the way philosophers have generally treated the Rectorial Address is Orlando Pugliese's claim in "Heideggers Denken und der Nationalsozialismus," in *Zur Philosophischen Aktualität Heideggers*, ed. Dietrich Papenfuss and Otto Pöggeler (Frankfurt: Klostermann, 1991), 368, that "it strikes one as grotesque to place the Rectorial Address at the center of a projected collection of more than one hundred volumes of Heidegger's writings." For a good discussion of the ideological context of the Rectorial Address in 1933, see Rainer Alisch, "Heideggers Rektoratsrede im Kontext," in *Deutsche Philosophen 1933*, ed. W.F. Haug (Hamburg: Argument, 1989), 69–98; and George Leamann, *Heidegger im Kontext*.

address seriously and reading it as a condensed and concentrated expression of Heidegger's most enduring philosophical themes. This short text will, I contend, function as a kind of philosophical manifesto for Heidegger, containing in nuce the broad outlines of his sweeping history of being and his mythic vision of a German *Sonderweg* rooted in a profound affiliation with the Greeks. Moreover, it will function as a veritable lexicon of Heidegger's mythic-political language of the 1930s, a lexicon that draws heavily from Nietzsche. I want to put forth a reading of this text that clearly situates Heidegger's program of university reform, political revolution, and metaphysical upheaval within its proper Nietzschean context so that we can grasp both the political nature of his reading of Nietzsche and the Nietzschean character of his interpretation of politics. By paying close attention to the strategic movements within this text, I want to read Heidegger's commitment to, and confrontation (*Auseinandersetzung*) with, National Socialism as an exercise in Nietzschean rhetoric which deploys the language of *mythos* to establish a new meaning for Germany's future.

To understand in a genuine way the mood of Heidegger's Rectorial Address, we need to situate it within its own historical context. As we saw in chapter 1, Heidegger had been writing about a "futural" coming (*das Kommende*) for the German *Volk*—his Weimar vision of the Pauline *parousia*—since *The Fundamental Concepts of Metaphysics* lectures in 1929. This advent of a new form of German *Dasein* would, however, take time (or so Heidegger believed, until the early months of 1933).

Then came the unexpected *Machtergreifung*. Caught in the generational mood of euphoric self-renewal (a mood whose intensity within German history was matched only by the feverish outburst of patriotic nationalism in the first days of war in August 1914), Heidegger embraced the moment of revolutionary possibility as a way of instituting the foundation for another beginning. If other Germans responded to the National Socialist takeover with "a widely held feeling of redemption and liberation from democracy" and felt relief that an incompetent and petty-minded government would no longer be left to solve the profound crisis of the times, Heidegger concerned himself with greater issues.[2] He interpreted the events of early 1933 not as a political transfer of power, but as an epochal shift within being itself, a radical awakening from the slumbers of Weimar politics as usual.

He writes to Elisabeth Blochmann in late March of 1933 that the political revolution is really only a "first awakening"—a preliminary indication of a kind of Pauline "wakefulness" reconfigured in a National Socialist context. But what truly matters "in the present world-moment [*Weltaugenblick*] of Western events," he tells her, is the resolve "to prepare ourselves

---

2. Sebastian Haffner, *Von Bismarck zu Hitler* (Munich: Knauer, 1987), 219, cited in Safranski, *Ein Meister aus Deutschland* (Munich: Hanser, 1994), 270–271.

for a second, more profound revolution" (HBB: 60–61). Four days later he writes to Jaspers in the same expectant mood: "as obscure and questionable as many things are, so I sense more and more that we are growing into a new reality and that an epoch has become old. Everything depends upon whether we prepare the proper place of combat [*Einsatzstelle*] for philosophy and help bring it to language" (HJB: 152).

But what would this "second" revolution entail? How would it effect the kind of sweeping changes necessary for an epochal shift within being? In that "world-moment" of March 1933, Heidegger believed that it would mean nothing less than "the total transformation [*völlige Umwälzung*] of our German *Dasein*" and the fulfillment of the longstanding dream that the German *Volk* become themselves authentically by embracing their own future as destiny (HCW: 52/NH: 150).

Heidegger was not alone in conceiving of revolution in totalizing terms. In his study, *The European Revolutions and the Character of Nations* (1931), Eugen Rosenstock-Huessey explained, "when we speak here in this book of *revolution*, we mean only those who wanted to introduce into world history once and for all a new principle of life, that is a total transformation [*Totalumwälzung*] [of existence] . . . Revolutions worthy of the name want to provide a new impulse for the whole world and communicate a new order of things."[3] But if Heidegger shared with Rosenstock-Huessey a belief in the power of revolution to transform the whole of existence, he radically denied his pointed contention that "all genuine revolutions are world revolutions." For Heidegger, the revolution of 1933 was most emphatically a German revolution; what was at stake in the new revolutionary situation was the *Dasein* of the German *Volk*.

The topic of a communal form of *Dasein* had already been taken up by Heidegger in section 74 of *Being and Time* in conjunction with the theme of authentic historicity. There Heidegger had put forth the argument that "fateful [*schicksalhafte*] *Dasein* essentially exists as being-in-the-world in being-with others"; this basic condition, Heidegger determined, comprised "the destiny [*Geschick*] . . . of the community, of the *Volk*" (BT: 352/SZ: 384). By 1933, the topic of a shared destiny becomes a constant refrain in Heidegger's lectures and writings, culminating in the conviction that the German *Volk* has been granted a privileged status in the history of the West. In the summer semester of 1933, this presumption is then transformed into a full-blown eschatology about a *völkisch*-political *parousia*. There, in "Die Grundfrage der Philosophie," Heidegger writes: "the other beginning of philosophy and its future will not be created sometime or somehow from world-reason; it will only be realized by a *Volk*, as we be-

---

3. Eugen Rosenstock-Huessey, *Die europäische Revolution und der Charakter der Nationen* (Stuttgart: Kohlhammer, 1960), 5.

lieve: by the Germans—not by us, but by those who are coming" (FarG: 195). Only through the *Volk* and its shared sense of destiny could the pathway to another beginning be opened. This belonging together of *Volk* and the power of beginning was not, however, unique to the Germans. At the very beginning of philosophy, the same archaic logic applied, a logic whose very power derived from the *arche* itself. As Heidegger put it, "there is no such thing as the beginning of philosophy insofar as *the* philosophy does not exist. Rather, the beginning of philosophy is and remains Greek" (FarG: 195). As the *Volk* who belonged to the first beginning, the Greeks expressed the power of originary thinking; as the *Volk* who had been charged with the task of inaugurating an other beginning, the Germans would have to forge an essential connection to their Greek predecessors.

Heidegger's constatory affirmation of the Germans as a *Volk* bound to the *arche* had deep roots in Fichte's claims from his *Addresses to the German Nation* (1808) that the Germans were an *Urvolk* (originary people).[4] For Fichte, this originary identity of the Germans was a characteristic shared only by the Greeks; in his *Addresses,* he contends the Germans are "a *Volk* that has the right to call itself simply *the Volk.*" In the summer of 1934, in "On Logic as a Question concerning Language," Heidegger took up Fichte's inquiry and posed the question anew: "What is a *Volk?*"

> We are *a Volk* and not *the Volk.* We have spoken of *Volk* without saying what we mean by that. *What is a Volk?* We come to use the term "we" in a decisive way. But whether we belong to a *Volk* or not is not a matter of our preference. We cannot decide concerning our descent. But what is this decision about?— What is a *Volk?* What is decision?—these are two essentially related questions. (L: 20)

Heidegger goes on to characterize the standard ideas of *Volk* based on racial and biological considerations. He then begins to focus on the problem of "decision" which he interprets as essential to the authentic constitution of a *Volk,* since only in decision-making can *Dasein* become authentic: "there is a connection between authentic decision-making and true being-oneself." "Authentic decision-making," Heidegger contends, "is a deciding about oneself which, out of the struggle of the one who judges (*Kampfrichter*), makes one into what one should be" (L: 30). The decision confronting the German *Volk* appears to Heidegger as one concerning its history and/as its future. In a speech of November 11, 1933 (delivered at an election rally in Leipzig to decide whether to withdraw from the League of Nations), Heidegger told his fellow university professors:

> The German *Volk* has been summoned [*gerufen*] by the *Führer* to vote; the *Führer,* however, is asking nothing from the *Volk.* Rather, he is giving the *Volk*

4. Fichte, *Reden an die deutsche Nation* (Hamburg: Meiner, 1978), 106.

the possibility of making, directly, the highest free decision of all: whether the entire *Volk* wants its own *Dasein* or whether it does *not* want it. Tomorrow the *Volk* will choose nothing less than its future. (HCW: 49/GA 16:190)

In this historical decision to withdraw from the League of Nations, Heidegger had located what he terms "the outermost limit of the *Dasein* of our *Volk*." "And what is this limit? It consists in that originary demand of all being that it keep and save [*retten*] its own essence." The essence of the German *Volk* is something that has been granted to them not by other nations but by their own historical affinity to the Greeks since, as Heidegger would later formulate it, "the German, like the Greek, is called [*berufen*] to poetizing and thinking" (P: 167/GA 54: 250). As the one who had been "called," the fate of the *Volk* lies in its "clear will to self-responsibility," a will that through work (*Arbeit*) would win back for the *Volk* its original state of "rootedness" (*Bodenständigkeit*) (HCW: 50/GA 16: 190–191). This will to a true *Volksgemeinschaft*, Heidegger claims, "will make this *Volk* hard towards itself" and will also serve to bring about "the awakening [*Aufbruch*] of a youth who are growing back to their roots [*Wurzeln*]." By regaining a sense of its own rootedness, the *Volk* will, at the same time, "win back the *truth* of its will to existence, for truth is the revelation of that which makes a *Volk* certain, clear, and strong in its actions and knowledge." As Heidegger pursues the question of truth and its relation to the German *Volk*, he turns to a consideration of science (*Wissenschaft*) and of its origin.

Science, he claims, "is bound to the necessity of a *völkischen Dasein* that is self-responsible." But there is more. Science, especially a *völkisch* form of science, has nothing to do with the technical research and training that defines the various disciplines of learning. In its most genuine form, *völkische Wissenschaft* "renounces the idolization of all rootless [*bodenloses*] and powerless thinking"; it demands rather "the originary courage either to grow or to be destroyed in confrontation [*Auseinandersetzung*] with being." Again, what emerges from this confrontation is a kind of originary setting-asunder of being and beings, a Heraclitean play between concealment and revelation that belongs only to those who are "strong" and "hard" enough to confront the danger of the originary. In this willingness to confront danger—which he argues is but another name for "questioning"—Heidegger finds the courage of Nietzsche's Zarathustra.[5]

---

5. Friedrich Nietzsche, *Nietzsche in seinen Briefen* (Leipzig: Kröner, 1932), 334. There Nietzsche writes to Franz Overbeck about the thought of eternal recurrence, "the thought that splits the history of humanity into two halves." Nietzsche confides to his friend that he will need "courage to bear such a thought." When conjoined with Jünger's affirmation of the warrior's hardness and Schlageter's readiness to die for the fatherland, Nietzsche's thoughts about courage and danger become distorted. What rules instead is the rhetoric of *Kampf* and

For us, questioning is not the unconstrained play of curiosity. Nor is questioning the stubborn insistence on doubt at any price. For us, questioning means: exposing oneself to the sublimity of things, and their laws; it means not closing oneself off to the terror of the untamed and to the confusion of darkness. To be sure, it is for the sake of this questioning that we question, and *not* to serve those who have grown tired and their complacent addiction for comfortable answers. We know: the courage to question [means] to experience the abysses of *Dasein* and to endure the abysses of *Dasein*. (HCW: 51/GA 16:192)

In this portrait of the *Volk* as a community who embraces questioning in all its dangers and who collectively affirms its own essence in and through its inquiry into the essence of truth, Heidegger returns to his constant theme: the destiny of the Germans in the history of the West. What is at stake for Heidegger in the rhetorical *topos* of "questioning" is the very identity of the German *Volk* as the *Volk* who will come to its essence only through a future return to its origins. This return is itself determined in and through the relation of the German *Volk* to the Greeks: "the Greeks, to whom Nietzsche said, the Germans alone were equal" (HBB: 52). This originary affinity between the Greek and the German *Volk* becomes determinative for Heidegger's own ontological politics in the 1930s. It will mark his whole discussion of the essence of truth as *aletheia,* of science (*Wissenschaft*) as *philosophia,* of rootedness (*Bodenständigkeit*) as autochthony, of confrontation (*Auseinandersetzung*) as *polemos,* and of the other beginning as a futural *arche.* But this appropriation of the Greek beginning was not direct or immediate. It came to Heidegger through Fichte, Hegel, Hölderlin, and especially Nietzsche. The Greeks of Heidegger's German *mythos* were Nietzschean figures who affirmed hardness, danger, freedom, power, struggle, and destiny. I will return to consider this Nietzschean mediation of the Greek *arche* in a later chapter, but for now I want to make a more specific point. The Greeks functioned for both Heidegger and Nietzsche as the decisive figures in a re-thinking of Western history at its roots. But where Nietzsche appropriated Greek values in the spirit of individual autonomy and self-overcoming, Heidegger did so in the name of the community and of the *Volk.* And it is precisely this difference that will mark Heidegger's attitude toward politics in Germany during the 1930s.

In 1934, when Heidegger raised the question "who are we?" he was reacting against the bourgeois retreat into interiority and the private sphere of self-analysis. Against what he termed "addictive egocentrism" (*Ichsucht*) and "self-isolation" (*Selbstverlorenheit*), he turned to the *Volk* as a way of announcing a revolutionary break with the past and a new "awakening" (*Auf-*

---

heroism that becomes prominent in Heidegger's speeches of 1933–1934, collected in Schneeberger's *Nachlese zu Heidegger* (Bern, 1962), and GA 16.

bruch) to the originary politics of the future (L: 10). Reacting vehemently against Theodor Haecker's popular treatise *What Is Man?* (1933), a work which defined the essence of human being in terms of Christian anthropocentrism, Heidegger launched an assault against the bourgeois metaphysics of individuation and isolation. The essence of the human being, Heidegger insisted, was communal, bound up in history, language, and a belonging to the rootedness of tradition and the land. The question concerning the essence of human being was a question concerning the *Volk;* the essence of the *Volk,* in turn, was to be found in its readiness to affirm questioning itself as the root and ground of its own essence. But what was essential about this question had not yet been understood.[6] "Who are we?", Heidegger asked.

> This question must now, perhaps for the first time in this age, be posed as a question. Yet it is not all the same who poses the question. It is not something that has its source in a shrewd individual's clever notion; rather, there is a terrible necessity that surrounds it. The World War did not touch upon this question even once. Nor has the World War as a historical force begun to be integrated into the future. This decision concerning the war will be made in and through the decision about the trial human beings have been put through by this event. (L: 10)

But what kind of "trial" did the war present for the *Volk?* And how would the Germans respond to such a trial? Clearly, these questions were always directed at the future, and it was in response to future concerns that Heidegger offered his critique of Haecker, which was nothing less than a critique of Western metaphysics itself. What Heidegger identified in Haecker's work as the metaphysics of bourgeois-Christian individualism became for him an expression of the rootless nihilism that pervaded the modern Western tradition. The World War was merely an epiphenomenal occurrence; the roots of the crisis lay in the whole metaphysical tradition of scientific thinking that pervaded modern life. Understood in this way, Heidegger's lectures and addresses from 1933–34 about the *Volk,* work, youth, *Heimat,* and the university are, like the earlier essays, "What is Metaphysics?" (1929) and "On the Essence of Truth" (1930), responses to the problem of nihilism—now reconfigured within the new political situation. But Heidegger was not content with merely responding to the times, since, as he put it: "the only really enduring philosophy is the philosophy

---

6. Theodor Haecker, *Was ist der Mensch?* (Leipzig: Hegner, 1933). For a discussion of Heidegger's critique of Haecker, see Ott, *Heidegger: Unterwegs,* 255–259 and IM: 142–144/EM: 109–111, where Heidegger writes: "To be sure, there are books today entitled: 'What is man?' But the title merely stands in letters on the cover. There is no questioning. . . ."

which is truly of its time, but that means, has command of its time" (HBB: 144).[7]

Heidegger's extended discourse on "The *Volk*" was an attempt to respond to Nietzsche's critique of nihilism within modernity. Confronted by a world in which all values have been de-valued and where the death of God leaves a void that cannot be filled, Heidegger challenges a whole *Volk* to become authentic (like Schlageter) by responding to the call of conscience that he interprets as a call to embrace the terror of genuine questioning. By posing in its own way (even while it is "on the march") the disquieting, non-bourgeois Parmenidean question concerning being—"why are there beings at all, and why not rather nothing?"—the *Volk* is simply raising the question: "who are we?" (BW: 112/WM: 19; L: 10). This coupling of *Volk* and questioning becomes an explicit theme in the Rectorial Address where Heidegger attempts to forge a deeper connection between the *Volk* and the nature of *Wissenschaft*. Hence, in the Rectorial Address, Heidegger writes:

> If we will the essence of science in the sense of *the questioning, unsheltered standing firm in the midst of the uncertainty of the totality of being*, then *this* will to essence will create for our *Volk* a world of the innermost and most extreme danger, i.e., a truly *spiritual* world. For "spirit" is neither empty acumen, nor the noncommittal play of wit, nor the busy practice of never-ending rational analysis nor even world reason; rather, spirit is the determined resolve to the essence of being, a resolve that is attuned to origins and knowing. And the *spiritual world* of a *Volk* is not its cultural superstructure, just as little as it is its arsenal of useful knowledge and values; rather it is the power that comes from preserving at the most profound level the forces that are rooted in the soil and blood of a *Volk*, the power to shake most extensively the *Volk's* existence. A spiritual world alone will guarantee our *Volk* greatness. For it will make the constant decision between the will to greatness and the toleration of decline the law that establishes the pace for the march upon which our *Volk* has embarked on the way to its future history (RA: 33–34/SdU: 14).

Heidegger's eschatological reading of the "world-moment" of 1933 will get played out in *völkisch* terms throughout the Rectorial Address. In an era where the very idea of a "world" war carried with it apocalyptic overtones, Heidegger will turn his attention to re-forming the German discourse about the future in terms of the *Volk* and its relationship to *Geist*, *Wissenschaft*, *Wesen* and the forces that are rooted in earth and blood. For

7. Heidegger makes this statement in a letter to the Prussian Minister of Culture, Adolf Grimme, on May 10, 1930. There he provides his own reasons for declining the first call to Berlin for the chair in philosophy; Heidegger was called a second time in 1933, and his response was delivered in the form of the radio address "Why Do We Stay in the Provinces?" In 1923, Husserl had also received a call to leave Freiburg and take over the chair in Berlin once occupied by Ernst Troeltsch, but he also declined (HBB: 230).

Heidegger, Spengler's crisis-narrative about "the decline of the West" pointed to a genuine danger for Germany: the radical nihilism of Western values that Nietzsche had already diagnosed.

But Spengler's crude reliance upon biological-morphological metaphors had diverted attention from the genuine source of the problem. The only authentic possibility for renewal and regeneration lay in a "revolutionary awakening" (*Aufbruch*) that would "break out" of the rigid, calcified structures of metaphysical thinking that had occluded any attempt to recover the primordial sources of thinking. These primordial sources, rooted both in the autochthony of the earth and in the lost patrimony of the ancient Greeks, would need to be retrieved by the *Volk* with a "primordially attuned knowing [*wissende*] resoluteness toward the essence of being." This resolute retrieval of the first beginning of the West became for Heidegger the distinguishing mark of the authentic National Socialist revolution. Beyond the "merely" political revolution undertaken by Hitler and the party, this "second revolution" alone could achieve "the total transformation of German *Dasein*." Only then would the crisis of Western nihilism and rootlessness be overcome, opening the path to a "futural" beginning for the Germans (and for the West). All of these preconditions come into play in Heidegger's Rectorial Address where they form a nexus of intersecting concepts. But even as Heidegger began to deploy these concepts, the axiomatics and thematics of his Address came back to the situation of German science at the university.

As Heidegger saw it, the regeneration of the West (and with it, as its most fundamental precondition, the "total transformation of German *Dasein*") required a renewal of *Wissenschaft* as well as a radical reorganization of the site of *Wissenschaft* at the university. During the early part of 1933, Heidegger became preoccupied with the idea that "the true revolution had to come from the university."[8] If the university were merely an institutional center for research and teaching, a bureaucratic vortex within which various disciplines intersected in a geographical space, a convenient assemblage of specialties without a spiritual center, then the term "*Universität*" would become an empty and hollow word. But Heidegger sought to rethink the meaning and vocation of the German university back to the question of its essence. What was "essential" about the German university had been lost; only through a resolute retrieval of its essence in accordance with its origin in archaic Greek thinking could the crisis situation of the West in the world-moment of 1933 be resolved. "Everything is at stake this time," Heidegger wrote to Elisabeth

---

8. Georg Picht, "Die Macht des Denkens," in *Antwort: Martin Heidegger im Gespräch*, ed. Günther Neske and Emil Kettering (Pfullingen: Neske, 1988), 176.

Blochmann in those revolutionary days of 1933. "I will not let up in this struggle [*Kampf*]" (HBB: 70).

II. THE ESSENCE OF THE GERMAN UNIVERSITY

Heidegger's Rectorial Address attempted to take up the struggle for the essence of science, now understood as a struggle for the essence of the German university. And, indeed, Heidegger's turn to the question of essence was itself undertaken in a spirit of struggle. Like many of his other National Socialist colleagues (especially Baeumler, Heyse, and Krieck), Heidegger sought to place the university in the vanguard of revolutionary change. In the crisis moment of 1933, these philosophers, committed to the metaphysics of a German *Sonderweg*, could all agree with Heyse's contention that "the German revolution is a unified metaphysical act of German life that expresses itself in every area of German *Dasein*"—especially the university.[9] By affirming the spiritual leadership of the university, these philosophers hoped to lead the German *Volk* into a new epoch of national unity where, through determined struggle, a new community would emerge to transform the history of the West. Heidegger shared this vision of the German university and became dedicated to fulfilling its spiritual mission. As a philosopher, he was convinced that philosophy must lead the attack on the old, encrusted structures of traditional practice. The way in which Heidegger formed his critique of the university was, however, decisive not only for his own political activity; it also helped to shape his entire thought path far beyond 1933. In this sense, the Rectorial Address needs to be read not merely as a document of Heidegger's political convictions, but as a manifesto that expresses his most fundamental philosophical positions.

That said, it is important to place this manifesto within its own political context. Hans Sluga's insightful *Heidegger's Crisis: Philosophy and Politics in Nazi Germany* has helped to do this by situating the Rectorial Address within the context of other prominent academic addresses and lectures in the months following the Nazi takeover. Sluga convincingly demonstrates that Heidegger's address was only one of many delivered in those enthusiastic days of spring 1933 committed to the idea of a philosophical restructuring of society through a reformulation and radical revolution of the university and the sciences. As Sluga puts it:

9. Hans Heyse, "Geleitwort," *Kant Studien* 40 (1935): i–ii. For details on Heyse's involvement at the University of Göttingen after 1936, see Hans-Joachim Dahms, "Aufstieg und Ende der Lebensphilosophie: Das philosophische Seminar der Universität Göttingen zwischen 1917 and 1950," in *Die Universität Göttingen unter dem Nationalsozialismus*, ed. Heinrich Becker and H.J. Dahms(Munich: Saur, 1987), 169–199.

The philosophers, already involved in a struggle over their place in the continuum of knowledge, felt that they could not let the moment pass without getting involved in what promised to be a total reorganization of German life. Some thought it imperative to get involved in order to restore German philosophy to its rightful place. Others thought it equally urgent to assure a place for their own new thinking. They all set out to show that they and they alone could define the ontological order on which the emerging political order could be grounded.[10]

What emerged from this generational preoccupation with reorganization and reform was "a climate of intensified struggle between the philosophical schools over which of them represented the true philosophy of National Socialism, which of them had properly identified its inner truth and greatness."[11]

What is remarkable, in retrospect, is how modish Heidegger's Rectorial Address truly was. In a speech delivered two weeks before Heidegger's, Alfred Baeumler also drew upon the mythic language of *arche* and *Anfang*, boldly announcing that "a new epoch is beginning," an epoch in which the German *Volk* would be presented with "the mission [*Auftrag*] . . . to organize the world anew."[12] Drawing upon the ancient Greeks as a source for *völkisch* renewal, Baeumler tells his audience: "we are certain to come closer to the Greeks than we ever have before if we but educate ourselves according to the law of our own essence [*Wesen*]." Heidegger will take up Baeumler's challenge in his own way by framing the question of national renewal in terms of the question of essence which he then redirects toward his own project. Thought essentially, the question concerning the essence of the *Volk* becomes for Heidegger a question concerning the essence of the university. This turn to the question of essence is then undertaken as a way of affirming philosophy as the proper place for the beginning of a *völkisch* revolution rooted in the problem of essence itself. For in Heidegger's labyrinthine logic, the question of essence will get rethought as a problem of essential questioning. In questioning itself, Heidegger will locate the hidden sources for a return to the archaic Greek practice of *philosophia*, a practice that he designates as the ground and root for "the total transformation of German *Dasein*." In and through the careful practice of authentic philosophizing, Heidegger will attempt to seize the *kairos* moment of revolutionary upheaval and undertake "to lead the leader" (*den Führer führen*).[13]

10. Sluga, *Heidegger's Crisis*, 201.
11. Ibid., 229.
12. Baeumler, *Männerbund*, 136–137.
13. This claim that Heidegger wanted "to lead the leader" is the product of second-hand conversations and suppositions. Pöggeler argues that Heidegger wanted to "educate" the Führer rather than "lead" him, *Neue Wege mit Heidegger*, 204.

Seeing himself as "the born philosopher and spiritual leader of the new movement," Heidegger turned to a diagnosis of Germany's spiritual ills. As his guide, he chose Nietzsche.[14] Ever since the winter of 1929/30, Nietzsche's analysis of the crisis of Western nihilism had shaped Heidegger's view of the German future. The Rectorial Address employed Nietzsche's formula of "the death of God" to critique the modern German university and its practice of *Wissenschaft*. But Nietzsche's critique went deeper. In *The Gay Science,* Nietzsche had railed against "the tyranny of truth and science" with its grave and somber practices of positivist research, calling instead for an "alliance of laughter and wisdom" (GS: 92, 74; KSA 3: 390, 370). In an aphorism entitled "We Homeless Ones," Nietzsche tried to situate the experience of nihilism in an age of scientific certitude:

> Among Europeans today there is no lack of those who are entitled to call themselves homeless in a distinctive and honorable sense: it is to them that I especially commend my secret wisdom and *gaya scienza.* For their fate is hard, their hopes are uncertain; it is quite a feat to devise some comfort for them—but what avail? We children of the future, how *could* we be at home in this today? We feel disfavor for all ideals that might lead one to feel at home even in this fragile, broken time of transition; as for its "realities," we do not believe that they will *last.* The ice that still supports people today has become very thin; the wind that brings the thaw is blowing; we ourselves who are homeless constitute a force that breaks open ice and other all too thin "realities." (GS: 338/KSA 3: 628–629)

Nietzsche will offer a response to this "fragile, broken, time of transition [*Übergangszeit*]" that rejects German nationalism and racism and affirms instead the solitary existence of one who, like Zarathustra, lives on mountains, apart from the mass:

> Humanity! Has there ever been a more hideous old woman among all old women—(unless it were "truth": a question for philosophers)? No, we do not love humanity; but on the other hand we are not nearly "German" enough, in the sense in which the word "German" is constantly being used nowadays, to advocate nationalism and race hatred and to be able to take pleasure in the national scabies of the heart and blood poisoning that now leads the nations of Europe to delimit and barricade themselves against each other as if it were a matter of quarantine. For that we are too open-

14. Pöggeler, "Heideggers politisches Selbstverständnis," 34, reports that in May of 1933, the Freiburg economist Walter Eucken (who was opposed to Heidegger's rectorial aims) claimed that "Heidegger gave the impression that he wanted to carry out things according to the principle of the *Führer* system. Clearly, he saw himself as the born philosopher and spiritual leader of the new movement and as the only truly great thinker since Heraclitus." Ott, *Heidegger: Unterwegs,* 164–165.

minded, too malicious, too spoiled, also too well informed, too "traveled": we far prefer to live on mountains, apart, "untimely," in past or future centuries, merely in order to keep ourselves from experiencing the silent rage to which we know we should be condemned as eyewitnesses of politics that are desolating the German spirit by making it vain and that is, moreover, *petty* politics: to keep its own creation from immediately falling apart again, is it not finding it necessary to plant it between two deadly hatreds? *must* it not desire the eternalization of the European system of a lot of petty states?

We who are homeless are too manifold and mixed racially and in our descent, being "modern men," and consequently do not feel tempted to participate in the mendacious racial self-admiration and racial indecency that parades in Germany today as a sign of a German way of thinking and that is doubly false and obscene among the people of the "historical sense." We are, in one word—and let this be our word of honor—*good Europeans*, the heirs of Europe, the rich, oversupplied, but also overly obligated heirs of thousands of years of European spirit. (GS: 339–340/KSA 3: 630–631)

Clearly, Nietzsche's "good Europeans" were not the spiritual ancestors of Heidegger's mythic Germans; in no sense did they derive their spiritual power from "the forces that are rooted in the soil and blood of a *Volk*" (HCW: 33–34; SdU: 14). Hence, though Heidegger derived much of his critique of modernity from Nietzsche—especially his critique of *Wissenschaft*—he did not share Nietzsche's view of "petty politics."

III. SELF-DETERMINATION, SELF-ASSERTION, AND LEADERSHIP

Heidegger's "Self-Assertion of the German University" comes to us as a carefully packaged text. When we read it, the political overtones of its language color its philosophical arguments; but even when read within this register, its overall meaning is difficult to discern. What emerges instead is a standard portrait of Martin Heidegger as National Socialist rector crusading to place the stamp of the movement upon the university. Ironically, this was not the reaction it generated on May 27, 1933, among the Freiburg faculty and student body. As Heidegger himself admitted in his letter to the De-Nazification hearings after the war:

Only very few clearly understood what this title ["The Self-Assertion of the German University"] meant in the year 1933 . . . The address was not understood by those whom it concerned; neither was its content understood, nor was it understood that it states what it was that guided me during my term in office in distinguishing between what was essential and what was less essential and merely external . . . The Rectorial Address was spoken into the wind and forgotten the day after the inaugural celebration. During my rectorate, not one of my colleagues discussed any aspects of the address with me. They moved in the tracks of faculty politics that had been worn out for decades. (RFT: 22, 25; SdU: 29–30, 34)

But did the blame for this misunderstanding lay with the audience or with Heidegger? I would argue that in some sense Heidegger intended his address to be obscure, since the more arcane the message, the more space it would provide for him to effect radical change.[15] On May 27th, who understood what "self-assertion" meant? Who could have discerned in the very title of this address a confrontation with the forces of revolution that ruled the day, forces that Heidegger hoped to form and shape into his own *Gestalt* of the German future? And who could have detected the obscure reference to Nietzsche that lay hidden in the wordplay of the title?

In many ways, "The Self-Assertion of the German University" serves as the Heideggerian version of Nietzsche's *Thus Spoke Zarathustra: A Book for Everyone and No One*. Obscure, hermetic, and at times impenetrable, its language appears, on the surface at least, to be easily assimilated by listeners and readers. As an address for everyone, it borrows from the standard National Socialist lexicon of power-force-struggle-fate-destiny-mission-leader-community-decision-*Volk*-command-service-bond-discipline-battle-and will (to limit the list). But it employs this standard NS argot in a way that proved incomprehensible to most of its listeners. It was certainly not surprising that after hearing the address, the NS Minister of Culture and Education for Baden, Otto Wacker, labelled it the expression of a "private National Socialism" (RFT: 23/SdU: 30). But if we could even overcome the sheer logical incongruity of a "politics of the private," what would this mean for Heidegger's vision of the German university and, ultimately, of the German future?

Heidegger had joined the NSDAP on May 1, 1933, in a public ceremony (ten days after having been elected the rector of the University of Freiburg). His decision was made on the basis of political conviction, not careerist opportunism. From the very beginning, his private reading of world events had convinced him of the utter bankruptcy of the liberal democratic government during the Weimar period. What he hoped to find in National Socialism was a remedy for the disease of European nihilism that had bequeathed to the West the inexorability of its own decline. Later, in a letter to Hans-Peter Hempel from September 19, 1960, Heidegger admitted that in an age of economic and political crisis he had hoped that "National Socialism would both acknowledge and assimilate all the constructive and productive forces" of the age and open up

15. Against Heidegger's self-serving postwar claim that the Rectorial Address was quickly forgotten, Safranski's research shows that the speech was published twice more in the NS period and was well received in the party press. See *Ein Meister aus Deutschland*, 291.

the possibility of a new beginning.[16] In his very first lecture of the summer semester of 1933, held on May 4 (some three weeks before his Rectorial Address), he announced to an overflowing auditorium what this new beginning would entail. "German academic youth today," Heidegger proclaimed,

> finds itself in the midst of a revolutionary awakening [*Aufbruch*]. It stands before its vocation [*Berufung*] and lives from the will to find discipline and education, which will make it ready and strong for the spiritual and political leadership conferred upon it as its mission [*aufgetragen*] for the sake of coming generations. (NH: 27)

As a lifelong academic committed to a radical refashioning of the German university, Heidegger's commitment to National Socialism was always determined by his position as a philosophy professor. What, for him, the movement entailed was its inaugural power to initiate a "leap out of our own present," as he put in his lectures "On the Essence of Truth" (GA 34: 10). For those who became seduced by the political opportunities of the present and who missed the essentially "futural" meaning of the National Socialist revolution, Heidegger had little patience. It was clear to him that not everyone could grasp "the inner truth and greatness of this movement" (IM: 199/EM: 152). For those who had ears to hear, Heidegger's *kerygma* proclaimed the advent of a National Socialist *parousia*. But not all those in the "party" understood the "movement," and not all who listened to the message grasped its inner meaning and "essence." Heidegger's Rectorial Address could only be properly grasped by those who understood the mission (*Sendung*) and the task (*Auftrag*) of the German *Volk* and who were willing to be led by a philosopher who, as professor and rector, would show them the way. Understood in this sense, Heidegger's earliest speeches in praise of National Socialism should, at the same time, be recognized as critical encounters (*Auseinandersetzungen*) about its "inner meaning." We need to conceive this in two ways: first, as an *Auseinandersetzung* with the political-institutional structures of party, state, and nation, and, second, as a critical departure from the other National Socialist philosophers who were attempting to steal the fire of revolution and consign it to their own hearth. In a decisive way, these two confrontations were focused on the thought of Nietzsche.

In a letter that Heidegger sent to Stefan Zemach on March 18, 1968, he claimed that his Nietzsche lectures of 1936–1940 were delivered in such a way that "every listener clearly understood them as a fundamentally critical confrontation [*Auseinandersetzung*] with National Socialism" (GA 40:

16. Safranski, *Ein Meister aus Deutschland,* 269.

233). And in his report to the De-Nazification Committee of 1945, he maintained that he had "entered still more clearly into confrontation and into spiritual resistance [*geistigen Widerstand*] [with National Socialism], through a series of Nietzsche courses and talks beginning in 1936 and continuing until 1945" (DDP: 540–541). The self-promotional character of these claims notwithstanding, I would argue that (at least in the two senses mentioned above) Heidegger's work on Nietzsche did constitute an authentic *Auseinandersetzung* with National Socialism, officially understood. But the provenience of this confrontation is not 1936 but rather the Rectorial Address of 1933, written as a battle-piece against the standard NS—*Nietzschebild* (image of Nietzsche). Above all else, it was in Nietzsche's name that Heidegger undertook his own *Kampf* against what he termed "the new and the old" (RFT: 16/SdU: 22).

Heidegger's lexicon and thematics, his question-frame and his mode of execution in the Rectorial Address, were dependent upon his idiosyncratic reading of Nietzsche and his *Auseinandersetzung* with other Nietzsche commentators within the party. In a significant sense, and owing to its unique political climate, the Rectorial Address can be read as a condensed version of the six volumes of lecture courses that Heidegger delivered between winter 1936/37 and winter 1944/45. Clearly, the thematics will shift, but the underlying dynamic will remain constant: Heidegger will rethink his commitment to National Socialism and to a German future in and against his critical confrontation with Nietzsche. What this signifies is that as Heidegger grows more critical of Nietzsche's reading of Western history and philosophy, his position vis-à-vis "official" National Socialism will also shift. What we need to keep in mind, despite Heidegger's claim that "all essential philosophical questioning is necessarily untimely [*unzeitgemäss*]," is how unremittingly timely, how inextricably tied to the times [*zeitgemäss*] Heidegger's work truly is. To read his Parmenides lectures from 1942/43, for example, apart from the context of the Nazi defeat at Stalingrad, is to miss their fundamental significance. Like Nietzsche, the teacher of the untimely, Heidegger strives to be at odds with his time, to set himself into spirited confrontation with the forces of modernity—even as he falls back into line with the spirit-negating homologies of his Nazi colleagues.

In his battle-piece "Schopenhauer as Educator," Nietzsche levied a devastating critique upon contemporary German university culture. "Kant," he argued:

> clung to the university, submitted to authority, sustained the pretense of religious faith, put up with colleagues and students; so it is only natural that his example has begotten university professors and professorial philosophy . . . But many stages in the emancipation of the philosophical life are

still unknown among the Germans . . . That "truth," however, of which our professors chatter so much, appears a mousy little creature from whom nothing unruly or exceptional need be feared—a cozy, good-natured little thing who constantly assures all the established powers that she will cause nobody any trouble; after all, she is only "pure science" [*reine Wissenschaft*]. In sum, I would say that philosophy in Germany must more and more forget about being "pure science." (UO: 173/KSA: 1: 351)

The model for philosophers must be the ancient Greeks, Nietzsche insisted, for they knew how to affirm life. But this was not so straightforward a command, since for Nietzsche, "living at all means to be in danger" (UO: 180/KSA 1: 360). Heidegger's Rectorial Address follows Nietzsche in this dual affirmation of danger and of the Greeks as the way out of the wizened, desiccated university culture built in the spirit of scientific objectivity and devotion to scholarly detail. Like Nietzsche, Heidegger wants to overturn the mandarin ideal of teaching and research and affirm in its stead the spirit of dangerous questioning and danger itself. But where Nietzsche ultimately rejects the university, seeing it as an institution that stifles creativity and cultural reform, Heidegger turns to it as the *topos* of essential-primordial thinking. For him, the university must be in the vanguard of the coming revolution or it will fail.

In this sense, Heidegger's Rectorial Address also breaks with Nietzsche by affirming the educational legacy of German idealism, especially that of Fichte, whose role within the Address will prove decisive for the way that Heidegger will read Nietzsche's critique of modernity. In his own Rectorial Address at the newly founded University of Berlin, delivered on October 19, 1811, Fichte would raise the decisive question: "What then is the University?" For him, the answer is clear: the university is the place for "the spiritual education of our race," providing the *Volk* with a means of "fulfilling its destiny." Given its formative role in the determination of the *Volk*, it is hardly surprising that Fichte will declare the university to be "the most important institution and the holiest thing which the human race possesses."[17] In the midst of a national awakening, Fichte will look to the university as a source of leadership and national determination (*Bestimmung*). But Fichte will impress upon his listeners that "if a university is to achieve its purpose and be truly what it pretends to be, it must be left to itself thenceforward; it needs, and rightly demands, complete external freedom, academic freedom in its widest sense." In the midst of another national awakening, Heidegger will confront this same issue as he tries to work out the tension between Fichte's affirmation of the university and

17. J. G. Fichte, "Concerning the Only Possible Disturbance of Academic Freedom" (1812), in *The Educational Theory of J. G. Fichte,* trans. G. H. Turnbull (London: Hodder & Stoughton, 1926), 263–264.

Nietzsche's denial of its value. Had Heidegger followed Nietzsche on this path of denial, he would undoubtedly have also rejected Fichte's powerful myth of the Germans as an *Urvolk*. But since he does embrace this myth of the originary, the consequences for his reading of the German university (and its self-assertion) will be decisive—not only for the university but for the German *Volk* as well.

In the moment of national resurgence, Heidegger will look to the university as a way of overcoming the economic, social, and political ills plaguing Germany. It will be in and through the university's self-determination and its responsibility to its calling that Heidegger will position his critique of the old order. But this Fichtean lexicon of self-determination (*Selbstbestimmung*), responsibility (*Verantwortung*) and calling (*Berufung*) that carries with it the whole legacy of idealist metaphysics and its commitment to spirit (*Geist*), will get appropriated by Heidegger and be transformed into a messianic form of National Socialism. Only by following the call of its inner essence—which lies at the origin of Western thinking—will the university (and by extension, the *Volk*) be able to overcome the deracination that afflicts both higher learning and the German people. Nietzsche had already diagnosed the maladies of rootless nihilism that afflicted modernity, but he understood that the university had become so entangled in the metaphysical structures of the modern world that it could no longer serve as a springboard for Dionysian revolt. Like the German *Volk* from which it had grown, the university represented the most egregious form of presentism, a kind of self-congratulatory reflex of contemporaneity. Regrettably, Heidegger will fall victim to the worst kind of presentism in the world-moment of 1933, expending his considerable philosophical energy on an affirmation of the NS order.

Ten days before Heidegger's address, the newly appointed chancellor Adolf Hitler, in a brilliant tactic of deception, turned the Wilsonian principle of "the right of peoples to self-determination" (*Selbstbestimmungsrecht der Völker*) against the Western democracies. In his famous *Friedensrede*, Hitler called for a national re-awakening of the *Volk*, a homecoming for those who had lost their self-respect, while at the same time allaying foreign fears about German military expansion. Heidegger's Rectorial Address took up Hitler's theme of self-determination and, by way of a circuitous invocation of Fichte, returned to the Nietzschean problem of self-assertion.

For those who heard it, Heidegger's address must have been difficult to follow. The logic of the discourse is at times involuted and impenetrable; one is confronted at all turns by the force of epideictic language and locution. The effect is at times dizzying. From the distance of our own time, we can detect reasons for this confusion. For one, the incongruities between the Nietzschean lexicon and the National Socialist thematic prove at times jarring. But the difficulty of understanding lies more in the dissonance between the various layers of the text: Plato and Clausewitz, Fichte and Schlageter, Nietzsche and Hitler. The Rectorial Address is a palimpsest written over with the signatures of the Pre-Socratics and Hölderlin, of German idealists and Nazis. At root, it is a radical rethinking of the essence of *Wissenschaft* on the model of Humboldt and Fichte's bold and innovative attempt to found the University of Berlin (1810) on a new principle of scientific learning.

Heidegger opens "The Self-Assertion of the German University" by addressing the issue of the self, which begins with Heidegger, the rector:

> Assuming the rectorship means committing oneself to leading this university *spiritually and intellectually*. The teachers and students who constitute the rector's following will awaken and gain strength only through being truly and collectively rooted in the essence of the German university. This essence will attain clarity, rank, and power, however, only when the leaders are, first and foremost and at all times, themselves led by the inexorability of that spiritual mission [*Auftrag*] which impresses onto the fate of the German *Volk* the stamp of their history. (RA: 29/SdU: 9)

To unpack the logic of this condensed argument we need to rephrase the problem: who is the rector himself? what is the "self" of the university? how are these questions related to the *Volk* itself?

The rector himself is the leader (*Führer*) of the university, the self who takes upon himself the commitment to leadership. As Charles Scott has pointed out in his insightful essay on the address, the rector is also the head (*Haupt*) of the university.[18] [Scott will offer a reading that makes much of the interplay between *Haupt*, *Behauptung* (assertion), and *Enthauptung* (decapitation) in the Rectorial Address and in the De-Nazification report.] In Scott's analysis, "how the university is 'headed' is a preoccupation of the address." Since the university reforms of Humboldt in the early nineteenth century, the rector was understood to be the first among equals; the university was conceived as a collegial community whose power derived from a common mission, not a single individual. Heidegger's address offered a decisive challenge to this Humboldtian ideal, placing the question of leadership at the head of the discussion. For Heidegger, the rector was both the leader and the head of the university; thus, as he composed his plan for a new constitution, submitted to the educational ministry in Karlsruhe, he re-emphasized the power of the rector (*Führer*) over the academic senate, the chancellor, and the deans.[19] This

---

18. Charles Scott, "Heidegger's Rector's Address," 237–264 and RFT: 22/SdU: 30.

19. Ott, *Heidegger: Unterwegs*, 191–192, and David F. Krell, *Daimon Life: Heidegger and Life-Philosophy* (Bloomington: Indiana University Press, 1992), 142–147. See also the crucial documents on university reform from *Martin Heidegger und das 'Dritte Reich,'* ed. Bernd Martin (Darmstadt: Wissenschaftliche Buchgesellschaft, 1989), 170–176.

bold plan constituted a radical rejection of the neo-humanist ideal of democratic leadership by the university senate. But it also represented a fundamental break with the whole mandarin *Bildungsideologie* of *Geist* and *Idee*. In this he was at one with Alfred Baeumler who, in his inaugural address at Berlin on May 10, had attacked the traditional humanism of scholars like Eduard Spranger, the mandarin pedagogue. Baeumler put forth an argument about the new "political" university against the humanist tradition of Schleiermacher, Humboldt, and Fichte: "an institution of higher learning which in the very year of revolution speaks of leadership by *Geist* and *Idee* and not of leadership by Adolf Hitler and Horst Wessel is unpolitical . . . Hitler is not less than the *Idee*, he is more than the *Idee*—for he is real."[20] By placing the rector himself at the very head of the university, Heidegger, in his opening paragraph, was announcing a complete break with the longstanding traditions of German academic governance and placing himself firmly (with Baeumler) as a supporter of the new National Socialist *Führerprinzip*.

What Heidegger affirmed as the ground for his "spiritual leadership [*geistige Führung*]," however, was not his own authority (understood as a kind of Weberian "charismatic leadership"), but rather "the essence of the German university" itself. Moreover, by placing emphasis on "spiritual" rather than "political" leadership, Heidegger subtly alluded to his own notion of a "second revolution" that would prove "deeper" than the mere political takeover by the party (SL: 571/HBB: 60). What would lead "the students and teachers who constitute the rector's following" is the essence of the university itself which can, however, only attain power when the rector, in turn, is led by the inexorability of the spiritual mission bequeathed to the German *Volk* as its destiny. This metaphysical conjoining of spirit and essence at the axis of German destiny will powerfully shape the style and thematics of the entire address. From the very outset, the language of the address is rhetorical rather than constative; questions are posed, challenges are levied, everywhere there is a sense of urgency and purpose. Every page announces a dramatic call to the German people to return to its originary essence in and through a radical rethinking of the university's mission within national life. The rector's role, then, is to lead by following, to lead the *Volk* into the realm of questioning—which is itself the very essence of spiritual life. Through questioning, Heidegger hopes to awaken the university community and to lead it back to its roots in the essence of the university. Like the Schlageter speech delivered the previous day, the Rectorial Address will speak of roots and destiny in the martial language of battle and struggle.

Heidegger asks his audience: "do we know who we ourselves are? . . .

20. Baeumler, *Männerbund*, 126–127.

Can we know that at all . . . ?" And he puts forth a response: "we" cannot know ourselves merely by an acquaintance with the present conditions of the university nor by studying its history. We can only come to know ourselves through the hardness (*Härte*) of self-limitation, which requires a willing and asserting of ourselves. But what is self-assertion?

IV. THE ARCHEOLOGY OF SELF-ASSERTION

One of the more impenetrable parts of the address that the university audience heard on that festive Saturday in May of 1933 must have been the term "self-assertion" (*Selbstbehauptung*). Clearly the word rendered the effect of an active, energetic, resolute, and perhaps even martial commitment to the university's mission. What was the university's role to be in the new social and political order? Should it wait passively for the politically appointed ministers in Karlsruhe and Berlin to promulgate plans for bureaucratic reorganization and reform? Not at all. Rather, the university needed to actively assert its own role by returning to its essence, an essence that could not be grasped through the traditional humanistic path of scholarship or historical erudition, but only through a self-assertive willing of that essence in and through *philosophia*. In this sense, the very title of the address concealed a battle cry against: (1) the bureaucratic state apparatus of education; (2) the traditional Humboldtian model of university life; (3) the non-philosophical faculties within the present university structure; (4) the non-spiritual forces within German culture who sought to take charge of and direct the revolutionary energies of the moment; and (5) that part of the *Volk* who had forgotten the authentic roots of its own essence in spirit and in the Greeks.

However, the choice of the title concealed another decisive move, the decision to invoke Nietzsche as the spiritual center of the address. Although Nietzsche is named only once in the Rectorial Address, his signature signs for the whole argument and provides the discourse with its explicitly framed questions. What animates Heidegger's discussion in the address is the Nietzschean analysis of Western culture in terms of crisis, specifically the crisis of nihilism. But what proves even more decisive for Heidegger's way of proceeding is the crisis-narrative of Western history and philosophy that he inherits from Nietzsche, a narrative whose axial figure is Plato. If, for Nietzsche, Plato is the first metaphysician, the thinker who breaks with the Pre-Socratic spirit of *agon* (*Wettkampf*), *polemos* (*Auseinandersetzung*), and *eris* (*Streit*), then it is in and against his influence that Greek philosophy should be read. As Nietzsche put it in *Philosophy in the Tragic Age of the Greeks*: "The activity of the older philosophers . . . tended toward the healing and purification of the whole . . . thus did the philosopher protect and defend his home [*Heimat*]. But later, beginning with Plato, the philosopher becomes an exile and conspires against his native land [*Vaterland*]" (PTAG: 35/KSA 1: 810). Heidegger will apply Nietzsche's crisis-narrative to his own reading of Western history as nihilism, finding in Nietzsche himself "the last metaphysician." The whole argument of the Rectorial Address depends upon this figuration of Plato and Nietzsche as beginning and end, as *arche* and *eschaton* of Western metaphysics. This narrative structure will inform Heidegger's own reading of "essence" and especially the essence of *Wissenschaft*, since it is Heidegger's contention that genuine science is not *scientia* but *philosophia* and that genuine philosophy is Pre-Socratic in its essence. Hence, when Heidegger draws upon the name of Nietzsche in the Address, it is within the cluster of this idea-nexus. At the end of Western metaphysics, Nietzsche stands as a heroic figure who announces the closure of one epoch and the inauguration of another:

> And if our ownmost existence itself stands on the threshold of a great transformation; if it is true what the last German philosopher to passionately seek God, Friedrich Nietzsche, said: "God is dead"; if we must take seriously the abandonment of man today in the midst of being, what then does this imply for science? (RA: 33/SdU: 13)

What Heidegger does not make clear to his audience, but what determines the very logic of his investigation, is this axial status of Plato (at the beginning) and Nietzsche (at the end), leaving the present generation as one in the midst of transition (*Übergang*), which Heidegger then determines as the only way out of the West's decline (*Untergang*). As Heidegger put it in one of his political speeches, "The University in the National Socialist State": "Those of us today stand in the struggle [*Erkämpfung*] for a new reality. We are only a transition [*Übergang*], only a sacrifice [*Opfer*]. As warriors in this battle [*Kämpfer dieses Kampfes*], we have to be of hard stock [*ein hartes Geschlecht*], one that no longer clings to anything of its own, one that commits itself to the ground [*Grund*] of the *Volk*" (GA 16: 772). Heidegger's reference to "the death of God" then becomes a shorthand expression for this whole narrative understanding of Western history in terms of beginnings and ends. It is this self-same narrative structure that Heidegger will appropriate as the foundation for his Nietzsche lectures a few years later. In those very lectures, Heidegger would attest that the expression "'God is dead' is not an atheistic doctrine but the formula for the fundamental experience of an event in Western history" (GA 43: 193). But, given the context of the Rectorial Address, how is this crisis-narrative inscribed in the term "self-assertion"? And what does self-assertion have to do with Nietzsche?

Although Heidegger never explicitly defined self-assertion in his Rectorial Address, nor offered an account justifying its usage, the way he positioned the term within the conceptual nexus of other Nietzschean expressions such as will (*Wille*), force (*Kraft*), power (*Macht*), battle (*Kampf*), danger (*Gefahr*), necessity (*Not*), greatness (*Grösse*), fate (*Schicksal*), and others, helped to reinforce its close connection to will to power. As Heidegger put it, "the self-assertion of the German university is the originary, common will to its essence . . . The will to the essence [*Wille zum Wesen*] of the German university is the will to science [*Wille zur Wissenschaft*] as the will to the historical spiritual mission of the German *Volk* as a *Volk* that knows itself in its state. Science and German fate must *at the same time* come to their essential will to power [*im Wesenswille zur Macht kommen*]" (RA: 30/SdU: 10, translation altered).

The Nietzschean character of this language is unmistakable, but what is less obvious is the Nietzschean wordplay in Heidegger's use of the term "*Selbstbehauptung.*" Before he introduces this term proper, he prefaces it with a rhetorical display of word-cognates that share the same prefixes (Selbst-) and suffixes (-ung), all clustered around the notion of a self. Hence, Heidegger uses the terms "self-administration" (*Selbstverwaltung*), "self-reflection" (*Selbstbesinnung*), "self-limitation" (*Selbstbegrenzung*), finally leading up to the term *Selbstbehauptung.* Nested within this word-cluster is the subtle trace of the term *Selbsterhaltung* (self-preservation), a term that Nietzsche employs in *The Gay Science* to delimit the meaning of "will to power." Darwinian self-preservation, Nietzsche contends, is a mark of disease, not health; it is something one attaches to the sickly temperament of the scholar whose only life-expressions take the form of taxonomies, tables of categories, systems of files, and the like. And it is precisely within the rhetorical matrices of scholarship and the scholar that Nietzsche locates his discussion of self-preservation:

> *Once more the origin of scholars.*—The wish to preserve oneself is the symptom of a condition of distress, of a limitation of the really fundamental instinct of life which aims at *the expansion of power* and, wishing for that, frequently risks and even sacrifices self-preservation. It should be considered symptomatic when some philosophers—for example, Spinoza who was consumptive—considered the instinct of self-preservation decisive and *had* to see it that way; for they were individuals in conditions of distress [*Notlagen*] . . . and in nature it is not conditions of distress that are *dominant* but overflow and squandering, even to the point of absurdity. The struggle for existence is only an *exception*, a temporary restriction of the will to life. The great and small struggle always revolves around superiority, around growth and expansion, around power—in accordance with the will to power which is the will of life. (GS: 291–292/KSA 3: 585–586)

In his own discussion of *Selbsterhaltung* in the Nietzsche lectures, Heidegger conjoins it to the question of *Selbstbehauptung,* paronymously as it were, finding a kindred root in the phenomenon of will to power. Self-assertion is rooted in will to power, Heidegger claims; it is the plenary expression of the will's overflowing energy. Hence, just as will to power is not a willing "toward" something external to it (viz., power) but is itself, as power, nothing other than the actuality of willing, so too, Heidegger argues, self-assertion does not involve the assertion of something that the self does not have, but is rather the assertion of that which it already is, namely, its essence. Self-preservation, by way of contrast, becomes so ensnared within the reigning order of whatever is at hand that it loses any fundamental connection to its essence. It is within this context of the will to power—and its relation to self-preservation and the problem of essence—that Heidegger defines self-assertion:

> To will is to want to become stronger. Here too Nietzsche speaks by way of reversal and at the same time by way of defense against a contemporary trend, namely, Darwinism. Let us clarify this matter briefly. Life not only exhibits the drive to self-preservation, as Darwin thinks, but also is self-assertion. The will to preservation merely clings to what is already at hand, stubbornly insists upon it, loses itself in it, and so becomes blind to its proper essence. Self-assertion, that is, wanting to remain on top at the head [*im Haupt*] of things, is always a return to the essence, to the origin. *Self-assertion is originary [ursprüngliche] transformation of what is essential.* (Ni: 60–61/GA 43: 70, translation altered)

In this brief gloss on the problem of self-assertion, Heidegger forcefully identifies its Nietzschean patrimony. Taken literally, *Selbstbehauptung*, understood as "self-heading," is the placing of the self at the head of things in order to transform it at its essence—or, at its origin [*Ursprung*]. Self-assertion is thus a kind of strategical deployment of the self in the service of an *Ursprungsphilosophie*—and it is this privileging of the origin as the basis of all philosophy (as archeology, as genealogy, and as a return to the Pre-Socratic sources of Western philosophy) that places a Nietzschean stamp on Heidegger's entire thought, especially his political work of the early 1930s. More narrowly conceived, however, we need to ask about the implications of this *Ursprungsphilosophie* for the Rectorial Address and for Heidegger's collectivist understanding of the "self" in the German university's self-assertion.

By interpreting self-assertion as will to power and as "the originary transformation of what is essential" (*Wesensverwandlung*), Heidegger comes to two fundamental insights that intersect at the axis of origin. First, by conceiving of "will itself . . . [as] simultaneously creative and destructive," Heidegger breaks with the Darwinian tradition of self-preservation that understands will only in terms of its creative power, forgetting all the while its essential connection to the destructive. Second, by rejecting this Darwinian model of self-preservation in favor of an originary self-assertion, Heidegger succeeds in breaking with the whole linear, evolution-ary, and progressivist metaphysics of history that forces the destiny of the German *Volk* into the frame of a Hegelian narrative about "progress in the consciousness of freedom."[21] Against this developmental, historicist model of time, Heidegger will follow Nietzsche's path by inverting the Hegelian narrative of progress by means of a return to the origin. In this way the setting forth (*Aufbruch*) into the future (which Heidegger sees as the essential meaning of the National Socialist revolution) will depend upon a radical break (*Bruch*) with the past that enables the *Volk* to reap-propriate its essence by way of a circular return.[22] This movement toward essence then is construed by Heidegger as a kind of *Heimkehr* or "home-coming." And although the course of this movement is at times labyrinthine and confusing, Heidegger makes one thing clear: the path to the future can only be followed by an essential self-assertion that asserts its own self in and through its return to the origin.

What emerges from Heidegger's involuted logic of return is an arche-ology of self-assertion that offers an account (*logos*) of the origin (*arche*) which, at the same time, functions as a *mythos* for a future *Heimkehr*. Nietzsche would, of course, reject the *völkisch* implications of this read-ing of self-assertion, finding in the communal affirmation of the will an otiose expression of will to power. For him, the communitarian impulse represented the vulgar and banal form of a herd mentality that rejected all creative impulses in favor of an unbridled self-negation and -destruc-tion. And yet, Heidegger would always read this differently. His Hölder-linian dream of establishing a new German future by returning to the essence of the *Volk* would place his work at radical odds with Nietzsche. For Heidegger, the necessity of self-assertion was always the task of the *Volk*. And the only proper path to self-assertion lay in radical question-ing, a task that could best be carried out, or so Heidegger thought, at the university. But how was the self-assertion of a *Volk* related to the task of the self-assertion of the German university? And how could the uni-versity fulfill the Hölderlinian demand to return to the essence of the *Volk*? Heidegger put forward a response to these questions by reframing them as different ways of posing the question: What is the essence of the university?

21. G.W.F. Hegel, *Vorlesungen über die Philosophie der Weltgeschichte* (Hamburg: Meiner, 1970), 63.
22. On the figural meaning of *Bruch, Aufbruch, Ausbruch, Durchbruch, Einbruch,* and other cognates in Heidegger, see the insightful articles by Frank Edler, "Philosophy, Language, and Politics: Heidegger's Attempt to Steal the Language of the Revolution in 1933–34," *Social Research* 57, no. 1 (1990): 197–238, and "Heidegger's Interpretation of the German 'Revolu-tion'," *Research in Phenomenology* 23 (1993): 153–171. Edler discusses the rich context of this conceptual nexus in Hölderlin, Scheler, von Hellingrath, Krieck, and others.

V. THE ESSENCE OF SCIENCE AS *PHILOSOPHIA*

Heidegger's complex argument in the Rectorial Address hinges upon a series of fundamental assertions whose own metaphysical ground is merely rhetorically addressed, never "essentially" uncovered. But if, as Heidegger made clear in the Nietzsche lectures, self-assertion is nothing other than "essential-assertion" (*Wesensbehauptung*) (or, assertion of the essence), then the self-assertion of the university means the assertion of its essence. And here Heidegger turns the question of essence back upon the historical foundations of the Humboldt university and its taxonomic division of the sciences. As far back as the War Emergency Semester of 1919, Heidegger had railed against the deadening effects of university life upon authentic existence. At the very outset of those lectures, he claimed that "today we are not ripe enough for *genuine* reforms in the realm of the university . . ." (GA 56/57: 4). In this same spirit, he writes to Elisabeth Blochmann in 1918, lamenting "the sickly confusion in the programmatic reform proposals and theories about 'the essence of the university'" (HBB: 7). Heidegger's assault upon the sclerotic, calcified institutions of higher learning continued throughout the Weimar years, culminating in his lecture course of the summer semester of 1929 in which he chose the explicit theme "Introduction [*Einführung*] to Academic Studies." The academic *Führer* who would lead his students into the problem of academic studies opened the semester by pronouncing that "academic study today has become questionable." Students, he claimed, are possessed of "the knowledge that despite the greatest accomplishments of their science, something essential is lacking."

> The whole of science and genuine learning do not even come into view for those who are studying. The university is more and more taking on the character of a department store where knowledge gets dispensed as if it were just another present at hand object. The university has become a trade school. The faculties of law and medicine especially are cut off from the university without a thought and set up as if they were independent trade schools. . . . Today at the university aren't we missing what is essential? Haven't we all lost the sense of community and of something shared in common which we as students should have? Can academic study still be grasped in this way as a totality? Can it maintain the proximity to the world which it should have? This characteristic sense of existing within the totality of the world, which academic studies once was (and should be), needs to be awakened once again. . . . We need to attempt to grasp science and philosophy in their essential being while, at the same time, keeping in view their unity. (GA 28: 347–348)

During this period Heidegger had put forth a devastating critique of the disciplinary boundaries that prevailed at the university. He especially challenged the conventional division of research into the separate "fields" of the natural sciences (*Naturwissenschaften*) and human sciences (*Geisteswissenschaften*) that dominated the philosophical work of the Neo-Kantians and the Dilthey school.[23] But Heidegger also challenged the burgeoning prestige of the new social sciences, such as psychology, sociology, and anthropology, as well as the modish forms of National Socialist "folk science" (*völkische Wissenschaft*) and "politicized science" (*politische Wissenschaft*). None of these so-called "sciences" had achieved the measure of self-reflection, self-limitation, or self-administration that Heidegger considered fundamental to the constitution of a genuine science. They merely represented the rise of a technical model of learning that had rendered the traditional Humboldtian ideal of *Bildung* superfluous and nugatory.

To supplant this humanist ideal of education, National Socialist philosophers such as Ernst Krieck and Alfred Baeumler had proposed their own plans for university reform. Krieck shared Heidegger's concern that the German university "no longer has a unified basis and a singular direction of meaning." Against the widespread dispersion of knowledge into specialized, technical fields that isolated the individual and turned him into a mere "specialist," Krieck, in his Rectorial Address, proposed a "unified *völkisch*-political worldview." As he saw it,

> Above all, a new philosophy needs to be developed from the problems and tasks of each academic discipline, a philosophy which will meaningfully bring together the multiplicity of these disciplines under a unified worldview, like arches under the dome of a great cathedral. Such a new philosophy would establish a unified goal for all scientific work across the boundaries of the academic disciplines—thus achieving a total worldview out of the interweaving of individual details. . . . In this way, the university will be able to fulfill its task of national-political education.[24]

Baeumler too argued that in the revolutionary moment of the present, science would have to undergo revision. "The university of the future will be political," Baeumler assured his audience, "because it is grounded in the political character of science, a science that is in itself political insofar as it will always set itself against other spiritual forces. . . ."[25] But if Heidegger shared with his colleagues Krieck and Baeumler a zeal for pedagogical reform and revolution, he broke with them over the issue of how to implement these changes. Heidegger supported the notion that science must have its roots in the *Volk*, but he could not support the idea of a National Socialist *völkische Wissenschaft*. Nor could he condone the attempts made by the party and state to politicize scientific research or to force its

23. See Charles Bambach, *Heidegger, Dilthey, and the Crisis of Historicism* (Ithaca: Cornell University Press, 1995).

24. Ernst Krieck, *Die Erneuerung der Universität* (Frankfurt: Bechhold, 1933), 9.

25. Baeumler, *Männerbund*, 145.

inquiry within the frame of a racial-biological metaphysics. The essence of the university, Heidegger contends, is rooted in science; however, science in its present form at the university is a mere semblance of what it originally was. In this sense, the Rectorial Address takes up, in reconstituted form, the basic argument from "What is Metaphysics?" that "the rootedness of the sciences in their essential ground has atrophied" (BW: 96/WM: 2). Against the prevailing tendency to identify science with its contemporary forms and practices, Heidegger calls for a radical rethinking of the essence of science in terms of its original roots which he then locates in the ancient Greek practice of *philosophia*.

Genuine *Wissenschaft* in this originary sense is not mere evident and self-certain knowledge on the model of *scientia;* it has, rather, the character of what Plato in the *Theaetetus* termed *thaumazein* or "wonderment." "The beginning [*arche*] of all wisdom [*philosophia*] lies in wonderment [*thaumazein*]," Socrates tells the young Theaetetus, a claim that Heidegger will seize upon in his Rectorial Address as he seeks to reshape the German university in accordance with this Platonic truth (*Theaetetus*, 155d). *Thaumazein*, or what Heidegger termed "the initial wondering perseverance in the face of what is," constitutes the root, the beginning, and the *arche* of genuine science (RA: 33/SdU: 13). And it is only by retrieving the wonder of that originary beginning that the German *Volk* can come to its own concealed essence. But Heidegger poses a decisive question to his audience: how can we experience this originary essence? "We" can experience it, Heidegger tells them,

> . . . only if we again place ourselves under the power of the beginning of our spiritual-historical existence. This beginning is the departure, the setting out [*Aufbruch*] of Greek philosophy. That is when, from the culture of one *Volk* and by the power of that *Volk*'s language, Western man rises up for the first time against *the totality of what is* and questions it and comprehends it as the being that it is. All science is philosophy, whether it knows it and wills it or not. All science remains bound to that beginning of philosophy and draws from it the strength of its essence, assuming that it still remains at all equal to this beginning. (RA: 31/SdU: 11)

This decision to place itself under the power of the *arche* marks the *Volk*'s commitment to the task of self-assertion. But the essence of science as *philosophia-thaumazein* cannot be retrieved without a profound commitment to radical questioning as the source of this self-assertion. The *Volk* must be willing to embrace "questioning itself [as] . . . the highest form of knowledge" (RA: 33/SdU: 13). If the *Volk* does genuinely appropriate this Greek legacy of radical questioning as the source of its science, then it will be able to disrupt the reign of metaphysical science over its own destiny. In lieu of the comfortable, encapsulated spheres of technical learning at the university, the *Volk* would then be able to pursue science in its intimate connection to *Dasein,* rather than as a career choice. By providing the sciences with a common aim and by unifying them in the name "of all the world-shaping forces of humanity's historical existence," the *Volk* comes to a decision about its most fundamental identity, which is another way of posing the question concerning spirit (*Geist*). For Heidegger, "spirit is the primordially attuned, knowing resoluteness toward the essence of being" (RA: 33/SdU: 14); it is the power that is rooted in the soil and blood of a *Volk.* Only a spiritual world can guarantee the *Volk* greatness—but will the *Volk* choose this greatness or will it passively accept decline? The decision facing the *Volk*—whether to assert its own originary rootedness in Greek *thaumazein* or to accept the rootless reign of the sciences and their centrifugal forces of dispersion—posed, in a reconstituted form, the same choice that Heidegger outlined in 1929 between the rootedness (*Bodenständigkeit*) of German spiritual life or its increasing Judification.[26] Each alternative constituted a fundamental choice about the German future: Athens or Jerusalem? Which path would the *Volk* follow—the rootedness of the *arche* or the rootlessness of Jewish modernism?

For Heidegger, the choice was always clear. Like Nietzsche, "who revert[ed] to the beginning of Western philosophy," Heidegger would always choose the road to Athens (Ni: 19/GA 43: 22). In the world-moment of 1933, Heidegger exhorted the German *Volk* to engage in a heroic struggle to assert itself against the rootless nihilism of the modern world. Self-assertion would take the form of a *Kampf;* it would involve a battle against the levelling forces of the present to win back the originary beginning for the future. In this sense, the Rectorial Address needs to be read as a battle cry, a piece of martial rhetoric whose invocation of the *Volksgemeinschaft* as a *Kampfgemeinschaft* serves notice that the decision to win back the greatness of the Greek beginning will require the heroic resoluteness of a Schlageter (SdU: 18). "The beginning still *is,*" Heidegger insists.

> It does not lie *behind* us as something long past, but it stands *before* us. The beginning has—as the greatest moment, which exists in advance—already passed indifferently over and beyond all that is to come and hence over and beyond us as well. The beginning has invaded our future; it stands there as the distant decree that commands us to recapture its greatness.
>
> Only if we resolutely obey this decree to win back the greatness of the beginning, only then will science become the innermost necessity of our existence. Otherwise, science will remain something in which we become involved purely by chance or will remain a calm, pleasurable activity, an activity free of danger, which promotes the mere advancement of knowledge.

26. *Die Zeit,* December 22, 1989, 50.

> If, however, we obey the distant decree of the beginning, then science must become the fundamental event of our spiritual existence as a *Volk*. (RA: 32–33/SdU: 12–13)

The task of this *Kampfgemeinschaft* is "to realize the original and full essence of science . . . decreed in the distant past" (RA: 36/SdU: 16). But as Heidegger had already made plain in his Plato course from 1931/32, essence could never be derived from a phenomenon through scientific inquiry of the traditional sort; it could only be won through confrontation (*Auseinandersetzung*) and struggle (*Kampf*) (GA 34: 92). The self-assertion of the German university would demand a Heraclitean sensitivity to the strife-yielding play of *aletheia*, a Nietzschean will to mastery over oneself in and through the *agon* with others, and a Jüngerian commitment to total mobilization whereby all private concerns would be prescinded through public service to the *Volk*. What the Germans faced in 1933 was not merely an administrative question about university reform but a decision about the destiny of the Occident. "Here, in this place, in this lecture hall," as Heidegger put it in his discussion of university reform in 1921, the German *Volk* would have to make the decision that Nietzsche had prepared for them: either to accept the nihilism of decline or to return to the greatness of the ancient Greeks (GA 61: 63). If the Volk wished to accept the challenge of this decision, however, it would have to assert itself through a resolute will to the *archontic* essence of science, an essence whose being (*ontos on*) was rooted in the beginning (*arche*). In other words, the destiny of the *Volk* and, in turn, the destiny of the West, was made dependent upon the fundamental tenets of *Ursprungsphilosophie*. And therein lay its danger.

The *Kampf* for the *arche* would be dangerous; it would require that the teachers of the university "advance to the outermost post," "stand their ground," and "find new courage." It would also require that the students be "on the march," mindful of the need for "struggling ever anew for its spiritual world." In this mutually determinative struggle of the two forces, the will to self-assertion would emerge.

> The teachers' will to essence must awaken to the simplicity and breadth of the knowledge of the essence of science and grow strong. The students' will to essence must force itself into the highest clarity and discipline of knowledge and must shape, through its demands and determinations, the engaged knowledge of the *Volk* and its state and incorporate this knowledge into the essence of science. Both wills must ready themselves for mutual struggle. All capacities of will and thought, all strengths of the heart, and all capabilities of the body must be developed *through* struggle, must be intensified *in* struggle, and must remain preserved *as* struggle. . . . [S]truggle alone will keep this opposition open and implant within the entire body of teachers and students that fundamental mood out of which self-limiting self-

assertion [*sich begrenzende Selbstbehauptung*] will empower resolute self-reflection [*Selbstbesinnung*] to true self-administration [*Selbstverwaltung*]. (RA: 37–38/SdU: 18–19)

For those who had heard the Schlageter speech the day before, these martial references to "*Kampf,*" "courage," and the Jüngerian virtues of the warrior, came as no surprise. Nor did the reference to Clausewitz (amidst the other citations from Nietzsche, Plato, and Aeschylus) seem as jarring as it might appear today. The *Kampfgemeinschaft* of the university would have to engage in battle with the forces of decline, a battle that would transform the university from its present identity as a trade school into its "futural" mission of providing a site for originary questioning. As the vanguard of a "second," ontological revolution, Heidegger's self-asserting German university would lead the German *Volk* back to its roots. But this commitment to the original essence of science as the proper task of the university would demand a threefold bond from the German *Volk*, a bond that would demand the end of the careerist, trade school model and the beginning of a new ideal of public service.

VI. PLATO'S *STAAT* AND HEIDEGGER'S *VOLK*

Part of Heidegger's aim in offering a new model of public service involved making philosophy the very center of university existence. If, at the founding of the Humboldt university in 1810, philosophy had provided the model for university study, by 1933 the situation had changed dramatically. The growing prestige of the natural sciences, the technical demands of an industrial economy, and the bourgeois predilection for the safe, comfortable careers of law, medicine, and business had all combined to dethrone philosophy from its erstwhile status as queen of the sciences. Fichte's *Wissenschaftslehre*, Hegel's *Phenomenology of Spirit*, and Kant's *Critique of Pure Reason* had long lost their office of providing a metaphysical foundation for the sciences. Philosophy, in short, had definitively ceased to be a *scientia scientiarum* or a science of science itself. And yet Heidegger's Rectorial Address set forth the bold proposal to reposition philosophy at the very center of university life by making it a new kind of *Wissenschaft*. In order to carry out this program, however, Heidegger deemed it necessary to free philosophy from its moorings in academic theory and allow it free reign in the realm of questioning. This radical approach to philosophy as an open path of questioning rather than a fixed system of doctrine, was something that the young Heidegger had already learned from Plato and Aristotle.

In his 1921/22 course, *Phenomenological Interpretations to Aristotle*, Heidegger indicated that genuine philosophy is an experience rather than a theory; it offers us "not the saving coast but the leap into the tossing boat where everything hangs upon getting hold of the sail line and looking to the wind . . . Stable ground [*der feste Boden*] lies in laying hold of questionability" (GA 61: 37).[27] And in 1923/24, Heidegger opened his lecture course, "Introduction to Phenomenological Research," by declaring, "it is my conviction that philosophy is at an end" (GA 17: 1). Traditional Neo-Kantian philosophy as an academic *Kathederphilosophie*, offering rostrum-style pronouncements was dead; even from the early Freiburg days Heidegger had launched an assault against the insular theoretical world of the traditional university. But in his courses on Plato, especially the one from 1931/32, "On the Essence of Truth," Heidegger had uncovered a hidden understanding of Greek *theoria* as something other than mere theory. In the Platonic understanding of *theorein* as the highest form of life (*bios theoretikos*), Heidegger located the possibility of overcoming the dichotomy between theory and praxis that reigned throughout the academy. This chasm between the theoretical and the practical had poisoned the very ideal of scholarly comportment bequeathed to the German university by the neo-humanist tradition of the Humboldt era. But Heidegger sought to rethink the theory/praxis relation. From the 1928/29 Freiburg course, "Introduction to Philosophy," Heidegger had understood Aristotle's *Nicomachean Ethics* (1176b–1177b) to mean that "the fundamental theoretical attitude is the highest. Why? . . . The fundamental theoretical attitude is that kind of *praxis* in which the human being can be authentically human. It is proper to note that *theoria* is not merely a particular kind of *praxis* but the most authentic kind of all" (GA 27: 174). The crisis of modern science, however, lay in its inability to recover the authenticity of this praxis. "The contemporary scholar," Heidegger writes, "has distanced himself from the origin." Hence, any attempt by the neo-humanist mandarins to renew the ideal of the Greeks "remains a feeble matter for scholars who can perhaps flock around a journal—*Antike*—but none of this gets to the roots of contemporary existence" (GA 27: 167).[28]

By May of 1933, Heidegger's appropriation of the Platonic-Aristotelian *bios theoretikos* would be wedded to a *völkisch* understanding of the *Politeia*. For Plato, the *polis* was to serve as the site of philosophical education or *paideia*. Indeed, within the history of the West, the *Republic* functions as a model of authentic education, since it presents *philosophia* not as a kind of theoretical *Bildung* but as a dialogic, interactive praxis of incessant ques-

27. Theodore Kisiel's translation here gets to the heart of Heidegger's life-long preoccupation with "experience"; see Theodore Kisiel, *The Genesis of Heidegger's "Being and Time"* (Berkeley: University of California Press, 1993), 233.

28. For details on Jaeger's journal *Die Antike*, see Donald O. White, "Werner Jaeger's 'Third Humanism'," 282–285.

tioning. Philosophy here is presented as "the longer path" rather than as "the saving coast" (*Republic* 504c; GA 61: 37). "*Paideia* is not *Bildung*," Heidegger claims, "but *hemetera physis*, that which holds sway as our ownmost being" (GA 34: 114). But philosophical *paideia* is also set forth in *The Republic* as a praxis whose aim is leadership of the polis: the formation of the philosopher-king. In the context of the Rectorial Address, *paideia* would become, in accordance with another etymological root of *hemetera*, a *hemetera physis* of the fatherland and the *Heimat:* "that which holds sway over our homeland."[29] In accordance with this polis-centered *paideia* of Plato, Heidegger seek to rethink the roots of the National Socialist state in terms of the originary Greek understanding of science as *philosophia* and to place the university at the center of the "second, deeper revolution." Plato's presence in the Rectorial Address thus comes to signify the deep affinity between the German mission of rescuing the West through *Wissenschaft* (in its essential form) and the originary Greek founding of Western science as *philosophia*. Beyond this, however, Plato also comes to symbolize a new vision of the National Socialist state.

Most scholarship on Plato in Germany between the early nineteenth century and the Great War had been dominated by the contributions of Friedrich Schleiermacher, Ulrich von Wilamowitz-Moellendorff, and by the Neo-Kantian philosophers, Eduard Zeller and Paul Natorp.[30] Generally, philological studies focused on the unity and development of the Platonic system, while philosophical work concentrated on the meaning and significance of Plato's epistemology and metaphysics. Within these studies Plato came to be regarded as a humanist, a Kantian, a metaphysician, and the founder of an enduring theory of ideas. By the time of Heidegger's

29. *Benselers Griechisch-Deutsches Wörterbuch*, 385, translates *hemetera* as "unser Land, unser Vaterland, unsere Heimat" (our land, our fatherland, our homeland).

30. For a history of the German interpretation of Plato, see E.N. Tigerstedt, *Interpreting Plato* (Stockholm: Almquist & Wiskell, 1977); Hans-Joachim Krämer, *Plato and the Foundations of Metaphysics* (Albany: SUNY Press, 1990); and Ada Hentschke and Ulrich Muhlack, *Einführung in die Geschichte der klassischen Philologie*. Paul Natorp's study of 1902, *Platos Ideenlehre* (Darmstadt: Wissenschaftliche Buchgesellschaft, 1961) was decisive for the Neo-Kantian reading of Plato that Heidegger and his NS contemporaries were trying to dismantle: Kurt Hildebrandt, *Platon: Der Kampf des Geistes um die Macht* (Berlin: Bondi, 1933) and Carl Vering, *Platons Staat* (Frankfurt: Englert & Schlosser, 1932). Part of what Heidegger attempts in GA 34 and the Rectorial Address is a rethinking of the whole tradition in terms of a new, "futural" *arche* that will transform the originary Greek experience of truth opened up in Plato's Allegory of the Cave and in the Pre-Socratics. As Hildebrandt put it in his essay "Das neue Platon-Bild," *Blätter für deutsche Philosophie* 4 (1930): 190–202. "A new portrait of Plato can emerge only if a new man emerges first." This standard NS commitment to "the new man" became a staple of the academic right. But the use and abuse of Plato for political purposes in the early Nazi years was also typical. Carl Vering exemplifies this position in the preface to *Platos Dialoge in freier Darstellung* (Leipzig: Freytag, 1935), vii–viii. In 1935, Vering writes: "the hopes which ten years ago gave me the courage to attempt to introduce congenial readers (especially German youth) to the intellectual world of the great political philosopher, Plato, have been fulfilled in an unexpected way through the national revolution of 1933."

Rectorial Address, however, this situation changes dramatically. A new *Platonbild* emerges within Germany that shifts attention away from the traditional dialogues and the theory of ideas; now most academic energy is directed toward a political reading of *The Republic, The Laws,* and *The Seventh Letter.*[31] Reacting against the paralytic spirit of the older generation's historicism and positivism, Werner Jaeger puts forth a reading of Plato that attempts to make *The Republic* a new and vital form of political *paideia* for the Germans. Like Heidegger, he unearths a unique spiritual kinship between the Greeks and Germans which, he claims, manifests itself in the primordial affinity of *paideia* and *Bildung.* "When a Greek says 'education' [*paideia*]," Jaeger writes, "he means something different than what other nations mean, namely, what the German language calls '*Bildung*', which has the feel about it of something deeply Greek. And it appears as if he could not think at all otherwise."[32]

In the charged political atmosphere of the moment, Plato becomes a "crisis-philosopher," as Kurt Hildebrandt, a member of the George Circle, put it.[33] Against the traditional interpretations put forth of him as a meditative sage or as an aesthetic humanist, Plato's new role (in Hildebrandt's words) is to become a "prototype for the Germans of a saviour in times of dissolution and destruction." Moreover, the schema for the salvation of the Germans is thought to be prefigured in *The Republic.* As Hans Heyse attests in his Rectorial Address, Plato's *Politeia* offers "an originary form of the idea of the *Reich* . . . As Plato's philosophy takes the fundamental values of Greek *Dasein* as its starting point and culminates in the *Politeia* (thereby creating the originary form of philosophy and science)—so our philosophy and science takes as its starting point the fundamental values of Teutonic-German man (manifested once again in the war) in order to attain its highest rank in the idea and reality of the *Reich.*"[34] Carl Vering, the editor of a popular version of Plato's *Der Staat,* also drew a portentous comparison between the archetype of Plato's *Republic* and the destiny of the German *Volk:* "the same fate also broke forth upon our German fatherland and so we stand before the task which Plato put before us—to embark upon the reconstruction of the state and of a new culture from

---

31. For an informative history of the *NS Platonbild,* see Teresa Orozco, *Platonische Gewalt: Gadamers politische Hermeneutik der NS-Zeit* (Hamburg: Argument, 1995), and her essay "Die Platon-Rezeption in Deutschland um 1933" in *'Die Besten Geister der Nation': Philosophie und Nationalsozialismus,* ed. Ilse Korotin (Vienna: Picus, 1994), 141–185.

32. Werner Jaeger, "Antike und Humanismus," in *Humanistische Reden und Vorträge* (Berlin: de Gruyter, 1937), 115.

33. Kurt Hildebrandt, "Das neue Platon-Bild," 190: "Plato is a model of the savior in times of dissolution and destruction." Teresa Orozco, *Platonische Gewalt,* 40–44.

34. Hans Heyse, *Die Idee der Wissenschaft und die deutsche Universität,* 12. Heyse, like many of his NS contemporaries (including Heidegger), invokes Plato as a way of grounding the "originary" essence of the German *Volk* in a Greek beginning or *arche.*

the ruins of a great past."[35] This new political reading of Plato was expressed in a series of works whose very titles manifested a challenge to the traditional *Platonbild:* Adolf Rusch's "Plato as Educator of German Men," Hildebrandt's *Plato: the Struggle of Spirit for Power,* Herbert Holtorf's "Plato: the Selection [*Auslese*] and Formation [*Bildung*] of Leaders [*Führer*] and Warriors," and Joachim Bannes' *Hitlers Kampf und Platons Staat.*[36]

Within National Socialist political philosophy, Plato became a model for the analysis of the "total state" which would mobilize its youth in the service of a pedagogical-political revolution. As Hildebrandt put it, "for that which we today call 'the total state' there is no more perfect figuration than Plato's *Politeia.*"[37] In Plato's discussion of *paideia,* these NS philosophers found a prototype for racial breeding (*Zucht*), biological selection (*Auslese*), and the education of leaders (*Führer*) who would serve as the new guardians of a state organized according to Plato's tripartite division of labor in *The Republic.* Ernst Krieck went so far as to invoke Plato as a model of education for the SS: "no one has known the power of the muses as deeply as Plato, who once again can become our teacher. For the education of those in the *Bünde,* in the state youth groups, in the *Reichswehr,* and in the military squadrons of the SA, the SS, and the *Stahlhelm,* this education modeled on the muses has become a necessity."[38] Plato's heroic, anti-democratic, elitist vision of a new political order had been transmitted to the Germans as a way to reorganize their society in deep kinship with their spiritual predecessors. As a philosopher who could teach the Germans that everything is governed by struggle, Plato became indeed a "thinker in a time of need."

Heidegger's only explicit reference to Plato in the Rectorial Address came at the very end when he cited the now famous line: "*ta . . . megala panta episphale . . .* " ("all that is great stands in the storm . . .") (*Republic,* 497d). But the signature of Plato was imprinted on almost every page of the text. In the very opening paragraph, the discussion of "spiritual leadership" (*geistige Führung*) takes up the question of the philosopher-king now recast to fit the situation of the German university. Heidegger's crucial decision to root his discussion of spiritual leadership in terms of the university's essence rather than its present historical appearance also shows Plato's influence. Moreover, Heidegger's reconfiguration of the *bios*

35. Carl Vering, *Platos Dialoge,* vii.
36. Adolf Rusch, "Plato als Erzieher zum deutschen Menschen," *Humanistische Bildung im nationalsozialistischen Staat,* 9 (1933): 44–49; Kurt Hildebrandt, *Platon: Der Kampf des Geistes um die Macht;* Herbert Holtorf, *Platon: Auslese und Bildung der Führer und Wehrmänner* (Berlin: Teubner, 1934); and Joachim Bannes, *Hitlers Kampf und Platons Staat* (Berlin: de Gruyter, 1933).
37. Kurt Hildebrandt, "Anmerkungen," in *Der Staat* by Platon (Leipzig: Kröner, 1935), 364.
38. Ernst Krieck, *Musische Erziehung* (Leipzig: Armanen, 1933), i.

theoretikos as something more originary than mere theory; his rethinking of *Wissenschaft* as *philosophia* and of *philosophia* as *thaumazein;* his determined insistence on an understanding of philosophy as a heroic stance of resolute struggle rather than as an academic form of ceaseless research and self-preoccupied careerism—all these reinforce the Platonic character of the Rectorial Address. But what clearly marks Heidegger's National Socialist-Platonic view of the university is his blueprint for concrete university reform in the threefold bond of German students to "the *Volksgemeinschaft,* . . . the honor and destiny of the nation, . . . [and] the bond . . . to the spiritual mission of the German *Volk*" (RA: 35/SdU: 15). It is with this ambitious proposal for the radically "national" and "social" *völkisch* university that Heidegger attempted to become the Platonic leader of the German nation, the philosophical *Führer* to lead the *Führer.*

Heidegger's National-Socialist retrieval of the *Politeia* repeated Plato's tripartite division of labor between workers/farmers; soldiers/auxiliaries; thinkers/philosophers. For Heidegger the future of German society depended upon a recovery of this threefold scheme in the form of a resolute commitment to service (*Dienst*) in the name of the *Volk.* But this service can only be performed in turn when the students, in an act of determined self-assertion, "place themselves under the law of their essence and thereby delimit this essence for the very first time" (RA: 34/SdU: 15). Alluding to the idealist tradition of Kant and Fichte, Heidegger affirms that "giving the law [*nomos*] to oneself [*autos*] is the highest freedom." But the autonomy of Heidegger's discourse is wedded to a Platonic vision of a total state where freedom does not lie in the arbitrary sphere of individual liberty. Heidegger has in mind, rather, Jünger's notion of "total mobilization" whereby "each individual life becomes ever more unambiguously the life of a worker."[39]

Heidegger claims that in an age of unbridled nihilism the only possibility for genuine freedom lies in service to the state. He then proposes that this new concept of freedom will enjoin students to three equiprimordial bonds. "The three bonds—*through* the *Volk to* the destiny of the state *in* its spiritual mission—are *equiprimordial.* The three forms of service that follow from them—labor service [*Arbeitsdienst*], military service [*Wehrdienst*], and knowledge service [*Wissensdienst*]—are equally necessary and of equal rank" (RA: 36/SdU: 16). Heidegger argues for the equiprimordial status of the three bonds within German society and against any hierarchical scheme of organization since (in good National Socialist fashion) he wants to think of the state not as a mere political entity but as a *völkische Gemeinschaft* whose very essence consists in its spiritual

39. Ernst Jünger, "Total Mobilization," in *The Heidegger Controversy,* ed. Richard Wolin (New York: Columbia University Press, 1991), 128.

mission. What this mission entails, as the Rectorial Address repeats several times, is the recovery of the spirit of antiquity for a radical renewal of the German *Volk* in and through its self-assertion of spiritual kinship with the Greeks. In itself, this definition of the German mission was not unique. We have seen how various other prominent philosophers and philologists had transformed the idea of "spiritual mission" into their own cultural-political programs. Still, the core of these programs was always educational. As Werner Jaeger put it in the introduction to his three-volume history of Greek culture, *Paideia:*

> Physically and intellectually . . . our history still begins with the Greeks. I have therefore called our own group of nations Hellenocentric. By "begins" I mean not only the temporal commencement, but also the *arche*, the spiritual source to which, as we reach every new stage of development, we must constantly revert in order to reorient ourselves. That is why throughout our history we always return to Greece. . . . Yet our kinship with Greece is not merely racial, however important the racial factor may be in understanding the nature of a *Volk* . . . [it is] based on a true and active spiritual kinship.[40]

This supposed spiritual kinship between the Greeks and the Germans, whose cultivation figures like Jaeger, Heyse, Baeumler, Hildebrandt, and Heidegger posited as the most pressing task of the German *Volk*, became the basis of a National Socialist revolutionary consciousness. In *Mein Kampf*, Hitler himself had argued that "the struggle that rages today concerns great goals: a culture is fighting for its existence, one that joins together millennia and embraces Greece and Germany together."[41] Heidegger's archetype for the coming National Socialist revolution—the ontological one, not the political revolution that Hitler had deemed "over" in 1934—was the tripartite social blueprint of *The Republic,* given a Nietzschean and Jüngerian stamp.

Where Plato had clearly privileged the philosopher kings as the highest estate over the workers and soldiers, Heidegger, with his *völkisch* and heroic values, wished to see the philosopher as co-original or equiprimordial with the other two groups. For him, equiprimordiality defined the proper balance between these three classes, since what animates their service is not their own goals but the spiritual mission [*geistigen Auftrag*] of the *Volk* that then guides the destiny of the nation. Clearly, those who had been regularly attending Heidegger's lectures must have been struck by the mention of *Wissensdienst* as co-original with *Arbeits-* and *Wehrdienst*. The Plato lectures of 1931/32 had clearly privileged the philosopher over the worker and the soldier, seeing in the prisoner who escaped the cave, beheld the sun, and then returned back again, a heroic figure who represented the highest ideal of the *polis:* radical questioning.

40. Werner Jaeger, *Paideia* (New York: Oxford University Press, 1965), 1: xv–xvi.
41. Adolf Hitler, *Mein Kampf* (Munich: Zentralverlag der NSDAP, 1936), 470.

Moreover, Heidegger's whole manner of proceeding in the Rectorial Address gave precedence to the university (over the factory and the barracks) as the vanguard of the second revolution. It was only within the university that the essence of the *Volk* (through a radical rethinking of the essence of *Wissenschaft*) could be uncovered. In the Rectorial Address, Heidegger continued to insist that "the highest realization of genuine practice" was theory. And yet this seems to go against his claims about the equiprimordiality of the three services. How should we understand this? Clearly, part of Heidegger's emphasis is rhetorical; he means to offer, as a new National Socialist rector, an account of the university that accords with the "social" aspects of the national revolution. But we can also detect in this discussion a way of dismantling the outmoded structures of insular academic theorizing that plagued the neo-humanist Humboldt university.

Armed with a new martial rhetoric and with Jünger's analysis of the worker, Heidegger wanted to revolutionize the standard forms of self-definition that plagued the Weimar university. In Jünger's Nietzschean reading of modern society, work reshapes individual and communal life by reconfiguring it as will to power. The worker is no longer a mere appendage to the technological drive of productive forces but has forged "a new relationship to the elemental energies, freedom and power, which is uniquely his."[42] As Nietzsche put it in his notebooks from the 1880s: "From the future of the worker.—Workers should learn to feel like soldiers . . . in possession of power" (WP: 399/WM: 506).

In his Rectorial Address Heidegger genuinely sought to revolutionize university life by forcing it within the question-frame of the total state. Yet as he continued to privilege philosophy as the only authentic possibility for national renewal, Heidegger also sought to bring it in line with his *völkisch, heimatlich,* and heroic values. In this way, he could drive the philosopher from the library and the classroom and compel him to confront the national task of work-service in dedication to the state. As he would later put it in a speech to a group of recently employed workers in the National Socialist labor service:

> *Wissenschaft* is not the possession of a privileged class of citizens, to be used as a weapon in the exploitation of the working people. Rather, *Wissenschaft* is merely the *more rigorous* and therefore *more responsible* form of that knowledge which the entire German *Volk* must seek and demand for its own historical existence as a state. . . . *In its essence,* the knowledge of true *Wissenschaft* does *not* differ *at all* from the knowledge of the farmer, the woodcutter, the miner, the artisan. For knowledge means: *to know one's way*

42. Ernst Jünger, *Der Arbeiter,* 78.

around in the world into which we are placed, as a community and as individuals . . . all work is *as work* something spiritual [*Geistiges*]. . . . The accomplishment of a miner is no less spiritual than the activity of a scholar. . . . For this reason, neither for you nor for us can the will to build a living bridge remain any longer an empty, hopeless wish. This will, *to consumate the creation of jobs by providing the right kind of knowledge,* this will must be our innermost certainty and never-faltering faith. For in what this will wills, we are only following the towering will of our *Führer.* (HCW: 57–60/NH: 200–202)

Even as Heidegger preached the Nietzschean gospel of will to the National Socialist workers, however, his own rhetorical demarcation of the workers as "you" and the scholars as "us" betrayed his Platonic sense of elitism. What Heidegger sought in his scheme of three binding commitments and three forms of participatory service was a way of rethinking the traditional bourgeois model of class society along *völkisch* lines. But he also wanted to take seriously the military component of armed service as a way of heroicizing the academic life. What lay behind the Platonic blueprint for German revolution was a Nietzschean will to vitality that would shatter the paralytic molds of the old Humboldt university and would, through a kind of Dionysian self-assertion, retrieve the spirit of awed wonderment that marked ancient Greek *thaumazein,* making it the foundation of a new national existence. Heidegger's "private" National Socialism, nourished at his cabin in Todtnauberg, was now becoming public. But the *kerygma* of his call to service found an echo only in the private cave of Zarathustra's isolation, not in the public cave of Plato's polis. What remained most distinctive about Heidegger's call was that its quasi-religious, martial voice, intoned in the language of myth, failed to unify the three forms of service into "*one* formative force."

VII. THE *PHILOMYTHOS* AND THE MYTH OF HEROIC GREATNESS

It would be unfair to delimit the breadth of influences upon Heidegger's thinking and to find in Plato alone the genuine source for Heidegger's vision of a new Germania. Clearly, the mythic force of his private *Volksreligion* of the "national" and the "social" could be located in Hölderlin, the Youth Movement, and the cult of Schlageter, as well as in the traditions of *Heimat,* hearth, and the hero. But it is difficult for a reader of the Rectorial Address not to be confused by the jarring incongruencies in Heidegger's thematics and language—especially the disjunctions between Plato and Clausewitz, the *völkisch* and the martial, the *Heimat* and the battlefield, the awe of *thaumazein* and the will of self-assertion. As one of Heidegger's former students, Karl Löwith, so incisively put it, after hearing the speech "one was in doubt whether one should start reading Diels' *Pre-Socratics* or enlist in the SA."[43] What marks the internal dynamic of this address is its chiasmic crossing of two powerful philosophical sources—Plato and Nietzsche—at precisely the center of another chiasm, that between *philosophia* and *mythos*. Within this vertiginous configuration, myth itself comes to dominate the movement at the axis of intersection, since it shifts the address' focus from Nietzschean self-assertion and a politics of the will to Platonic *thaumazein* and the philhellenic recovery of originary science. At the same time, the address seeks to infuse this self-assertive, philomythic understanding of the university with a Jüngerian energy that marshals this selfsame "will to essence" in the service of a Platonic vision of the polis.

Heidegger himself knew of the Aristotelian conjunction of *mythos* and *thaumazein* at the beginning of the *Metaphysics* where Aristotle declared:

> It is because of wondering [*thaumazein*] that men began to philosophize and do so now. First, they wondered at the difficulties [*aporon*] close at hand; then, advancing little by little, they discussed difficulties also about greater matters . . . Now a man who is perplexed and wonders considers himself ignorant (whence a lover of myth [*philomythos*], too, is in a sense a philosopher [*philosophos*], for a myth is composed of wonders [*thaumasion*]) (*Metaphysics*, 982b).[44]

Heidegger's own reading of the National Socialist movement was deeply mythic. He sought in a sense to make the originary myth of philosophy as wonderment the emergent force of a new *mythos* about *Wissenschaft* and the *Volk*. At the heart of this vision was Plato, since it was in *The Republic* that the defining myth of Western philosophy was related: the allegory of the cave as the *mythos* of a different kind of truth whose essence could only be wrought from the combative play of/within *aletheia*. In the Rectorial Address, Heidegger sought to recapture the power of that *mythos* as the essence of the *polis* itself and to refound the NS state in the image of Platonic *thaumazein*. By rethinking the essence of truth in terms of *paideia*, and by making *paideia* the foundation of the new state, Rector Heidegger hoped to become the new philosopher-king/*Führer* of a "*völkische polis*." But the very incongruency of that expression—the impossible conjunction of the German adjective and the Greek noun—made Heidegger's vision an impossible one to realize. Instead, the *Volksreligion* of the *Heimat* is left behind in Heidegger's failed "academic summer camp" project [*Wissenschaftslager*] at Todtnauberg in 1934.[45]

Still, the Rectorial Address asserts the myth of *aletheia* as the highest

43. Karl Löwith, *My Life in Germany*, 34.

44. Aristotle, *The Metaphysics*, trans. Hippocrates Apostle (Grinnell: Peripatetic Press, 1979), 15.

45. Hugo Ott, *Martin Heidegger: Unterwegs*, 214–223.

goal of the *polis,* the animating force of Western philosophy, science, and education, a myth whose realization depends upon the will to self-assertion carried out by the German university. As the *philomythos* of the political, Heidegger realizes, however, that the essence of truth is itself governed by *Kampf,* struggle, conflict, strife, and *polemos.* This essence can only be won through a battle-hardened will to self-assertion. Plato's myth depends upon Nietzsche's will. *Wesensverwandlung* (the transformation of the essence) emerges through *Selbstbehauptung* (self-assertion) (GA 43: 70). As the last Greek philosopher of the philomythic tradition, Plato stands as a figure poised on the threshold of a metaphysical turning; as "the last German philosopher," Nietzsche stands at the end of metaphysics itself. But at the end of a metaphysics bound to the metanarrative of nihilism, "when the spiritual strength of the West fails and the West starts to come apart at the seams, when this moribund pseudocivilization collapses into itself, pulling all forces into confusion and allowing them to suffocate in madness," Heidegger reaffirms myth as the heart of the *polis* (RA: 38/SdU: 19).

As he brings his address to closure, Heidegger poses again the fundamental question of his *kerygma:* "Do we will the essence of the university or do we not will it?" Out of the *polemos* between following and leading, a struggle that carries within itself—if it is authentic—the possibility of "resistance" (*Widerstand*), Heidegger finds the will to carry forth the new beginning. As he asserts in his rhetorically framed *epilogos:*

> We can only fully understand the glory and greatness [*Grösse*] of this new beginning [*Aufbruch*], however, if we carry within ourselves that profound and far-reaching thoughtfulness upon which the ancient wisdom of the Greeks drew in uttering the words:
> *ta . . . megala panta episphale . . .*
> "All that is great [*Grosse*] stands in the storm [*Sturm*] . . ." (Plato, *Republic,* 497d) (RA: 38–39/SdU: 19)

At the very end of his remarks, in a rhetorical gesture itself marked by a polemical politics of citation, Heidegger gives breath, if in an indirect way, to the animating spirit of Plato that runs throughout his address. Clearly, the final effect of the language is itself *stürmisch,* marked by the turbulent storms of rhetorical self-assertion and the will to essence. The Platonic dispensation to the German *Volk,* Heidegger seems to be saying, can only be received by those steeled in the storm of essential conflict. But this simple gesture of citation, the turning back upon the origin to retrieve the power of the inaugural, becomes itself both a Rosetta stone and a palimpsest for understanding the dynamics and thematics of the Rectorial Address.

In the most basic sense, Heidegger's translation from Plato's Greek violates the meaning of the original text. In a self-assertive act of hermeneutic violence, Heidegger lays the Greek word *episphales* upon his own Nietzschean anvil and forges from its original Greek meaning of being "in danger," "prone to a fall," "at risk," "precarious," a new language of heroism and self-assertion.[46] Etymologically, *episphales* derives from the Greek prefix "*epi-*" (upon, toward, over) and the Greek verb stem "*sphallo*" ("to cause to fall," "throw down," "trip-up"). But Heidegger finds in this term the heroic language of *Sturm*, battle, conflict, and *polemos*. "Standing in the storm," in this new Heideggerian context, means something like enduring the Heraclitean conflict within the essence of truth. But, as ever in Heidegger's retrieval of the Greeks, there is also the dual legacy of *Kampf* and *Heimat*. In its original context within book 6 of Plato's *Republic*, this passage describes Socrates' response to Adeimantus' charge that philosophers are unsuited to rule the polis. The discussion then takes up the question: "Which of today's cities could accommodate the philosophic nature?" Adeimantus: "What are you getting at?" Socrates: "How a philosophic city can prevent its own destruction. All great things are precarious constructions; as the proverb says, fine things are hard" (*Republic* 497c-d).[47] Or as Schleiermacher translated it in the standard German edition: "*Denn alles Grosse ist auch bedenklich . . .*" ("for everything great is also worthy of question").

Instead of appropriating the standard translations, and with them the conventional interpretations, Heidegger boldly sets forth a violent reading of Plato's text that emerges out of the conflict between the traditional understanding of the *polis* and a National Socialist will to the new beginning. What this new beginning demands of the German *Volk* is the will to question the traditional reading of *Wissenschaft* and its essence, philosophy and its heritage, the Greeks and their greatness. Only a *Volk* that wills this will to question, that asserts itself resolutely in its commitment to service, that endures the *Kampf* of future oriented conflict can call itself "great." In this rhetorical emphasis on "greatness" and "all that is great," Heidegger repositions Plato within his own Nietzschean world of will.

At root, Heidegger's inquiry into Platonic greatness yields a Niet-

---

46. Henry Liddell and Robert Scott, *A Greek-English Lexicon* (New York: American Book Company, 1897), 557. *Benselers Griechisch-Deutsches Schülwörterbuch*, 323, translates *episphales* as "zum Fallen geneigt," "unsicher," and "gefährlich," which matches the Liddell-Scott renderings almost exactly. The *Menge-Güthling Griechisch-Deutsches Wörterbuch* (Berlin: Langenscheidts, 1957), 276, is very close to this as well. Most standard dictionaries would hardly support Heidegger's philological rendering of the original Greek here. And yet when considered within the Nietzschean-Jüngerian context of the Rectorial Address and the Schlageter speech, we can understand why Heidegger was inclined to lay his translation of Plato's *Politeia* on the Procrustean bed of his own martial-philosophical commitments.

47. Plato, *The Republic*, trans. R. W. Sterling and W. C. Scott (New York: Norton, 1985), 186–187.

zschean archeology of self-assertion. What is truly great for Heidegger is the philosophical virtue of radical questioning, a trait that Heidegger associates with the ancient Greeks and that Nietzsche finds in Zarathustra. What is Nietzschean "greatness?" In *Ecce Homo*, Nietzsche writes:

> The species of man that [Zarathustra] delineates, delineates reality *as it is:* he is strong enough for it—he is not estranged from or entranced by it, he is *reality itself,* he still has all that is fearful and questionable in reality in him, *only thus can man possess greatness.* (EH: 100–101/KSA 6: 370)

At the end, Heidegger's chiasmic crossing of Platonic *thaumazein* and Nietzschean greatness yields a new philomythic understanding of the German *Volk* that returns to the same mythic constellation of *Kampf* and *Heimat* that we encountered in our reading of the Schlageter speech. Only that *Volk* which can, in Tyrtaeus' words, "stand steadfast, with both feet rooted firmly on the ground," rooted in the earth (*Boden*) and the *Heimat,* a *Volk* committed to the myth of *Bodenständigkeit,* is capable of standing fast in the storm of modern nihilism. Heidegger's Rectorial Address ends by taking up again the myth at the beginning of the Western tradition: the philosopher as hero and as leader. At the axis of intersection between Athens and Todtnauberg, Plato and Nietzsche, *thaumazein* and will to power, Heidegger reclaims the oldest myth of the philosopher as hero to inaugurate a revolutionary *Aufbruch.* Rector Heidegger, as the Schlageter of spirit, would take up this legacy with renewed vigor until his withdrawal from leadership in the fall of 1934. What follows is his own Nietzschean *Auseinandersetzung* with the political forces that brought about an end to his Platonic dream of reshaping the *polis* in the image and likeness of the philosopher.

We need to look at this shift in Heidegger's stance more carefully as a way of grappling with his Nietzsche lectures in the winter of 1936/37. But we also need to understand how Nietzsche helped to provide Heidegger with a decisive metanarrative about the shape and contours of the Western philosophical tradition and of Europe's place within that narrative. For what determines Heidegger's mythic understanding of the West is the role that Europe plays in the recovery of the Greek inauguration and the mission of the German future.

The Geo-Politics of
Heidegger's *Mitteleuropa*

He who always searches for the ground, perishes.

—FRIEDRICH NIETZSCHE
KSA 13: 562

The beginning is always what is greatest.

—MARTIN HEIDEGGER
EM: 12

I. HEIDEGGER'S *URSPRUNGSPHILOSOPHIE*

Part of what we have seen in Heidegger's geo-philosophy of 1933–34 is its abiding preference for origins. The myth of the origin—in Plato, in the Pre-Socratics, in the Greek language—is played out in terms of its connection to the earth, the native soil, rootedness, the homeland, and other encoded formulations that reinforce Heidegger's exclusionary *mythos* of Graeco-Germanic autochthony. In the political speeches of 1933–34, we uncovered a double form of this mythic autochthony: a *political* form rooted in the native earth (Schlageter's *Heimat, Bodenständigkeit,* the Alemannic soil) and an *ontological* form rooted in the chthonic realm of Greek myth (the gods of Hölderlin and W.F. Otto, the Tyrtaeus of Jaeger's "subterranean philosophy," the archaic logic of the Pre-Socratic thinkers). If the political form of Greek autochthony was bound to the legacy of Erichthonius, the founder of Athens sprung from the earth, its ontological form was bound to the chthonic sources of Pre-Socratic thinking sprung from the *arche* of being itself.[1] For Heidegger, the double legacy of this origin or *Ur-sprung*—the political and the ontological, the German and the

---

1. This deep connection between the founder of Athens and his autochthonic heritage can be seen in his very name—*eri* + *chthonos* (Gk.), where *eri* is an inseparable prefix augmenting the effect of the earth. For a guide to the historical background of the Greek myth of autochthony and its connection to Erichthonius, see *Der Kleine Pauly,* ed. Konrat Ziegler and Walther Sontheimer (Munich: dtv, 1979), 2: 356; Nicole Loraux, *The Children of Athena* (Princeton: Princeton University Press, 1993), 37–71; and Timothy Ganz, *Early Greek Myth* (Baltimore: Johns Hopkins University Press, 1993), 233–235. For the etymological ties, a helpful source is Hjalmar Frisk, *Griechisches Etymologisches Wörterbuch* (Heidelberg: Carl Winter, 1973), 557.

Greek, the *Bodenständigkeit* of the *Volk* and the *arche* of the Pre-Socratics—helped to shape the contours of his thinking in the crucial years of the National Socialist revolution during the 1930s. What he had hoped for in the *Aufbruch* of 1933 was the retrieval of the first beginning of Greek thought, an *arche* whose power and force was so deeply rooted in the Western tradition that, given the proper maieutic care of a new rector, it might be capable of giving birth to another, "futural" *arche* in the German homeland. This hope was at the center of Heidegger's Rectorial Address and its insistent claim that "the beginning still *is*. It does not lie *behind us* as something that was long ago, but stands *before us*" (RA: 8/SdU: 12–13).

As Heidegger's other political speeches from 1933–1934 made eminently clear, this "other" beginning would come to the Germans only if, in a *Kampf* both with and for their forgotten Greek patrimony, they could reclaim the lost power of the origin. But Heidegger's *mythos* of the *arche* went even deeper. To this ontological *mythos* of a German rootedness in Greek thought, Heidegger wedded the political *mythos* of the *Volk* and its "centuries-long and irreplaceable rootedness [*Bodenständigkeit*] in the Alemannic-Swabian soil" (DE: 11). The Rectorial Address expressed in its most condensed form both aspects of the Heideggerian *mythos* of rootedness: as Pre-Socratic *arche* and as Alemannic *Bodenständigkeit*. From the rectorial pronouncements of May 1933 until Heidegger's *Spiegel* interview of 1966 and beyond, this myth of Graeco-Germanic rootedness functions as a kind of hermeneutical cipher for Heidegger's encrypted utterances concerning art, technology, poetry, politics, nihilism, the history of philosophy, and the destiny of the West.

This chapter explores the ways in which Heidegger deployed this myth of autochthony in offering his own account of Germany's place within "the historical destiny of the West" (EdP: 31–41; IM: 42/EM: 32). Heidegger's work of the 1930s offered a reading of Western history grounded in a political narrative about the history of ontology. But this reading was also marked by an eschatological anxiety about the future of Europe and about Germany's position within that future. Looking back over the two thousand, five-hundred year history of the West (a narrative that begins with the Pre-Socratics and excludes Egyptian and Mesopotamian culture), Heidegger reads it as the history of nihilism, as an Adamic fall from originary *aletheia*. In light of this ontological history, Heidegger sees his own age as facing a profound crisis about the destiny of the West. Painfully aware of the voguish prescriptions offered by Weimar sociologists with their clichés about anomie, rootlessness, and crisis, Heidegger insists that the crisis about which he writes is not of recent provenance. Its ontological roots go back to Pindar, Sophocles, Heraclitus, and Parmenides. But this mythic *Ursprungsphilosophie* is also intimately connected to the world of Heidegger's politics, a connection that can be drawn as far back as Heidegger's early Marburg lectures and his response to the heated political crisis in the Ruhr during 1923–1924.[2]

In early December of 1924, Heidegger delivered a series of lectures on Aristotle's *Rhetoric* against the background of the French occupation of the Ruhr area. French troops were deployed to collect reparations in the form of coal and steel since Germany, in the midst of a crippling depression, had been unable to make good on the financial debt incurred by the Treaty of Versailles. In 1923, Schlageter had given his life in the cause of resistance and by the time of Heidegger's lectures Germans were determined to stand up to what they perceived as French aggression. Within the context of this volatile political crisis, Heidegger lectured on the origins of Greek ontology and its battle (*Kampf*) for truth. Even here in 1924, Heidegger's myth of political and ontological rootedness comes into play. In his lecture, entitled "Dasein und Wahrsein nach Aristoteles," Heidegger raises the question: "Does truth really find its ground in judgment, or has it been uprooted and displaced from a more native soil [*Bodenständigkeit*]?"[3]

Against the background of the Ruhr crisis, Heidegger makes a direct connection between the political struggle waged by the Germans against their foreign invaders and the ontological struggle waged by the early Greek philosophers over the question of being. "The *Ruhrkampf*," Heidegger claims, "must become the *Titanenkampf* [*gigantomachia*] over being once fought by the great Greek philosophers, which we Germans are destined to make into our *Kampf.*" This fateful yoking of politics and ontology at the axis of autochthony will emerge again in the decisive 1930 lecture "On the Essence of Truth." There Heidegger will once again connect the Greek experience of *aletheia* to the rootedness of the native soil (*Boden-*

2. Jürgen Habermas, *The Philosophical Discourse of Modernity* (Cambridge: MIT Press, 1989), 151–160, and Theodor Adorno, *Philosophische Terminologie* (Frankfurt: Suhrkamp, 1973), 150–151; both offer penetrating accounts of Heidegger's *Ursprungsphilosophie*. Yet Habermas too easily dismisses this as a kind of sentimental, nostalgic yearning for origin associated, on the one hand, with romantic metaphysics and, on the other, with a National Socialist drive for authoritarian control. Moreover, Habermas never pursues the question of how these two topics interrelate in any systematic way, especially within the context of Heidegger's geo-politics. For an insightful discussion of Heidegger's philosophy of the origin, see John Pizer, *Toward a Theory of Radical Origin* (Lincoln: University of Nebraska Press, 1995), 129–167.

3. Theodore Kisiel, "Situating Rhetoric/Politics in Heidegger's Practical Ontology (1923–1925: The French Occupation of the Rhine)," *Existentia* 9 (1999): 11–30. Kisiel's essay provides a rich source for tracing the theme of autochthony (*Bodenständigkeit*) back to this early lecture from 1924. I would like to thank Professor Kisiel for his help in finding key sources for my analysis here. See also Theodore Kisiel, *The Genesis of Heidegger's "Being and Time"* (Berkeley: University of California Press, 1993), 281–286. The text of this piece with the title "Wahrsein und Dasein (Aristoteles Ethica Nicomachea Z)" is scheduled to be published in GA 80: *Vorträge* by Klostermann.

ständigkeit) that finds expression in the *Heimat*.[4] Although the later drafts of this crucial essay suppress the fact that Heidegger originally delivered this lecture to a congress whose theme was "Festigung der Heimat" ("Strengthening the Homeland"), we have first-hand accounts that situate it clearly within the thematic nexus of "rootlessness" and *Bodenständigkeit*. This same litany of themes—rootedness, autochthony, homeland, the German struggle against foreign oppression in the service of truth—gets played out again in the Schlageter tribute of May 1933, in the Langemarck speech commemorating the fallen war dead from November 1933, in the "Creative Landscape" address of March 1934, in the lectures on logic during the summer of 1934, and in the lectures on Hölderlin of winter 1934/35. In his discussion of Hölderlin's "Germania" and its connection to Heraclitean thought, Heidegger expresses in the most succinct manner possible the implications of this political-ontological autochthony. "The 'fatherland,'" Heidegger affirms, "is being [*Seyn*] itself" (GA 39: 88, 93, 104–105). But "the earth of the homeland" is not simply a natural region demarcated by the boundaries of settlement, nor is it a mere geographical or political enclosure measured by the science of cartography. Rather, the earth is there for the gods, as well, and, Heidegger claims, "insofar as the earth is a homeland, it opens itself up to the power of the gods."

This chthonic force of the earth comes to play a determinative role in forming Heidegger's *mythos* of ontological-political autochthony. During the 1930s, Heidegger would continue to draw upon the chthonic sources of Greek ontology for his understanding of German politics. However, Heidegger's understanding of the subterranean, chthonic power of Greek thought came to him through the work of Hölderlin and Nietzsche. "These two," Heidegger claimed, "knew the Greek beginning in a more originary way than all previous epochs" (BQP: 110/GA 45: 126). If Hölderlin's poetry opened up the hidden sources of Pre-Socratic thinking, then Nietzsche's philosophy uncovered the subterranean depth of Dionysian experience. As Nietzsche put it in a note from the *Nachlass:*

> There can be no doubt that the Greeks sought to interpret the ultimate mysteries of 'the destiny of the soul' . . . on the basis of their Dionysian experiences: here is the great depth, the great silence in all matters Greek—*one does not know the Greeks* as long as this hidden, subterranean [*unterirdische*] entrance still lies submerged. Importunate scholars' eyes will never see anything in these things, however much scholarship still has to be employed in the service of excavation. Even the noble zeal of such friends of antiquity as

4. For some textual sources linking politics and ontology to the theme of autochthony in "On the Essence of Truth," see NH: 12–13; Heinrich Berl, *Gespräche mit berühmten Zeitgenossen* (Baden-Baden: Bühler, 1946), 62–68; and Kisiel, "Situating Rhetoric," 18.

Goethe and Winckelmann here has something unpermitted, even immodest about it. (WP: 541/KSA 11: 681–682)

Nietzsche came to represent the philosopher who held the key to opening up the hidden, chthonic sources of the originary Greek *arche*. In his first set of lectures on Nietzsche in 1936/37, Heidegger insisted that "Nietzsche is the first—if we discount for the moment Hölderlin—to release the 'classical' from the misinterpretations of classicism and humanism" (Ni: 127/GA 43: 149). And to emphasize his disdain for the academic classicism of Germany's "Second Humanism," Heidegger even cites Nietzsche's acerbic claim that "it is an amusing comedy, which we are only now learning to laugh at, which we are now for the first time *seeing*, that the contemporaries of Herder, Winckelmann, Goethe, and Hegel claimed *to have rediscovered the classical ideal*" (WP: 447/KSA 13: 132).

Since the late eighteenth century, German poets, aesthetes, and thinkers had all been gripped by a kind of preoccupation with ancient Greek culture, a preoccupation that led in myriad ways to what has been termed "the tyranny of Greece over Germany."[5] In an age where German culture was developing without the framework of a unified nation state, a range of philosophers and writers asserted their own national ideals in terms borrowed from their visions of antiquity.[6] Within the context of this German Hellenomania, heightened by the invasion of Napoleon in 1806, Fichte, Hegel, and their contemporaries came to draw upon the myth of a singular Graeco-German affinity rooted in both language and *Heimat*.[7] Fichte went so far as to claim that the Germans constituted an *Urvolk* (or "originary *Volk*") much like the Greeks. For these philosophers the path to an essential German identity—what Heidegger might have termed "the self-assertion of the Germans"—lay in its originary connection to the Greek. This myth of Graeco-Germanic affinity dominates German thought in the nineteenth century, putting its stamp on the whole movement that we now term the "Second Humanism" of Goethe, Schiller, Herder, and Schlegel. Even the founding of the highly influential University of Berlin in 1810 is influenced by this whole set of cultural assumptions. As Walther Rehm put it in his study *Griechentum und Goethezeit*: "Within German cultural life the belief grew ever stronger that without the relation to Greek antiquity it would be impossible to shape one's own life and to attain a genuinely German form of humanity."[8]

5. E. M. Butler, *The Tyranny of Greece over Germany* (Boston: Beacon Hill, 1958).
6. Josef Chytry, *The Aesthetic State: A Quest in Modern German Thought* (Berkeley: University of California Press, 1989).
7. G. W. F. Hegel, *Vorlesungen über die Geschichte der Philosophie*, vol. 18 of *Werke* (Frankfurt: Suhrkamp, 1971), 173–176; and Johann G. Fichte, *Reden an die deutsche Nation* (Hamburg: Meiner, 1978), 72, 106–107.
8. Walther Rehm, *Griechentum und Goethezeit* (Bern: Francke, 1952), 229.

But this idealized portrait of Greece also took the form of a cultural and political struggle on the part of Germans to assert their own autochthonous identity against the French spirit of Enlightenment and the Latinity of both Gallic and Roman Catholic culture.[9] In this spirit of struggle against the poisonous influence of French *civilisation,* German *Kultur* asserts itself against what Fichte called "the deadly foreign spirit."[10] In carrying out this self-assertive struggle, the Germans prove themselves to be essentially connected to the Greeks who, within their philosophy, analogously put aside (in Hegel's words) "the foreign origin."[11] By excluding the "other," non-German (that is, Latin) influences from their *mythos* of a German future, these thinkers will set the tone for the later National Socialist appropriation of Greek antiquity expressed by philosophers like Alfred Baeumler, Hans Heyse, Kurt Hildebrandt, and others. In his essay "Hellas und Germanien," Baeumler reprises the Fichtean litany that "in the recovery of Hellenic culture for the West . . . the German racial soul has started back on the path to itself."[12] Like Fichte, Baeumler too manages to uncover "an originary, genuinely German relation to Greek culture that is incomprehensible to other nations."[13] In a powerful way, Baeumler's gesture of retrieval and reappropriation will restate the Neo-humanist credo of a special kinship between the Germans and the Greeks. It will zealously assert the political autonomy of the German *Volk* through the reclaiming of its cultural-linguistic autochthony in the soil of antiquity.

In many ways the cultural chauvinism evident in Baeumler's essay was hardly exceptional. Mandarin humanists such as the nineteenth-century scholar Ulrich von Wilamowitz-Moellendorff had also repeated the standard conceit that "only the German understands the best of Hellenic cul-

9. Hellmut Sichtermann, *Kulturgeschichte der klassischen Archäologie* (Munich: Beck, 1996) offers an insightful account of German Philhellenism as does the book by Suzanne Marchand, *Down from Olympus: Archeology and Philhellenism in Germany, 1750–1970* (Princeton University Press, 1996). See also Martin Bernal, *Black Athena,* vol. 1, *The Fabrication of Ancient Greece, 1785–1985* (New Brunswick: Rutgers University Press, 1987), 281–316. These sources are also helpful for tracing the German vision of Greece in the modern era: Ulrich von Wilamowitz-Moellendorff, *History of Classical Scholarship* (Baltimore: Johns Hopkins University Press, 1982); J. E. Sandys, *A History of Classical Scholarship,* vol. 3 (Cambridge: Cambridge University Press, 1908); Ada Hentschke and Ulrich Muhlack, *Einführung in die Geschichte der klassischen Philologie* (Darmstadt: Wissenschaftliche Buchgesellschaft, 1972); *Altertumswissenschaft in den 20er Jahre,* ed. Hellmut Flashar (Stuttgart: Steiner, 1995); and Ute Preusse, *Humanismus und Gesellschaft* (Frankfurt: Peter Lang, 1988). Given the dominance of Greek culture over German thinking from Winckelmann to Heidegger, this list can only touch on a few of the historical sources. I have learned a good deal, however, from Vassily Lambropoulos' book, *The Rise of Eurocentrism* (Princeton: Princeton University Press, 1993).

10. Fichte, *Reden an die deutsche Nation,* 115.

11. Hegel, *Vorlesungen über die Geschichte der Philosophie,* 174.

12. Alfred Baeumler, "Hellas und Germanien," in *Studien zur deutschen Geistesgeschichte* (Berlin: Junker & Dünnhaupt, 1943), 295.

13. Baeumler, "Nietzsche und der Nationalsozialismus," in *Studien zur deutschen Geistesgeschichte,* 285.

ture."[14] And yet Baeumler's National Socialist retrieval of antiquity was fundamentally different than either the staid classicism of the academic mandarinate or the idealist Philhellenism of Germany's "Second Humanism." What Baeumler sought in the tradition of the ancient world was not the Apollonian clarity of Enlightenment reason and harmony but the irrational, elemental, archaic, and subterranean forces of Dionysian myth. It was in this chthonic realm of Greek mythic thought—transmitted by Nietzsche—that Baeumler located the archaic sources for the cultural and political rebirth of Germany. Baeumler's "hope for the hastened rebirth of Hellenic culture from the depths of German being" was tempered, however, by his belief that such a rebirth could not come forth of its own power. On the contrary, he understood that the experience of the chthonic would be "difficult to attain."[15] Through what he termed "the most violent exertions of the Germanic racial soul," Baeumler insisted that for Germany to find its own cultural identity it would need to "reconquer the Hellenic world."[16] In this "decisive battle" to reclaim its lost patrimony, the German *Volk* would need to affirm what Baeumler variously termed its "originary kinship" or "racial affinity" with the ancient Greeks. And, like Heidegger, Baeumler believed that the hidden depths of this originary, Graeco-German affinity were understood only by Nietzsche and Hölderlin:

> Nietzsche's discovery of Greek culture *before* Pericles and Socrates is one that emerged out of his deepest instinct. This indeed constituted Nietzsche's most important historical discovery, one that remained foundational for him until the very end. From it followed, by necessity, everything else: the rejection of Christianity together with the rejection of the Roman-humanist tradition. That is the historical meaning of the concept "Dionysos." From this standpoint Nietzsche opened up once again the whole problem of Western history—exactly as Hölderlin had done in his final hymns.[17]

In Nietzsche's "discovery" of the chthonic depths of Dionysian will to power, Baeumler unearths a turning point in the history of the West—and in Germany's position within that history. What seemed especially crucial was that the deep and abiding connection that bound the Greek and German peoples be recovered in its originary and primordial sense, something that had not been achieved in the academic classicism of the Neo-humanists and their ideal of *Bildung*. The Graecophilia of the Neo-humanists seemed to Baeumler nothing less than another kind of

14. Ulrich von Wilamowitz-Moellendorff, "Griechische und Römische Persönlichkeit," *Wiener Blätter für die Freunde der Antike* 2 (1925): 92.

15. Baeumler, "Nietzsche," in *Studien zur deutschen Geistesgeschichte*, 252–255.

16. Baeumler, "Hellas und Germanien," 295; *Nietzsche: Der Philosoph und Politiker* (Leipzig: Reclam, 1931), 92.

17. Baeumler, *Studien zur deutschen Geistesgeschichte*, 250–251.

Roman attempt at taking over the Greek legacy without genuinely under-standing its essential power. "Rome" signified for Baeumler the bureau-cratic, organizational style of centralized state administration animated by an urban, mercantile spirit bent on conquest and expansion. This Roman drive for conquest was not, however, born out of an agonal love for con-test and confrontation; it was rather animated by the imperial drive for colonization and the businessmen's need for new markets.[18] Roman cul-ture was nothing more than "the externalized form of Greek culture," something "superficial" and "decorative."[19] And yet the Roman legacy had exerted an enormous influence on the history of the West and had formed Europe in the image of a Latin and Christian culture. The result, Baeumler claimed, was the triumph of nihilism.

Baeumler believed, however, that the dominance of Latinate culture was coming to an end and that a new epoch was dawning that would bring about the rebirth of the Germanic *Volk*. For this rebirth to occur, the *Volk* would need to reappropriate the originary chthonic legacy of Greek myth bequeathed to it by Hölderlin and Nietzsche. "The German politics of the future," Baeumler contended, "will be unthinkable without the element of Hölderlin and Nietzsche."[20] In Baeumler's view, if the Germans would heed Nietzsche's critique of the nihilism of Christian-Roman civilization laid out in *The Will to Power,* they might yet become "the *Führer* of Europe." Writing in 1931, Baeumler poses the question:

> What would Europe be without the Nordic Germans? What would Europe be without Germany? A Roman colony. . . . Germany can exist in its world-historical form only as the Greater Germany. It has only the choice of being the anti-Roman power of Europe or of not being at all. . . . Only a Nordic Germany, the Germany of Hölderlin and Nietzsche, can be the creator of a Europe that will be more than a Roman colony. Nietzsche belongs not to the world of Bismarck but to the epoch of the Great War. The German state of the future will not constitute a sequel to the work of Bismarck; it will, rather, be created out of the spirit of Nietzsche and of the Great War.[21]

Baeumler's spirited attack against the nihilistic influence of Roman cul-ture became a staple of National Socialist thinking in the 1930s. "Rome" became a symbol of the rootlessness of urban life, of universalism, *Zivili-sation*, cosmopolitanism, comfort, bourgeois security, and philistine learn-ing. The *Pax Romana* signified for Baeumler the triumph of a slave moral-ity that had forgotten the Heraclitean joy of battle: *Kampf, polemos,* and

18. Baeumler, *Nietzsche: Der Philosoph und Politiker,* 90–97, 104, 122, 182–183; "Nietzsche," in *Studien zur deutschen Geistesgeschichte,* 257–258; and "Der Kampf um den Humanismus," in *Politik und Erziehung* (Berlin: Junker & Dünnhaupt, 1937), 65–66.

19. Baeumler, *Studien zur deutschen Geistesgeschichte,* 251.

20. Baeumler, *Nietzsche: Der Philosoph und Politiker,* 182.

21. Ibid., 182–183.

eris.[22] Only by reclaiming the Hellenic love for the *agon* and the originary Germanic passion for *Kampf* would Europe be saved from the leveling influences of Roman (i.e., Christian, Enlightenment, bourgeois, nihilistic) culture. Baeumler was insistent that Europe could be saved only by Germany—and that Germany could be saved only by what he termed its "drive to self-assertion [*Selbstbehauptung*], to power, to victory."[23] The fulfillment of this Germanic self-assertion took the form of "the German spirit's journey homeward to itself and to its originary Dionysian home [*Urheimat*]"—a journey whose passage would need to be completed "without the transmission of Latin culture."[24]

If Baeumler's analysis of Roman and Greek culture strikes us today as tendentious, chauvinistic, and marked by the bellicose style of geo-political aggression, that is because it so perfectly reprises the violent style of National Socialist thinking, a style to which Heidegger himself fell victim in the decisive year of 1933. Heidegger's own analysis of the history of philosophy drew upon the storehouse of clichés that were part of Baeumler's intellectual world: the search for an autochthonous affinity linking Greek and German culture; the identification of Rome as the source for the rootlessness and nihilism of Western history; the appeal to Hölderlin for forging a chthonic bond between the Greek gods and the German *Volk;* the pressing into service of Nietzsche for a decision abut the crisis of nihilism confronting the German nation; the commitment to a masculinist lexicon of *Kampf, agon,* battle, conquest, and the hero; a reading of German history in terms of destiny, fate, and decision.

All of these mythic propositions of Graeco-Germanic affinity and of the Roman occlusion of the Greek beginning find their way into Heidegger's thought. Upon reading the work of Baeumler, Heyse, Hildebrandt, Krieck, and others, we can see how Heidegger's encrypted history of Western ontology reveals, despite his vigorous protestations to the contrary, an essential affinity to the views propagated by his own National Socialist contemporaries. Such an attempt to locate Heidegger's *Ursprungsphilosophie* in the mythic world of National Socialist discourse should not, however, be construed as an effort to flatten out the complex bends and turns on Heidegger's path of thinking. On the contrary, I want to offer a reading of Heidegger's work that attends to the nuances and idiosyncrasies of its language, style, and thematics. But I also want to address the all too common tendency to read Heidegger solely on his own terms or in conversation with those "great" thinkers whom he deems worthy of mention. I will argue that Heidegger's work cannot be properly understood without

---

22. Ibid., 67.
23. Ibid., 93, and Baeumler, *Politik und Erziehung,* 53.
24. Baeumler, *Studien zur deutschen Geistesgeschichte,* 258; *Politik der Erziehung,* 53.

attending to the deep-rooted myth of political *and* ontological autochthony that he shares with other National Socialist thinkers. This myth helps to determine Heidegger's understanding of Germany as a nation "caught in a pincers. Situated in the center [*Mitte*]," confronting a "great decision regarding Europe" (IM: 38/EM: 29). This is not to say that Heidegger's philosophy can be reduced to myth, however; clearly, he sets out to craft a careful and rigorous language that attempts to destructure the Western tradition's own mythic discourse about truth. Nonetheless, in Heidegger's discussion of the German nation and its relation to Europe, I think we can find traces of a political mythology of the *Volk* bound to the generational thinking of the German right. In this chapter I want to look critically at Heidegger's notion of "Europe" and at his rhetorical tropics of "destiny," "fate," and "the history of the West." Part of my argument is that, unlike many studies of Heidegger that focus either on the political or the ontological axis of his thought, I want to examine the roots of Heidegger's myth of autochthony in both its political *and* ontological configurations. To get a sense of how much of this mythic configuration was drawn from contemporary sources, I want to first look a bit more closely at Baeumler's interpretation of Germany's role in the history of the West before proceeding to a discussion of Heidegger's own geopolitics in his 1935 lectures, *Introduction to Metaphysics,* and his 1936 essay, "Europe and German Philosophy."

II. *EUROPA* AND THE HISTORY OF THE WEST

Baeumler's chthonic history of Western philosophy, a history that privileged the agonal, the heroic, the masculine, the Greek, and the Teutonic, was itself the product of a *völkisch* reading of Hölderlin and Nietzsche. For Baeumler, these two German legends had irrevocably altered the way modern Germans could approach and understand the Greeks. Through what he termed their "Germanic Hellenism," Baeumler claimed that both Nietzsche and Hölderlin had authorized a "re-conquest of the Hellenic world." In their reading of Greek culture, he argued, "the decisive battle has begun."[25]

> Our century has to confront the question: which values is the West willing to draw upon in shaping its future? We are certain that only a value-system which, in its essential characteristics, has an affinity with the Hellenic is capable of rending Europe from its anarchy of values. The discovery of the Hellenic world signifies nothing less than the presentiment of a new epoch.

25. Baeumler, *Studien zur deutschen Geistesgeschichte,* 295–296.

In the *Aufbruch* of 1933, Baeumler repeats his thesis that "a new epoch is beginning."[26] From his world-historical perspective, he interprets the National Socialist Revolution as an assault upon the foundations of European values and as an end to their epochal hegemony. As he sees it, "Europa" as a cultural entity was created out of the "synthesis" of three fundamental historical traits: "Christian inwardness, Roman culture, and the scientific spirit." And what made Nietzsche great was his untiring *Kampf* against the humanistic impulses of this cultural synthesis. By rejecting the Roman, Christian, Enlightenment values of bourgeois comfort, sterile contemplation, and the ideal of the "theoretical man," Baeumler maintained that Nietzsche had cleared a path for the originary retrieval of Greek values. But this retrieval could only be achieved through an act of essential self-assertion, an act that would assert the Germans' own primordial bond to the Greeks and would, in turn, constitute an assertion of their own essence as a *Volk*. In this sense, self-assertion (*Selbstbehauptung*) for Baeumler became synonymous with the Nietzschean understanding of will-to-power as a drive toward one's essence. In Baeumler's curious logic, since the essence of the Germans lay in their primordial affinity with the Greeks—and since Hölderlin had been the first to understand this affinity—one would be authorized to read "*The Will to Power* as a commentary on Hölderlin's poetry."[27] Within Baeumler's epochal-originary history of Europe, Nietzsche, Hölderlin, and the Greeks all became precursors of the National Socialist attack on the old Europe. In his 1934 address, "Nietzsche and National Socialism," which repeats his assault on "the theoretical man," "the *vita contemplativa* of the monk," and "bourgeois individuality," Baeumler valorizes "the daring of the deed," which he reinscribes within the symbolic world of National Socialism. "Today, if we see German youth march under the sign of the swastika," Baeumler claims, "we are reminded of Nietzsche's *Untimely Meditations* where for the first time German youth is called upon. It is our greatest hope that the state remains free for them today. And if we call to them: 'Heil Hitler'—so at the same time we are saluting Friedrich Nietzsche."[28] What made Baeumler's Nietzschean reading of German history even more relevant to his National Socialist contemporaries, however, was the way he juxtaposed its untimely critique of European values with the all too timely theme of the Great War.

If in the Nietzschean-Hölderlinian retrieval of the Greeks Baeumler found the seed for "the beginning of a new epoch in European history,"

26. Ibid., 137 and 249.
27. Ibid., 249, and Baeumler, *Nietzsche: Der Philosoph und Politiker*, 93, for the reference to *Selbstbehauptung*.
28. Baeumler, *Studien zur deutschen Geistesgeschichte*, 289, 294.

then in the outbreak of the Great War he found its flower.[29] By transposing his analysis of ancient Greek hero worship and the cult of the dead to the fallen German soldiers on the battlefields of Langemarck and Verdun, he is able to marshal his Nietzschean critique of European values in the service of a chthonic reading of Western history. In Baeumler's crisis-narrative, "The Great War signifies a turning point in the history of the West," one whose genuine meaning can only be grasped by the Germans. By virtue of their membership in the "historical community of fate [*Schicksalsgemeinschaft*]," the Germans can understand the war as a decisive battle against the Roman values of private life, urban culture, cosmopolitan enlightenment, and humanistic learning.[30] In this sense, Baeumler interprets the meaning of the Great War in communal terms as part of a larger German destiny that can only be deciphered world-historically. Now the meaninglessness of the carnage is granted a meaning. The singular death of the infantryman who perishes in the irrational, chthonic tumult of battle becomes part of a communal self-assertion to win back for the Germans the originary legacy bequeathed to them by the Greeks. From this chthonic origin Baeumler unearths a deeper, more primordial understanding of history. Baeumler asks: Why did these young Germans die?

> They died for a reality and only when we ourselves feel *bound* through them to this same reality are we able to speak of them and their death. The reality for which they fell is called—*Germany.* Not the empirical Germany, as it was, but that other Germany that is more genuine and real and that has been laid down in the depths of our history, that is what they have confirmed through their death.[31]

Baeumler's reference to an "other" Germany in the context of an address on the Great War gave voice to that longstanding hope expressed by the Hölderlin scholar, Norbert von Hellingrath, of a "secret Germany": a Germany of the future whose innermost Germanness lay in its hidden affinity to the Greek past.[32] According to this cryptic account, "Germany"

29. Baeumler, *Politik und Erziehung*, 51. This same kind of commitment to the warrior ethos of the Great War can be seen in the writings of Ernst Jünger from the 1920s and in Werner Jaeger's essay on "Tyrtaios über die wahre *Arete*," *Sitzungsberichte der Preussischen Akademie der Wissenschaften zu Berlin* (1932): 537–568. For an excellent discussion of the Jaeger connection, see Frank Edler, "Heidegger and Werner Jaeger on the Eve of 1933: A Possible Rapprochement?" *Research in Phenomenology* 28 (1998), 122–149.

30. Alfred Baeumler, *Männerbund und Wissenschaft* (Berlin: Junker & Dünnhaupt, 1943), 19 and 23.

31. Ibid., 19.

32. Norbert von Hellingrath, *Hölderlin-Vermächtnis* (Munich: Bruckmann, 1936), 124–125. For an account of "Das geheime Deutschland," see also J. M. Ritchie, *German Literature under National Socialism* (London: Croom Helm, 1983), 3–20; Peter Gay, *Weimar Culture* (New York: Harper & Row, 1970), 46–69; Karlhans Kluncker, *"Das geheime Deutschland": Über*

becomes the name for a future homeland whose essence and spirit could never emerge in the materialist, bourgeois, epoch of individual fate. Hence, the Germans are called upon to renew their identity as a *Schicksalsgemeinschaft* by excavating its hidden sources from their Hellenic past, thereby preparing Germany for the return of the ancient gods. Consequently, when Baeumler writes that "the Great War leads us back to the sources of our history" and "the World War directs our view back not to decades but to centuries," he is pointing to the origins of such a belief. But he is also offering an encrypted narrative of Western history marked by the mythic vision of a secret Germany promulgated by Hölderlin and Hellingrath, a narrative that fashions politics mythically and myth politically.[33] In one version of the myth, it is the fallen Hellingrath killed at Verdun who points the way to the future; in another, it is Nietzsche whose doctrine of will to power is discerned in the entrails of the Great War. This perception that (as Werner Sombart put it) "the War of 1914 . . . is Nietzsche's war" dominates the intellectual world of Alfred Baeumler and his National Socialist contemporaries.[34] It fosters a vision of the German past and future that reconfigures history as myth and as destiny. As Baeumler himself expressed it: "the origin of all development lies in myth. Myth precedes all history; myth *determines* history."[35]

Heidegger's work, I want to argue, cannot properly be understood without situating it within this mythic world of a secret Germany whose future hopes lie in the Nietzschean-Hölderlinian transmission of a chthonic Greek *arche*. Like Baeumler, Heidegger will read both Nietzsche and Hölderlin against the background of the Great War, finding in their work—and especially its connection to the Greeks—the sources for Germany's metaphysical *Sonderweg* in European history. As part of this *Sonderweg* thesis, Heidegger will grant to the Germans a privileged status as the only *Volk* capable of understanding the Greeks. This singular kinship to Greek culture (especially in its form as Heraclitean *polemos*, Sophoclean *agon*, or Pindaric celebration of heroic death) will lead Heidegger to privilege *Kampf, Auseinandersetzung*, and *Selbstbehauptung* as essential historical traits in the life of a nation. It will also help to establish a metaphysical link between Heidegger's ontological myth of autochthony and his political one. That is, it will serve as the copula between the Greek experience of being and the German yearning for a homeland, a pairing whose unity is

Stefan George und seinen Kreis (Bonn: Bouvier, 1985). Heidegger too came under the influence of the nationalist ideals of the George Circle and gave a copy of his 1929 inaugural lecture to Friedrich Gundolf. He even mentions to Elisabeth Blochmann, in a letter from December of 1929, that he had a "very nice talk with Gundolf" in Heidelberg, HBB: 34.

33. Baeumler, *Männerbund und Wissenschaft*, 27–28.
34. Werner Sombart, *Händler und Helden* (Munich: Duncker & Humblot, 1915), 53.
35. Alfred Baeumler, *Das mythische Weltalter* (Munich: Beck, 1965), 199.

brought together in Heidegger's understanding of the Great War. The Great War functions within Heidegger's work as the source for his Hölderlinian-Nietzschean reading of German history in terms of destiny. Moreover, I would maintain that it provides the rich cultural background for his notions of autochthony and the homeland, as well as for his belief in the unique spiritual mission of the German *Volk*.

III. HEIDEGGER, SCHELER, AND THE "METAPHYSICS OF WAR"

In April of 1934, Heidegger resigned from his post as rector and turned his full attention to lecturing. His first course in the summer of 1934, entitled *Logik*, returned to the thematic nexus of the Rectorial Address by raising the question of German identity. "*Who are we?*" asked Heidegger, a question that he posed over and over again during the course of the semester (L: 6–16, 24; cf. GA 38: 65). His answer to this question was drawn less from the realm of "logic," however, than it was from the cultural fundament of the German experience in the Great War. "We stand," Heidegger proclaimed, "within the being of the *Volk*." He then went on to argue that the essence of the *Volk* could not be defined by census-takers, cartographers, or civil administrators. "A census counts the population and to be precise it counts only that certain part within the borders of the state; those of German extraction who live outside these borders do not belong to the *Volk* in this sense, yet those who are alien to the ancestral line are counted." In other words, as Heidegger began to formulate his notion of German identity, he wanted to include within the *Volk* those Germans in the Sudetenland, in Posen, in Danzig, in West Prussia, and in the Alsace who had been politically excluded by the terms of the Versailles Treaty. He also appeared to be concerned about those people living inside Germany (i.e., Jews) who were *Stammesfremde* or "alien to the ancestral line or genealogical stock of the *Volk*."

What determines Heidegger's understanding of the *Volk* here is not, however, its racial composition but its relation to language, history, and autochthony. Employing the "authentic" language of the Great War, Heidegger speaks of the *Volk* in terms of its *Kameradschaft* and declares that it is only through the act of making an authentic decision that "we" genuinely belong to the *Volk*. He tells his students, "What we will is to prepare the possibility of moving from a decision to resoluteness . . . In resoluteness we are transported into futural happening [*Geschehen*]" (L: 24–34). Employing terms drawn from section 74 of *Being and Time,* Heidegger links the identity of the *Volk* with "the fateful destiny [*das schicksalhafte Geschick*] of *Dasein* in and with its 'generation'" (BT: 352/SZ: 384). He argues that the individual fate of *Dasein* is not only bound up in its being-with others (*Mitsein*) generationally; it is also determined by its occurrence-with others (*Mitgeschehen*) in the form of a *Gemeinschaft* as a *Volk*. This shared sense of fateful being-with others Heidegger terms "destiny" or *Geschick* and insists that it is not the mere aggregate of monadic subjects who happen to live together at the same time or within a shared political space. Rather, destiny is determined by a community's resoluteness in relation to its own language and to its own history. In this sense, "fateful destiny can be explicitly disclosed in retrieve [*Wiederholung*] with regard to its being bound up with the heritage handed down to it. Retrieval first reveals to *Dasein* its own history" (BT: 353/SZ: 386). Concretely, this means that the identity of a *Volk* is constituted in and through its relation to history, understood as destiny. Again, borrowing the language of the Great War, Heidegger claims that the destiny of a *Volk*, a destiny tied to the power of language and tradition, must be fought for: "In communication and in battle [*Kampf*] the power [*Macht*] of destiny first becomes free."

In the context of his lectures in the summer of 1934, Heidegger will draw upon these veiled references to the martial language of *Kampf* and *Macht* and situate them within a powerful reading of German historical destiny. What history means for Heidegger will be determined by the relationship of a *Volk* not merely to its past but also to its future:

> It is questionable whether entering into history means entering into the past.—If a *Volk* steps into history, it steps into the future. If it steps out of history, it no longer has a future. It enters *into* history (the past) insofar as it steps out of history (the future). (L: 42)

Given this "futural" emphasis, Heidegger will argue that "Negroes are also human beings, though they have no history." And yet, according to his Germanocentric reading, "when the airplane brings the *Führer* to Mussolini then history happens"(L:40). What constitutes history then is its relation to the *Volk;* what will come to determine the destiny of the *Volk* is its relation to the "soil of the earth" (*Erdboden*), the native soil from whence springs German autochthony. The earth, he tells his listeners, cannot be reduced to a mere geological phenomenon for observation. Rather, "the history of the *Völker* finds its place in the soil [*Boden*] and *Völker* make history in that they first create space and soil. Making, however, is not producing.—The *Volk* is made through history." History becomes in this sense "not an object but the being of the *Volk*" (L: 70). And yet the path to the self-assertion of the German people had been blocked by what Heidegger perceived as his generation's loss of its own identity and essence. The historical forces unleashed by the Great War had hardly been understood. Germany as a nation was created out of the conflicts and struggles of the war; its destiny was determined by the outcome of the peace. And yet, Heidegger lamented, "The World War as an historical power has still not been integrated into the future at all" (L: 10).

Heidegger's vision of German destiny had been formed and shaped by his own generational experience of the Great War.[36] Like so many other German mandarins of that era, Heidegger came to believe in what Max Scheler termed "the genius of war." Rejecting pacifism as the last refuge of the coward, Scheler contended that peace posed a threat to the moral and intellectual condition of the soul as well as to "the vitality of the *Gemeinschaft.*" "Only war and nothing other than war could heal and put an end to the constitutive dangers . . . posed to culture and *ethos.*"[37] In his book, *The Genius of War and the German War* (1915), Scheler praised war as a civilizing process and as the great *stimulans* of life. War, he claimed, was the "dynamic principle of history"; peace, on the other hand, was its "static principle." Consequently, Scheler viewed war not as the outbreak of mere rage or violence but as a spiritual force that helped to shape the destiny of a *Volk*. In the agonal conflict between two nations, a *Volk* was thrown back upon its own history, forcing it to confront its concealed essence. As Scheler put it: "Every war is a return to the creative origin from whence the state sprung forth." In this confrontation with the origin, the *Volk* is galvanized into a *Schicksalsgemeinschaft* ("community of fate") and begins to understand its mission. It is in terms of the destiny and mission of the German *Volk* that Scheler framed his understanding of *agon, Kampf, Auseinandersetzung*, and *polemos* as a "metaphysics of war." The upshot of this agonal metaphysics was to see the "genius" of the Great War as a stimulus to the "firm foundation of a much deeper *Gemeinschaft* of the European Central Powers—Germany and Austria—in which the solidarity of Europe's Western powers against Asia is prepared."

Scheler's originality notwithstanding, his vision of a German *Schicksalsgemeinschaft* battling to assert itself in the middle of Europe against the mercantile spirit of England (and later, America) and in opposition to the barbarous threat posed by Asia, was hardly original. Like other German academics such as Werner Sombart, Rudolf Eucken, Johann Plenge, Paul Natorp, and Ernst Troeltsch, Scheler was committed to a form of *völkisch* nationalism that glorified *Kampf* as a principle of German self-manifestation. These nationalist thinkers, whose common ideological program has often been characterized by the term "the ideas of 1914," all believed in

36. Domenico Losurdo, *Die Gemeinschaft, der Tod, das Abendland: Heidegger und die Kriegsideologie* (Stuttgart: Metzler, 1995); and Julian Young, *Heidegger, Philosophy, Nazism* (Cambridge: Cambridge University Press, 1997).

37. Max Scheler, *Der Genius des Krieges und der Deutsche Krieg* (Leipzig: Verlag der weissen Bücher, 1915), 103, 17, 113–117.

the singularity of German destiny and in the *Volk*'s special "mission" (*Sendung*).[38] They greeted the war as a turning point in the history of the West and saw it as a great opportunity for Germany to establish its spiritual leadership within Europe. Most could agree with Scheler's contention that "this is the greatness of the world-historical situation: that this un-precedented war is either the beginning of European rebirth or the be-ginning of its atrophy! There is no third possibility!"[39] Caught in the middle as "that currently isolated European middle nation," Germany's destiny was, in Scheler's words, "to attain the role of being the source of European rebirth."[40] Scheler's vision of Germany as a nation caught in the middle, forging its future destiny through its *Kampf* against West and East, would come to fruition in the postwar era as a *mythos* for German rebirth.

Ernst Krieck, in the preface to *Die deutsche Staatsidee,* would return to Scheler's insight about the Great War as the turning point of German des-tiny. Writing in 1934, Krieck looks back and declares: "We are standing be-fore the same great task that began in the Great War"—the formation of a unified German *Volk.* In what he terms the *Frontbildung* of the war, Krieck discerns "the emergence of a supra-personal, communal form of life which manifests a revolutionary principle: the formation of a space of des-tiny [*Schicksalsraum*] for all fellow Germans."[41] In this *Schicksalsgemeinschaft* of the *Volk* who have put behind them personal aspirations, class preju-dices, and religious differences, Krieck locates the genesis for "the break-through of 1933." For him, nothing is clearer than that "the triumphal movement of National Socialism has its genuine origin and wellspring in the Great War." Like Alfred Baeumler, Kurt Hildebrandt, Christoph Sted-ing, and many other National Socialist ideologues of his day, Krieck de-tected in the war the outlines of a powerful *mythos* for rethinking Ger-many's destiny at the center of Europe, a *mythos* that Heidegger too would retrieve and place at the center of his own "metaphysics of war."

In his own political speeches of this same period, Heidegger too will seize upon the image of the Great War for his figuration of National So-

---

38. For an account of the "Ideas of 1914," see Kurt Flasch, *Die geistige Mobilmachung: Die deutsche Intellektuellen und der Erste Weltkrieg* (Berlin: Fest, 2000); Fritz Ringer, *The Decline of the German Mandarins* (Cambridge: Harvard University Press, 1969), 180–199; Hartmut Fries, *Die grosse Katharsis* (Konstanz: Verlag am Hockgraben, 1994), 1: 206–220; Johann Plenge, *1789 und 1914: Die symbolischen Jahre in der Geschichte des politischen Geistes* (Berlin: Springer, 1916); Klaus von See, *Die Ideen von 1789 und die Ideen von 1914* (Frankfurt: Athenaion, 1975); and Rudolf Kjellén, *Die Ideen von 1914* (Leipzig: Hirzel, 1915). Heidegger too, like Scheler, Sombart, Natorp, Kjellén, and others, was convinced that the German "mission" in 1914 was to defeat the liberalism of 1789. For a different, albeit complementary, assessment of Heidegger's position, see Hans Sluga, *Heidegger's Crisis* (Cambridge: Harvard University Press, 1993), 75–100.
39. Scheler, *Der Genius des Krieges,* 308.
40. Max Scheler, *Krieg und Aufbau* (Leipzig: Verlag der weissen Bücher, 1916), 20.
41. Ernst Krieck, *Die deutsche Staatsidee* (Leipzig: Armanen, 1934), 1–3.

cialist revolution, interpreting it as a historical challenge to the future identity of the *Volk*. "The new spirit of community as camaraderie . . . this 'spirit of the front' [*Frontgeist*] became the determining force in the preparation of the National Socialist revolution" (GA 16: 300). In a memorial address delivered on the twenty-fifth anniversary of his Gymnasium graduation, Heidegger reflects back on his former classmates who are absent from the class reunion, those who died sacrificing their lives in the Great War. Employing the same epideictic language as in his Schlageter memorial address, Heidegger tells his fellow classmates, "our comrades died an early death; this early death was, however, the most beautiful and greatest death. The greatest death because it dared to be the most supreme sacrifice for the fate of the *Volk*" (GA 16: 279–283). As the years pass, Heidegger continues, we make the death of our comrades an object of personal memory, something that we recall in retrospect, that sinks ever more assuredly into the past and whose continued existence, we convince ourselves, depends upon our own effort at recollection. "And yet that is all a delusion. For the Great War is *only now* coming upon us. The awakening of our dead, the two million casualties from out of the endless graves, the graves that extend themselves like a secret wreath around the borders of the Reich and of German Austria, this awakening is only now beginning. The Great War is only today becoming for us Germans—and for us first among all *Völker*—a *historical* reality of our *Dasein*, for history is not what has been, nor is it what is present. History is, rather, the futural and our mandate for the futural." What the war has yielded, Heidegger proclaims, is nothing less than the question of the essence of the *Volk* and its relation to its future as a way of confronting its past. In the strictest of terms, the war has posed the question: "which *Volk* has summoned the inner strength to remain equal to the great test from the Great War that only now has come forth and become manifest[?] This is the question put to the *Völker* concerning the originary character of their national order. . . ." Heidegger draws his remarks to a close by making a decisive connection between the strength demanded of the *Volk* in its confrontation with the Great War and the philosophical legacy of Heraclitus. To be originary as a *Volk*, Heidegger implies, means that a *Volk* be able to confront its history spiritually as a *polemos* that both engenders new possibilities and preserves tradition. Out of this polemical confrontation with its heritage, the *Volk* takes upon itself the mission of recovering its own origin:

> From us is demanded: enduring courage, clear knowledge, genuine standards, belief in the mission of the *Volk*. The Great War must be spiritually conquered by us in such a way that battle (*Kampf*) becomes an *inner law* of our *Dasein*. Here we take over in a new way that deep wisdom spoken by

Heraclitus, one of the earliest and greatest thinkers of the Greeks, that *Volk* with whom we have an ancestral kinship (*stammverwandten*) and an essential affinity. This Heraclitean saying is one that we usually know only in its worn-out and truncated form. Hence we usually say "strife is the father of all things." But the Greek text reads: *polemos panton men pater esti, panton de basileus, kai tous men theous edeixe tous de anthropous, tous men doulous epoiese tous de eleutherous* (fragment 53). Conflict is the begetter of all things—of all things, however, also their ruler—; and indeed some it manifests as gods, others as humans. Some it makes appear as slaves, others as masters. (GA 16: 283)

From within this Heraclitean interpretation of the world as strife and conflict, Heidegger would come to an understanding of the German *Volk* as that *Volk* whose inner affinity to the Greeks placed it in a decisive position for deciding the future history of the West. The Great War had placed all the European nations before the impending question "concerning the health of a *Volk's* life-impulse, concerning its power to resist historical decline." "We stand in the midst of this decision," Heidegger claims; "and our generation [*Geschlecht*] is the transition and the bridge. . . . Our generation—in secret fellowship with our dead comrades—is the bridge to the spiritual-historical conquest of the Great War" (GA 16: 281–284). In these reflections on the Great War we can find traces from the powerful cultural movements of the period—the camaraderie of the Youth Movement, the communal ideals of *völkisch* nationalism, the martial heroism of the right, and the cultural messianism of those thinkers committed to the "ideas of 1914."

Drawing on the postwar writings of Spengler, Jünger, Carl Schmitt, and W.F. Otto, Heidegger will transform the "ideas of 1914" into his own onto-poetic fable of German autochthony spun from the primordial-ancestral sources of a hidden Greek *arche*. In Heidegger's work of the 1930s, the "metaphysics of war" will get played out as a philosophical reflection on Heraclitean *polemos* and Nietzschean *Kampf*. In a later chapter, I want to look at how this use of martial rhetoric affects Heidegger's reading of Nietzsche; here, I want to restrict my discussion to the way the language and metaphysics of war shapes Heidegger's understanding of Germany as a nation "caught in a pincers," situated at the center of Europe.

IV. THE POLITICS AND METAPHYSICS OF AUTOCHTHONY:
BLOCH AND ROSENZWEIG

Given the choices open to German philosophers in the postwar era, Heidegger's embrace of the "ideas of 1914" was certainly not inevitable. Within the same era, Ernst Bloch (a German-Jewish Marxist) rejected what he perceived as the poisonous effects of the German *Sonderweg* thesis—especially its cavalier dismissal of "the ideas of 1789" and their commitment to rationality, individual liberty, and the universal role of law.[42] Whereas Heidegger followed Scheler, Sombart, and Krieck in embracing the nationalist dream of a "world-mission" for the German *Vaterland*, Bloch turned to a pan-European, international ideal for Germany: a "European Germany" and a "European *Vaterland*."[43] Like Heidegger, Bloch found in antiquity the sources for his vision of the German future. But where Heidegger stubbornly followed Hegel, Hölderlin, and Fichte in privileging the Greek origin in his figuration of Germany destiny, Bloch nominated his Hebrew forebears as a more proper model for fostering the democratic values of a new Germany. Rejecting the *Sonderweg* thesis with its logic of a historically unique, solitary path of German development, Bloch looked to the German past for traces of another Germany, of a path not taken. He found in the Fichte of 1806, the author of *Characteristics of the Present Age*, a cosmopolitan vision of European unity at odds with the provincial nationalism of the *Addresses to the German Nation* of 1808.[44]

Against the Fichtean-Heideggerian principle of *Bodenständigkeit* with its martial exclusion of non-autochthonous peoples, Bloch affirms what he deems the more fundamental Fichtean principle of "German freedom and democracy" with its cosmopolitan inclusion of all peoples, autochthonous or not.[45] Going back through German history, Bloch outlines the suppression of this democratic ideal in the Prussian drive for geographical expansion and political conquest. He interprets the Franco-Prussian War of 1870 as a power move to form a unified national state under Prussian hegemony. This power play by Bismarck, he claims, crushed the democratic hopes of the bourgeois revolution of 1848 by fostering a nationalist program of imperial-military expansion, the inevitable result of which was the outbreak of the Great War. Ironically, however, this newly formed German national state was hardly a unified nation. Prussia and Swabia were never truly integrated in any meaningful way—except politically. In this sense, Heidegger's Hölderlinian rhapsodies about the "Alemannic soil" can be read as the expression of a certain provincial love of the native earth rather than as the declaration of a nationalist ideologue. Nonethe-

---

42. Besides the works by Kjellén, Plenge, and Sombart on this theme, Max Scheler also wrote a seminal essay, "1789 und 1914," *Archiv für Sozialwissenschaft und Sozialpolitik* 42, no. 2 (1916–1917): 586–605.

43. For a perceptive analysis of Ernst Bloch's Pan-European vision, see Manfred Riedel, *Tradition und Utopie: Ernst Blochs Philosophie im Licht unserer geschichtlichen Denkerfahrung* (Frankfurt: Suhrkamp, 1994), 11–67.

44. J. G. Fichte, *Characteristics of the Present Age* (London: Chapman, 1847), and Riedel, *Tradition und Utopie*, 56–61.

45. Ernst Bloch, *Kampf, nicht Krieg: Politische Schriften, 1917–1919* (Frankfurt: Suhrkamp, 1985), 233.

less, Heidegger's discourses on *Bodenständigkeit* did have national implications. As the product of a lower middle-class, Alemannic heritage, Heidegger naturally rejected the urban, cosmopolitan world of Bloch's Jewish upbringing. Moreover, his myth of the *Vaterland* choked off all possibilities of following Bloch's "other" path for Germany: the path of a utopian, cosmopolitan ideal of an international "community of the spirit." Nonetheless, in Bloch's messianic vision of the "true Germany" of the spirit (in opposition to the nationalist vision of a "secret Germany" of the soil) we can recover the powerful sources for a critique of Heidegger's geo-philosophy of the earth as *terra*—(territory) and as *chthonos* (the chthonic, subterranean, *unterirdische* forces of rootedness).[46]

As we look more closely at Bloch's implicit critique of Heideggerian autochthony, we can see how his twofold origin as German and as Jew points him in the direction of another origin—one that rejects the singularity of the *Vaterland* for the plurality of a European homeland.[47] Like Nietzsche, Bloch rejects the Germanic mania for nationalism and instead embraces the ideal of a cosmopolitan *Europa* as a worthier goal for German philosophy. Within this same postwar context, another messianic German Jew, Franz Rosenzweig, joins Bloch in offering a devastating critique of German nationalism and its ideal of autochthonous destiny. In his *Star of Redemption* (1921), Rosenzweig points to the treacherous implications of Hellenic autochthony for the German community and challenges its axiomatics of land, territory, earth, soil, roots, and indigenous home. Drawing upon the *arche/re'shiyth* of his own Judaic heritage, Rosenzweig questions the logic of geo-philosophy and its privileging of the soil as the basis of political community. In a fragment entitled "Peoples and their Native Soil," that serves as a kind of manifesto against autochthony, Rosenzweig writes:

46. In chapter 5, I will push this Heideggerian connection to the earth even further, tracing it back to Baeumler's writings on the tellurian, the chthonic, and the myths of the ancients. In their book, *What Is Philosophy?* trans. Hugh Tomlinson and Graham Burchell (New York: Columbia University Press, 1994), Gilles Deleuze and Felix Guattari offer an account of Heidegger's metaphysics of the earth as a form of "geo-philosophy." As they put it, within Heidegger's work "the history of being or of the earth is the history of its turning away, of its deterritorialization in the technico-worldwide development of Western civilization started by the Greeks and reterritorialized on National Socialism," 95. Part of what I want to stress is the subterranean form of thinking—what W.F. Otto, in *Die Götter Griechenlands* (Frankfurt: Klostermann, 1987), 189, terms the "unterirdische Wohnstatt" or "subterranean dwelling place"—that helps to form the complex world of myth and politics that informs Heidegger's thinking.

47. Bloch's early work, though open to the "international," still has a decidedly Eurocentric focus; the peoples of Asia and Africa have not yet emerged as themes for Bloch here, especially in his essay "Bodenständigkeit als Blasphemie," *Politische Messungen* (Frankfurt: Suhrkamp, 1970), 74–82.

The peoples of the world are not content with the bonds of blood. They sink their roots into the night of earth, lifeless in itself, but the spender of life, and from the lastingness of earth they conclude that they themselves will last. Their will to eternity clings to the soil and to the reign over the soil, to the land. The earth of their homeland is watered by the blood of their sons, for they do not trust in the life of a community of blood, in a community that can dispense with anchorage in solid earth. . . . For while the earth nourishes, it also binds. Whenever a people loves the soil of its native land more than its own life, it is in danger that . . . in the end the soil will persist as that which was loved more strongly, and the people will leave their lifeblood upon it. In the final analysis, the people belong to him who conquers the land. It cannot be otherwise, because people cling to the soil more than to their life as a people. Thus the earth betrays a people that entrusted its permanence to earth. The soil endures, the peoples who live on it pass. . . .

And so, in contrast to the history of other peoples, the earliest legends about the tribe of the eternal people is not based on indigenousness [*Autochthonie*]. . . . To the eternal people home is never home in the sense of land, as it is to the peoples of the world who plough the land and live and thrive on it, until they have all but forgotten that being a people means something besides being rooted in a land. The eternal people has not been permitted to while away time in any home. It never loses the untrammeled freedom of a wanderer.[48]

Rosenzweig's critique of the political implications of autochthony unraveled the bond between *Volk* and soil, *Gemeinschaft* and *Bodenständigkeit*, that Heidegger had established in the political speeches of his rectorate. But by framing his narrative within the terms of ancient Jewish history, rather than those of originary Greek philosophy, Rosenzweig also set forth a formidable critique of Heidegger's Hellenic history of being. Geopolitically, he challenged the territorialist-imperial logic of a "metaphysics of war" that guided European political history. Onto-archeologically, he burst asunder the self-evident assumption of a Graeco-Germanic *arche* that ruled over all aspects of Western philosophy. Both politically and ontologically, Rosenzweig's *Star of Redemption* undermined the fundamental tenets of autochthonous metaphysics that sustained Heidegger's entire project. In the Jewish experience of exile and estrangement and in the ordeal of wandering and diaspora, Rosenzweig found the traces of a path not taken, a path whose outlines had been covered over and occluded by the roots of Graeco-German tradition. From its earliest tales of Eden, Babel, Ur, Egypt, and Babylon, Jewish history had been marked by the phenomenon of expulsion and rootlessness. Abraham's lament—"I am a stranger and a

48. Franz Rosenzweig, *Star of Redemption*, trans. William Hallo (Boston: Beacon Press, 1972), 299–300; *Stern der Erlösung* (Frankfurt: Suhrkamp, 1996), 332–333.

sojourner . . ." (Genesis 23:4)—had foretold of future travail. But the Jewish people had found succor in the tribal bonds of their shared history and language—and in what Rosenzweig termed its "blood-community" since, as he claimed, "only blood gives present warrant to the hope for a future."[49] Tragically, Rosenzweig's notion of a blood-community would be turned against him by Nazi ideologues in the years following his death in 1929. And yet despite his own racial metaphysics of blood, Rosenzweig would offer a powerful critique of autochthonous metaphysics in his emphasis on language and/as destiny. Heidegger too would turn to language as the source of *völkisch* destiny and poetic homecoming. In the lectures on Hölderlin in 1934/35, he would write: "language as such constitutes the originary essence of the historical being of human being" (GA 39: 67). And yet Heidegger's understanding of language—precisely as it intersects his political reading of Hölderlin—would reinforce the logic of autochthony that denies the possibility of an "other" path as formulated by the Jewish-Germans Rosenzweig and Bloch. The last century has witnessed the devastating effects of autochthonous metaphysics upon Western and non-Western cultures alike. The mere procession of names—Rwanda, Croatia, Palestine, Cambodia, Auschwitz—gives testimony to the effects of racial exclusion on those groups designated as allochthonous or non-originary. Heidegger's violent and exclusionary metaphysics of *völkisch* autochthony can be situated in the same tradition. What, I would argue, has not been widely recognized is how powerfully this form of metaphysics continues on in Heidegger's work—even after the collapse of National Socialism.

From the Rectorial Address in 1933 until the end of the war, Heidegger would cling to his geo-philosophical *mythos* of a German *Sonderweg* and of an appointed mission for the German *Volk*. As he lost faith in the revolutionary effects of National Socialism, he abandoned his aggressive, volitional commitment to the myth and began to divest himself of the language of self-assertion, *Kampf, Wille, Dienst, Frontgemeinschaft,* and other politically laden terms. After 1938, Heidegger will begin his own *Auseinandersetzung* with National Socialism which he begins to see as caught up within the selfsame metaphysics of will, technology, and domination that characterizes all modern subjectivity. But throughout this entire period, continuing right through the last published text from 1976, Heidegger will still cling to the old metaphysics of the earth, the land, the native soil, and rootedness that he outlined in the Schlageter speech and the Rectorial Address. Even the turn to the Eckhartian language of *Gelassen-*

---

49. Rosenzweig, *Star of Redemption,* 299; *Stern der Erlösung,* 332. Read against the background of Rosenzweig's work, Heidegger's writings of the 1930s betray a clear political message: only those who share in the autochthonic bond to the Greeks can genuinely experience the truth of being. All others are mere "foreigners"—ontologically and politically.

heit in the 1940s and '50s will still reveal the underlying metaphysics of *Bo-denständigkeit*, autochthony, and the Alemannic soil that pervades Heidegger's work of the 1930s. Whether Heidegger confronts the question concerning technology, the poetry of Trakl, Rilke, and George, or the matter of building-dwelling-thinking, his question-frame will be marked by the same conceptual nexus of rootlessness, homelessness, and deracination as in his earlier political writings. If, in 1929, Heidegger finds the danger to the "native and indigenous [*bodenständige*]" German spirit in its "increasing Judification," by 1955 he situates it in the "calculative thinking" spawned by the metaphysics of the modern age.[50] And yet, despite the muted effect provided by his softer accent and his new conciliatory tone, the underlying message remained the same. In the 1955 address, "Gelassenheit," delivered to his Alemannic countrymen in Messkirch, Heidegger raised the question:

> Is there still a life-giving homeland [*wurzelkräftige Heimat*] in whose ground [*Boden*] man may constantly stand rooted, that is, be autochthonic [*ständig steht, d.h., boden-ständig ist*]? Many Germans have lost their homeland, have had to leave their villages and towns, have been driven from their native soil. . . . We grow more thoughtful and ask: What is happening here—with those driven from their homeland no less than with those who have remained? Answer: the *rootedness*, the *autochthony* [*Bodenständigkeit*], of man is threatened today at its core. Even more: the loss of rootedness is caused not merely by external circumstances and fates, nor does it stem only from the negligence and superficiality of man's way of life. The loss of autochthony springs from the spirit of the age into which we were all born.[51]

As Heidegger begins to trace the history of this loss of autochthony, he turns to a discussion of the emergence of calculative thinking which, he asserts, "developed first in the seventeenth century and indeed in Europe and only in Europe." From first to last, Heidegger will designate Europe as the source of Western metaphysical thinking and as the center of the West, designations whose ground and logic are never seriously argued for philosophically but rather are simply assumed and taken as self-evident. If we are to understand this turn in Heidegger's thinking toward Europe rather than Germany and toward *Gelassenheit* rather than self-assertion, we will need to consider it within the metaphysics of earth, land, soil, and roots that constitute Heideggerian autochthony. This belief in rootedness as the indispensable source for our genuine relation to being—a notion that has emerged in the environmentalist literature around Heidegger—

---

50. Heidegger's letter to Victor Schwoerer of October 20, 1929, was published for the first time in *Die Zeit*, no. 52 (December 22, 1989), 50. Martin Heidegger, *Discourse on Thinking* (New York: Harper & Row, 1966), 46; *Gelassenheit* (Pfullingen: Neske, 1988), 12.

51. Heidegger, *Discourse on Thinking*, 48–50; *Gelassenheit*, 15–17.

is hardly an innocuous article of faith.[52] It proves just as essential for Heidegger's political decisions as for his eco-poetic reveries about "nearness" (*Nähe*), "dwelling" (*Wohnen*), and the "homeland" (*Heimat*). But it also functions as a central element in Heidegger's own construction of the history of philosophy, a construction that has powerfully shaped the way continental philosophy is practiced both in Europe and America.[53] In the postwar period, during his time of exile from university teaching, Heidegger will retreat from his aggressively Germanocentric politics of self-assertion and try to salvage his career by employing a more broadly inclusive "European" rhetorical style. In the period from May of 1933 until May of 1945, however, Heidegger will cling to a reading of Western history and philosophy that is purely Germanocentric in all its essentials—from the way it understands the development of metaphysics in the Greeks to the way it constructs an interpretation of European politics or the way it elides Romans, Jews, and other cultural groups. As we have seen, despite his stature as the most original thinker of his epoch, Heidegger's Germanocentric philosophy of being was hardly unique. All too uncritically it affirmed the arsenal of clichés that were part of the war generation's response to the tensions of European geo-politics.

As Germany's crisis grew ever more intense, Heidegger fell back upon this storehouse of conservative doctrine as a guide for understanding the rootlessness and deracination that he saw everywhere around him. In two of Heidegger's texts from the years 1935 and 1936—*An Introduction to*

52. Michael Zimmerman has emerged as perhaps the most thoughtful Heideggerian to embrace the notion of "deep-ecology" and his *Contesting Earth's Future: Radical Ecology and Postmodernity* (Berkeley: University of California Press, 1994), 91–149, attempts to address the question of Heidegger's National Socialism and its implications for a philosophy of the earth. Others like Bruce Foltz, *Inhabiting the Earth: Heidegger, Environmental Ethics, and the Metaphysics of Nature* (Atlantic Highlands: Humanities Press, 1995), Ladelle McWhorter, ed., *Heidegger and the Earth: Essays in Environmental Philosophy* (Kirksville: Thomas Jefferson University Press, 1992), and Dolores La Chapelle, *Earth Wisdom* (Los Angeles: Guild of Tutors Press, 1978), while offering helpful assessments of Heidegger on the question of ecology, never really come to terms with his political legacy. Part of what I want to stress is that we read Heidegger "selectively" at our own peril—whether the topic is ecology, technology, poetry, art, architecture, music, religion—or even "philosophy."

53. Part of my critique of Heidegger's influence on contemporary continental philosophy follows from the choice of topics, themes, problems, and framing questions that dominate the program lists of the American Philosophical Association and the Society for Phenomenology and Existential Philosophy and that characterizes the course offerings and required reading lists of many continentally focused graduate programs in the United States. "Plurality" and "diversity" should be taken seriously in regards to the history of philosophy as well. Perhaps we can also include into the conversation about continental philosophy figures such as Rosenzweig, Bloch, and Löwith, figures whose work is marginalized in the programs of the APA and SPEP. Essays by Simon Critchley, "Black Socrates? Questioning the Philosophical Tradition," *Radical Philosophy* 69 (Jan./Feb. 1995): 17–26, and by Robert Bernasconi, "Heidegger and the Invention of the Philosophical Tradition," *Journal of the British Society for Phenomenology* 26, no. 3 (1995): 240–254, have questioned the mosaic of structures that have formed the "field" of continental philosophy as an academic discipline.

Metaphysics and "Europa und die deutsche Philosophie"—we can find the outlines of his argument about this need for rootedness and autochthony. By following the logic of his account in these texts, we might begin to see how decisive the problem of autochthony was, and not only for his understanding of German politics but also for the way he framed the history of Western philosophy.

V. THE METAPHYSICS OF *MITTELEUROPA*

Baeumler's essay, "The Meaning of the Great War" (1929), had established the significance of the National Socialist conceit that the Germans constituted "the *Volk* of the European middle [*Mitte*]."[54] In another essay, entitled "The Dialectic of Europe," Baeumler had also proffered the standard NS view that the Germans' turn toward self-assertion—what he called "the homecoming of the German spirit"—signified nothing less than "the beginning of a new epoch in European history."[55] Heidegger too, like Baeumler, Scheler, Krieck, Spengler, and other conservative-nationalist thinkers, came to understand Germany as a nation caught in the middle, situated at the center of a Europe which was itself situated at the center of a historical conflict between America and Russia. As the center of the center, Germany would occupy a pivotal position both geographically, within Europe, and historically, within the destiny of the West. In both his Freiburg lecture course from the summer of 1935, *An Introduction to Metaphysics,* and in a talk delivered in April of 1936 at the Bibliotheca Hertziana in Rome, entitled "Europa und die deutsche Philosophie," Heidegger attempted to offer a geo-philosophical reading of Western destiny that hinged on understanding the significance of this metaphysics of "the center" (*Mitte*)—both for Germany and for Europe.

In *Beyond Good and Evil,* Nietzsche characterized the German *Volk* in one of his aphorisms as a *"Volk der Mitte"*—"a people of the center/middle"— even as he spoke with trepidation about the prospect of "the Germanization of all Europe" (BGE: 174–175; KSA 5: 184–185). By 1934, the National Socialist Nietzsche revival had wholly transformed—or rather, transmogrified—this Nietzschean characterization. Now Baeumler began to interpret Nietzsche as the prophet of a Germanic-Nordic Europe that would overturn its Roman-Christian legacy. In his words, "before Nietzsche's very eyes appeared the old task of our race: the task to be *Führer* of Europe." And another National Socialist Nietzschean, Ernst Horneffer, in his book *Nietzsche as Herald of the Present,* wrote that in the Nietzschean self-assertion of

54. Baeumler, *Männerbund und Wissenschaft,* 4.
55. Baeumler, *Politik und Erziehung,* 51.

the German will lay "the *Schicksalsfrage* [question of destiny] of the future."[56] Baeumler and Horneffer found in the *Selbstbehauptungswille* of the German *Volk* (its will to self-assertion) the measure of its destiny and the source of its National Socialist identity, something that Heidegger too would embrace. But where these philosophers interpreted that destiny in terms of a "great politics" of racial conquest and imperial expansion, Heidegger focused on the ontological meaning of German destiny. He would, from the very beginning, view these crudely political values as merely part of the external casing of National Socialism. But Heidegger was not concerned with the external. He sought to uncover "the inner truth and greatness" of National Socialism—something that he believed was intimately bound up with the ancient Greek question about the meaning of being (IM: 199/EM: 152). In its decision to overcome the rootlessness of Western metaphysics and reclaim Germany's lost homeland at the center of the center, National Socialism appeared to Heidegger as the authentically German response to the historical crisis of Europe.

One cannot properly understand *An Introduction to Metaphysics* without situating it within this constellation of themes. Heidegger reads European history metaphysically and, in turn, reads metaphysics through the lens of European history. As he begins his analysis of German destiny, he positions it in terms of his own "metaphysics of the middle." That is, he understands Germany *spatially* as the nation caught in the middle, lying at the heart of Central Europe. Here he follows the lead of the political economist Franz Naumann whose work *Mitteleuropa* (1915) set forth the geopolitical terms of a German-dominated Central Europe.[57] But Heidegger also conceives of Germany *temporally* as the nation caught in the middle between Europe's past and future, between its forgotten Greek *arche* and its undecided German *eschaton*. At one point in his lectures of 1934/35 on "Germania," he alludes to Hölderlin's verse about "the center/middle of time" (*die Mitte der Zeit*) which, he claims, "first emerges on the ground of the earth out of the genuine origin [*Herkunft*] and the creatively grasped future [*Zukunft*]" (GA 39: 290). Moreover, consonant with the "ideas of 1914," Heidegger sees Germany as the nation called to save Europe and the West from its own metaphysical self-destruction, a destruction that can be averted only if the Germans recover the lost roots of Greek *aletheia*. In

---

56. Baeumler, *Nietzsche: Der Philosoph und Politiker,* 182; and Ernst Horneffer, *Nietzsche als Vorbote der Gegenwart* (Düsseldorf: A. Bagel, 1934), 43.

57. Franz Naumann, *"Mitteleuropa"* (Berlin: G. Reimer, 1915). For a broader discussion, see Jörg Brechtefeld, *"Mitteleuropa" and German Politics* (New York: St. Martin's Press, 1996), and Henry Cord Meyer, *"Mitteleuropa" in German Thought and Action, 1815–1945* (The Hague: Nijhoff, 1955). In his interview of 1966 in *Der Spiegel,* Heidegger states that his political views of 1933 were developed along the lines of Naumann's—although this can also be understood as a retroactive attempt to make his position seem more politically acceptable, SI: 270/*Antwort:* 84.

his 1936 lecture, "Hölderlin and the Essence of Poetry" (held only six days before the "Europa" talk), Heidegger speaks of Hölderlin as the poet of a "*Zwischenbereich,*" or "a realm in-between" the gods and the *Volk.* But he also understands him as a poet who thinks beyond the limits of temporal boundaries, penetrating into the very "middle of being" (*Mitte des Seins*). In this way he grasps his own era in terms of a new temporality that accords with his poetical insight into the middle of being. Heidegger writes that for Hölderlin "this is the destitute time because it stands under a twofold temporal absence: in the no-longer of the gods who have fled and the not-yet of the one who is coming" (EHD: 47).[58] On the basis of this reading of Hölderlin, Heidegger comes to see Germany as a nation standing spatially and temporally in the middle, caught between past and future, lying between East and West. If it were to avoid being inundated by the sweeping forces at the vortex of the modern world, Germany would have to confront the crisis at the center of Europe. For Heidegger this meant coming face to face with the rootlessness of Europe's own history and with the forces of political and technological change that threatened Europe's very existence.

Heidegger's reading of Europe is offered as a response to the crisis of the West whose external signs had already been made manifest in the conflagrations of the Great War. In a superficial way, Spengler had already pointed to the most obvious features of the crisis: the growing alienation of modern life, the sterility of the urban metropolis, the soullessness of commercial *Zivilisation,* the decadence of modern values. In his early Freiburg lectures from 1919–1923, Heidegger had criticized Spengler for his crude reduction of historical facticity to the mechanical patterns of a cultural morphology. As a contemporary representative of what Heidegger termed "inauthentic historical consciousness," Spengler had reduced future oriented happening to mere "calculation," as if "the not-yet" could be brought before us in advance as something "present" (GA 63: 56). From his 1920 lecture in Wiesbaden on the *Decline of the West* until his winter 1942/43 course, *Parmenides,* Heidegger would continue to characterize Spengler's work as "cheap," "concocted," "coarse," and marked by "notorious ignorance and the journalistic superficiality of the vulgarly educated modern rabble" (P: 56, 113/GA 54: 82, 168; GA 59: 16).[59] But these carping expressions of mandarin petulance aside, Heidegger found in Spengler's work traces of an autochthonic metaphysics of the German future in

58. In his poem, "Germania," Hölderlin also refers to Germania within "die Mitte der Zeit," between past and future. Friedrich Hölderlin, *Hyperion and Selected Poems,* ed. Eric Santner (New York: Continuum, 1990), 214–215; Hellingrath will also draw on this Hölderlinian view of the *Vaterland* and its connection to the earth in *Hölderlin-Vermächtnis,* 147–154.

59. For details about the unpublished Wiesbaden lecture, see Kisiel, *The Genesis of Heidegger's "Being and Time,"* 553.

harmony with his own geo-philosophy. In the following passage from *Parmenides,* we can see the deep ambivalence in Heidegger concerning Spengler's critique:

> Only to an age which had already forsaken every possibility of thoughtful reflection could an author present such a book, in the execution of which a brilliant acumen, an enormous erudition, and a strong gift for categorization are matched by an unusual pretension of judgment, a rare superficiality of thinking, and a pervasive frailty of foundations. This confusing semischolarship and carelessness of thinking has been accompanied by the peculiar state of affairs that the same people who decry the priority of the biological thinking in Nietzsche's metaphysics find contentment in the aspects of decline in the Spenglerian vision, which is based throughout on nothing but a crude biological interpretation of history. (P: 56/GA 54: 82–83)

Even as he rejected Spengler's biologism—and his biologistic reading of Nietzsche—Heidegger discerned in Spengler's analysis of Western history a way of uniting Nietzsche's critique of European nihilism with the conservative-nationalist ideas of destiny, *Mitteleuropa,* and the "metaphysics of war." This he found in Spengler's discussion of autochthony and the native soil. As in his criticisms of National Socialist racial thinking, however, Heidegger would assail the basic principles of biologism and try to bring the focus back to *Bodenständigkeit.* Where Spengler prattled on about "the physiognomy of culture" and "the cyclic organs of cosmic existence," Heidegger dismissed this as the specious blather of an over-educated schoolmaster.[60] But where he spoke of "earth-boundedness," "the power of the land" and "the roots of being," Heidegger found echoes of his own autochthonous history of Western destiny. Spengler's language was tied to the generational *Kulturkritik* of the German mandarinate, a language that Heidegger found modish and reductive. In his bifurcated categories of soul vs. intellect, *Kultur* vs. *Zivilisation,* organic vs. mechanical, *Gemeinschaft* vs. *Gesellschaft,* Spengler offered a feuilletonistic philosophy of history that drew on the language of sociology. Heidegger himself, while spurning this language of binary opposition, was not immune to the conservative impulses that generated it. In fact, he transformed them into his own inimitable style of *Ursprungsphilosophie.* But when Spengler located the reasons for the decline of culture in the phenomenon of rootlessness, Heidegger recognized a historical critique with profound epochal significance.

For Spengler, "the man of the land and the man of the city are different essences"; in the city, "separated from the power of the land—cut off from it even by the pavement underfoot—being becomes more and more languid, sensation and reason more and more powerful . . . All art, all reli-

---

60. Oswald Spengler, *The Decline of the West* (New York: Knopf, 1979), 1: 101, 2: 5.

gion and science become slowly intellectualized, alien to the land, incomprehensible to the peasant of the soil. With civilization there sets in the climacteric. The immemorially old roots of being are dried up in the stone-masses of its cities."[61] Attentive to the historical effects of deracination, Spengler claims that "when being is sufficiently uprooted . . . there suddenly emerges—the sterility of civilized man." In this new historical type—the nomadic "parasitical city dweller"—Spengler finds the symbol of a decadent political-economic order: the rootless capitalist. By conceiving of money "as an inorganic and abstract quantity, entirely disconnected from the notion of the fertile earth and from the values of originary life," the modern city dweller had become cut off from the source of historical destiny. As part of his critique, Spengler pointed to the rootless effects of democracy, capitalism, and the urban marketplace. Following Nietzsche's critique of democratic values, Spengler interpreted politics as a form of will to power. The leveling of values and the rootlessness brought on by democratic culture appeared to him as threats to the future of Germany. For him, the destiny of a people was determined by its "tendency to take root in a landscape." In this sense, by understanding politics as "the blind cosmic drive to validity and power that . . . remains bound up with the earth, the 'home'-land," Spengler attempted to transform Nietzsche's "great politics" into a politics of the earth.[62]

Heidegger rejected most of Spengler's Nietzschean observations about politics, but he did have sympathy for Spengler's overall project of conjoining Nietzsche's history of European nihilism with a politics and philosophy of the earth. If, as a stateless wanderer, Nietzsche himself was immune to the politics of autochthony, Spengler, as a committed philosopher of the state, was intent on refashioning Nietzsche's *Kulturkritik* into the frame of a nationalist metaphysics of the earth. We can find traces of this attempt in Spengler's discussion of peasant life and in the rootedness it offers. In this passage from *The Decline of the West*, we can discern the same emphasis on roots, soil, landscape, and native ground that we saw in Heidegger's Schlageter speech and in "Creative Landscape":

> [The peasant] roots in the earth that he tends, the soul of man discovers a soul in the countryside, and a new earth-boundedness of being, a new feeling, pronounces itself. Hostile nature becomes the friend; earth becomes *Mother* Earth. Between sowing and begetting, harvest and death, the child and the grain, a profound affinity is set up. A new devoutness addresses itself in the chthonic cults to the fertile earth that grows along with man. . . . The peasant's dwelling is the great symbol of settledness. It is itself plant, thrusts its roots deep into its "own" soil . . . this is the condition precedent of every

61. Ibid., 2: 92, 103 and 1: 32.
62. Ibid., 2: 113, 440.

Kultur, which itself in turn grows up out of a mother-landscape, and renews and intensifies the intimacy of man and soil. . . . Only in *Zivilisation* with its giant cities do we come again to despise and disengage ourselves from these roots. Man as civilized, as *intellectual nomad,* is again wholly microcosmic, wholly nameless. . . . Today at the end of this *Kultur,* the rootless intellect ranges over all landscapes and possibilities of thought. But between these limits lies the time in which a man held a bit of soil to be something *worth dying for.*[63]

Spengler's radical emphasis on rootlessness as a source of European ni-hilism struck Heidegger as an important supplement to Nietzsche's meta-physical critique of Western history. But he also gleaned something else from Spengler—a way to think of German destiny in terms of an overall history of the world, what Spengler would call *Weltgeschichte,* and what Hei-degger would transform into *Seynsgeschichte.* Like Spengler, Heidegger thought eschatologically; indeed, his whole way of reading Hölderlin from 1934–1945 was alive to the eschatological dimension of destiny, fate, and "end" that he uncovered in Spengler's writings. As part of this eschatolog-ical style of thinking, Heidegger understood the Germans as a *Volk* whose essence was futural, or rather, as a *Volk* whose identity was bound up in the futural retrieval of the *arche* and the homeland. "Homecoming," Heideg-ger wrote in one of his Hölderlin essays, "is the future of the historical essence of the Germans" (EHD: 30). In Spengler's world-historical figura-tion of German destiny as a struggle for rootedness, belonging, and per-manence at the center of Europe, Heidegger found traces of his own geo-philosophical account of *Mitteleuropa.* Again, like Spengler he understood Germany's position as a *Kampf* or struggle for self-assertion between Rus-sia on the East and England/America on the West. And yet, within his own metaphysics of the middle, Heidegger would interpret Spengler's dis-course about "fate" and "roots" differently. Where Spengler spoke of fate in terms of end, decline, and biological death, Heidegger would speak of it in terms of *homecoming,* the arrival of the last god, and eschatological "world-darkening." And where Spengler invoked the language of earth, soil, and landscape to point to the origin of culture, Heidegger would de-velop his own lexicon of *Bodenständigkeit,* autochthony, and rootedness to recover the hidden *arche* of being. Both Spengler and Heidegger under-stood the crisis of modernity in terms of myth—even if they configured their myths differently. And each found in Nietzsche's language of ni-hilism the sources for uncovering the roots of the myth. What defined their various efforts to offer a diagnosis of Europe's cultural crisis was their attempt to wed the pan-European vision of Nietzsche to their own nation-alist visions of a *Mitteleuropa* dominated by Germany. It is this nationalist

63. Ibid., 2: 89–90.

vision of *Mitteleuropa* that comes alive in Heidegger's *Introduction to Metaphysics,* where we find an analysis of the spiritual decline of the West read through the lens of Nietzschean nihilism and committed to a metaphysics of the middle and to a metaphysics of autochthony.

VI. HEIDEGGER'S IDEA OF EUROPE IN *INTRODUCTION TO METAPHYSICS*

Heidegger's *Introduction to Metaphysics* opens as a philosophical reflection on the question: "Why are there beings rather than nothing?" As he continues with his lecture he comes back to this question often, reframing it within different contexts—grammatical, etymological, logical, historical, aesthetic. But in the first chapter of this work he also locates the question politically and he does so by considering it within the context of Nietzsche's remark that "the highest concepts" are nothing but "the last trail of smoke of evaporating reality" (IM: 36/EM: 27; KSA 6: 76). In 1935, Heidegger will again take up being as a forgotten question, an issue he raised in *Being and Time* and in his Freiburg inaugural lecture of 1929, "What Is Metaphysics?" (BT: 1/SZ: 2). However, Heidegger will also raise a historical theme that remains unquestioned and obscured in the long academic treatise *Being and Time*—the question of Europe in relation to the question of the West. Now when Heidegger asks, "is 'being' a mere word and its meaning a vapor or is it the spiritual destiny of the West?" he situates it within a whole nexus of concerns about destiny, rootedness, autochthony, and eschatology that will shape his work until the very end of his life (IM: 37/EM: 28). In this new political form, Heidegger will take up the question of German destiny as a decision about how to interpret the essence of truth—a theme from his original 1930 lecture, "On the Essence of Truth." There, in the context of a discussion about the province of Baden and the theme of *Heimat,* Heidegger would make a fateful connection between the experience of Greek *aletheia* and the rootedness of Alemannic autochthony. In a *völkisch* reading of *Sein* that wanted to recover the forgottenness of being by retrieving a hidden Greek *arche,* Heidegger would point to a shared Graeco-German affinity for autochthony as a way out of the nihilism afflicting the West. By 1935, Heidegger would, on the basis of this autochthonic reading, interpret the Germans as a *Volk* with a spiritual mission to move the West out of its constricted sphere of technological-imperial concerns and into the realm of originary reflection. From the fundamental ontology of *Being and Time* with its concern for an individuated *Dasein* who shares a world with others, Heidegger would turn to an archaic politics focused on the *Volk* at the metaphysical center of being. The stakes were not small.

Baeumler too had understood the Germans as a "*Volk* of the European middle/center" and Hellingrath and George had already spoken of the necessity of a German mission, so Heidegger was hardly breaking new ground in *Introduction to Metaphysics.*[64] Whereas these earlier thinkers had framed their remarks in wholly Germanocentric terms, however, Heidegger sought to offer an account of the entire history of the West as he understood it. The scope of his interpretation was broadly Nietzschean as it attempted to grasp the present crisis of Europe within the history of Western ontology. In that sense, his new political reading of European destiny was still anchored to the old mythic account of Greek philosophy. Here again we find the intersection of the political and the ontological in the form of a deep-rooted desire to return to the homeland: ontologically, to philosophy's archaic Greek homeland and, politically, to Germany's future oriented homeland of a *Volk* rooted in its past. As the nation caught in the middle of those ancestral and futural *archai*, Germany would serve as the spatial and temporal middle of a world-historical decision. As he reframed this decision at the axis of a political-ontological intersection, Heidegger would again take up the familiar discourse about a "metaphysics of the middle." But he would situate it within Nietzsche's familiar trajectory of the course of European nihilism:

> This Europe, in its ruinous blindness forever on the point of cutting its own throat, lies today in a great pincers, squeezed between Russia on one side and America on the other. Seen metaphysically, Russia and America are both the same: the same desperate frenzy of unbridled technology and of the rootless [*bodenlos*] organization of the average human being. (IM: 37/EM: 28)

Heidegger goes on to provide examples of this rootless, desperate kind of metaphysical existence. He points to the all too familiar ontic situation of modern life: the transformation of every form of existence into a "resource"; the flattening of temporality into its consumable form as "news" (where political assassination and symphony concerts come to us simultaneously via radio [—and, now television]); the heroization of boxers and other sports figures, and the vulgarization of the individual into "mass man." All these forms of existence indicate to Heidegger the desperate plight of modern *Dasein* which, because of its pathological dependence on the need for novelty, variety, speed, simultaneity, and the instantaneous, has lost its ability to experience time within an ontological context. As a result of this frenzied preoccupation with the "new"—understood

64. Baeumler, *Männerbund und Wissenschaft*, 4; Hellingrath, "Hölderlin und die Deutschen," *Hölderlin Vermächtnis*, 123–154.

through its Latin roots as mode, *modus, modernus* or the "modern"—"time as history has vanished from the *Dasein* of all *Völker*" (IM: 37–38/EM: 28–29). This condition of rootlessness, disintegration, and spiritual decay had already been diagnosed by Nietzsche in *The Will to Power.* There, in a chapter entitled "On the History of European Nihilism," under the heading "On the History of Modern Darkening [*Verdüsterung*]," Nietzsche prefigured the metaphysical crisis of the West that Heidegger sought to address (WP: 40/WM: 50–51). As Heidegger put it:

> The spiritual decline [*Verfall*] of the earth is so far advanced that *Völker* risk exhausting that last reserve of spiritual energy that enables them just to see and assess this decline as such (in respect to the destiny of 'being'). This simple observation has nothing to do with cultural pessimism and, of course, with optimism either; for the darkening of the world [*Verdüsterung der Welt*], the flight of the gods [*die Flucht der Götter*], the destruction of the earth, the transformation of human beings into a mass, the hateful suspicion of everything that is creative and free have reached such proportions throughout the earth that such infantile categories as pessimism and optimism have long become ludicrous.
>
> We are caught in a pincers. As the *Volk* situated at the center we experience the sharpest pressure, as the *Volk* with the most neighbors we are the *Volk* in the greatest danger, and with all this we are the metaphysical *Volk*. But this *Volk*, as certain as we are of this vocation [*Bestimmung*], will only be able to forge a destiny [*Schicksal*] from it if it creates *in itself* a resonance, a possibility of resonance for this vocation and conceives its tradition in a creative way. All this implies that this *Volk* as a historical people places itself and thereby the history of the West out of the center of its futural happening into the originary realm of the powers of being. If the great decision concerning Europe is not to be reached on its road to annihilation, then it can only be reached through the unfolding of new historically *spiritual* forces from out of the center (IM: 38–39/EM: 29, translation altered).

On one level, the political message of this 1935 text seems clear: Germany is a country which, because of its geographical location, stands in danger. And one might well expect this kind of nationalistic outburst on the part of a National Socialist partisan. But Heidegger's references to "the darkening of the world," "the flight of the gods," "the destruction of the earth," and to a distinctively German "vocation" all carry a special significance for him as he attempts to characterize the crisis of the West. They are written in an encoded language suffused with the geo-political clichés of Spengler, Scheler, Baeumler, Hellingrath, Krieck, and other metaphysicians of "war" and of the "middle" who force the language of Nietzsche ("*Verfall,*" *Verdüsterung der Welt*"), Hölderlin ("*Die Flucht der Göt-*

ter"), and Fichte (*"Die Bestimmung des Menschen," "Schicksal"*) into the hardened frame of their own Germanocentric metaphysics.[65]

Heidegger was not immune to such rhetorical pyrotechnics; on the contrary, his vision of Germany as a nation caught in the middle would retrace the imperialistic designs of 1914 and adumbrate the two-front war of 1941–1945. This geo-politics, re-configured as geo-philosophy, would transform Spengler's prophetic claim that "before us stands a last spiritual crisis that will involve all Europe and America" into an archeo-eschatological reading of the West rooted in a politics and ontology of the autochthonous.[66] This geo-philosophy has oftentimes been misconstrued by Heidegger scholars as constituting a temporary mistake on Heidegger's part, a kind of lapse in judgment or a regrettable, even reprehensible, fall into the world of politics and ideology. But what needs to be considered in this context—especially in the 1935 lectures—is the deep and abiding connection between Heidegger's political commitment to an autochthonous German *Volk* at the center of Europe *and* his ontological decision to read the history of Western philosophy on the basis of another kind of autochthony—namely, the indigenous, rooted, *subterranean* origin of Greek philosophy that ruled over the history of the West. At the crossing of these two autochthonic themes, Heidegger's philosophy will be formed in the crucial years 1933–1938. In this sense, we need to begin to understand how Heidegger's discourse concerning Europe is hardly a subsidiary concern, a mere political diversion amidst an ontological critique of modernity. Rather, as I hope to show, it helps form the very shape and structure of his ontological approach.

VII. THE VIOLENCE OF THE UNCANNY: *ANTIGONE* AND THE GERMAN *VOLK*

In a work that raises the question "How does it stand with being?" what are we to make of the persistent focus on questions of the political and on the vocation of the German *Volk*? How are we to reconcile the ontological

---

65. Nietzsche, KSA 9: 90 and KSA 12: 62, 122; Hölderlin, *Hyperion and Selected Poems*, 210–211; and Fichte, *Reden an die deutsche Nation*, 58, and *Die Bestimmung des Menschen* (Hamburg: Meiner, 1962). Heidegger is hardly alone in his political appropriation of Nietzsche, Hölderlin, and Fichte. In chapter 5, I will offer a fuller analysis of the National Socialist *Nietzschebild*. For a National Socialist *Hölderlinbild*, see Werner Bartscher, *Hölderlin und die deutsche Nation* (Berlin: Junker & Dünnhaupt, 1942); Kurt Hildebrandt, *Hölderlin: Philosophie und Dichtung* (Stuttgart: Kohlhammer, 1939); and *Hölderlin: Gedenkschrift zu seinem 100. Todestag*, ed. Paul Kluckhohn (Tübingen: Mohr, 1943). Also, to get a sense of how Fichte was manipulated by National Socialists, see two collections of his work edited for political effect: Fichte, *Rufe an die deutsche Nation*, ed. Hans Schmoldt (Berlin: Eher, 1943); and Fichte, *Politik und Weltanschauung: Sein Kampf um die Freiheit*, ed. Wolfram Steinbeck (Stuttgart: Kröner, 1939). See also Arnold Gehlen, *Deutschtum und Christentum bei Fichte* (Berlin: Junker & Dünnhaupt, 1935).

66. Spengler, *Decline of the West*, 1:424.

question of "the fate of 'being' " and the political question of "the fate of Europe" (IM: 38, 42/EM: 29, 32)? For the Heidegger of *Introduction to Metaphysics*, these questions are not reconciled but set into confrontation with one another in terms of an extended meditation on the question about "the fate of the earth" and the decision by the German *Volk* "to retrieve the beginning of our historical-spiritual *Dasein*, in order to transform it into the other beginning." As Heidegger sets out to raise anew the question of being in all its ontological power, he is thrown back upon the political vocation of the Germans and their willingness to transpose themselves "into the originary realm of the powers of being." This means, above all, engaging/confronting the ancient Greeks and their primordial experience of being in the *polis,* an experience whose metaphysical force is most powerfully expressed, Heidegger will claim, in the first stasimon of Sophocles' tragic play *Antigone.*

As he comes to consider *Antigone* within the *Introduction to Metaphysics,* Heidegger does not proceed directly to his reading of the play but rather first situates it at the crossroads of two other pressing concerns: the question concerning the essence (*Wesen*) of being and the question concerning the essence of the human being. Moreover, this discussion about the *Antigone* chorus is put forward as a kind of excursus on the traditional Parmenidean question concerning the relation of "being and thinking." But, Heidegger warns, "the division of 'being and thinking,' which has long since become pale, empty and rootless, no longer allows us to recognize its origin unless we go back to its beginning" (IM: 141/EM: 108). Our usual inclination to divide the world into our pre-made Cartesian categories of "subject" and "object" no longer allows us to think of being and thinking in an originary way. For this we need to go back to the *arche* of the tradition before the metaphysical signatures of Plato, Aristotle, and their Latin-Christian doxographers covered over and concealed the original word of Parmenides. Only in this polemical confrontation or *Auseinandersetzung* with the origin can the human being think the relation of being and thinking in an originary way. As Heidegger will put it:

1. The determination [*Die Bestimmung*] of the essence of the human being [*des Menschen*] is *never* an answer, but essentially a question.
2. The asking of this question and its decision are historical, not merely in a general sense; rather, this question is the essence of history.
3. The question of who the human being is must always be posed in an essential connection with the question of how it stands with being. The question of human being is not an anthropological question but a historically meta-physical question (IM: 140/EM: 107).

This "historically meta-physical question" about the human being's relation to being comes to Heidegger through the reflections of Fichte's work, *Die Bestimmung des Menschen,* which poses the question about the "determination" of the human being as a question about *Bestimmung* in the sense of "destiny" and "vocation."[67] Like Fichte, Heidegger will interpret the essence of the human being as a question concerning history and our proper relation to a community and a *Volk.* But he will pose this question in Parmenidean terms as well and will claim that "what Parmenides's saying expresses is a determination of the essence of the human being from out of the essence of being itself" (IM: 144/EM: 110). This saying—*to gar auto noein estin te kai einai* (usually translated "thinking and being are the same")—became the guiding principle of Western philosophy precisely at the time when its original meaning was no longer understood. The truth of this originary saying loses its power just as it is grasped as what is constantly present for a subject. This metaphysical category of "constant or standing presence" (*ständige Anwesenheit*) is "what underlies, what is present," i.e., "substance" in the Latin sense of what stands (L. *stans*) under (L. *sub*) (IM: 202/EM: 154). In an effort to twist himself free of this encrusted metaphysical tradition of standing presence, Heidegger will put forward a reading of Parmenides' saying that wants to rethink the static metaphysics of "standing" with a Sophoclean meditation on the originary meaning of "standing" (*stehen, ständig, beständig*) in its relation to "standing forth" or *ent-stehen,* thought in its Greek sense as *physis.* As Heidegger will put it, "*Physis* is *standing-forth* [*Ent-stehen*], a self-emerging that arises from [*sich heraus-stehen*] what is concealed thus bringing the concealed to a stand [*Stand*] for the first time" (IM: 14–15/EM: 12).

Drawing on the paronomasic range of the stem *stehen* (and its etymological derivatives), Heidegger will reposition his guiding question in *Introduction to Metaphysics,* "Why are there beings rather than nothing?" to read—"how does it stand with being?" On the basis of this inquiry, he will rethink the meaning of truth not as an eternal category but as a *historical* process of conflict, confrontation, and retrieval. Hence, Heidegger will claim, "Originary truths of such magnitude can only be held fast if they constantly [*ständig*] unfold in a still more originary unfolding; not, however, merely through their application or invocation. The originary remains originary only if it has the constant [*ständig*] possibility of being what it is: Origin as springing-forth" (IM: 145/EM: 111). Here Heidegger will claim that thinking and being do not stand there opposite one another as constant entities that do not change. On the contrary, they be-

---

67. J. G. Fichte, *Die Bestimmung des Menschen* (Hamburg: Meiner, 1962). Fichte will come to understand "Bestimmung" not merely as an epistemological "determination" by a subject but as an ethical-historical call of destiny, a vocation in its deepest sense. A good example of the National Socialist interpretation of Fichte can be found in Franz Böhm, *Anti-Cartesianismus: Deutsche Philosophie im Widerstand* (Leipzig: Meiner, 1938), 261–269. See also IM: 38/EM: 29.

long together in a reciprocal way and must be worked out anew within the historical situation that emerges. It is against this ontological background that Heidegger will offer his reading of the crisis of Europe by way of an excursus on the problem of Sophocles' *Antigone*. "The question of how it stands with being," Heidegger will claim, "reveals itself as the question of how it stands with our *Dasein* in history, the question of whether we *stand* in history or merely stagger. From a metaphysical point of view, *we are staggering*" (IM: 202/EM: 154). In his interpretation of the *Antigone* chorus, Heidegger finds a way of initiating a counter-movement to this process of historical-metaphysical staggering by offering a critique of the metaphysics of constant presence. Here Heidegger will rethink the meaning of what is *ständig* by grasping it not as a permanent condition but as the name for what needs to be constantly reinterpreted. Above all, Heidegger will claim, the essence of truth lies not in its status as what is permanent (*status* understood here in its Latin sense as "manner of standing"), but as what is constantly (*ständig*) unfolding from out of the possibilities of a tradition. In political terms this means, concretely, that the possibilities for a *Volk* lie in its ability to negotiate the tensions in its tradition between what is permanently rooted in the earth (*boden-ständig*) and how this permanent rootedness needs to be constantly repositioned within the newly emerging conditions that confront it. Rootedness and autochthony in this sense demand a confrontation between the permanence of the past and the possibilities of the future as they collide within the historical moment opened up in the present. Heidegger will uncover the hidden power of these possibilities in his creative confrontation with the text of the *Antigone* chorus.

As Heidegger himself will claim, the purpose of his interpretation is to "attempt to gain a stance [*Stand*] in the midst of the whole [of being] in order to measure [*ermessen*] who the human being is according to this poetic discourse" (IM: 148/EM: 114). But, in an age itself measured by the mediocre and average (*mittelmässig*), what would constitute the proper standard (*Massstab*) according to which (*demgemäss*) we might begin to recuperate an authentic possibility for the *Volk*? How might a *Volk* combat what is simply of its own time (*zeitgemäss*) that thwarts the possibility of its creative unfolding? And wherein would such untimely (*unzeitgemäss*) possibilities derive their energies? In 1935, Heidegger turns to the early Greek poetic-philosophical legacy of Parmenides-Heraclitus-Sophocles as a way of initiating a movement of thinking that will cut through the detritus of the Roman tradition that became definitive (*massgebend*) for the Western tradition. In this movement of recuperating the originary Greek experience of *physis*, Heidegger will come to understand the human being in conjunction with Sophocles' *Antigone* ode as *to deinotaton*—"the uncanniest," the one who, in the most intense way of all beings, feels himself not at home amongst other beings. As Heidegger expresses it, "the human being is *to deinotaton,* the uncanniest of the uncanny [*das Unheimlichste des Unheimlichen*]. . . . The Greek word *deinon* has that uncanny ambiguity with which Greek discourse takes the measure of [*ermessen*] the counter-turning confrontations [*gegenwendigen Aus-einander-setzungen*] of being" (IM: 149, 8, 13/EM: 114, 6, 11). In this "taking the measure of" being, in and through the ambiguities and counter-turning possibilities of what language measures, Heidegger finds a way of determining the essence of human being in and against the interpretation/determination of being as such. But again, this understanding of "essence" (*Wesen*) is thought of less as a permanent condition than as a constant possibility in the sense of *Ständigkeit.* The measure or *Mass* of human being is its ability to constantly recreate itself in terms of the ambiguous possibilities afforded to it in its confrontations with being. In this uncanny strife/contest/*agon* with being, the human being opens up a space within being and engenders history. Precisely at this point of intersection between the measure of human being (*Massstab*) and the constancy (*Ständigkeit*) provided by the human being's lost home within being, Heidegger hopes to find a ground upon which to stand, one that will serve as a home for German *Dasein.* In so doing he seeks to overcome the crisis of nihilism diagnosed in the untimely philosophy of Nietzsche.

The *Antigone* ode proves to be an excellent source for recuperating this kind of creative reading, since it offers as its focal concern the plight of the human being as the one who is most essentially not at home in being. This condition of homelessness is not, however, the simple product of a historical trend or sociological process; it is rather the very condition of human being as such, an ontological fundament, not a merely ontical characteristic. How then, given this ontological order, can the human being secure a historical dwelling place upon the earth? And how might the choral ode from *Antigone* offer some insight into this problem?

In an effort to wrest from the ode the possibility of a new historical abode for the Germans, Heidegger will set upon a violent interpretation of the Sophoclean text since he believes that only through violence can the creative possibility of finding/founding a home be realized. This violence, *pace* Heidegger, is not arbitrary in any sense, however; it is of the essence of being itself. Accordingly, if the essence of being is itself violent, then only if the human being understands and experiences herself as violent can she authentically unfold her being (IM: 139, 156–164/EM: 106, 120–125). In the opening stanza of the first choral ode in *Antigone,* this violence will be interpreted as being bound up with the Sophoclean definition of the human being as "the uncanniest," *to deinotaton.* The human being is uncanny because she is the violent one—uncanny in a double sense:

On the one hand *deinon* means the terrible, but not in the sense of petty terrors. . . . The *deinon* is the terrible in the sense of the overpowering sway [*überwältigenden Waltens*] which compels panic fear, true anxiety as well as collected, silent awe that vibrates with its own rhythm. The violent [*das Gewaltige*], the overpowering is the essential character of the sway [of being] itself. . . .

But on the other hand *deinon* means the violence in the sense of the one who needs to use violence, who not only has violence at his disposal but does violence [*gewalt-tätig*] insofar as using violence is the basic trait not only of his doing but also of his *Dasein*. . . . Beings as a whole, as the sway, are the overpowering, *deinon* in the first sense. The human being is, however, *deinon* first because he remains exposed to this overpowering sway, because he belongs to being in an essential way. But at the same time the human being is *deinon* because he is the violence-doer in the sense designated above. . . . The human being is the violence-doer, not aside from and along with other attributes but solely in the sense that by virtue of and in his violence-doing [*Gewalt-tätigkeit*] he uses violence [*Gewalt*] against the overpowering [*Über-wältigende*]. Because he is doubly *deinon* in an originarily united sense, he is *to deinotaton*, the most violent: violence-doing in the midst of the overpowering. (IM: 149–150/EM: 114–115)

This tension within the definition of human being between his violence-doing against being and the violence of being itself will come to characterize for Heidegger the uncanny condition of human existence upon the earth. What is uncanny is the fundamental violence of being as a whole, a violence in and through which human being itself comes to being. But what is even more uncanny—and, in Heidegger's view as he reads Sophocles' ode, the most uncanny or uncanniest—is the violence exercised by human beings in their efforts to master, subdue, and control the violence of being. Heidegger will grasp this violent tension in metaphysical terms as the fundamental tension between what Sophocles calls *techne* and *dike*. *Techne* in this metaphysical sense does not mean "technique," "skill," or "method of production"; it signifies rather a way of disclosure that opens up being itself in its determinate form as a particular being. *Techne* makes manifest the unmasterable power and sway of being: humans navigate the violent sea, they scale the most formidable of mountains, they sedulously turn the earth over in a proper season to produce a harvest, they tame the wild beasts and yoke them to their given tasks. All these forces are subjugated in and through the violence of *techne*. Against this subjugation, and determining it in an originary way, however, is the overarching structure of *dike*, which Heidegger (abjuring the traditional German translation of *dike* as "*Gerechtigkeit*" or "justice") will translate as *Fug* or "fugal jointure," that overpowering structure of being that compels all beings to adapt to, fit in (*einfügen*), and comply with (*sichfügen*) the enjoining structure (*das fügende Gefüge*) of being. In this vision of being as a kind of organizing matrix that brings all beings together contrapuntally in a fugal structure, where opposition and conflict serve as unifying forces that allow divergences to converge even as they become mutually implicated in their difference, Heidegger will put forward his own vision of the *polis* as the site of openness for the contests, conflicts, antagonisms, and enjoining oppositions of the violence-doing (*Gewalt-tätigkeit*) of *techne* and the overpowering fugal jointure of *dike*. The consequences for his reading of the *Antigone* are profound.

Now Heidegger will dispense with the traditional ethical-political-juridical readings of the play as a struggle concerning obedience to a legal order, following one's conscience, or initiating/suppressing anarchy. For him, *Antigone* will present itself as the working-out in language of the contrapuntal forces of human being that find their way violently into a fugal order that joins together and enjoins the oppositional aims of human beings like Creon and Antigone. On this reading the violence of opposition between *techne* and *dike* is worked out in and against the *polis* as the site for the opening-up and unfolding of history. This process of disclosure requires a daring and a self-assertion that first can create a breach or *Bresche*, an opening in the battle formation against the standard and conventional understanding of the world. Only when one can confront the world through daring and violence will it become open for the creative possibility of history. Only as historical can a *Volk* survive. But the founding of the *polis*, much as the creative-revolutionary act of transforming the conventional order of the *polis*, requires violence. "The violence-doing of poetic speech, of thinking projection, of building configuration, of state-creating action is not an application of faculties that the human being has, but a taming and disposing of the violent forces by virtue of which beings open themselves as such insofar as the human being marches [*einrückt*] into them" (IM: 157/EM: 120). In the historical situation of 1935, Heidegger will understand the *Antigone* chorus as the concealed metaphysical cipher for coming to terms with the political situation of the German *Volk*. What is required for an authentic relation to the *polis* is not a constitution, a legislature, a judicial order, or a compact affirmed by each member of the nation-state. Rather, genuine political order demands a daring, violence-initiating act by a founder—either a state-founder or an artist, a poet or a thinker who can lead (*führen*) the *Volk* or who might dare to become a leader (*Führer*) through an intro-duction (*Ein-führung*) into the metaphysical truths of the *dike/techne* conflict.

Even after the failure of his rectorate in April of 1934, Heidegger will still harbor the hope that he might be able to provide the philosophical leadership for the "second" German revolution to follow the first initiated by Adolf Hitler. In August of 1934, he will present a plan to the NS Ministry for Science and Education for setting up a *Dozentenakademie* to train university teachers. According to Heidegger's proposal, the academy is to offer a new model of authentic "political" existence in an "educational life-community." As Heidegger will put it, "The *vita communis* of the teachers and students is ensured through the rigor of the daily order and the simplicity of one's life-conduct, through the natural alternation of scientific work, relaxation, concentration, war games, physical work, marching, sport, and festivals" (GA 16: 308–309). In a lecture delivered at the same time, Heidegger will also put forward his vision of the German state embodied by a political vision of *Führung:*

> The essence of the National Socialist revolution consists in the fact that Adolf Hitler has put into effect the new spirit of community and raised it to a formative power in the new order of the *Volk*. The National Socialist revolution is therefore not the external take-over of an existing state power through the growth of a party that has attained its position. It is, rather, the inner re-education of the whole *Volk* to the goal of willing/wanting its own unanimity and unity. Insofar as the *Volk* wills/wants its own determination, it acknowledges the new state. The authority of this state is the responsible enforcement of that will of the *Führer* to which the obedient trust of the *Volk* empowers its leading [*Führung*]. The state is not a mechanical instrument of the law which is established alongside economics, art, science, and religion. On the contrary, the state signifies the vital order ruled throughout by the reciprocal interplay of trust and responsibility, an order in and through which the *Volk* realizes its own historical *Dasein*. (GA 16: 302)

This vision of the state as a vital order in and through which the *Volk* instantiates its historical *Dasein* comes close to the idea of the *Fug* that animates the *Antigone* chorus. Here the state is understood not as a merely legal or political apparatus but as the enjoining structure that brings beings to form in and through its "formative power." To rephrase the political question—what is the proper relation of a *Volk* to a state?—metaphysically, we need to ask: "how does it *stand* with the state?" In what sense does the state *instantiate* the *Dasein* of the *Volk?* In 1933–34, in a seminar entitled "On the Essence and Concept of Nature, History, and the State," Heidegger raises these questions as a way of posing the question about the essence of the political.

> What then is the space of a state? For the state is not a construction of spirit nor a sum of laws nor a verbal constitution, but is essentially related to and marked by space. The space of a state is in a certain sense the space of the autochthonous people, understood as the operative range of its interaction in trade and traffic, commerce and communication, thus the "reach" of its power (*Be-reich*), the "realm" of its regime and rule (*Reich*). We call this space a land, territory, sovereign domain, dominion. It is in a sense the fatherland, which is not to be confused with a home. Viewed externally, home is in most cases a narrower region of the state's space, and it need not have

anything at all to do with the state. Each involves entirely different relations. We can speak of the state only when the will to extension, the interaction generally called traffic and trade, is added to autochthony. I have a home because of birth, I am tied to it by way of natural powers. Home finds its expression in the nativity of autochthony and the sense of being bound to a place. But nature makes man autochthonous only when it belongs to the people as an environment, a surrounding world of which that man is a member. A home becomes the mode of being of a people only when it enters into the wider interaction of trade and traffic, commerce and communication, when it becomes a state. Peoples or their offspring who do not move beyond their home ties to their proper mode of being, the state, are in constant danger of losing their status as a people and entering into decline. This is also the great problem of those Germans who live outside the borders of the Reich. They have a German home but do not belong to the state of Germans, to the Reich, and so are without their proper mode of be-ing. By way of summary, we can thus say that the space of a people, the people's ground, reaches as far as the branches of this people have found a home and have become autochthonous such that the space of the state, its territory, arrives at its boundaries through traffic and trade, through its interaction at a distance, in the expanse of the world.[68]

As he lays out his vision of a German geo-politics in 1935, Heidegger will draw on these insights into the metaphysical relation of a state to a *Volk* and will transform his political reading of autochthony into an archaic-ontological account of the history of the West. As he offers his reading of a Germany "caught in a pincers. Our *Volk*, standing in the center . . . ," he will think of German destiny as being bound up with the fate of Antigone as she confronts the political order of Creon (IM: 38/EM: 29). The uncanniest being of all, homeless and out of joint, violently striving through a willful act of self-assertion aimed at mastery, this human being as *deinon*, as *unheimlich*, as the one without a home, is the German *Volk* striving to find a home at the center of a European order marked by the dictates of legal-political control and dominion—the Treaty of Versailles (what in the NS argot of Heidegger's day was called simply "*das Friedens-diktat*," "the dictated peace"). Against this dictatorship of Western European liberalism and the Wilsonian principle of "self-determination" (*Selb-stbestimmungsrecht der Völker*), the German *Volk* would, like Antigone, offer determined resistance. Following Fichte's notion of a special path of destiny, or *Sonderweg*, for the German *Volk*, Heidegger would come to understand the concept of *Selbstbestimmung* as one that compelled the *Volk* to determine itself (*sich selbst bestimmen*) in the sense of its destiny (*Bestimmung*),

---

68. Theodore Kisiel, "In the Middle of Heidegger's Three Concepts of the Political," in *Heidegger and Practical Philosophy*, ed. F. Rauffoul and D. Pettigrew (Albany: SUNY Press, forthcoming), 149–150. I want to thank Professor Kisiel for providing me with a copy of this piece in manuscript form.

on the basis of its unique vocation (*Bestimmung*) (GA 16: 189, 193, 201, 221, 767–768). As he comes to envision the destiny of the *Volk*, he will draw on the same language of fugal interplay that marks the *Antigone* chorus. Thus he will speak of "the vital structure [*Gefüge*] of the state" that helps "the *Volk* to win back its autochthony" and he will claim that "the state is the resuscitating and unifying structure [*Gefüge*] in which the *Volk* enjoins itself [*sich fügend*] to set out all the great powers of human being." In the "realization of the developing state in which the German *Volk* finds its true destiny and vocation [*Bestimmung*]," Heidegger will find the same principle as in the creative work of art. This he calls "the concealed law of all being—that all genuine reality is preserved only in and through the human being's power of sacrifice [*Opferkraft*]." All creative transformation and preservation—in poetry and thinking, in religion and in politics—demands sacrifice.

In his Hölderlin lectures of 1934/35 delivered just before the 1935 course on *Introduction to Metaphysics*, Heidegger spoke of the power of sacrifice as that which "first, foremost, and before all else creates the space for community" (GA 39: 73). Here he was thinking of the sacrifice made by "the soldiers at the front" who, through the sacrifice of their death, prepared the ground for the re-emergence of a home for the German *Volk*. Later in his lectures he finds this same creative power in the poetry of Sophocles. "The *Antigone* poetry of Sophocles is as poetry a founding [*Stiftung*] of the whole of Greek *Dasein*, for poetry as a projection of be-ing [*Entwurf des Seyns*] (rootedness and rescue) grounds human *Dasein* upon the earth in the face of the gods. Poetry as founding secures the ground of possibility so that the human being can settle upon the earth at all, settle between the earth and the gods—that is, become historical, which means: to be a *Volk*. What the human being, once it is settled, then pursues and snatches up may be counted as a gain; but his authentic be-ing—altogether settled, being rooted in the soil [*Boden ständig zu sein*]—this dwelling is grounded in and through poetry, that is, it is 'poetic'" (GA 39: 216). This kind of "poetic dwelling," instituted by Sophocles and Hölderlin, constitutes what Heidegger will call "'politics' in its supreme and authentic sense" (GA 39: 214). As he turns his attention more fully to an analysis of *Antigone*, Heidegger will follow up on his interpretive link between poetic dwelling, sacrifice, and the power of being rooted in the soil. Like Antigone, the German *Volk* lies exposed at the center of a political order that seeks to bring it into line with its authoritarian decrees. And, like her, they must learn to embrace the power of sacrifice, that power that risks the loss of the home even as it raises its victims—Schlageter, the heroes of Langemarck—to the heights of greatness in their sacrifice that creates a new home for the *Volk*.

Antigone comes to represent for Heidegger that human being who defies the technical-rational dominion of state-order for a more genuine form of community and for a more authentic relation to the earth. Although he never provides specific details about the course of the action in the play, his overall commitment to the sacredness of the earth as an organizing theme offers clues to a Heideggerian reading rooted in the "authentic politics" of the *Volk*. As the basis for such a reading, it is imperative to recall how one of the most pointed contrasts in the play is Creon's and Antigone's conflicting definitions/interpretations of the earth. Creon defines it as "land" in the sense of the space of "political territory"; Antigone, on the contrary, will think of it as the "homeland" and as the place for the dwelling of the gods (chthonic) and for the burial of the dead in accordance with the divine order of things. She understands, given the recent deaths of her parents and her two brothers, that human life is a way station or middle-point between the earth and the sky. Antigone's fate is to pose the question for human beings: what is our proper and authentic relation to the earth? How are we to properly honor the earth as a place of divine sanctuary? If we follow her in understanding the earth as the originary source of all being, as the space within and against which human beings confront their own limits within the order of *physis,* then the question about the earth becomes a question about the possibility of historical dwelling and the destiny of a *Volk.* At least that is how Heidegger will proceed as he lays out his reading of *Antigone* as a poetic meditation on the problem of the *polis.* In Heideggerian terms, Creon grasps the *polis* as something crudely political, as something defined by authority, control, and dominion. He becomes a model for the kind of untrammeled Cartesian self-assertion and voluntarism of the modern subject armed with *techne.* Creon's *polis* is out of touch with the powers of the earth which, in line with the opening lines of the first *stasimon,* he thinks of as a "resource," something that can be controlled, subdued, and mastered through the plough, the soil, the yoke, the web, and the other instruments of calculative *techne.* This attempt at "dominion over the earth," what Heidegger will term *Erdherrschaft,* will only focus on the surface of the earth and not on its chthonic depths that harbor and conceal the rooted powers of the gods that allow for genuine autochthonous grounding in a community.

Deracinated and out of touch with the earth, Creon stands as a figure of modern Cartesian subjectivity, isolated, lacking all ties to a community, and grappling with the nihilism of his own failed projections. On the basis of this characterization, Heidegger will come to his own geo-political and ontological account of a post-Versailles Germany lying at the center, exposed to its enemies in Europe and confronted by the nihilism of *Seinsvergessenheit* ("the oblivion of being"). On Heidegger's reading, Germany does not exist as a cartographically determined nation-state, arranged (*eingefügt*) by treaties or the outcome of wars; it is, rather, a mythic Hölderlinian homeland, the *topos* of a futural myth of return, of that space of projected hope that has its roots in the soil of the native earth as a place of dwelling, a place for the historical unfolding of the *Volk* where *polis* meets *Gemeinschaft* at the axis of Graeco-German autochthony.

This reading of *Antigone* breaks sharply with the traditional ethical-political reading of Hegel that wants to understand the play as the supersession of a one-sided opposition between divine and human law, the private and the public, that affirms centralized state power. Heidegger's ontological reading will reject the Hegelian movement toward harmony-reconciliation and will instead affirm the irreconcilability of tragic opposition and conflict. Hence, Heidegger will not try to read the choral ode's opposition between the one who is "highest in the *polis*" (*hypsipolis*) and the one "who is city-less" (*apolis*) as simply representing the positions of Creon and Antigone respectively. Rather, Heidegger will opt for a more violent reading that sees both Creon and Antigone as embracing those ontological characteristics of the *deinon* that make them both "wonderful" and "terrible" at the same time. What proves to be most uncanny about each is their measureless excess that goes beyond the measure of law to the violence of being itself. This *seynsgeschichtliche* politics of the earth, a politics that transforms the calculative, Cartesian politics of Versailles into the originary, rooted politics of the *Volk*, will become for Heidegger the hidden, authentic meaning of the *Antigone* chorus as the poetic expression of a different kind of state-founding. In the historical moment of 1935, Heidegger will dare to attempt a philosophical expression of state-founding that translates Antigone's ethos of sacrifice into a National Socialist community built on the sacrifices of the Great War. Caught in the nets of the National Socialist euphoria for revolutionary awakening, Heidegger will claim that "the highest actualization of human be-ing happens in the state."[69]

The nineteenth-century theory of state, which focused on the status of its "sovereignty," where the "highest power" is "apprehended as the essence and expression of the state," proved itself in his eyes to be a form of rule that "knows nothing about itself." A model of state rule that grants the highest power to one (mon-archic) or to the few (olig-archic) merely demonstrates the bankruptcy of Creon's principle of rulership. The Western model of the democratic state offers nothing but a "counter phenomenon" to this principle since it simply shifts sovereignty to the people, thus going to the other extreme. It remains, however, caught up within the

---

69. Theodore Kisiel, "In the Middle of Heidegger's Three Concepts of the Political," 149–152. The selections from this piece draw on Heidegger's unpublished seminar from WS 1933–1934, "On the Essence and Concept of Nature, History, and the State."

logic of the "contra," since it replicates the monarchic principle of sovereignty even if in an inverted way. But the will to political power cannot genuinely occur if it is tied to the arbitrary rulership of a single figure bent on coercion. "The true effectuation of a will does not come by coercion but by awakening the same willing in the other." "The will of the leader [*Führer*] first of all re-creates the others into a following out of which a *Gemeinschaft* arises. It is out of this vital solidarity of followers to leader that sacrifice [*Opfer*] and service [*Dienst*] arise, and not from sheer obedience and institutional coercion." The *Führerstaat*, the state where the actualization of a *Volk* happens in and through the carrying out of its will by a *Führer*, represents the highest possibility of *Dasein:* to become what it is in a *Gemeinschaft*, through sacrifice and service. As that human being who understands that the individual is nothing without sacrifice, nothing without its irrevocable bond to community, Antigone becomes the model of the National Socialist will to the political against the politics of monarchic coercion. The power of the *arche*, the concealed force of the ruling origin, cannot be forced into the frame of a single will; it cannot be reduced to a singular *mon-arche*. It can only unfold in and against a structure (*Gefüge*) that enjoins (*fügt*) the will of the *Volk* to comply with (*sich fügen*) the archaic forces of being in all their overpowering violence. This unfolding depends upon sacrifice, a sacrifice that may demand the loss of the individual through destructive violence. Antigone, Schlageter, the heroes of Langemarck, Hölderlin, and Nietzsche all risked the extreme, all wound up re-enacting the cycle of Sophoclean tragic destiny—of being at one and the same time both *hypsipolis* and *apolis*. These figures are revered by their communities, becoming "highest in the city," because through their sacrifice they helped engender the future destiny of their communities. They risked becoming "city-less" and without a home because their incursions into the heart of the *polis,* incursions that were violently creative, pushed beyond the limits of the reigning order of their day.

Heidegger was all too aware of the dangers of "overstepping" the limits of *physis*. He had learned through the figures of Antigone and Oedipus that insight into the concealed essence of being would bring self-destruction. And yet in the upward surge of his National Socialist enthusiasm for the second "ontological" revolution that would follow upon the first "political" one, Heidegger would forget the lessons of the very texts he was deciphering. In his rigid stance of solidarity with Hitler, he would wind up re-enacting the same arrogant stance as Creon. Instead of genuine re-sistance [*Wider-stand*] to the coercion of National Socialism, Heidegger would take his stand as a loyal German partisan, arrogating to the Germans alone the bonds of unity with the ancient Greeks. In his affirmation of a singularly German form of community, a community itself formed through exclusion, banishment, and, ultimately, annihilation, Heidegger would reprise the same singular willfulness as Antigone and the same exclusionary violence as Creon. In so doing he would complete the cycle of hybristic self-assertion and tragic blindness that marks the texts of his beloved Sophocles. Heidegger's venture, like Creon's, would founder on its own violent incursions into the realm of the *polis,* leaving him as a philosophical prince who had transgressed his own principles, a thinkerly monarch whose own attempts at rule end by violating the sacred province of the *arche.*

VIII. NIETZSCHE'S "GREAT POLITICS," HEIDEGGER'S PETTY POLITICS

Heidegger's discussion of Sophoclean tragedy in *Introduction to Metaphysics* would be so positioned in the text that it would serve as a poetical refrain on the questions raised in its opening chapter on the problem of the German *Volk.* There Heidegger called the Germans "the metaphysical *Volk*" and admonished them to "move itself . . . beyond the center of their future happening into the originary realm of the powers of being." He then added: "If the great decision concerning Europe is not to lead to annihilation, then it can only be made through the unfolding of new historical-*spiritual* forces from out of the center" (IM: 38–39/EM: 29). To mobilize the necessary forces for this "vocation" (*Bestimmung*), Heidegger would draw on the lessons of Nietzsche and his doctrine of "great politics." Consequently, we should not be surprised by Heidegger's sustained excursus on European political geography in a work ostensibly dedicated to metaphysics. The Nietzsche lectures of 1936/37 will carry forward this Heideggerian vision of German geo-politics, but the outlines for such a vision are already in place by the summer of 1935.

Nietzsche developed his notion of great politics in the 1880s as a response to the leveling effects of democratic politics that he perceived throughout Europe. But he also coined the term as a kind of mocking inversion of what was then called "great politics"—namely, the imperialist-expansionist program of Bismarck who, during 1884–85, brutally forged a colonial German empire on the continent of Africa. Against this kind of crude *Machtpolitik,* Nietzsche's ironically termed "great politics" proposed an international, transnational style of politics that would point beyond the "petty politics" of nationalism and particularism and engage a new Pan-European ideal of culture. Deeply critical of Bismarck's petty "blood and iron" aggression, Nietzsche called for a new ruling caste in Europe, "a species of man that does not yet exist: 'the masters of the earth'" (WP: 503/ WM: 640). This new aristocracy of artists, creators, philosophers, and disciples of Dionysus were to set upon the task of transforming the slave values of democratic culture and instituting a new order of rank: a spiritual elite of commanders and legislators. It was Nietzsche's hope that this European-wide battle for control would accelerate the effects of nihilism and usher in a crisis of such proportions that the old order would no longer be able to stand. As he dramatically expressed it in *Ecce Homo:* "I know my fate. One day there will be associated with my name the recollection of something frightful—a crisis like no other before on earth, of the profoundest collision of conscience, of a decision against everything that until then had been believed in, demanded, sanctified. I am not a man, I am dynamite. . . . Only after me will there be *great politics* on earth" (EH: 96–97/KSA 6 365–366). In the wake of this great *Kampf* for power, Nietzsche maintained that Europe would be confronted with a final decision about its own existence: to decline into the pettiness of nationalist expansion and *völkisch* self-assertion or to will the great politics of transvaluation.

As he puts forward the ideal of "the Good European," however, Nietzsche is reminded of the German nationalists and the *völkisch* ideologues—"the buffoons of politics"—who have fought against the ideal of European unity. The Germans, Nietzsche writes, are responsible for "this sickness and unreason *the most inimical to culture* there is, nationalism, that *névrose nationale* with which Europe is sick, that eternalizing of the petty-state situation [*Kleinstaaterei*] of Europe, of *petty* politics: they have deprived Europe itself of its meaning, of its *reason*—they have led it into a blind alley.—Does anyone except me know a way out of this blind alley? . . . A task great enough once again to unite the *Völker*? . . ." (EH: 90–92/KSA 6: 359–360). In the spirit of great politics, Nietzsche understands Germany as a country without *esprit*, without the ability to understand the need for profound change. The German longing for national power, Nietzsche claims, has been a disaster: "In the history of European culture the rise of the *Reich* signifies one thing above all: a displacement of the center of gravity" (TI: 74/KSA 6: 106). If Europe is to rid itself of the sickly, diseased, and atrophied instincts of its petty-political past, Nietzsche argues, it will need to confront the dangers of nationalism and come to terms with another menacing threat: Russia, "that monstrous empire-in-between [*Zwischenreich*] where Europe, as it were, flows back into Asia" (BGE: 138/KSA 5: 139–140). For Nietzsche, the hope is that this menacing threat to the East will galvanize Europe "to *acquire one will* by means of a new caste that would rule Europe, a protracted terrible will of its own which would be able to project its goals millennia hence—so that the long-drawn-out comedy of its petty states [*Kleinstaaterei*] and the splintered will of its dynasties and democracies should finally come to an end. The time for petty politics is over: the very next century will bring with it the struggle for mastery over the whole earth [*den Kampf um die Erd-Herrschaft,*]—the *compulsion* to great politics" (BGE: 138/KSA 5: 140).

Part of Nietzsche's call for a new great politics against the traditional "great" politics of Bismarck involved an understanding that a world revolution was necessary to combat the forces of democracy, socialism, and Americanism that threatened Europe. As Heidegger began to form his own analysis of politics in the 1930s, he takes up some of Nietzsche's most prominent themes. Like Nietzsche, Heidegger too will offer a blistering critique of democracy as a possible course for Europe. In a selection from his first set of Nietzsche lectures from 1936/37 (which he omitted from the 1961 edition published in the Adenauer era), Heidegger writes: "Europe still wants to cling to 'democracy' and does not want to learn to see that this will be its historical death. For democracy is, as Nietzsche clearly saw, only a degenerate form of nihilism" (GA 43: 193). And Heidegger will also take up Nietzsche's critique of socialism as a leveling process carried out by the rabble. As he begins to formulate his own geo-political version of *Mitteleuropa*, however, Heidegger will set out to tailor Nietzsche's critique of Russia and America to his own National Socialist perspective. According to this new view of Europe, Heidegger sees Germany threatened on the West by England and America and on the east by Russia. In its superficial outlines, this vision follows Nietzsche's own harsh assessment of American and Russian culture, but with one crucial difference: whereas Nietzsche persisted in his grudging admiration for Russian fatalism and its aristocratic traditions, Heidegger saw only the threats of Bolshevism.

In Heidegger's hands, Nietzschean great politics will function as a means to justify Germany's rejection of Anglo-American democracy and Soviet Communism—both of which Heidegger interprets as rootless and nihilistic. But Heidegger will also try to adapt this version of great politics to Scheler's analysis of Germany's geo-political situation in *The Genius of War*. There Scheler outlined his vision of Germany as a nation caught in the middle between "English-American capitalism" and an "expanding Russian empire."[70] And even though Scheler's book was written before the Bolshevik Revolution of 1917, it still strikes Heidegger as relevant in its basic structural principles. As Heidegger begins to lay out his analysis of a Germany "caught in a pincers," he falls back on Scheler's metaphysics of war and its notion of a German mission within Europe and of a "European mission against the East that surges against it." When read through the lens of Nietzsche's great politics, however, Scheler's geo-political analysis will be transformed into a geo-philosophical examination of the question of nihilism. Now, Nietzsche's analysis of great politics and Scheler's metaphysics of war are brought together in a remarkable kind of spiritual geography that will function as the background for Heidegger's interpretation of European nihilism. Before I turn to a discussion of Heidegger's

---

70. Scheler, *Genius des Krieges*, 248–249.

use of Nietzschean terms such as *Weltverdüsterung* ("the darkening of the world") or *Verwüstung* ("devastation") to describe Europe's nihilistic condition, however, I would like to consider briefly the political geography of Germany in 1935 when *Introduction to Metaphysics* was first written.[71]

As we have seen throughout our study, Heidegger was preoccupied with the problem of the "threatening deracination [*Entwurzelung*] of the West," a process that took many forms: as loss of a spiritual connection to the Greeks, as *Seinsvergessenheit,* as the loss of autochthony and the homeland (DE: 20). But in political terms there were other more tangible losses as well. As part of the Versailles settlement imposed by the Allied powers in 1919, Germany was forced to accept the loss of Alsace and Lorraine, Danzig, and parts of Western Prussia and to endure the French occupation of the Ruhr for a period of time. As a result of these changes, at least twelve million Germans were now living outside the borders of the Reich in 1935.[72] Moreover, with the collapse of the old Austro-Hungarian monarchy and the re-drawing of so many national boundaries according to Wilson's principle of self-determination, there now appeared four new states on Germany's borders, leaving a power vacuum at the center of Europe. When Heidegger described the Germans in *Introduction to Metaphysics* as "the *Volk* with the most neighbors," he was alluding to this new political situation. But he was also lamenting the plight of the twelve million *Reichsdeutsche* who had lost their autochthonous identity as rooted Germans and were now threatened by the rootlessness of technological-political calculation and forced to live under new national flags. Heidegger's vision of *Mitteleuropa,* then, was heavily determined by concrete political realities. It was not merely a composite that was cobbled together from the remnants of Hölderlin's poetics, Nietzsche's metaphysics, and Scheler's ideology of war.

For Heidegger, questions of metaphysics were inherently political. But all too often the basis of Heidegger's politics was hardly grounded philosophically. Instead Heidegger drew on the storehouse of clichés available to any Baden schoolboy who had passed his *Abitur* examination, as we can

71. Nietzsche employs the language of *Verwüstung* and *Wüste* in KSA 4: 380, 385; KSA 6: 382; and *Verdüsterung* in KSA 11: 433, 571; KSA 12: 122; KSA 13: 169, 449.

72. Brechtefeld, *"Mitteleuropa" and German Politics,* 48. Even in 1955, after the devastating effects of a second world war, Heidegger will still return to his old litany about displaced Germans: "Many Germans have lost their homeland, have had to leave their villages and towns, have been driven from their native soil. Countless others whose homeland was saved, have yet wandered off. . . . What is happening here—with those driven from their homeland no less than with those who have remained? Answer: the *rootedness,* the *autochthony* [*Bodenständigkeit*] of the human being is threatened today at its core. Even more: the loss of rootedness is caused not merely by circumstance and fortune, nor does it stem only from the negligence and superficiality of humanity's way of life. The loss of autochthony springs from the spirit of the age into which all of us were born," DT: 48–49/G: 15–16.

see in his interpretation of "Americanism."[73] Leaning on the staple of pronouncements from Hegel, Burckhardt, Nietzsche, Scheler, Jünger, Rilke and others, Heidegger deemed America (by which he meant the United States) a land without history, a culture without roots, a people held in the deadening grip of total mobilization, preoccupied by size, expansion, magnitude, and quantity (IM: 46/EM: 38). Unaware of the autochthonic Mesoamerican culture of the Aztecs, Mayans, and Chibchas, Heidegger's "metaphysical" interpretation of American technology came from a second-hand reading of Burckhardt and Rilke—a mere projection of European fears and ambivalence about its own culture transposed onto the New World.[74] In his *Introduction to Metaphysics,* Heidegger translates this *Amerikabild* into a critique of "intelligence," "calculation," "planning," and technological mobilization. Read within the context of his geo-philosophical account of *Mitteleuropa,* Americanism symbolizes rootlessness, deracination, the loss of autochthony and of any meaningful connection to the earth. Metaphysically, it mirrors the program of Russian Communism. In this sense, Heidegger will interpret both America and Russia as nations that represent the unbridled nihilism of modern life, a nihilism that he will term "*Weltverdüsterung.*"

Caught in the middle between the technical cleverness of America and the regulatory production of Russia, Germany alone stands as the last hope for a "mobilization of the powers of being as such and as a whole" against the merely technical mobilization of resources, capacities, and potentials. Only by raising the question of being as a spiritual task, as a kind of national will to self-assertion can the effects of Americanism and Communism be countered, Heidegger claims. "Asking the question of being is one of the essential and fundamental conditions for an awakening of spirit and hence for an originary world of historical *Dasein*. It is indispensable if the peril of world-darkening [*Weltverdüsterung*] is to be forestalled and if

73. A German *Abitur* is the qualifying examination for university admission taken at the end of one's *Gymnasium* training, the classical humanist ideal of German secondary education.

74. Heidegger's anti-Americanism was prominent throughout his life—and was tied intimately to his political-ontological understanding of autochthony: HHI: 54–55, 65, 70, 90, 143, 153/GA 53: 68, 80, 86, 112, 179, 191; PLT: 113/H: 268–269; QCT: 135, 153/H: 87–88, 103–104; BQP: 50/GA 45: 54–55; BC: 77/GA 51: 92; GA 52: 10–11, 27, 35, 80; GA 65: 149; GA 67: 150; SI: 280–281/Antwort: 105–106. In his book, *The Invention of the Americas,* trans. Michael Barber (New York: Continuum, 1995), Enrique Dussel offers a powerful critique of Hegelian-Heideggerian Eurocentrism and puts forward a reading of Amerindian autochthony as a different way of understanding European colonization. Detlev Peukert, "'Americanism' versus *Kulturkritik,*" in *The Weimar Republic,* trans. Richard Deveson (New York: Hill & Wang, 1992), 178–190, provides some background on situating the German discourse on "Americanism" in its own political and cultural context. Again, read contextually, Heidegger's rants against America betray the same right-wing tendencies as other thinkers of the *Sonderweg*. Heinz D. Kittsteiner, "Heideggers Amerika als Ursprungsort der Weltverdüsterung," *Deutsche Zeitschrift für Philosophie* 45 (1997): 599–617.

our *Volk* at the center of the West is to take on its historical mission" (IM: 50/EM: 38). But here Heidegger situates the problem of *Weltverdüsterung* in the ontico-political realm of autochthony. At the end of his discussion about the pincers of America and Russia, Heidegger tells his students, "To ask 'how does it stand with being?' means nothing less than to *retrieve* the beginning of our historical-spiritual *Dasein* in order to transform it into an other beginning. This is possible. It is indeed the crucial form of history because it begins in the fundamental event. . . . Through our questioning we enter into a landscape within which our fundamental prerequisite is— to win back the rootedness [*Bodenständigkeit*] of our historical *Dasein*" (IM: 39/EM: 29–30). Here, as throughout his discussion of *Mitteleuropa*, Heidegger develops his own archeo-eschatological vision of German politics, a politics whose roots lay in a hidden Greek beginning and whose destiny is to forge the historical possibility of an "other" beginning: the future oriented homecoming of the Germans. Between these two beginnings, Heidegger will interpret the present as a time of transition, an *Übergang* rather than an *Untergang*.[75] And he will nominate Nietzsche as the thinker of this transition.

In his eschatological zeal to translate the politics of Central Europe into the ontology of ancient Greece, Heidegger seizes upon Nietzsche's analysis of European nihilism as his guide. Where Nietzsche spoke of *Verdüsterung*, or "darkening," as a sign of the decadence and declining vitality of post-Enlightenment European culture, Heidegger turns this into a lament about deracination. And where Nietzsche employed a variety of metaphors to communicate his sense of the listlessness and exhaustion of the West—*Verdüsterung, Verwüstung, Verdunkelung*, among others—Heidegger will follow suit.[76] Heidegger becomes so enamored of this apocalyptic, chiliastic language of "darkening," "devastation," and "eclipse" that from 1935 onwards his works will reflect a preference for Nietzschean images of world-transfiguration. He will speak of *Weltverdüsterung, Weltverwüstung, die Verfinsterung der Welt, Weltnacht, die Verelendung der Erde, Verdunstung, Verblendung*, to cite only the most prominent.[77] Like Nietzsche, Heidegger

75. Playing on the Nietzschean trope of *Übergang*, or "transition," a way of rethinking Spengler's classic discourse on *Untergang*, or "decline," Heidegger understands his own time as a Hölderlinian-Nietzschean decision about the end of the West in its confrontation with the beginning, BQP: 109–110, 169/GA 45: 125–127, 196.

76. Nietzsche employs the term *Verdüsterung* and its cognates in KSA 1: 346; KSA 2: 627; KSA 3: 73, 136, 347, 573, 582; KSA 5: 44, 125, 156, 258, 302; KSA 9: 90; KSA 10: 518, 600; KSA 11: 571; KSA 12: 95. He will draw on the language of *Verwüstung* (and cognates) in KSA 1: 74, 200, 264, 295, 478, 486, 488, 771, 776; KSA 4: 380, 381, 385; KSA 6: 383, 388; KSA 7: 343, 348, 399; KSA 13: 305, and on that of *Verdunkelung* in KSA 1: 200.

77. Heidegger will draw heavily on this Nietzschean rhetoric—of *Verwüstung* in GA 50: 86; GA 53: 68; GA 66: 156, 175; GA 67: 38, 107, 143, 146–150; GA 69: 43, 47, 73, 94, 96; GA 77: 210–216, 229, 233–236, 238–241; of *Verdüsterung* in EM: 29, 34, 38; H: 248–249, 253, 294, 300; NII: 395; GA 65: 119; HBB: 92; of *Weltnacht* in H: 248–249, 294, 300; of *Verfinsterung* in

finds in these metaphors a way of countering the light-metaphysics of the European Enlightenment. And he transforms these metaphors into an overarching critique of America, Russia, and the calculative-technological imperative that he sees threatening both Europe and the West. Heidegger's work of the 1930s and '40s is replete with variations on this fundamental theme. By the time of the Second World War, however, Heidegger will have abandoned the defense of "spirit" that is so prominent in the *Introduction to Metaphysics* lectures. And yet he will nonetheless remain committed to the same geo-philosophical reading of *Mitteleuropa* derived from his understanding of Nietzsche's great politics as in his earlier works.

In an era when National Socialist philosophers like Baeumler, Horneffer, and Hildebrandt were arguing that Nietzsche's "good European" was really nothing else but a "master of the earth" and that Nietzsche's goal was "not pacificism and cosmopolitanism but the great war for the German *Volk* to become *Führer* in Europe," Heidegger will fall victim to his own "private" National Socialist interpretation of Nietzsche.[78] Now Nietzsche will be brought in line (in the sense of a philosophical *Gleichschaltung*) with a *völkisch*-nationalist account of Germany as a nation granted the mission of "saving" the West. Hardly anything could be farther from Nietzsche's design. In *Beyond Good and Evil,* Nietzsche writes of the German attempt "to Germanize the whole of Europe" as something worthy of ridicule and contempt. He then puts forward the ideal of "the good European" as an antidote to the poison of "national agitations, patriotic palpitations, and floods of various archaicizing feelings...." (BGE: 175, 171/KSA 5: 185, 180). He then adds: "Indeed, I can imagine dull, sluggish races which, even in our fast-moving Europe, would need half a century to overcome such atavistic attacks of patriotism [*Vaterländerei*] and soil addiction and be restored to reason, I mean to 'good Europeanism'." For Nietzsche, nationalism, *Heimatpolitik, Bodenständigkeit,* and soil addiction were all to be understood as external symptoms of an underlying disease that had brought Europe to its feet—the sickness of nihilism. And yet Heidegger, who concurred with Nietzsche on the diagnosis of Europe's condition, broke with him on the matter of a proper cure.

Rejecting the notion of the good European, Heidegger embraced the petty politics of the *Volk* and reframed Nietzsche's critique of nihilism to accord with the standard National Socialist nostrums about geo-politics that he shared with his contemporaries. When he spoke in *Introduction to*

HBB: 100; NII: 394; GA 67: 253; of *Verblendung* in NII: 393; of *Verdunstung* in EM: 27, 39, and of *Verelendung* in a 1971 letter to Hans Kock, cited in *Die Frage nach der Wahrheit,* ed. Ewald Richter (Frankfurt: Klostermann, 1997), 63.

78. Kurt Hildebrandt, "Die Idee des Krieges bei Goethe-Hölderlin-Nietzsche," in *Das Bild des Krieges im Deutschen Denken,* ed. August Faust (Stuttgart: Kohlhammer, 1941), 406, and Baeumler, *Nietzsche: Der Philosoph und Politiker,* 176–177.

Metaphysics about the Germans as "the *Volk* with the most neighbors" who were at the same time "the *Volk* in the greatest danger" and *"the* metaphysical *Volk,"* Heidegger was expressing his most fundamental philosophical convictions: about Germany's position within *Mitteleuropa,* about the threat of Americanization as the most dangerous form of nihilism, about Graeco-German metaphysics as the basis of an essential ontico-political form of autochthony. Although Heidegger would abandon the aggressively nationalistic rhetoric of the *Volk* in the years after 1938 and turn his attention to a subtle critique of National Socialist attempts at world domination and "mastery over the earth," he would still cling to the basic principles of his geo-philosophy of rootedness in the native soil.

As we read Heidegger under the changed conditions of our own postmodern predicament, we may be inclined to dismiss this side of his work—and indeed there are compelling reasons why we should. But before we do so we need to recognize the effects such principles had in their own time. Perhaps part of the problem can be traced back to Heidegger's own preference for roots—and for staying at home. Until the 1950s, Heidegger rarely traveled to foreign countries, and when he did his stays were brief.[79] Unlike Nietzsche, who lived most of his adult life abroad, traveling back and forth like a nomad from Sils Maria to Nizza, from Basel to Rapallo, from Lake Silvaplana to Venice and Turin, Heidegger preferred the indigenous soil of the Black Forest and the landscapes of the Alemannic countryside. Whereas Nietzsche wrote most of his important books in different cities in Switzerland, Southern France, and Northern Italy, Heidegger composed almost all of his work after 1929 at his peasant cottage in Todtnauberg and at his house near Freiburg. And as reductionist as biographical detail can be, these differences between the philosopher of the wandering and itinerant Zarathustra and the thinker of homeland, rootedness, and native soil should not be left out of consideration.

To end this chapter's focus on Europe and German destiny, I want to consider a short essay that Heidegger composed in Rome during his brief stay there in 1936 while he was delivering the lecture "Hölderlin and the Essence of Poetry."[80] In this short piece we see Heidegger at work framing

79. Heidegger was invited to visit Japan for an extended stay in the 1920s but declined—presumably out of concern for his family. But his fear of the foreign, the non-native, the allochthonous must have also played a significant role in his decision. He did visit Amsterdam, Rome, and in the 1960s, after much delay and a few false starts, he finally traveled to Greece and wrote a journal, *Aufenthalte,* about his stay there. After his ten-day trip to Rome in 1936, he complains to Jaspers that the whole time he was "confused, exasperated, and infuriated," HJB: 161. Through the intercession of Jean Beaufret, he did make a number of trips to France in the 1950s to lecture and to visit Provence, but before 1945 he does not often leave Germany.

80. Heidegger wrote "Europe and German Philosophy" while in Rome in May of 1936—although the basic ideas are a summary of his early essay, "On the Essence of Truth."

his Germanocentric history of philosophy in ways that can apply to all of Europe—and to the history of the West. Without insulting his Italian hosts by subjecting them to the egregious nationalism of his *Sonderweg* metaphysics, Heidegger restates the geo-philosophical thesis of *Introduction to Metaphysics* more cryptically. Instead of situating the problem of autochthony politically in terms of *Mitteleuropa,* he now offers to his foreign audience an ontological argument for *Bodenständigkeit* that engages the world of ancient Greece.

IX. "EUROPE AND GERMAN PHILOSOPHY" (1936)

In his *Introduction to Metaphysics,* Heidegger challenged what he would later call "the Americanization of language"—namely, its tendency to become instrumentalized by the technical demands of business, commerce, and media—and turned his attention to the poetic-philosophical speech of Sophocles and Heraclitus for a pathway out of the nihilistic crisis facing both Germany and the West (GA 52: 10). As he put it, "because the destiny of language is grounded in the temporally particular *relation* of a *Volk* to *being,* the question of *being* will become for us bound up with the question of *language*" (IM: 51/EM: 39). In his 1936 Rome lecture "Europe and German Philosophy," Heidegger will reframe the question about Europe's destiny in terms of a retrieval of the language of the Greeks.

Heidegger delivered this speech to the Kaiser-Wilhelm-Institut on the eighth of April in 1936. Just one month earlier, Hitler had marched his troops into the demilitarized Rhineland arrogantly violating the treaties of Versailles and Locarno in an attempt to restore a measure of German autonomy in Europe. In the wake of this action, the German Foreign Office had alerted other governments that Hitler's decision should be understood as a reaction to the French pact with the Soviet Union whose effect was to isolate Germany at the center of Europe, hence posing a threat to its national security.[81] Given this concrete set of circumstances, Heidegger's metaphysical vision of a Germany caught in the pincers between Russia and the West seemed on the verge of becoming a political reality.

This fear of a threat from the East became a dominant motif in Heidegger's 1936 address. In his opening remarks, Heidegger laid down the basic framework for his argument:

Our historical *Dasein* experiences with increasing distress and clarity that its future is tantamount to a naked either/or: either Europe's rescue or its destruction. The possibility of rescue, however, demands two things:
1. The preservation of the European *Völker* against the Asiatic.

81. Gordon Craig, *German History, 1866–1945* (New York: Oxford University Press), 689.

2. The overcoming of their own deracination and fragmentation.
Without this overcoming such preservation cannot be realized. (EdP: 31)

As in the *Introduction to Metaphysics* lectures, here Heidegger understood the situation of Europe eschatologically as a crisis that would determine the very future of Europe—and of the West. The causes for the crisis were both of recent provenance (the nihilism engendered by the Great War, the rise of Americanism, the threat from Russia and Asia, the instrumental force of language and technology, etc.) and of long-standing origin (the *Seinsvergessenheit* of Western philosophy, the Platonic-Aristotelian transformation of Pre-Socratic *aletheia*, the rootlessness of Roman culture). As he saw it, in order to overcome this crisis and to preserve Europe against the ancient threat of a barbarian invasion from the East, a "historical transformation of *Dasein*" was necessary. This "transformation" (*Wandel*) was not to be understood as a "blind thrust into an undetermined future but rather as a creative confrontation [*Auseinandersetzung*] with all of previous history—its essential structures and epochs." Heidegger grasps this confrontation with history as something akin to the essential disclosure that occurs in the process of creating an art work. As the work sets itself in place against the formal limits of its technical-equipmental traits, it bursts asunder the utile, thingly structures that define it, thus opening itself to the conflict or *Streit* that makes art possible. In "Europe and German Philosophy," Heidegger understands the future of Europe in much the same way as a *Streit* with the history of the West concerning the definition of truth. Only insofar as a *Volk* takes upon itself the task of "enduring" the essential conflict within truth—understood as conflict itself—can it come to know "what it is" (EdP: 32). "Only by virtue of the truth of this knowledge," Heidegger writes, "does a *Volk* come into the nearness [*Nähe*] of its origin. Out of this nearness emerges the soil [*Boden*] upon which a standing [*Stehen*] and a persistence is possible: true autochthony [*Bodenständigkeit*]." Only in the autochthonic standing within tradition can the *Volk* "prepare and institute the great turn of European history."

Heidegger's address determines the notion of "Europe" in ways that radically alter the question-frame of his contemporaries. In fact, the address can be read as an assault upon the scientific-humanistic model of Europe laid down by Kant in his famous essay "Perpetual Peace" (1795). Kant's cosmopolitan ideal of a "universal community" and an "international state that would necessarily continue to grow until it embraced all the peoples of the earth" was offered in the spirit of a scientific-rational solution to the problem of warfare.[82] In the years following the Great War, the spirit of Kant's cosmopolitan proposal was endorsed by the supporters

82. *Kant's Political Writings*, ed. Hans Riess (Cambridge: Cambridge University Press, 1970), 105–107.

of the League of Nations. But it was also adopted in varying ways by the old European humanist tradition as well. In 1919, Paul Valéry proposed a humanist defense of Europe in his essay "The Crisis of the Mind." In this postwar atmosphere, Valéry offered a diagnosis of Europe's spiritual crisis that recognized the same threats Heidegger would notice: "democracy, the exploitation of the globe, and the general spread of technology, all of which presage a *deminutio capitis* for Europe."[83] Looking at these threats to Europe, Valéry posed his own either/or: ". . . must these be taken as absolute decisions of fate? Or have we some freedom *against* this threatening conspiracy of things?" For Valéry, the moral and intellectual greatness of Europe consisted in its commitment to Christianity, humanism, and what he termed "the European spirit." What concerned him was the impending prospect of a collapse in European pre-eminence, the loss of Europe's position as the cultural-political-economic-metaphysical center of the modern world. The ultimate question for Valéry was thus:

> Will Europe become *what it is in reality*—that is, a little promontory on the continent of Asia? Or will it remain *what it seems*—that is, the elect portion of the terrestrial globe, the pearl of the sphere, the brain of a vast body?[84]

Valéry's humanistic defense of European cultural hegemony over Asia and the developing non-Western world was animated by a belief in the technical and intellectual superiority of the Enlightenment legacy bequeathed by Kant and his successors. But Valéry was also spurred on by his belief in the Latin legacy of European culture that he located in the Roman Catholic tradition and in Roman classical humanism. Heidegger would, of course, opt for a different patrimony for Europe: the Graeco-Hellenic legacy. But even here Heidegger's decision to select Greece as the originary site for European self-definition was carried out in such a way that it challenged the standard appeal to the Greek legacy. Heidegger's teacher, Edmund Husserl, had also offered an analysis of Europe's spiritual-intellectual crisis that looked to ancient Greece as a way out of the crisis facing the West. In his 1935 lecture, "Philosophy and the Crisis of European Humanity," Husserl too saw Europe being confronted by an imminent threat to its very existence and, like Heidegger, he too believed that Greek philosophy would need to play a more determinative role in Europe's future were it to endure. As Husserl put it, "within European civilization, philosophy has constantly to exercise its function as one which is archontic for the civilization as a whole."[85] As "archontic," philosophy

83. Paul Valéry, "The Crisis of the Mind," in *History and Politics,* trans. Denise Folliot (New York: Bollingen, 1962), 36, 326.

84. Ibid., 31.

85. Edmund Husserl, *The Crisis of European Sciences and Transcendental Phenomenology,* trans. David Carr (Evanston: Northwestern University Press, 1970), 289.

would regain its function as a guiding force within European culture and reaffirm the Greek spirit of philosophical inquiry. But the similarity between Heidegger and Husserl ends there. Where Heidegger turned to the Greeks as the archontic source for his subterranean, chthonic excurses on *Volk, Heimat,* and *Bodenständigkeit,* Husserl found in Greek thinking the sources for "free and universal theoretical reflection" that would serve as a model for a "supranational" ideal of reason. Only through this commitment to the universal form of science as something rational and free would Europe be able to survive. In Husserl's words:

> There are only two escapes from the crisis of European existence: the downfall of Europe in its estrangement from its own rational sense of life, its fall into hostility toward the spirit and into barbarity; or the rebirth of Europe from the spirit of philosophy through a heroism of reason that overcomes naturalism once and for all. Europe's greatest danger is weariness. If we struggle against this greatest of all dangers as "good Europeans" with the sort of courage that does not fear even an infinite struggle, then out of the destructive blaze of lack of faith, the smoldering fire of despair over the West's mission for humanity, the ashes of great weariness, will rise up the phoenix of a new life-inwardness and spiritualization as the pledge of a great and distant future for man: for the spirit alone is immortal.[86]

Husserl's response to the crisis of European existence posed a simple choice: either Europe would fall into a form of barbarism and attack the legacy of rationality *or* it would reaffirm the spirit of rational inquiry and save the West. Philosophy itself was a model of the kind of universal, rational attitude of thought that would help Europe to make this crucial decision. Unlike Heidegger, however, Husserl insisted that philosophy was not something peculiarly Greek or German; it was never something "limited to the home nation." Quite to the contrary, Husserl claimed, "unlike other cultural works, philosophy is not a movement of interest which is bound to the soil of the national tradition. Aliens, too, learn to understand it and generally take part in the immense cultural transformation which radiates out from philosophy."[87] What characterized philosophy in its archontic function as guide for European culture was its universality and its theoretical approach to "objective truth."

As Heidegger began to formulate his own analysis of Europe's spiritual crisis, he offered a radical contrast to Husserl's Pan-European, rational ideal. In two dramatic ways Heidegger challenged the Kantian premises of Husserl's ideal portrait of Europe. Firstly, he rejected its cosmopolitan, universal model of "European supranationality" as rootless and as a grave

---

86. Ibid., 299.
87. Ibid., 286.

danger to Europe's very survival. Secondly, he contested Husserl's reading of Greek philosophy as something universal, rational, scientific, and theoretical. For Heidegger, *thaumazein* was not merely a pre-theoretical habit of thought which opened up the path for "the *theoria* of genuine science." It was itself, rather, the philosophical comportment whose retrieval and recovery was essential if the West were to grasp truth essentially—that is, not as an assertoric proposition or rational conclusion but as the very play of concealment/unconcealment whose essence lay hidden in the Greek experience of *aletheia*. Both politically and ontologically, Heidegger characterized Husserl's definition of Europe as something rootless and un-Greek. Against Husserl's "ideas of 1789," Heidegger raised the specter of the ideas of 1914. It was precisely in Germany's autochthonic affinity with Greek philosophy—its rootedness in the *arche* of the Greek experience of being—that there lay any hope for the rescue of the West from its imminent collapse. If Valéry and Husserl defined Europe in terms of its scientific-humanist mission for all of humanity, Heidegger defined it ontologically and politically in terms of genuine autochthony.

Already in his Rectorial Address, Heidegger had attempted to show that a retrieval of the Greeks was essential to the future of the West. There he had claimed, however, that access to the *arche* of Greek thought would be difficult since the Western tradition of scientific rationality had covered over and occluded the genuine sources of Greek philosophical questioning. Still, throughout the Rectorial Address, Heidegger stresses the need for such a retrieval designating Germany as the sole nation capable of retrieving the Greek *arche*. As the privileged nation, Germany has a "historical mission" to save the West at a time "when the spiritual strength of the West fails and the West starts to come apart at the seams" (RA: 38/SdU: 19). And yet, though there are two references to the West (*Abendland*) and twenty-seven references to Germany in this decisive speech, there is no mention of Europe at all. How are we to account for the radical divergence in language between the Rectorial Address and the Rome lecture? Did Heidegger experience another kind of *Kehre* between 1933 and 1936, a "European" turn as it were, a shift from the Germanocentric vision of the rector to a Pan-European perspective? And can we locate in this shift a fundamental turn in Heidegger's understanding of German nationalism?

Part of the differences between these two speeches can be traced to the rhetorical demands placed upon Heidegger as a foreign speaker delivering an address in Rome. When he was asked to deliver another lecture in 1937 to the International Descartes Congress in Paris, Heidegger responded by composing an essay, "Wege zur Aussprache," which dealt with the topic of establishing an understanding between France and Germany.[88] Like the Rome address, this 1937 essay focused on the crisis facing the West—"the threat of complete deracination"—and pointed to the early Greeks as the source for overcoming the present situation. Because the essay was addressed to a French audience, however, Heidegger refrained from any unilateral affirmation of the privileged German mission to save the West. Instead, Heidegger reverted to the same strategy that he employed in his Rome lecture—he framed the problematic of the Rectorial Address in the language of a Western rather than of a merely German mission. In this short six-page essay, Heidegger refers to the West (and its cognates) nine times; by contrast, he refers to Germany only four times and always in a binary relation with France. The whole rhetorical focus is on the "historical-spiritual formation of the West" (DE: 15). And, as in "Europe and German Philosophy," Heidegger directs his remarks at the threat posed to Europe by "the Asiatic." Referring to the Greeks, Heidegger writes: "only by virtue of its fierce but creative confrontation [Auseinandersetzung] with what was most foreign to it and most difficult—the Asiatic—did this *Volk* grow up in the short course of its historical uniqueness and greatness" (DE: 21). By defining Europe through and against its relationship to Asia, and by constructing an interpretation of Greece as the "counter-Asiatic," Heidegger attempts an autochthonic history of Western culture carried out in the name of a political-ontological privileging of Graeco-German affinity.

In this sense Heidegger's idea of Europe functions as the name for a specific philosophical-historical interpretation of Western culture rather than as a merely geographical designation. Valéry had posed a timely question: was Europe to become merely "a kind of cape of the old continent, a western appendix to Asia" or was it to remain the technological-industrial "brain" guiding the development of world civilization?[89] In 1936 Heidegger prepared his own response—Europe was neither to become a mere appendix to Asia nor to remain as the name of a technical-instrumental project of Cartesian world domination. Rather, Europe's task was to retrieve its genuine identity, an identity whose own roots lay in the first

88. Heidegger never actually delivered this address in Paris because of political intrigues focusing on his desire to head the German delegation—and the decision by the Ministry in Berlin to choose Heyse as the head. In a letter to Friedrich Metz, the rector of Freiburg, Heidegger explains that his original plan was to write an essay challenging "the dominant liberal-democratic interpretation of science" that permeated the French delegation and to help in preparing an "effective and powerful German delegation," FarG: 330. The essay was originally published in a decidedly political work, *Alemannenland: Ein Buch von Volkstum und Sendung*, ed. Franz Kerber (Stuttgart: J. Engelhorns, 1937), 135–139. Kerber, the mayor of Freiburg at the time, had also been editor in chief of the Nazi journal *Der Alemanne;* see Rüdiger Safranski, *Ein Meister aus Deutschland: Heidegger und seine Zeit* (Munich: Hanser, 1994), 376.

89. Valéry, *History and Politics*, 312, 31.

beginning of Greek thought.[90] Contra Valéry, Heidegger defined Europe not as a mere promontory off the mainland of Asia but as the name of a metaphysical history of being. In this way, Heidegger's discourse about Europe offered a mythic framework within which to anchor his concepts of *Mitteleuropa* and *Bodenständigkeit*, helping him to find a way of rooting his own philosophemes in the archaic soil of the Greeks. Within the context of this new "Europa"-rhetoric, the old problems of *Verwüstung, Verdüsterung*, and the flight of the gods were now re-framed as questions about Europe's relation to the first Greek beginning. Despite this self-consciously stylized rhetoric about the European sources of renewal and transformation, however, Heidegger's underlying argument was still marked by the *völkisch* language of autochthony. To properly understand the axiomatics of Heidegger's lecture, then, we will need to translate this new rhetorical language using the Rosetta stone hewn from the hard rock of Schlageter's Black Forest quarry. And if we read "Europe and German Philosophy" with an eye for this encoded message, we will find there a virtual catalog of Heidegger's most enduring philosophical themes.

In its most basic sense, Heidegger's address functions as a kind of rhetorical paralepsis; that is, it makes its point by an act of indirection. It brings its theme to the center by omitting it or by disregarding it entirely. Hence, as he looks back upon the history of Europe and seeks a way to preserve it against the incursion of the Asiatic and to overcome its rootlessness and fragmentation, Heidegger simply omits mentioning two of Europe's most fundamental traditions: Roman Catholicism and Roman humanism. In a speech delivered in Rome about Europe's past and future, Heidegger consciously elides all references to Roman and Latin culture in a paraleptic attempt to emphasize his point: only through a return to Greek thought can the West be saved. In a lecture of about ten-octavo page length, Heidegger will spend six pages focusing exclusively on Greek thought and on explicating three Greek words: *physis, logos*, and *aletheia*. As he constructs his argument, he will emphasize the Greek origins of European thought and he will claim that "the fundamental position of Western philosophy" was determined by the Platonic-Aristotelian transformation of Heraclitean-Parmenidean *aletheia*. Such a transformation, he will maintain, "determined the fate of Western philosophy in the centuries that followed" (EdP: 38). Nowhere are there Latin references to be found. Nor are any other European languages brought into consideration; the only non-German figure mentioned is Descartes and then only pejora-

90. EHD: 177. Jacques Derrida, *The Other Heading: Reflections on Today's Europe*, trans. Pascale-Anne Brault and Michael Naas (Bloomington: Indiana University Press, 1992), 19–34, 111–118. Derrida offers a critique of Heideggerian geo-philosophy configured as a "spiritual geography"—especially as a contrast to Valéry.

tively as someone whose thinking effected a mathematization of being. Heidegger tells his listeners that only by retrieving the archaic Greek experience of *aletheia* can European deracination be overcome. And yet the only people capable of such a task are the Germans. Standing on Roman soil, situated at the crossroads of Christian/humanist tradition, speaking in a library built during the efflorescence of Renaissance humanist culture, Heidegger opts for a mythic Hellenic patrimony for the West and boldly determines that the fate of Europe will depend on the readiness of the Germans to reclaim that patrimony and affirm a Graeco-Germanic form of autochthony.

What proves distinctive about "Europe and German Philosophy" when considered against this background is the way that Heidegger goes about grounding that autochthony. In his Rectorial Address, in the political speeches, in the Hölderlin lectures, and in *Introduction to Metaphysics,* Heidegger will consistently reaffirm the indigenous bond that unites the German *Volk* with the Greeks. In all of these works we can detect an intimate connection between the political rootedness of the *Volk* in the native soil and their ontological rootedness in archaic Greek thought. In Heidegger's own archeo-eschatological scheme of thinking laid down in the Rectorial Address, the history of the West was determined by the Greeks at the origin and would be decided by the Germans at the end. In this way, the notion of autochthony would take on the function of connecting the first beginning of Greek thought with that other "futural" beginning of German destiny. But, in the Rome lecture, Heidegger elided all reference to a political form of *völkisch* autochthony in favor of an ontological form, thus abandoning the rhetoric of a geo-philosophical *Sonderweg* for the Germans. And yet, if read carefully, one can see how this philosophical discourse on *aletheia* succeeds in constating the political autochthony of the Germans by contesting the Roman heritage of Europe. As in most of Heidegger's philosophical prose from the '30s, much depends on how we interpret his use of the collective pronoun "we." "Who are we?" Heidegger often asks in his lectures.[91] In the *Logik* lectures of summer 1934, Heidegger writes: "Who are we ourselves? Answer: the *Volk*"; "we stand in the being of the *Volk*" (L: 54, 16). And again in *Beiträge,* Heidegger raises the question "who are we?" and tells his audience that this question can never be genuinely engaged "as long as we do not grasp the essence of philosophy as meditation on the truth of being [*Seyn*]" (GA 65: 49).

At the close of his "Europe and German Philosophy," Heidegger will reaffirm the *völkisch* meaning of this "we" as the name of a communal des-

91. For various constructions and configurations of Heidegger's pointedly political question of "who are *we?*" see: GA 29/30: 6–10, 103, 407–408, 413–414; GA 34: 6, 45, 76, 119–122; GA 39: 49–50, 70–71, 77, 165, 174–177; GA 45: 109, 188–190, 226; GA 65: 48–54, 100, 125, 245, 265, 300, 303, 318, 322; GA 66: 153; L.: 6, 8, 10, 12, 20, 26, 36, 54, 66, among others.

tiny for the West. "Insofar as we once again ask the *fundamental question* of Western philosophy from a *more originary* beginning, we stand in the service of *the* task which we designate as the rescue of the West" (EdP: 40). In the encoded language of his autochthonous reading of Western history, "Europe" becomes the name of a destiny whose roots lie in the Greeks and whose future lies in the readiness of the Germans to excavate those roots and thereby reshape Europe's future. This lecture can hardly be read then as Heidegger's attempt to shift the focus from his Germanocentric reading of history. On the contrary, by availing himself of a new European rhetoric, Heidegger confirms the determining role of the German *Volk* in recovering the archontic legacy of the Greeks. As in the "Wege zur Aussprache" essay a year later, here Heidegger will emphatically reject what in a 1933 speech he termed *Weltverbrüderung* (the kind of "world brotherhood" associated with the ideas of 1789) for an exclusionary, *völkisch* reading of both Europe and the West (NH: 145). Even his interpretation of ancient Greek philosophy here is formed by his exclusionary emphasis on autochthony.

Against Nietzsche's view of Greek philosophy as an eclectic, supranational phenomenon with elements of Egyptian, Indian, Persian, and other Middle Eastern and Oriental influences, Heidegger will project his own National Socialist vision of autochthony back onto the Greeks and insist on the *European* origin of Greek thought against the threat of incursion from Asia Minor.[92] By appropriating Ephesus, Miletus, Samos, and other city-states to his Europocentric vision of Greece, Heidegger succeeded in suppressing the Asian element and re-reading the *arche* of Western history in terms of his own *mythos* of Graeco-German affinity. Europe begins, for Heidegger, in the Greek attempt to suppress the Asiatic and to assert its rootedness in the chthonic. And Europe's future consists in his eyes in the parallel German attempt to preserve itself against these same barbaric Asian forces (now in the form of Bolshevism and Russian technocracy) and to assert its rootedness in the chthonic Greek tradition.

Throughout the 1930s and '40s, Heidegger will turn to the lexicon of his 1936 lecture for a way of reframing his understanding of the history of being. He will draw upon the language of *Bodenständigkeit, Verwüstung, Entwurzelung,* and *Streit* to analyze the rootlessness and devastation that he uncovers in European nihilism. Now the term "*Europa*" will serve as a name designating what the West has become in its planetary phase of world

---

92. In WP: #1050, Nietzsche explicitly points to the Asiatic roots of Greek philosophy, KSA 13: 225. Heidegger will, of course, contest the Asiatic and will insist on the European origin of Greek thinking. For Heidegger's assault on the Asiatic, see GA 13: 21; FCM: 73/GA 29/30: 110; GA 39: 133–134; EdP: 31; DE: 21. In Ni: 22–23, 104–105/GA 43: 24–25, 122, Heidegger will reject any "Egypticism" within Nietzsche and will, in his analysis of the famous Böhlendorff letter, reject any Asian element in Hölderlin.

domination. And the term "*Abendland*" will become a code word for the *Seynsgeschichte* of the West.[93] In the years following this 1936 lecture, Heidegger will often use the terms "Europe" and "the West" interchangeably without any clear difference, and yet at other times he will employ them as names for *Seynsgeschichte* (*der Abendland*) and *Seinsvergessenheit* (*Europa*).[94] As we reflect on the idiosyncratic language of Heidegger's writings, we would do well to remember its encoded prescripts and its underlying message about the threat of deracination and the loss of a homeland. Heidegger's ontology cannot be reduced to mere nostalgia. Its labyrinthine structure and its earnest language of etymological pirouettes were offered in a difficult, critical, thoroughly rigorous style that abjured the romantic longing of *schwärmerische Heimsucht* and Odyssean *nostos*. And yet the genuine sources for Heidegger's *Ursprungsphilosophie* should be sought not only in Pre-Socratic philosophy, Hölderlinian poetry, and the design of a Greek temple. We also need to consider the powerful effect of the quotidian influences on Heidegger's thought that were part of the political culture whose lineaments he so often sought to cover over and deny.

In this sense, I would argue that Heidegger's ontological narrative of the West in terms of *Seynsgeschichte* needs to be read as an expression of his own fiercely Germanocentric emphasis on autochthony in its most political form. What Heidegger locates in the Greeks is an ontological justification for political-cultural exclusion. This is no mere ancillary concern. It becomes, rather, the guiding trope in formulating Heidegger's widely influential history of philosophy. The logic of this schematic history is already laid out in 1934/35 in "Hölderlins Hymnen: 'Germanien' und 'der Rhein'" where Heidegger traces the lineage of Graeco-Germanic thought back to Heraclitus and his alleged attempt to cleave all ties to the Asiatic. As Heidegger explains:

> Hölderlin too stands under the power of Heraclitean thinking. Under this selfsame power there also comes a later one: Nietzsche. Properly speaking, Meister Eckhart stood under this power at the beginning of German philosophy. The name Heraclitus is not the title of a Greek form of philosophy that long ago expired. Neither is it a formula for a hackneyed form of cosmopolitan humanity. It is, rather, the name of an originary power of Western-German historical *Dasein* and indeed in its confrontation [*Auseinandersetzung*] with the Asiatic." (GA 39: 133–134)

Insofar as Asia represents the "other" of Graeco-Germanic *Dasein*, it stands as a name for the barbaric, the rootless, the allochthonic—those

---

93. Heidegger PM: 257–258; WM: 169.
94. For various references, see EP: 90/VA: 77; FCM: 69/GA 29/30: 104; EGT: 17/H: 300; EHD: 177; PM: 257/WM: 169.

whose roots are not indigenous but who come from an/other place.[95] For Heidegger, Asia comes to signify pure alterity, the otherness that threatens the preservation of the homeland. Greece, on the other hand, will connote the home itself as the last birthplace of the German *Volk*, the native soil (*chthonos*) from whence the *Volk itself* (*autos*) was sprung. By clinging to his mythic construction of the Alemannic earth as the ground and origin of Western and European history, and by locating the *arche* of that myth in the autochthony of Greek thought, Heidegger helped to foster and perfect the longstanding tradition of German spiritual-cultural hegemony that had begun with Winckelmann. But he also succeeded in granting philosophical legitimacy to a model of Western thought that was radically xenophobic, exclusionary, and racist (if not in any biological sense). By turning his attention away from Rome, Jerusalem, Asia Minor, and both Russia and America, Heidegger came to promote a pernicious Graeco-German form of philosophical autochthony that would in the end prove far more dangerous to Europe's future than the threats he outlined in "Europe and German Philosophy." When Heidegger writes in 1942, after the American entry into the Second World War, that "we know today that the Anglo-Saxon world of Americanism has resolved to annihilate Europe, that is, the homeland [*Heimat*], and that means: the commencement of the Western world," he merely confirms this (HHI: 54/GA 53: 68). For him, the "other" (here defined as Americanism) can only mean "ahistoricality and self-devastation [*Selbstverwüstung*]" which he interprets as a "renunciation of the commencement."

What Heidegger brings to light in his Rome lecture is how this American renunciation of the first Greek beginning yields nothing less than the eclipse, the devastation, and the forgetting of being. Against this nihilistic movement of devastating the earth, despoiling the homeland, and uprooting all ties to the beginning, Heidegger will read the history of Europe as a narrative whose ending is still undecided and whose fate still remains bound to the either/or of: the preservation of Europe (Germany, the homeland, *das Volk*) against the Asiatic (all that is "other," the American act of ahistoricality, Russian Communism) *or* its devastation by the forces of *Verwüstung*, *Verdüsterung*, deracination, and nihilism. The great irony within Heidegger's logic of exclusion is that he sees the only possible way out of the final dissolution of Western *Seinsvergessenheit* as an act of remembrance dedicated to retrieving the West's hidden origin. The history of our century has, contra Heidegger, revealed the dangers of all violently exclusionary forms of national, racial, and cultural self-assertion. But Heidegger seems to have missed this crucial point. Precisely at a time

---

95. On the notion of the allochthonic, see Lambropoulos, *Rise of Eurocentrism*, 215–216.

when the long history of German and European imperialism was being unmasked as destructive and nihilistic in both its political and philosophical practices, Heidegger pushed ahead with his program of an ever more exclusionary form of thinking.

Writing in 1961 in the midst of the French struggle over decolonization, Frantz Fanon announced in *The Wretched of the Earth* that "the European game has finally ended; we must find something different."[96] As a West Indian of African descent who suffered under the French rule in Martinique, Fanon questioned the system of exclusion that had granted the French political and economic power over a colonial empire. But he also challenged the philosophical principles of exclusion that made such imperialism possible. "For centuries," Fanon writes, the Europeans "have stifled almost the whole of humanity in the name of a so-called spiritual experience. Look at them today swaying between atomic and spiritual disintegration. . . . Europe now lives at such a mad, reckless pace that she has shaken off all guidance and reason. . . . It is in the name of the spirit, in the name of the spirit of Europe, that Europe has made her encroachments, has justified her crimes and legitimized the slavery in which she holds four-fifths of humanity. Yes, the European spirit has strange roots."[97]

Like Fanon, Heidegger understood that Europe was "running headlong into the abyss."[98] But where the former colonial understood the need for difference, Heidegger sought the way out of Europe's crisis by authorizing a more narrowly constricted form of identity. Clinging to his myth of German autochthony, Heidegger turned to ancient Greece as a way of legitimizing his practice of exclusion. And yet he was certainly not unique in doing so. It became a staple of National Socialist philosophy to enlist the Greeks in the service of the German revolution and to find in Germany a "new Hellas."[99] But Heidegger's myth of autochthony was not merely an extension of his National Socialist commitments. For him, the politics of National Socialism were but an expression of his longstanding aspiration to be at home in the native soil of the earth. "We" can only be saved, Heidegger tells his students, his Roman audience, his readers, if we make the decision to retrieve the Greek origin. Heidegger never abandons this position. Long after he has given up faith in official National Socialism, he retains his faith in the homeland. Even through the difficult postwar years when he realizes that the homeland is no longer possible as a political con-

96. Frantz Fanon, *The Wretched of the Earth* (New York: Grove Press, 1968), 312.
97. Ibid., 311–313.
98. Ibid.
99. Baeumler, for example, will write his essay "Hellas und Germanien" in the same spirit, *Studien zur deutschen Geistesgeschichte*, 295–311. See also *Deutsche Klassiker im National-sozialismus*, ed. Claudia Albert (Stuttgart: Metzler, 1994), 233–248.

figuration, Heidegger persists in his hopes for a future oriented *Heimat.* He still dreams the dream of a "Germania" sprung forth of itself from the archaic Greek earth with the help of the poetic language of *mythos:* a language of an origin lost and of an origin to come.

In "Europe and German Philosophy," Heidegger provides the outlines of this myth and frames his discussion in terms reminiscent of his 1930 Karlsruhe lecture "On the Essence of Truth." This short lecture offers in nuce the whole structure of the elaborately developed myth of ontological autochthony that Heidegger found in the early Greeks. I would like to explore the origins of this Graeco-Germanic connection by turning to a fuller analysis of "On the Essence of Truth" and considering it within the context of Heidegger's own use and abuse of Greek thought for his archeo-eschatological history of the West. In a decisive sense, it is this mythic bond to the Greeks that will persist in Heidegger's work and will spur him to uncover a metaphysical *Sonderweg* in Western history on whose basis he will continue to assert a political *Sonderweg*—even if after 1945 he will be forced underground by a new political set of circumstances.

CHAPTER FOUR

Heidegger's Greeks and the Myth of Autochthony

The veneration of classical antiquity . . . is a splendid example of Don Quixotism. . . . One imitates something purely chimerical and chases after a wonderworld that never existed. One cannot understand our modern world if one does not grasp the uncommon and monstrous influence of sheer fantasy.

—FRIEDRICH NIETZSCHE
KSA 8: 121

The beginning of our history is the Greeks.

—MARTIN HEIDEGGER
BC: 13/GA 51: 16

I. THE POLITICS OF THE ANTI-POLITICAL

Heidegger's work of the 1930s was marked by a persistent yearning to recuperate the Greek beginning for his own age. In his Rectorial Address, he could claim that "the beginning still *is*. It does not lie *behind* us as something long past, but it stands *before* us. . . . The beginning has invaded our future" (RA: 32/SdU: 12–13). Indeed, at the end of his address, he told his listeners that "we" can only grasp the greatness of this new beginning if we can come to understand the words of Plato in the *Republic:* "all that is great stands in the storm" (*Republic,* 497d). After the failure of his rectorate in 1934 and by the beginning of his first Nietzsche lectures in 1936/37, Heidegger will have distanced himself from the official party program of National Socialism. And yet in many ways, despite this distance, Heidegger's recovery of Greek philosophy—especially its archaic core in the Pre-Socratics—will be carried out in the name of a purer form of National Socialist thought, a recovery that will have already recognized its greatness. By 1937, Heidegger will have moved decisively away from the aggressive, self-assertive nationalism of his Rectorial Address, a nationalism that depended upon the *stürmisch* recovery of Platonic greatness, to embrace a more originary form of politics: the politics of the *arche.* But just how extensive a shift was involved in this turning from the aggressively martial rhetoric of the Rectorial Address and its invocation of Plato to the more auroral, archaic language of the late 1930s and its mythic recovery of the Pre-Socratics is still to be determined.

Otto Pöggeler, one of the first scholars to have had access to the extensive *Nachlass* collection, has claimed that by 1938 Heidegger begins to have serious doubts about the National Socialist program. After this time he views the National Socialist push for world domination by means of technology as part of the selfsame drive to "world devastation" carried out by other Western nations.[1] In his notebooks from the period after the *Beiträge* (during 1938–1939), Heidegger identifies devastation as a kind of "dominion over beings" and as a form of "the forgetting of being" (GA 66: 156). And he argues that in the age of technology, "the subjectivity of humanity frames itself in its purest form in the nation" (GA 66: 172). Already in the winter of 1937/38, Heidegger raised questions about the "race research" carried out by Nazi scientists and technicians, as well as about the growing emphasis on folklore and ethnology at the German universities—all of which he labeled "positivism." In notes to his seminar "The Threat of Science," Heidegger expressed disgust at the government's plan to collapse the universities into the technical colleges (BdW: 14–15, 22–27). He confesses in his notes that his ambitions as rector were riddled with errors, and he even acknowledges that "the moment of a genuine beginning and of a transformation is gone." And yet he attempts to work underground as it were, even stating at one point, "yes, we now need to don the mask of the 'positivist' so that we will be mistaken for another." In this kind of position as an underground critic of the regime and of its disastrous form of university politics, Heidegger raises the question—what should our stance be? " 'Resignation'? No. Blindly affirming everything? No. Conformity? No. Only: Constructing in advance of our time [*Vorausbauen*]." This kind of philosophical *Vorausbauen* is Heidegger's encoded term for preparing the possibility of an "other beginning," as he later puts it. Even the Nazis' attempt to abolish philosophy by reducing the number of academic chairs and university positions cannot succeed in undermining Heidegger's hopes for an other beginning. "Philosophy cannot be abolished because it is not something that can be procured. Since it is not something of the kind that one can 'organize,' it follows that it is also not something that can be abolished through organization." At the very end of his notes, Heidegger remarks: "The

1. Otto Pöggeler, "Von Nietzsche zu Hitler?: Heideggers politische Optionen," in *Annäherungen an Martin Heidegger*, ed. Hans Schäfer (Frankfurt: Campus, 1996), 98–99. Pöggeler's thesis here repeats an argument he makes in "Den Führer führen? Heidegger und kein Ende," *Philosophische Rundschau* 32 (1985): 26–67; "Heidegger's Political Self-Understanding," in *The Heidegger Controversy*, ed. Richard Wolin (New York: Columbia University Press, 1991), 198–244; *Philosophie und Nationalsozialismus—am Beispiel Heideggers* (Opladen: Westdeutscher Verlag, 1990); and the third, expanded edition of *Der Denkweg Martin Heideggers* (Pfullingen: Neske, 1990), 370–371.

Germans abolishing philosophy (with the aim of reclaiming the essence of the *Volk*) is world-historical suicide."

In a letter to Jaspers after the war, Heidegger tells his former friend that "in the years 1937 and 1938 I hit rock bottom. . . . We saw the war coming . . . then came the persecution of the Jews and everything approached the abyss. We never believed in 'victory'—and if victory had come *we* would have been the first to fall" (HJB: 201). Heidegger's hyperbole and self-mythification notwithstanding, his other writings from the period offer evidence of a serious critique of Nazi party ideology.[2] In *Beiträge zur Philosophie (Vom Ereignis)* he claims it is "pure nonsense to say that experimental research is Nordic-Germanic" (GA 65: 163). And in his Nietzsche lectures of 1940, he subtly critiques the Nazi war effort as an attempt to gain "absolute dominion over the earth": "it is not enough that one possess panzers, airplanes, and communications equipment; nor is it enough that one has at one's disposal men who can service such things; it is not even sufficient that man only master technology as if it were something neutral, beyond benefit and harm, creation and destruction, to be used by anybody at all for any ends whatsoever" (Niii: 116–117)/GA 48: 205). What does ultimately matter for Heidegger in 1940 (as in 1976) is the possibility of preparing the ground for an understanding and experience of the essence of truth in its originary form.

By the end of the Second World War, Heidegger will have long abandoned the aggressive nationalistic rhetoric of his Rectorial Address. Instead of embracing the *stürmisch* language of the Address with its emphasis on battle, struggle, service, will, self-assertion, and the resolve of those who stand firm, Heidegger will turn to the Eckhartian language of detachment and letting be. In a text written in the waning days of German collapse, Heidegger puts forward the notion that in the face of the current devastation within Germany one needs "to learn simply to wait until our own essence has become noble and free enough to join us to the secret of this destiny [*Geschick*] in a way that accords with it [*schicklich*]" (GA 77: 216–217). But as the "Evening Dialogue in a Prisoner of War Camp in Russia between a Younger and an Older Man" progresses, it becomes clear that Heidegger's discourse about waiting (*Warten*) should not be confused with the subjective posture of a-waiting or expectation (*Erwarten*). On the contrary, Heidegger writes that "in pure waiting we wait for nothing"—not "the" nothing but a

2. The evidence from the *Gesamtausgabe* offers to those with an eye for detail a portrait of Heidegger as a committed nationalist rooting for a German victory at Stalingrad in P: 77/GA 54: 114 and then being disappointed in defeat. GA 55: 181 also gives evidence of Heidegger resuscitating the Schlageter myth of "readiness for death" for the fatherland. His postwar explanations of detachment need to be read with care—and skepticism. Heidegger did offer a critique of Nazi racial-political ideology, but he still kept faith in the essential "truth and greatness" of "the" movement.

waiting that is marked by the absence of expectation. In this experience of pure waiting, Heidegger finds a way to endure and even to accept "the devastation that settles over the earth of the homeland."

During this period of mourning, fear, and utter defeat, Heidegger finds a way to reclaim his earlier work and to transform its heavily nationalistic message into a new vision of Germanness. What is remarkable in this "Evening Dialogue" (written in the very last days of the war and dated May 8, 1945, one day after Germany's surrender) is how amidst the mood of despair and uncertainty Heidegger can still think of the Germans as a future oriented *Volk*—albeit in a markedly different sense than he did in 1933. From the horizon of defeat he sees the Germans—whom he had earlier labeled "the *Volk* of poets and thinkers"—as the *Volk* who must now learn to wait:

> Younger Man: Perhaps the poets and thinkers of a *Volk* are nothing other than those who wait in the noblest way. . . .
>
> Older Man: Then the *Volk* of poets and thinkers would be in a unique sense the *Volk* who waits . . .
>
> Younger Man: . . . Is waiting for what is to come not perhaps authentic thinking? I have an unmistakable feeling that the healing we are experiencing does not derive from our being personally freed from any inner necessity. Healing comes from our knowing that, as those who wait, we are the first to begin to enter into the still withheld essence of our defeated *Volk*.
>
> Older Man: You mean that insofar as we are becoming those who wait we first become Germans?
>
> Younger Man: I not only mean that, I've known it since early this morning. And yet we will not become Germans as long as we resolve to find 'the German' in an analysis of our supposed 'nature.' Caught in such intentions we only chase after the national. . . .
>
> Older Man: Why do you speak so vigorously against the national? (GA 77: 234–235)

As the dialogue draws to a close, the older man will claim that "nationality is nothing other than the pure subjectivity of a *Volk*"—and the younger man will reply: "The essence of subjectivity lies in the fact that the human being, the individual, groups, and the human race rise up in order to throw themselves back upon their own resources and assert themselves [*sich behaupten*] as the ground and measure of all that is real." For the Heidegger of 1945, this unbridled form of self-assertion—which in 1933 he identified as the key to "the historical–spiritual mission of the German *Volk* as a *Volk*"—is now understood to be intimately bound up with the whole phenomenon of devastation (*Verwüstung*), desolation (*Verödung*), and abandonment (*Verlassenheit*) (RA: 30/SdU: 10; GA 77: 212–215). Now he too sees Hitler's version of National Socialism as a crude, destructive form of subjectivist thinking aimed at world domination and the conquest of the earth. And yet, despite the obvious contrast between the texts of 1933 and those of 1945, we need to be extremely careful in addressing the question of a "shift" or "turn" in Heidegger's thought.

As we come to consider the issue of a genuine shift in Heidegger's thought, we need to be wary of attaching too much significance to the merely external signs of change.[3] I would argue, for example, that although Heidegger's advocacy of "waiting" and "detachment" in the waning hours of the war might appear to us as the sign of a radical shift from the pro-Hitler speeches of 1933–1934, in a deeper sense it constitutes nothing of the sort. Seen from the position of Heidegger's own ontological narrative of Western history as *Seynsgeschichte*, nothing has changed. If Heidegger now begins to recognize the dangers, if not horrors, of Nazism, we should be wary of reading into this a renunciation of his earlier political views. What has transpired here in the intervening twelve years is not a *volte face* on the question of National Socialism but an awareness of the terrible failure of a particular version of it in its organizational, technocratic, administrative, and military-political form. Heidegger's critique of Western history in terms of subjectivity, technicity, world dominion, devastation, and rootlessness remains in place. But now he comes to view Nazism as a force of complicity in the epoch of "the abandonment of being" rather than as a counterforce to the "darkening of the world," as he had in the *Introduction to Metaphysics* of 1935, when he still spoke of "the inner truth and greatness of this movement" (GA 77: 213; IM: 45, 199/EM: 34, 152).

Just as in his 1935 reading of Germany as a nation "caught in a pincers, situated in the center," in 1945 Heidegger still sees "the Germans as the center and the heart of the West" (GA 77: 244). The political conditions have changed but the metaphysical ones remain. Now the Germans—ever the *Volk* of the future, the "futural" *Volk*—will have to learn the waiting game; now their historical destiny as the *Führer* of the West will have to take a different form. And yet, even as he surrenders his political dreams and his erstwhile hopes for national self-assertion, he does not renounce his faith in the elect status of the Germans. In spite of all the physical destruction brought on by the bombing raids and the tank assaults, Heidegger will still nourish his faith in the metaphysical calling of the Germans as the *Volk* chosen to save the West from the onslaught of devastation. "The

3. For a record of Heidegger's statements on defending his rectorship, see "Das Rektorat 1933/34: Tatsachen und Gedanken" in SdU: 21–43, which is translated by Lisa Harries in *Martin Heidegger and National Socialism: Questions and Answers*, ed. Günther Neske and Emil Kettering (New York: Paragon House, 1990), 15–32. Also see the "Documents from the Denazification Proceedings Concerning Martin Heidegger," trans. Jason Wirth, *Graduate Faculty Philosophy Journal* 14, no. 2 and 15, no. 1 (1991): 528–556, as well as the documents collected in *Martin Heidegger und das Dritte Reich*, ed. Bernd Martin (Darmstadt: Wissenschaftliche Buchgesellschaft, 1989), 186–212, and documents on the *Lehrverbot* in GA 16: 367–448.

war is over," Heidegger writes in May of 1945, "nothing has changed, nothing is new. On the contrary . . . the *devastation* continues" (GA 77: 241). As in his *Germania* lectures of 1934, in which Heidegger speaks of "the *Vaterland* as the historical being [*Seyn*] of a *Volk*," in 1945 he will still cherish the same dream—only now under different conditions and within a different rhetorical register. Heidegger continues to draw upon the *völkisch* language of rootedness, autochthony, homeland, and earth to frame his new postwar analysis of devastation, but by now he has long since abandoned the overtly political-martial language of will, hardness, *Dienst, Kampf, Aufbruch* (revolutionary departure or setting forth), and self-assertion. When he does invoke the term "*Volk*," it is only by way of criticism—as in the "Evening Dialog" where he equates it with "pure subjectivity," and in the Parmenides lectures where he equates *Volkheit* and *Volk* with "subjectivity and egoicity" (GA 77: 235; P: 137/GA 54: 204).[4] But there is a conceptual shift as well.

In the "Germania" lectures, Heidegger will draw upon the classical shibboleth of the Germans as "the *Volk* of poets and thinkers" and adapt it to his contemporary political rhetoric about the *Aufbruch* of the Germans (GA 39: 134). In this same context, he will reaffirm the political meaning of the German revolution of 1933. When Hölderlin speaks of "the fatherland," Heidegger writes, "he means the 'land of the fathers', he means us—this *Volk* of this earth as historical, in its historical being. This being [*Seyn*], however, is founded poetically [*dichterisch gestiftet*], configured by thinking [*denkerisch gefügt*], and placed in knowledge, and rooted in the earth and historical space by the authorship of the one who founds the state" (GA 39: 120). Again in these lectures, Heidegger will underline "the powers of poetry, thinking, and state-founding" as essential for the historical unfolding of the essence of the *Volk*. As he sees it, poetry, thinking, and state-founding are necessary for the authentic historical *Dasein* of a *Volk* to emerge (GA 39: 144, 41). In the very next semester (summer of 1935), Heidegger will situate his discussion of the three "powers" of poetry, thinking, and state-founding in an analysis of the poetry of Sophocles, the thinking of Heraclitus, and the state-founding [sic] of Oedipus (IM: 106–165/EM: 81–126). Moreover, he will insist on seeing these three powers as the tripartite expression of "a single, creative self-assertion [*Selbstbehauptung*]" indigenous to Greek (and German) being.

After the defeat at Stalingrad in the bitter winter of 1942–43, however, Heidegger's geo-political configuration of German destiny comes to a painful end. No longer will he put forward a *political* vision of the *Vaterland*. Instead, he will rethink what in 1934/35 he termed "the Greek-Ger-

---

4. For example, in the "Letter on Humanism" PM: 260/WM: 172, Heidegger equates self-assertion with subjectivity.

man mission" by putting an ever greater emphasis on the other two powers of the German *Volk:* poetry and thinking.[5] Now Heidegger will abjure
the language of geo-politics and resurrect his myth of a German *Sonderweg*
by reframing it in terms of a Hölderlinian retrieval of Greek poetry and
thinking. The myth of state-founding is carefully excised. In its wake, Heidegger will stress the poetic-philosophical dimension of Germany's special mission to the West, interpreting it not as the present task of the Germans (as he did in the Rectorial Address) but rather as something distant
and "futural" that stands before them. Following the lead of Hölderlin,
Heidegger will say that to be German is to be "futural." And to be future
oriented, according to this selfsame logic, is to stand in proximity to the
origin of Greek poetry and thinking. What the Germans are, Heidegger
intimates, can never be accounted for in terms of their present identity.
They can only be imagined in terms of the future, and their future, in
turn, can only be conceived through a retrieval of their ancient Greek patrimony. Heidegger will cling to this Hölderlinian myth of a future oriented German homeland throughout the difficult days of the war. Even
after the terrible destruction and loss at Stalingrad and the setbacks on the
Eastern Front and North Africa, Heidegger will persist in clinging to his
exclusionary myth of Graeco-Germanic affiliation. In the summer of
1944, as the German collapse appears ever more imminent, Heidegger
tells his students:

> At the moment we can only have a presentiment of this: . . . that the destiny
> of humanity and of different peoples is deeply rooted in the particular rela-
> tion of the human being to the respectively appearing or self-denying
> essence of unconcealment—that is, truth. . . . If we consider that the
> essence of truth revealed itself in the West for the first time and in a deter-
> minative sense to the Greeks, then we can recognize to what extent the des-
> tiny that became Greece is nothing past or antiquated—nothing we can
> term 'antiquity'—but rather a still undecided coming that we Germans
> alone, first, and for a long time to come, can and must think, both with the
> Greeks as well as against them. (GA 55: 204)

By May of the next year, Heidegger will have fully extinguished all traces
of political activism from his myth of a German future. In its stead he will
insist on an ever more originary, ever more primordial attunement to the
poetic-philosophical *arche* of the Greeks.

Agnes Heller has focused attention on this dimension of Heidegger's
thought and has argued that, in the winter of 1942/43, "Heidegger called
upon his students to accept an apolitical, anti-political thinking that he

---

5. Heidegger, GA 50: 102 and P: 77, 167/GA 54: 113–114, 250.

traced back to the Greeks."[6] In her thoughtful reading, Heller contends that Heidegger interprets Plato and Parmenides as anti-political thinkers who dispense with the "political" meaning of the *polis* in order to put forward the founding myth of *aletheia*. In many ways, Heller has pointed to a significant shift in Heidegger's work, a shift that I would argue can already be discerned in the years 1937–38.[7] But in her haste to identify this "new" anti-political stance in Heidegger, Heller has missed an important nuance (and here she is emblematic of a whole tendency in Heidegger scholarship). In 1942 and after, Heidegger does not embrace an anti-political style; rather, his politics go underground (literally: in a turn to the chthonic). Henceforth, Heidegger will advocate a new politics of the anti-political: an originary politics of the *arche* that dispenses with, extinguishes, and deracinates the aggressively nationalist dimension from the old politics of the earth, the homeland, the soil, and the fatherland. In the name of the old poetic-philosophical myth of autochthony, Heidegger will now assert that "the essence of power is foreign to the *polis*" (P: 91/GA 54: 135). Now the roots of the homeland will be protected from the threatening incursions of a political rhetoric saturated with National Socialist slogans about "work," "service," "folk community," and the politics of will and self-assertion. What will emerge in the next two and a half years is a language of German autochthony stripped of all geo-political references. And yet, the same structural principles will remain in place.

In effect, Heidegger will reaffirm the *ontological* sources of German autochthony—its unique mission to save the West, its singular affinity to the Greek *arche*, its distinctive identity as the *Volk* who comes to itself in and through a confrontation with its poets and thinkers—even as he dispenses with the *political* sources of his myth. Or rather, Heidegger will now deploy

6. Agnes Heller, "Parmenides and the Battle of Stalingrad," *Graduate Faculty Philosophy Journal* 19, no. 2, and 20, no. 1 (1997): 247–262. No simple position can be taken on Heidegger's attitude toward politics during the Nazi era. Julian Young's claim that after 1935 Heidegger abjured National Socialism strikes me as a misconception that leads to the kind of apologetics practiced by Heidegger himself, *Heidegger, Philosophy, Nazism* (Cambridge: Cambridge University Press, 1997), 5. Young argues, for example, that "neither the early philosophy of *Being and Time*, nor the later, post-war philosophy, nor even the philosophy of the mid-1930s . . . stand in any essential connection to Nazism." Yet he does not really consider the works of other National Socialist philosophers like Baeumler, Heyse, Krieck, Hildebrandt, and others, to see whether this holds true. Heller's work is far more thoughtful and merits real consideration. Still, I would argue that Heller's essay doesn't really address the subtle shifts in Heidegger's politics from 1933 to 1939 to 1942 to 1944 that I think essential for coming to terms with his reading of the early Greeks.

7. Already in the lectures from WS 1937/38, "Basic Questions of Philosophy," Heidegger speaks of the need for "what is revolutionary"—but this is now four years after the political revolution of 1933 and the hopes of the Rectorial Address, BQP: 39/GA 45: 41. After 1938, he will become dissatisfied with the official NS party order and will try to cultivate his own more originary NS politics of autochthony.

the old myths of political autochthony in their concealed form as myths of ontological autochthony that renounce all traces of political self-assertion, even as they summon the "powers" of poetry and thinking for a recuperation of the first beginning. At this critical juncture in the history of the German *Volk* and in his own thinking, Heidegger will sever—at least rhetorically—the bond between political and ontological autochthony that we have been tracing in the Rectorial Address, the Schlageter speech, the "Germania" lectures, the Rome lectures, and in the *Introduction to Metaphysics*. After 1938, the aggressive political character of Heidegger's writing will be tempered by his growing awareness that the Nazis' form of National Socialism is but another example of devastation and world dominion. Even as Heidegger turns away from interpreting the essence of politics as something "political," however, can we in any sense speak of this as a shift in Heidegger's fundamental position? Is the turn from a language of will and self-assertion to one of waiting and releasement genuinely the mark of a "confrontation" with and "spiritual resistance" against National Socialism, as Heidegger himself maintained in his letter to the Freiburg Rector on November 4, 1945?[8] Should we even place an emphasis on Heidegger's own position vis-à-vis National Socialism, as if by inquiring into the particulars of his correspondence, course lectures, official activities, and the like we could uncover his genuine political position? Or is this project not perhaps fraught with its own metaphysical assumptions about politics that would hardly be able to determine the essential jointure of the political and the ontological that unifies Heidegger's thought path? In a fundamental sense, we need to ask: How can we can account for a change in Heidegger's political position if he continues to embrace the selfsame myth of ontological autochthony that animated his earlier political writings? In other words, how can we speak of a shift or a turn in Heidegger's thought from 1933 to 1945 if there is no essential break with his earlier conception of the history of philosophy and of the West—and of Germany's position within that history?

In this chapter, I want to focus attention on these questions by considering Heidegger's use and abuse of the longstanding myth of Graeco-German autochthony. I especially want to direct attention to the ways in which Heidegger's understanding of Greek myth and philosophy helped to shape both his politics of the *arche* as well as his later anti-political politics of the German future. As part of my plan for helping to excavate the sources of Heidegger's ontological politics, I want to establish a context within which to situate its myth of Graeco-German affiliation, its au-

---

8. Heidegger, "Documents from the Denazification Proceedings," 540–541. Despite the shift in rhetorical emphasis from that of will and self-assertion to a language of waiting and releasement, the essential vision of an autochthonic homeland does not change. It simply will be displaced poetically through a future directed Hölderlinian homecoming.

tochthonic retrieval of the archaic, and its chthonic archeology of the future. In order to do so, I will need to consider how Nietzsche's interpretation of Pre-Socratic philosophy, Hölderlin's vision of a Greek theophany, and the National Socialist reception of Plato helped to shape Heidegger's own politics of the *Aufbruch* in 1933, as well as his poetics of homecoming in the years after he lost his political faith. At the root of all these purported shifts, turns, and transformations, however, lies Heidegger's founding myth of autochthony.

II. HEIDEGGER'S ELEGY OF *ALETHEIA* AND THE GREEK BEGINNING

In his Karlsruhe lecture of 1930, "On the Essence of Truth," Heidegger laid the groundwork for all his later ontological politics. Clearly, as Theodore Kisiel has persuasively argued, we can find traces of the new language of Greek autochthony as far back as the Aristotle lectures of 1924.[9] There Heidegger will pose the question: "Does truth really find its ground in judgment, or has it been uprooted and displaced from a more native soil [*Bodenständigkeit*]?" In the original Karlsruhe lecture, Heidegger will again come to understand truth not as a matter of mere agreement between a subject and an object nor as a valid description of states of affairs that can be adequately represented through propositional statements. Instead, Heidegger will come to understand truth as disclosure, as the insight into the radical finitude of *Dasein* as that being whose existence is marked by the "da" as the open space for its own possibilities. But he will also move outside the sphere of traditional anthropocentrism and see disclosure as a function of entities themselves in their being. Simply put, Heidegger will now come to stress the non-human dimension of disclosure (a subtle shift from the human-focused phenomenology of *Being and Time*) as something intimately bound up with the very movement of being. In "On the Essence of Truth," he will seize upon this insight into the disclosive character of being and make it the cornerstone of his own thought. Henceforth, Heidegger will come to understand being as a playful process of turnings and reversals, concealment and revelation, closure and dis-closure, whose radically hidden character has been suppressed, forgotten, misprisioned, and contested by the long succession of Western philosophers since Plato. Consequently, Heidegger will deem it necessary to rewrite the history of philosophy in order to reclaim what he characterizes as the originary truth of being—*aletheia*.

Aletheia is a Greek word that is traditionally translated as "truth." In the standard lexica of Heidegger's day, it was also translated as "correctness"

---

9. Theodore Kisiel, "Situating Rhetoric/Politics in Heidegger's Practical Ontology (1923–25: The French Occupation of the Ruhr)," *Existentia* 9 (1999), 17.

(*Richtigkeit*), "veracity" (*Wahrhaftigkeit*), "genuineness" (*Aufrichtigkeit*), and "reality" (*Wirklichkeit*).[10] As part of his shift from the *Dasein*-centered ontology of *Being and Time* (that laid waste to the epistemological project of Neo-Kantian philosophy), Heidegger comes to translate *aletheia* in what he now determines to be its more originary sense as "unconcealment" or *Unverborgenheit* (PM: 144/WM: 84). Already in winter of 1929/30, Heidegger had written concerning *a-letheia*:

> In linguistics, the 'a' is termed alpha-privative. It expresses the fact that the word before which it is placed lacks something. In truth beings are torn from concealment. Truth is understood by the Greeks as something stolen, something that must be torn from concealment in a confrontation in which precisely *physis* strives to conceal itself. Truth is innermost confrontation of the essence of the human being with the whole of beings themselves. . . . It is not simply there; rather, as a revealing, it ultimately demands the engagement [*Einsatz*] of the whole human being. Truth is rooted in the fate of human *Dasein* as something it is part of. (FCM: 29/GA 29–30; 43–44)

In his original Karlsruhe lecture, Heidegger will think through the rootedness of truth in its most fundamental sense as rooted in the native soil of the Alemannic homeland and as rooted in the *arche* of the Western philosophical tradition. And he will find in the Pre-Socratic notion of *aletheia* an *arche* of his own. Already in *Being and Time*, Heidegger had attempted a deconstruction or de-structuring (*Abbau*) of the Western philosophical tradition. Now, however, he will reconceive that tradition by measuring it against the originary experience of *aletheia*:

> If we translate *aletheia* as 'unconcealment' rather than 'truth', this translation is not merely 'more literal;' it contains the directive to rethink the ordinary concept of truth in the sense of the correctness of statements and to think it back to that still uncomprehended disclosedness and disclosure of beings.

In this effort to rethink truth back to originary disclosure, Heidegger will likewise rethink Western history, especially its "beginning:"

> History begins only when beings themselves are expressly drawn up into their unconcealment and conserved in it, only when this conservation is conceived on the basis of questioning regarding beings as such. The origi-

10. Heidegger's tendency to play fast and loose with standard translations from the Greek is all too well known. Still, he depended upon the lexica of his day for philological background. I have checked three standard Greek-German editions from Heidegger's day for translations of *aletheia*: Adolf Kaegi, ed., *Benselers Griechisch-Deutsches Schulwörterbuch* (Leipzig: Teubner, 1904), 33; Menge-Güthling, *Enzyklopädisches Wörterbuch der griechischen und deutschen Sprache* (Berlin: Langenscheidt, 1913), 34; Franz Passow, *Handwörterbuch der griechischen Sprache* (Leipzig: Vogel, 1841), 97.

nary disclosure of beings as a whole, the question concerning beings as such, and the beginning of Western history are the same; they occur together in a 'time' which, itself immeasurable, first opens up the open region for every measure. (PM: 144–45/WM: 84–85)

In his original 1930 lecture, Heidegger had especially stressed the intersection of philosophy, history, and being at the *arche* of the tradition, when *aletheia* emerged from its hiddenness:

This threefold of the commencement [*Anfang*] of philosophy, the beginning [*Beginn*] of human history, and the first manifesting of nature as such—in its originary sense as *physis*—this threefold occurs together in the same world-moment.[11]

For Heidegger, the discourse concerning *aletheia* signifies not merely another historical narrative about the path of philosophy's development and its interpretation of being as *physis*. What emerges, rather, is a powerful narrative about the pilgrimage of truth through the whole of Western history, an elegiac retelling of philosophy's oldest myth about its origins and of Germany's relation to the myth. On the basis of this dynamic reading of truth as *aletheia*, Heidegger will rethink both the beginning and end of Western history, its *arche* and its *eschaton*. He will now focus attention not merely on the ontological condition of Western *Dasein* as historical; rather, he will read the history of the West itself ontologically, as a narrative of being's pilgrimage through, in, as, and of, time.[12] By the middle of the 1930s, Heidegger will even coin a new term to characterize his ontological reading of Western history on the basis of *aletheia* and *arche: Seynsgeschichte*, or the history of "be-ing." In *Beiträge*, Heidegger will offer an extensive reading of *Seyn* as the name designating the possibility of thinking the truth of "be-ing" from the position of "another beginning"—an *arche* of the future.[13] But even from the time of the Karlsruhe lecture, this new understanding of being in terms of archaic *aletheia* will help Heidegger to

11. To my knowledge, the editors of the *Gesamtausgabe* do not have plans to publish the original, *völkisch* version of "Vom Wesen der Wahrheit" from July, 1930, delivered at the Karlsruhe conference on "Festigung der Heimat" ("Strengthening the Homeland"). I have, however, consulted an early draft delivered on December 11, 1930, in Freiburg, in the possession of the Herbert Marcuse Archive in Frankfurt. The citation here is taken from this text, 0012.01 catalog number, page eight. For references to the earlier version, see NH: 9–13 and Heinrich Berl, *Gespräche mit berühmten Zeitgenossen* (Baden-Baden: Bühler, 1946), 61–68.

12. As part of his turn, or "Kehre," from the anthropocentric language and framing question of *Being and Time*, Heidegger will rethink the classic problem of historicity in Dilthey and Count Yorck von Wartenburg. Now, instead of focusing on the historicity of *Dasein*, Heidegger will turn his attention more pointedly to the historicity of *Sein*, rethought as a grand narrative of *Seynsgeschichte*.

13. Heidegger, GA 65: 3–4, 55, 175–186, to cite only some of these references in *Beiträge*, and GA 66: 83–106, 217–222.

find an ontological ground for his own political form of autochthony. Now German rootedness in the native soil will be reinforced by Greek rootedness in the originary truth of disclosure. This crossing of German and Greek roots in a discourse about truth and its beginnings will prove decisive for Heidegger through the 1930s and after. During this period, Heidegger's entire narrative history of Western philosophy will be shaped by privileging autochthony as the source of "greatness" (as he puts it in the Rectorial Address) and "salvation" (in the language of the "Europe" piece and the Heraclitus lectures) (HCW: 38/SdU: 19; EdP: 31, 40; GA 55: 108, 181). As autochthonous, the Greek *arche* will serve as the source, the inception, the root of Germany's identity. But the power of the Greek *arche* will not be limited to its determination of the past. In an essential sense, Heidegger will rethink the *arche* as futural as well and this will come to determine his hopes for the German people—even in the face of defeat in 1945.

In his Plato lectures of 1931/32, similarly entitled "On the Essence of Truth," Heidegger began to make this connection between the Greek beginning and the future oriented greatness of the Germans, a theme he would transform into the leitmotif of his Rectorial Address. If we think of the beginning merely as a point of entry or as something primitive, he writes, we will miss its inceptive power and remain in the grip of the inessential. "In everything inessential and without consequence the beginning is that which can be overcome and is overcome; hence, in the inessential there is progress! In the essential, however, there where philosophy belongs, the beginning can never be overcome—not only not overcome, but never even attained. In the essential, the beginning is the unattainable, that which is greatest, and because *we* no longer grasp anything of this beginning, everything in our country has fallen utterly to ruin" (GA 34: 15). After the National Socialist takeover, the beginning will be rethought as a revolutionary *Aufbruch,* or new departure, that will transform German historical existence.

In the early 1930s, this *arche*-discourse is marked by the language of violence and self-assertion.[14] A decade later, the martial references will be

14. In his lecture course from WS 1931/32, "Vom Wesen der Wahrheit," Heidegger offers a portrait of the philosopher as a heroic figure who, through an "act of violence" (*Gewalttat*), frees his fellow prisoners from the cave of political and cultural oppression, much as Plato's philosopher does in *The Republic* (514a-521c), GA 34: 80–81. Heidegger re-emphasizes that liberation from the cave must involve violence and that "the liberator must be a man of violent action." In the *Introduction to Metaphysics,* Heidegger also seizes on the theme of violence, or *Gewalt,* in his interpretation of Sophocles' choral ode from *Antigone.* He argues that the character of the human being as *deinon,* ("terrible/wonderful") can also be understood as violent. The poet, the thinker, the statesman—all are uniquely aware of the uncanny power of violence that lies at the heart of *physis* (IM: 157, 162, 164, 176/EM: 120–121, 124, 125, 134).

At the conclusion to his Hölderlin lecture from WS 1934/35, Heidegger asserted, "The

elided, yet Heidegger will still insist on the exclusive privileging of the Germans as the sole inheritors of the Greek patrimony. Employing the same rhetorical trope of Graeco-German autochthony as in the Rectorial Address, in 1943 Heidegger will claim that "the Germans and only the Germans can save the West in its history" (GA 55: 108). And, in 1945, he will persevere with his mythic designation of the Germans as the *Volk* who, like the Greeks, can be called "the *Volk* of poets and thinkers" (GA 77: 233).

As ever, Heidegger's myth of a German future will be authorized by the Greek *arche*. To read him in terms of this *arche* and to designate the "archaic" as decisive for Heidegger's thought path is already to have put forward a definite interpretation of his work. Much depends on just how keenly we want to excavate the depths of this kind of thinking—to initiate a kind of archeology of Heidegger's *arche*. If we read the *arche* narrowly as a definitive historical point of origin or as the temporal beginning of Greek political/philosophical experience, we will have missed Heidegger's meaning. *Arche* functions in Heidegger's work as the name designating the twofold character of the beginning: on the one hand, it names the origin as such as the source of all emergence or incipience; on the other, it designates the power that comes to presence in the origin itself. In this latter sense, the origin is understood as an *Ur-sprung* or "originary leap" out of history and its rosary bead model of sequential time. Rejecting the historicist tendency to fetishize the origin as the root cause of historical phenomena, Heidegger will instead interpret the *arche* in its etymological sense (from the Greek verb *archein* which means "to rule or govern") as the "ruling origin" of being.[15] As Heidegger defines it, the *arche* in this sense is not a temporally prior point of origination whose significance lies in its status as a precursor or antecedent. Rather, the *arche* derives its

---

violence of be-ing [*Seyn*] . . . must once again and in a genuine way come to question," GA 39: 294. Given his philosophical preoccupation with violence and the power of "bringing forth" the hiddenness of being, we need to look at Heidegger's practice of textual or hermeneutical violence more carefully. Heidegger self-consciously set out to violate the academic practices of his generation in an effort to unleash the hidden power of the poetic word that lay hidden beneath the scholarly apparatus of footnotes, textual citation, indexing, and philological accuracy that marked the study of Hölderlin, Nietzsche, and the ancient philosophers. Already in *Being and Time*, section 63, Heidegger will point to the necessity of doing violence in one's interpretive activity. For more references to violence in Heidegger's work, see GA 39: 66, 190, 292; GA 47: 304; GA 66: 16, 68, 420; GA 69: 76, 217; IM: 149–164/EM: 114–125; HHI: 63, 90/GA 53: 77, 112; EGT: 19, 57/H: 303, 343. This list is by no means exhaustive.

15. In his Nietzsche lectures from SS 1937, Heidegger writes: "Philosophy inquires into the *arche*. We translate that word as 'principle.' And if we neglect to think and question rigorously and persistently, we think we know what 'principle' means here. *Arche* and *archein* mean 'to begin.' At the same time, they mean to stand at the beginning of all; hence, to rule. Yet this reference to the designated *arche* will make sense only if we simultaneously determine that *of* which and *for* which we are seeking the *arche*." And, he will note, "to inquire into the *arche* . . . is metaphysics," Nii: 187, 189/GA 44: 208–209, 211–212.

power from, or rather unfolds its power as, something "futural [*zukün-ftig*]." In the winter of 1937/38, Heidegger writes: "The *futural* is the *beginning of all happening*. Everything is enclosed within the beginning. Even if what has already begun and what has already become seem forthwith to have gone beyond their beginning, yet the beginning—apparently having become itself something past—remains in power and abides, and everything futural comes into confrontation with it. In all genuine history, which is more than the mere sequence of events, futurity is decisive" (BQP: 35/GA 45: 36). In his political heyday, Heidegger will advocate a radical and revolutionary appropriation of the *arche* as the source of a ruling origin marked by a commitment to leadership (*Führerschaft*), service (*Dienst*), and struggle (*Kampf*). As late as 1937, Heidegger will write: "the original and genuine relation to the beginning is the revolutionary which, through the upheaval of the habitual, once again liberates the hidden law of the beginning" (BQP: 35/GA 45: 37).

After the conflagrations of *Kristallnacht* in November of 1938, however, Heidegger will take a step back from the revolutionary pronouncements of his earlier work. As we will see in the next chapter on Nietzsche, Heidegger will grow increasingly skeptical concerning the political metaphysics of power and will put forward a devastating critique of the political as an extension of modernist metaphysics in its Cartesian form. In his notebooks from 1938–1940, entitled *Die Geschichte des Seyns,* Heidegger will claim, "'power' must be removed immediately from the framework of 'political' observations and attitudes and factions. 'Power' can only be inquired about in its essence metaphysically. And only then if the essence of metaphysics is recognized and its beginning (starting point)—thus its completion—is experienced" (GA 69: 66). Heidegger will now read the history of being in terms of a new non-violent ethos of what he will term *Ereignis,* the mutual appropriation of humanity and being. This new framework of *Seynsgeschichte* will extend to Heidegger's interpretation of the political realities of his own day, including the political machinations of Stalin and Russian Communism.

Heidegger will contend that Communism is not merely a form of state power, a political worldview, or an economic doctrine; rather, he will see it as a metaphysical disposition of modern humanity that represents the end of the first beginning. "The 'dominion' of Communism is the end of the first beginning of the history of be-ing. The sudden rupture of the end of this history is the other beginning. In the first beginning be-ing prevails essentially [*west*] as emergent opening (*physis*); in the other beginning be-ing prevails essentially as the event of appropriation [*Ereignis*]" (GA 69: 213). In every sense, Heidegger's interpretation of Western history and of Germany's place within that history will be shaped by this myth of the beginning, the myth of the Greek *arche* that as the originary commencement of Western being rules over and governs its future. This myth of the *arche* as the myth of *aletheia* will function as the ontological justification for Germany's political status—in 1933, as the *Volk* "on the march . . . to its future history" and, in 1945, as the *Volk* "who still constantly waits for what is coming" (HCW: 34/SdU: 14; GA 77: 234). Even after the war, Heidegger will rehabilitate the myth in his reading of Anaximander as a way of ontologically redeeming a defeated Germany in a time of danger.[16]

Through all of the political turmoil, the myth of the *arche* will come to legitimate the linkage of Graeco-German autochthony and thus confirm Germany's elect status as the *Volk* chosen to save the West. Hence, despite the appearance of a kind of retreat from the *Sonderweg* power politics of his Nazi speeches, Heidegger will persevere in his commitment to German dominion, albeit now in a selectively ontological form. Abjuring Hitler's political conquest of Europe as the expression of a Cartesian will to domination, Heidegger will now turn to a discourse about *arche, aletheia, Seynsgeschichte,* and the Greek beginnings that attempts to colonize the West not as political-martial *Lebensraum* but as the space of ontological dominion. In the name of an Athenian autochthonic privilege— we are the genuine "children of the earth," the only ones with a true homeland, hence we shall rule—Heidegger will legitimate the German claim to privilege and domination as something granted to them by being itself.[17] This is not a racial metaphysics of the blood but a spiritual metaphysics of rootedness: in the soil and in the Greek beginning. Heidegger himself will claim "the *thought* of race, that is to say, calculating with race has its source in the experience of being as subjectivity and is not a 'political' issue. Race-breeding is a path of self-assertion [*Selbstbehauptung*] for the purpose of mastery" (GA 69: 70). In denying a biologistic metaphysics of blood, however, Heidegger will affirm a mythic metaphysics of autochthony. But what are the sources of this myth of autochthony that grants the Germans ontological privilege? How did Heidegger come to accept the power of this myth as the source of his history of being? Why did Heidegger choose the Greeks as his model for privilege and autochthony? And how did they come to function as the name for the archaic power of being itself? Heidegger's decision to read Western historical experience narrowly through the optic of a Greek genealogy rather than ecumenically as the story of interchange between both Occident and

16. Heidegger, EGT: 54/H: 339 and PM: 257/WM: 169, where Heidegger speaks of "nearness to the source" precisely in 1946. Despite the postwar tone of "internationalism," we can find traces of Heidegger's Germanocentric interpretation of Anaximander more clearly expressed in BC: 9, 81–106/GA 51: 11, 94–123.

17. See, for example, the article by Nicole Loraux, "Myth in the Greek City: The Athenian Politics of Myth," in *Greek and Egyptian Mythologies,* ed. Yves Bonnefoy, trans. Wendy Doniger (Chicago: University of Chicago Press, 1992), 40–46.

Orient, Hellenic and Hebraic, Athens and Jerusalem, has proven a dangerous one, given the history of our century. We need to look more critically at the sources of Heidegger's myths so that we can read Heidegger's postwar writings about the ecological shepherding of being and the rustic poetry of Hebel and Mörike in their proper context. I want to excavate the sources of Heidegger's myth of autochthony in the Greeks in order to rethink its domineering status as an underground version of the old 1933 myth of a "secret Germany."

III. THE ATHENIAN MYTH OF AUTOCHTHONY AND ITS GERMAN FATE

It would certainly be foolhardy to deny the pervasive influence of Greek or German culture in the formation of the West's own identity. Graeco-German thought has provided some of the most essential structures of self-definition that have shaped the grand narrative of Western history. And yet such an acknowledgment is not inherently tethered to a logic of exclusion and a metaphysics of autochthonic affinity, as it is in Heidegger's. Nonetheless the use and abuse of Greek philosophy for purposes of affirming a metaphysics of cultural exclusion, privilege, and hegemony did not commence with Heidegger. Already in his *Lives of Eminent Philosophers* from the early third century C.E., Diogenes Laertius underscored the singularly Greek origin of philosophy and excluded any trace of "barbarian" influence:

> There are some who say that the study of philosophy had its beginning among the barbarians. They urge that the Persians have had their Magi, the Babylonians or Assyrians their Chaldaeans, and the Indians their Gymnosophists; . . . If we may believe the Egyptians, Hephaestus was the son of the Nile, and with him philosophy began. . . . These authors forget that the achievements which they attribute to the barbarians belong to the Greeks, with whom not merely philosophy but the human race itself began.[18]

Diogenes' claim about the Greek origin of philosophy was itself rooted in another powerful myth about the Greeks as the very autochthons of human being. This discourse about Greek autochthony is virtually inseparable from that concerning the origins of philosophy. But in order to grasp the political function of the myth we need to consider its own origins.

The Greek myth of Erechtheus went back to ancient times and is first

18. Diogenes Laertius, *Lives of Eminent Philosophers*, trans. R. D. Nicks (Cambridge: Harvard University Press, 1959), 3–5. See also the insightful article by Robert Bernasconi, "Philosophy's Paradoxical Parochialism," in *Cultural Readings of Imperialism*, ed. K. Ansell-Pearson (New York: St. Martin's, 1997), 212–226.

made mention of by Homer.[19] Erechtheus, who is often confused with Erichthonius and perhaps originally identical with him, was a mythic king of Athens, the first ruler, the *archon* of the *arche*.[20] As his name indicates, he was of chthonic origin, born of the earth itself. In one telling of the myth, Erechtheus was the product of a failed assault by Hephaestus on Athena who rejected the god's advances, leaving his seed to fall upon the earth. The earth, in turn, became impregnated by the seed and in due time produced a son, a "child of the earth," half-human and half-serpent, who was cared for and protected by Athena. In some versions of the myth, he is even considered a serpentine or quasi-serpentine deity.[21] But it is not until the political turmoil of the fifth century that Erechtheus is transformed by the Athenians into a human ancestor-king who is the progenitor of a line of Athenian kings.[22] In an era of foreign invasion and internecine conflict with other Greek city-states over Athens' right to imperial rule, the Athenians will reframe the myth of Erechtheus to confirm their status as autochthonous "children of the earth," as those chosen to rule on the basis of their autochthonic origins.

In her masterful study of Athenian political self-formation, *The Invention of Athens,* Nicole Loraux argues that this myth of Athenian autochthony, which claimed that "the Athenians came first," will function as a justification for Athens' claim to political hegemony.[23] According to the

19. Homer, *The Iliad,* trans. Richmond Lattimore (Chicago: University of Chicago Press, 1961), book 2, lines 546–547. Timothy Ganz, *Early Greek Myth* (Baltimore: Johns Hopkins University Press, 1993), 233–247, offers an account of the Athenian myth of Erechtheus and Erichthonius and their relation to the theme of autochthony.

20. *The Oxford Classical Dictionary,* ed. N.G.L. Hammond and H.H. Scullard (Oxford: Clarendon Press, 1970), 405–406.

21. Philip Mayerson, *Classical Mythology in Literature, Art, and Music* (Glenview: Scott, Foresman, 1971), 172–173.

22. Vincent Rosivach, "Autochthony and the Athenians," *Classical Quarterly* 37 (1987): 294–306; John Peradotto, "Oedipus and Erichthonius: Some Observations on Paradigmatic and Syntagmatic Order," *Arethusa* 10 (1977): 85–101. See also W. Blake Tyrrell and Frieda Brown, *Athenian Myths and Institutions* (New York: Oxford University Press, 1991); and *Greek Tragedy and Political Theory,* ed. J. Peter Euben (Berkeley: University of California Press, 1986). In her article from this collection, "Myths and the Origins of Cities: Reflections on the Autochthony Theme in Euripides' *Ion,*" 252–273, Arlene Saxonhouse argues that Athenian autochthony proved to be both xenophobic and aristocratic. When the democratic element came to the fore in the late fifth century B.C.E., it had to confront the tensions between its male egalitarian ethos and its tradition of autochthonic privilege and exclusion. Women, slaves, and foreigners were, of course, excluded in this Athenian community—but so were other Greek city-states. The fantasy of patrilineal succession will dominate Athenian political discourse throughout this period. Heidegger would certainly have knowledge of these autochthonic sources and, like Nietzsche and Burckhardt, would unfailingly reject the democratic turn within Athens as an expression of decline.

23. Nicole Loraux, *The Invention of Athens,* trans. Alan Sheridan (Cambridge: Harvard University Press, 1986), 1–2, and *Born of the Earth: Myth and Politics in Athens,* trans. Selina Stewart (Ithaca: Cornell University Press, 2000).

myth, "the Athenians are 'unique among men' in all their exploits. Their uniqueness extends even to their origin: their autochthonous birth isolates them from the motley descendants of Pelops, Cadmus, Aegyptus, Danaus, and so on." But the myth will also function as a way to subjugate other non-autochthonous Greeks and to exclude them from political participation in the life of the city. In Loraux's view, the original myth of autochthony will "give the Athenians an aristocratic image of themselves" and will authorize rhetors like Lysias and Isocrates to "praise the Athenians for being born from their soil [and] . . . to bring out their nobility, which finds expression in the frequent opposition between the vulgar mass and the elite of the autochthones."[24] As Isocrates put it in *Panegyricus:*

> We did not become dwellers in this land by driving others out of it, nor by finding it uninhabited, nor by coming together here a motley horde composed of many races; but we are of a lineage so noble and so pure that throughout our history we have continued in possession of the very land which gave us birth, since we are sprung from its very soil.[25]

Aristotle too in the *Rhetoric* (1360b) will make a fundamental link between noble birth (*eugeneia*) and autochthony, claiming that "noble birth means that the members of a race or a city are sprung from the soil [*autochthonas*] or ancient [*archaious*]."[26] And Plato in the *Republic* (414b–415d) will have Socrates put forward a case for the "Noble Lie," a myth about the autochthonous birth of the city's ruling elite.

All of these Greek accounts of autochthony will be marked by the exalted claim that they alone among men were the first and that, on the basis of their archaic origins, they constituted an elect or chosen race who deserve to rule. The political uses of the myth were especially prominent in Athenian drama during the struggle with Sparta in the Peloponnesian War, but even afterwards, in the midst of defeat, the myth became serviceable as a rhetorical tool for enhancing Athens' position in Hellas.[27]

Given their tentative status as a late-developing political nation, it is hardly surprising that the Germans will appropriate the myth of originary kinship with the Greeks to sanction their own historico-metaphysical *Son-*

24. Loraux, *The Invention of Athens,* 149–150.

25. Isocrates, "Panegyricus," in *Isocrates,* trans. George Nolin (Cambridge: Harvard University Press, 1954), 1: 132–133.

26. Aristotle, *The "Art" of Rhetoric,* trans. J. H. Freese (Cambridge: Harvard University Press, 1975), 48–49. In his lectures from SS 1924, "*Grundbegriffe der aristotelischen Philosophie,*" Heidegger will take up this theme of autochthony in Aristotle and open a discussion of *Bodenständigkeit.* See the unpublished text of this course in the Herbert Marcuse Archive of the Stadt-und Universitätsbibliothek, Frankfurt am Main, #0005.01, 9 and 105.

27. For reference to autochthony in fifth-century Athens, see "Ion," in *Euripides,* vol. 4, ed. A. S. Way (Cambridge: Harvard University Press, 1980), lines 20, 30, 589; and "Acharnians," in *Aristophanes,* vol. 1, ed. B. B. Rogers (Cambridge: Harvard University Press, 1930), line 1076.

derweg in Western history. During the late eighteenth and early nineteenth centuries, this myth of Graeco-German autochthony will be set in place by Winckelmann, Humboldt, Schiller, Fichte, Hölderlin, and others, with the aim of establishing a new German cultural identity. As Walther Rehm asserts in his classic study, *Griechentum und Goethezeit,* there now develops a generational faith that "only through the Greeks can one pass into the heart of the Germans."[28] The tenets of this myth will function in a variety of ways: as the authorization of a new aesthetic religion; as the source of an authentic German homecoming; as the model for a path of cultural development that will rescue the Germans from the excesses of Latinity and Enlightenment; as the sign of German superiority over other nations owing to their Hellenic rootedness, and as the foundation for a new myth about the German future. On the basis of their shared autochthonic heritage, the Germans will now claim to be pre-eminent among nations since, as Humboldt put it, "the Germans possess the undeniable merit of being the first to have truly understood and profoundly experienced Greek culture."[29]

In a land divided by the different political jurisdictions of various states, duchies, principalities, kingdoms, provinces, and free cities, German poets, philosophers, and artists fused their yearnings for cultural unity into an image of a Germany reborn out of its filial bond to ancient Hellas. Philhellenism took many forms, but it flourished in Germany as a way of projecting the hopes for future unity back onto a past that was fragmented, unstable, and marked by political and religious divisions. In this sense, the original myth of Graeco-Germanic autochthony functioned as a way for Germany to reconstitute itself culturally in response to the political incursions launched by Napoleon in the first years of the nineteenth century.

Especially in *Addresses to the German Nation* (1808), delivered in French-occupied Berlin, we see Fichte marshaling the myth of autochthony for political effect. On the basis of a perceived affinity between the Greeks and the Germans in terms of their language and their shared fate as nations unified by culture rather than politics, Fichte will declare the Germans an *Urvolk* or "originary people."[30] They alone, Fichte will declare, are charged with a spiritual mission to rescue Europe. In this sense, Fichte will attempt to repatriate the Germans on the soil of antiquity in an effort to establish their elect status. But Fichte will also deploy the myth of autochthony as a way of excluding the non-German from his new cultural

28. Walther Rehm, *Griechentum und Goethezeit* (Bern: Francke, 1952), 367.

29. Hellmut Sichtermann, *Kulturgeschichte der klassischen Archäologie* (Munich: Beck, 1996), 157.

30. Johann G. Fichte, *Reden an die deutsche Nation* (Hamburg: Meiner, 1978), 106, 139, 214, 60.

politics of the originary. What separates the Germans and the non-Germans, Fichte will claim, is that "the Germans remained in their original dwelling places of the ancestral stock while the others emigrated elsewhere; the Germans preserved the original language of the ancestral stock while the others adopted a foreign language." In this invidious comparison between the native and the foreign, the autochthonous and the allochthonous, the German and the non-German, Fichte will reprise the ancient Greek practice of designating the "other," i.e., non-Greek, as "barbarian."

In a culture where one's own national identity is precarious because of foreign invasion, lack of political stability, and the emergence of cosmopolitan, enlightened values, this turn to the myth of Graeco-German autochthony takes on an important function—politically and otherwise. Much as the Athenians themselves, these late eighteenth and early nineteenth-century Germans will invoke the myth of autochthony as a way to assert their own national ideals and hopes for the future. In this sense, German Philhellenism will fulfill a variety of functions in a culture that seeks to reaffirm its own sense of rootedness in a period of foreign threats and assaults. By the time of Heidegger's Rectorial Address in 1933, the rhetorical context of political rootedness would be radically altered. And yet, despite all the changes symbolized by the dates 1848, 1871, and 1918, the logic of German autochthony will persist. Politically, the failed democratic ideals of the Frankfurt Parliament, the blood and iron tactics of Bismarck, the drive to world power in von Tirpitz and Kaiser Wilhelm II, the "stab in the back" legend promulgated by Ludendorff—all of these pointed to a radically different ideal of national identity. Culturally, the interpretation of antiquity undertaken by Bachofen, Burckhardt, Rohde, Nietzsche, and others succeeded in undermining the neo-classical model of Greece that had dominated the work of Germany's Second Humanism. Now these scholars' recovery of the chthonic element in archaic Greek religion, tragedy, and philosophy initiated a new understanding of antiquity that rejected the political uses of the older humanist myth. And yet, through all of these political and cultural changes, the myth of autochthony endured. Before I turn to a fuller consideration of Heidegger's use of this myth, however, I want to explore some of the ways it was appropriated by Heidegger's National Socialist colleagues in the 1930s for their own political visions of the German future.

IV. PLATO IN A BROWN SHIRT

To identify oneself with the Greeks as an originary *Volk* became, as we saw with Fichte, an orthodox German strategy for establishing a logic, a rhetoric, a metaphysics, a poetics, and, above all, a politics of autochthony. By authenticating their own identity as the "children of the earth," the Athenians had both inaugurated and authorized a vision of their past that proved politically useful.[31] By resuscitating this original Athenian myth and making it the basis for their own authorization of a new political future, the German Philhellenes set into place the foundations of a new myth of Graeco-German affinity. The effects of this retrieval were profound, extending into our own century and leaving their mark upon German academic life in powerful ways. Only the uses and abuses of the myth undertaken by the German professoriate during the National Socialist era has led succeeding generations to challenge the authority of this Philhellenic legacy. During the postwar era, German scholars have been forced to reconsider the ways in which the myth of Greek origins has both sanctioned and legitimized the most brutal and barbarous acts in the name of political exclusion.[32]

The Greeks—the first among races, that race "with whom not merely philosophy but the human race itself began," to repeat the myth of Diogenes Laertius—distinguished between themselves and others by virtue of their native autochthony. On the basis of this aboriginal distinction and in the name of an archaic authority conferred upon them in and through it, they divided humanity into two groups: "humanity properly speaking, composed of Greeks and of all those who speak Greek, and the others, the *barbarians*, those who talk gibberish, since there is but one language worthy of the name-Greek."[33] By virtue of this radical elision of all non-Greeks from the realm of the authentically human (i.e., Greek), Hellenic culture carried out the most tautologically pure form of self-assertion imaginable. The philosophical power of this kind of radical self-assertion would not be lost on Heidegger. In the summer of 1933, only weeks after his fateful Rectorial Address, Heidegger would reenact this originary Greek act of tautological self-assertion and exclusion in his lectures on "*Die Grundfrage*

---

31. Nicole Loraux, *The Children of Athena,* trans. Caroline Levine (Princeton: Princeton University Press, 1993); Jacques Derrida, *The Politics of Friendship,* trans. George Collins (London: Verso, 1997). Loraux and Derrida offer readings of autochthony that retrieve the *political* origins of autochthonic myth. Derrida will also point out that "the bond between the political and autochthonous consanguinity" can lead "to the worst symptoms of nationalism, ethnocentrism, populism, even xenophobia," 99–100).

32. For works dealing with the connections between the Greeks and National Socialism, see Volker Losemann, *Nationalsozialismus und die Antike* (Hamburg: Hoffmann & Campe, 1977); Suzanne Marchand, *Down from Olympus: Archeology and Philhellenism in Germany, 1750–1970* (Princeton: Princeton University Press, 1996); Teresa Orozco, "Das philosophische 'Bild der Antike' und der NS-Staat," *Das Argument* 32 (1990): 556–558; and Paul Böckmann, "Hellas und Germanien," in *Von Deutscher Art in Sprache und Dichtung,* vol. 5, ed. F. H. Ehmcke (Stuttgart: Kohlhammer, 1941), 341–404.

33. This is part of the argument made by Marc Froment-Meurice, *That Is to Say: Heidegger's Poetics,* trans. Jan Plug (Stanford: Stanford University Press, 1998), 25.

der Philosophie." German destiny, Heidegger would claim, is bound up with the task of recuperating the Greek beginning for a German future. "The German *Volk* is placed before the alternative: either it becomes itself or the world falls into barbarism. The question which we are dealing with in this lecture, this question is nothing other than preparing for the decision ... whether we will become a *Volk* or be overcome by some form of barbarism" (FarG: 194). Confronted by this binary alternative, Heidegger's response was clear: like the Greeks before them, only the Germans could circumvent the onslaught of an allochthonic barbarism. Like philosophy itself, which was originarily Greek and would have been unthinkable in a world of barbarism, the possibility of a German future depended on the purity of ontological kinship. Heidegger's message repeated the logic of autochthonic exclusion: only those who speak Greek (German) would be able to think philosophically. Even after the war and the collapse of his political hopes of autochthony, Heidegger would repeat the message of 1933. In the *Spiegel* interview of 1966, he would once again invoke the spirit of Fichtean exclusion. Asked by his interviewer whether he still believed that the Germans had specific qualifications for confronting the problems of the modern age, Heidegger replied: "Yes. . . . I am thinking of the special inner affinity of the German language with the language of the Greeks and with their thinking. This has been confirmed to me again and again by the French. When they begin to think they speak German. They insist that they could not get through with their own language."[34]

Here we can see that, long after the bombs had fallen on the streets of Freiburg near where he delivered his Rectorial Address, the same place where he earnestly invoked the Greeks in the name of a National Socialist revolution, Heidegger would still fall back upon the hidden power of the Greek *arche.* And yet the war would affect the form of the old myth. Already in the *Letter on Humanism* from 1946 we can detect a transformation. Now Heidegger's use of the Greeks will be circumscribed by a postwar retreat from a political form of Germanocentrism. In its stead, Heidegger will rely heavily on the linguistic affinity of Greek and German as a way of smuggling the myth of autochthony into the new postwar order—a kind of political correctness, post-Nazi style. But anyone familiar with the historical particulars of Heidegger's corpus can detect in his systematic rejection of Roman *humanitas* and Latin humanism the marks of the selfsame metaphysics of exclusion as in his National Socialist addresses. All of the tenets of the originary myth of *aletheia* with its peremptory rejection of all things Roman (i.e., Christianity, Renaissance Humanism, Italo-French-Gallic culture) are firmly in place. What we are left with is a catalog of as-

---

34. Martin Heidegger, "Spiegel Interview," in *Martin Heidegger and National Socialism,* 63; *Antwort,* ed. G. Neske (Pfullingen: Neske, 1988), 107–108.

sertions about Graeco-German affinity that cannot simply be dismissed as provincial schoolbook clichés but need to be understood as systematic expressions of a metaphysics of exclusion, a metaphysics of "race," that is as threatening as any "mere" biologism. In this sense, Heidegger's shift from the martial activism of 1933 to the passive "waiting" of 1945 needs to be understood as a shift in emphasis rather than as a shift of fundamental convictions. From 1938 and after, Heidegger will remain committed to his myth of Graeco-German autochthony even as he begins to understand National Socialism as bound up in the selfsame ethic of rootless nihilism and imperial domination as the metaphysically bankrupt Romans.

During this same period, Heidegger will also interpret Plato differently as he attempts to refine the twists and turns in his narrative history of the fate of Greek *aletheia*. Now he will situate the great shift in the interpretation of *aletheia*—from the experience of unconcealedness to the determination of truth as *homoiosis* (the "agreement" between subject and object)—in Plato's own work and reinterpret the history of metaphysics on the basis of this distinction. In doing so, Heidegger will recruit Plato as the first "humanist" and as the initiator of the end of the tragic age of the Greeks. In accordance with this shift, Heidegger will deem only the Pre-Socratics and the Greek tragedians as part of the archaic origins of Western thinking. This new interpretation of Plato is in many ways a departure from the one Heidegger put forth in "On the Essence of Truth" (1931/32) and the Rectorial Address. In these early years, Plato will provide Heidegger with his own model of philosophical praxis, an ideal one can find in the conclusion of the Rectorial Address: the philosopher as the heroic man of action who must withstand the storm of public criticism. In an unusually subtle reading of Plato's myth of the cave-dweller in the *Republic* (514a-521c), Heidegger will retrieve one of the essential truths of his philosophical thought path: the understanding of philosophy as something inseparable from myth. Myth becomes a staple of Heideggerian discourse. It functions as a name designating the originary, the primordial, the incipient, the inaugural, the archaic, and the autochthonic. And it becomes part of the essential language that Heidegger will draw upon in summoning his history of being as *aletheia* (P: 89/GA 54: 131). As Heidegger will put it in his *Introduction to Metaphysics*: "Originary history is . . . , if it is anything, mythology" (IM: 155/EM: 119).

But the uses of Platonic mythology were hardly unique to Heidegger. During the 1930s in Germany, the name "Plato" became synonymous with a National Socialist ideal of political self-assertion that would radically alter the portrait of Plato embraced by the older academic establishment. In place of the Neo-Kantian Plato, who was esteemed as a logician, a metaphysician, and an epistemologist, the National Socialist Plato will appear as a political philosopher of the state. Now, from out of the musty seminar rooms and the crowded lecture halls, a new Plato will emerge who will become the advocate of a reconstituted German *Reich* and whose works will be read in terms of Germany's contemporary political situation. National Socialist philosophers such as Ernst Krieck, Alfred Baeumler, Hans Heyse, Kurt Hildebrandt, Joachim Bannes, Herbert Holtorf, and others will now put forward "the new view that Plato is not an unworldly scholar but rather a statesman."[35] As Heyse put it in his 1936 inaugural lecture at Göttingen, "Plato starts with the question, which is not an arbitrary theoretical standpoint but rather springs from the historical necessity of a whole *Volk*... What does the genuine ontological and axiological constitution of the Greek man consist of? [...] Plato answers: the state—more precisely, the historical life of the Hellenic *polis*... and as Plato's philosophy proceeds from the fundamental values of Greek *Dasein* and reaches its height in the state, thereby creating the originary model for philosophy and science, so too our philosophy and science proceeds from the fundamental values of our Germanic-German *Dasein* in order to attain its highest rank and value in the idea and reality of the new *Reich*."[36] But Hildebrandt went even further. He took Plato's philosophical writings from the years after the Peloponnesian War as an index of the German situation after 1918 and argued that "the situation of Hellas after the victory of Lysander [404 B.C.E.] corresponds to the situation of Europe after the Peace of Versailles."[37]

Plato will now become the name designating a new reading of the Graeco-German myth of autochthony. And autochthony will now be in-

35. *Platons Vaterländische Reden*, ed. Kurt Hildebrandt (Leipzig: Meiner, 1936), 189. Teresa Orozco has done important work in situating the Plato reception of the 1930s within its National Socialist context. Her book, *Platonische Gewalt: Gadamers politische Hermeneutik der NS-Zeit* (Hamburg: Argument-Verlag, 1995) tries to position Gadamer's seemingly apolitical form of hermeneutics within its historical epoch, an effort that at times overstates its case. Nonetheless, I would argue that Orozco's work on the Platonic threads within NS philosophy has important implications for Heidegger's thought. Orozco summarizes her overall argument in a short piece, "Die Platon-Rezeption in Deutschland um 1933," in *"Die Besten Geister der Nation": Philosophie und Nationalsozialismus*, ed. Ilse Korotin (Vienna: Picus, 1994), 141–185.

36. Hans Heyse, "Die Aufgabe der Philosophie in der neuen Universität," in *Volk und Hochschule im Umbruch*, ed. Artur Schürmann (Berlin: Stalling, 1937), 47–49. In his Rectorial Address of December 4, 1933, *Die Idee der Wissenschaft und die deutsche Universität* (Königsberg: Gräfe & Unzer, 1935), 12, Heyse, like Heidegger, will take Plato as his model for reform of the German university—and German national existence. Heyse will contend that "the *Republic* is the originary form of the idea of the Reich."

37. Kurt Hildebrandt, ed., *Platon: Der Staat*, trans. A. Horneffer (Stuttgart: Kröner, 1955), ix–x. Hildebrandt published this edition in 1955 as part of a process of rehabilitating his reputation as a crude Nazi apologist. He made careful changes in this later edition, changes that covered over the racial metaphysics of the original 1933 edition, also published by Alfred Kröner, but in Leipzig. For example, in the 1955 edition all allusions to Hitler and "pure blood" are elided. For references to these topics, see pages x–xi and xxii–xxiii in the 1933 edition.

terpreted in the most radically political way possible: as a myth justifying German political-racial supremacy in the name of a violent exclusion of the barbaric "other." These German ideologues will turn to Plato as a way of legitimating their own vision of German national and racial supremacy. Part of their strategy will be to reassess the entire Platonic corpus in light of the doctrine of political and racial autochthony. In this new system of classification, Plato's most important works will be those dealing with the origins of the Athenians as children of the earth. To correspond with this new *Platonbild*, Hildebrandt will either translate or edit those works that demonstrate the genuinely political dimension of Plato's work. In one of his editions, entitled *Platons Vaterländische Reden (Plato's Discourses on the Fatherland)*, Hildebrandt will lay out for his readers the contemporary significance of Plato's dialogues. Within this scheme, the *Apology* becomes a discourse about the degeneracy of a democratic Athens that has abandoned the principles of rank and exclusion; the *Crito* will be interpreted as an attack on the apolitical element within the state, whereas the *Menexenus* will be read as an affirmation of eugenics and racial purity.[38]

If an earlier generation of scholars, led by Schleiermacher and Wilamowitz von Moellendorff, could question the authenticity of the *Menexenus,* or view it merely as an exercise in satire, that could only mean that they had missed its essential message. Hildebrandt insisted that these merely academic readings could not fathom "the most profound need of the *Volk* after the Great War whose hearts opened for a simple truth: pathos for the fatherland. In a deeply moving sense our own fate now bursts forth in Plato's discourse."[39] Not only was the *Menexenus* the authentic work of Plato, but above all of his other works it constituted "the true introduction to the *Republic*."[40] For Hildebrandt, the *Menexenus* becomes a key text because in it "Plato differentiates the idea of an eternal Athens from the degenerate Athens of the present."[41] In this Platonic distinction, Hildebrandt will find a model for his own distinction between the ideal of a "Secret Germany" and the degenerate democracy of Weimar. This practice of separating the pure from the degenerate was hardly a new one in the history of German Hellenomania. On the contrary, it was at the root of Germany's myth of an archaic Greek origin. In his *History of Ancient Art*

---

38. Hildebrandt, ed., *Platons Vaterländische Reden*, 7–76.

39. Ibid., 63.

40. *Platon: Der Staat* (1933 edition), xxiii.

41. *Platons Vaterländische Reden*, 65. Hildebrandt's work weds the National Socialist politics of race and autochthony to a Platonic ideal of *eugeneia*. On Hildebrandt's reading, Plato's *Republic* can be read—indeed *should* be read—as a strong reaction against the mixing of autochthonous, racially pure Athenians and the allochthonous, racially mixed inhabitants of the seaport city of Piraeus. Plato's dialogue appears to him as an example of an "originary Hellenic" impulse, not a utopian one. See Kurt Hildebrandt, *Platon: Der Kampf des Geistes um die Macht* (Berlin: Bondi, 1933), 227.

(1764), Winckelmann had already laid down the fundamental law of Graeco-German autochthony: "to seek the source itself and return to the beginning in order to find truth, pure and unmixed."[42] A century later, Jacob Burckhardt would revive the Winckelmannian myth of the *arche* in his lectures entitled *Griechische Kulturgeschichte*. Burckhardt became intrigued by the Attic myth of autochthony and its relation to the telluric forces within the Greek homeland. But even as he explored the topic of "an originary autochthonous population . . . dwelling still in the very place where once the human race originated with them," Burckhardt never exploited the myth for the purpose of political dominion.[43] In the hands of Hildebrandt and his National Socialist colleagues, however, Winckelmann's aesthetic ideal of an *arche* and Burckhardt's historical account of autochthony would be transformed into a racial myth of Graeco-German kinship, purity, and exclusion. And the philosophical source for this racial myth would be found in Plato.

In the *Menexenus* (which is really a recollection by Socrates of a funeral oration delivered by Aspasia), Plato writes about Athenian nobility of birth and its relation to autochthony:

> Now as regards [the Athenians'] nobility of birth [*eugeneias*], their first claim thereto is this—that the forefathers of these men were not of immigrant stock, nor were these their sons declared by their origin to be strangers in the land sprung from immigrants, but children of the earth, sprung from the soil [*autochthonas*], living and dwelling in their own true fatherland. (237b)

> So firmly rooted and so sound is the noble and liberal character of our city, and endowed with such a hatred of the barbarian, because we are pure-blooded Greeks, unadulterated by barbarian stock. (245d)[44]

By binding noble birth and indigenous origin to the notions of eugenics and autochthonic exclusion, Plato will construct his ideal of an eternal Athens, an ideal that will serve as the foundation of Graeco-Germanic

---

42. Johann Joachim Winckelmann, *Geschichte der Kunst des Altertums* (Vienna: Phaidon, 1936), 321.

43. Jacob Burckhardt, *Griechische Kulturgeschichte* (Leipzig: Kröner, 1930), 1: 22–23. Burckhardt's conservative politics never veered into the dangerous waters of racial exclusion and militant nationalism.

44. Plato, *Menexenus*, trans. R. G. Bury (Cambridge: Harvard University Press, 1942), 341–343 and 369 for the Loeb Classical Library edition. I have also found it both helpful and illuminating to consult the standard German translation of Plato by Schleiermacher in Platon, *Werke* (Darmstadt: Wissenschaftliche Buchgesellschaft, 1990), 2: 231–233, 255.

affinity. Or so Hildebrandt will argue. Athens' "bond to the autochthony-myth of the origin establishes the racial purity of Attica."[45] And as a pure bred Athenian writing for a generation threatened by the influx of metics from within and barbarians from without, Plato wanted to "praise noble birth and *eugeneia*." As Hildebrandt put it, "Plato's pride in Athens is racial and race, in turn, is cherished as the originary breeding come forth from the landscape! How could he have presented this *völkisch* idea more purely and more powerfully than through the ancient Athenian myth of autochthony? Only the Attic race is originally born from the earth itself."[46] And the parallels with Germany concerning the threat of racial mixing seem obvious to Hildebrandt. Whoever considers the Greek response to the collapse of Athens after the Peloponnesian War, "thinks at the same time of Europe's ingratitude to Germany in 1919. To such a person it appears as if Plato were speaking directly about our circumstances. Since no *Volk* stands as close to Hellenic poetry, art, and philosophy as the Germans, we cannot deny that the political events of our time are directly bound in a spiritual sense to those described in the *Menexenus*."[47]

In their own discourses concerning a Graeco-German bond, Heyse, Krieck, and Baeumler will find similarly in Plato the model of National Socialist revolution. For these party members, Plato's "postulates of racial breeding and racial hygiene [serve] as the natural foundation of state education."[48] In Krieck's view, "race" and "blood" become "spiritual values" for Plato: "noble blood, the embodiment of noble races, and the best of human stock signify the biological foundation of everything spiritual." Baeumler too will find the elements of a new racial-political model of education in Plato's political philosophy. In his inaugural lecture of 1933 at the University of Berlin, Baeumler will speak out against the Neo-humanist appropriation of antiquity that had formed the nineteenth-century vision of Graeco-German affinity. If "the Neo-humanist portrait of the Greeks was determined by art and science," Baeumler argues that "our modern vision of the Greeks is determined by the *polis*." As he puts it, "if the life that lies before us will be a life in the state, a political life, then it is also a Greek life." As the model of this new political form of German exis-

45. *Platons Vaterländische Reden*, 69. Hildebrandt also offers a political-racial reading of autochthony in his full-length study, *Platon: Der Kampf des Geistes um die Macht*, 145-146. There he argues that Athens had to shape its own identity and freedom by setting itself up against the "barbarians." Plato did not "shrink from finding the pure idea of a Hellenic Greece of genuine blood—the 'race'—in Attica. He presented this thought in a highly impressive way in the ancient Attic myth of autochthony [*Autochthonie*], of being sprung forth from the earth."

46. *Platon: Der Staat* (1933 edition), xxii.

47. *Platons Vaterländische Reden*, 68.

48. Ernst Krieck, *Philosophie der Erziehung* (Jena: Eugen Diederichs, 1930), 119, 116.

tence, Baeumler cites the "greatest book on education in the Greek world: Plato's *Republic*."[49]

V. THE POLITICS OF HELLENOMANIA

What emerges from these National Socialist readings of Plato is a unified sense that the Platonic *polis* can provide a model for a more authentically German form of existence. Part of their plan will be to use Plato in the service of a National Socialist *Aufbruch* that will re-establish an originary connection between the Germans and their Greek ancestors, a connection that they believed was lost in the historicist Philhellenism of the nineteenth century. Baeumler will prove himself a tireless critic of the established academic industry of Hellenomania. The Neo-humanist emphasis on interiority, aesthetic sensibility, the cultivation of personal taste, and the bourgeois pride in *Bildung* will strike him as an exercise in pettifoggery and self-aggrandizement. In his battle-piece, "*Der Kampf um den Humanismus*" (1935), Baeumler will unleash an assault against the Neo-humanist tradition that challenges its aesthetic view of history:

> National Socialism has an *immediate* and *direct* relation to Greek civilization based on the concept of race. This relation is not one mediated by classicism or humanism. In Greece we find pure Nordic blood, not blood mixed with the Etruscan or other Oriental stock as in Rome. The anti-humanist movement is bringing this *immediate* relation to Greek civilization into the present. We have a tradition of relating to antiquity—but it is not the humanist one. It is the tradition of Winckelmann, Hölderlin, and Nietzsche. Knowledge of this immediate relation between Greek and German culture confirms the accuracy of the racial view of history.[50]

Baeumler's Nordic ideology aside, Heidegger too would join his National Socialist colleagues in recruiting Plato for the new German revolution. As we saw in the Rectorial Address, Heidegger employed Plato's scheme of a tripartite division within the *polis* as the model for his three forms of service to the state: labor, military, and knowledge service. And he too would yoke the meaning of Plato's political philosophy to the National Socialist rhetoric of *Kampf*—especially the *Kampf* versus humanism that, in light of the changed political circumstances after the war, Heidegger would reframe into his famous "Letter on Humanism." But there were other parallels as well. Hans Heyse found in Plato's political philosophy "the fundamental values of our Germanic-German *Dasein*" and sought "to 'rewrite' history . . . so as to gain a new relationship to the Greeks (this

---

49. Alfred Baeumler, *Männerbund und Wissenschaft* (Berlin: Junker & Dünnhaupt, 1943), 137.

50. Alfred Baeumler, *Politik und Erziehung* (Berlin: Junker & Dünnhaupt, 1937), 64–65.

Volk whose affinity with us is both natural and elective), and to its highest representative—Plato."[51] And, like Heyse, Heidegger too turned to Plato as a model for Graeco-German affinity and for a new *mythos* of the German future. Especially in the early 1930s, Plato became for him the authority legitimating the elect status of the Germans as the *Volk* chosen to save the West by reclaiming originary Greek *aletheia*. Moreover, Plato also became an important source for confirming Heidegger's vision of Graeco-German autochthony. Unlike Hildebrandt, Baeumler, Krieck, and Heyse, however, Heidegger rejected the biological link between Greeks and Germans. For him, what established the "special inner relationship" between the two peoples was not blood or race but the metaphysical affinity of their languages and their shared experience of rootedness in the earth. Already in the summer of 1930, Heidegger could claim that "only our German language still corresponds to Greek in terms of its philosophical character of depth and creativity" (GA 31: 51). And as far back as the summer semester of 1924, in his lectures on Aristotle, Heidegger was insisting that "we need to win back the sense of rootedness and autochthony [*Bodenständigkeit*] that was alive in Greek philosophy."[52]

Contra Hildebrandt, Heidegger did succeed in dislodging the racial metaphysics of *eugeneia* from the ontological rootedness of the *autochthon*. And yet even as he broke with the crude biologism of his National Socialist contemporaries, we can find in Heidegger's persistent commitment to the myth of a special Graeco-German affinity the elements of a National Socialist metaphysics of race—grounded in autochthony rather than in biology. To raise this question is not to engage in the practice of guilt by association, however—as if because Heidegger shared Baeumler's rejection of Latin humanism and German Philhellenism, Krieck's commitment to a special German mission, Heyse's belief in the natural kinship between Greeks and Germans, and Hildebrandt's exclusionary metaphysics of autochthony, he too can be labeled a bona fide Nazi. It is, rather, to situate Heidegger's tendentious retrieval of Greek metaphysics in its proper context and to acknowledge the political origins of his idiosyncratic form of Hellenomania. Even Heidegger's own denials about his

51. Hans Heyse, *Idee und Existenz* (Hamburg: Hanseatische Verlagsanstalt, 1935), 296–297.

52. Martin Heidegger, *Grundbegriffe der aristotelischen Philosophie*, unpublished lectures SS 1924, from the Herbert Marcuse Archive in the Stadt-und Universitätsbibliothek in Frankfurt am Main, #0005.01, 6. Heidegger would transform the categories of Aristotelian rhetoric into a confrontation with the French authorities occupying the Ruhr area. This rhetorical move is comparable to the one Heidegger made in his 1924 speech "Dasein und Wahrsein nach Aristoteles"; see Theodore Kisiel, "Situating Rhetoric/Politics in Heidegger's Practical Ontology," 11–30. Kisiel succinctly states the essential question of the lecture: "Does truth really find its ground in judgement, or has it been uprooted and displaced from a more native soil (*Bodenständigkeit*)?" In SS 1924, Heidegger will raise the same question—with all its political connotations as well.

"political" use of the Greeks in the *Ister* and *Parmenides* courses should not dissuade us from understanding the fundamentally political context of his myth of the Greek *arche* and of his *Seynsgeschichte*. As Heidegger himself will argue in 1942:

> The polis. Today—if one still reads such books at all—one can scarcely read a treatise or book on the Greeks without everywhere being assured that here, with the Greeks, 'everything' is 'politically' determined. In most of these "research results" the Greeks appear as pure National Socialists. This overenthusiasm on the part of scholars seems not to even notice that with such 'results' it does National Socialism and its historical uniqueness no service at all, not that it needs it anyway. These enthusiasts are now suddenly discovering the 'political' everywhere. . . . (HHI: 79–80/GA 53: 98)

But as Heidegger would emphasize in the *Parmenides* lectures:

> The essence of the *polis*, i.e., the *politeia*, is not itself determined or determinable 'politically.' The *polis* is just as little something 'political' as space itself is something spatial. The *polis* itself is only the pole of *pelein*, the way the being of beings, in its disclosure and concealment, disposes for itself a 'where' in which the history of a human race is gathered. Because the Greeks are the utterly unpolitical *Volk*, unpolitical by essence, because their humanity is primordially and exclusively determined from being itself, i.e., from *aletheia*, therefore only the Greeks could, and precisely had to, found the *polis*, found abodes in which the gathering and preserving of *aletheia* happens. (P: 96/GA 54: 142)

And yet despite Heidegger's all too obvious rejection of the political dimension of National Socialism, especially its ideology of world domination bound up with the metaphysics of *Machenschaft* and *Gestell*, we should try to understand how powerfully Heidegger's work was affected by it. Years after the war, particularly in the 1962 notebooks from his first tour of Greece (*Aufenthalte*) and in his 1967 address to the Academy of Sciences and Arts in Athens, Heidegger continued to embrace the mythology of an archaic Greek beginning marked by the originary ruling power of *aletheia* that shapes Western destiny.[53] Near the end of the journal describing his last days in Greece in 1962, Heidegger will write:

> Modern technology and the scientific industrialization of the world relentlessly dispatch themselves, extinguishing every possibility of sojourning.

> Nevertheless the strange conclusion of my Greek tour in Delphi, though it was already timely, was not a departure from Greece. While the ship steered

53. Martin Heidegger, *Aufenthalte* (Frankfurt: Klostermann, 1989); and "Die Herkunft der Kunst und die Bestimmung des Denkens," in *Distanz und Nähe*, ed. Petra Jaeger and Rudolf Lüthe (Würzburg: Königshausen & Neumann, 1983), 11–22.

its way out of the Corinthian Gulf into the Ionian Sea, the whole of ancient Greece transformed itself into a single, self-contained island against all other known and unknown worlds. The departure became an arrival. What transpired and brought with it the warrant of its enduring character was the sojourn of the departed gods opening itself to remembrance. (A: 33)

And, in a 1966 letter to Hannah Arendt, written from the pastoral landscape of the cabin in Todtnauberg, Heidegger would succinctly restate the myth of *aletheia* that he drew upon in *Aufenthalte:* "In the meantime my three sojourns in Greece with Elfride—in part cruises, in part living in Aegina—have borne testimony to this one thing, which even now can barely be thought: that *A-Letheia* is not merely a word or the matter of etymologizing but the still reigning power of presence in all beings and things. And no technological structure [*Ge-stell*] can thwart it [*verstellen*]" (AHB: 153).

The eco-poetic and pastoral quality of this prose notwithstanding, we need to begin to see what is genuinely at stake in Heidegger's discourse on the Greeks. The pastoral images of rootedness in the landscape that we saw deployed in Schlageter's funeral oration; the Hölderlinian song of the lost homeland; the departed gods that pervaded the lectures on "Der Ister" and the discussions of "Germania"; the Platonic discourse about rootedness in the earth that found its way into the Rectorial Address and the lectures, *On the Essence of Truth;* and the Pre-Socratic idyll about the still enduring power of *aletheia* that animated the *Parmenides* lectures—all these need to be rethought in terms of their own political, cultural, and rhetorical landscape. These Heideggerian "topics for thought" are not merely elegiac variations on the innocent myth of Arcadia now transplanted into the Alemannic soil of the Black Forest. On the contrary, they constitute the subterranean or chthonic depth-dimension of a National Socialist metaphysics of racial exclusion and superiority that will be dislodged from the biological sphere of *eugeneia*, blood, and consanguinity even as it is reconfigured rhetorically in the pastoral language of autochthony. Such a maneuver is political to the core, even if it engages in a rhetoric of the anti-political. And the logic of autochthony is always marked by such exclusion. Autochthony affirms the privileged status of one group while at the same time designating the allochthonous groups as the "other." Heidegger's elegiac reveries about the homeland, rootedness, the Alemannic soil, and German affinity with the Greeks are all marked by the binary logic of inclusion and exclusion. The non-Greek, the non-German, the "Roman," the "Jew," the female, the "Asian," the "liberal," the "humanist," the "American," the "Senegal Negro," the "barbarian" are all figurations of a philosophy that is committed to a myth of hierarchy and exclusion, an ontological *Sonderweg* of German self-assertion that endures even after the martial rhetoric of Nazi self-assertion recedes from view.[54]

Indeed, I am arguing that Heidegger's use of the Greeks is always political—even if after 1938 his rhetoric of Hellenomania was resolutely configured in the language of the apolitical. We can find traces of such subtle maneuvering in those texts written just after the war when Heidegger was desperately trying to rehabilitate his work in light of the teaching ban imposed on him by the De-Nazification committee. For example, in his short essay, "The Anaximander Fragment" (1946), Heidegger adopts the rhetorical posture of "stubbornly insisting on thinking Greek thought in Greek fashion." Nonetheless, he assures his readers, "in our manner of speaking, 'Greek' does not designate a particular *Volk* or nation, nor a cultural or anthropological group. What is Greek is the dawn of that destiny in which being illumines itself in beings and lays claim to a certain essence of the human being; that essence unfolds historically as something fateful, safeguarded by being and released without ever being separated from it" (EGT: 25/H: 310). And yet Heidegger's "Greeks" do not merely designate the name of a Western destiny; they also authorize and legitimate a cultural form of racism. In the name of an originary axis of Graeco-German kinship, affinity, patrimony, ancestry, and descent, whose ground is never really examined in a philosophically rigorous fashion, Heidegger simply announces the dawn of a new destiny. Considered systematically, Heidegger's historical narrative of the West, rethought and reconfigured in terms of recuperating an originary Greek *arche* for a "futural" German *eschaton,* is predicated upon the purity of Greek myth and its still reigning power. In truth, however, the Greek homeland that Heidegger sought to retrieve never really existed. As Philippe Lacoue-Labarthe has put it, "Heidegger, following Hölderlin's practice directly, 'invents' a Greece which has never actually seen the light of day: repetition in the Heideggerian sense is repetition of what has not occurred."[55]

Heidegger often underscored the fact that the Greeks, "his" Greeks, were difficult to recover, given the occlusions and subterfuges of the nineteenth-century industry of German academic Philhellenism that covered over their originary character. As he put it in 1937/38, only Hölderlin and Nietzsche were capable of inaugurating a proper retrieval of the Greek

---

54. One could put together a veritable catalog of citations from Heidegger's *Gesamtausgabe* about his targets of criticism. For a partial list, see: GA 56/57: 72–73; L: 38; Niii: 69/GA 47: 134, on the "Senegal Negro" and the African tribe. On Heidegger's attitude toward America, see: GA 45: 54–55; GA 52: 10–11, 27, 35, 80; GA 53: 68, 80, 86, 112, 179, 191; GA 55: 107; GA 65: 149; GA 67: 150; PLT: 113/H: 268–269; SI: 280–281/Antwort: 105–106; QCT: 135, 153/H: 87–88, 103–104, and IM: 37, 42, 45, 50/EM: 28, 32, 34, 38. On his attitude toward the Asian, see GA 13: 21; GA 29/30: 110; GA 39: 133–134; GA 43: 24–25; DE: 21; EdP: 31.

55. Philippe Lacoue-Labarthe, *Heidegger, Art, and Politics* (Oxford: Blackwell, 1990), 58.

arche, only "these two knew the Greek beginning in a more originary way than all previous epochs" (BQP: 110/GA 45: 126). And yet, in some essential sense, Heidegger's retrieval of the Greeks has as many affinities with the work of Hildebrandt and Baeumler as it does with that of Hölderlin or Nietzsche. Within Heidegger's thought, the very topology of the Greek world signified a political program of re-writing the history of the West in accordance with *völkisch* principles. As part of this process, Heidegger would rethink these principles in terms of their *principia,* now freed from the Latinate metaphysics of the *princeps* (prince, ruler) and translated as and through the *arche.*[56] Given the emphasis that Heidegger placed upon the *arche,* we would do well to inquire about its status within his work—even as we deconstruct it down to its political roots. *Arche* functions as the name of a myth: the desire for pure origin, primordiality, incipience, inauguration, dawn, and commencement. Reconfigured in the encoded language of Greek autochthony, however, Heidegger's discourse on the Greek term "*arche*" will come to signify the metaphysical movement of dominion, power, command, ascendancy, and rule. Even in its etymological sense, *arche* connotes the ruling power of origination.[57] For Heidegger, *arche* rules in the name of a higher *princeps* that authorizes a hierarchical ordering of nations, *Völker,* races, languages, cultures, and states on the basis of a chimerical archaicism: the primacy of the Greeks. Within this system of signifiers, the term "Greek" will function as the historical name for the *arche* itself. And the *arche,* in turn, will function as the mythical source for rethinking the history of the West in terms of this hierarchical system. In this sense, we can speak of a politics of the *arche,* a politics which, as a way of ordering three thousand years of Western history, will transfer ontological sovereignty from the Greeks to the Germans in the name of an archaic and primordial ruling origin. The very language of such a project will invoke the power of the mythic.

VI. THE POLITICS OF A SINGULAR *ARCHE*

Plato himself knew that in the founding of the *polis* myth plays an important role. In his own philosophical tale about the origins of the *polis* in the *Republic,* Plato has Socrates forge his own myth about the autochthonic origin of its citizens. As Socrates begins to construct his city-in-speech, he tells Glaucon that the most pressing task of the wise legislator is to convince the citizens of their shared autochthonic kinship:

---

56. Reiner Schürmann, *Heidegger on Being and Acting: From Principles to Anarchy,* trans. Christine-Marie Gros (Bloomington: Indiana University Press, 1986), 106–114.
57. Hjalmar Frisk, *Griechisches Etymologisches Wörterbuch* (Heidelberg: Carl Winter, 1973), 1: 158.

I shall try to persuade first the rulers, then the soldiers, and then the rest of the city that all the training and education they have received from us are actually products of their own imaginations, just the way it is with a dream. In truth, they were the whole time deep within the earth being given form and feature. . . . When the process was complete, they were all delivered up to the surface by their mother earth, whence it comes that they care for their land as if it were mother and nurse and feel bound to defend it from any attack. Likewise do they regard their fellow citizens as brothers, born of the same soil, children of the selfsame earth. (*Republic* 414 d–e).[58]

For Plato, as for Heidegger, the repatriation of the Greek *polis* on the soil of an archaic earth constituted a mythic substitution of autochthony for the consanguinous bond of blood and race.[59] In this mythic turn, Plato proffered an autochthonous form of *eugeneia* practiced with the philosophical art of *mythos*. As in Heidegger, there is a threat to the mythic purity of the *polis* in the form of a mixed population of citizens and foreigners. When Socrates "goes down to the Piraeus" at the beginning of the *Republic,* he will confront a foreign goddess and a procession of non-Athenians. And yet Plato does not condemn the foreign as such; he is not threatened by the Athenian equivalent of a "Judification of the German spirit,"[60] whereas Heidegger clearly is. By carefully attuning ourselves to the rhetorical dynamics and strategic deployment of this Platonic myth of autochthony in a new German context, we can begin to decipher Heidegger's encoded references to rootedness, *arche,* and origin as political claims to exclusion, de-limitation, and dominion. Those of us who read Heidegger for his powerful insights into the historical shifts within the Western tradition need to begin to look more critically at the effects of his mythic formulations on our own philosophical practices. And we especially need to rethink Heidegger's interpretation of the Greeks.

As is clear to anyone who has studied Greek culture in systematic fashion, Heidegger's portrait of "the Greeks" is wildly oversimplified. In his own earnest haste to rethink Greek history in terms of a *Seynsgeschichte* rooted in *aletheia,* Heidegger often forgets his own insight that there is not "one" Greece but rather many. As a result, he sometimes winds up conflating the Pre-Socratic concern for the *arche* with the Athenian myth of autochthony. We can find the traces of this tendentious and hermeneutically violent style of reading in Heidegger's choice of topics for his lecture courses. After 1933, Heidegger's focus on Greek philosophy is limited to a

58. Plato, *The Republic,* trans. Richard Sterling and William Scott (New York: Norton, 1985), 113; and *Platon: Der Staat,* 109.

59. Marc Shell, *Children of the Earth: Literature, Politics, and Nationhood* (Cambridge: Harvard University Press, 1993), 147. Shell also argues that the "Noble Lie" of Socrates about national kinship is part of the "fiction of common autochthony," 12.

60. Compare my comments in chapter 1, section 5. See also notes 37–41 in this chapter for Hildebrandt's National Socialist view.

discussion of three Pre-Socratic thinkers—Anaximander, Parmenides, Heraclitus—and beyond that only to Plato and Aristotle. Within his mythic history of Western thought there are, however, only three "primordial" thinkers. As Heidegger put it in the *Parmenides* lectures: "the first primordial thinker was named Anaximander. The two others, the only others beside him, were Parmenides and Heraclitus" (P: 2/GA 54: 2). In the name of an originary history of being, Heidegger dispenses with the merely "historical." Instead, following Nietzsche's injunction in *Untimely Meditations* to interpret the past only out of the vitality of the present, he attempts to free history from the noxious malady of historicism that he sees poisoning the modern interpretation of antiquity.[61] In this process, Heidegger will shift emphasis from Nietzsche's focus on the present to his own Germanocentric myth of the future:

> The beginning never allows itself to be represented or considered in historiography. . . . Historiographical [*historische*] considerations attain only the past and never reach the historical [*das Geschichtliche*]. . . . The historical is not the past, not even the present, but the future. . . . *The future is the origin of history. What is most futural, however, is the great beginning.* (BQP: 38–39/GA 45: 40–42)

Within this "futural" scheme, what is not primordial becomes merely historiographical. Hence, thinkers such as Anaximenes, Empedocles, Democritus, Anaxagoras, or Zeno—all of whom, within Heidegger's *seynsgeschichtliche* narrative, fail to think primordially—are excluded from consideration. Moreover, the whole Hellenistic tradition of philosophy is rendered nugatory with one stroke. In a sweeping gesture of dismissal, Heidegger will boldly reconfigure the history of philosophy from his writing desk in Todtnauberg.[62] Asian philosophy will not even be seriously addressed. However, it is within the realm of early Greek history and culture that Heidegger's contributions appear to be most hermeneutically violent. The rhapsodic meditations on the Greek dawn that pervade Heidegger's work characteristically simplify the historical evidence. In excavating the "essential" sources of Greek *aletheia*, Heidegger will conflate Pre-Socratic *arche* with Athenian autochthony. The term "archaic" will now designate an experience rather than an epoch. In keeping with the tenor of this approach, Heidegger will likewise employ the word "Greek" as a term

61. Friedrich Nietzsche, *Untimely Meditations*, trans. R.J. Hollingdale (Cambridge: Cambridge University Press, 1983), 94/KSA 1: 293–294. Unfortunately, I have not been able to read Heidegger's lectures from WS 1938/39 since they are still being edited by Hans-Joachim Friedrich. They are scheduled to appear as volume 46 of the *Gesamtausgabe* under the title *Nietzsches II. Unzeitgemässe Betrachtung.*

62. Rainer Martin has put forward a thoughtful critique of Heidegger's Graecophilic history of being in his book *Heidegger Lesen* (Munich: Fink, 1991), especially chapter 4, "Die Griechen," 153–226.

of approbation rather than description. Historical and cultural differences between sixth-century B.C.E. Ephesus and fourth-century B.C.E. Athens are flattened out and ignored. In the process, the decisive cultural shift from an oral to a written culture will be reconfigured as the transition from primordial *logos* to instrumentalist logic. And Heidegger will brook no opposition. Writing in the *Introduction to Metaphysics* against a modern tradition that has forgotten primordial *logos*, Heidegger declares:

> If we wish to combat intellectualism seriously, we must know that intellectualism is only an impoverished modern offshoot of a development long in the making, namely the position of priority gained by thought with the help of Western metaphysics. It is important to curtail the excrescences of modern day intellectualism. . . . The misinterpretation of thought and the abuse to which it leads can be overcome only by authentic thinking that goes back to the roots—and *by nothing else.* (IM: 122/EM: 93)

Heidegger will continue to insist on the primacy and ruling power of the *arche.* But as Nietzsche himself might have put it, which *arche?* The autochthonic *arche* of Athenian rootedness? The Pre-Socratic *arche* of *aletheia?* The Platonic *arche* of a *polis*-sustaining *mythos?* The Heraclitean *arche* of a primordial *logos* constituting an eternal order that manifests itself in discourse? The Anaximandrian *arche* of a primordial origin that marks the inauguration of Western thinking? The Oedipal *arche* of a double birth, both of blood and soil, whose very emergence reveals a hidden conflict between the chthonic forces that destroy the *polis* and the autochthonic forces that sustain it? These are choices about which Heidegger was not always clear. For him, the power of the *arche* was at first political, then anti-political. And yet, as we saw even in his anti-political phase, his myth of the origin was always bound to the fate of the *polis,* rethought as the German *Volk.*

However, Heidegger was also not unaware of the multiple possibilities/potencies lying within the origin itself. His was no mere monarchic interpretation of the *arche.* In one of his notebook drafts from *Besinnung,* Heidegger speaks of "an interpretation of the history of be-ing" that acknowledges "the multiplicity of *archai*" (GA 66: 405). And perhaps in this Heideggerian recognition of the plurality of beginnings, and of the need for their constant supplementation and proliferation, we can find possibilities for philosophical thinking that undermine the Heideggerian threat of Graeco-Germanic rule.

In his texts from the early 1920s, the young Heidegger was keen on insisting that "the philosopher . . . is precisely the genuine and constant 'beginner,'" someone for whom the task of truth was ever underway, constantly demanding the interpretive elasticity of Aristotelian *phronesis* (GA

61: 13).[63] And, in many ways, what marks Heidegger's entire thought path is its attention to this spirit of constant beginning. Within Heidegger's thinking, within the hidden folds of unfolding *aletheia*, there are hints, pointers, traces, indications that can be read to work against Heidegger's own sometimes violent understanding of the *arche* as the Pre-Socratic inception of a National Socialist history of being. Heidegger himself would claim that "the *arche* means, at one and the same time, beginning and dominion" (PM: 189/WM: 317). But, as Reiner Schürmann reminds us in his reading of Aristotle, we are left to decide how to deploy our own philosophical representations of the *arche,* since "the origin is said in many ways."[64] There is not a single, univocal, isomorphic *arche* within the Western tradition, but rather multiple *archai* that allow for alternative ways of interpreting the origin(s) of a tradition. Heidegger's work offers us both the possibility of homology and of heterology, of exclusionary Graeco-Germanic autochthony and of an an-archic counter-movement to dominion, hierarchy, and the politics of the *Führer*-principle. What I have tried to uncover in both the political and "anti-political" writings is the dangerous commitment to autochthony that threatens to undermine all possibilities of reading Heidegger's work in an anarchic spirit, in ways that challenge the authoritarian myth of a singularly "Greek" ruling origin. Through all of our readings of Heidegger and the promise of more volumes to come, we need to remember that there are other possibilities that lie hidden within the tradition.

Levinas, for example, has challenged this myth of autochthony by calling into question the very principle of geographic rootedness. Like Franz Rosenzweig, who claimed that "being a people means something besides being rooted in a land," Levinas argued that "the chosen home is the very opposite of a root. It indicates a disengagement, a wandering."[65] And it was precisely this commitment to rootedness as a political form of division and exclusion that Levinas found dangerous. As he told an interviewer in 1982, "For me, Heidegger is the greatest philosopher of the century, perhaps one of the very great philosophers of the millennium; but I am very pained by that because I can never forget what he was in 1933 . . . he has a very great sense for everything that is part of the landscape; not the artistic landscape, but the place in which man is enrooted. It is absolutely not

---

63. John van Buren, *The Young Heidegger* (Bloomington: Indiana University Press, 1994), 324–341 and 391–397, focuses on the theme of "constant beginning" in Heidegger's thought.

64. Schürmann, *Heidegger on Being and Acting,* 95–97.

65. Franz Rosenzweig, *Star of Redemption,* trans. William Hallo (Boston: Beacon Press, 1972), 300; Emmanuel Levinas, *Totality and Infinity,* trans. Alphonso Lingis (Pittsburgh: Duquesne University Press, 1969), 172.

a philosophy of the émigré! I would even say that it is not a philosophy of the emigrant. To me, being a migrant is not being a nomad. Nothing is more enrooted than the nomad. But he or she who emigrates is fully human: the migration of man does not destroy, does not demolish the meaning of being."[66] Since Heidegger's very understanding of the history of being was dominated by a myth of rootedness, of the ruling power of Graeco-German autochthony, it becomes essential for Levinas to contest its underlying logic and historical dominance. In one sense, however, this task of contestation and resistance to the myth of autochthony had already been initiated by Nietzsche well before the critique proffered by Levinas.

Nietzsche never succumbed to the Platonic desire for either a pure origin or an origin of purity. Neither did he fall victim to the racial myths of an Aryan link between Greeks and Germans. If later so-called "Nietzscheans," such as Baeumler, Hildebrandt, or Heyse, would attempt to wed Nietzsche's interpretation of antiquity to a racial eugenics rooted in autochthony, they did so in violation of Nietzsche's own thought. Not only did Nietzsche contest the doctrine of Graeco-Germanic autochthony on political grounds, viewing it as a crude and vulgar form of nationalist blood-politics, he also rejected it as bad philology, seeing it as part of "an utterly castrated and mendacious study of the classical world" (UO: 329/KSA 8: 19). On Nietzsche's reading, "the" Greeks were not a single race or people; nor were they the "first" originary culture, the only truly earth-born humans. Rather, Greek culture was the product of a creative intermixture between various Asian, Near Eastern, and Hellenic influences.

> *Earliest inhabiting* of Greek soil: people of Mongolian origin, worshippers of trees and snakes. A fringe of Semites along the coast. Thracians here and there. The Greeks took all these elements into their own bloodstream, along with gods and myths (several of the Odysseus stories are Mongolian). . . . What are "racially pure" Greeks? Can't we simply suppose that Italic peoples, mixed with Thracian and Semitic elements, became *Greek*? (UO: 387/KSA 8: 96)

What Nietzsche draws from his study of antiquity is less an insight into an imagined primordial *arche* than an awareness that what we find in the Greeks is what we project onto them. In this sense, he sees the German

---

66. Emmanuel Levinas, *Entre Nous: On Thinking-of-the-Other,* trans. M. Smith and B. Harshav (New York: Columbia University Press, 1998), 117. Levinas is at pains to grapple with the ontological meaning of otherness or alterity—but, unlike Heidegger, he is not threatened by it, nor does he seek to exclude the other. On the contrary, in the face to face encounter of one human being to another, Levinas finds the source of ethical responsibility.

image of Hellas as one marked by the fervent desire for cultural identity, an impulse that in Heidegger's work will be refashioned into a German search for a homecoming.

Nietzsche understood these romantic longings for the homeland to be part of the German malady of nationalism. And he was wary of any attempts to support such impulses by turning to an archaic or originary source of German national or racial supremacy. In one of his notebooks from 1875, he remarks, "How far removed from the Greeks one has to be to attribute to them the stupid notion of autochthony as does [Karl Otfried] Müller" (UO: 368/KSA 8: 70).[67] And yet Heidegger will attempt, purportedly in the spirit of Nietzsche, to initiate precisely such a reading of the Greeks. Yoking his own Hölderlinian form of homecoming to the myth of autochthony, Heidegger will attempt to uncover the subterranean and chthonic Nietzsche, the Nietzsche who found in Pre-Platonic philosophy the sources for a profound transformation and deconstruction of the project of modernity. And, in Heidegger's hands, the Nietzschean injunction "to discover now the fifth and sixth centuries" will be employed as a weapon to combat the modernist metaphysics of *techne* in the name of an archaic primordiality (UO: 342/KSA 8:34).

VII. THE PRE-SOCRATIC RENAISSANCE IN WEIMAR

Nietzsche's work proved decisive for Heidegger, especially during the period from 1936–1945 when he offered no less than six courses on topics such as the will to power, the eternal recurrence, metaphysics, art, history, epistemology, and the problem of European nihilism. The effect of this extended confrontation with the matter of Nietzsche's philosophy was extraordinary. But perhaps the single most decisive aspect of Nietzsche's work to influence Heidegger was its interpretation of the Greek world. If we wish to trace this influence, we will need to understand just how powerfully Nietzsche's chthonic, subterranean, *unterirdische* appropriation of Greek tragedy, poetry, and Pre-Socratic philosophy shaped Heidegger's own approach to the Greeks. Besides Hölderlin, no one helped to form Heidegger's vision of the mythical Greek *arche* as much as Nietzsche. But as always in speaking of Heidegger and his relation to the tradition, the lines of influence are never direct. As Hölderlin came to Heidegger through the poetic-nationalist influence of von Hellingrath, the German Youth Movement, and the postwar "Hölderlin-Renaissance," Nietzsche's

---

67. Nietzsche will put forward a similar argument against autochthony in PTAG: 301/KSA 1: 806.

work came to him through the George Circle, Jünger, and the generational consciousness of the Great War.[68] There is another decisive influence as well, the one exercised by Nietzsche on German classical philology during the 1920s.

Nietzsche's effect upon Weimar Germany's intellectual life was profound, capped by the appearance of a new twenty-three volume edition of the *Werke* by Musarion Verlag in 1920, the publication of Ernst Bertram's *Nietzsche: Versuch einer Mythologie* (which went through six editions between 1918 and 1922), and the printing of Spengler's *Decline of the West*, which succeeded in popularizing Nietzsche's thought in broad academic circles.[69] Especially in the field of classical philology Nietzsche's impact was dramatic. In the course of a decade, a new generation of classical scholars weaned on Nietzsche would help to transform the study of Pre-Socratic philosophy by reclaiming its archaic power from the palimpsestic erasures of Christian, humanist, and Enlightenment culture. As a result of their efforts, a new field of study emerged: Pre-Socratic thought. In Glenn Most's words, "in the decade after the Great War studies on the earliest Greek philosophers were without a doubt marked by a boom as never be-

68. Reading Heidegger reading Hölderlin or Nietzsche becomes a very different enterprise when one's lens is focused from the position of a late twentieth-century American observer rather than from that of a German observer in the 1930s. The same, of course, holds true for Heidegger's interpretation of Plato or the Pre-Socratics. Some helpful sources for tracing the NS *Hölderlinbild* include: Alessandro Pellegrini, *Friedrich Hölderlin: Sein Bild in der Forschung* (Berlin: Walter de Gruyter, 1965); Claudia Albert, "Hölderlin," in *Deutsche Klassiker im Nationalsozialismus* (Stuttgart: Metzler, 1994), 189–248; and Werner Bartscher, *Hölderlin und die deutsche Nation: Versuch einer Wirkungsgeschichte* (Berlin: Junker & Dünnhaupt, 1942). For a consideration of the NS *Nietzschebild*, see S. F. Oduev, *Auf den Spuren Zarathustras* (Berlin: Akademie, 1977); Steven Aschheim, *The Nietzsche Legacy in Germany, 1890–1990* (Berkeley: University of California Press, 1992); Heinz Malorny, "Friedrich Nietzsche und der deutsche Faschismus" in *Faschismus-Forschung*, ed. Dietrich Eichholtz (Berlin: Akademie, 1980), 279–301; and Hans Langreder, *Die Auseinandersetzung mit Nietzsche im Dritten Reich*, diss. University of Kiel, 1971.

69. The Musarionausgabe of Friedrich Nietzsche, *Gesammelte Werke*, 23 vols. (Munich: Musarion Verlag, 1920–1929) provided a second, more aesthetically produced edition of the works that went beyond the Naumann edition published under the auspices of Elisabeth Förster-Nietzsche. At the same time, the Kröner Verlag in Leipzig was producing a Taschenausgabe for popular use. Clearly, reading Nietzsche was becoming all too chic. Adding to Nietzsche's popularity was Ernst Bertram's study, *Nietzsche: Versuch einer Mythologie* (Bonn: Bouvier, 1989), originally published in 1918 by Bondi in Berlin, that became standard reading for the literary establishment of Weimar. As a member of the George Circle, Bertram sought to portray Nietzsche as a kind of prophet of *Germanentum*, an anti-democratic figure who expressed the hopes of a secret Germany. For more on the George Circle's relation to Nietzsche, see Kurt Hildebrandt, *Wagner und Nietzsche: Ihr Kampf gegen das Neunzehnte Jahrhundert* (Breslau: F. Hirt, 1924); Ernst Gundolf and Kurt Hildebrandt, *Nietzsche als Richter unserer Zeit* (Breslau: F. Hirt, 1923); Wilhelm Kusserow, *Friedrich Nietzsche und Stefan George: Ein Vergleich* (Berlin: n.p., 1927); Heinz Raschel, *Das Nietzsche-Bild im George-Kreis* (Berlin: de Gruyter, 1984), and Frank Weber, *Die Bedeutung Nietzsches für Stefan George und sein Kreis* (Frankfurt: Peter Lang, 1989).

fore and seldom thereafter."[70] Besides a new edition of Hermann Diels's pioneering 1903 compilation, *Die Fragmente der Vorsokratiker,* three other collections of Pre-Socratic fragments appeared during these years. Now, for the first time in German culture, Pre-Socratic philosophy became an important intellectual concern for the present, a new way of reconceiving the foundations of the old order and of offering the possibility of cultural renewal. In the spirit of Nietzsche's *Kulturkampf* against the German middle-class world of state, religion, and *Bildung,* these philologists sought to free the writings of Heraclitus, Parmenides, Empedocles, and Zeno from their prosaic status as "classical" texts and began to experience them within a new cultural context. In this sense, their Nietzschean appropriation of the archaic was carried out as a struggle against the dominance of the older philological establishment, embodied by Nietzsche's old nemesis, Ulrich Wilamowitz von Moellendorff.[71]

Heidegger was, of course, part of this new generation of academics whose interest in Pre-Socratic thought was stimulated by the influence of Nietzsche. Like his colleagues from the field of classical philology and philosophy—Ernst Hoffmann, Julius Stenzel, Karl Reinhardt, Walter F. Otto,

---

70. Glenn Most, "*Polemos Panton Pater:* Die Vorsokratiker in der Forschung der Zwanziger Jahre," in *Altertumswissenschaft in den 20er Jahren,* ed. Hellmut Flashar (Stuttgart: F. Steiner, 1995), 87. Most has also written a broad-ranging article on the notion of the "archaic," entitled "Zur Archäologie der Archaik," *Antike und Abendland* 35 (1989): 1–23; taken together, these two pieces present a penetrating account of the German preoccupation with antiquity, the archaic, and the origin. During the 1920s in Germany, there was something of a "Pre-Socratic mania," Most argues. Besides the Diels edition (which went through a third and fourth edition in 1922), there were also editions of Pre-Socratic fragments in the 1920s compiled by Wilhelm Nestle, *Die Vorsokratiker in Auswahl* (Jena: Eugen Diederichs, 1922); K.W. Schmidt, *Die Vorsokratiker: Eine Auswahl für den Schulgebrauch* (Berlin: Weidmannsche Buchhandlung, 1924); Michael Grünwald, *Die Anfänge der abendländischen Philosophie: Fragmente und Lehrberichte der Vorsokratiker* (Zürich: Artemis, 1925).

For some historical perspective, see Hans-Georg Gadamer, "'Die Griechen, unsere Lehrer': Ein Gespräch mit Glenn W. Most," *Internationale Zeitschrift für die Philosophie* (1994): 139–149.

71. Heidegger's reception of Pre-Socratic thinking in the 1920s takes place within this overall transformation in philology that began with Nietzsche's battle with Wilamowitz and the older generation of classicists. Of course, Heidegger will take a different path, and yet his turn toward the Pre-Socratics depends upon the Nietzschean retrieval carried out by Otto, Reinhardt, and their generation. Uvo Hölscher will argue, for example, in "Die Wiedergewinnung des antiken Bodens: Nietzsches Ruckgriff auf Heraklit," *Neue Hefte für Philosophie* 15–16 (1979): 156–182, that Diels fashioned his translations of Heraclitus' texts to conform with Nietzsche's aphoristic style of composition. Heidegger will, in turn, read Heraclitus through his own Nietzschean lens. For an account of the history of philology from the hermeneutic model of the Second Humanism through Nietzsche, Wilamowitz, Jaeger, and their successors, see Ada Hentschke and Ulrich Muhlack, *Einführung in die Geschichte der klassischen Philologie* (Darmstadt: Wissenschaftliche Buchgesellschaft, 1972). On the Wilamowitz-Nietzsche debate, see William M. Calder III, "The Wilamowitz-Struggle," *Nietzsche-Studien* 12 (1983): 214–254; and M.S. Silk and J.P. Stern, *Nietzsche on Tragedy* (Cambridge: Cambridge University Press, 1981), 90–109.

and others—Heidegger found in Nietzsche's chthonic reading of the Pre-Socratics the source for a new way of approaching the history of philosophy. Despite his claim that Nietzsche's "interpretations of the [Pre-Socratic] texts are commonplace throughout, if not superficial," Heidegger still deemed Nietzsche's retrieval of the archaic as decisive for the German future (EGT: 14/H: 298). In the standard nineteenth-century German histories of philosophy, the Pre-Socratics were assigned the secondary function of preparing the groundwork for the later philosophical achievements of Socrates, Plato, and Aristotle. But, in his early work from 1873, *Philosophy in the Tragic Age of the Greeks*, Nietzsche effected a dramatic shift. Unlike the traditional historians, Nietzsche did not relegate the Ionian and Eleatic philosophers to the status of mere forerunners. Instead, he viewed them as originary thinkers who expressed the profound depths of Greek tragic consciousness. Reversing the standard nineteenth-century practice of privileging Plato and the tradition of Platonism, Nietzsche came to value these Pre-Platonic thinkers above their successors. "Ever since Plato," he claimed, "philosophers lack something essential in comparison to the republic of creative genius from Thales to Socrates" (PTAG: 34/KSA 1: 809–810).

In his lectures on the *History of Philosophy*, Hegel had divided early Greek thought into three stages: from Thales to Anaxagoras, from the Sophists to Socrates, and from Plato to Aristotle.[72] As a result, he determined that thinkers like Anaximander, Heraclitus, and Parmenides constituted merely a preliminary stage in the progressive development of Greek thought. This stage-theory was later adopted by prominent nineteenth-century historians of philosophy such as Eduard Zeller, Wilhelm Dilthey, Friedrich Überweg, and Wilhelm Windelband.[73] The outlines of this approach, however, go as far back as Aristotle, who proposed such a model in the *Metaphysics*, and Cicero, who replicated it in the *Tusculan Disputations*.[74] This ingrained tradition of consigning the Ionian-Eleatic

72. G.W.F. Hegel, *History of Philosophy*, trans. E.S. Haldane (Atlantic Highlands: Humanities, 1983), 1: 165, and *Vorlesungen über die Geschichte der Philosophie* (Frankfurt: Suhrkamp, 1971), 1: 189.
73. Eduard Zeller, *A History of Greek Philosophy: From the Earliest Period to the Time of Socrates*, 2 vols., trans. S.F. Alleyne (London: Longmans, Green, 1881); Wilhelm Dilthey, *Grundriss der allgemeinen Geschichte der Philosophie* (Frankfurt: Klostermann, 1949); Friedrich Überweg, *Grundriss der Geschichte der Philosophie* (Berlin: Mittler, 1912); and Wilhelm Windelband, *Lehrbuch der Geschichte der Philosophie* (Tübingen: Mohr, 1948).
74. For Aristotle's division, see *Metaphysics*, trans. Hugh Tredennick (Cambridge: Harvard University Press, 1936), 16–48 (983b–988a); and Cicero, *Tusculan Disputations*, trans. J.F. King (Cambridge: Harvard University Press, 1989), 430–437. This fundamental division of ancient Greek philosophy has dominated our own century as well, so much so that now the post-Aristotelian period of Greek thought has been relegated to its current status as a subdivision for classicists and specialists in ancient philosophy. Heidegger did not initiate this scheme of classification but his tendentious ordering and decisive elisions from the cor-

philosophers to positions as mere seers, cosmologists, poets, sages, or mythographers became standard practice in the academic world of the late nineteenth century. When Nietzsche attempted to carry out his own vitalist retrieval of this archaic tradition, he fell back upon the older model. Like Hegel, Nietzsche would argue that "with Plato something wholly new begins" (PTAG: 34/KSA 1: 809). Accordingly, Nietzsche's determination of "a gap, a break in development" between Socrates and earlier thinkers can hardly be considered original (HAH: 124/KSA 2: 217). In many ways it reinscribed the same "Pre-Socratic" tradition of Aristotle, Cicero, Hegel, Schleiermacher, and the German philological establishment. But the way Nietzsche worked out the consequences of this break did effect a genuine change in perception. Nietzsche's vision of a self-sustaining artistic culture in the sixth and fifth centuries B.C.E. had a considerable effect in undermining Aristotle's teleological model of Greek philosophy as a linear, progressive movement from archaic *mythos* to rational *logos*. And the way Nietzsche contested the marginalizing of the Pre-Socratics in academic philology did ultimately initiate a new kind of retrieval of archaic Greek culture that would transform the German relation to antiquity.

Nietzsche's break with the Aristotelian-Hegelian model of Greek thought indeed proved so decisive that in Tilman Borsche's words, "it authorizes us to speak of Nietzsche's 'invention' of the Pre-Socratics."[75] While we may balk at such an exalted claim and acknowledge that Nietzsche was not the first to "discover" the archaic, chthonic, ecstatic dimension in Greek experience, nonetheless, we still have to recognize that he was the first to have made this reading culturally decisive for the modern era. More powerfully than either Burckhardt or Rohde, Nietzsche transformed the German reception of the Greeks that had been dominated by the "Second Humanism" of Goethe, Schiller, Lessing, Winckelmann, Humboldt, and their contemporaries.[76] It was his Dionysian assault on Winckelmann's Apollonian ideal, that sculptural image of serene beauty and static harmony, that proved decisive in the shift from a classical model of Greece to an archaic one. As Nietzsche put it in one of his notebooks from 1888, "the concept 'classical'—as Winckelmann and Goethe had formed it, not only did not account for the Dionysian element but excluded it from itself" (KSA 13: 235). In this sense, Nietzsche's interpreta-

---

pus of ancient philosophy has had a deleterious effect on contemporary philosophical study—especially among American continental philosophers.

75. Tilman Borsche, "Nietzsches Erfindung der Vorsokratiker," in *Nietzsche und die philosophische Tradition*, ed. Josef Simon (Würzburg: Königshausen & Neumann, 1985), 1: 81.

76. Burckhardt, chapter 3 of *Griechische Kulturgeschichte*, vol. 1 and Erwin Rohde, "Dionysische Religion in Griechenland," chapter 9 of *Psyche* (Tübingen: Mohr, 1902). See also Sichtermann, *Kulturgeschichte der klassischen Archäologie*, 121–165; 224–247.

tion of the Pre-Socratic era as "archaic" constituted a kind of anti-classicism, an untrammeled attack on the traditional German image of fifth-century Athens as the apogee of ancient Greek culture.[77] In the wake of this anti-classical construction of the archaic, philologists such as Hermann Diels, Wilhelm Nestle, Hermann Fränkel, and Karl Reinhardt carried out a hermeneutic archeology of early Greek texts that helped to consolidate a Nietzschean revolution in the study of ancient philosophy. Now there began a new academic reception of archaic thought that helped to move it from the margins of a specialized discipline to the very center of intellectual concern. As Glenn Most has argued, with the publication of Diels' *Fragmente der Vorsokratiker* (an edition that provides the first complete German translation of fragments that previously had only been available in Greek or Latin), a Heraclitean *Kulturkampf* against the older order begins. "From now on Heraclitus no longer belongs to the disciplinary world of philology, rather he has (also) become a German-speaking author."[78] And, given the implicit and explicit parallels between their work, "during the nineteen twenties Heraclitus and Nietzsche were looked upon as the two most important Pre-Socratics. Heraclitus was understood—not always consciously—as a Greek Nietzsche and Nietzsche as a German Heraclitus."

The effect of Nietzsche's Dionysian retrieval of the Pre-Socratics upon the generation of Weimar academics was profound. And Heidegger was no exception. Like Nietzsche, Heidegger undertook his archaic reading of the Pre-Socratic tradition in the spirit of revolutionary reform. His aim was not, however, a *Kulturkampf* in Nietzsche's sense, but a radical recovery of lost, hidden, and forgotten possibilities. Where Nietzsche sought to rescue Greek archaic culture from the grammar lessons of the *Gymnasium* and make it a vital part of German cultural reform, Heidegger attempted to experience the Greek *arche* as a kind of adumbration of German destiny. Hence, in his reading of the Anaximander fragment, he could still rail against the Platonic-Aristotelian interpretations of the archaic in which "classical and classicist representations prevail" (EGT: 14/H: 297). Heidegger's assertion in the Rectorial Address that "the beginning still *is*" captures perfectly this Nietzschean spirit of an anti-classical affirmation of powers latent within the *arche*. Long after the revolutionary moment of 1933 had receded, however, Heidegger would continue to draw upon

77. Hubert Cancik has written a series of works dealing with Nietzsche and the archaic—and with the reception of Nietzsche in the 1920s: *Nietzsches Antike* (Stuttgart: Metzler, 1995); *Philolog und Kultfigur: Friedrich Nietzsche und seine Antike in Deutschland* (Stuttgart: Metzler, 1999); "Der Nietzsche-Kult in Weimar (I)," *Nietzsche-Studien* 16 (1987): 405–429; and "Der Einfluss Friedrich Nietzsches auf klassische Philologen in Deutschland bis 1945," in *Altertumswissenschaft in den 20er Jahren*, 381–402.

78. Most, *"Polemos Panton Pater,"* 106–108; Hermann Diels, *Fragmente der Vorsokratiker*, 3 vols., ed. Walther Kranz, 18th ed. (Zurich: Weidmann, 1992).

Nietzsche's insight into the living force of the archaic for the present and future. In his 1967 lecture, "The Origin of Art and the Destination of Thinking," Heidegger would claim that, "historiographically considered, the Greek world is indeed past. But historically, when it is experienced as our destiny, it remains even now and becomes ever again something present. . . . For the beginning of a destiny is the greatest. It rules in advance over everything that comes after it."[79]

Heidegger's turn to the Pre-Socratics in the early 1930s follows upon his Nietzschean *Kehre* in the *Fundamental Concepts of Metaphysics* (1929/30). But it also proceeds from his direct engagement with the classical philology of the day, especially those works that constituted part of the Pre-Socratic renaissance in Weimar. Through the pioneering work of Frank Edler, we now know how closely tied to the writings of Pre-Socratic philologists like Karl Reinhardt, Ernst Hoffmann, Julius Stenzel, and Kurt Riezler, Heidegger's project truly was.[80] What these philologists set out to achieve was a portrait of the archaic thinkers that freed them from the categorical system of Aristotle and the doxographical constructions of later Aristotelians. In Aristotle's scheme, thinkers such as Heraclitus, Anaximenes, and Empedocles were all classified as "physicists," philosophers who conceived of *physis* both as substance and as first cause (*Metaphysics*, 983–984). But in his ground-breaking study, *Parmenides und die Geschichte der griechischen Philosophie* (1916), Reinhardt put forth a reading of Parmenides as a thinker-poet (*Denker/Dichter*) whose fundamental concern was the relation between language and ontology.[81] Throughout the 1920s and 1930s, Reinhardt would attempt to bring together his interpretation of archaic thought with the poetry of Hölderlin and George, the philosophy of Nietzsche, and the tragedies of Sophocles—concerns that Heidegger would share in his own work.[82]

Ernst Hoffmann also took part in the generational critique of the older doxographical approach to the Pre-Socratics. In his 1925 work, *Die Sprache und die archaische Logik*, Hoffmann contested the standard thesis that Pre-Socratic thought was defined by a philosophy of nature, understood as

79. Martin Heidegger, "Die Herkunft der Kunst und die Bestimmung des Denkens," 11–12.

80. Frank Edler, "Heidegger and Werner Jaeger on the Eve of 1933: A Possible Rapprochement?" *Research in Phenomenology*, 28 (1998): 122–149.

81. Karl Reinhardt, *Parmenides und die Geschichte der griechischen Philosophie* (Frankfurt: Klostermann, 1985). Reinhardt's father had studied classical philology at Basel with Nietzsche; this influence can be detected in the Parmenides book, especially its attention to Pre-Platonic thought.

82. Karl Reinhardt's works include: *Vermächtnis der Antike* (Göttingen: Vandenhoeckh & Ruprecht, 1960); *Sophocles*, trans. Hazel and David Harvey (New York: Barnes & Noble, 1979); *Die Krise des Helden* (Munich: dtv, 1962). For references to Reinhardt in Heidegger's work, see GA 22: 51, 63–64, 230; HBB: 29; BT: 494/SZ: 223; AHB: 123, 125; IM: 107–108/EM: 82.

physis (substance).[83] In his view, besides offering an account of nature, these early thinkers also put forward a philosophy of culture and language. Focusing on what he termed an "archaic" logic—a form or *Gestalt* of ancient thought that is "still tied to the material through which the philosophical *eidos* wants to come to expression—viz., language"—Hoffmann sought to uncover the originary sources of later Platonic and Aristotelian logic and to direct philosophical attention back to the problem of *logos,* now understood not merely as metaphysical reason but as language.[84] In the *History of Ancient Philosophy* that he published with Ernst Cassirer, Hoffmann offered an interpretation of the "history of Greek philosophy as the history of 'Logos' attempting to find itself."[85] Heidegger himself had problems with Hoffmann's approach, seeing it as still too caught up with the teleological model of analysis and too tied to Cassirer's Neo-Kantian philosophy of culture. Moreover, he saw Hoffmann's decision to read Aristotle as a kind of "Ur"-Neo-Kantian epistemologist as wholly bound to the metaphysics of the mandarinate order.[86] And yet Hoffmann's work was part of a generational turn to the archaic in German academic philosophy that established the context for a renewed study of Pre-Socratic thought that would prove so decisive for Heidegger. In working through the metaphysical residue in the work of Reinhardt, Hoffmann, Stenzel, and Riezler, Heidegger would come to find the "authentic" meaning of the archaic in his own ontology of the originary, the primordial, and the autochthonic. Nonetheless, the structural parallels between Heidegger's desire for a radical recovery of the Greek beginning and the aims of his colleagues in classical philology and philosophy were not coincidental.

In an academic address delivered in 1930, "What is Living and What is Dead in the Philosophy of Classical Antiquity?," Julius Stenzel sought to recover the living, vital element in ancient thought for contemporary philosophy, thereby freeing it from its traditional status as a specialized field for trained classicists. Emphasizing the need to retrieve the classics for his own generation, Stenzel declared, "the Germans have had time and again to lose antiquity and then 'gain it anew in order to possess it'. . . . Thus even today we are seeking a new relationship to antiquity in which perhaps Greek philosophy is even more significant than the other areas of an-

83. Ernst Hoffmann, *Die Sprache und die archaische Logik* (Tübingen: Mohr, 1925).

84. Ibid., viii.

85. Ernst Cassirer and Ernst Hoffmann, *"Die Geschichte der antiken Philosophie,"* in *Lehrbuch der Geschichte der Philosophie,* ed. Max Dessoir (Berlin: Ullstein, 1925), 7.

86. In HJB: 50, Heidegger makes a brutal comment to Jaspers about Hoffmann's lecture in Spring 1925 at the "Berliner Tagung der Freunde des Gymnasiums": "your colleague Hoffmann . . . made the most pathetic impression on all of us and we all wondered how such a man could attain a chair in a philosophy department." See also EGT: 14/H: 297 for a veiled reference to Hoffmann and his notion of "archaic logic."

cient culture."[87] But Stenzel did not aim at a mere revival of ancient culture or a repetition but at a "creative rebirth of ancient thoughts out of a new vitality," one that "seeks to rediscover directly the true ancient world and thereby the beginning, the origin of the whole history of culture." In his *Metaphysik des Altertums* (1929), Stenzel attempts a kind of "*Destruktion* of Eleatic metaphysics" and warns against the Neo-Kantian tendency to view Pre-Socratic thought as a mere stage on the way toward an objective, rational science of nature.[88] Rejecting Werner Jaeger's identification of *logos* with modern logic (which he sees as an anachronism that suppresses "the ontological side" of *logos*), Stenzel makes a strong case for understanding the Greek interpretation of being as something that "lies beyond the division between subject and object." And he also argues for a reading of the *arche* as both a temporal point of beginning and as a principle of ruling origin that determines all that proceeds forth from it. Moreover, in his discussion of Socrates, he characterizes him as a philosopher "rooted in the earth of the homeland."

Clearly, these were topics and themes that Heidegger too would take up, even if in a very different way and for more politically focused reasons. But when Heidegger announces in his lecture course of summer 1932, *Der Anfang der abendländischen Philosophie (Anaximander und Parmenides)*, that "the beginning is not something primitive but rather the simplicity of everything that is great," he is giving voice to a generational *leitmotif* expressed in the works of Stenzel, Hoffmann, Reinhardt, and others. Like them, Heidegger too would argue that the archaic philosophy of the Greek world did not merely constitute a preliminary stage of mythic speculation on the path to rational enlightenment. Rather, it initiated an originary form of thinking whose philosophical power had been covered over and concealed by the palimpsestic reinscriptions of Platonic and Aristotelian metaphysics.[89]

VIII. HEIDEGGER, NIETZSCHE, AND GERMAN PHILHELLENISM

In a powerful and dramatic way, Nietzsche's revolution in the study of Pre-Socratic philosophy in Germany helped to lay the groundwork for Heidegger's own revolutionary recovery of the archaic. Like Nietzsche, Hei-

---

87. Julius Stenzel, "Was ist lebendig und was ist tot in der Philosophie des klassischen Altertums?" in *Kleine Schriften zur griechischen Philosophie* (Bad Homburg: Gentner, 1966), 300–301; and Frank Edler, "Heidegger and Werner Jaeger," 132–133.

88. Julius Stenzel, *Metaphysik des Altertums* (Munich: Oldenbourg, 1931), 6, 9–10, 29, 83–84.

89. Martin Heidegger, *Der Anfang der abendländischen Philosophie*, unpublished lectures SS 1932 from Herbert Marcuse Archive in the Stadt-und Universitätsbibliothek in Frankfurt am Main, #0029.01, 9. This set of lectures is scheduled to be published as volume 35 of the *Gesamtausgabe*.

degger would put forward a reading of Pre-Socratic thought as essentially tragic, as an experience of truth marked by *Kampf.* But Heidegger never followed Nietzsche's own lead in understanding the texts of the archaic period as expressions of personal character and genius. Rather, he sought to interpret them as poetic sources that both augured and inaugurated the path of Western destiny, originary attestations to the dawning power and the ruling potential of a hidden Greek *arche.* Where Nietzsche found in the fragments of the archaic period traces of a Dionysiac experience of the world in all its aesthetic forms, Heidegger found only a text-centered model of truth, one that relegated *aletheia* primarily to the realm of poetic composition and a writerly form of art. One need only compare the aesthetic world of Nietzsche's *Birth of Tragedy* to Heidegger's "Origin of the Work of Art" to get some sense of the difference in style. Nietzsche's focus on the multiform realm of Greek tragic performance as a visual, tactile, auditory experience marked by the fluid motion of dance, song, and speech demonstrates his concern for a fully developed phenomenological work of art as *Gesamtkunstwerk.* Heidegger's focus on the fixed visual forms of architecture and painting, however, expressed less the rich, polymorphous experience of Greek tragic art than it did a static, calcified model of text-centered philology projected back onto Greek forms. Like the other philologists of the Pre-Socratic renaissance, Heidegger felt more at home in the texts of Hölderlin than in the temples of Artemis or Athena. Because he lacked any genuine archeological experience on Greek soil, he confected his own archeology of Hellas modeled not on sculpture, architecture, or painting, but on the paratactic constructions of Hölderlin. In this way, Heidegger translated the fragments of Anaximander, Heraclitus, and Parmenides, using Hölderlin's own paratactic model of translation as his guide. But since he insisted that what he sought to retrieve was not the fixed meaning of an ancient text but the fluid possibilities of a future oriented German homecoming, we can see how his philologically-inspired model of Greek *aletheia* might be understood as problematic, if not contradictory.

Heidegger's image of Hellas cannot easily be reduced to one source. As we have seen in our considerations of the political, philological, and historical context of Heidegger's thought, the range of influences on his interpretation of the Greeks was broad and diverse. Still, Heidegger always acknowledged the primacy of Hölderlin and Nietzsche, "the two who had the deepest experience of the end of the West . . . and could transform it in their creative work through their concomitant reflection on the beginning of Western history" (BQP: 109/GA 45: 126). For him, the Greek beginning was never a historical event that could be recovered in any historiographical sense. Rather, it was always understood as an indication of future possibilities whose shape and form had been prepared historically in the work of Hölderlin and Nietzsche. Nietzsche had already indicated as much in his characterization of Western history as a *historia abscondita* ("hidden history") which could never be accounted for retrospectively according to the principles of scientific history. As Nietzsche himself would put it, "Perhaps the past is even now still essentially undiscovered!" (GS: 34/KSA 3: 404).

For Nietzsche, the Greek beginning had long receded from view, its Dionysian power stifled by the incursions of the Christian-humanist-Enlightenment traditions. The Greek philosophers of the tragic age had been driven underground, forced back to the subterranean cave of the Boeotian soothsayer, Trophonius, whose underground lair had once been the site of philosophy's chthonic birth (PTAG: 33/KSA 1: 808).[90] By the time Nietzsche had pointed to these subterranean sources of pre-Socratic thought, however, Winckelmann's Apollonian ideal of "noble simplicity and tranquil grandeur" had already overdetermined the way of conceiving Germany's relation to antiquity. By offering a highly visual and aesthetic portrait of the Greek world that was compatible with the Apollonian values of the Enlightenment, Winckelmann succeeded in establishing the fundamental tenets of German Philhellenism. In the process, Nietzsche argued, he would also contribute to the idealization of Hellas and the cultivation of a humanist sensibility whose historical effect was to occlude any genuine access to the chthonic sources of Pre-Socratic thought. Without this chthonic tie, no German could be expected to grasp the depths of genuinely archaic experience. As Nietzsche put it in a notebook entry from 1885: "*one does not know the Greeks* as long as this hidden subterranean [*unterirdische*] entrance lies blocked and obstructed" (WP: 541/KSA 11: 681).

Heidegger's own relation to German Philhellenism was determined in large measure by this Nietzschean caveat against Neo-humanist classicism. As we have seen in chapter 1, already in 1933 Heidegger had writ-

90. In his early treatise, *Philosophy in the Tragic Age of the Greeks*, Nietzsche describes the ancient philosopher as a "chance wanderer . . . walking as it were out of the cave of Trophonius," PTAG: 33/KSA 1: 808. This obscure reference to the cave of Trophonius as the site and source of philosophic wisdom would become determinative for Nietzsche, opening him up to the subterranean, chthonic sources of Pre-Socratic thought. Not much has been made of this connection in Nietzsche scholarship although Frederick Hotz's "Nietzsche's Unmodern History of Philosophy" (Ph.D. diss., University of Texas–Dallas, 2000) makes some important strides in that direction. Heidegger never truly grasped this Trophonian dimension of Nietzsche's early work, tied as he was to a textual rather than performative model of Greek chthonic philosophy. However, the oracle of Trophonius represented to Nietzsche much more than an academic reference to an archaic source; for him it came to signify the creative power of Greek existence itself as a model by which to measure the joyless routine of German academic life. For references to Trophonius, see Pausanias, *Guide to Greece*, trans. Peter Levi (Hammondsworth: Penguin, 1971), 1: 393–396 and 2: 179–180; *The Oxford Classical Dictionary*, 1097; and, *Der Kleine Pauly: Lexikon der Antike*, vol. 5, ed. Konrat Ziegler (Munich: dtv, 1979), 987–988.

ten to the German classicist Werner Jaeger about the need for "subterranean philosophizing" in the area of ancient thought as a way of bringing about a new German instauration.[91] But the hidden implications of a subterranean, chthonic form of thinking in Heidegger's work would not become manifest until his lecturers on Nietzsche and Hölderlin. Nietzsche's influence was decisive. But Hölderlin's image of Hellas—mediated through the political interpretations of Hellingrath—would also come to shape Heidegger's vision of Graeco-German affiliation in terms of a mythic crossing of Pre-Socratic philosophy and National Socialist politics. Like Hölderlin himself, Heidegger would employ the figure of Hellas as a way of asserting his own political hopes-even if the spirit animating those hopes was decidedly different. Where Hölderlin's retrieval of Greek "subterranean fire" was undertaken as an affirmation of the French revolutionary spirit of 1789, Heidegger's recovery of the archaic emerged from out of the reactionary politics of 1914 and 1933.[92] And it was this spirit of political reaction that marked Heidegger's own reading of Hölderlin.

In his first lecture course on Hölderlin from WS 1934/35, Heidegger chose to focus on the hymn "Germania," which he read as a poetic proclamation of "the 'fatherland' as the historical be-ing of a *Volk*" (GA 39: 120). On the basis of Hölderlin's call for the futural return of the gods, Heidegger spoke of the fatherland as the site of a new beginning for Germany, the homeland where the *Volk* would be able to root itself in the earth. What was necessary for the preparation of such a beginning was a recovery of the archaic experience of being (*Sein*) as be-ing (*Seyn*), an experience that had been adumbrated in the poetry of Hölderlin and the thought of Heraclitus. "Hölderlin stands under the power of Heraclitean thought," Heidegger proclaimed (GA 39: 133–134). And, on the basis of this inner connection to the Greek *arche*, he insisted, "Hölderlin established in advance the new inaugural necessity that awaits us." Heidegger's rhetorical strategy to both juxtapose and conjoin Heraclitus and Hölderlin, Hellas and Germania, the first beginning and the future directed beginning, would get played out in a variety of ways over the next twelve years. From 1934 to 1946, Heidegger would devote three lecture courses to Hölderlin's work and deliver numerous addresses on his poetry, all the

91. See chapter 1, n. 51, and Edler, "Heidegger and Werner Jaeger," 123–125.
92. Like Hellingrath before him, Heidegger would willfully disregard the leftist revolutionary element in Hölderlin and would dismiss all of his sympathy for the republican ideals of the French Revolution. Instead, he would follow the dangerous politics of the George Circle in deeming Hölderlin as the poet of a secret Germany. For the Hölderlin reference to "unterirdisches Feuer," see Friedrich Hölderlin, *Sämtliche Werke*, ed. Norbert von Hellingrath and Friedrich Seebass (Berlin: Propylaen, 1922), 2: 198. For Hölderlin's link to the French Revolution, see Gerhard Kurz, *Mittelbarkeit und Vereinigung: Zum Verhältnis von Poesie, Reflexion, und Revolution bei Hölderlin* (Stuttgart: Metzler, 1975).

while turning to him as the poetic source for his mythic history of being.[93] Over the course of this period, Hölderlin will be invoked as the poet of the fatherland, the muse of a new politics of *Kampf*, the founder of a mythic German ontology of the *arche*, and the voice of national homecoming. By 1946, however, in the climate of post-war de-Nazification, Heidegger will alter his strategy of invoking Hölderlin as the symbol of German political renewal and instead will point to him as "proof" of his own anti-political interpretation of Greece and Germany. Explicitly rejecting the martial nationalism of his "Germania" lectures, with their emphasis on Hölderlinian images of "Death for the Fatherland," Heidegger will now interpret Hölderlin as a poet of the international. In his "Letter on Humanism," Heidegger will write:

> ... when Hölderlin composes 'Homecoming" he is concerned that his 'countrymen' find their essence. He does not at all seek that essence in an egoism of his people. He sees it rather in the context of a belongingness to the destiny of the West. But even the West is not thought regionally as the Occident in contrast to the Orient, nor merely as Europe, but rather world-historically out of nearness to the source. . . . 'German' is not spoken to the world so that the world might be reformed through the German essence; rather, it is spoken to the Germans so that from a destinal belongingness to other peoples they might become world-historical along with them. The homeland of this historical dwelling is nearness to being (PM: 257–258/WM: 169)

In this move from an explicitly political reading of the homeland in the "Germania" lectures to an anti-political one that finds the meaning of *Heimat* in an unmediated "nearness to being," Heidegger will attempt retroactively to absolve himself of his former political affiliations. But he will also attempt through a bold act of self-interpretation to influence the philosophical reception of his work. Heidegger will now view his own lectures on Hölderlin as mythic constructions of a German future that incorporate the destiny of the *Volk* into the destiny of other nations. As part of this work of hermeneutic self-explication, Heidegger will put forward a new politically cleansed reading of his work on the Greek tradition. In this sweeping attempt at autoexegesis, Heidegger will now try to cover over his

---

93. The three lecture courses from WS 1934/35, WS 1941/42, and SS 1942 are included in the *Gesamtausgabe* as GA 39, GA 52, and GA 53. Four different lectures are gathered in EHD and others in GA 75. But, there are also numerous references to Hölderlin in other lecture courses as well. Some of the better commentaries on the Heidegger-Hölderlin relationship include: Kathleen Wright, "Heidegger and the Authorization of Hölderlin's Poetry," in *Martin Heidegger: Politics, Art, and Technology*, ed. Karsten Harries and Christoph Jamme (New York: Holmes & Meier, 1994), 164–174; Marc Froment-Meurice, *That is to Say: Heidegger's Poetics*, 80–148; Christopher Fynsk, *Heidegger, Thought, and Historicity* (Ithaca: Cornell University Press, 1986), 174–229; and Susanne Ziegler, *Heidegger, Hölderlin und die "Aletheia"* (Berlin: Duncker & Humblot, 1991).

autochthonic politics of the Greek *arche* by transforming it into an eco-poetic evocation of the advent of being and a timely warning about the dangers of unbridled technology.[94] Despite Heidegger's rhapsodic invocations of Hölderlin, Heraclitus, and the Greek beginning in these postwar writings, it will not be difficult to detect the selfsame politics of Graeco-German autochthony as in the writings of 1933.

IX. SOPHOCLES, HÖLDERLIN, AND THE POLITICS OF HOMECOMING

Perhaps the best source for locating this shift from an explicit politics of the *arche* to an anti-political discussion of the homeland can be found in Heidegger's 1942 lecture course, *Hölderlin's Hymn: "The Ister"*. The *Ister* lectures become decisive for tracing this shift since they provide an essential point of contrast to the earlier work of 1933–35 when Heidegger actively supported National Socialist politics. Like the 1934/35 lectures on *Hölderlin's Hymns: 'Germania' and 'The Rhein'*, the *Ister* lectures follow the path of a hermeneutical trajectory that attempts to locate the essence of the political in the concealed message of Hölderlin's late river hymns. As ever, Hölderlin remains for Heidegger the poet of the national—but now "the national" will be rethought as something apart from nationalism, as the locality of human dwelling in the homeland. The *Ister* lectures will also mark an important shift in Heidegger's work about the relationship of German politics to Greek tragedy. Just as in the *Introduction to Metaphysics* of 1935, the *Ister* work will focus on the first choral ode from Sophocles' *Antigone*. But now, in 1942, Heidegger will interpret the ode not as a reflection on the Greek *polis* as the site for the unfolding of *human* history, but will read it as a concealed message on the unfolding of a *history of being* as the historical destiny of the West.

Through a kind of originary hermeneutics, Heidegger will focus on the hidden meaning of the Greek phrase *to deinon*, which occurs in the opening line of the first stasimon of Sophocles' tragedy.[95] On the basis of this singular term, Heidegger will *determine* the fundamental meaning of

---

94. On Heidegger's complex art of cover-up, see the insightful book by Reinhard Mehring, *Heideggers Überlieferungsgeschick: eine dionysische Selbstinszenierung* (Würzburg: Königshausen & Neumann, 1992).

95. Sophocles, *Antigone*, trans. Andrew Brown ((London: Aris & Phillips, 1987), line 332. Heidegger's commentary in IM: 146–165/EM: 112–126 and HHI: 51–122/GA 53: 63–152 provides a significant contrast between the political mood of 1935 and that of 1942. For Hölderlin's translation of *Antigone*, see *Sämtliche Werke*, 5: 1–2, 183–260. See also Karl Reinhardt's translation of Sophokles, *Antigone*, 6th ed. (Göttingen: Vandenhoeckh & Ruprecht, 1982), originally published in 1942; Kathleen Wright, "Grenzen der Weisheit: Heideggers Sophokles-Interpretationen 1935/1942," in *Weisheit*, ed. Aleida Assmann (Munich: Fink, 1991), 537–546; Th. Oudemans and A. Lardinois, *Tragic Ambiguity: Anthropology, Philosophy, and Sophocles' "Antigone"* (Leiden: E. J. Brill, 1987); and George Steiner, *Antigones* (Oxford: Clarendon Press, 1986), 66–106, 131–135, 174–177.

Sophocles' play and, through it, the essence of human being within the bounds of the *polis*. He will begin by translating *to deinon* in a twofold sense as "the terrible" (*das Furchtbare*) and "the violent" (*das Gewaltige*)—two contending traits whose very oppositionality defines the contentiousness and strife that make up human being. According to this translation, human being is marked by a conflict between two kinds of power. On the one hand, such being is powerful "in the sense of the overpowering power [*überwältigenden Waltens*] which compels panic fear, true *Angst*." On the other hand, such being is powerful "in the sense of one who uses power, who not only disposes of power [*Gewalt*] but is violent [*gewalt-tätig*] insofar as the use of power is the fundamental trait not only of his action but also of his *Dasein*" (IM: 149–150)/EM: 114–115). On the basis of its violent, contentious identity, human being seeks to use its power by deploying its knowledge, craft, and technical skill (*techne*) in the service of mastery and dominion over being (*physis*). But it also confronts a limit to such mastery in the very order and governing structure (*dike*) of being itself. In this primordial conflict between the instrumental force of *techne* and the imperishable power of *dike*, Heidegger locates the source of the *Unheimlichkeit* (strangeness, uncanniness, homelessness) of human being.

As part of his attempt to read Sophocles in terms of the history of metaphysics, Heidegger will interpret *Antigone*, as he will *Oedipus Tyrannus*, as a play about the boundlessness of humanity's desire to wrest knowledge from the hiddenness of being. For him these plays come to represent the human attempt to force unconcealment (*a-letheia*) from concealment (*lethe*) in a violent gesture of mastery and control. In their various ways and in strangely different contexts, Oedipus, Antigone, and Creon will all come to symbolize the violent dimension of humanity's "struggle for being [*Kampf um das Sein*]" that defines "the great age of Greece" in terms of the power of "self-assertion" (*Selbstbehauptung*) (IM: 106–107/EM: 81). By 1942, however, after his fateful encounter with Nietzsche and (through him) with National Socialism, Heidegger will abandon the violent politics of *Kampf* and self-assertion for another kind of politics: the politics of the anti-political. Now Heidegger will rethink the essential conflict in Sophocles' choral ode from *Antigone* as the tension and strife that manifests itself within being as a whole. As in 1935, Heidegger will focus attention on the Greek *polis* as the site or place of human historical happening. But now he will lay emphasis on the relation of history to the homeland and on the homeland itself as the very source of Graeco-German destiny.

Following Sophocles' insight in the *Antigone* chorus, Heidegger will claim that "the human being [is] the uncanniest [*unheimlichste*] being" and that "human beings are, in a singular sense, not homely, and that their care is to become homely" (HHI: 71/GA 53: 87). By translating Sophocles' term *to deinon* as "*das Unheimliche*" ("the unhomely"), Heideg-

ger will commit to a hermeneutic strategy that will shape his whole reading of Hölderlin and of German politics. Now the condition of being unhomely will be understood as something tied to the fundamental condition of human being itself. Ontologically speaking, he will claim, human
beings are like Antigone. They too share the fate of being uncanny. And,
like her, they too stand alone amidst beings facing the uncanny prospect
of being without a home. But this sense of "unhomeliness" (as Heidegger
terms it) is not simply one form of uncanniness among others. On the
contrary, it expresses the uncanniness of human being as such, the uncanniness of that being who alone among all other beings is not at home
within being itself. In this state of tension between not being at home and
yearning for a home, Heidegger will locate the source of Greek tragic art,
a source whose power he will find again only in the poetry of Hölderlin. As
Heidegger will claim, Hölderlin's river hymns—especially the late hymn
"The Ister," which is first published in an edition by Norbert von
Hellingrath—come to express the ontological tension within human
being that was revealed in Sophoclean tragedy.[96]

In his 1942 lectures, Heidegger will designate Hölderlin's Ister hymn as
the poetic site of an ontological-political homecoming. But the path of
this homeward journey will be twisted and hard to follow. Part of the difficulty involved in this task lies in the poem itself, part in Heidegger's
hermeneutically violent reading of the poem's meaning. Rejecting the
standard literary-aesthetic approach to Hölderlin that treated the river
hymns merely as symbols of the change, transformation, and becoming of
nature, Heidegger will interpret them as the poetic-ontological expressions of a Germanocentric metaphysics of history. On Heidegger's reading, Hölderlin's naming of the German river "Danube" (*Donau*) by the
Greek name of "Ister" (*Istros*) signals a problem of relating identity and
difference, sameness and the foreign as an act of hermeneutic translation
and relocation. Translation, for Heidegger, will never be reduced to the
mere act of verbal transposition or equivalency; words are not only translated but are relocated (*übersetzt/übergesetzt*) to another context. Hence his
re-translation of Hölderlin's German translation of Sophocles' Greek
choral ode will itself enact a kind of ontological-poetic relocation of archaic Greek culture on German soil. That is, it will attempt to bring into
language the uncanny relation of a Greek homeland to a German one.
And Heidegger will hazard this kind of ontological-poetic confrontation
(*Auseinandersetzung*) precisely in his reading of the Ister hymn. Writing in
1942, he will carry out this hermeneutic confrontation with Hölderlin in

---

96. What made this ontological link to the Ister ever more significant for Heidegger was
that this poem had been published for the first time by Hellingrath who also provided the
title, HHI: 2, 14/GA 53: 2, 15.

the midst of another kind of historico-political confrontation—the World War.

In his lecture course, Heidegger will seize upon the river imagery in "*Der Ister*" as a way of rethinking the relation of Greece and Germany— both spatially and temporally—in terms of a political metaphysics. Spatially, the river Danube runs its course from west to east, from its source in Donaueschingen (near Heidegger's own Black Forest home) to its mouth in the Black Sea (not far from the ancient Greek colonial city of Istros). This transcontinental journey from the upper Danube across *Mitteleuropa* to the lower Danube at the very limit of Europe itself appears to Heidegger as an encrypted narrative about German destiny at the axis of intersection between west and east, modern and ancient, end and origin, German and Greek. For even as it transects the geographical-spatial boundaries of distant cultures, the Ister also transgresses their historical-temporal limits. Hence, what becomes involved for Heidegger in Hölderlin's designation of the Danube as "Ister" is nothing less than the rethinking of Graeco-German kinship against the poisonous influence of Roman culture. The Romans had two distinct names for the one river. They called the upper Danube "Danuvius" and the lower, "Ister." But Hölderlin will see them as one, and will reverse the Latin suppression of the Greek origin by reclaiming it for the Germans. Thus, in the third stanza of his poem, Hölderlin will write:

> Yet almost this river seems
> To travel backwards and
> I think it must come from
> The East.
> Much could
> Be said about this.[97]

Employing the figure of chiasmic reversal, Hölderlin will write as if the genuine origin of the Ister lay in the east, at its Greek source, rather than in Germany. Such a reversal will violate the logic of geography by reconfiguring the source of the river according to a metaphysics of history. Or so Heidegger will claim.

In his poem, Hölderlin will then reverse the Roman strategy of dividing the river in two. Now he will reclaim the original Greek name of the river for the upper half and, in so doing, reconnect the original name to the river's source, as if the genuine provenance of the Ister were in Greece

---

97. Friedrich Hölderlin, *Hyperion and Selected Poems*, ed. Eric Santner (New York: Continuum, 1990), 270–271; *Sämtliche Werke*, 4: 221.

rather than Germany. For Heidegger, the meaning of this reversal will be all too clear. On his reading, the Ister flows hesitantly at its source—precisely at the source—because the very motion of the surging force outward toward the east is met by a countersurge or pull that is ruled over by the power of the origin itself—the homeland (HHI: 143/GA 53: 178). It is as a poem that celebrates the originary power of the homeland that Heidegger will read *"Der Ister."* But there is another reason why "the Ister whiles by the source and is reluctant to abandon its locale." "It dwells near the origin because it has returned home to its locality from its journeying to foreign parts." In this sense, it comes to expression as the unity of both the dwelling place within the homeland and the journeying from it, understood as the unity of becoming homely and being unhomely (HHI: 164/GA 53: 202). This becoming homely in and through the encounter with the strange, foreign, and unhomely enacts for Heidegger what he terms "the law of history," the tenets of which were originally set forth in a letter written by Hölderlin to his friend Casimir Ulrich Böhlendorff on December 4, 1801.

Hölderlin writes to his friend on the eve of his departure for France, a trip that he undertakes because, as he says, "they [the Germans] have no use for me." By traveling to a foreign land, Hölderlin apparently hopes to locate the sources for a more genuine homeland in which he can reclaim the lost origin of the German nation. But even before offering his thoughts on France, Hölderlin will focus on the meaning of ancient Greece for his task. As he tells Böhlendorff:

> We learn nothing with more difficulty than to freely use the national. And, I believe that is precisely the clarity [*sic*] of the presentation that is so natural to us as is for the Greeks the fire from heaven. For exactly that reason they will have to be surpassed in beautiful passion . . . rather than in that Homeric presence of mind and talent for presentation.
>
> It sounds paradoxical. Yet I argue once again . . . [that] in the progress of education the truly national will become the ever less attractive. Hence the Greeks are less master of the sacred pathos, because to them it was inborn, whereas they excel in their talent for presentation, beginning with Homer, because this exceptional man was sufficiently sensitive to conquer the Western *Junonian sobriety* for his Apollonian empire and thus to veritably appropriate what is foreign.
>
> With us it is the reverse. Hence it is also so dangerous to deduce the rules of art for oneself exclusively from Greek excellence. I have labored long over this and know by now that, with the exception of what must be the highest for the Greeks and for us—namely, the living relationship and destiny—we must not share anything identical with them.
>
> Yet what is familiar must be learned as well as what is foreign. This is why the Greeks are so indispensable for us. It is only that we will not follow them

in our own, national [spirit], as I said, the *free* use of *what is one's own* is the most difficult.[98]

As Hölderlin understands it, what is proper or natural for a *Volk*—what is *das Eigene*—can be appropriated [*angeeignet*] only when it is experienced in and as the other or the foreign. A culture's return to itself can only take place in and through its journey outward. What is "natural" for the Germans—what is their own, what they are born to—is what Hölderlin alternately calls "the clarity of presentation" and "Junonian sobriety." What is foreign, strange, and other for them is what he variously terms "fire from heaven" and "sacred pathos." The only way the Germans can genuinely come to appropriate what is natural for them, according to this logic, is to journey southward, retrieving fire from heaven (the sacred pathos of Greeks), thus making the clarity of presentation properly their own. As Hölderlin sets about to appropriate the foreignness of ancient Greek culture, he chooses as his strategy for retrieval an originary style of translation. Rejecting Winckelmann's aesthetic classicism with its ideal of order and mimesis, Hölderlin sets out to penetrate to the core of Greek tragic art through jarring, often violent translations of Pindaric and Sophoclean forms. By reappropriating archaic conventions of syntax and grammar whose paratactic, discontinuous structures appeared to the reader as fragmented and incomplete, and by then juxtaposing them with a frighteningly literal style of translation, Hölderlin produced an effect of disjunction and dislocation—what the *Antigone* chorus had termed "uncanny." Moreover, in his use of archaic etymologies that ruptured the smooth surface of meaning provided by a "classical" text, Hölderlin pointed to the roots of a different homeland for the Germans: the *Heimat* of Sophoclean language.

Heidegger would ultimately find in these various Hölderlinian strategies of rupture, disjunction, and violent transgression a model for his own understanding of Graeco-German affinity. And, as prototypes of a radical style of cultural retrieval, they would prove decisive in helping him to articulate the underlying meaning of Germany's historical journey toward homecoming. Following the logic of Hölderlinian poetics, Heidegger will argue in the Ister lectures that the law of exchange outlined in the Böhlendorff letter applies to the destiny of the German nation as well: "What for the Greeks is their own is what is foreign to the Germans; and what is

---

98. Friedrich Hölderlin, *Essays and Letters on Theory*, trans. Thomas Pfau (Albany: SUNY Press, 1988), 149–150; *Sämtliche Werke*, 3: 319–320. Heidegger will refer to the Böhlendorff letter in a number of contexts: GA 39: 136, 290–294; Ni: 103–104/GA 43: 122; GA 52: 135; HHI: 124–125, 135–137/GA 53: 154–155, 168–170; EHD: 82, 86–88, 157–158. This is only a partial list.

foreign to the Germans is what is proper to the Greeks" (HHI: 124/GA 53: 154). In various contexts and in diverse ways, Heidegger will return to this theme of historical homecoming throughout his Hölderlin lectures and essays.[99] Indeed, it will form the very basis of his understanding of the "Ister" as a river poem that articulates the law of historical homecoming as a journey outward from the source and home. As Heidegger puts it:

> The law of being homely as a becoming homely consists in the fact that historical human beings, at the beginning of their history, are not intimate with what is homely, and indeed must even become unhomely with respect to the latter in order to learn the proper appropriation of what is their own in venturing to the foreign, and to first become homely in the return from the foreign. The historical spirit of the history of a humankind must first let what is foreign come toward that humankind in its being unhomely so as to find, in an encounter with the foreign, whatever is fitting for the return to the hearth. For history is nothing other than such return to the hearth. (HHI: 125/GA 53: 156)

In this reading of the hearth as the source of historical homecoming, Heidegger will find the axis of his own ontological-political reading of German history. The hearth, Heidegger will claim, is but another word for "being." And yet the hearth can also be read as the site or stead of being-homely, of coming to determine the center of the home, as the place for human dwelling. As the uncanniest of all beings, Antigone leaves the hearth and home to take up the task of burying her brother. Still, despite her movement outward away from the home, in an uncanny way she preserves the home by seeking to shelter her dead brother under the earth away from the edicts of the *polis* that threaten his burial. In this sense, Antigone succeeds in carrying out the law of Hölderlinian homecoming: only by leaving her home does she ultimately succeed in sustaining it. Only by journeying outward from the hearth is she able to preserve it. What is preserved, however, is not the familial hearth within the homeland but the chthonic, subterranean sources of the hearth that lie buried under the earth in both a cave and a crypt.

Heidegger's Ister lectures will attempt to reclaim these chthonic elements in the story of Antigone for a new reading of German homecoming, one that is marked by a concern for the hearth as the source of an ontological-political philosophy of rootedness and autochthony. On Heidegger's reading, rootedness in the earth will become the decisive measure of a genuine historical homecoming that marks the point of affinity between the Germans and their Greek ancestors. As he conceives

---

99. Heidegger raises the issue of historical homecoming as a way of thinking through the Böhlendorff letter and relating it to his overall vision of Graeco-German autochthony.

it, Hölderlin's poetry comes to express this chthonic longing of the Greek tragic hero to return to the earth and its roots as to a lost home. Heidegger even indicates as much in the lecture course on the *Ister* and in his 1943 address "Homecoming," where he explicitly links Hölderlin's poetry to the chthonic sources of the earth: to "the soil of the native land" and "the soil of the homeland" (EB: 267/EHD: 29).[100]

Underlying Heidegger's ontological thematization of the German homeland as the hearth and the source of being, however, was a decidedly political reading of the National Socialist project as it stood in 1943. By then, Heidegger had long become disillusioned with the National Socialist attempt to dominate the earth through the violent use of *techne*. After the German failure at Stalingrad in the winter of 1942/43, he began to attack National Socialism from within, as it were, setting up in its place the hope for a German future that was committed to the homeland as the source of autochthonic regeneration. Now he saw National Socialism as a hindrance to the realization of such a future. In his "Homecoming" essay, Heidegger will appeal to those Germans who have committed themselves to a kind of "inner emigration" from the Nazi regime, those who understand that the historical reality of National Socialism has succeeded only in destroying the roots of the homeland. In place of his erstwhile political commitment to the regime, Heidegger will now take up in a more self-consciously "anti-political" way his old Hölderlinian *Volksreligion* of *Heimat*, hearth, and rootedness. Writing from this position of inner emigration, Heidegger will pose the question to those Germans who no longer find a home on German soil:

> Supposing then that those who merely reside on the soil of the native land are not yet those who have come home to their own in the homeland; and supposing also (apart from the merely fortuitous possession of home-bred things and of one's own life) that to the poetic essence of homecoming there belongs a sense of being open to the origin of the joyous—supposing *both* these things, then are not those sons of the homeland who (though far from the soil of the homeland) gaze into the serenity of the homeland that lights up for them and who devote themselves to a discovery that is still spared them, are these sons of the homeland not squandering their lives on an errand of sacrifice? Are they indeed not the nearest kindred of the poet? (EB: 267/EHD: 29–30; translation altered)

100. In EB: 267/EHD: 29, Heidegger writes of "those who only reside on the soil of the native land [die auf dem Boden des Geburtslands nur Ansässigen . . . sind]." But he indicates there that mere residence does not have the ontological status of genuine homecoming. Heidegger's discourse on the *Ansässigen* may have deeper roots in Jacob Burckhardt's *Griechische Kulturgeschichte*, 1: 22–23, in which Burckhardt refers to the Athenian claim to power and rule as being "aboriginal" or "sprung from the soil"—in German, *uransässig* and *bodenentsprossen*. Heidegger seems to favor the *uransässig* here against the mere *Ansässigen*.

In a gesture of spiritual expatriation, Heidegger will now rethink the problem of "becoming homely" (*Heimischwerden*) in terms of his new condition of inner political exile. If, in 1934, Heidegger could exhort ethnically German students who lived outside the borders of the Reich to come to Germany "not only to absorb themselves in German science but to become homely [*heimisch werden*] in the German motherland and the German *Volksgemeinschaft*," by 1943 he will have abandoned such eager hopes. Now he will claim that genuine homecoming "consists solely in the people of the country becoming homely [*heimisch werden*] in the still-withheld essence of the home" (NH: 212; EB: 245/EHD: 14).[101] The difference in perspective was dramatic. In the early years, he still believed in the nationalist dream of a Greater German Reich that would include all ethnic Germans within its borders. By 1943, however, Heidegger will come to think of the "authentic" Germany as something still-withheld, still "futural," an ideal at odds with the crudely biologistic imperialism of the Third Reich. And yet, in some important sense, the logic of Heidegger's ontological politics will not have changed at all. He will still enlist Hölderlin in the service of a *völkisch* homecoming, only now he will defer the politics of this homecoming to an indefinite future instead of committing himself to an ideal of political self-assertion in the present. In a move that is subtle and elusive, Heidegger will now define homecoming archaically as "the return into the nearness of the origin [*arche*]" (EB: 258/EHD: 23). And, with this move toward the archaic, he will have established the essential conditions for an anti-political reading of the homeland as the ontological ground of the *polis*.

As Heidegger will maintain, genuine homecoming for the Germans can only occur in and through the historical retrieval of the Greek *arche*. But, since the original Greek *arche* is itself a mythic product of German yearning rather than the emergence into presence of a genuinely historical phenomenon, we need to become more skeptical about the putative "Greek" sources of Heidegger's narrative. Heidegger's "Greece," like Hölderlin's, can never be recovered since, as Philippe Lacoue-Labarthe has argued, "it never took place."[102] In Heidegger's thinking, as in that of German Philhellenism, "it became necessary also to 'invent' a Greece

101. In a speech he delivered on January 22, 1934, entitled "National Socialist Education," Heidegger outlines what he thinks is necessary for a German *Volksgemeinschaft*: "to know to what point urbanization has brought the Germans, how they would be returned to the soil and the country through resettlement, to know what is entailed in the fact that eighteen million Germans belong to the *Volk* but, because they are living outside the borders of the Reich, they do not belong to the Reich," HCW: 56/NH: 200/GA 16: 233. Clearly, Heidegger dreamed of one day reuniting all members of the *Volk* into a single nation bound by their autochthonic links to an ancestral past.

102. Philippe Lacoue-Labarthe, *Typographies*, trans. Christopher Fynsk (Stanford: Stanford University Press, 1998), 246.

which had up to that point remained unimitated, a sort of metaphysics of Greece, if you will, which would allegedly be at the foundation of Greece itself (but which then also ran the risk of never really having taken place in itself)."[103] Our recognizing these mythological sources of Heidegger's Graecomania is crucial to an understanding of his work, but we also need to see how the mythologization of the Greek *arche* was carried out politically, even when it was done in the name of an anti-political reading of the *polis*. And this is especially true for Heidegger's use of Hölderlin.

As the war appeared to be lost, Heidegger invoked the poetry of Hölderlin as a way of rethinking the German mission in the world. When the self-assertion of panzers and air strikes failed, Heidegger called for a different ideal of German destiny. In the midst of the desolation spawned by the war, Heidegger hoped that Germany might emerge as the nation capable of saving the West by taking up its lost identity in the Greeks. And for help in recruiting the Germans to such a task Heidegger turned to Hölderlin. Heidegger did not, however, think of Hölderlin primarily as an emissary of spiritual homecoming or as an envoy of poetic rebirth for the German language. Rather, I would argue, Heidegger's philosophical engagement with Hölderlin was *always* political. When he deploys the innocent language of "homecoming," "the uncanny," "poetic dwelling," "the hearth" and "commencement," he attempts to carry out his political designs by other means through an encoded discourse that works both as a subtle critique of historical National Socialism and as an urgent call for the instantiation of a more properly authentic National Socialism. What emerges from a careful scrutiny of this language—even the later eco-poetical language of the fourfold with its poignant elegy about "the gods who have fled"—is nothing less than the mythification of a poet for political purposes. This political use and abuse of Hölderlin as a "poet in a destitute time" can hardly be thought of as unique. On the contrary, it can be traced back to and situated in a specific historical and cultural moment: the postwar German reception of Norbert von Hellingrath's philological researches on Hölderlin.

X. NORBERT VON HELLINGRATH'S MYTH OF A SECRET GERMANY

As a member of the George Circle, Hellingrath came to see Hölderlin as more than a great poet who had been slighted and had fallen out of favor because of shifting literary tastes. For Hellingrath, Hölderlin became the embodiment of George's new ideal: the poet as *Führer*. In his office as the

---

103. Philippe Lacoue-Labarthe, *Heidegger, Art, and Politics*, 79; see also two other works by Lacoue-Labarthe and Jean-Luc Nancy, "The Nazi Myth," *Critical Inquiry* 16 (1990): 291–312, and *Retreating the Political*, ed. Simon Sparks (London: Routledge, 1997).

leader of the *Volk*, the poet would "gaze beyond his time, proclaim the future, and . . . prepare a new arrival of the gods on earth."[104] Hellingrath's writing offered then not merely another career-advancing publication; it sought rather to make Hölderlin the prophet and founder (*Stifter*) of a new German future, what Hellingrath termed "a secret Germany." In Hellingrath's eyes, the standard bourgeois reflex to identify the Germans as "the *Volk* of Goethe" was itself the product of the realist-naturalist aesthetic that had flourished in the nineteenth century and had relegated Hölderlin to the status of a minor poet. But Hellingrath sought to challenge this complacent attitude:

> I call us "the *Volk* of Hölderlin" because it is of the very essence of the Germans that their innermost burning core (which lies infinitely deep beneath the surface of its sedimented crust) can only come to light in a *secret* Germany. This innermost core expresses itself through human beings who, at the very least, must be long dead before they are recognized and find a response; in works that will always impart their secret only to the very few, saying nothing to most, and wholly inaccessible to non-Germans. Indeed, this is true because this secret Germany is so certain of its inner value . . . that it makes no effort to be heard or seen. . . . Hölderlin is the greatest example of this hidden fire, of this secret *Reich*, of this still unrecognized coming into being of the divine burning core.[105]

Hellingrath's portrait of Hölderlin was marked by a deeply aesthetic impulse to create spiritual values that would save Germany from the vulgar materialist impulses of the technological order. To carry out this aesthetic quest, he enlisted Hölderlin, the translator of Pindar and Sophocles, the poet of Graeco-German homecoming. But Hellingrath was no *völkisch* ideologue. As a member of the George Circle and as the son of a German general, Hellingrath harbored little affection for the values of hearth and home. His real aim involved fostering a kind of aesthetic education that would create an aristocracy of culture and spirit against the leveling influences of German bourgeois life. To this end, he helped to confect an image of Hölderlin modeled on the *mythos* of an archaic Greece. As Hellingrath put it, "Hölderlin's turn to the Fatherland is only the direct consequence of his Greek being"; "he exalts the Greek past as a German future."[106] As part of this effort, Hellingrath focused on Hölderlin's disjointed and at times violent translations of Pindar and Sophocles, transla-

104. Norbert von Hellingrath, *Hölderlin: Zwei Vorträge* (Munich: Hugo Bruckmann, 1922), 31–32. For a portrait of Hölderlin as poetic *Führer* see the study by the George Kreis member Max Kommerell, *Der Dichter als Führer in der deutschen Klassik* (Berlin: Bondi, 1928).

105. Ibid., 16–17. In Hellingrath's testament here to the image of a "secret Germany," we find the afflatus for Heidegger's own political vision.

106. Norbert von Hellingrath, "Vorrede" to his edition of Hölderlin's *Sämtliche Werke*, 4: xiii, xii.

tions whose innate affinity to archaic forms proved to Hellingrath that "today, alone among all languages, the German language may be compared to the ancient [Greek]."

What emerged from Hellingrath's editorial labors and scholarly writing was nothing short of a full-fledged "Hölderlin Renaissance" within German culture. Now Hölderlin would be recruited in the name of various cultural and political initiatives from both the right and the left.[107] But Hellingrath's own interpretations proved more fertile for thinkers from the right, including, of course, Heidegger. Heidegger would follow other right-wing Hölderlin enthusiasts like Kurt Hildebrandt, Paul Böckmann, and Berthold Vallentin in reaffirming the essential truth of "Hölderlin's overly bold proclamation, incomprehensible to a whole century, of the originary Greek-German essence."[108] From Hölderlin's notoriously difficult and impenetrable poetic style, these thinkers would conjure an image of the bard as a committed German nationalist, one whose love for the homeland was rooted in the deeply primordial link between archaic Greece and modern Germany. Hildebrandt, for example, would embrace the fantasy of a future directed German Reich embodied in the National Socialist "idea of the Fatherland." As part of this strategic use of the poet for blatantly political ends, Hildebrandt would seize upon the myth of the *arche* and the thought of Heraclitus as indications of the racial-linguistic-autochthonic bond between Germania and Hellas. At one point in his 1939 book, *Hölderlin,* he went as far as to interpret the poet's line from "The Migration"—"Yet I long for the Kaukasos!"—as a call for racial purity between two Caucasian groups: "the Hellenic race" and "the Germans . . . [who were] just as purely Aryan."[109] Hellingrath's own reading of Hölderlin was not overtly racial in the style of Hildebrandt. Nevertheless, it did establish the kind of deeply nationalist context for interpreting Hölderlin's work that would influence the postwar generation through the era of National Socialism. Moreover, it helped to legitimate the practice of hermeneutic violence in Hölderlin studies that Heidegger would reprise in his own work.

Hellingrath's researches shaped Heidegger's interpretations in a num-

---

107. For an account of this shift see Helen Fehervary, *Hölderlin and the Left* (Heidelberg: Carl Winter, 1977); Henning Bothe, *"Ein Zeichen sind wir, deutungslos": Die Rezeption Hölderlin von ihren Anfängen bis zu Stefan George* (Stuttgart: Metzler, 1992); Claudia Albert, "'Dient Kulturarbeit dem Sieg?': Hölderlin-Rezeption von 1933–1945," in *Hölderlin und die Moderne,* ed. Gerhard Kurz (Tübingen: Attempto, 1995), 153–173; Heinrich Kaulen, "Der unbestechliche Philologe: Zum Gedächtnis Norbert von Hellingraths (1888–1916)," *Hölderlin Jahrbuch* 27 (1991): 182–208; and also those works listed in note 68 of this chapter.

108. Berthold Vallentin, "Winckelmann," in *Der George Kreis,* ed. Georg P. Landmann (Stuttgart: Klett-Cotta, 1980), 370; and Paul Böckmann, *Hölderlin und seine Götter* (Munich: Beck, 1935).

109. Kurt Hildebrandt, *Hölderlin: Philosophie und Dichtung* (Stuttgart: Kohlhammer, 1939), 246–247.

ber of ways. As late as his 1950 essay, *"Hölderlins Erde und Himmel,"* Heidegger would write: "Somewhere Kant makes an observation, the spirit of which is: it is easy to discover something after one has been taught where to look. In relation to Hölderlin, Norbert von Hellingrath remains for us just such a teacher" (EHD: 152). Hellingrath's first decisive move was to shift attention away from Hölderlin's early poems and his novel *Hyperion* (1797) and instead to place emphasis on the late hymns and elegies as well as on the translations of Sophocles and Pindar. By claiming Hölderlin as a late descendent of Hellenic ancestry and as a formidable nationalist, Hellingrath effected a kind of interpretive revolution in Hölderlin studies. When he later died as a twenty-eight year old infantryman at Verdun (1916), there quickly emerged a nationalist myth which sought to unite the poetic yearning for a return to the homeland with the ethic of sacrificial death in service of the Fatherland. It is in this spirit that Heidegger would later write that Hellingrath's editions "hit us students like an earthquake" (OWL: 78/GA 12: 172). Hellingrath offered to young Germans of the postwar generation a wholly mythic vision of the poet of myth. Obscuring the genuine political context of Hölderlin's work and its democratic support for the revolutionary ethos of 1789, Hellingrath transformed Hölderlin into a right-wing nationalist in conformity with the "ideas of 1914." In his one-sided account, Hölderlin emerged as the poet who offered the Germans an authentic path to national self-assertion by way of a "holy marriage" between Germania and Hellas.[110] On this reading, Hölderlin's significance for German culture hinged upon his role in "prophesying to the German *Volk* their elect status and their imminent fulfillment."[111] In raising the poet to such an elevated position, however, Hellingrath also managed to alter the status of his work. Hölderlin's abundant references to "Asia" and "the Asiatic" were either suppressed or made to conform to the Hellenocentric vision of George. Hölderlin's romantic attachment to his local, Swabian environs was now seen as evidence of a burgeoning nationalism. And his many references to the earth, the land, the soil, and the native ground were understood as expressions of a chthonic longing for rootedness in the German landscape. More significantly, Hölderlin's poetry will now be read, not as rhapsodic or elegiac verse, but as a kind of "metaphysics of history," a reading of German politics in terms of myth, destiny, and redemption.[112] This Hellingrathian vision of a "secret Germany" possessed of a unique historical mission will dominate Heidegger's own political reading of Hölderlin.

Like Hellingrath, Heidegger will conflate Hölderlin's use of myth with

---

110. Stefan George, "Das Hellenische Wunder," in *Der George Kreis*, 87.
111. Hellingrath, "Vorrede," xi.
112. Bothe, *"Ein Zeichen sind wir, deutungslos,"* 112.

his own mythologization of Hölderlin as political prophet. In the process, he will rend Hölderlin's work from its historical context and refashion it to conform to his own *Sonderweg* metaphysics of German autochthony. And he will do all this in the name of an "essentially more primordial" reading of the texts, even as he shifts his own interpretation of Hölderlin from the aggressive nationalism of 1933–34 to the self-serving "internationalism" of 1946.[113] When Hölderlin, in concert with Hegel and Schelling, wrote in "The Oldest System-Program of German Idealism" (1796) that "we need a new mythology . . . mythology must become philosophical in order to make the *Volk* rational and philosophy must become mythological in order to make philosophers sensual," he was advocating a "new religion" of reason inspired by the revolution in France.[114] But, when Heidegger advocated his own *Volksreligion* of *Heimat*, hearth, and homeland, he was far removed from the Swabian context of 1797. His mythic call for a "secret Germany . . . that still lives through all the misery of the *Volk*" conjured a very different image of political order, one that justified Germany's elect status among nations on the basis of its autochthonic relation to the Greeks(GA 16: 290). Within this selfsame logic of autochthony, the Böhlendorff letter, the translated choral ode from *Antigone*, the late river hymns, the Pindar renderings, all came to enact for Heidegger the Hölderlinian law of homecoming by way of an encounter with the foreign. Now, even the conflagrations of a world war could be reconciled to the logic of poetic destiny. As the poet of the Greek beginning, de-historicized beyond all recognition, the Hölderlin of Heidegger's imagination will come to legitimize Germany's metaphysical task of preparing the "other" beginning for the elected *Volk*. But this historical task is never conceded as something inevitable. The Germans will need to work to excavate the hidden, buried, archaic, and chthonic roots of German destiny in that "other" Greece, the Greece of Winckelmann, Karl Otfried Müller, Burckhardt, Hölderlin, Hellingrath—and Nietzsche, always Nietzsche, for Heidegger's mythology of German destiny within the history of the West would be unthinkable without Nietzsche. And yet, as with Hölderlin, the Nietzsche of Heidegger's writings is not simply the author of specific his-

---

113. Compare, for example, Heidegger's nationalist sentiments from WS 1934/35 about Hölderlin as the poet of the *Vaterland*, GA 39: 120–123, with his remark from 1946 about Hölderlin's status as the poet of the Occident whose writings need to be read "not patriotically, or nationalistically, but in terms of the history of being," PM: 257/WM: 168. For a record of von Hellingrath's influence on Heidegger, see *Martin Heidegger/Imma von Bodmershof Briefwechsel, 1959–1976*, ed. Bruno Pieger (Stuttgart: Klett-Cotta, 2000).

114. Hölderlin, *Essays and Letters on Theory*, 155–156. This short programmatic essay, which has been variously attributed to Schelling and Hegel, was not included in the original Hellingrath edition of the *Sämtliche Werke*. My reference to the German text derives from the later edition: Friedrich Beissner and Jochen Schmidt, eds., F. Hölderlin, *Werke und Briefe* (Frankfurt: Insel, 1969), 2: 648–649.

torical texts. He is, rather, a mythic figure transmitted to Heidegger through the work of a preceding generation, a prophet outlining a historical metaphysics of Western destiny rather than a mere philosopher. "Nietzsche," like "Hölderlin," becomes the name of a way to read history mythically in terms of an inner, originary bond to the Greek *arche*. In order to follow the path of Heidegger's thought from the Rectorial Address in 1933 to the De-Nazification hearings of 1945, we will have to account for the enduring presence of Nietzsche in this work and trace the shifts in the movement from political mythology to a mythology of the anti-political.

CHAPTER FIVE

Heidegger's "Nietzsche"

Above all, do not confound me with what I am not.

—FRIEDRICH NIETZSCHE
EH: 3/KSA 6: 257

The political revolution cannot be separated from the spiritual revolution.

—ALFRED BAEUMLER
Alfred Rosenberg und der Mythus des 20. Jahrhunderts

I. SELF-STAGING THE NIETZSCHE LECTURES

When in 1961 Heidegger finally got around to organizing the extensive lecture notes and essays drawn from his courses on Nietzsche from 1936/37 to 1944/45, he came to view them as constituting a kind of résumé of his own philosophical development. As he put it in the "Foreword" to *Nietzsche:* "Considered as a whole, the publication aims to provide a view of the path of thinking that I followed from 1930 to the 'Letter on Humanism' (1947)" (Ni: xvi/NI: 10).[1] For a German audience eagerly awaiting the unfinished "second part" of *Being and Time,* the publication of this massive two-volume collection—it is 1155 pages in length—came to be thought of as a kind of second *magnum opus,* an impression that Hei-

---

1. Throughout this chapter, I will cite the *Gesamtausgabe* version of the Nietzsche lectures to provide the original citations for David Krell's four-volume translation of Heidegger's *Nietzsche* (San Francisco: Harper & Row, 1979–1987). At various times, I will also cite the original 1961 edition of *Nietzsche* (Pfullingen: Neske, 1961) in two volumes to show the differences between the original manuscript version and the later published version. As in all matters of Heideggerian textuality, however, we need to be very careful about taking anything for granted. The GA version cannot in all cases be taken as the simple original. Heidegger revised and edited these texts himself before handing them over to his editors, and only someone familiar with the arcana of Heideggerian orthography may be able to follow the scribblings, erasures, deletions, and palimpsestic additions from the author of "the Last Hand"—as the advertising brochure from the Klostermann citadel puts it. My purpose in juxtaposing certain passages from GA 43, 44, 47, 48, and 50 with passages from NI and II will be to show how Heidegger sought to cover over or transform the meaning of a sentence or paragraph—or to elide politically incriminating sentiments—with the aim of presenting, via the cultivated style of a *"raffinierte Selbstinszenierung"* (an "ingenious self-staging"), a politically cleansed version of the originals. For anyone wishing to follow the path of this *Selbstinszenierung,* it would be instructive to read the texts of 1936/37–1944 against those of 1961, with an eye toward the political differences between Nazi Germany and the Federal Republic.

degger himself sought to convey. These two volumes, in their tastefully understated salmon-colored dust jackets, were intended to reinforce an impression of serious philosophical weight; they were to be received as a veritable masterwork by the reigning German master.[2] Few people of the time, however, were in a position to understand the complex and artful style of philosophical self-presentation that went into the publication of this text. With a kind of guileful legerdemain, Heidegger succeeded in directing not only the way his works would be published, but, more significantly, the way they would be interpreted and understood. By using his own *imprimatur* to advance a work that would serve as a guide to following his path of thought—from the first masterwork of 1927 (*Being and Time*) through the thorny period of 1933–1945 and on to postwar writings such as *Holzwege* (1950), *The Principle of Reason* (1957), and *On the Way to Language* (1959)—Heidegger succeeded in controlling to an unusual degree the reception and dissemination of his thought (a practice that continues even today in the managed style of the *Collected Edition* of his works).[3] By collating manuscripts in unhistorical fashion, eliding delicate passages that might offend, revising with an eye to political correctness, and juxtaposing to alter contexts, Heidegger engineered a kind of wildly successful "cover-up" of his own political affiliations and views, so much so that it was not until the Heidegger centenary of 1989 that this whole style of self-presentation came under widespread scrutiny.[4] Those of us who read Heidegger today read him in a very different way than his audience did in 1961.

2. Heidegger did publish a number of books during the 1950s—*Holzwege* (1950), *Einführung in die Metaphysik* (1953), *Was heisst Denken?* (1954), among others [for a bibliographical list, see William Richardson, *Heidegger: Through Phenomenology to Thought* (The Hague: Martinus Nijhoff, 1963), 675–680], but none of these constituted a "major" work on the scale of *Being and Time*. Throughout the German university world at the time, there was much talk about a second magnum opus, and when Heidegger published his two-volume *Nietzsche*, it was received as the long-awaited major work. Even the design of the book jacket, with its unofficial title *heidegger/nietzsche*, presented this work as a confrontation between two thinkers whose names alone constituted an *Auseinandersetzung*.

3. No one has written more incisively about the philological and philosophical problems of the *Gesamtausgabe* than Theodore Kisiel. For his critique of the vision, planning, and production of the Heidegger corpus, see "Heidegger's *Gesamtausgabe*: An International Scandal of Scholarship," *Philosophy Today* 39 (1995): 3–15; "Edition und Übersetzung: Unterwegs von Tatsachen zu Gedanken, von Werken zu Wegen," in *Zur philosophischen Aktualität Heideggers*, ed. Dietrich Papenfuss and Otto Pöggeler (Frankfurt: Klostermann, 1992), 3: 89–107. See also Daniel Dahlstrom, "Heidegger's Last Word," *Review of Metaphysics* 41 (1988): 589–606.

4. The most prominent books dealing with the political dimension of Heidegger's work that came out between 1987–1990 include Hugo Ott, *Martin Heidegger: Unterwegs zu seiner Biographie* (Frankfurt: Campus, 1988); Victor Farias, *Heidegger und der Nationalsozialismus*, trans. Klaus Laermann (Frankfurt: S. Fischer, 1989); Jacques Derrida, *De l'esprit: Heidegger et la question* (Paris: Editions Galilée, 1987); Philippe Lacoue-Labarthe, *La fiction du politique* (Paris: C. Bourgois, 1990); and Richard Wolin, *The Politics of Being* (New York: Columbia University Press, 1990). Otto Pöggeler also issued a third edition of his seminal work, *Der Denkweg Martin Heideggers* (Pfullingen: Neske, 1990) to coincide with this period of scandal and discourse. Pöggeler's "Nachwort zur dritten Auflage," 337–410, proves ultimately to be more insightful

In his insightful work, *Heideggers Überlieferungsgeschick,* Reinhard Mehring has analyzed this Heideggerian practice of guileful self-presentation and has argued that we need to begin to look more critically at the manner and order of Heidegger's publications. By following what Mehring has termed Heidegger's *"Selbstinszenierung"* (style of self-staging, self-production, theatrical self-presentation), we are finally in a position to begin unraveling the complex skein of philosophical themes, historical topoi, authorial directives, editorial suturings, and metaphysical leitmotifs that comprise the *Nietzsche* volumes. The task is an enormous one, however, and it will certainly require the work of many hands. In this last chapter, I would like to focus on Heidegger's writings on Nietzsche from 1936 to 1945, seeing them as variations on the theme of political and ontological autochthony that we have been following in our discussion of Heidegger's political writings, Rectorial Address, Hölderlin lectures, courses on the Pre-Socratics, and essay on "Europe and German Philosophy." Part of the problem in reading the Nietzsche lectures, I will argue, reflects their unique style of delivery and composition. Far from offering a "unified" approach to the philosophy of Nietzsche from a "Heideggerian" perspective, these lectures offer a textual record of the shifts, turns, deviations, and spirals that take place in Heidegger's thought in the crucial years from 1936 to the end of the war. In their very manner of publication, we can see how Heidegger was at pains to cover over these delicate detours and spiraling turns on his path of thought.[5] In 1961, he wanted to present these lectures

---

on the topic of Heidegger's political views than his earlier works on Heidegger. During this same period of approximately three years, there also appear two important collections of documents, speeches, letters, and personal reminiscences focusing on Heidegger's political activities: *Antwort: Martin Heidegger im Gespräch,* ed. Günther Neske and Emil Kettering (Pfullingen: Neske, 1988) and *Martin Heidegger und das "Dritte Reich,"* ed. Bernd Martin (Darmstadt: Wissenschaftliche Buchgesellschaft, 1989). Richard Wolin's edition of *The Heidegger Controversy* (New York: Columbia, 1991) follows a year later. Then the American reception of Heidegger's politics begins in earnest.

5. Unfortunately, the English language translations of the 1961 *Nietzsche* edition do not help to clarify matters. David F. Krell may have been hampered by copyright problems or by the plans of Harper & Row in his four-volume edition of Heidegger's *Nietzsche.* At any rate, what he produced is an edition that corresponds neither to volumes GA 43, GA 44, GA 47, GA 48, and GA 50 in Klostermann's *Gesamtausgabe* nor to those of the Neske edition. It is its own edition, one that offers Heidegger's Nietzsche to an American audience on Krell's terms. Nii, for example, includes the essay "Who Is Nietzsche's Zarathustra?" (1953) from VA: 101–126, but Krell leaves out "Die Metaphysik als Geschichte des Seins" (1941), "Entwürfe zur Geschichte des Seins als Metaphysik" (1941), and "Die Erinnerung in die Metaphysik" (1941)—all of which were included in Joan Stambaugh's translation of *The End of Philosophy* (New York: Harper & Row, 1973), 1–83. This approach to Heidegger's Nietzsche lectures made it hard for American readers to read Heidegger historically—and critically. Krell did provide some helpful analysis in his afterwords to each volume, but they were still not critical enough of Heidegger's fundamentally National Socialist views. For a criticism of the Krell edition, see Frank Schalow, "The *Gesamtausgabe* Nietzsche: An Exercise in Translation and Thought," *Heidegger Studies* 9 (1993): 139–152. Schalow does not, however, address the National Socialist sources of Heidegger's *Nietzschebild.*

as part of his own autobiographical struggle with the history of meta-physics conceived as a history of be-ing (*Seyn*). By focusing on the meta-historical narrative of being's eventful pilgrimage through and as time, Heidegger hoped to deflect attention away from the historical circum-stances of the lectures themselves. As he presents them, these essays, lec-tures, notebook entries, and rough drafts constitute nothing less than a "confrontation" or *Aus-einander-setzung,* with "*the matter [Sache]*" of think-ing (Ni: xv/NI: 9):

> The task of our lecture course is to elucidate the fundamental position within which Nietzsche unfolds the guiding question of Western thought and responds to it. Such elucidation is needed in order to prepare a con-frontation with Nietzsche. If in Nietzsche's thinking the prior tradition of Western thought is gathered and completed in a decisive respect, then the confrontation with Nietzsche becomes one with all Western thought hith-erto....
>
> Confrontation is genuine criticism. It is the supreme way, the only way, to a true estimation of a thinker. In confrontation we undertake to reflect on his thinking and to trace it in its effective force, not in its weaknesses. To what purpose? In order that through the confrontation we ourselves may be-come free for the supreme exertion of thinking. (Ni: 4–5/NI: 13)

Through his confrontation with Nietzsche, Heidegger hoped to pro-vide a detailed, comprehensive, and critical account, not only of Nietz-sche's thought, but of the history of Western philosophy as a whole. But he had other motives as well. Heidegger dispensed with the idea of offering another well-researched, scholarly monograph on the particulars of Nietz-sche's philosophy. Instead, he came to view Nietzsche meta-historically as a name representing the consummation of Western metaphysical think-ing in its final stages. "Nietzsche," Heidegger argues, "is the *last metaphysi-cian* of the West. The age whose consummation unfolds in his thought, the modern age, is a final age. This means an age in which at some point and in some way the historical decision arises as to whether this final age is the conclusion of Western history or the counterpoint to another beginning. To go the length of Nietzsche's path of thinking to the will to power means to catch sight of this historical decision" (Niii: 8/NI: 480). Heideg-ger delivered these lines originally in his summer 1939 course, "Nietzsches Lehre vom Willen zur Macht als Erkenntnis." In his 1961 edition, these lines are almost identical—and yet, considered hermeneutically, their meaning becomes radically different. In the context of the earlier draft, Heidegger's history of the West was understood eschatologically from the position of a Hölderlinian vision of the German future. The history of be-ing [*Seynsgeschichte*] was not merely thought as a matter of metaphysical consummation or ontological unfolding; it was also grasped, quite decisively, as a matter of political destiny.[6] The history of being was narrated as a process of decline, decay, darkening, and devastation—a movement away from the ontological rootedness of the Pre-Socratic *arche*.[7] Only through the overcoming of this epochal rootlessness might the West be saved. This epochal rootlessness, in turn, could only be overcome through the "creative power" of the German *Volk*.[8] Only the Germans, that *Volk* of thinkers and poets, had the power to retrieve the force of the first Greek beginning and prepare the path for the arrival of another beginning. All of Heidegger's references to *Ankunft* ("arrival"), *Zukunft* ("future"), and *der kommende Gott* ("the coming god") betray this eschatological outline of Western history. The Germans' affinity with their Greek philosophical ancestors would serve as the foundation for a new rootedness in the Alemannic soil. Ontological autochthony, when crossed with political autochthony, would lead to "the salvation of the West" (EdP: 40).

Heidegger expressed such sentiments in clear terms in three different essays from 1936–1937: "Europa und die deutsche Philosophie," "Die Bedrohung der Wissenschaft," and "Wege zur Aussprache." There he spoke about "the threat to the West of its utter deracination [*Entwurzelung*]," of Europe's need of "overcoming its own deracination and fragmentation," and of the necessity of a *Volk* "to enter into proximity to its origin," thereby attaining "true rootedness and autochthony [*Bodenständigkeit*]" (DE: 16; EdP: 31–32). When Heidegger spoke in 1939 about "the historical decision" that Nietzsche's work posed, he was situating this decision in terms of the nihilism that he saw threatening the modern age. For him, the modern configuration of nihilism was but another expression of rootlessness. And, in an essential sense, it was this threat of rootlessness that made it imperative for the German *Volk* to enter into proximity with its Greek origin. The *mythos* of a rootedness in the Greeks, when wedded to what Heidegger termed "a centuries-long and irreplaceable

6. In his notebook entries from 1938–1940, Heidegger writes: "'the history of be-ing [*Seyn*],' is the name for the attempt to put the truth of being as appropriative event back into the word of thinking . . . ," GA 69: 5. In another passage from *Besinnung*, he explains that "the first history of being [*Sein*], from *physis* to the 'eternal recurrence,' is a declining beginning. The course of this history remains hidden, however. . . . Because the beginning can only be experienced in an incipient way, it is only from out of the other beginning of the history of be-ing [*Seynsgeschichte*] that the first beginning and its history can come into openness—though never into the realm of the public," GA 66: 223. For Heidegger, the question of *Seynsgeschichte* was always political—precisely where he denies the "political" dimension, as in HHI: 79–87/GA 53: 97–108 and P: 88–97/GA 54: 130–144.

7. Here, as elsewhere, Heidegger's lexicon of *Verwüstung, Untergang, Verfinsternis, Vernachtung*, and *Verdüsterung* can be traced back to Nietzsche. See chapter 3, notes 74 and 75.

8. Heidegger will focus on the power of the *Volk* to "rescue" Germany in DE: 20; GA 55: 108; GA 65: 54, and EdP: 40.

rootedness in the Alemannic-Swabian soil," would yield the essential foundation for Heidegger's Graeco-Germanic *Ursprungsphilosophie* (DE: 11).

Throughout the Nietzsche lectures, Heidegger will come back to this mythic reading of Western history in terms of its Greek origin. In fact, he will read Nietzsche's fundamental critique of modernity in and against its relation to the Pre-Socratics. As he will put it, "Nietzsche's philosophy is the end of metaphysics, inasmuch as it reverts to the beginning of Greek thought" (Nii: 199/NI: 464). Moreover, Heidegger will find in Nietzsche's recovery of this *arche* an axial point for understanding the entire tradition of Western thought: "the consummation of metaphysics as the essential fulfillment of modernity is an end because its historical ground is itself a transition to the other beginning. The other beginning does not leap outside the history of the first, does not renounce what has been, but goes back into the grounds of the first beginning" (Niii: 182/NII: 29). This whole discourse about beginning and end, *arche* and *eschaton,* will shape the very contours of Heidegger's philosophical narrative about the history of being from the 1930s onward. What will emerge from this metaphysical-historical crossing of archeology as eschatology is an *Ursprungsphilosophie* with a decidedly Nietzschean stamp, one that will interpret the modern age as nihilism and will locate the origins of nihilism in the Platonic decline from the Pre-Socratic origin. This Nietzschean genealogy will leave its mark on the lectures, essays, notes, and drafts that come together in Heidegger's *Nietzsche* of 1961.

In 1936 Heidegger's privileging of the Greek *arche* was never solely metaphysical, however. It was always tied to his decidedly political reading of the German future in terms of the myth of autochthony. In this sense, Heidegger's *Ursprungsphilosophie* is not to be understood as a mere atavistic or nostalgic yearning for the past. It was, on the contrary, future-directed and bound up with a Hölderlinian vision of homecoming that still lay ahead for the German *Volk.* As Heidegger himself would later put it in "A Dialogue on Language": "Origin or provenance [*Herkunft*] always remains that which comes toward us as future [*Zukunft*]" (OWL: 10; GA 12: 91). Here Heidegger went farther than Nietzsche in assigning a political meaning to his philosophy of origin and transforming it into a way of reading the present situation of Germany in the 1930s and '40s. Hence, Heidegger can tell his students: "To this day Nietzsche has not been understood. His fate is the fundamental happening of our history."[9] During the 1930s, Heidegger was unequivocal when using the collective pronoun "we" and the genitive adjective "our"—he was referring to the German

---

9. Martin Heidegger, "Der Anfang der abendländischen Philosophie," unpublished lectures from SS 1932 in possession of the Herbert Marcuse Archive of the Stadt-und Universitätsbibliothek, Frankfurt am Main, #0029.01, 9.

Volk as an autochthonous group. By 1961 the political and historical circumstances had changed dramatically.

After his ordeal with the De-Nazification Committee in December 1945 when he lost his teaching position, Heidegger was desperate to rehabilitate his philosophy and reclaim his chair at Freiburg. Anyone who reads his "Letter on Humanism" (written 1946, published 1947) in light of his difficulties with the French authorities in Baden can glean this message.[10] After Heidegger was granted emeritus status in 1949 and began teaching again in the winter of 1951–52, he experienced a kind of institutional rehabilitation, so much so that by the end of the decade Heidegger had succeeded in re-establishing his position as Germany's foremost philosopher.[11] The publication of the *Nietzsche* volumes in 1961 now reaffirmed this status. But we read these texts poorly if we fall victim to the all too common habit of reading them out of context. Through a choreographed effort of autoexegetical cleansing and purging, Heidegger presented these volumes to the public as "proof" of his apolitical motives during the Nazi era. By positioning Nietzsche and the problem of nihilism in the context of a centuries-long philosophical debate about Plato, Descartes, Aristotle, Hegel, and Kant, Heidegger made it appear as if his genuine topic was simply "*the matter* of thinking"—understood as a purely intraphilosophical narrative about "the history of being." In this way, he could offer various perspectives on the thought of Nietzsche as a focal point for the history of metaphysics.

But Heidegger's motives were not purely philosophical—either in 1936–45 or in 1961. In our reading of Heidegger's lectures on Hölderlin, his *Introduction to Metaphysics,* and in his other speeches, we have seen a persistent hybridization of the ontological and the political. As part of our inquiry we have seen how, for Heidegger, ontological autochthony (the *mythos* of a primordial origin or Pre-Socratic *archē*) becomes inextricably bound to political autochthony (the *mythos* of an ancestral homeland rooted in the earth). We have also seen how Heidegger's *Ursprungsphilosophie* comes to function as "geo-philosophy"—a form of thinking that thinks the "origin" or *Ursprung* in terms of the earth as autochthonous ground. From this critical perspective we have been able to see how Heidegger's history of being gets played out as a narrative about German homecoming. But the text of 1961 tries to narrate a different story.

There Heidegger seeks to conceal his earlier commitment to political autochthony by reverting to a strategy of elision and omission. As part of

---

10. Compare, for example, Heidegger's passages from GA 39: 4, 290–294, with PM: 257–260/WM: 168–172. See also Anson Rabinbach, "Heidegger's *Letter on Humanism* as Text and Event," *New German Critique* 62 (1994): 3–38.

11. Ott, *Heidegger: Unterwegs,* 334–340.

this strategy he will omit passages critical of "democracy," elide a reference to his Rectorial Address, and attempt to render his lectures ahistorical by placing them in the "timeless" context of philosophical-historical analysis. The conflation of genres (lectures, essays, notes) in the main text and the editorial arrangement of the material contribute to this overall effect. Nor does Heidegger seek to situate his volumes in their original hermeneutic context of the 1930s. He self-consciously omits references to his contemporaries and to the reigning Nietzsche scholarship of that time. Only in the very first lecture course will he even mention the work of Alfred Baeumler or Karl Jaspers—and he will nowhere reference the important book of 1935, *Nietzsche's Philosophy of the Eternal Recurrence of the Same*, by his Jewish student, Karl Löwith.[12] Part of Heidegger's strategy can doubtless be traced back to his demand that his work be considered only against the "great" philosophers of the tradition and not be placed in any merely academic context. But we also need to appreciate just how carefully Heidegger choreographed the production of the *Nietzsche* volumes to cover over any trace of his own involvement in the politics of National Socialism.[13] That Nietzsche became a kind of cause célèbre for National Socialist thought in the 1930s can hardly be denied. Part of my argument here will be to try to read Heidegger's original Nietzsche lectures in their appropriate National Socialist context.

I want to engage Heidegger's arguments about nihilism, modernity, will to power, metaphysics, the transvaluation of values, and the eternal return of the same, not only as elements of an intra-philosophical history of being, but also as intra-party sorties in a generational *Kampf* about Nietzsche's "proper" relation to National Socialism. By situating Heidegger's lectures in this generational context and by reading them as part of an ongoing struggle with philosophers such as Alfred Baeumler, Kurt Hildebrandt, and Ernst Horneffer, I want to show how deeply imbedded they were in the political metaphysics of National Socialism. On my reading, Heidegger's Nietzsche lectures did indeed constitute a "confrontation (*Auseinandersetzung*) with National Socialism"—but in a very different sense than that claimed by Heidegger. To follow the path of this *Auseinandersetzung* signifies nothing less than to uncover the political foundation of Heidegger's history of being.

12. Heidegger's reference to Baeumler from SS 1937 in GA 44: 229 will, for example, be eliminated in the 1961 edition. At the same time Heidegger ignores Karl Löwith's book *Nietzsches Philosophie der ewigen Wiederkunft des Gleichen* (Berlin: Die Runde, 1935).

13. Just as an example, Heidegger's SS 1937 lectures employ the term "Kultur-Rasse" when describing a theme from Spengler, GA 44: 106. In the 1961 edition, Heidegger has changed it to "Kultur," Nii: 101/NI: 360. These kinds of minor changes abound; taken together they constitute a self-conscious practice of political cleansing.

II. HEIDEGGER'S "CONFRONTATION" WITH NIETZSCHE

At the very outset of his first Nietzsche lecture in 1936, "Nietzsche: The Will to Power as Art," Heidegger leaves no doubt about his hermeneutical relation to his subject. The task of the lectures, he tells his listeners, will be "to prepare a confrontation [*Auseinandersetzung*] with Nietzsche," so that "the confrontation with Nietzsche becomes a confrontation with all Western thought hitherto" (Ni: 4/GA 43: 5). To ensure that the rhetorical effect of his interpretation will not be missed, Heidegger goes on to underline the significance of this "confrontation" by repeating the term ten times within three paragraphs. But what did Heidegger seek to convey in his confrontational reading and how are we to interpret it? More significantly, for our purposes, how did the meaning of this confrontation change between 1936 and 1961? And how are we to measure such a change? Before we can even begin to answer these difficult questions, however, we will need to become more attentive to Heidegger's rhetorical use of the term *Auseinandersetzung* as a way of unifying his lecture courses. We will also need to direct attention to the changing meaning of this confrontation in its different rhetorical contexts.

When Heidegger first used the term *Auseinandersetzung* to characterize his reading of Nietzsche in the winter of 1936/37, he was drawing on the archeo-teleological lexicon that he developed in his reading of ancient Greek philosophy. In its standard colloquial sense, *Auseinandersetzung* can be rendered to mean "debate," "discussion," "dispute," "quarrel," "contest," "settling of accounts," or "altercation," among other possibilities. The range of meanings extend from a sober analysis or examination of a topic to a violent struggle or clash.[14] Etymologically, however, the term means something like a "placing" or "setting" (*setzen*) things "apart-from one another" or separating them out from one another (*auseinander*). The simple translation of *Auseinandersetzung* as "confrontation" misses this decisive element of *reciprocal* determination in the play of back and forth, to and fro. For Heidegger this decisive form of playful interaction as a "setting-asunder-of-one-element-from-another" was hardly a matter of terminological dispute. It lay at the heart of all originary thinking and offered a pathway for reconfiguring the essence of truth. In his 1931/32 lecture on Plato's "Allegory of the Cave," Heidegger writes:

> *Aletheia* is not merely the openness of a being, it is rather in itself a setting-asunder [*Auseinander-setzung*] (now we can grasp the alpha privative more clearly). . . . To the *essence* of truth *belongs* untruth.

14. *The New Wildhagen German Dictionary* (Chicago: Follett, 1965), 106, and *Cassell's German English Dictionary* (New York: Macmillan, 1978), 65–66.

Unconcealment, the overcoming of concealing, does not genuinely happen if it is not in itself an originary struggle [*Kampf*] against hiddenness. An *originary* struggle (not a polemic): that means a struggle which itself first *creates* its enemy and opponent and brings it into its *sharpest opposition.* Unhiddenness is not simply the one shore and hiddenness the other. Rather, the essence of truth as unconcealment is the bridge. Better: it is the *building of a bridge from* one side *against* the other (GA 34: 92).

In the early 1930s, Heidegger deploys the term *Auseinandersetzung* in a decidedly martial context in conjunction with the terms *Kampf, Streit, Polemik,* and *Macht* to communicate something of the originary struggle he unearths in the essence of Greek *aletheia.*[15] Although he never uses this term explicitly in his Rectorial Address, we can hear echoes of it in his references to "struggle," "battle," and "essential opposition" (*Wesensgegensatz*) throughout that speech (HCW: 36–39/SdU: 18–19). This polemical-martial understanding of *Auseinandersetzung* is even more pronounced in Heidegger's violent translation of a passage from Plato's *Republic* at the conclusion of his speech. When Heidegger declares at the end that "All that is great stands in the storm," he rhetorically reaffirms the heroic language of will, battle, conflict, *Sturm* and *polemos.* As I argued in chapter 2, "standing in the storm" here means nothing less than enduring the Heraclitean conflict within the essence of truth. In this sense, *Auseinandersetzung* becomes another kind of self-assertion—not of an isolated subject but of a historical *Volk.* By winter of 1934/35, this kind of *völkische Auseinandersetzung* will emerge full-scale in Heidegger's interpretation of Heraclitus as "the name of an originary power in Western-German historical *Dasein* . . . in confrontation with the Asiatic" (GA 39: 134).

In *Introduction to Metaphysics* (1935), Heidegger will explicitly link *Auseinandersetzung* to a translation of fragments B53 and B80 of Heraclitus. Within this context *Auseinandersetzung* will serve as a German translation of Heraclitean *polemos:*

> The *polemos* named here is a strife [*Streit*] that holds sway before everything divine and human; it is not war [*Krieg*] in the human sense. First and foremost, according to Heraclitus, this struggle [*Kampf*] allows what is essential to come into opposition by setting itself apart from itself [*auseinandertreten*], thus letting position and stance and rank first come into relation in what is present. In such setting itself apart, clefts, intervals, expanses, and jointures open themselves up. In con-frontation [*Aus-einandersetzung*] there emerges a world. (Confrontation neither divides nor even destroys unity. It forms this; it is gathering-*logos.* *Polemos* and *logos* are the same) (IM: 62/EM: 47, trans. altered).

15. Compare, for example, passages from GA 34: 66, 92, 325 with those from GA 39: 125–126, 135–136, in which Heidegger will use the term *Auseinandersetzung* in passages alongside terms such as *Kampf, Gegnerschaft, Widerstreit, Gewalt,* and other martial terms.

In various contexts and in a range of passages, Heidegger will employ the term *Auseinandersetzung* as a guiding word for thinking the proper relation of Germany and Greece and for posing the question of the first beginning as it relates to the other beginning. Because it expresses the primordial strife within the originary Greek experience of the essence of truth, *Auseinandersetzung* becomes a crucial term for thinking the relation between the first and the other beginning (GA 65: 58; 181–188; 205–206).[16] As Heidegger himself puts it in one of his drafts from *Besinnung*: "*Con-front-ation* [*Aus-einander-setzung*]: that between metaphysics in its history and the thinking of the history of be-ing [*seynsgeschichtliches Denken*] in its future" (GA 66: 80). Only in the confrontation with the first Greek beginning would the Germans be able to think the other beginning. But this confrontation was not only *ontological,* in that it would have to rethink the history of being; it would also be *political* in that such a confrontation would involve a genuine *Auseinandersetzung* with European history and Germany's place within that history.

Heidegger expressed as much in his 1936 address, "Europe and German Philosophy," where he argued that "the preservation of the European *Völker* from the Asiatic" could only be achieved by a "creative confrontation with the whole of its history hitherto" (EdP: 31–32). Only in this confrontation with its history could "a *Volk* come into the proximity of its origin" and achieve "genuine autochthony [*Bodenständigkeit*]." In his 1937 address, "Wege zur Aussprache," Heidegger repeated his claim that the only path to overcoming the "threatening deracination of the West" lay in the "creative confrontation with the strangest and most onerous— the Asiatic" and with "the historical world of the early Greeks" (DE: 20–21). Through this confrontation and it alone would the *Volk* be in a position to attain "historical singularity and greatness." By reading the destiny of the *Volk* as a matter of creative confrontation, and by interpreting this confrontation as an indices to the history of the West, Heidegger succeeded in linking his narrative of *Seynsgeschichte* to his myth of German political autochthony. *Auseinandersetzung* within this political context would be thought as the German "setting-itself-apart" from the European traditions of liberalism, democracy, enlightenment, and Anglo-French political institutions, as well as from Russian Communism and Asian barbarism. In a kind of Heraclitean confrontation with democracy from the West and with Communism from the East, the Germans would assert themselves as the autochthonous *Volk,* rooted in the homeland and in the Greek philosophical tradition. This inscription of German destiny on the palimpsest of Greek philosophy would become a determinative theme in all of Hei-

16. For an illuminating discussion on *Auseinandersetzung,* see Gregory Fried, "Heidegger's *Polemos,*" *Journal of Philosophical Research* 16 (1990–1991): 159–195.

degger's work during the 1930s, shaping the framing questions of his thinking.

When Heidegger spoke of *Auseinandersetzung,* he was invoking a whole constellation of themes clustered around the rhetoric and axiomatics of autochthony. But autochthony itself would always be determined by Heidegger as a kind of *Auseinandersetzung* with German history as a crucial turning point in the history of being. The epoch of unbridled technological nihilism could only be worked through if the Germans would remain rooted in the earth and not fall victim to the Americanization of the West. In a decidedly confrontational sense, Heidegger's lectures on Nietzsche attempt to lay out a path of recovery from this historico-metaphysical malady by reconfiguring the history of metaphysics in line with a new German future. But the Nietzsche lectures also constitute a running commentary on the effects of nihilism upon the German *Volk* and on its need to confront its own destiny in the form of a historical decision. When Heidegger writes in the summer of 1939 that the "thoughtful confrontation with Nietzsche" means coming to terms with the modern age as a "final" age, he is framing this confrontation precisely as a historical decision (Niii: 8/GA 47: 8). If we seek to grasp the political meaning of this confrontation, we will need to attend to Heidegger's rhetorical discourse about *Auseinandersetzung* throughout his Nietzsche lectures and writings from 1936 to 1945 and later, from 1961.

Heidegger's decision to use the term *Auseinandersetzung* as a pivotal theme in his lectures was itself Nietzschean. What he sought to convey by it was something of the rich philosophical depth of Heraclitean *polemos.* He also hoped to draw on the whole Nietzschean rhetoric of battle, struggle, contest, challenge, duel, feud, and competition conveyed in the terms *agon, Wettkampf, Wettstreit,* and *Gegensatz.*[17] Nietzsche himself developed the term *Wettkampf,* or "contest," from his reading of early Greek tragedy, poetry, rhetoric, philosophy, and music. In one of his notebook entries from 1871, he writes that his aim is "to develop the concept of the contest [*Wettkampf*] out of Heraclitus" (KSA 7: 400). But Nietzsche thought of the contest as a metaphysical principle for understanding the whole cultural world of Pre-Platonic Greece: its athletic games in Homer, its cosmic principle of strife in Hesiod, its rhetorical debates among the Sophists, its rhapsodic element in Pindar, its dialectical component in the Socratic *elenchus* and in the Platonic symposium, as well as its many forms and appearances in the theological cults, the martial competitions, and the political struggles. Nietzsche's *Birth of Tragedy* can indeed be read as an extended cultural meditation on the meaning of the contest not only as a

17. For some Nietzschean uses of the terms *Gegensatz, agon, Wettkampf,* and *Wettstreit,* see KSA 1: 25, 783–792; KSA 7: 399–407; KSA 12: 331.

Greek aesthetic principle, but also as a way of reconstituting a decadent German culture after the political triumphalism of the Franco-Prussian war. As Nietzsche put it in his essay, "Homer on Competition" (1872), "the aim of agonistic education was the well-being of the whole, of state society" and was not primarily thought of in individual, subjective terms.[18] Even later in his notebooks from the time of *Zarathustra* (ca. 1883), Nietzsche would link the principle of the contest to a martial form of community. "Solitude is necessary for a time, so that a being may be wholly penetrated and cured—and thus become hard. A new form of community: Militantly asserting itself [*sich kriegerisch behauptend*]. Or else the spirit becomes feeble. . . . War between different thoughts! And their armies! (But without gunpowder!). . . . The contest as principle" (KSA 10: 515).

Heidegger would draw upon this Nietzschean principle of martial self-assertion (*Selbstbehauptung*) in his Rectorial Address where he called for a new form of community for the *Volk*—one rooted in an originary bond with the early Greeks. "Stand[ing] on the threshold of a great transformation," the German *Volk* would, Heidegger declared, need to confront the essential truth about "the abandonment of modern humanity in the midst of beings" proclaimed in Nietzsche's phrase "God is dead" (RA: 8/SdU: 13). Only then would they be able to win back the greatness of the Greek beginning and prepare the possibility of another beginning in a German future. Heidegger would never abandon his myth about the greatness of the *arche* lying in the future. Nor would he jettison his attachment to Nietzsche's principle of *Wettkampf* as a necessary element in the preparation of an archaic future. "Essential opposition" (*Wesensgegensatz*) would be a determinative force both ontologically and politically; the Rectorial Address was offered as a way of galvanizing these forces in Germany into a *Kampfgemeinschaft* so that (in Heidegger's words) "our *Volk* fulfills its historical mission" (RA: 12–13/SdU: 18–19).

By the time Heidegger began his Nietzsche lectures he had settled on the term *Auseinandersetzung* as a way of expressing this Nietzschean-Heraclitean power of opposition, contestation, and strife as an organizing principle for his own work, as well as for understanding Nietzsche and the history of Western philosophy. The failure of the rectorate had dampened Heidegger's enthusiasm about taking an active role in shaping and molding the forces of opposition within German society. In a letter to Karl Jaspers in July of 1935, Heidegger writes about "two thorns in my flesh: the confrontation [*Auseinandersetzung*] with the faith of my youth and the failure of the rectorate" (HJB: 157). This deep sense of personal defeat

18. Friedrich Nietzsche, "Homer on Competition," in *On the Genealogy of Morality*, ed. Keith Ansell-Pearson (Cambridge: Cambridge University Press, 1994), 192. See also KSA 1: 789.

brought to an end Heidegger's Platonic dream, so evident in the Rectorial Address, of reshaping the polis in the image and likeness of the philosopher.

As he stands at the podium in October of 1936 and lays out the structure of his argument, Heidegger will begin a confrontation with those forces within Germany that undermined this Platonic dream. And he will use his Nietzsche lectures as a way of asserting his own philosophical vision of a more perfect National Socialist Germany—precisely in and through a confrontation with National Socialism and with the reigning National Socialist interpretation of Nietzsche. In this sense, Nietzsche becomes for Heidegger the name of a topic (*Sache*) for thinking: the confrontation with modernity as an epoch of nihilistic uprootedness. Such a confrontation not only thinks of the modern era as an age of transition between the end of metaphysics and the beginning of a postmetaphysical style of thinking. It also rethinks the present in terms of an archaic future. This old dream of the George Circle—to reconstitute an uprooted Germany by means of an archaic retrieval of Hellas—would be reframed and repositioned by Heidegger as an *Auseinandersetzung* with his NS contemporaries over the meaning of will to power for a German polity. If many of his colleagues in philosophy, like Baeumler, Heyse, Hildebrandt, Richard Oehler, Heinrich Härtle, Ernst Horneffer, and Friedrich Würzbach embraced a Nietzschean metaphysics of will and struggle in the service of technological domination, Heidegger thought otherwise.[19] He offered an alternative version of a "secret Germany" against this "*Kampfes-und Willensmetaphysik*" and he invoked the name "Nietzsche" as a way of undermining the standard National Socialist vision of politics and of German futurity.[20]

From 1936–45, the name "Nietzsche" will signify for Heidegger a whole complex of mutually implicated and reciprocally countervailing forms of *Auseinandersetzung*: of Heidegger with Nietzsche's philosophy; of Nietz-

19. The list of books written by National Socialist partisans on the thought of Nietzsche is too long to include here. Some of the most prominent include the propaganda piece *Nietzsche und der Nationalsozialismus* (Munich: Zentral Verlag der NSDAP, 1937) by Heinrich Härtle; Ernst Horneffer, *Nietzsche als Vorbote der Gegenwart* (Düsseldorf: A. Bagel, 1934); Richard Oehler, *Friedrich Nietzsche und die deutsche Zukunft* (Leipzig: Armanen, 1935); Friedrich Würzbach, *Nietzsche und das deutsche Schicksal* (Berlin: Bondi, 1933); Alfred Baeumler, *Nietzsche: Der Philosoph und Politiker* (Leipzig: Reclam, 1931); Alfred Baeumler and Kurt Hildebrandt, eds., *Nietzsches Werke*, 4 vols. (Leipzig: Reclam, 1931).

20. Ernst von Aster, "Nietzsche-Einflüsse und Nietzsche-Renaissance," in *Die Philosophie der Gegenwart* (Leiden: A.W. Sijthoff, 1935), 239. For an interpretation of the National Socialist *Nietzschebild*, see Manfred Riedel, *Nietzsche in Weimar: Ein deutsches Drama* (Leipzig: Reclam, 1997); Martha Zapata Galindo, *Triumph des Willens zur Macht: Zur Nietzsche-Rezeption im NS-Staat* (Hamburg: Argument, 1995); Hans Langreder, "Die Auseinandersetzung mit Nietzsche im Dritten Reich," Ph.D. dissertation, University of Kiel 1971; and Gerhard Lehmann, "Friedrich Nietzsche und die Nietzschebewegung der Gegenwart," in *Die deutsche Philosophie der Gegenwart* (Stuttgart: Kröner, 1943), 183–204. See also chapter 3, note 68.

sche's philosophy with the history of metaphysics; of Heidegger with the history of metaphysics in and through Nietzsche; of Heidegger with other Nietzsche commentators; and, above all, of Heidegger with National Socialism (in and through his confrontation with Nietzsche, with other Nietzsche commentators, and with the history of Western metaphysics). When Heidegger speaks of confronting a "historical decision" in the Nietzsche lectures, he is alluding to this complex concatenation of historico-philosophical *Auseinandersetzungen* that intersect in Germany in the 1930s and '40s around the name and topic of "Nietzsche." When he resuscitates this topic in 1961, however, he will attempt to simplify this complex of themes by reducing it to a purely intra-philosophical discourse.

III. HEIDEGGER AND THE METAPHYSICS OF EDITORIAL PRACTICE

When he published his Nietzsche lectures in 1961, one of the passages that Heidegger sought to alter concerned a reference to the "splendid book by Kurt Hildebrandt, *Wagner and Nietzsche: Ihr Kampf gegen das 19. Jahrhundert*" (Ni: 89/GA 43: 105).[21] As a member of the George Circle and later a committed Nazi, Hildebrandt had argued that "the most fruitful and characteristic idea with which Nietzsche considered the Greek world is that of the *agon,* and of the contest [*Wettkampf*]."[22] Drawing on Hildebrandt's interpretation, Heidegger too would seize upon the centrality of the Greek *agon* for Nietzsche and transform it into a *Wettkampf/Auseinandersetzung* with National Socialism. Indeed, throughout the late 1930s and early '40s, Heidegger would find himself in constant conflict with the official Nazi party organ of intellectual affairs, *Das Amt Rosenberg,* over the production of a new *Historisch-Kritische Ausgabe* (HKA) of Nietzsche's work. The details of this conflict help to provide the background necessary for understanding the Nietzsche lectures. In May of 1934, just after his resignation as rector, Heidegger visited the Nietzsche Archives in Weimar.[23] Eighteen months later, on the recommendation of Walter F. Otto, he is selected to become an official member of the editorial board

21. Given Kurt Hildebrandt's unambiguous support of the Nazi regime, it is hardly surprising that Heidegger would omit the word "splendid" from his reference to Hildebrandt's *Wagner und Nietzsche: Ihr Kampf gegen das Neunzehnte Jarhhundert* (Breslau: E. Hirt, 1923) in his 1961 edition. Compare GA 43: 105 with NI: 106.

22. Kurt Hildebrandt, *Nietzsches Wettkampf mit Sokrates und Plato* (Dresden: Sibyllen, 1922), 7.

23. Marion Heinz and Theodore Kisiel, "Heidegger's Beziehungen zum Nietzsche-Archiv," in *Annäherungen an Martin Heidegger,* ed. Hermann Schäfer (Frankfurt: Campus, 1996), 103–136. This article contains a good deal of historical information on Heidegger's workings with the Nietzsche editorial commission for the HKA, including excerpts from hitherto unpublished letters of Heidegger.

working on the HKA.[24] From 1936–1938, Heidegger visited the archive twice yearly to attend meetings of all the board members and discuss editorial guidelines, lay down methodological principles, and try to coordinate the work of preparing a thoroughly "historical-critical edition" of Nietzsche's writings that would go beyond the earlier Naumann, Kröner, and Musarion editions.[25]

Heidegger had serious doubts about joining the HKA commission and was persuaded only because of what he perceived as the *philosophical* necessity of preparing a new edition of Nietzsche's *Nachlass*. On one of his earlier visits, he had met Nietzsche's sister, Elisabeth Förster-Nietzsche, and her cousins, Richard and Max Oehler, all of whom had been deeply involved in constructing a fascist interpretation of Nietzsche's work that affected its textual integrity.[26] Förster-Nietzsche had worked hard to confect a myth of Nietzsche as a Teutonic prophet and seer, a kind of anti-Moses figure who would affirm a racially pure, anti-Semitic Aryan order. Richard Oehler was her handpicked servant who carried out this enterprise. In order to fulfill her petit bourgeois dream of enshrining her brother in a pantheon of German prophets, Förster-Nietzsche convinced Hitler to endorse the building of a Nietzsche Hall in Weimar that would serve as a permanent home for the archive, as well as a cultish site for Nietzsche pilgrims and enthusiasts. Oehler also planned a Nietzsche-Zarathustra monument replete with snake and eagle to complement the proposed shrine. The whole effect of this quasi-religious idolatry struck Heidegger as repulsive and wholly out of character with the spirit of Nietzsche's thought. Given the financial restrictions under which the archive had to work, Heidegger was vehement in declaring that the money would be better spent in supporting the historical-critical work of the commission rather than in building a new cult shrine. In a letter from February 28, 1937, Heidegger writes to Oehler: "Even today I can only characterize

24. Marion Heinz, "Nachwort," GA 44: 252–253. There are also details on Otto and Heidegger in the Heinz and Kisiel, "Heideggers Beziehungen zum Nietzsche-Archiv," 106–108; and Farias, *Heidegger und der Nationalsozialismus*, 348.

25. For details about the institutional connections between the HKA and das Amt Rosenberg, see Zapata, *Triumph des Willens zur Macht*, 182–200. The HKA had as its aim the establishment of both a historical and critical edition of Nietzsche's writings. Because the Naumann edition of the *Grossoktavausgabe, Nietzsches Werke*, 15 vols. (Leipzig: Naumann, 1894–1904) [hereafter: GOA], prepared by Elisabeth Förster-Nietzsche, was deemed philologically and historically uncritical, as were the later revised editions of *Nietzsches Werke*, 20 vols. (Leipzig: Kröner, 1901–1926) and the *Musarionausgabe* of Nietzsche, *Gesammelte Werke*, 23 vols. (Munich: Musarion, 1920–1929), the editorial committee of the HKA sought to offer a new edition that would present Nietzsche's *Nachlass*, especially the texts from the uncritical work, *Wille zur Macht*, GOA, vols. 15–16, in its historically proper form. For a history of the Nietzsche archives, see David Marc Hoffmann, *Zur Geschichte des Nietzsche-Archivs* (Berlin: de Gruyter, 1991); for a discussion of the *Will to Power*, see Wayne Klein, *Nietzsche and the Promise of Philosophy* (Albany: SUNY Press, 1997), 181–199.

26. Riedel, *Nietzsche in Weimar*, 22–51.

this situation as a disgrace and a scandal."[27] But Heidegger had other, more fundamental, criticisms of Oehler and the commission.

What genuinely preoccupied Heidegger in his work with the HKA was the preparation of a new edition of *The Will to Power* which had been published originally in 1901 by Nietzsche's sister and Peter Gast, with help from Ernst and August Horneffer.[28] In this first edition, there were 483 aphorisms organized in four parts. In the second edition of 1906, this number more than doubled, expanding to 1,067 entries. By the time Heidegger joined the commission in 1935, Baeumler's inexpensive edition of *Der Wille zur Macht*, published by Alfred Kröner, had succeeded in making this book—one that was never published by Nietzsche himself—into one of the most important philosophical texts of the twentieth century.[29] Baeumler's own book on Nietzsche from 1931 served to reinforce the perception of *The Will to Power* as an essential text.[30] Heidegger shared Baeumler's view about the centrality of *The Will to Power* in understanding Nietzsche's work, though he had a different vision about how to publish it. Hence, he sought to work for a new edition that would rearrange, supplement, and thematically transform this text according to his own philosophical interpretation. From 1936–1938, as he was delivering his lectures on the will to power and eternal recurrence, Heidegger became actively involved in planning the whole Nietzsche *Nachlass* from 1884–1888. His letters to the main editor of the HKA, Karl Schlechta, about the ordering and dating of aphorisms show that he was concerned with producing what he considered to be a more philosophically unified edition. It was this unwavering commitment to a *philosophical* rather than a merely historical-critical or philological edition that animated his efforts. His aim, in short, was to produce a new Nietzsche edition of *The Will to Power* in line with his own reading of Western philosophy as *Seynsgeschichte*. As Heidegger conceived it, these editorial decisions were not merely bureaucratic or technical ones; the Nietzsche Commission's work would help to determine the *Nietzschebild* in Germany for the next generation. Hence, Heidegger deemed it imperative that he be involved in preparing the new edition.

Heidegger had already been exposed to the profound philosophical

27. Heinz and Kisiel, "Heidegger's Beziehungen zum Nietzsche-Archiv," 112.

28. In her "Vorwort" to the first edition of *Wille zur Macht* (1901), Elisabeth Förster-Nietzsche writes that "volume 15 [of the GOA] is to be seen as the culmination of the years-long, laborious, and conscientious work of the editors: Peter Gast and Ernst and August Horneffer," GOA, vol. 15, p. xxii. She claims, in a wholly disingenuous way, that "I myself am not the editor of this volume but at best a collaborator in the most unassuming way."

29. Friedrich Nietzsche, *Der Wille zur Macht*, ed. Alfred Baeumler (Leipzig: Kröner, 1930). This handy *Taschenausgabe* helped to make this confection of notebook entries into one of the essential philosophical "texts" of the century. Baeumler himself considered WM to be "Nietzsche's philosophical magnum opus," 699.

30. Baeumler, *Nietzsche: Der Philosoph und der Politiker*, 46–59.

implications of editorial practice through his work on Max Scheler's *Nachlass*. After Scheler's death in 1928, Frau Scheler had organized a committee, composed of Heidegger, W. F. Otto, Nicolai Hartmann, Kurt Riezler, and others, with Richard Oehler as its head. Indeed, Heidegger was convinced that the model for such a *Nachlass* should be Nietzsche's *Will to Power* since it was organized around the themes of metaphysics rather than around the problems of anthropology.[31] Oehler's anthropological interpretation won the day, however, and wound up shaping the Scheler reception in the years that followed. Heidegger was, of course, deeply critical of such a trend. He likewise expressed dismay about editorial principles in his comments on the Diels edition of the Pre-Socratics that had created such a stir during the 1920s. In his lecture course of 1932, "Der Anfang der abendländischen Philosophie," Heidegger will criticize the ordering system of Diels' text and argue that "the ordering of fragments must be determined according to an essential understanding of the whole of [Parmenides'] poem."[32] This was no small matter. Eleven years later, in his Heraclitus lectures from the summer of 1943, Heidegger would return to his criticism of the Diels edition. In his comments challenging Diels' decision to place the famous Logos-fragment first, we can find important parallels to his criticism of the Nietzsche edition planned by the HKA. Heidegger claimed that the taxonomical ordering of writings by librarians and editors will never get at the "essential" matter for thinking:

> More essential than having the text of a thinker completely preserved and intact is that we ourselves, even if only from a distance, are able to gain a relation to that which is to be thought in the thinking of a thinker. We strive not for a philological-historical proficiency that brings to completion the reconstruction of a text. Rather, we attempt to prepare ourselves so that the still to be transmitted word comes upon us from out of its essential center. The elucidation of fragments, if it is to be thoughtful . . . must experience what is to be thought. Whether and to what extent this succeeds can neither be proven in advance nor calculated afterwards as a "success." What is to be thought is not anything "objective"; this thinking is not anything "subjective." The differentiation between object and subject has no place here. This is something foreign to the world of the Greeks and, above all, to the realm

31. Heinz and Kisiel, "Heideggers Beziehungen zum Nietzsche-Archiv," 108–109. At this early period, Heidegger still viewed WM as something worthy of imitation. In a letter dated May 25, 1932, to the head of the Scheler edition, Richard Oehler, Heidegger writes: "In the process of working through all the material I am ever more convinced that the only possible model for publishing [the Scheler edition] is Nietzsche's *Will to Power*. . . ." By WS 1936/37, Heidegger became convinced that a new edition of WM was desperately needed, as he makes plain in a letter from November 12, 1938, to Richard Leutheusser, a member of the HKA, 113–114.

32. Heidegger, "Der Anfang der abendländischen Philosophie," 18 (unpublished ms. from Herbert Marcuse Archive, cited in note 9).

of originary thinking. . . . Hence there is little need to provide lengthy as-
surances that we do not imagine that what we present is "the only true Heraclitus" for all times. It will suffice if our pointing toward a path for interpreting Heraclitus' word has a glimmer of truth to it—that which illumines
(GA 55: 38–39).

For Heidegger, the philosophical meaning of editorial practice would
get played out in his interpretation of the Pre-Socratics throughout his
life. As he saw it, the originary character of these texts had been covered
over by the complex historical process of textual transmission and editorial reconstruction. Diels' edition was hardly the first to have contributed
to this state of affairs. Much more lay in the balance, however, than mere
philological precision or scholarly exactness; the very future of Western
history was at stake. The German *Volk* was confronted by an essential decision: either to recover these archaic sources in an originary way or to consign them to the status of antiquarian writings whose fate would be left to
exegetes and scholiasts. In this sense, we need to understand Heidegger's
critique of Diels' method and style of redaction not as a scholarly-aca-
demic quibble, but as another strategy in his archeo-eschatological history
of being. Precisely because the Diels' edition was, in Heidegger's words,
"so widely accepted today as authoritative," it needed to be challenged in
its fundamental ontological assumptions. Hence, Heidegger would argue
that Diels' whole system of ordering, arranging, and presenting the fragments was "absurd" because of its own hidden and unspoken metaphysical assumptions. As Heidegger put it in his 1943 course:

> If in this lecture we follow a different way of ordering the Heraclitus frag-
> ments, then that does not mean that we think we are reconstructing these
> forever lost texts in a better way. What we deem important is this alone: that
> we come into relation with what holds sway in incipient thinking in such a
> way that we experience it as that-which-is-to-be-thought. Provided that what
> is incipient, however, holds sway over all that proceeds from it and is in ad-
> vance of it, then what is incipient is not something that lies behind us.
> Rather, it is one and the same with what comes before us and towards us in
> a mysterious turning [*geheimnisvollen Kehre*] (GA 55: 43).

Even in matters of editorial practice, Heidegger would always come
back to the fundamental truth of the *arche*-philosophy that he laid out in
this Rectorial Address. Against the positivist-philological metaphysics of
scholarly practice, Heidegger would put forward his myth of an archaic future, a future whose realization would depend on the recovery of what is
"essential." As with his myth of autochthony, Heidegger's practice of
philosophical editing would seek to excavate a more originary, subterranean text hidden beneath the surface of the published, tradition-trans-

mitted work. Only through this practice of deconstructive (and violent) excavation would we come into the proximity of essential history—what Heidegger would term *Seynsgeschichte*. It was this hidden thematic of an archaic-futural narrative of being that sustained his criticisms of Diels, the Scheler *Nachlass,* and the Nietzsche edition.

At first, during the years 1934–1937, Heidegger will attempt to work within the institutional framework of the HKA and the archives to effect a change in the reigning interpretation of Nietzsche throughout Germany. Because of a series of events in 1937–1938 involving an attempt by Das Amt Rosenberg to control his own work and the work of the HKA, however, Heidegger will turn his critique of the Nietzsche commission's editorial practice against "official" National Socialism itself. The details of this turn mark an important point both within the Nietzsche lectures themselves and within Heidegger's attitude toward National Socialism. Thus in the years after this turn, the Nietzsche lectures will indeed constitute an *Auseinandersetzung* with National Socialism, one that clearly breaks from the enthusiastic support of 1933. Now Heidegger will deploy his narrative of an archaic future against the National Socialist order that he once believed to be the vanguard of such a future. But Heidegger will hardly give up on his essential reading of National Socialism. On the contrary, he will cling ever more firmly to the belief that his own autochthonic version of "Freiburg National Socialism" constitutes the only "originary" (i.e., "archaic-futural") form of NS thinking left.[33] The dynamic of this shift will be intricate and hard to follow.

At first, Heidegger will recruit Nietzsche as his comrade in arms in confrontation with National Socialism, a process that will last until roughly the winter of 1938. After that time, however, he will experience a shift in thinking and will begin to see Nietzsche as merely a forerunner of the fallen and inessential versions of National Socialism: ones that have succumbed to the metaphysics of will to power and technological dominion over the earth. In this new constellation of the political, Heidegger will now see official National Socialism as a pure form of Nietzschean will to power—and as a typical expression of modern nihilism. We will need to look at these turns and shifts in Heidegger's thinking and, in conjunction with his practice of transgressive reading and hermeneutic violence, see

33. This is a phrase used by Carl von Weizsäcker, "Begegnungen in Vier Jahrzehnten," in *Erinnerung an Martin Heidegger,* ed. Günther Neske (Pfullingen: Neske, 1977), 245–246. Von Weizsäcker remembers a student in the winter of 1933–1934 telling him: "Freiburg National Socialism was devised in the entourage around Heidegger. In private they would say 'the true Third Reich has still not begun but is yet to come.'" Throughout his life, Heidegger will keep alive this hope of a secret National Socialist vision of German homecoming. One sees traces of this in SI: 62–63/ANT: 107–108.

how they determine the very basis of his *Auseinandersetzung* with Nietzsche and, through him, with National Socialism.

In 1936/37, Heidegger will interpret Nietzsche as a manifestation of "Western fate and as the one who expresses our collective sense of who we are" (GA 43: 281). In a passage deleted from the 1961 edition, Heidegger will even go so far as to argue that "this last of the great Western thinkers . . . returns so decisively to the beginning of Western philosophy as no essential thinker before him" (GA 43: 4–5). By 1942/43, the situation will have changed dramatically. Now Heidegger will contend that "Nietzsche's thinking . . . [is] as remote as possible from the essence of truth as *aletheia*," and he will further maintain that Nietzsche's philosophy is "utterly un-Greek," i.e., inessential (P: 158; 94/GA 54: 235; 139). But how are we to account for this decisive change? What has transpired in the ensuing five and a half years that can offer some indication of this apparent *volte-face*? And how are we to measure the transition between the affirmative meaning of Heidegger's "confrontation" in the early Nietzsche lectures with the censorious stance of the later ones? What can have led Heidegger to interpret Nietzsche as the consummate modern nihilist in 1940 when only a few years earlier he was presenting Nietzsche's aesthetics as a definitive countermovement to nihilism (Ni: 73/GA 43: 86)?

As in most matters of Heidegger's thinking, the answers are hardly simple or self-evident. Part of the reason lies in the complex historical circumstances of 1939–1940 with the outbreak of the Second World War. But part of the reason also lies in Heidegger's decision to break with "official" National Socialism. After the war Heidegger sought to conceal this genuinely *political* dimension of the Nietzsche lectures through a series of revisions, rectifications, redactions, and evasions. If we are to follow the twists and turns on this path of thinking, we will need to recognize the breadth of Heidegger's hermeneutic violence. This violence extends not only to his transgressive style of reading Nietzsche's philosophical texts and transposing them to his own *seynsgeschichtliche* context. It also manifests itself in Heidegger's postwar interpretations and explanations of his earlier writings and lectures on Nietzsche.

When the war ended and as he was facing scrutiny about his own political affiliations and complicities from the De-Nazification Committee in Freiburg, Heidegger began in earnest to engineer a philosophical cover-up. In these tense months in late 1945 and early 1946, he was hardly alone in his attempt to rewrite the past.[34] Many former Nazi academics were scrambling to put forth a credible version of their recent political allegiances. In two documents written in late 1945, Heidegger offers a politi-

---

34. Ott, *Martin Heidegger: Unterwegs*, 291–327.

cal defense against the charges of the committee, framed as a kind of self-styled Socratic *apologia*. In a letter to the rector of Freiburg University, Heidegger will explain his position vis-à-vis National Socialism as follows:

> Beginning in 1936 and continuing until 1945 I entered still more clearly into confrontation [*Auseinandersetzung*] and into spiritual resistance [*geistigen Widerstand*] through a series of Nietzsche courses and lectures. Of course, Nietzsche could never be lumped together with National Socialism since—apart from what is fundamental—his position against anti-Semitism and his positive stance towards Russia rule out such an identification. On a higher level, however, the confrontation with Nietzsche's metaphysics is the confrontation with nihilism, a nihilism which, in its political form, ever more clearly shows itself as fascism.[35]

And in his 1945 draft, "The Rectorate 1933/34: Facts and Thoughts," Heidegger will claim that his early seminars on Ernst Jünger and Nietzsche served as a "confrontation" with what was coming.[36] Over twenty years later, in his "Spiegel Interview" (1966), Heidegger would continue to draw on this carefully sculpted legend abut his "spiritual resistance" in the Nietzsche lectures. In response to a question about his relationship to the NSDAP, Heidegger would contend: "The lectures on Nietzsche began in 1936. All of those who could hear heard that this was a confrontation with National Socialism."[37] And in a letter from March 1968 to Stefan Zemach in Jerusalem, Heidegger writes that "my stance towards National Socialism at that time [1935] was already unambiguously antagonistic. . . . [As evidence] I would like to point to my Nietzsche lectures from 1936–1940 which every listener understood clearly as a fundamentally critical confrontation with National Socialism" (GA 40: 233). And yet in his introduction to the two-volume *Nietzsche* edition of 1961, Heidegger will suppress the political character of this confrontation by avoiding all reference to National Socialism even as he will revive the rhetoric of *Auseinandersetzung* for a new politically cleansed confrontation with Nietzsche. This editorial gesture of suppression and elision can hardly be thought of as something casual or inessential.

In the changed political climate of 1961, Heidegger will seek to revive his *mythos* about an archaic Graeco-German future as a way to save the West—only now he will reposition it within a different political configura-

35. Martin Heidegger, "Documents from the Denazification Proceedings," trans. Jason Wirth, *Graduate Faculty Philosophy Journal* 14, no. 2 and 15, no. 1 (1991): 540–541, translation altered.

36. Martin Heidegger, "The Rectorate 1933/34: Facts and Thoughts" in *Martin Heidegger and National Socialism*, ed. Günther Neske and Emil Kettering, trans. Lisa Harries (New York: Paragon, 1990), 18/SdU: 24.

37. Heidegger, SI: 51, 53/ANT: 93, 95.

tion. In this new rhetorical register, the *Auseinandersetzung* alluded to in the text will now be understood as an intra-philosophical confrontation between Heidegger and Nietzsche on the guiding question of Western thought. By working through his own philosophical confrontation with Nietzsche, Heidegger will attempt to show that the problems of the postwar world are part of a centuries-long narrative of Western history. The nihilism that confronts us in the forms of urban dislocation, psychological anomie, and the anxieties about an atomic holocaust are only recent expressions of a more fundamental planetary phenomenon: the uprooting and deracination of human existence from the earth. Heidegger's Nietzsche lectures attempt a critique of modern rootlessness and devastation (what Nietzsche termed *Verwüstung*) by positioning them within a philosophical narrative about the history of being (KSA 6: 382; GA 50: 86). The *mythos* about autochthony and German destiny is now presented as a meditation on rootlessness as a phenomenon of Western technological domination. In this form, as a critique of modern Western nihilism, Heidegger hopes to lay the groundwork for his postmetaphysical reflections on *Ereignis* and the other beginning that he takes up in the *Beiträge* (1936–1938). Yet what will be suppressed here, of course, is the wholly political dimension of this confrontation as it was played out in the 1930s. By arguing, for example, that his confrontation with Nietzsche *began* in 1936 (after the failure of the rectorate), Heidegger gives the impression that these lectures signaled the beginning of his break with National Socialism, thus obscuring the role that Nietzsche played in his decision to join Hitler in 1933 and in the composition of the Rectorial Address.

Part of my argument here will be to show how deeply implicated in the specifics of a National Socialist worldview Heidegger's original Nietzsche lectures truly were. This will involve positioning these lectures within their own historical context and attempting to see them, not as documents offering "spiritual resistance" to National Socialism, but as exhortations setting forth a heresiology of National Socialist calumnies. I will read Heidegger's Nietzsche lectures as his radical and, at times, audacious effort at establishing a more originary form of National Socialist thinking in and through his confrontation with Nietzsche. At first, he will attempt to use his confrontation with Nietzsche as a way of purging the heresies of other Nietzsche commentators such as Baeumler, Hildebrandt, Oehler, Härtle, and Ernst and August Horneffer.[38] By the time his lecture cycle is over in 1944, however, Heidegger will have long abandoned his search to work within the established National Socialist framework. After 1940, Heidegger will see Nietzsche as implicated in the selfsame metaphysical struc-

---

38. August Horneffer, *Nietzsche als Moralist und Schriftsteller* (Jena: Eugen Diederichs, 1906), and also note 19 in this chapter.

tures of unbridled subjectivism and technological domination as the Nazis themselves. Now he will define his role as that of the outsider. Wholly alienated from the institutional and political machinations of National Socialist will to power, Heidegger will begin to craft a new identity as the prophet of an "essential" form of National Socialism at odds with the inessential versions being promulgated by other NS philosophers. As in the years 1929–1933, before the ascent of Hitler, Heidegger will once again go underground and try to recover the subterranean sources for a new German future. And he will turn to Hölderlin's poetry as a source for reclaiming the hidden power of this authentic Germany. At the same time, Nietzsche's status as the herald of the German future will be decidedly altered. Now, in the summer of 1942, Heidegger will claim that Nietzsche denies the archaic power of the Greek world for the Roman metaphysics of will and domination (HHI: 54–55/GA 53: 67–68). Within this configuration, Heidegger will fall back upon the old Hellingrathian myth of a secret Germany as the only possible pathway out of the devastation and world-darkening brought on by the Second World War. Now he will show how the planetary war threatens autochthony and the homeland and reveals itself as bound up with "the ultimate American act of American ahistoricality and self-devastation. For this act is the renunciation of commencement [das Anfängliche] and a decision in favor of that which is without commencement." In the wake of this planetary confrontation with the forces of nihilism, Heidegger's Nietzsche lectures will turn their critique back against Nietzsche himself, defining him ultimately as the consummate nihilist. What began as a confrontation *with* Nietzsche about the power of the Greek *arche* in shaping the German future now becomes a polemic *against* Nietzsche as a thinker who is wholly modern and utterly un-Greek (P: 43, 94/GA 54: 63, 139).

As he began his lectures in 1936, Heidegger sought to work through the guiding question of Western metaphysics by confronting Nietzsche's thought as a guide for questioning itself. After the developments of 1937–1938, however, Heidegger will break with the official institutional forms of National Socialist thought and he will even use Nietzsche as his guide for this break. And yet, by 1940, Heidegger will begin to see Nietzsche's philosophy as an example of the selfsame metaphysics of will and domination that contaminated the purity of the original German revolution of 1933. The occasion of Heidegger's turning away from National Socialism can be traced to a few developments in 1937–1938; the ground of the turn from Nietzsche, however, lies in the dynamic and thematics of Heidegger's "turn" itself. Before inquiring into the structural dynamics of this turn, we will need to situate Heidegger's views back into the historical context of 1937.

IV. HEIDEGGER'S "CONFRONTATION(S)" WITH NATIONAL SOCIALISM

To speak of Heidegger's *Auseinandersetzung* with National Socialism demands a brief accounting and recounting of his own philosophical position within the National Socialist order.[39] Heidegger clearly had problems with the official ideological positions of the Nazi hierarchy linked to the offices of Das Amt Rosenberg (responsible for "surveillance of the whole spiritual-ideological indoctrination and education of the NSDAP") and to Walter Gross' Bureau of Racial Doctrine. As Hugo Ott has shown, Heidegger was intricately involved in skirmishes within these official quarters about matters of intellectual freedom, publication, and ideological conformity.[40] That Heidegger had pursued a path of confrontation and opposition to this hierarchy can be traced in the historical documents. But there is also an unwritten record that needs to be exhumed from under the pile of lectures and manuscripts that poses as the definitive "Edition of the Last Hand." Rainer Marten, one of Heidegger's former students, has contributed to this project of exhumation in his critical writing on "Heideggers Geist."[41] Marten writes of visiting Heidegger at his cabin in Todtnauberg, the site of the essay "Creative Landscape" that offers a philosophical rhapsody on the virtues of autochthonic rootedness. As he enters Heidegger's study and looks out the window onto the majestic valley below, Marten reflects for a moment on a matter of essential absence, of what is no longer present: "the carved swastika that embellished the well outside the philosopher's window until the end of the war." After May of 1945, Heidegger will, of course, have effaced all signs of this originary symbol of the fourfold and of archaic cosmology. But the traces of its power will persist even into Heidegger's last years. What he confronted in his *Auseinandersetzung* with National Socialism was the ideological-institutional character of the Nazi worldview that became the focus of his subterranean assaults on the official party apparatus. But, as Marten's anecdote indicates, even through the dark years of the war, Heidegger retained an elemental faith in the symbolic power of the National Socialist myth whose image adorned the stone well at Todtnauberg until 1945.

---

39. For an account of Heidegger's Nietzsche interpretation within the reigning National Socialist view, see Otto Pöggeler, *Philosophie und Nationalsozialismus — am Beispiel Heideggers* (Opladen: Westdeutscher Verlag, 1990), and "Heidegger, Nietzsche, and Politics," in *The Heidegger Case: On Philosophy and Politics*, ed. Tom Rockmore and Joseph Margolis (Philadelphia: Temple University Press, 1992); George Leamann, *Heidegger im Kontext* (Hamburg: Das Argument, 1993); and Hans Sluga, *Heidegger's Crisis: Philosophy and Politics in Nazi Germany* (Cambridge: Harvard University Press, 1993).

40. Ott, *Martin Heidegger: Unterwegs*, 242.

41. Rainer Marten, "Heideggers Geist," in *Die Heidegger Kontroverse*, ed. Jürg Altwegg (Frankfurt: Athenäum, 1988), 225–243.

One year after Hitler's panzers invaded Poland, Heidegger begins a draft of "Nietzsche's Metaphysics" in September of 1940. In his introductory remarks, he will make a powerful claim that "the consummation of the modern age unfolds its history . . . on the basis of Nietzsche's metaphysics" (Niii: 190–191/GA 50: 7–8). He will then go on to analyze this history in terms of what he calls both a "proximate" goal and a "most distant" goal. The proximate goal is an analysis of the German situation in 1940 in the midst of a world war where "the struggle for world domination [*Kampf um die Erdherrschaft*] and the unfolding of the metaphysics that sustains it bring to fulfillment an epoch of the earth and of historical humanity." In this "struggle for power over the earth itself," Heidegger will identify the boundless and rootless metaphysics of Cartesian subjectivity that finds expression in Nietzschean will to power. On his reading, the National Socialist attempt to subdue the earth through the power of unbridled *techne* merely fulfills the historical logic of Nietzschean metaphysics. But within his analysis of Nietzsche's thought, Heidegger will ultimately point to another "most distant" goal of his meditation: preparing the path for recovering the autochthonic power of rootedness *in* the earth rather than extending the technological power of dominion *over* the earth. As he interprets it, "the contest [*Streit*] is no longer a struggle [*Kampf*] to master beings. . . . Now the contest becomes a confrontation [*Auseinandersetzung*] between the power of beings and the truth of be-ing [*Seyn*]." Here Heidegger will transform his earlier *Auseinandersetzung* with Nietzsche into a confrontation and conflict with the National Socialist metaphysics of world (and earth) domination that he sees all too clearly prefigured in Nietzsche's work.

As he turns the Nietzsche lectures into a "confrontation between the power of beings and the truth of being," Heidegger will have decisively broken with National Socialism as a form of political metaphysics. Instead, he will seek to offer a rooted form of Freiburg National Socialism as his "most distant goal." As Heidegger puts it in late summer 1940, "in terms of chronological order, of course, the goal remains infinitely far from the demonstrable events and circumstances of the present age. But this merely means that it belongs to the historical remoteness of another history" (Niii: 191/GA 50: 8). And, as the war progresses and the situation becomes worse, Heidegger's hopes for a future-oriented National Socialism will become ever more separated from the reality of the Nazi regime. But the war was hardly the single cause for his break. Heidegger's crisis of confidence in official National Socialism can be traced back to his difficulties with Das Amt Rosenberg in 1937–1938.

In a letter to Jaspers from 1950, Heidegger wrote that "in the years 1937 and 1938 I hit rock bottom" (HJB: 201). The Reich Ministry of Education in Berlin had conspired to keep Heidegger from leading the German delegation attending a Descartes Congress in Paris in 1937.[42] In that same year, Heidegger delivered an address to the science and medical faculty at Freiburg that warned of the "inner threat" that contemporary science posed to "essential knowledge." In his private notes, he warns of the impending NS plan to transform the universities into technical colleges useful to industry and "technical-practical-political" demands. Moreover, he reacts strongly against the party's attempt to eliminate philosophy, since philosophy is fruitless and without any political relevance. In his notes he writes: "the reduction in the number of academic chairs, the cancellation of positions for philosophy scholars—that is no loss. That is something wholly in order and has long been called for. But to want to strike 'philosophy' itself with this is ludicrous. . . . For the Germans to abolish philosophy with the aim of attaining the essence of the *Volk*—that is world-historical suicide!" (BdW: 27, 8, 14). In conjunction with this process, he laments that with the rise of pseudo-disciplines, such as racial, *völkisch*, and "political" science, the university has lost all connections to essential thinking.[43] And, in the midst of all these rising tensions, his essay on "The Age of the World Picture" (1938) is denied publication.[44] Later he will report that in the summer semester of 1937 his Nietzsche course was under surveillance by the SS.[45] Within this context of political surveillance, Heidegger's own work with the Nietzsche Commission will likewise come under the scrutiny of Das Amt Rosenberg.

In 1938, Alfred Grunsky, the main reviewer for philosophy in Rosenberg's office, published a review deeply critical of the editorial practices of the HKA. Grunsky argued that the work of the Nietzsche edition was marked by an excessive philological precision and attention to insignificant detail that violated the spirit of Nietzsche's creative enterprise. As a result, Das Amt Rosenberg demanded that the next edition of the HKA published by the commission first be sent to their office before receiving final approval. Heidegger was livid. He told Richard Oehler that he could not abide this censorship and surveillance of the commission's work, which he claimed needed a free hand to "secure the work of Nietzsche . . . for the German *Volk* and the future of the West."[46] Heidegger's protest was registered with the members of the commission but, owing to both political and economic pressures, they succumbed to the demands of the Amt

42. Rüdiger Safranski, *Ein Meister aus Deutschland: Heidegger und seine Zeit* (Munich: Hanser, 1994), 374–376; *M. Heidegger and National Socialism*, 32, 52; Ott, *Martin Heidegger: Unterwegs*, 263–278.

43. Heidegger, BdW: 22 lists *Volkskunde*, *"Raumforschung*,*"* and *Rassenlehre* as examples of this kind of pseudo-science.

44. Otto Pöggeler, "Von Nietzsche zu Hitler?" in *Annäherungen an Heidegger*, ed. Hermann Schäfer (Frankfurt: Campus, 1996), 98.

45. Heidegger, "The Rectorate 1933/34," 31/SdU: 41.

46. Heinz and Kisiel, "Heideggers Beziehungen zum Nietzsche-Archiv," 120–125.

Rosenberg. Soon thereafter, Heidegger would retreat to his "private" confrontation with National Socialism through his Nietzsche lectures: "this was to be expected; thereafter, any collaboration with the commission became impossible—just work for Nietzsche's opus independent of the edition." Heidegger stopped attending HKA meetings and conferences and finally withdrew from the commission officially in 1942.

Institutionally, this break with the HKA signified another step in Heidegger's withdrawal from public life in the Third Reich. But Heidegger's confrontation with official National Socialism had already been underway in more systematic fashion in his courses on Nietzsche. His break from the commission merely formalized this state of affairs. As in his experience with the rectorate, Heidegger discovered that the institutional forms of the National Socialist order were incompatible with his myth of an archaic future for the *Volk*. At no point during his work on the HKA did Heidegger seek to secure a philologically rigorous, scholarly edition; his aim was to bring Nietzsche in line with his own narrative about the history of being and the essence of truth. In this sense, Heidegger's Nietzsche lectures sought to achieve a kind of *seynsgeschichtliche Gleichschaltung*.[47] What other National Socialist commentators had missed in their overemphasis on the racial, biological, anthropological, and pseudo-political dimensions in Nietzsche's thought was its essential connection to the hidden history of being. As Heidegger put it at the opening of the lecture cycle: "we can never succeed in arriving at Nietzsche's philosophy proper if we have not in our questioning conceived of Nietzsche as the end of Western metaphysics and proceeded to the entirely different question of the truth of being" (Ni: 10/GA 43: 15). Through his editorial activity at the HKA, Heidegger came to the conclusion that the heart of this hidden history lay in ovo in Nietzsche's *Nachlass*, especially book 3 of what had been crudely put together under the title of *The Will to Power*.[48] And he determined that these posthumous notes, when ordered, organized, and decoded according to an "essential" reading, would provide a key for understanding this hidden history.

V. HEIDEGGER, BAEUMLER, AND THE NATIONAL SOCIALIST INTERPRETATION OF NIETZSCHE

What Heidegger sought to offer in his Nietzsche lectures was an analysis of Germany's contemporary situation conceived according to Nietzsche's

47. This kind of *seynsgeschichtliche Gleichschaltung* or "bringing into line with the history-of-being" was at the heart of Heidegger's "Freiburger Nationalsozialismus."

48. For Heidegger's critical comments on the editing of Nietzsche's *Will to Power*, see Ni: 9–11/GA 43: 11–14; Nii: 82–84, 150–165/GA 44: 86–88, 157–173; Niv: 11/GA 48: 19–20.

diagnosis of the modern age as an epoch of nihilism. His aim in this regard was hardly unique. In his 1931 book, *Nietzsche: Der Philosoph und Politiker*, Alfred Baeumler had likewise offered a vivid portrait of Nietzsche as the diagnostician of European nihilism and had traced the crisis back through the turbulence of the Great War to its roots in the Western tradition, beginning with Plato. Like Heidegger, Baeumler too positioned his critique in terms of the thought of Heraclitus, Plato, the Latin humanists, Descartes, Hölderlin, and Nietzsche. And he sought to combat the rootlessness of modern bourgeois democratic culture by offering a Nietzschean philosophy of heroic nihilism that would galvanize the *Volk* into a revolutionary and ecstatic consciousness of their rootedness in the German earth and in the Greek tradition. Moreover, like Heidegger, he too understood the contemporary situation as one of impending crisis for the Germans, one in which they would be faced with a crucial decision about the historical destiny of the West. I would like to concentrate on Baeumler's reading of Nietzsche in this section because it seems to me that his ideas constitute a kind of intellectual and philosophical nexus within which National Socialist ideology will develop in the 1930s—a nexus to which Heidegger's thought is intimately bound. Rhetorically, conceptually, and ideologically, Heidegger and Baeumler share much in common.

Before the revolutionary moment of 1933, Heidegger had come into contact with Baeumler and a relationship grew that went beyond mere academic formality. The two went hiking together near Dresden in 1932, and the next summer Heidegger invited Baeumler to his cabin in Todtnauberg for a visit. What originally brought the men together, however, was their shared concern for the archaic and chthonic sources of Greek culture and its relevance for contemporary Germany. Heidegger had written to Baeumler in 1928 expressing admiration for the latter's lengthy introduction to a recent volume of Bachofen's writings on the ancient world.[49] In his essay dealing with the archaic and mythic sources of Western culture, Baeumler set out the principles of a chthonic philosophy of history, a project that caught Heidegger's attention. Drawing on what Bachofen termed "tellurism"—the archaic principle that sees the essential meaning of human life as rooted in and arising from the earth or soil (derived from the Latin noun "tellus," meaning "earth" and the Greek verb "tello," meaning "to come forth, arise")—Baeumler focused on the meaning of the earth in the formation of ancient culture. For Baeumler, human history was not the product of a telos-directed Hegelian dialectic but was rather the outcome of a tremendous struggle, or *Kampf*, between what the ancient Greeks had termed the Olympian and the chthonic deities. As he put it, "what has found its expression in these terms are pow-

49. Hans Sluga, *Heidegger's Crisis* (Cambridge: Harvard University Press, 1993), 151.

ers which have always determined human *Dasein*—and always will. . . . Out of the conflicts between them there emerges history."[50] By focusing on these chthonic sources of ancient Greek culture, Baeumler attempted to underscore the central meaning of struggle, conflict, opposition, and contest for understanding human history, a theme that seemed to him all the more significant given the chthonic powers that had been unleashed in the recent struggles of the Great War. Rejecting Winckelmann's fable about the noble simplicity and tranquil grandeur of Hellenic culture, Baeumler put forward a forceful account of the subterranean, telluric, and chthonic elements that shaped the archaic world of the Greeks and that lay dormant in the modern epoch. Only by recovering the originary power of these chthonic forces, Baeumler argued, could the Germans defeat the new Olympian forces of Enlightenment, democracy, liberalism, and internationalism that threatened to destroy modern Europe. As Baeumler saw it, the war in Europe had come to represent the symbolic struggle between archaic rootedness and modern rootlessness that would determine the destiny of the Germans. And to make a more forceful case for his argument about the meaning of conflict and struggle within German history, he turned to the writings of Nietzsche.

In the Bachofen introduction, Baeumler drew a connection between these two former Basel University colleagues who transformed the ingrained intellectual practices of historicism, positivism, and Hegelian dialectics that dominated the nineteenth-century German university world. Both Bachofen and Nietzsche sought to overcome the nineteenth-century academic view of antiquity by excavating the archaic sources of the Greek world that lay hidden in myth, symbol, and the primordial phenomenon of tragic art. In Baeumler's view, it was this mythic construction of the past that provided the key for decoding the hidden or chthonic history of the Greek world that had been covered over by the palimpsestic inscriptions of classical and Christian culture. "Myth *determines* history," Baeumler insisted; "every interpretation of history rests upon myth."[51] And yet Baeumler maintained that despite Nietzsche's deep insight into this hidden history, he had missed a decisive feature of ancient culture that Bachofen had stressed: the elemental power of the subterranean, the chthonic, and the telluric. As he saw it, Nietzsche had simply failed to understand the "cult of the dead and the chthonic powers. The whole world of chthonic religion remains from beginning to end outside the sphere of his knowledge and interest. He lacks all sense for the soil, the earth, the cult, the locality, the heroes, and the underworld." For Nietzsche's thought to become integral to the coming German revolution, it would need to be

---

50. Alfred Baeumler, *Das mythische Weltalter* (Munich: Beck, 1965), 20.
51. Ibid., 297, 199, 257.

supplemented and reconceived according to this chthonic dimension of history. Or so Baeumler thought. And between 1926 and 1933 Baeumler set out to coordinate the work of Nietzsche with this chthonic tradition in the name of a new cultural-political myth: *das Volk*.

"If we wish to understand what culture is," Baeumler writes, "we will need to find the life-roots of the *Volk*. One can comprehend a plant only in terms of the root that clings to the earth. In this same way one can grasp the culture of a *Volk* only from the roots of its collective life."[52] By under- scoring the significance of roots, homeland, ancestry, soil, and nation, Baeumler attempted to bring Nietzsche's thought into line with the *völkisch* element of the new National Socialist worldview. In his Rectorial Address, Heidegger too would organize his thoughts around the thematic nexus of Nietzsche, the Greeks, National Socialism, and the chthonic "forces that are rooted in the soil and blood of a *Volk*" (HCW: 34/SdU: 14). And, like Baeumler, he too would put forward a new communal ideal of *völkisch* life that would help usher in a National Socialist revolution. For both men, bourgeois individuality and the Cartesian philosophy of the subject signaled a decline in German life. As Baeumler put it, "liberal cul- tural thought ends in the glorification of museums and libraries, concert halls and theatres as the sites in which human beings find themselves 'spir- itually enriched'." But these bourgeois ideals of the interior spiritual life merely end in "a new kind of barbarism." Only the communal life of Na- tional Socialism, Baeumler contends, "places human beings once again in an essential relation to . . . an originary order of things." Since Nietzsche too had fallen victim to "modern subjectivism," Baeumler maintained that his work on the early Greeks needed to be rethought in line with a communal interpretation of archaic Greek life: "the Greek (at least in the archaic period) is not an 'individual'; he is a member of the *polis*, a mem- ber of a religious community."[53] In his influential book, *Nietzsche: Der Philosoph und Politiker*, Baeumler will endeavor to present an image of Nietzsche as a philosopher of the communal life in the *polis*.

After his own *völkisch* political awakening in the late 1920s, Baeumler will see Nietzsche as the prophet and herald of a new communal German identity. As part of his approach, he will stress the autochthonic roots of this identity in the ancient Germanic soil. Distinguishing carefully be- tween the originary Germanic (*germanisch*) and the modern German (*deutsch*), Baeumler will argue that the Roman-Christian-humanist influ- ences of Western culture have covered over and concealed "the subter- ranean Germanic strata of German being"—i.e., the communal au-

52. Alfred Baeumler, *Politik und Erziehung* (Berlin: Junker & Dünnhaupt, 1937), 124–125.
53. Baeumler, *Das mythische Weltalter*, 272–273.

tochthonic bond of blood ancestors. In his view, it was Nietzsche's great service to have launched a cultural assault against Roman-Christian culture in the name of a Graeco-Germanic bond and to have broken with the old bourgeois ideal of a German "culture-state" composed of poets and thinkers. In its stead, Nietzsche sought "to lead [*führen*] the Germans to a form of great politics."[54] Other scholars had missed the significance of these communal and political elements in Nietzsche's thought, Baeumler stressed, because they lay hidden in the labyrinthine architecture of Nietzsche's unfinished drafts and notebooks. But Baeumler was convinced that through an originary Germanic reading of these sources, with an eye toward their inner connection to the National Socialist worldview, they could be recovered in their essential form. What would be required in this kind of essential recovery would be that Baeumler himself become (in Martha Zapata's words) "a co-author" with Nietzsche in bringing to fruition the hidden meaning of these texts.[55] As Baeumler put it, "whoever wants to assess Nietzsche's work needs to take up the logical task of fitting together all of its parts, a task for which Nietzsche himself did not find time."[56]

In this regard, Nietzsche's fragmentary, incomplete work seemed to Baeumler a kind of Pre-Socratic philosophy *redivivus*. Much as Diels needed to bring together the fragments of Heraclitus in a systematic way to provide a key for understanding ancient texts, Baeumler considered it necessary for a modern editor to fit Nietzsche's system together from out of its disjointed parts. In the process of working out this system, Baeumler came to think of Nietzsche's own philosophy as Heraclitean rather than Dionysian. And, in Heraclitus' teaching that "struggle [*Kampf*] is the father of all things," Baeumler found the core of Nietzsche's thought: "to see the world and man as Heraclitean means for Nietzsche . . . asserting oneself [*sich behaupten*] in this struggle or perishing [*untergehen*]." Against the impending threat of decline or *Untergang,* a threat made all too poignant by Spengler, Baeumler raised the necessity of a German form of communal self-assertion, what Heidegger in his Rectorial Address termed *"Selbstbehauptung."* To fulfill this task and to prepare the German *Volk* for its new Heraclitean challenge, Baeumler turned his attention to producing a new edition of Nietzsche, organized around "essential" themes. Besides editing a new eight-volume set of Nietzsche's work with Alfred Kröner publishers in Leipzig and writing all new introductions and afterwords, Baeumler also edited two new editions of the *Nachlass*—with new section headings emphasizing the political themes of "Society and State," "Socialism and

---

54. Baeumler, *Nietzsche: Der Philosoph und Politiker,* 88, 166.
55. Zapata Galindo, *Triumph des Willens zur Macht,* 85.
56. Baeumler, *Nietzsche: Der Philosoph und Politiker,* 14–15.

Democracy," "Germany and Europe," "The Counter-movement," and "The Crisis of Europe."[57] As Baeumler would make all too clear in his introduction to the Kröner *Werke*, what was involved in these editions was not mere philology or historical erudition. Rather, they "opened up once again the whole problem of Western history—exactly as Hölderlin had done in his final hymns." By presenting the thoughts of Nietzsche within their own properly political context, Baeumler hoped to show how Nietzsche prefigured National Socialism and how, through a careful editorially cleansed version of his texts, the self-aware reader might begin to understand the dawn of a German revolution. In essence, Nietzsche's work constituted a kind of ferocious Heraclitean *Wettkampf* with the nihilistic forces of modern European history and culture.

Heidegger too will become ensnared in this same National Socialist constellation of ideas in the early 1930s. Like Baeumler, he will attempt to prepare the German *Volk* for a revolutionary rebirth through a reading of Nietzsche, the Pre-Socratics, and Hölderlin. He will also underscore the significance of editorial labor for bringing forth the hidden but essential meaning of German history. This shared commitment to anti-liberal, anti-Roman, anti-humanist, and anti-Enlightenment ideas that pervades the work of both Baeumler and Heidegger is hardly a coincidence. It reflects a common faith in the National Socialist ideology of postwar heroic nihilism and militant self-assertion that reigned in the Germany of the early 1930s. In the spirit of a mythic-archaic bond with the early Greeks, both Heidegger and Baeumler called for a renewal of the German *Volk*. On the basis of this alleged primordial autochthonic bond, both set forth an essential reading of Western history and philosophy organized and directed by their own violent interpretations of Heraclitus, Plato, Sophocles, Hölderlin, and Nietzsche. And, in the process, both offered a devastating critique of Rome, Latin humanism, medieval Christianity, the subjectivism of Descartes, the Anglo-French Enlightenment, modern democracy, and the non-autochthonous peoples of the earth. To contemporary Anglo-American readers, these similarities may appear uncanny or perhaps arbitrary. But for those who have read the contemporary academic sources from the 1920s and '30s in Germany they reconfirm a certain political-philosophical version of National Socialism.

The work of Baeumler and Heidegger reflects a specific generational

---

57. Baeumler was virtually indefatigable in producing a new, more aggressively National Socialist version of Nietzsche's writings for public consumption. Besides producing two separate editions of the *Werke*—the eight-volume *Dünndruck Ausgabe* of Nietzsche's *Werke* (Leipzig: Kröner, 1930–1931) [see vol. 1, xx, for the reference to Hölderlin's final hymns] and the twelve-volume *Taschenausgabe* of Nietzsche's *Werke* (Leipzig: Kröner, 1930–1932), Baeumler also edited two different collections of aphorisms from the *Nachlass*: F. Nietzsche, *Die Unschuld des Werdens*, 2 vols., ed. Alfred Baeumler (Leipzig: Kröner, 1930) and *Nietzsches Philosophie in Selbstzeugnissen*, 2 vols., ed. Alfred Baeumler (Leipzig: Reclam, 1931).

affinity for the chthonic, the rooted, the telluric, the mythic, and the archaic that expresses itself in the paradoxical yearning for a new instauration of things—what, in the torturous political discourse of the age, was termed "conservative revolution." Heidegger's discourse about a first beginning and an other beginning betrays this same paradoxical yearning to rethink history in terms of both its end (eschatology) and its origin (archeology). His reading of Nietzsche becomes simply another way of expressing this generational leitmotif. This does not mean that we can reduce Heidegger's *Nietzsche* solely to the level of generational assumptions and clichés, however. Yet finally we need to see how generationally rooted Heidegger's narrative of *Seynsgeschichte* truly was and how its rhetorical turn to the subterranean philosophy of the early Greeks was an encoded discourse about a National Socialist politics of autochthony. Like other conservative revolutionaries, Heidegger embraced the new postwar ethos of will and power (marked by an unyielding commitment to masculinity, heroism, hardness, danger, courage, and daring) that was popularized in both the writings of Ernst Jünger and the cult of Schlageter.[58] Moreover, he also embraced the conservative revolutionary critique of modern technology, rootless capitalism, and political liberalism that defined the entire movement. To this constellation of themes he added a *völkisch* penchant for communal and corporative existence, an ideal whose roots lay in the German Youth Movement's valorization of the *Bund* and its repudiation of bourgeois individualism. Both Baeumler and Heidegger were politically committed to a National Socialist revolution in the spirit of Nietzsche—and yet, ultimately, given Heidegger's ontological presuppositions, a break proved to be inevitable. Still, these two thinkers shared a fundamental faith in the conservative revolutionary commitment to Nietzsche as the herald and prophet of a new German future that would be ushered in through a philosophical politics of *Kampf*, destiny, and self-assertion.[59]

58. For an account of the Conservative Revolution, see Rolf Peter Sieferle, *Die Konservative Revolution* (Frankfurt: S. Fischer, 1995); Roger Woods, *The Conservative Revolution in the Weimar Republic* (New York: St. Martin's, 1996); and *La 'Révolution Conservatricè' dans Allemagne de Weimar*, ed. Louis Dupeux (Paris: Éditions Kimé, 1992). For a critical account of the masculine ethos in and around Heidegger, see Patricia Huntington, *Ecstatic Subjects, Utopia, and Recognition: Kristeva, Heidegger, Irigaray* (Albany: SUNY Press, 1998), 33–76; and Klaus Theweleit, *Männerphantasien*, 2 vols. (Frankfurt: Rowohlt, 1978). Part of the problem with reading Heidegger is that many of his editors, publishers, commentators, and disciples read him monochromatically in terms of a great conversation with the Western tradition. August Wiedmann's fascinating book, *The German Quest for Primal Origins in Art, Culture, and Politics* (Lewiston: Edwin Mellen, 1995), situates Heidegger in a far richer polychromatic context and helps us to see the prevalence of generational leitmotifs in his work.

59. Alfred Baeumler, *Alfred Rosenberg und der Mythus des 20. Jahrhunderts* (Munich: Hoheneichen, 1943), 70. As Baeumler puts it, "world history cannot be understood as an 'imaginary' development to an imaginary goal; it is, rather, the concurrent struggle and self-assertion [*Selbstbehauptung*] of myths that give form to being." Baeumler too will draw on the rhetorical power of *Selbstbehauptung* for his Nietzschean reading of a National Socialist Ger-

VI. NAZI BIOLOGISM AND HEIDEGGERIAN AUTOCHTHONY

In his radio address of April 1933, "Das Volk und die Gebildeten," Baeumler told his audience that it was Nietzsche who led German philosophy to the discovery that "the human being is a political being."[60] And, in his interpretations of Nietzsche, Baeumler made it clear that at the very center of Nietzschean thought lay the doctrine of "great politics." Baeumler argued that to the German *Volk*, Nietzsche had posed "the ancient task of our race: the task of being the leader [*Führer*] of Europe."[61] In their distinctive ways, both Heidegger and Baeumler will turn to the thought of Nietzsche as a way of interpreting and legitimizing their versions of the National Socialist revolution. And, to a remarkable degree, their work becomes paradigmatic for German academic philosophy during the thirties as it attempts to define itself as National Socialist in and through its relation to Nietzsche.[62] In this sense, writing about Nietzsche for this generation becomes itself a political act. Baeumler's own work explicitly argues for reading Nietzsche as a political philosopher of the state, and, after 1933, this reading becomes a definitive index of the reigning National Socialist view of Nietzsche. Baeumler will put forward a convincing portrait of Nietzsche as a philosopher of heroic will to power who sees the world systematically in terms of a Heraclitean play and contest of vital and degenerate forces. According to this reading, there is only one center to Nietzsche's work and that lies in his doctrine of will to power, a doctrine whose centrality had been missed by earlier commentators, since it had been most clearly expressed in the *Nachlass* rather than in works that Nietzsche published during his lifetime. By rearranging his written notes according to this new systematic center and by reading will to power as both the key to a new philosophy of the subject and to a new politics of the *Volk*, Baeumler concluded that he had found the basis of a proto-National Socialist philosophy for the German nation. At last, here in Nietzsche's

many: *Politik und Erziehung*, 27, 48, 53; *Nietzsche: Der Philosoph und Politiker*, 15, 93, 179; *Weltdemokratie und Nationalsozialismus* (Berlin: Duncker & Humblot, 1943), 12, 19–20: "All being wants to assert itself. It is a law of the living that at the depths of being there is a longing for self-assertion that can never be surrendered in favor of some kind of universality." Baeumler also speaks powerfully about the connection between Fichte's *Reden an die deutsche Nation* and German *Selbstbehauptung* in an essay entitled "Philosophie" in *Deutsche Wissenschaft: Arbeit und Aufgabe* (Leipzig: Hirzel, 1939), 32–33.

60. Alfred Baeumler, *Männerbund und Wissenschaft* (Berlin: Junker & Dünnhaupt, 1943), 114.

61. Baeumler, *Nietzsche: Der Philosoph und Politiker*, 182.

62. The status of Heidegger and Baeumler within the National Socialist order can be traced in the work of Zapata Galindo, Oduev, and Aschheim—see note 68, chapter 3, and note 20 in this chapter. See also Sluga, *Heidegger's Crisis*; Karl Jaspers, *Nietzsche: Einführung in das Verständnis seines Philosophierens* (Berlin: de Gruyter, 1950); and Karl Löwith, *Nietzsches Philosophie der ewigen Wiederkehr des Gleichen*, 199–225.

philosophy of will to power lay the solution for reconciling the will of the individual and of the political community. In terms of the individual subject, Baeumler defined will to power as the pure assertion of will *as* power. For Baeumler, the subject's goal was not the accretion of power that it did not yet have, but the expression of power that it already was. Such a subject had little in common with the passive, inward-directed, theoretical construct of Cartesian ego-metaphysics. On the contrary, Baeumler's Nietzschean subject expressed the masculine-*bündisch* values of self-assertion, warriorly courage, and communal allegiance. In political terms, this new fascist subject of will and self-assertion became the model for a Heraclitean struggle of power politics that would place the German state at the center of a reconfigured Europe. In its essence, then, "Nietzsche's philosophy of will to power is [a] philosophy of politics."[63] Much as Bismarck, Frederick the Great, and the Ottonian emperors, Nietzsche sought to assert the power of the German *Volk* as a decisive political force at the center of Europe.

Within the context of the German ressentiment against France during the Weimar period, Baeumler's political interpretation of Nietzsche struck a nerve. Now Nietzsche's philosophy of will to power could be read as a metaphysical justification for refusing to accept the humiliating Treaty of Versailles. Moreover, it could also be interpreted as a call for a strong German leader who could set aright the destructive triumph of democratic, liberal, and communist forces that had been ushered in by the Great War. But as *Nietzsche: Der Philosoph und Politiker* made clear, the roots of these German-French conflicts went back beyond July of 1914 to the ideas of 1789 and Rousseau's pusillanimous "feminism," and, ultimately, to the imperial Roman origins of Franco-Gallic culture.[64] It was this Franco-Roman version of the state, Baeumler argued, that Nietzsche always rejected, not the state itself in its Germanic, self-assertive form. Readers who had not grasped the inner political unity of Nietzsche's *Nachlass* fragments had failed to consider this hidden but essential dimension. Again, the work of editing and organizing proved to have deep metaphysical significance—a message that was hardly lost on Heidegger, though he was no mere follower. Heidegger would concur with Baeumler's contention that the *Nachlass* was at the heart of Nietzsche's genuine philosophy and that, when read properly, it could be thought to harbor a hidden political-metaphys-

---

63. Martha Zapata Galindo offers a persuasive account of Baeumler's notion of a masculine heroic subject, going so far as to speak of Baeumler's *"Selbstbehauptungssubjekt," Triumph des Willens zur Macht*, 88–92; and Alfred Baeumler, *Studien zur deutschen Geistesgeschichte* (Berlin: Junker & Dünnhaupt, 1943), 292.

64. Baeumler, *Nietzsche: Der Philosoph und Politiker*, 113–115. Within Baeumler's heroic-masculine lexicon, "feminism" denotes a lack of courage and an unmanly, cowardly bearing and attitude.

ical meaning. But here, as elsewhere, Heidegger would go his own way and, in the process, transform his reading of Nietzsche into a *grand récit* of the whole Western tradition.

Baeumler had argued that the state was a "heroic manifestation . . . , a structure of supremacy and mastery . . . , the means and expression of the struggle for the highest power."[65] "This is what is alive in Nietzsche," he insisted, "even there, indeed precisely there, where he speaks out against the state and precisely there where he attacks Germany. This too is what lives in the hymns of Hölderlin." What lay at the foundation of this heroic-Hölderlinian conception of the state and made it possible, he claimed, was Nietzsche's philosophy of will to power as a form of political self-assertion. To draw forth such a reading from the texts, however, required that Baeumler first embrace a hermeneutics of violence that would utterly disregard their context—and, as in other matters of textual violation, he proved himself fit for the task. Hence, in one passage Nietzsche writes, "the various moral prejudices have until now not been traced back to the existence of the genus 'man.' Rather, they have been traced to the existence of a '*Volk*,' a 'race,' etc.—and indeed from *Völker* who wanted to assert themselves [*sich . . . behaupten*] against other *Völker*" (KSA 11: 141). On the basis of this passage, Baeumler concludes that Nietzsche was advocating a kind of *völkisch* self-assertion. As he reads it, "insofar as the individual takes upon himself the demands of the *Volk*, his strength grows; insofar as he is part of the tension between world-historical entities, he pursues the path to greatness. For all active natures, this path leads to the state." As Nietzsche himself put it in one of his notebook entries: "A new form of community: warriorly self-assertion [*sich kriegerisch behauptend*]" (KSA 10: 515). For Baeumler, the hidden subtext to Nietzsche's agonal metaphysics of power lay in a political metaphysics bound up in "the Greek . . . drive to self-assertion, power, and victory."[66] Out of this Nietzschean political philosophy, Baeumler will develop a racial metaphysics of history that will elide all Roman, Christian, Franco-Gallic, and Oriental influences in the name of Graeco-German racial autochthony and Germanic self-assertion.

Heidegger will draw upon Baeumler's fundamental categories of interpretation in his own work on Nietzsche. But where Baeumler offers a metaphysics of *Kampf* grounded in race, blood, genetics, and heredity, Heidegger will reject what he perceives to be the crudely biological premises of this vision for a more essential, ontologically grounded metaphysics. Baeumler's and Rosenberg's "myth of the blood" strikes Heidegger as something fundamentally incompatible with Nietzsche's whole way

65. Ibid., 179–181.
66. Ibid., 73.

of thinking.[67] Moreover, the Nazi discourse about Nietzsche's "alleged biologism" appears to Heidegger as but another manifestation of nineteenth-century positivism presented in the form of a cultural worldview. Going back to the lecture "On the Essence of Truth" and the Rectorial Address, Heidegger had attempted to rethink the German conception of *Wissenschaft* according to its originary Greek essence as *aletheia*. He even went so far as to equate the primordial sense of *Wissenschaft* with "knowledge of the *Volk* . . . , knowledge of the destiny of the state . . . , together with the knowledge of the spiritual mission" (HCW: 36/SdU: 16). But the Nazi conception of *Wissenschaft*, promulgated at the university in the form of "political" science, racial lore (*Rassekunde*), racial doctrine (*Rassenlehre*), *völkische Wissenschaft*, and what Krieck termed "*völkisch-politische Anthropologie*," seems to Heidegger but a pale version of the originary Greek practice of science as *philosophia*.[68] The essays of 1937 and 1938—"Die Bedrohung der Wissenschaft" and "The Age of the World Picture"—will develop a formidable critique of this inauthentic kind of science. However, it is in the Nietzsche lectures that Heidegger offers perhaps his most incisive account of National Socialist science and its racial-biological metaphysics.

As ever, Heidegger will rethink the measure of science in terms of originary autochthony; that is, he will reflect on the ground of modern science as it relates to the primordial Greek experience of *aletheia*. In his words: "science and reflection on the specific field are both historically grounded on the actual dominance of a particular interpretation of being, and they always move in the dominant circle of a particular conception of the essence of truth. In every fundamental self-reflection of the sciences, it is always a matter of passage through metaphysical decisions that were either made long ago or are being prepared now" (Niii: 44–47/GA 47: 64–68). But biologism gets stuck in the nineteenth-century metaphysics of science that came to be known as "positivism." Positivism defines truth not in terms of historical experience but as the representation of an objective state of affairs by a subject. It carries out its Cartesian project of securing truth within its method by apprehending beings as objects present at hand that can be transformed by the privileged subject into a secure picture or *Bild*. And, on the basis of its scientifically secured research, it organizes beings themselves into a world picture (*Weltbild*). Science itself thus fulfills the Cartesian dream of making human beings "the masters and possessors of nature."[69]

67. Baeumler speaks of the "myth of blood" in *Alfred Rosenberg*, 71; and Härtle, *Nietzsche und der Nationalsozialismus*, 55–64.

68. Ernst Krieck, *Völkisch-Politische Anthropologie*, 3 vols. (Leipzig: Armanen, 1938).

69. Rene Descartes, *Discourse on Method*, trans. Donald Cress (Indianapolis: Hackett, 1993), 35; Heidegger, QCT: 116–154/H: 69–104.

This critique of modern science as positivism has all too often been read in terms of an eco-poetic, deep-ecological critique of technological devastation and dominion that Heidegger offered in the spirit of Eckhartian *Gelassenheit*. But there were other, more politically charged sources for his critique and those who would read Heidegger carefully should attend to them as well. In the midst of his debate about Nietzsche's "alleged biologism," Heidegger sought to offer a critique of Nazi science and racial metaphysics in an effort to affirm a more originary, ontological-autochthonic form of inquiry and questioning. As we have seen throughout our reading, this form of ontological autochthony was from the start ultimately bound up with a German metaphysics of destiny that would be hard to reconcile with Eckhartian detachment and meditative calm. And yet Baeumler too would invoke the name of Eckhart to secure his own National Socialist version of truth, a rhetorical move that Heidegger would also make.[70] Hence, when we read the Nietzsche lectures as a critique of biologism, race, and the metaphysics of blood and consanguinity, we need to remember that Heidegger's rejection of these principles was grounded in what he deemed a more fundamental form of communal identity— namely, autochthony. Like other National Socialist thinkers, Heidegger too would exclude the Hebrews, the Romans, the Asians, the non-Europeans, though he would do so not on the basis of race or blood, but owing to what he perceived as the missing autochthonic link to the first Greek beginning. Exclusion for Heidegger thus became a matter of metaphysical rather than biological origin.

If other Nietzsche commentators reduced the thought of will to power to a Darwinian drive for survival, Heidegger insisted on interpreting it ontologically as "the fulfillment of Western metaphysics" (Niv: 59/GA 48: 104). In his words, "when Nietzsche thinks beings as a whole . . . he is not thinking biologically. Rather, he grounds this apparently merely biological world picture *metaphysically*" (Niii: 46–47/GA 47: 66–68). What other National Socialists took to be essential for Nietzsche—namely, biology— Heidegger views as mere "foreground" and as a matter of subjective impression. But Heidegger warns: "whether one votes yes or no on Nietzsche's 'biologism,' one always gets stuck in the foreground of his thinking. The predilection for this state of affairs is supported by the form of his own publications. His words and sentences provoke, fascinate, penetrate and stimulate. One thinks that if only one pursues one's impressions one has understood Nietzsche. We must first unlearn this abuse that is supported by current catchwords like *biologism*. We must learn to 'read.'"

---

70. Baeumler, *Alfred Rosenberg*, 83–84. See also Fritz Giese, *Nietzsche: Die Erfüllung* (Tübingen: Mohr, 1934), 139, which links Rosenberg and Hitler to Eckhart and eternal recurrence; and Hans Heyse, *Idee und Existenz* (Hamburg: Hanseatische Verlagsanstalt, 1935), 219–220.

Clearly, as Heidegger read it, Baeumler's work had failed to move beyond the foreground.

Heidegger would challenge Baeumler's biologistic reading of Nietzsche, not only as science and metaphysics, but also as a form of politics. And he would extend this critique to Baeumler's overall philosophy of heroic realism grounded in Nietzschean will to power. For Baeumler, will to power meant the deployment of vital energy in line with the Heraclitean principle of struggle, conflict, and war. As he defined it, "will to power is not a will that has power as its goal or that 'strives' after power. . . . The will only wills/wants itself."[71] In this sense, "will to power does not strive after any goal but is itself eternal becoming that knows no goal. This becoming is a struggle [*Kampf*]." As part of this metaphysics of will and struggle, Baeumler will argue that Nietzsche's genuine philosophy expresses an ultimately political motive to rethink human history along the lines of power and to affirm a Nordic-masculine-heroic form of dominion. Hence, on the basis of Nietzsche's philosophy of will, which he redefines as a "philosophy of politics," Baeumler will attempt to rethink will to power in explicitly statist terms and "to ground the state in race."[72] Heidegger too will argue that "what the will wills/wants it already has" and, like Baeumler, will underscore the Heraclitean principle of struggle (QCT: 77/H: 216). Both men will also agree that the bourgeois interpretation of Nietzsche in terms of "values" will hardly suffice and that only those schooled in the originary, revolutionary politics of National Socialism will be able to "read" Nietzsche properly. In this sense, both would concur with the NS ideologue Hans Kern that "whoever stands outside of this revolution and does not know what it desires and where it comes from, will never be able to comprehend Nietzsche."[73]

Yet Heidegger would ultimately break with Baeumler on the question of politics precisely as it related to the NS revolution. As he saw it, Baeumler's emphasis on racial-political themes had blinded him to the ultimate metaphysical significance of will to power. For Baeumler, will to power meant a political will to domination and triumph that would be brought about by the Nordic warrior fighting for the self-assertion of the German *Volk*. Heidegger, on the contrary, always thought of the political revolution as the groundwork and preparation of the metaphysical revolution—hence, he deemed Baeumler's Nietzsche works as inessential in that they had reduced Nietzsche's metaphysics primarily to a form of politics. Nowhere was this more evident, Heidegger would claim, than in Baeumler's decision to jettison the thought of eternal return. In his Nietzsche

71. Baeumler, *Nietzsche: Der Philosoph und Politiker*, 46–47.
72. Baeumler, *Studien zur deutschen Geistesgeschichte*, 292.
73. Hans Kern, "Nietzsche und die deutsche Revolution," *Rhythmus: Monatschrift für Bewegungslehre* 12 (1934): 146.

book, Baeumler had interpreted eternal return as a kind of theological vestige that needed to be excised from the corpus of Nietzsche's work. As he put it, "in terms of Nietzsche's system, this thought is of no consequence. We have to view it as the expression of a highly personal experience. It has no connection to the thought of will to power and indeed, when thought through to its end, it bursts asunder the coherence of the philosophy of will to power. . . . Through the thought of eternal return everything becomes subjective."[74] Moreover, Baeumler maintained that this doctrine had the inevitable effect of rigidifying Nietzsche's dynamic and playful notion of Heraclitean becoming by turning it into a hardened category of Platonic being.

Heidegger will come into confrontation with Baeumler's reading, however, by attempting to think eternal return and will to power *together* as the heart of Nietzsche's metaphysics. For him, Baeumler's decision to elide the doctrine of eternal return betrays a fundamental misreading, not only of Nietzsche's philosophy, but of the history of philosophy as a whole and, by extension, of National Socialism's place within that history. Eternal return, he will argue, is not a manifestation of subjective thought but a philosophical doctrine that challenges the foundations of subjectivism by seeing it as the ultimate form of nihilism. In this sense, it serves as a counter-thought to nihilism in that it reduces all values to nothing and forces us to confront a world without any ultimate goal for beings. It thus poses a fundamental decision for the European world: whether to succumb to the subjective nihilism of our Cartesian mastery and domination of the earth *or* to recover our chthonic roots in the earth as part of a political-ontological revolution. As such, the doctrine of eternal return becomes for Heidegger an essential part of Nietzsche's reading of modernity as an epoch of nihilism and as the age of critical decision and confrontation. Because Baeumler reads Nietzsche's philosophy solely in terms of National Socialist theory, he misses the historical significance of eternal recurrence for the decision about nihilism. As Heidegger will write, "Nietzsche's doctrine of eternal recurrence conflicts with Baeumler's conception of politics. It is therefore 'without importance' for Nietzsche's system" (Niii: 22–23/GA 43: 25–26). In the end, Heidegger will conclude that "Baeumler does not grasp metaphysically, but interprets politically."[75]

In contrast to Baeumler, Heidegger attempts to "grasp metaphysically" through an interpretation of politics. Because Baeumler's portrait of Nietzsche had placed the racial-political doctrines at the forefront and

---

74. Baeumler, *Nietzsche: Der Philosoph und Politiker,* 80.

75. As testimony to his blatantly political reading of Nietzsche, Baeumler will write: "the key to understanding all of Nietzsche's concrete demands and goals lies in his interpretation of the state," *Nietzsche: Der Philosoph und Politiker,* 88.

had interpreted nihilism primarily in these terms, it wound up underplaying the ontological dimension of his thought. For Heidegger, this proved to be its most egregious flaw. In lieu of Baeumler's blatantly statist-political interpretation, Heidegger pointed to Nietzsche's reversal of Platonism and of Platonic structures of knowledge within Western philosophy as the more essential path for the present generation. For him, the recovery of a Pre-Socratic notion of truth from beneath these structures held forth the only genuine hope of a permanent revolution for the German *Volk*, more permanent than any overtly political action or biological-racial doctrine could offer. And yet, despite his critique of these racial-biological-political-statist interpretations, Heidegger's decision to read Nietzsche within an elegiac *Seynsgeschichte* repeated many of the same rhetorical gestures employed by Baeumler: the use of Greek philosophy in interpreting the National Socialist revolution; the invidious positioning of Roman imperialism against the Greek *polis* as a way of defining a genuinely autochthonous German *Volksgemeinschaft;* the turn to a *mythos* of the archaic and originary for legitimating a vision of the "futural"; the pressing into service of Nietzsche for a decision about the crisis of nihilism confronting the German nation; the commitment to a masculinist ethos of heroic will, struggle, *Kampf,* greatness, and self-assertion born out of the spirit of the Great War; a totalizing vision of history in terms of destiny, fate, and justice (*Gerechtigkeit*); a conservative-revolutionary critique of the modern epoch rooted in the values of the homeland, the earth, the soil, roots, and autochthony. If we are to understand Heidegger's own characterization of the Nietzsche lectures as constituting an *Auseinandersetzung* with National Socialism, then we need finally to recognize how deeply rooted these lectures are in the political ideology that they seek to contest.

At stake for Heidegger in his writings on Nietzsche from 1936–1944 was nothing less than the viability of the National Socialist revolution itself and of its decided failure to enact the hopes of ontological renewal promised at the outset. National Socialism put forward the hope of totalizing history, of rendering all hitherto existing structures, ideas, traditions, and institutions meaningful only in relation to its own future directed narrative of political rebirth, renewal, reversal, and revolution. Heidegger's own narrative of a history of being, marked at opposing ends by a "first" and an "other" beginning, aimed at transposing this National Socialist narrative onto the history of the West now understood ontologically, and not just politically. Everything was at stake in this bold initiative, not merely a statist regime. Hence, the confrontation needed to be attuned to the shifting political registers of meaning within the German *Volk*—and Heidegger did not shy away from putting forward his own most revolutionary narrative of ontological rebirth.

VII. HEIDEGGER'S EARLY NIETZSCHE LECTURES

"Nietzsche" was not a new topic for Heidegger as he commenced his lecture course in the winter of 1936–37. He had already engaged Nietzsche's "On the Uses and Disadvantages of History for Life" in his discussion of historicity from *Being and Time* and in winter 1929/30 had taken up Nietzsche's pairing of the two ancient deities of art, Dionysus and Apollo, for an analysis of what he termed "the contemporary situation."[76] Moreover, in his Rectorial Address, Heidegger had given prominence to Nietzsche's proclamation about the death of God, and in *Introduction to Metaphysics* (1935) had alluded to Nietzschean metaphysics at crucial points in his lectures.[77] Nietzsche had been important to Heidegger as a philosophical partner in dialogue, going all the way back to his student days in Freiburg where he had listened to lectures given by his dissertation director, Heinrich Rickert, on Nietzsche and the problem of values. Rickert had a distinctly Neo-Kantian reading of Nietzsche that positioned him in the great tradition of axiology going back to Plato's metaphysics. For him, Nietzsche was not a revolutionary thinker who had initiated a radical transvaluation of all values; rather, Nietzsche was just an epigone of Kant. Where Kant had understood values in terms of science, Nietzsche had reduced them to the unscientific level of will. Still, Rickert argued that Nietzsche was part of a Kantian tradition that had transformed the nineteenth century. "Now problems of value become crucial; indeed, the fundamental questions of philosophy now attain the status of questions of value where earlier they had been defined as questions of being."[78] Rickert even goes so far as to argue that "Nietzsche's principal thesis concerning the being of the world—the doctrine of eternal return—is only comprehensible as an answer to the question of value. Only that human being who can 'endure' this doctrine stands as the one who attains the highest level of value."

As he begins his own Nietzsche lectures, Heidegger will attempt to reverse Rickert's decision to privilege value over being—only now he will focus his attention on the contemporary form of value-philosophy: the

---

76. Heidegger, BT: 362/SZ: 396–397; FCM: 72–74/GA 29/30: 107–110.

77. Heidegger, RA: 33/SdU: 13; IM: 4, 12, 13, 17, 36, 39, 106, 126, 199, 203/EM: 3, 10, 14, 27, 28, 30, 80, 96, 152, 155. How seriously Nietzsche affected Heidegger's thought in this period can be seen from the exergue to his SS 1931 lecture course, *Aristotle's Metaphysics, Theta 1–3*, trans. Walter Brogan and Peter Warnek (Bloomington: Indiana University Press, 1995), xvi/GA 31: 1. There Heidegger writes "the inner will of this course can be characterized by a word from Nietzsche;" he then cites a passage from aphorism 419 of Nietzsche's *Will to Power*.

78. Heinrich Rickert, "Die deutsche Philosophie von Kant bis Nietzsche," unpublished lectures from the University of Heidelberg, ms. 31, 8–23; this is an earlier version from WS 1917/18 of ms. 160. My thanks to the Universitätsbibliothek in Heidelberg for providing me with a copy of this manuscript.

National Socialist worldview. What Heidegger undertakes here is a bold and decisive reconfiguring of the contemporary NS view of Nietzsche away from questions of "value" (politics, culture, ideology, worldview) toward the primordial understanding and experience of being. As early as 1935, Heidegger had expressed his longing to overcome NS value-philosophy by means of an ontological revolution: "the works that are being peddled about nowadays as the philosophy of National Socialism but have nothing whatever to do with the inner truth and greatness of this movement (namely, the encounter between global technology and modern man)—have all been written by men fishing in the troubled waters of 'values' and 'totalities'" (IM: 199/EM: 152).[79] Heidegger then speaks of Nietzsche's own "entanglement in the thicket of value-representation and his failure to understand its questionable origin." But even as he echoes Rickert's earlier reading of Nietzsche as axiologist, Heidegger will transform it into his own inimitable version of the history of philosophy rethought as a new Adamic myth of ontological decline and fall.

In "The Will to Power as Art," Heidegger sets to work developing a reading of the philosopher that grows out of a close interpretation of specific texts. Here and in the lectures from 1937, "Nietzsche's Fundamental Metaphysical Stance in Western Thinking: The Eternal Return of the Same," Heidegger will privilege certain passages from the *Nachlass* and employ them in an effort to establish a kind of hierarchy between unpublished and published works. On this basis he then puts forward an ontological interpretation of Nietzsche's aesthetics and doctrine of eternal return that confronts the established biological, psychological, and anthropological readings of such topics. In the unpublished texts, Heidegger will find a kind of alternative and hidden history of truth that had gone undetected by most Nietzsche commentators, a narrative along the lines of what Nietzsche in the *Gay Science* termed a *historia abscondita*. Speaking about such a tradition, Nietzsche wrote: "Every great human being exerts a retroactive force: for his sake all of history is placed in the balance again, and a thousand secrets of the past crawl out of their hiding places—into *his* sunshine. There is no way of telling what may yet become part of history. Perhaps the past is still essentially undiscovered! So many retroactive forces are still needed!" (GS: 104/ KSA 3: 404). Following Nietzsche's insight, Heidegger will burrow beneath the accumulated layers of philosophical sediment and attempt to excavate the hidden sources

79. Heidegger added the note in parentheses about global technology in the 1953 edition of *Einführung in die Metaphysik*, another attempt at altering the textual record of the NS years by the author of "the Last Hand." For a critical commentary on Heidegger's editorial practice in IM, see Jürgen Habermas, "Mit Heidegger gegen Heidegger Denken: Zur Veröffentlichung von Vorlesungen aus dem Jahre 1935," reprinted in *Philosophisch-Politische Profile* (Frankfurt: Suhrkamp, 1981), 65–72.

of a subterranean and chthonic style of thinking that he believed was covered over by Western metaphysics.

In his first lecture series on Nietzsche, Heidegger will sketch an outline of this hidden history of truth by reading Nietzsche as a stimulus for a retroactively focused hermeneutics of the *arche*. Turning back to Plato through the metaphysical accretions of Platonic and Kantian aesthetics, Heidegger will seek to uncover the hidden essence of art in the Pre-Platonic experience of truth as unconcealment. In this experience, he will locate the source and the guiding directive for his own ontotheological history of the West along Nietzschean lines. In "The Will to Power as Art," Heidegger will acknowledge that the sources for this history derive from notes in Nietzsche's *Nachlass* of 1888 and his section from *Twilight of the Idols*, entitled "How the 'True World' Finally Became a Fable" (WP:305–306/WM: 386–387/KSA 13: 370–371, 270–271; TI: 50–51/KSA 6: 80–81). In this lecture series, Heidegger's task is to reconceive the problem of art from within this history by taking up Nietzsche's claim that art constitutes a genuine countermovement to nihilism (Ni: 75–76/GA 43: 88). For Nietzsche, the whole Western metaphysical tradition is marked by the Platonic imperative to define truth as something supersensuous, incorporeal, and numinous. Within this Platonic tradition, art itself will be thought of as mimetic, as something that produces or brings forth a mere likeness or appearance of what is true. Not surprisingly, art will thus be thought of as subordinate to truth within the Platonic tradition, because it can only provide a simulacrum of the true in a transitory form rather than an instantiation of the true itself as idea. Nietzsche, of course, will put forward a devastating critique of Plato's metaphysics as nihilism and will insist in no uncertain terms that "art is *worth more* [*mehr wert*] than truth" (WP: 453/WM: 578/KSA 13: 521). In this move to define art in terms of value (*Wert*), however, Heidegger will conclude that Nietzsche himself remains firmly tied to the metaphysics of truth that he seeks to contest and overcome.

From his earliest notebook drafts of 1870–1871, Nietzsche had written: "my philosophy: inverted Platonism [*umgedrehter Platonismus*]" (KSA 7: 199). In his early attempt to interpret art as sensuous, corporeal, and ecstatic, Nietzsche comes to understand his philosophy not only as an inversion of Platonism but also as an overcoming of the metaphysics of the supersensuous that spawned it. His "fable" about "the history of an error" from 1888 simply reconfirmed this view. Heidegger would, however, interpret Nietzsche's thought differently. For him, Nietzsche's alleged "inversion" (*Umdrehung*) of Platonism never succeeds in "twisting free of" (*Herausdrehung*) those metaphysical categories of permanent presence, enduring selfsameness, and constant immutability that constitute Platonic metaphysics. Rather, Nietzsche's attempt to think art as "the highest form of will to power" and as its "supreme configuration" merely replicates the inherent Platonic bias toward permanence as a condition of truth—only now in the form of a "value" (GA 67: 47; Ni: 218/GA 43: 271). Nietzsche's inversion—rethought as transvaluation (*Umwertung*)—thus ends up reinscribing the codex of Platonic metaphysics on the truth tablets of the Western philosophical tradition. Despite his criticism of Nietzsche's position, however, Heidegger will go to great lengths to salvage Nietzsche's fundamental project as a way of countering this tradition.

Even as he will argue that Nietzsche's mere inversion/reinscription of Platonism does not genuinely uncover the hidden essence of truth within Western philosophy, Heidegger will at the same time strive to recuperate Nietzsche's fundamental insight into art as a way of raising again the question of being as *aletheia*. In these early Nietzsche lectures, Heidegger will now seize upon the ontological implications of art to put forth his own *völkisch*-political reading of truth, a reading that, as we have already seen, he developed in his original lecture "On the Essence of Truth" from the *Heimattag* at Karlsruhe in 1930.[80] Going back to this decisive lecture, Heidegger had argued that truth is never simply present in and of itself; it is "not a feature of correct propositions that are asserted of an 'object' by a human 'subject' and then 'are valid' somewhere . . . ; rather, truth is disclosure [*Entbergung*] of beings through which an openness essentially unfolds [*west*]" (PM: 146/WM: 86). What proved decisive here was the realm of the hidden, the concealed, the closed—what Heidegger termed *Verborgenheit* or "concealment" from the German verb *bergen* ("to shelter" or "to hide") and the noun *Berg* ("mountain").[81] Because the Western metaphysical tradition had forgotten this hidden and concealed dimension of truth and had relegated it to the realm of non-presence, it could never reclaim the primordial Heraclitean insight into truth as the mutually determinative play and contest between concealment and unconcealment. But Heidegger understood Heraclitean strife as essential to the unfolding of truth from out of its hiddenness, and he determined to put forward an account of the history of truth that would not forget the ontological significance of concealment, sheltering, and hiding. As he fashioned his own political rhetoric in 1933, he would bring together the ontological significance of *Verborgenheit* with the etymological root of the *Berg* as "sheltering mountain." In his Schlageter memorial speech, Heidegger would contrast the

80. Schneeberger, NH: 9–13. In one of his original drafts for "Vom Wesen der Wahrheit" (December 11, 1930), Heidegger will draw on the language of *bergen* and its cognates, "Unverborgenheit" and "Entborgenheit" to translate the play of unconcealment/concealment that he finds in the ancient Greek notion of *aletheia*. References are to be found in the draft of this text in the Herbert Marcuse Archive of the Stadt-und Universitätsbibliothek, Frankfurt am Main, #0012.01, 7.

81. *Cassell's German-English Dictionary*, 100–101.

"hero's native mountains" (*Heimatberge*) with his "hardness of will" and his "inescapable destiny" (HCW: 41–42/NH: 48–49). And, in his rhapsodic paean to rustic life, "Creative Landscape," Heidegger would again draw on the elemental power of the *Berg* as something essential to the life and will of the *Volk* (HMT: 27–30/DE: 9–13).[82] The topography of the landscape here would be described as something inextricably bound up with the destiny of the German people. The language of *Berg* and *bergen* would thus become linked not only rhetorically but also ontologically and politically. The "centuries-long and irreplaceable Alemannic-Swabian rootedness and autochthony [*Bodenständigkeit*]" in the soil and mountain landscape of the Black Forest would function here as the very ground of possibility for recovering another kind of "centuries-long and irreplaceable" form of autochthony: the hidden and *verborgene* dimension of Pre-Socratic *aletheia*. The consequences of this bond between political and ontological autochthony would emerge more powerfully, however, in Heidegger's reflections on art.

In his 1935 lecture, "The Origin of the Work of Art," Heidegger developed the language of *Berg, bergen,* and *entbergen* into a full-scale series of paronomasic variations on the root stem "*berg*": *das Bergende, die Verbergung, die Verborgenheit, die Unverborgenheit,* and others (H: 7–68). By defining the work of art in terms of strife, contest, *agon,* and *polemos,* Heidegger sets out to dispel the modern notion that art is merely an object produced by a subject. In his view, the work of art sets into work the unfolding of the essence of truth from out of its origin or *arche,* a process that commences with the strife between what seeks to remain hidden, sheltered, or concealed and what strives for disclosure, openness, and unconcealment. As Heidegger puts it, this strife between concealment (*Verborgenheit*) and unconcealment (*Unverborgenheit*) will get played out as an opposition between earth and world:

> The setting up of a world and the setting forth of earth are two essential features in the work-being of the work. They belong together. . . . The world is the self-opening openness of the broad paths of the simple and essential decisions in the destiny of a historical people. The earth is the spontaneous forthcoming of that which is continually self-secluding and to that extent sheltering and concealing [*Bergenden*]. World and earth are essentially different from one another and yet are never separated. The world grounds itself on the earth, and earth juts through world. Yet the relation between world and earth does not wither away into the empty unity of opposites unconcerned with one another. The world, in resting upon the earth, strives to surmount it. As self-opening it cannot endure anything closed. The earth,

82. For a brief, clear discussion of Heidegger's notion of *Bergung* ("sheltering") and its relation to truth see Richard Polt, *Heidegger: An Introduction* (Ithaca: Cornell University Press, 1999), 149–151.

however, as sheltering and concealing, tends always to draw the world into it-self and keep it there. (BW:172/H:36–37)

By thinking the art work in terms of the strife between earth and world and by focusing on the "sheltering and concealing" aspects within this strife, Heidegger succeeded in refashioning the chthonic and subter-ranean philosophy that he developed in the early 1930s in dialogue with Werner Jaeger, W. F. Otto, and Alfred Baeumler.[83] Especially in his con-stant references to the earth as a source of concealment and hidden power, Heidegger will attempt to evoke the chthonic dimension of ar-chaic Greek thinking. And he will do so by focusing on the originary power of art to bring to presence the hidden character of *physis*. In this move to rethink art as strife and to concentrate on its hidden essence, Heidegger will raise the chthonic to an expressly ontological status.

In his original draft of "The Origin of the Work of Art" from 1931/32 he will explicitly link this ontological form of the chthonic to the political theme of autochthony. The work of art, within Heidegger's schema, func-tions as a way of bringing into relation the historical destiny of a *Volk* and its nearness or distance from its own origin. In this sense, it offers the possibil-ity of thinking the "futural" and the inaugural in terms of a historical deci-sion. Hence, Heidegger will ask: are we to frame our destiny in terms of the origin and see autochthonic rootedness in it? Or are we to pursue the root-lessness of technological dominion and mastery and sever our ties to the ori-gin? To answer these questions is to know who "we" are—and for Heidegger in the early 1930s the question of "who we are" was always thought in terms of an exclusionary form of political-ontological autochthony. At the very end of his original draft, Heidegger will pose the question:

> Are we in the vicinity [*Nähe*] of the essence of art as origin or are we not? And if we are not in the vicinity of the origin do we know this or do we not know it but merely stagger around carrying on the industry of art? If we do not know it then the first thing necessary is that we make it known. For clar-ity about who we are and who we are not is already the decisive leap [*Sprung*] into nearness to the origin [*Ursprung*]. Such nearness alone warrants a truly grounded historical *Dasein* as a form of genuine rootedness and au-tochthony [*Bodenständigkeit*] upon this earth. For—and here the word of Hölderlin provides closure:

83. This chthonic element in Heidegger's work has sources in Plato, Sophocles, and in Nietzsche's reading of the Pre-Socratics. But the more immediate sources for Heidegger are Baeumler's long introduction to J. J. Bachofen, *Der Mythus von Orient und Occident: Eine Meta-physik der alten Welt* (Munich: Beck, 1926), xxv–ccxciv; W. F. Otto, *Die Götter Griechenlands* (1929; Frankfurt: Klostermann, 1987); Werner Jaeger's "Tyrtaios über die wahre *Arete*," *Sitzungsberichte der Preussischen Akademie der Wissenschaft* 23 (1932): 537–568; and the *völkisch* tradition of *Bodenständigkeit* in Stifter, Hebel, and the Swabian folk poets. What is philosoph-ically significant here is how Heidegger weds this archaic-mythic discourse on the chthonic to a political form of metaphysics rooted in the autochthonic.

"Only with difficulty
Does what dwells near the origin, leave the source."[84]

For Heidegger the decision is clear. If the German *Volk* is to recover its originary rootedness in the earth, it will need to do so by way of a retrieval of its autochthonic bond with the archaic Greeks. But how is this to be done? How will the Germans be able to get out from under the nihilistic seal of ontological forgetfulness that plagues the modern world so that they might win back a measure of their authentic identity? In 1935–1936 Heidegger turns to art for his answers. He thinks that in the concealed power of the art work he might find a way of jump-starting the failed political revolution of 1933 that remained bogged down in the metaphysics of *techne* and its thematics of control, machination, dominion, and sovereignty.[85] Now he undertakes to rethink the relation between *physis* and *techne* as a kind of Heraclitean strife between earth and world, between the chthonic power of the archaic Greek gods who have fled and the enlightened Olympian forces of Cartesian rationality that embody clarity, light, and presence. In this new configuration of the archaic conflict between the chthonic gods and their Olympian descendants, Heidegger will find a mythic framework for interpreting the modern world. Like W. F. Otto,

84. Martin Heidegger, "Vom Ursprung des Kunstwerks: Erste Ausarbeitung," *Heidegger Studies* 5 (1989): 22. Heidegger never delivered the address in this form, as far as we know. The first public presentation was based on a second draft from 1935 now in possession of the Herbert Marcuse Archive at the Stadt-und Universitätsbibliothek, Frankfurt am Main, #0031.01. The first published version of this essay was in 1950 in *Holzwege*.

85. We can find traces of this same spirit of *völkisch* renewal in the National Socialist ecology movement. Raymond Dominick, *The Environmental Movement in Germany: Prophets and Pioneers, 1871–1971* (Bloomington: Indiana University Press, 1992), 86–118, provides helpful background for understanding the connections between the post-WWI German conservationists' longing for "national regeneration" and the beginnings of National Socialism. Konrad Guenther, a prominent German naturalist, argued, for example, that the Reich had collapsed, because "its foundation was not firmly rooted enough in the soil. . . . The ground upon which a *Volk* stands can only be the soil of the homeland. The more firmly it is rooted, the harder it is to uproot. . . . *Völker* who love their homeland defend it to the extreme and are unconquerable. But what does one love in the homeland? . . . One loves Nature!" As Guenther put it, either the Germans must become one *Volk* in nature and the landscape or they would become "cultural fertilizer for other nations." Guenther's fantasies about an *"Ur-Heimat"* as the creative source for the regeneration of the *Volk* were shared by other NS ideologues such as Walther Darré, Hitler's minister of agriculture, and Alfred Rosenberg, the director of the *Kampfbund für Deutsche Kultur.* In a kind of manifesto expressing the deepest values of the *Kampfbund,* an article from the party's central newspaper *Der Völkische Beobachter,* June 12, 1930, asserted: "In the midst of this apparently all-encompassing wave of internationalism, the greatest event of our time is the emergence of the new consciousness of the primordial deutsch-Germanic values of the soil, the new discovery of the deep rootedness of every culture and of all genuine, legitimate statehood in blood and soil (*Blut und Boden*)." Cited in Dominick, *The Environmental Movement in Germany,* 86, 93. We can see the same coupling of *Heimat, Bodenständigkeit,* and national renewal for the *Volk* in the preamble to the NS *Reichsnaturgesetz* of June 26, 1935, cited in Luc Ferry, *The New Ecological Order,* trans. Carol Volk (Chicago: University of Chicago Press, 1995), 101–102.

whose *The Gods of Greece* (1929) offered an interpretation of chthonic Greek religion as a primordial source for overcoming the rootlessness of Weimar modernism, Heidegger too would turn to the chthonic as a way of reframing the crisis of the German *Volk*.[86] But Heidegger would go beyond Otto in rethinking the whole history of the West in terms of a fall from an originary chthonic state of rootedness. And he would begin to think of this new ontological narrative of the fall as essential to the recovery of German greatness. For him, the selfsame struggle to recuperate the chthonic power of the earth that animates art is at work in the unfolding of an originary politics. In this sense, art and politics will be rethought as the relation of the chthonic and the autochthonic. *Bodenständigkeit,* as the conclusion to the original draft of "On the Origin of the Work of Art" makes clear, links the aesthetic and the political.

What is remarkable in this context is how Heidegger will colonize the aesthetic *as* the political by making the art work the necessary opening for a political commencement. That is, he will constitute the hoped for ontological revolution as dependent upon the founding power of essential art—even as, or rather precisely as, he begins to see the political revolution (of 1933) as having failed. This is what lay behind his well-known *Antigone* interpretation from *Introduction to Metaphysics* (1935). Here Heidegger will regard Antigone as a force of chthonic opposition to the rational and enlightened political order of Creon. He will put forward a reading of her as a kind of proto-National Socialist who strives to fight against the liberalism of the Weimar constitution (with its artificial legal order) by embracing the time-honored and eternal "law of the earth" (*nomous chthonos*).[87] It was this kind of chthonic interpretation of antiquity with an eye for its modern political meaning that Heidegger would also draw from Baeumler. In his introduction to the Bachofen edition, Baeumler would make an essential connection between chthonic art and politics by reading *Antigone* in terms of "the law of the ancient gods and of the subterranean (*Unterirdischen*), an eternal law that remains hidden from knowledge . . . and that stands in opposition to the proclaimed law of the state."[88] What emerges from this subterranean decoding of *Antigone* in

---

86. Walter F. Otto, *Die Götter Griechenlands,* 21. Otto speaks of the chthonic power of religion as something that is "erdgebunden" ("earth-bound") and "dem Element verhaftet" ("bound to what is elemental"). In RA, Heidegger speaks of "erd-und bluthaften Kräfte" ("forces that are rooted in the soil and blood"), a phrase with undeniably chthonic (and autochthonic) overtones, RA: 34/SdU: 18.

87. In his translation of line 368 from the choral ode, Karl Reinhardt will render this as "Gesetz der Heimat" ("law of the homeland"), thus forging a link between the chthonic and the homeland—*Antigone* (1942; Göttingen: Vandenhoeckh & Ruprecht, 1982), 43. Hölderlin will translate this same phrase as "Gesetze . . . der Erde" ("laws of the earth"), *Sämtliche Werke,* ed. Norbert von Hellingrath (Berlin: Propyläen, 1923), 5: 203; Heidegger will translate it as "Satzung der Erde" ("ordinance of the earth"), EM: 113.

88. Baeumler, *Das mythische Weltalter,* 234.

Baeumler's text is an interpretation of *earth* by Heidegger that is explicitly ontological. As Heidegger will indicate, the story of Antigone needs to be read in terms of the history of being. No psychological, ethnological, or anthropological conceptions will suffice (IM: 155/EM: 119). Viewed from within the crisis of *Seynsvergessenheit, Antigone* offers a powerful account of humanity's fall from an originary union with being into a state of deluded Cartesian mastery over the forces of *physis*. And when read as a fable about the "spiritual decline of the earth" and the dangers of modern *techne,* it becomes an essential link to understanding the political and spiritual mission of the German *Volk* (IM: 38/EM: 29).

Earth is no longer *chthonos,* no longer capable of providing the roots necessary for autochthony. Given the imperative of modern rationality, earth has become a "resource" for raw material, mere "territory" subject to public control, ownership, and disposition: its value determined by market forces and agribusiness and by the interlocking structures of real estate, tourism, and the culture industry. For Heidegger, the meaning of the parable is clear: like Antigone, the German *Volk* need to contest the modern forces of Enlightenment (Creon) by recovering their ancient bond to the earth. Only if, like her, they raise the fundamental question about the archaic-chthonic sources of their history can they, as Heidegger puts it, "win back a sense of rootedness and autochthony for historical *Dasein*" (IM: 39/EM: 30). Earth, then, becomes for Heidegger the primordial source for the possibility of authentic history. And because the work of art opens up this hidden dimension of the earth as origin, it becomes essential to the historical identity of a *Volk.* Heidegger himself would draw from this chthonic bond between art and earth an etymological connection between the homeland (*Heimat*) and the hidden (*heimisch*) ground of the origin (EHD: 92). "The homeland is the origin," Heidegger would declare; as political homeland for the *Volk* and as ontological ground for the work of art, the earth becomes the decisive realm for working out the destiny of the West within the history of being. Everything in Heidegger's work of the 1930s would turn upon this reading of the chthonic power of the earth and the autochthonic rootedness of the *Volk.* The discourse on art, the myth of the Greek beginning, the lectures on the history (and essence) of truth, the rhapsodies on Hölderlin, the confrontation with Nietzsche—all would in the end come back to the same originary question about the chthonic and the autochthonic.

In the name of this archaic myth of autochthony, Heidegger would put forward an *Ursprungsphilosophie* that authorized a privileged metaphysics of German destiny. On the basis of this myth, he would rewrite the history of the West as a narrative engendered by turns within the history of metaphysics. In lieu of the standard historical accounts that referenced Pericles, Caesar, Charlemagne, the Borgias, and Bismarck, Heidegger would offer a history read through the metaphysical contributions of Plato, Descartes, and Nietzsche. If the lectures on Nietzsche are to be read within their own context, then we need to see them as sorties in a struggle over the meaning of an autochthonic history of the West and of Germany's place within that history. What Heidegger will take from Nietzsche is his insight into the power of the chthonic and of its archaic Greek sources, since, as Nietzsche put it, "one does not know the Greeks as long as this hidden subterranean (*unterirdische*) entrance remains blocked" (WP: 541/WM: 686/KSA: 681). By reading Nietzsche's philosophy of art in terms of this subterranean or chthonic philosophy and by insisting on the superficiality of all biological-anthropological-psychological-axiological interpretations of Nietzsche's corpus, Heidegger sets out to rethink the National Socialist revolution as a radically Nietzschean countermovement to the nihilism of the modern world. Here, in his hybridization of art and "great politics," Heidegger seeks to galvanize National Socialism into an awareness of its historical mission: to "win back a sense of rootedness and autochthony for historical *Dasein.*"

It is easy to miss this underlying political metaphysics of autochthony in the lectures entitled "The Will to Power as Art," since they so rarely address the issue of politics in any explicit way. Part of this can be traced to Heidegger's own practice of editorial redaction and elision; part of it can be traced to the hermeneutical style of Heidegger's lectures themselves, especially their focus on textual rather than contextual explication. When the lectures were released in 1961, however, Heidegger deleted an important passage about art and its relation to Nietzsche's attempted "reversal" of Platonic metaphysics. In this later version, the political thematic is suppressed in favor of a purely ontological account of art. In the original lectures, however, Heidegger will place this passage about Nietzsche's great politics within the context of his own account of political autochthony and of the disastrous consequences of modern liberalism's rootlessness. There he will claim:

> Europe still wants to cling to 'democracy' and does not want to see that this would constitute its historical death. For democracy is, as Nietzsche clearly saw, only a degenerate form of nihilism; i.e., the devaluation of the highest values proceeds to such an extent that they remain merely 'values' without any form-giving force.... The phrase 'God is dead' is not an atheistic proclamation but a formula for the fundamental experience of an event [*Ereignis*] in the history of the West. I deliberately appropriated this phrase in my Rectorial Address of 1933.
>
> Only in light of this fundamental experience can Nietzsche's pronouncement 'My philosophy is inverted Platonism" be accorded its proper scope and significance. And it is only within this same broad horizon that we can interpret and comprehend the essence of truth (GA 43: 193).

In this passage, Heidegger succeeds in bringing together the various strands of his narrative of Western history. Nietzsche's attempt at an inversion of Platonism will be understood by Heidegger to constitute the last unwritten chapter in the history of truth. Now, by working through the metaphysical residue of Nietzsche's account of "How the 'True World' Finally Became a Fable," Heidegger attempts to arrogate Nietzsche's philosophy of art to his own chthonic history of truth and his autochthonic politics of the *arche*. Within this newly configured history the artwork becomes for Heidegger the setting-into-work of the truth of a *Volk*. By opening up a relation to truth in terms of the origin and by simultaneously preserving its hidden chthonic force, the artwork initiates a movement of recovery and recuperation that holds open the possibility of the essential self-assertion of the German *Volk*. That this possibility of self-assertion is an originary condition for the coming to presence of the work of art is something that Heidegger will maintain in both the "Origin" essay and the first Nietzsche lecture. In the strife and contest between earth and world that the artwork sets into motion, the event of truth reveals itself: "in essential strife the opponents raise each other into the self-assertion of their essence. The self-assertion of essence, however, is never the rigid insistence upon some contingent state of affairs, but an abandonment of self to the concealed originary provenance of one's own being. In strife each opponent transports the other beyond itself" (BW:173/H:37–38).

Again, in "The Will to Power as Art," Heidegger will come to understand Nietzsche's will to power as a kind of essential self-assertion, and he will grasp art as a modality of this self-assertion. Like the work of art whose chthonic power derives from the origin, "self-assertion [*Selbstbehauptung*], i.e., wanting to remain at the top, at the head [*Haupt*] of, is constantly a going back into the essence, into the origin. Self-assertion is originary transformation of the essence" (Ni: 61/GA 43: 70). In this interpretation, Heidegger will attempt to free the notion of self-assertion from any relation to a concrete individual self thought of as a bourgeois or Cartesian subject. He is at pains, rather, to reclaim its collective force and its corporative and communal identity. As he grasps it, the "essential will" (that is, will to power) does not assert a singular self but the originary essence of a self which is the *Volk*. Heidegger's meditation on art and the essence of truth thus finds its authentic meaning in the transformation of a merely subjective will into a self-assertive communal will toward the origin. What remains hidden in the life of a *Volk* is precisely this originary essence that has been covered over and occluded by the individualizing tendencies of modern urban and industrial life. To confront the rootlessness of this modern form of subjectivity, Heidegger turns to the chthonic sources of his own tradition—but especially to Nietzsche whom he views as essential to "the task of the Germans to find their essence historically" (Ni: 104/GA

43: 122). What Heidegger will designate as his own task in 1936/37 is to deconstruct the history of aesthetics in the West back to its primordial ground in the chthonic. In the wake of this *Destruktion* of aesthetics back to the originary power of art, he will then undertake a recovery of the Greek *arche*. On this basis, and on this basis alone, can the hoped for ontological revolution take place. But it will first require a radical understanding of the political nature of essence, origin, will, truth, self-assertion, and autochthony. Like Antigone herself, Heidegger will attempt to rethink the meaning of the political state by turning to the hidden and concealed power of the earth as the primordial source for originary self-assertion. What will emerge from this attempt is the fateful dream of a political work of art as the bearer of an ontological revolution. But not all dreams come to fruition. As the possibility of a genuinely philosophical revolution receded, Heidegger would ultimately turn away from this Nietzschean dream of aesthetic-political self-assertion and embrace a more arcane and insular form of his own "Freiburg National Socialism."

By 1961 Heidegger would succeed in erasing most of the political traces from the corpus of his Nietzsche lectures. From within the new hermeneutical context of 1961, they read as if they were reflections from an ontologically attuned path of thinking that engaged only the originary questions of the Western tradition and not the ideological-political questions of the NS period. But, as we have seen, these lectures were political to the core—though not in the sense of politics as usual. What animated these diverse reflections on art, Platonism, and the will to power was a political ontology of the *arche* that both called for and justified a privileged metaphysics of German self-assertion. Later, of course, Heidegger would offer an elaborate denial when asked to "confront" the legacy of this metaphysical *Sonderweg*.[89] But in his own notes to the early Nietzsche lectures of 1936–38 Heidegger shows that he never deceived himself about his own relation to Nietzsche. There Heidegger writes that he does not seek to capture "the 'real Nietzsche' 'in itself'—no!" (GA 43: 276–282). Rather, he freely acknowledges that he engages Nietzsche in what he terms a *Kampfstellung* or "battle position" "in a *Kampf* for what is most essential." In this decisive *Kampf*, Nietzsche becomes for Heidegger a transitional figure who aids in "the preparations of those decisions that confront the West in this and in the coming century." But what was most "essential" was also decidedly political. The "renewal of the world through the salvation of the earth," as Heidegger put it in *Beiträge*, would not only involve the

89. This kind of denial can be found in Heidegger's letter to the Freiburg Rector of November 4, 1945. There Heidegger writes, "I entered still more clearly into confrontation and into spiritual resistance [*geistigen Widerstand*] through a series of Nietzsche courses and lectures beginning in 1936 and continuing until 1945." "Documents from the Denazification Proceedings," 540–541.

dismantling of Western aesthetics, it would also demand a radically at-tuned political will to the future (GA 65: 412). As Heidegger bore deeper into the roots of the Western tradition in his Nietzsche lectures, he would come to understand that Nietzsche's thought posed a threat to this dream of salvation. By the end of 1940, it became clear that only by "twisting free" of Nietzsche's National Socialist metaphysics of will as power could the ground be prepared for the authentic revelation of a "secret Germany."

VIII. THE METAPHYSICS OF WAR *REDIVIVUS*

Earlier in this chapter, we saw how 1938 would become a decisive year for Heidegger. The difficulties with Amt Rosenberg, the crisis within the Nietzsche Commission, the fallout from the Descartes Congress, the bru-tality of *Kristallnacht*—all came together to force Heidegger to rethink his fundamental relationship to National Socialism.[90] As he began his lec-tures "Nietzsche's Doctrine of the Will to Power as Knowledge" in the sum-mer of 1939, Heidegger began to understand both Nietzsche and National Socialism as names designating the consummation of Western nihilism. And, with the commencement of the Second World War, the lectures will begin to offer a year-by-year account of the bends and turns in Germany's political-military fortunes and of Heidegger's responses to them. Consid-ered within their own context, rather than as part of a self-orchestrated political cleansing project entitled *heidegger/nietzsche*, the lectures offer not "a" reading of Nietzsche, but plural, contradictory, multiform, and di-verse readings. Heidegger will turn from his earlier interpretation of Nietzsche as the thinker who "comes closer to the essence of the Greeks than any metaphysical thinker before him," and will ultimately come to view him as a metaphysician who "sees the Greek 'world' exclusively in a Roman way, i.e., in a way at once modern and un-Greek" (Niii: 113/GA 47: 207; P: 43/GA 54: 63). As part of this shift within the Nietzsche lec-tures, Heidegger will initiate a kind of "turning," or *Kehre*, away from the metaphysics of self-assertion, of will, and of "official" National Socialism.

It would be foolhardy and reductionist to try to locate the so-called "turn" (*Kehre*) of Heidegger's later thinking in this other turn within the Nietzsche lectures. All talk of a univocal, monotropic turning within Hei-degger's thought—whether it be the move away from a *Dasein*-centered ontology of everydayness toward a new understanding of the essence of truth, the turn from *Being and Time* to "On the Essence of Truth," the turn from *Sein* to *Seyn*, from will to *Gelassenheit*, from the metaphysics of pres-ence to the non-metaphysical thinking of *Ereignis*, from *Überwindung* to *Verwindung*, from the phenomenological to the political, or from the po-

90. See section 4 of this chapter and HJB: 201.

litical to the poetic—misses the fundamental character of what is ultimately at stake for Heidegger in the rhetorical figure of a "turning." One can find many so-called turns, twists, pirouettes, and sorties (*Einsätze*) on Heidegger's twisting and back-turning thought path. But each one will be reconfigured by Heidegger as a way of accounting for, or better, recuperating the dynamic of, a turning of and within the history of being. From out of the different political contexts of his life, Heidegger will rethink this turn within the history of being (that is, the turn away from and toward the originary truth of *aletheia*) in terms of his own reigning myth about the "secret Germany." Sometimes, as during the years 1946–1976, the myth will go underground and will take the form of a rhapsodic improvisation on the theme of the lost homeland. Other times, as in the 1930s, it will be explicitly linked to the destiny of the German *Volk*. But at all times throughout Heidegger's life the figure of a turning becomes a way of rethinking the myth of originary being in terms of the constraints and possibilities of the political moment. Hence, when Hannah Arendt propagates the myth that the Nietzsche volumes "contain lecture courses from the years 1936 to 1940, that is, the very years when the 'reversal' [*Kehre*] actually occurred," we need to be wary.[91]

As I have argued, one can indeed locate a change between the early and late Nietzsche lectures, a change that can be accounted for in at least two ways: first, a turn from the early text-focused lectures on art and eternal recurrence to the historically focused later pieces on European nihilism, the history of metaphysics, and the history of being; second, a turn from an early reading of Nietzsche's philosophy as constituting a countermovement to nihilism to a later one that sees it as the utmost expression of metaphysical nihilism. But this evident change or shift constitutes only one part of a larger shift within Heidegger's own political attitude toward National Socialism and toward his Hölderlinian dream of a German future. In one sense, Heidegger never really changed; he never abandoned his ontological myth of autochthonic rootedness. What changed was the way he interpreted that myth within the shifting political realities of the day. In 1936, Heidegger still believed in the power of Hitler's National Socialism to overcome the rootlessness of the modern world. In one passage from his Schelling lectures (deleted from the published edition after the war), Heidegger writes:

> The two men who, each in his own way, launched a countermovement to nihilism—Mussolini and Hitler—have both learned from Nietzsche in an essentially different way. But even with this they did not yet bring into play the authentic metaphysical range of Nietzsche's thought (GA 42: 40–41).

91. Hannah Arendt, *The Life of the Mind: Willing* (New York: Harcourt, Brace, Jovanovich, 1978), 2: 172.

What Hitler and Mussolini achieved in their own realms, politically, Heidegger wants to say, Nietzsche had already initiated in a far more original sense, metaphysically. Hence, Heidegger will argue in his early Nietzsche courses that Nietzsche's configuration of art and his thought of eternal return both constitute fundamental countermovements to metaphysical nihilism (Nii: 172/GA 44: 180). But even as he focuses on the historical-metaphysical dimension of Nietzsche's countermovement, Heidegger will at the same time configure this countermovement in concrete political terms as well. In this sense, Nietzsche's inversion of Platonism will be thought as the ontological counterweight to his doctrine of great politics. And the inversion of the numinous realm of *idea* and *eidos* will be juxtaposed to Nietzsche's rejection of democracy, liberalism, and the political tradition of Enlightenment subjectivity (GA 43: 190–196).

That Nietzsche's inversion of Platonism would be interpreted in this way by a philosopher committed to the communal ideals of National Socialism should hardly be surprising. In his own edition of Nietzsche's fragmentary writings, collected under the title *Die Krisis Europas,* Alfred Baeumler presents a portrait of Nietzsche as a virulently anti-democratic, anti-liberal thinker in search of a new German identity. In one of these aphorisms from a section that Baeumler entitles "The Countermovement," Nietzsche writes: "Thus far the Germans *are* nothing, but they will *become* something."[92] And, of course, Baeumler will draw his own conclusion that for the Germans to become who they are, they will need to forge "a countermovement against a Christian and democratic Europe." Heidegger will follow Baeumler here in configuring Nietzsche's philosophy as a countermovement to democratic liberalism. And, like Baeumler, he will come to read the destiny of the German *Volk* in and through this political reading. As we have seen, Heidegger had invoked Nietzsche and the Nietzschean language of will, power, *Kampf,* greatness, and self-assertion in his Rectorial Address. Over the next few years, Heidegger's whole approach to the issues and decisions of National Socialism would be guided by his confrontation with Nietzsche over the question of German destiny. By the time the war began, however, Heidegger would begin to rethink his connection to Nietzsche and to the language of self-assertion.

What emerges from Heidegger's early political speeches is an explicit attempt to combine this legacy of Nietzschean self-assertion with a *völkisch* language of roots, homeland, soil, earth, landscape, and autochthony. Much of my effort in preceding chapters has been directed at noticing the connections between this *völkisch* language of the earth and the political metaphysics that animates it. For anyone familiar with Nietzsche's work, this boldly conceived attempt to wed Nietzsche and the thematic of homeland

92. Baeumler, ed., *Nietzsches Philosophie in Selbstzeugnissen,* 188, 226.

seems wholly misguided, however. But Heidegger was deadly serious. He was determined to read Nietzsche as the philosopher of the chthonic, subterranean forces of primordial earth, the thinker who, in his recovery of archaic Greek thought, had provided an opening to the hidden power of *aletheia*. As part of his effort, he will cite Nietzsche's regard for the poet of the chthonic, Adalbert Stifter.[93] And in a kind of glissade of hermeneutical dexterity, Heidegger will attempt to rethink the essence of the German nation in terms of Stifter's chthonic rootedness (*Bodenständigkeit*) and Nietzsche's will to self-assertion (*Selbstbehauptung*). These two themes will be brought together to form a new National Socialist ethos of autochthonic destiny.

Heidegger's framing of German political destiny in terms of Nietzschean self-assertion parallels other National Socialist readings. For example, Ernst Horneffer in *Nietzsche as Herald of the Present* (1934) had already defined the will to self-assertion as necessary for deciding "the question about the destiny of the future."[94] And, in his political meditation, *World-Democracy and National Socialism*, Alfred Baeumler had placed the question of self-assertion at the forefront of Germany's political destiny. As Baeumler contended, "The being of the nation does not let itself be led by what comes from outside it. Nor does it fulfill this being by submitting itself to a higher form, rather it seeks its own configuration. Only by following the path of its own history does a *Volk* come to be itself; it never does so by implementing a prescribed universal standard. The fundamental tendency of a *Volk* is not a falling into line but a self-assertion."[95] Baeumler came to see in this Nietzschean will to self-assertion a philosophical principle that went beyond mere politics—or rather, that raised a certain form of politics to the level of an ontology: "All being wants to assert itself [*Alles Sein will sich behaupten*]. It is a law of life that the longing for self-assertion at the depths of being can never be renounced in favor of some kind of universality. The denial of the will to self-assertion is . . . in the realm of politics what theologians call 'The Fall of Man.' From time immemorial the essence of power has been seen to lie in self-assertion."

Heidegger too will find in the Nietzschean ideal of self-assertion a model for his own myth of German national identity along *völkisch* lines.

93. Heidegger mentions his fondness for Stifter in two letters to Elisabeth Blochmann, HBB: 45, 49. He writes to her: "In memory of this last Indian Summer and at the same time as something for quiet contemplation for the holiday I'm sending Stifter's *Nachsommer*. You know that Nietzsche loved this work above everything else," December 20, 1931. Heidegger also mentions Ernst Bertram's "Nietzsche, die Briefe Adalbert Stifters lesend," *Ariadne: Jahrbuch der Nietzschegesellschaft* (1925): 7–26. Bertram's *Nietzsche: Versuch einer Mythologie* (Bonn: Bouvier, 1989), 15, set out "to offer a mythology of the last great German and to capture something of what the historical moment [*Augenblick*] of our present in Nietzsche and as Nietzsche appears to be." Heidegger will imbibe something of the same drive toward mythification in his own Nietzsche lectures as that carried out by the George Circle.

94. Ernst Horneffer, *Nietzsche als Vorbote der Gegenwart* (Düsseldorf: A. Bagel, 1934), 43.

95. Baeumler, *Weltdemokratie und Nationalsozialismus*, 18–19, 12.

Nonetheless, Heidegger becomes ever more wary about the unbridled aggression and the authoritarian impulses that lie at the root of National Socialist *Machtpolitik*. As the war breaks out and as the German panzer divisions march eastward into Poland and westward into France, Heidegger begins to construe the efforts of the Nazi war machine as indications of a technological will to power that aims at subordinating the earth. As part of this process of what Heidegger ominously terms "machination" (*Machenschaft*), the earth will be reduced to a region for "planning, calculation, arranging, and breeding." With this push toward technical mastery comes the metaphysical dereliction, devastation, and destitution of historical nihilism. Beings now come to dominance as objects there for subjective manipulation and control, obliterating the archaic traces of whatever lies concealed or hidden. Now the hidden chthonic elements are forced into the full light of presence. In this way machination contributes to the historical process of the abandonment and forgetting of essential being and succeeds in bringing to completion the metaphysical epoch of *Seinsvergessenheit*. As Heidegger puts it in his notebooks from 1938/39: "The thinking of the World War from out of the beast of prey's highest will to power and the unconditionality of mobilization is in each case a sign of the completion of the metaphysical epoch. World wars as well as world peace (in its equivocal Christian-Jewish sense) signify corresponding forms of organized machination, which in this epoch already can no longer be means to any end or goal whatsoever. Neither can they be ends or goals in themselves but are rather that within which beings, and all that is real, have to reach completion . . ." (GA 66: 26–29).

In the face of this metaphysical process of machination, Heidegger will cling to his myth of chthonic and autochthonic origin. Unlike Baeumler, Horneffer, and other Nazi ideologues, however, Heidegger will abandon the rhetoric of aggressive political self-assertion in favor of a more subdued ideal. Hence, whereas Richard Oehler could militantly assert in *Friedrich Nietzsche and the German Future* that Germany's "compulsion toward great politics" would lead her to a "battle for dominion over the earth," Heidegger could only recoil from the crudely political tone of such a claim.[96] Yet Heidegger would never abandon his faith in the German mission or in the elected status of the *Volk*. Despite his critique of the Nazi imperative toward world domination, he patriotically supported the war effort and even came to endow each military success with metaphysical meaning. In his 1940 lectures, "Nietzsche: European Nihilism," Heidegger will claim that the German conquest of France needs to be interpreted not merely politically or militarily but rather in terms of a "mysterious law of history which states that one day a people [viz., the

96. Oehler, *Friedrich Nietzsche und die deutsche Zukunft*, 124–125.

French] no longer measures up to the metaphysics that arose from its own history" (Niv: 116/GA 48: 205). To put it simply, the French war effort was not up to the metaphysical task of carrying out Descartes' fundamental imperative of gaining mastery over beings through the method of representation. In these same lectures (in a passage that he deleted from the 1961 edition), Heidegger will arrogantly affirm the metaphysical supremacy of the German war effort: "From the viewpoint of bourgeois culture and intellectuality one might view the total 'motorization' of the *Wehrmacht* from the ground up as an example of boundless 'technicism' and 'materialism.' In truth, this is a metaphysical act which certainly surpasses in depth something like the abolition of 'philosophy.' This latter theme would only be a measure taken in the running of the schools and in education" (GA 48: 333). Hence, even though the National Socialist effort to abolish philosophy strikes Heidegger as ludicrous and destructive, on another, more essential level, he will affirm the military exploits of the National Socialist *Wehrmacht* in the most sympathetic terms.

Following this same logic, Heidegger will come to grasp the war as an ontological expression of epochal forces, as something necessary for the unfolding of German destiny. It will not occur to him to see this as bound up in any way with the adventitious effects of Hitler's mania or to construe it as an expression of economic, diplomatic, or social forces. For him, the war itself is but the historical appearance of Heraclitean strife at a decisive moment in the history of the West. And he will persist in interpreting the field campaigns and the air battles from within the frame and scaffolding of modern metaphysics in its Cartesian form. Hence, the war becomes the pure expression of a kind of technological will to power configured as unbridled self-assertion. Through the vagaries of both victory and defeat, Heidegger will continue to translate the German war experience into an ontological reverie about the future and destiny of the *Volk*. When, for example, British fighter planes bomb the imperiled French fleet at Oran in 1940, an event widely viewed as morally culpable, Heidegger will designate this action as an instantiation of Nietzschean "justice" and will to power (Niv: 144–45/GA 48: 264–265). And, in these same lectures, he will declare that "the securing of *Lebensraum* . . . is a metaphysical law of power" (GA 48: 141).[97] One year later, in the summer of 1941, while lec-

---

97. As Heidegger puts it: "Every mere '*preservation* of life' would already be a decline of life. The securing of *Lebensraum* (living space) is for the living being never a goal but only the means of intensifying life. Following this intensification the need for space grows again necessarily. This is a fundamental metaphysical law of *power itself* and not the obstinacy and caprice of those who hold power. Life—the reality of all realities experienced from out of the will to power as its fundamental character—is the drive towards the *intensification of life* and its enhancement, towards mastery, i.e. towards remaining dominant . . ." GA 48: 141. Heidegger deletes this passage from the 1961 edition.

turing on technology as "humanity's will to unconditional mastery over the earth," he will remark that "where one interprets the execution of this metaphysical will as a 'product' of selfishness or the caprice of 'dictators' and 'authoritarian states,' that reflects only political calculation and propaganda, or the metaphysical naïveté of a thinking that ran aground centuries ago, or both. Political circumstances, economic situations, population growth, and the like, can be the proximate causes and domains for carrying out this metaphysical will of modern world-history. But they are never the ground of this history and therefore never its 'goal' " (BC: 15/GA 51: 18). War is not merely a political struggle but a metaphysical *Kampf* about the underlying meaning of history.

In this sense, Heidegger's Nietzsche lectures can be read as a kind of updated version of Max Scheler's *The Genius of War and the German War* (1915) or Paul Natorp's *Germany's World-Calling* (1918), philosophical ruminations in the spirit of "the ideas of 1914."[98] Like these books, Heidegger's lectures interpret the German war in terms of an overall "metaphysics of war" that galvanizes the *Volk* into an awareness of its historical mission. Only within this *Schicksalsgemeinschaft* ("community formed by destiny"), these writers argue, can the genuine meaning of the military struggle be deciphered. That Heidegger should read the war tropologically as an indication of German destiny comes as no surprise to those who know of his great admiration for the war writings of Scheler, Natorp, and Jünger. Already in *Being and Time,* section 74, and in his Schlageter memorial address, we have seen how he seized upon the trope of struggle and *Kampf* for a philosophical reading of destiny.[99]

But it is in the Nietzsche lectures that the rhetoric of war will be employed as a way of organizing the history of the West metaphysically. Now Heidegger will appropriate the lexicon of Nietzschean metaphysics—strife, agon, will, struggle, power, dominion, force, justice, nihilism, the death of god, world-darkening, devastation—to put forward an ontologi-

---

98. Max Scheler, *Der Genius des Krieges und der Deutsche Krieg* (Leipzig: Verlag der weissen Bücher, 1915); and Paul Natorp, *Deutscher Weltberuf* (Jena: Eugen Diederichs, 1918). Both are examples of German chauvinism wedded to metaphysics.

99. In BT: 353/SZ: 386, Heidegger writes, "In communication and in struggle [*Kampf*] the power of destiny first becomes free." Within this context we might also place Heidegger's esteem for the vulgar military biography, Martin Sommerfeldt, *Hermann Göring* (Berlin: Mittler, 1933), which offered a heroic-mythological account of Göring's warriorly exploits. The book went through fourteen different editions in two years. Heidegger thought so highly of this book that he gave it as a present to the family of his art historian friend Hans Jantzen. Ott, *Martin Heidegger: Unterwegs,* 146–147. Sommerfeldt's chauvinistic lexicon of *Auftrag, Schicksal, Revolution, Deutschseins, Kampf, Gefahr, Grösse, Not, Sturm, Opfer, Macht, Helden, Kameraden, Heimat,* and *Entscheidung* rings all too clearly in the Schlageter memorial address of May 26, 1933, and the Rectorial Address of May 27, 1933. Perhaps Heidegger had read this as he was drafting these speeches? Sommerfeldt even cites Fichte in conjunction with the theme of a German *Auftrag—Hermann Göring,* 47.

cal interpretation of war that sees it primordially as a struggle of and for being. Within this Gestalt, the technology of destruction is grasped not merely as a contest for national supremacy or political-military advantage, but as a "struggle for world domination" in a Nietzschean sense. Citing Nietzsche's entry from the *Nachlass*—"The time is coming when the struggle for world domination will be carried on . . . in the name of *fundamental philosophical doctrines*"—Heidegger will claim that "the hidden unity of the 'fundamental philosophical doctrines' constitutes the essential jointures of Nietzsche's metaphysics. On the basis of this metaphysics, and according to the direction it takes, the consummation of the modern age unfolds its history" (Niii: 190–191/GA 50: 7–8).[100]

As Heidegger will contend, "the struggle for world domination and the unfolding of the metaphysics that sustains it bring to fulfillment an epoch of the earth's history and of historical humanity." But, if this epoch is coming to an end, then we are left in the difficult position of taking a stance in regard to this end. Should we allow the struggle for world domination to take place uncontested—or should we assert ourselves within this struggle and gain a measure of supremacy in the worldwide contest for dominion and control? This is the question of German historical destiny as Heidegger understands it. In the early years of his National Socialist commitment, Heidegger will embrace a political-ontological metaphysics of self-assertion. As he moves away from his enthusiastic support of NS organizational politics, however, he will alter the terms of his discourse. And yet one element of this discourse remains consistent. As in his Rectorial Address, Heidegger will always understand the meaning of National Socialism as a response to Nietzsche's fundamental teaching about the death of god. In the wake of the modern epoch's fundamental nihilism, Heidegger will retrieve Nietzsche's basic distinction between active and passive nihilism as a way of understanding the National Socialist revolution—and later, of the NS war effort. For Nietzsche, passive or incomplete nihilism merely repeats the older, life-negating values of otherworldly morality by playing them out in new, attenuated forms (e.g., socialism merely smuggles in Christian values under the greatcoat of political freedom). By contrast, active or complete nihilism hastens the decline of the old values and leads to the collapse of the structure that sustains these values, thus preparing or opening a space for their transvaluation (WP: 17–19/WM: 20–23/KSA 12: 350 and 476). Within this Nietzschean framework of questioning, Heidegger will come to see National Socialism as a form of active nihilism, an instantiation of what Baeumler termed "the 'countermovement' to a Christian-democratic Europe."[101]

---

100. For the Nietzsche citation, see KSA 9: 546. Baeumler also cites this passage in *Nietzsches Philosophie in Selbstzeugnissen*, 1: 217.
101. Ibid., 226.

As an authentic expression of Nietzschean will to power, then, National Socialism came to signify for Heidegger a totalizing strategy for organizing the energies of modern life. Unlike the political alternatives of Anglo-American democracy or Russian Communism that reinforced the nihilistic domination over the earth by means of *techne*, National Socialism appeared to Heidegger as a way of recovering the archaic power of the earth through a communal form of self-renewal. The outbreak of a war between these opposing forces only brought to the surface the underlying metaphysical tensions within the history of the West. As Baeumler would put it, "war is only an external form of the originary tensions that come into play with the historical *Dasein* of human beings."[102] Heidegger would continue to embrace this Heraclitean-Nietzschean-Schelerian metaphysics of war right through April of 1945—and beyond. But there would be a hitch. Until the winter of 1942, he would think of National Socialism as a form of active nihilism, celebrating the German victories and reading the progress of the war in terms of Nietzsche's metaphysical categories. But then came the devastating defeat at Stalingrad that shook Heidegger's confidence and forced him to rethink the German war effort and his faith in National Socialism as a countermovement to nihilism. He would still view the war as a "confrontation between the power of beings and the truth of being," but now he would see the Nazi war machine as itself bound up in the nihilism of machination and dominion. Only his own "private National Socialism," a National Socialism committed to the autochthony of a Greek *arche* and to German *Bodenständigkeit,* was authentic enough to provide a pathway out of the growing devastation brought on by the military conflict.

IX. PARMENIDES, STALINGRAD, AND THE MYTH OF ROMAN DECLINE

Heidegger's lectures from 1940–1944 provide a vivid example of the metaphysics of war rethought and repositioned in terms of Nietzsche's diagnosis of Western nihilism and Heraclitus' doctrine of logos. Taken as a whole, these lectures constitute a totalizing narrative of Western thought from Parmenides to Nietzsche that organizes the history of philosophy according to a political metaphysics of the homeland. In effect, Heidegger will colonize all of Western history as a province for German dominion. Ontology will be read here in and through the category of the political. Despite Heidegger's frequent and insistent allusions to Greek metaphysics, Cartesian methodology, and Nietzschean transvaluation, what will decisively form and determine his ontological history of the West are the ideas of 1914 read through the German experience of decline and devas-

102. Baeumler, *Alfred Rosenberg,* 28.

tation. Simply put, Heidegger's history of metaphysics shows itself, upon closer reading, to be an exercise in political philosophy. His Germanocentric emphasis does not merely express an imperial attitude that is culturally insensitive to other traditions; it is war by other means. In Heidegger's hands, the thesis of a *Sonderweg* of German politics is now given a metaphysical substrate and the "new order" of National Socialist politics is projected onto twenty-five hundred years of Western experience.[103] The Nietzsche lectures in particular come to embody the language of a metaphysics of war that reads the whole tradition from within the frame of the German war experience. That Heidegger would come to endow the war with primordial significance—not only for Germany but for the history of the West—is perhaps nowhere made as clear as in two letters he wrote in September of 1941 to the fiancée and the mother of a former student who died in battle. In these letters, we can find a measure of the metaphysical pathos that informed Heidegger's other, more philosophically engaged, language from the same period.

The language of these letters is clear and unostentatious. Abjuring the formal academic style for an elegiac, consolatory idiom, Heidegger nonetheless manages to frame these letters of condolence into metaphysical reveries about the fate of the German homeland. Alfred Franz had been a student of Heidegger's from 1937 until 1939 and had heard Heidegger's Nietzsche lectures firsthand before he was called into service and joined the German army. In September of 1941 Heidegger received word that Franz had been killed in combat in Russia. Touched by this event, he sat down to write about the death of his student in the encoded language of "sacrifice" and "necessity" that informed his earlier tributes to Albert Leo Schlageter and Norbert von Hellingrath. If Schlageter and Hellingrath represented for Heidegger the metaphysical tradition of self-sacrifice that gained expression in the Great War, Franz became for him a symbol of Germany's destiny thought in and through the metaphysics of war *redivivus*. In his letter to Franz's fiancée, Heidegger is brief and to the point. He writes that Franz was one of his best students and that he had expected much of him. He also speaks in a consolatory way about Franz and "the sacrifice of his young life."[104] But it is in the letter to Frau Franz, written on September 26, 1941 (his fifty-second birthday), that Heideg-

---

103. The phrase *"neue Ordnung"* (new order) became a term for the new political order, cribbed by NS ideologues from Nietzsche's *Will to Power*, aphorism 1055, WP: 544/KSA 11: 547. Baeumler also uses the term as his subtitle for *Weltdemokratie und Nationalsozialismus: die Neue Ordnung Europas als geschichtsphilosophisches Problem*, as does Heidegger in Niv: 56/GA 48: 73.

104. For the texts of these letters and a penetrating analysis of Heidegger's language of war, see Reinhard Mehring, *Heideggers Überlieferungsgeschick*, 90–102.

ger will draw on the metaphysical language of war that became so essential to his own philosophical project.

Heidegger will steer clear of any personal reflections in the standard sense. He employs, rather, a rhetoric of consolation nurtured on the hidden and essential language of Pre-Socratic philosophy and the heroic nihilism of Ernst Jünger. Franz, he tells the grief-stricken mother, was a young man "moved by an inner fire," someone whose life was marked by "reverence for what is essential." It is in terms of this reverence for the essential that "he remains present to us." Heidegger continues:

> For those of us left behind it is a difficult step to come to the knowledge that every one of these many young Germans who sacrifice their life with a still genuine spirit and reverent heart may be experiencing the most beautiful destiny [*Geschick*]. These men, who are intimately known by only a few friends, will once again awaken the Germans to their innermost calling [*die innersten Berufung des Deutschen*] of spirit and loyalty of heart indirectly and only after a century has passed. This hidden [*verborgene*] effect is more essential [*wesentlicher*] than any academic achievement that we might have expected from those who have fallen, no matter how important—had their lives been determined otherwise.[105]

Heidegger goes on to say that "there is a tradition of faithful commemoration that remains strong enough to transform loss into a gift." He then concludes by telling Frau Franz, "Every day brings greater need. But we must surmount it. And we are trying to bestow our sympathy upon all those who know that external successes are never able to overcome the necessity of pain."

In their own artful and persuasive way, Heidegger's letters of condolence restate the message of the Nietzsche lectures, albeit in a different rhetorical register. Like them, they offer a reading of the war as a metaphysical conflict about the destiny of the West and its struggle to reclaim what is "essential." What animates each is the attempt to understand the war as an expression of metaphysical nihilism, pitting the battle between Germany and the Allied Powers as one between the autochthonic rootedness of the *Volk* and the rootlessness of Communism and democracy. Within this larger framework, the elegy for Alfred Franz functions as a memorial tribute both politically and ontologically. On the one hand, it memorializes a brave German soldier who died fighting for "what is essential"; on the other, it commemorates the Greek experience of *aletheia* as the essential mode of historical disclosure and determination. In contemporary Europe, as in the ancient world of the Greek dawn, history unfolds as a struggle for either preserving or subverting the essence of truth.

105. Ibid., 91.

As the war progresses and as more German lives are lost, Heidegger will begin to reflect more intently on the significance of a single soldier's death and will turn to the Pre-Socratics for a measure of metaphysical consolation. The Parmenides lectures of winter 1942/43 will re-enact these fundamental themes of consolation and elegy but on a larger scale. They will portray the battle between Germany and its enemies not merely as a military struggle between two technologically equipped powers. Rather, they will construe it as a *Kampf* played out both for and within the history of being. In this sense, they offer an exegetical key to the political ontology that animates the Nietzsche lectures.

As Heidegger began this course in October of 1942, the German *Wehrmacht* was engaged in savage combat with the Soviet army in and around the city of Stalingrad. On the home front, the Freiburg Ordinarius conceived his lectures as philosophical sorties in a parallel struggle. What was at stake on the frozen ground near Stalingrad was the very destiny of the West, rethought elegiacally in terms of a lost autochthonic origin. What the German tank companies and artillerymen were executing on the ground, Heidegger attempted to effect in the classroom. By choosing for his analysis the fragments of a philosophical poem by Parmenides, Heidegger hoped to question the origin of the Occident as a viable historical force. Was the Occident at an end historically? Were the metaphysical potencies so rich and pervasive at the outset of this tradition now depleted and in decline? Would it be possible to resuscitate the hidden power of the Greek *arche* in the coming conflict? And how would the war affect the delicate metaphysical balance between inauguration and decline that marked the whole modern epoch? These were some of the questions that Heidegger would raise in his Parmenides course. But the archaic text of the Eleatic philosopher offered no easy answers.

Heidegger never wavered in his commitment to what was essential. His lifelong path of thinking may have taken many turns and twists, but it was always guided by the same fundamental myth of archaic experience and the healing power of autochthony that shaped his earlier *Wandervogel* years. The same chthonic forces that led Heidegger to rhapsodize about the *Fronterlebnis* of the Great War and the cult of Schlageter came to determine his reading of Parmenidean philosophy at the crossroads of the Second World War. As in his youth, Heidegger would fall back on the myth of a German mission to interpret the meaning and direction of the war, even if he no longer believed in the National Socialist version of that mission.[106] But, as the battle for Stalingrad turns and the Soviet divisions regroup and

---

106. In linking the idea of a German mission to the myth of the war experience, Heidegger shows himself to be at odds with Ernst Jünger. Jünger too valorizes war as a galvanizing experience of psychological will and determination, but he refrains from becoming involved in the same neo-romantic cult of *Volk*, sacrifice, and fatherland that Heidegger embraces.

finally repel the German offensive, the character of the mission will change. Now Heidegger will resign himself to the inevitable defeat of the German army and yet, out of the depths of his country's suffering, loss, and dismemberment, he will once again revive the Schlageter myth of self-sacrifice in service to the fatherland. In one of his notes to *Parmenides*, Heidegger will rethink the meaning of this suffering in terms of a grand narrative of being that positions the Germans alongside the Greeks as co-combatants in the *Kampf* for what is essential. Drawing on the rhetoric of *Auseinandersetzung* that he developed in the lectures on Nietzsche, Heidegger will insist that only by entering into a confrontation with the Greek *arche* can death on the battlefield be given its genuine significance and power. As he puts it:

> The beginning is primordial only when thinking is primordial and when man in his essence thinks primordially. This does not refer to the impossible task of repeating the first beginning in the sense of a renewal of the Greek world and its transformation into the here and now. On the contrary, it means to enter, by way of primordial thought, into a confrontation and dialogue with the beginning in order to perceive the voice of the disposition and determination of the future. This voice is only to be heard where experience is. And experience is in essence the suffering in which the essential otherness of beings reveals itself in opposition to the tried and usual. The highest form of suffering is dying one's death as a sacrifice for the preservation of the truth of being. This sacrifice is the purest experience of the voice of being. What is German humanity is that historical humanity which, like the Greek, is called upon to poetize and think, and what if this German humanity must first perceive the voice of being! Then must not the sacrifices be as many as the causes immediately eliciting them, since the sacrifice has *in itself* an essence all its own and does not require goals and uses! Thus what if the voice of the beginning should announce itself in our historical destiny? (P: 166–167/GA 54: 249–250).

One million people lost their lives in the conflict around Stalingrad between 1942 and 1943. Besides those who died in battle, there were others who froze or starved to death, or were murdered in camps of internment. Civilians and soldiers alike were forced to confront the brutalities of a war of technological devastation. From within Heidegger's metaphysics of war, however, the death toll merely confirmed what the lectures on Nietzsche had earlier proclaimed as nihilistic "world-darkening." What appeared as essential here was not bread or medical supplies nor even a word of compassion; what was "essential" was to recover the Greek beginning as a way of confronting the Russo-American threat of technological machination.

In one of his poignant fragments, entitled "Pages from the Exhumed Book," Edmond Jabès writes about the experience of exile and displacement. "The earth is an abyss," Jabès acknowledges; it provides no surety of rootedness. "The foreigner bears witness to the precariousness of taking root, rooted as he is in the ungrateful soil of his arbitrary future."[107] Challenging all discourse of patrimonial destiny and mission, Jabès traces the effects of exclusion and intolerance in all their deadly consequences, exposing the dangers of a metaphysics of race in all its biological and autochthonic forms. For him, the nationalist ethos of a *Volk*, a fatherland, and a communal and racial origin extinguishes in advance all possibility of genuine questioning by defining the origin as what "we" already are. But "origin means, perhaps, question," as Jabès reminds us. And questioning can never be privileged according to national provenance. Tragically, Heidegger did not think of the origin as Jabès did. He proceeded, rather, in imperious fashion to think it from within his own provincial worldview. Consequently, what emerged from his reflections on the Greek beginning was less a primordial discourse on the *arche* than a political affirmation of the German *Sonderweg*, thought metaphysically. Few texts make this as clear as the Parmenides lectures.

From within the safety and security of his enclosed Freiburg study, Heidegger reconfigures the map of Europe along ontological-political lines. Drawing on the longstanding tradition of anti-Latinity within German thought, he re-writes the history of the West in terms of an image of exclusion that conforms with his own Germanocentric predispositions. What had once been an aesthetic preference in Winckelmann is now turned into a metaphysical principle of German supremacy. But Heidegger will not succumb to the usual jingoism of political pamphleteers, nor will he indulge in the vulgarity of the racial ideologues. Instead, he will construct a metaphysical narrative of German ascendancy based on his reading of Fichte, Hölderlin, Scheler, Natorp, and the Pre-Socratics. And he will frame this narrative rhetorically as a struggle or *Kampf* between primordial Greek experience and derivative Roman culture.

Like other National Socialist philosophers such as Baeumler, Hildebrandt, Härtle, Heyse, and Rosenberg, Heidegger will uncover in Rome's historical legacy the sources of modern nihilism. Hence, where Baeumler can find in the Roman state a soulless drive toward centralization, accomplished through bureaucratic administration and engineering, Heidegger will detect a metaphysics of technical control, machination, and imperial dominion. And, where Hildebrandt will censure the Roman imperium for its racial mixing and cross-breeding, Heidegger will attack it for its embrace of universalism and its corresponding rootlessness. Yet there are profound points of agreement that bind these views together. Heidegger

---

107. Edmond Jabès, *A Foreigner Carrying in the Crook of His Arm a Tiny Book*, trans. Rosemarie Waldrop (Hanover, N.H.: University Press of New England, 1993), 34, 115.

will concur with Baeumler's analysis about "superficial, 'decorative' Roman culture" as a mere *imitatio* of the Greek, leading to its displacement and denigration.[108] He too will come to designate the "Romanizing" of the Greek world as something fundamentally barbaric, a historical process that has had tragic consequences for the West. Both men will, of course, resurrect an image of Nietzsche as the authentically German thinker who rejects the cultural tradition of *Romanitas* in all its various forms—especially as Christianity and Renaissance humanism. In this sense, they will esteem Nietzsche as the philosopher who seeks to overcome Romanism by recovering primordial Greek thought. Hildebrandt will go even further in his attacks on Roman culture by embracing a National Socialist philosophy of "racial hygiene" that rejects Roman miscegenation (with its "Negrification of the Volk") for an ideal Platonic community of "Aryan" citizens.[109] Härtle too will present a portrait of Nietzsche as a Nordic pagan opposed to Rome.[110] Like Hildebrandt, he will find no contradiction in simultaneously depicting Nietzsche as a descendant of Hellas and of Northern Europe. Richard Oehler will likewise contribute to this Nazified vision of Nietzsche as an anti-Roman thinker who rejects "the barbarian state" of imperial conquest.[111] By selectively reading Nietzsche according to their own political values, these philosophers will construct an image of Nietzsche at odds with the texts themselves, hardly an original idea in German Nietzsche scholarship. Going back to Nietzsche's own sister Elisabeth, the practice of textual editing and political promotion had gone hand in hand. Heidegger will, however, attempt something bolder and more magisterial.

On the basis of his own carefully crafted design of a history of being, Heidegger will rethink the relation of Nietzsche and Romanism according to his own changing political views. As a result, Nietzsche will be transformed from being a primordial Greek thinker who vehemently opposes Romanism to one who at long last is utterly un-Greek and wholly Roman. In itself, this change commands attention for the light it sheds on Heidegger's understanding of Nietzsche and Nietzsche's place within the history of philosophy. What is just as significant, however, is the way it helps to

---

108. Baeumler, *Studien zur deutschen Geistesgeschichte*, 251. On this theme see Gail Soffer, "Heidegger, Humanism, and the Destruction of History," *Review of Metaphysics* 49 (March 1996): 547–576.

109. *Platon: Der Staat*, ed. Kurt Hildebrandt (Leipzig: Kröner, 1935), xxxiii, 366. In his later 1955 edition of this same work published by Kröner in Stuttgart, Hildebrandt will delete all references to the "arische Rasse" and the "hellenische Rasse," 366. Moreover, he will rail against Roman "mechanized centralization" for the state. In his *Norm/Entartung/Verfall* (Berlin: Die Runde, 1934), 264–268, Hildebrandt will also focus on the problem of racial selection, or *Auslese*, and will develop an anti-democratic theory of "racial hygiene."

110. Härtle, *Nietzsche und der Nationalsozialismus*, 99–102.

111. Oehler, *Nietzsche und die deutsche Zukunft*, 18–20.

clarify Heidegger's inner relationship to National Socialism, from the time of his early Nazi years to the end of the war—and beyond.

Going back to his initial break with Roman Catholicism and its medieval Latin heritage, Heidegger was always wary of the ecumenical, universalist implications of Romanist culture. During the 1920s, he was still drawing on the rich philosophical vocabulary of Latin thinking—witness his hermeneutic gloss on the *Cura* fable from *Being and Time* (BT: 184–185/SZ: 197–199). After 1933, however, he will only reference Latin terms to provide evidence of their metaphysical poverty. In his 1935 essay, "The Origin of the Work of Art," Heidegger will begin to make a case for interpreting Roman culture as an epochal turning point in the history of truth. In the Latin translation and appropriation of Greek terms, he locates the beginning of "the rootlessness of Western thought" (BW: 154/H: 13). And, in the lectures of the same year that were published as *Introduction to Metaphysics,* he claims that the Latin translation of *physis* as *natura* initiates a way of thinking that "destroys our authentic relation to things" (IM: 13–14/EM: 11). The 1938 essay, "The Age of the World Picture," continues this assault against Roman thought by offering a genealogy of modern scientific calculation that traces its roots back through medieval Latin to Plato and Aristotle (QCT: 143–147/H: 94–98). In his notebook entries of 1938/39, entitled *Besinnung,* Heidegger will lament that "everything Greek is occluded by the Roman" (GA 66: 381,187, 195). Moreover, the translation of the Greek word *energeia* into Latin as *actus* will strike Heidegger as a signal of metaphysical decline: "the Romanizing of this fundamentally Greek metaphysical term brings to completion a thorough reinterpretation of the concept of being that is rootless." Within his overall narrative of the history of being, this Romanizing event will function as the basis for the Cartesian metaphysics of the *subjectum* that understands truth as *certitudo* (Niv: 96/GA 48: 181). More to the point, however, it will come to symbolize the metaphysics of will and self-assertion that Heidegger will associate with machination, dominion, technological control, and political deracination under the name "Americanism." Romanism *is* Americanism within Heidegger's ontological-political schema (HHI: 153/GA 53: 191). Hence, when America enters the war, Heidegger will see it as "the ultimate American act of American ahistoricality and self-devastation" and as a resolution to annihilate the homeland (HHI: 54/GA 53: 68). Within this mythic design, Heidegger will begin to interpret the Second World War as a Graeco-German struggle against a Romanist America and barbarian Russia.

Throughout the 1930s, Heidegger understood Nietzsche to be his co-combatant in this struggle against Roman influence in the West. As late as the summer of 1939, he will claim that in the battle between the Greek and the Roman, Nietzsche is definitely on the Greek side, in tune with the *arche:* "Nietzsche's interpretation of truth [is] . . . the most hidden and ex-treme consequence of the first beginning of Western thought" (Niii: 63/GA 47: 120). In his Nietzsche lectures of 1940, however, Heidegger will begin to read Nietzsche as a Roman thinker whose "metaphysics of will to power conforms only to Roman culture and Machiavelli's *The Prince*" (Niv: 165/GA 48: 297). Indeed, he will start to make a connection between the nihilistic effects of this rampantly Nietzschean will to power and the National Socialist embrace of machination and dominion. By the time of the lectures on Parmenides, Heidegger will complete this turn. In determined fashion, he will now develop a new encoded language, offer-ing a critique of National Socialist politics as a neo-Roman form of impe-rial domination in its planetary phase. The essence of the *polis,* he will claim, is nothing "political"; "the *polis* itself is only the pole of *pelein,* the way the being of beings, in its disclosure and concealment, disposes for it-self a 'where' in which the history of a human race is gathered" (P: 96/GA 54: 142). Only the Greeks experienced the aletheic dimension of the polis; the Romans' political form of the *res publica* and the *imperium* could never penetrate to this hidden realm. Given that modern Europe has been formed by the *imperium romanum* and the Roman Catholic medieval curia, it can hardly be surprising that the modern bureaucratic central-ized state has lost all sense of Greek political reality. The consequences for Europe's political future, Heidegger proclaims, are dire indeed. "That the Occident still today, and today more decisively than ever, thinks the Greek world in a Roman way, i.e., in a Latin, i.e., in a Christian way (as pagan-ism), i.e., in a Romanic, modern-European, way, is an event [*Ereignis*] touching the most inner center of our historical existence" (P: 45/GA 54: 66). What had once seemed to Heidegger to be the vanguard of a new po-litical *Aufbruch* to the Greek beginning now appears to him as another form of Romanism. The defeat at Stalingrad only confirms his metaphysi-cal view that "the historical state of the world we call the modern age . . . is founded on the event of the Romanizing of Greece" (P: 43/GA 54: 63).

X. HEIDEGGERIAN AUTOCHTHONY AT THE END OF THE WAR

By reading this turning point in German history in and through his con-frontation with Parmenides and by framing it within "the event of the Ro-manizing of Greece," Heidegger alluded to a new direction in his think-ing. But, behind all his encoded references to Roman (i.e., National Socialist) imperialism and his now open criticism of Nietzsche, had any-thing genuinely changed? Had the military defeats undermined his faith in the German "mission" to save the West? Hardly. Heidegger would still put forward his same myth about Graeco-German autochthony and the history of *aletheia;* only now it would be directed against both Nietzsche *and* National Socialism. Instead of using Nietzsche as a wedge to cleave off the noxious elements within the NS movement, now he will unambiguously identify Nietzsche with all of the political nihilism of National Socialism itself. What will emerge from this encounter is Heidegger's revised version of Hellingrath's old myth of a "secret Germany"—a vision of Graeco-Germanic autochthony that will sustain the dream of a future oriented beginning for the *Volk.* Adjusting to the new political-military conditions, Heidegger will now see the German defeat as inevitable, even as he continues to support the war effort with his two sons at the Eastern front. Throughout these difficult times Heidegger's new elegy of truth will continue to play out the old themes of the Rectorial Address but in a new form. Political autochthony, which Heidegger trumpeted in 1933 under the name of "German self-assertion," now recedes in favor of ontological autochthony—a strategy that continues in Heidegger's postwar writings.[112] The lectures on Parmenides mark this turn.

There Heidegger will once again introduce a chthonic thematics of earth, land, territory, ground, and soil that offers a view of politics rooted in the ontology of the earth. In a passage explicating a line from *The Iliad* (Book 23: 1.244) where Achilles speaks of burying his fallen companion Patroclus, Heidegger will offer a gloss on the Homeric phrase *Aidi keuthomai*—which he translates as *vom Geborgenwerden im Hades* ("of being hidden in Hades"). Drawing on the language of *bergen* and *verbergen,* as he did in the "On the Origin of the Work of Art," Heidegger will relate this term to the whole constellation of themes around the word *aletheia.* This reflection on Greek philology, by way of an excursus on the meaning of death in battle, will be related to the "essence of truth as unconcealment" and, by extension, to the concealment and hiddenness of the earth itself. Within Heidegger's overall meditation, the death of the fallen soldier becomes a way of rethinking the meaning of the earth. However, it will also function as a way to integrate the themes of death, battle, the subterranean, *aletheia,* anti-Romanism, the chthonic, and the autochthonic into a Graeco-German metaphysics of war at a turning point in Western history. Hence, Heidegger will write that in the Homeric conception of *Aidi keuthomai:*

> ... the earth itself and the subterranean come into relation with sheltering and concealing. The essential connection between death and concealment is starting to appear. For the Greeks, death is not a "biological" process, any more than birth is. Birth and death take their essence from the realm of disclosiveness and concealment. Even the earth receives its essence from this

112. Heidegger, PM: 244, 257, 260/WM: 152, 170, 172, and WCT: 29–32/WHD: 11–13.

same realm. The earth is the in-between, namely between the concealment of the subterranean and the luminosity, the disclosiveness, of the supraterranean (the span of heaven, *ouranos*). For the Romans, on the contrary, the earth, *tellus, terra,* is the dry, the land as distinct from the sea; this distinction differentiates that upon which construction, settlement, and installation are possible from those places where they are impossible. *Terra* becomes *territorium,* land of settlement as realm of command. In the Roman *terra* can be heard an imperial accent, completely foreign to the Greek *gaia* and *ge* (P: 60/GA 54: 88–89).

Within the historical moment of winter 1942–43, Heidegger's distinction between Greek *gaia* and Roman *terra* will get played out as a struggle between German rootedness and American-Russian rootlessness. As Heidegger presents it, the Second World War is, metaphysically considered, a death struggle for achieving a genuine relation to the earth. If the Allies win, the earth will become mere political territory to be disposed of and exploited like a Roman colony. As part of this push toward imperial dominion, the primordial, chthonic dimension of the earth will be covered over and suppressed, closing off any possibility of genuine rootedness in the homeland. At the same time, however, Heidegger also comes to deploy the rhetoric of anti-Latinity as a way of critiquing the National Socialist drive toward machination. Genuine autochthony, Heidegger seems to say, can only survive in the form of myth. Hence, from 1943 until the end of the war, Heidegger will focus attention away from the Romanizing influence of Nietzsche and the Nazis and turn his attention back to Parmenides and Heraclitus. The triumphal discourse on political autochthony will now recede in favor of an elegiac lament about the devastation of the earth.

In his *Feldweg-Gespräche* from the winter of 1944–45, Heidegger will continually return to the Nietzschean theme of the earth's devastation, or *Verwüstung,* as he lays stress on the ontological meaning of rootlessness (GA 77: 206–216). As the American-Russian victory appears ever more imminent, Heidegger will write: "the struggle over nihilism, for it and against it, is engaged on a field staked out by the predominance of the nonessence of nihilism. Nothing will be decided by this struggle. It will merely seal the predominance of the inauthentic in nihilism. Even where it believes itself to be standing on the opposite side, the struggle is everywhere and at bottom nihilistic—in the usual destructive sense of the word" (Niv: 239–40/NII: 384). To him, the war was not a moral struggle by the greatest generation of Americans against an evil Nazi menace. It was Roman nihilism harnessed to a new military garrison of terrible, frightening proportion: "'From humanity by way of nationality to bestiality (in brutality).' (Roman names!)" (GA 77: 243). In May of 1945, Heidegger concludes that "the war decides nothing." What matters is that "now for the first time the decision is being prepared—first and foremost—whether the *Germans* as the very center of the West deny their historical vocation and become sacrificed to foreign thoughts" (GA 77: 244). The geo-politics of the Nazi years go underground and in their stead Heidegger will begin to play on his shepherd's flute a new "song of the earth" that will transform the politics of autochthony into a pastoral roundelay about "building-dwelling-thinking."

As he retreats from his confrontation with Nietzsche and with National Socialism, Heidegger will begin to insulate himself politically from the excesses of the regime. His lectures on Heraclitus from 1943 take on an eschatological tone, viewing the present situation as ontologically rooted rather than as something political. "The planet is in flames," Heidegger proclaims; "the essence of humanity is out of joint. World historical reflection is something that can only come from the Germans—provided they can find and preserve what is 'German'" (GA 55: 123). And, in another passage, he writes:

> No matter how the external destiny of the West is configured, the greatest and most authentic test facing the Germans still lies ahead, a test in which the Germans will perhaps, against their will, be tested by those who are ignorant. This will be a test to see whether they, the Germans, are at one with the truth of be-ing [*Seyn*] and whether, beyond the readiness to die, they are strong enough to rescue what is originary, in all its unpretentiousness, against the petty-mindedness of the modern world.
>
> The danger that the 'holy heart of the peoples' of the West face is not that of decline [*Untergang*], but that we ourselves, confused and bewildered, submit to the will of modernity and get carried along by it. To stave off this disaster we will in the coming decades have need of thirty and forty year olds who have learned to think essentially (GA 55: 180–181).

Against the Roman threat of modernity, Heidegger would cleave to essential Greek thinking. In 1944, as he lectured on Heraclitus and the *Logos,* Heidegger would once again warn of the dangers of Roman culture and its ethos of aqueduct building, military conquest, and technical organization. At what he terms "a turning point in Western history," he still puts forward his myth of Graeco-German autochthony as his way of configuring the political and military events of the day. "In the present moment we can only foresee this: . . . that the destiny of the human race and its peoples is deeply rooted in the human being's relation . . . to the essence of unconcealment—that is, truth. . . . If we reflect that in the West it was the Greeks, first and foremost, who disclosed the essence of truth, then we can recognize to what extent the destiny that befell the Greeks is not something past and antiquarian that can be relegated to 'antiquity.' It is, rather, something that is undecided and still to come, something in and against which we Germans, alone and above all others for a long time to come, can and must think" (GA 55: 204). The metaphysics of Germany's *Sonderweg*, or "special path," is still alive and well even as Germany is collapsing all around him. Fearing the destruction of his manuscripts, Heidegger leaves Freiburg in the late fall of 1944 and retreats to the land of his forebears in Messkirch. On November 27, allied aircraft will wreak havoc on the city where only eleven years earlier Heidegger had proclaimed a "new beginning" for the German *Volk*. Spengler's vision of a "decline of the West"—or at least of a German-dominated West—seemed about to come true.

Yet despite the devastation in physical and human terms, and against the evident signs of a German decline, Heidegger continued to embrace his exclusionary myth of German supremacy. The war had proven nothing, Heidegger would claim. What would follow in the years of "peace" would simply be war by other means—a kind of permanent technological order of production, distribution, and total mobilization (EP: 103–109/VA: 91–97). In July of 1945, Heidegger writes to Rudolf Stadelmann (his Nazi colleague with whom he collaborated on the reforms of 1933–34): "Everyone now thinks of decline [*Untergang*]. But we Germans cannot perish [*untergehen*] because we have not yet arisen and must first persevere through the night."[113] The rhetorical pyrotechnics of 1933 had been supplanted by a more somber, meditative tone of reflection and equanimity but the message was the same. The myth of Graeco-German autochthony had survived even the horror of the death camps. Heidegger's new tone of *Gelassenheit* and his new identity as "the shepherd of being" would, at root, merely continue the old ontological politics of National Socialism by other, more poetic means. Now, as the De-Nazification Commission began to mount its investigation into his Nazi ties, Heidegger would begin to devise his new strategy of elusion and denial. After suffering a total breakdown, Heidegger went on the offensive, as he had done so often before, by writing.

In 1946, he drafts the "Letter on Humanism," "What Are Poets For?" and "The Anaximander Fragment"—all of which reformulate the themes of 1933 in a new, politically cleansed form. But despite his elisions of all references to the self-assertion of the one true *Volk*, these essays continue to promulgate the metaphysical *Sonderweg* of the early Nazi years even as they adopt the new politically correct tone of a "European"(rather than an essentially German) connection to the Greek beginning (BW: 218/H: 169). The same exclusionary ethos of anti-Latinity and anti-Americanism prevails (PLT: 113/H: 268; BW: 200–203/H: 151–154; EGT: 56/H: 342). As in the Heraclitus lectures, Heidegger would once again recuperate the

---

113. Ott, *Martin Heidegger: Unterwegs*, 157.

thematic of rescue and salvation from "the darkening of the world's night" (EGT: 17/H: 300; PLT: 91–92, 118, 142/H: 248–249, 273, 295). Even though he had been stripped of any soteriological hopes in a political sense, he still held fast to a Heraclitean form of rescue—"*sozein ta phainomena,* a rescue of that which shows itself" (GA 55: 398).

Throughout all of the changes wrought by the war, Heidegger's elegiac history of the West remained intact. Rescue would remain a privilege of the Germans, because it was granted to them as their autochthonic right. What made the planetary project of American dominion so metaphysically bankrupt was that it had no ancient roots, no autochthonic bond to an originary beginning. Heidegger's intense rejection of the Latin tradition and its Roman Catholic legacy can be traced back to this same inviolable prejudice in favor of rootedness. The Roman and Christian world knew nothing of the chthonic. The work of Walter F. Otto, Alfred Baeumler, and Werner Jaeger had taught Heidegger as much. But in his embrace of their chthonic religion of earth, rootedness, and soil, Heidegger fell victim to the selfsame forces of *Weltanschauung* and ideology that he so often disdained and found unworthy of genuine philosophical consideration.[114] He himself promulgated an "essential" history of being that, on further reflection and inquiry, turns out to be a geo-philosophical narrative about German history and politics, a metaphysical justification for a Messkirchian form of National Socialism. Hence, we should not be surprised to find that after the war—even after the undeniable revelations about Auschwitz, Treblinka, Bergen-Belsen, Theresienstadt, Buchenwald, Dachau, Sachsenhausen, and those other 'subterranean' topoi of terror, murder, and transgression—Heidegger would not recant his ideology of roots and soil nor its complicity in the National Socialist metaphysics of death. Instead, he will cling to a strategy of denial and will present his *Sonderweg* metaphysics in new shepherd's clothes.

Writing to his former student, Herbert Marcuse in 1948 about his political affiliations, Heidegger will argue:

- In my lectures and courses from 1933–44 I incorporated a standpoint that was so unequivocal that among those who were my students, none fell victim to Nazi ideology. My works from this period, if they ever appear, will testify to this fact.
- An avowal after 1945 was for me impossible: the Nazi supporters announced their change of allegiance in the most loathsome way; I, however, had nothing in common with them.
- To the charges of dubious validity that you express "about a regime that murdered millions of Jews, that made terror into an everyday phenome-

---

114. See for example Heidegger's comments in FCM: 1.2, 11, 172–174/GA 29/30: 1–2, 15–16, 255–258, for his disparaging remarks on *Weltanschauungsphilosophie.*

non, and that turned everything that pertains to the ideas of spirit, freedom, and truth into its bloody opposite," I can merely add that if instead
of "Jews" you had written "East Germans" [i.e., Germans of the eastern ter-
ritories], then the same holds true for one of the allies, with the difference that everything that has occurred since 1945 has become public
knowledge, while the bloody terror of the Nazis in point of fact had been
kept a secret from the German people. (HCW:163)

For him, the German defeat and reign of terror were simply re-appropri-
ated to the old mythic structures of *aletheia*, autochthony, and homecoming. Nietzsche was out. The Pre-Socratics and Hölderlin were still in, always and until the end. The old myth about a secret Germany had survived
the storm. Hadn't the conclusion to the Rectorial Address provided a hint
for those who had ears to hear?

Much could be said about Heidegger's disingenuous claim that his "lectures and courses from 1933–44" were "unequivocal" in their resistance to
"Nazi ideology." Anyone familiar with his practiced art of self-choreogra-
phy and autoexegetical purgation, a style that from first to last marks the
appearance, production, and editorial execution of "the *Collected Edition*
of the Last Hand [sic]," will already have dismissed such a claim as a form
of political apology.[115] Any genuine confrontation with Heidegger will
need to acknowledge this aspect of his style and how it has led to a kind of
self-perpetuating ethos of purely text-focused, intra-philosophical readings of his work. The industry of Heideggeriana abounds with examples of
just such a practice.[116]

Part of my effort in this book has been directed at reading Heidegger
within his historical context. Because Heidegger himself systematically
abandons the practice of indexing, footnoting, and providing any scholarly apparatus, those of us who read him are encouraged to forsake historical reference points and concentrate solely on the originary matter of
thinking. Given his own political affiliations and the threat posed by the
De-Nazification Commission and the French military authorities in
Freiburg after the war, this is hardly surprising. To accept this style of self-
choreographed presentation at face value, however, gives tacit assent to
an unhistorical mode of reading. My argument has been that Heidegger's
intra-philosophical history of being needs to be read historically within
the German political situation of the years after the Great War and leading
up to and through the period of National Socialism. I have focused primarily on Heidegger's work of the 1930s, because it seems to me that in
this early period Heidegger will lay out the essentials of his Graeco-Ger-

115. See note 3 in this chapter.
116. For the most telling examples, see *Heidegger Studies*, published by Duncker & Humblot in Berlin, which refuses to acknowledge the National Socialist milieu of Heidegger's
themes.

manic elegy of *Seynsgeschichte* in its most telling form. But the discourse on autochthony that begins in the Aristotle lectures from 1923–24, locating the phenomenon of *aletheuein* ('true-ing') in Schlageter's defense of the native soil, continues right through the 1950s and 1960s and helps shape Heidegger's eco-poetic idyll on the homeland and the dangers of technology. And, I would argue, it is this discourse that lies at the root of Heidegger's mythic history of being.

Heidegger was a chthonic thinker. Throughout his life, he was preoccupied by a longing for a subterranean, *unterirdische* philosophy of being with roots in the Greeks. The *Antigone* chorus' plea for thinking the *polis* in harmony with "the laws of the earth," Hölderlin's vision of "Germania" as "the daughter of holy Earth," Zarathustra's injunction to his audience to "remain true to the earth"—all of them come together in Heidegger's chthonic philosophy.[117] In 1971, Heidegger writes on the flyleaf to his 1938 essay, "The Age of the World Picture," an inscription to the sculptor Hans Kock that references the American moon-landing: "In the meantime: the astronautical impoverishment of the earth."[118] Clearly, the sexton's son from Messkirch had never dreamed of being airborne. Despite his admiration for Göring's feats of the air, Heidegger felt more of an affinity for the soil worked by his Alemannic ancestors.

In her essay of 1954, "Understanding and Politics," Hannah Arendt writes, "If we want to be at home on this earth, even at the price of being at home in this century, we must try to take part in the interminable dialogue with the essence of totalitarianism."[119] And yet part of the essence of totalitarianism is bound up with the discourse about the earth. Heidegger refused to acknowledge Arendt's demand to enter into dialogue with this essence, deeming it inessential when considered against the essence of truth. It falls to us, however, to take up this dialogue with renewed philosophical rigor and to challenge the logic of exclusion, privilege, and autochthonic identity that pervades Heidegger's thought. For all his rich philosophical acuity, Heidegger forgot to recognize the great insight of the hermeneutic tradition: truth does not arise from a singular point of origin or incipience; it emerges from out of the middle and in mediation with other hermeneutical claims, voices, and traditions. To read Heidegger hermeneutically is to read him in this context of historical dialogue against his own autoexegetical inclinations to conceal, suppress, and

117. Sophocles, *Antigone*, trans. Andrew Brown (London: Aris & Phillips, 1987), line 368; Friedrich Hölderlin, "Germania," in *Hyperion and Selected Poems*, ed. Eric Santner (New York: Continuum, 1990), 215; and Nietzsche, Z: 42/KSA 4: 15.

118. This inscription by Heidegger is cited in *Die Frage nach der Wahrheit*, ed. Ewald Richter (Frankfurt: Klostermann, 1997), 63.

119. Hannah Arendt, *Essays in Understanding*, ed. Jerome Kern (New York: Harcourt Brace & Co., 1994), 323.

elide. As Heidegger himself understood, philosophy too is historical. By engaging in a historical dialogue with the sources of Heidegger's tradition, we might help to initiate a historical confrontation with Heidegger's own thinking, a confrontation that seeks not to suppress or censure, but to challenge at its root any authorial attempt to provide directives on how to read what is 'there' for thinking.

Postscript

Technology tears human beings loose from the earth and uproots them. . . . I was frightened when I recently saw photographs of the earth taken from the moon. We don't need an atom bomb at all; the uprooting of human beings is already taking place.

—MARTIN HEIDEGGER
SI: 55/GA 16: 670

Given the specific focus of this study on Heidegger's geo-philosophical politics, I have concentrated my attention on those texts that Heidegger wrote between 1933 and 1945, the period of National Socialist rule in Germany. Clearly, in one sense, these dates are arbitrary historical markers whose significance should not be overestimated or given too determinative a role. Heidegger himself, as he came to reflect on his own thought path, would bypass these crude political markers and choose 1930 instead as the decisive year for following the *Kehre* of his thinking (PM: 250/WM: 208; Ni: xvi/NI: 10). In another sense, however, these dates are not arbitrary ones at all since their significance derives not from an external meta-narrative of politics and national affairs but from Heidegger's own vision of his philosophical role in the working out of German destiny. In 1933 he will be appointed as the new National Socialist rector of the University of Freiburg and will deliver a number of important addresses on the role and meaning of philosophy in national life. In 1945, after the devastating Allied air raid on Freiburg that forces him to flee the city, Heidegger will doggedly insist that "the war is at an end; nothing has changed, nothing is new, on the contrary" (GA 79: 241). But things will change. Now Heidegger will be confronted by an historical accounting of his own activities as rector and of his philosophical support for a regime of terror and extermination.

In the postwar years things would prove difficult for Heidegger. Besides facing a teaching ban imposed by the De-Nazification Committee of Freiburg and suffering a nervous collapse in early 1946 from the pressures of defending himself in public, Heidegger will also be subjected to a hostile critique from his former student, Karl Löwith, published in the French journal *Les Temps Modernes* (1946).[1] Over the next three years, Hei-

---

1. Karl Löwith, "Les implications politiques de la philosophie de l'existence chez Heidegger," *Les Temps Modernes* 14 (1946–1947); HCW: 167–185. Heidegger will also be criti-

degger will suffer the requisitioning of his house by French military authorities, the quartering of French soldiers in his family residence, and the ever present threat of having his personal library confiscated.

In the face of all these difficulties, and the all too real possibility of losing his government pension, Heidegger will prove himself resourceful. Through an alliance with the young French philosopher Jean Beaufret, Heidegger will begin the arduous work of rehabilitating his philosophical legacy. Owing to Freiburg's status as a municipality lying within the compass of French military jurisdiction, Heidegger perceives the link to Beaufret as one that might aid his cause. Given the French authorities' power to decide his fate, Heidegger's publication of the "Letter on Humanism," especially its attack on nationalism, seems particularly well timed (PM: 260/WM: 221). Spurred on by his success abroad at reclaiming his position of philosophical prominence, Heidegger resolves to take on a more active role at home and goes on the offensive, deciding to speak outside the halls of the university. In December 1949, the year of the Federal Republic's founding, he will begin a series of lectures on the question concerning technology that will continue over the next year at Bremen, Bühlerhöhe, and Munich (GA 79: 177). The Bremen lectures, as exercises in the fashioning of a new public identity freed from the taint of blood and soil politics, would provide the first move in the direction of a politically cleansed Heidegger reception within Germany.

Drawing on the image of Bremen as an old Hanseatic free city committed to the protection of free speech, Heidegger would position himself as the aggrieved independent thinker suffering under the ban of silence imposed by the De-Nazification Committee. In his opening remarks he refers back to a speech before the NS era, his lecture "On the Essence of Truth" (1930): "Nineteen years ago I gave a talk here and said things that only now are slowly beginning to be understood and have an effect. I took a risk then—and I will take a risk again today."[2] What Heidegger will risk is a bold attempt to rethink the essence of the modern world in terms of what he calls "*das Ge-stell*" (the enframing structure of modern technology that defines all being as standing presence). The danger that he sees threatening modern Western humanity comes in the form of technology's uncanny power to transform all beings into the form of "things" that are technically usable, available as standing reserve. As part of this world-transforming process of technical mastery, Heidegger claims, the being-

---

cized by Hannah Arendt in a 1946 article in *Partisan Review* where she claims: "it is rumored that he has placed himself at the disposal of the French occupational authorities for the reeducation of the German people," *Essays in Understanding*, ed. Jerome Kohn (New York: Harcourt Brace, 1994), 187.

2. Heinrich W. Petzet, *Encounters and Dialogues with Martin Heidegger*, trans. P. Emad and K. Maly (Chicago: University of Chicago Press, 1993), 55.

character of beings becomes occluded and ultimately forgotten. The "danger" that Heidegger points to in his question concerning technology is the danger of not even being aware that there is any danger posed by this technological transformation of being. And, as Heidegger makes clear, there is no more egregious example of this transformation than in the realm of language, especially scientific language. Under the pressure of the *Ge-stell,* language loses its poetic, auroral character and devolves into an instrumental agent in the production, delivery, and management of all oral and written discourse as "information." At the end of his lecture entitled "The Danger," Heidegger goes so far as to say that "the international character of scientific language is the strongest proof of its rootlessness and homelessness" (GA 79:66).

While most of Heidegger's arcane discourse must have been impenetrable for the non-academic audience gathered in Bremen, what did present itself clearly was the dramatic effect of the whole event: Heidegger was back and boldly confronting the essential questions of the day. Stripped of its endless neologisms and citations in Greek, Heidegger's discourse spoke clearly to the profound dangers that the atomic age posed to the newly-formed Federal Republic of Germany. What was decisive for him was to de-structure the political issues of the day—war guilt, the holocaust, the lightning-fast introduction of democratic values into German society, the proper relation of Germany to NATO and to the Soviet bloc—back into ontological questions about the essence of modern technology. And though he would never directly confront these issues in any traditional sense, he would offer hints and pointers by alluding to structural problems. For example, in his lecture on "The Thing," Heidegger would point out that, when traced to its Latin roots, "thing" means "res"—what stands in question. He then went on to explain that "*res publica* does not mean 'state' but rather that which publicly concerns everyone of a people and therefore is discussed in public" (GA 79:13). Never at home in the democratic world of the Weimar Republic, now Heidegger will put forward a critique of the Bonn Republic as well—though because of the nature of his former political ties, he will lay out his criticisms subtly. As part of his strategy, he will forego the *völkisch* nationalism from his earlier Nazi speeches and reconfigure it as a kind of rustic philosophy that draws on the imagery of earth, fields, and woodland paths. In his 1946 "Letter on Humanism," he was careful to reject the "egoism of [the] nation [*Volk*]" in favor of what he termed Germany's "fateful belongingness to the [other] nations" (BW: 241–242/WM: 169). And in the Bremen lectures he will qualify his remark about the rootlessness of the international language of science by telling his listeners that "this in no way signifies that rootedness and the native character of language are in the least bit vouchsafed and determined or even established by the merely national" (GA 79:66). Instead Heidegger will turn to a vigorous defense of "the homeland" (*Heimat*), a politically amorphous concept now stripped of any national-ist—or National Socialist—implications. In this office as a "public" philosopher warning against the planetary effects of technology, Heideg-ger will take on a new dramatic persona: the rustic shepherd of being. To reinforce this new identity as an eco-poetic philosopher of woodlands, landscapes, and country fields, Heidegger will publish an essay entitled "Fieldpath" (1949) and a book entitled *Woodpaths* (1950).[3] The effect of these publications will be to help establish a public conception of Heideg-ger as an apolitical country philosopher concerned with protecting the rustic character of the German landscape against the threats of homeless-ness and atomic devastation.

As he navigates the dangerous waters of postwar de-nazification and de-mocratization, Heidegger will begin to distance himself from any taint of fascist language and conceptuality—especially the Nazi discourse of the *Volk*. In this postwar era he will venture into the public realm for the first time with a new language of poetic thinking that he had privately devel-oped in his years of exile (both within the National Socialist order from 1939–1945 and during the banishment imposed by the De-Nazification Committee from 1946–1949). In his 1947 collection, *Aus der Erfahrung des Denkens*, Heidegger will call this new form of poetic thinking a "topology of being" that understands the concealed structure of what is as a four-fold: the place (*topos*) for the originary gathering (*logos*) of earth, sky, gods, and mortals (GA13: 84).

All of Heidegger's postwar writings will in some way address this ques-tion of situating philosophy topologically so that human beings can find their proper place within being. For Heidegger that means overcoming (*Überwindung*) the destructive effects of technology or, more properly, re-covering from (*Verwindung*) the metaphysics of the technological *Ge-stell* that has brought with it "devastation" (*Verödung*), "world-darkening" (*die Verdüsterung der Welt*), and the "flight of the gods" (GA13: 76; H: 248–295). As a way of allowing this recovery to take place, Heidegger will reject the anthropocentric language of voluntarism and attempt to let the Eckhart-ian comportment of *Gelassenheit* or "releasement toward things" help situ-ate the human being in its proper place or *topos* within the structure of being.[4] To come to such a place, Heidegger will claim, involves neither ac-tive achievement nor passive resignation. What is required instead is a

---

3. The publishing history of "Feldweg" can be traced in DE: 191. For *Holzwege*, see H: 344–345.

4. This is not to say that the discourse on *Gelassenheit* is solely a reaction to the postwar sit-uation of Germany. There are traces of "*Sein-lassen*" before 1945; see BT: 79/SZ: 84–85; PM: 144/WM: 83–84, and in BW: 171/H: 35 where Heidegger says "the work lets [*lässt*] the earth be an earth."

form of "persistent courageous thinking." As he puts it in a memorial address from 1955:

> We are the ones who think in this way if we know ourselves here and now as human beings who must find and prepare the path into the atomic age and both through it and out of it. If there awakens in us a releasement toward things and experiences for the mystery then we may come to a path that leads to a new foundation and ground. In this ground the creation of enduring works can touch new roots. In this way the truth of what Johann Peter Hebel says will surely be renewed in a different way and for a different epoch:
>> "We are plants which—whether we like to admit it to ourselves or not— must rise out of the earth in which we are rooted, if we are to blossom in the ether and bear fruit." (GA16: 529)

Held in his native village of Messkirch, this memorial address entitled "Gelassenheit" will find in the politically amorphous concept of the homeland a source of hope and future possibility for a German nation devastated by the effects of the Second World War, in whose wake "many Germans lost their homeland, had to leave their villages and towns and [became] exiles driven from their native soil." Living in a country confronted by the economic forces of agribusiness, the demographic shifts of a technological revolution, and the political pressures of a Cold War that flooded Central Europe with refugees, Heidegger will ask: "Does not the flourishing of any genuine, native work depend upon its rootedness [*Verwurzelung*] in the native soil of the homeland? . . . Is there still a powerfully rooted homeland in whose soil [*Boden*] the human being stands constant [*ständig*], that is, is rooted and auto-chthonic [*boden-ständig*]?" Heidegger then goes on to provide an answer or counter-word (*Antwort*) to his questions: "Answer: the *rootedness*, the *autochthony* [*Bodenständigkeit*] of contemporary humanity is threatened at its core. Even more: the loss of rootedness is not something caused by mere external circumstances or fortune. Nor is it due solely to the indolence and superficial lifestyle of human beings. The loss of autochthony and rootedness stems from the spirit of the age into which we all were born. . . . the atomic age" (GA16: 521–522).

In a series of speeches, lectures, informal talks, and memorial addresses—all centered on the themes of autochthony, rootlessness, the homeland, poetic thinking, and the writings of J.P. Hebel—Heidegger will put forward a radical critique of modern technology as a metaphysics of calculative thinking that threatens our potential "to bloom in the ether and bear fruit." Between 1954 and 1960, in Zähringen, Messkirch, Göppingen, Lörrach, and other small towns and villages in Germany and German-speaking Switzerland, Heidegger will alter, shift, transpose, and repackage his Hebel-interpretation to fit diverse rhetorical circumstances.[5] Through all of these varied discourses there will emerge a singular thematics of rootedness and autochthony that will echo the discourse concerning *Bodenständigkeit* from the years of Heidegger's political engagement with National Socialism. But within the concrete historical situation of Germany in the 1950s, this preoccupation with autochthony will take on a new and decisive function. Heidegger himself will even speak in his "Memorial Address" about what he terms a "new autochthony" (*"eine neue Bodenständigkeit"*) and urge his fellow countrymen to "give it a trial." He will intimate that "releasement toward things and an openness to mystery gives us the prospect of a new autochthony. This could one day even be appropriate for calling back the old, now rapidly vanishing autochthony in a changed form" (GA 16: 528).

In this call for a new autochthony that seeks to challenge the errancy of calculative thinking, Heidegger turns to Hebel's rustic ideal of the homeland for rescue and deliverance. Yet even as he despairs of being able to forestall the onslaught of democratization and its technological calculus of consumerism, Heidegger will embrace the hope of a poetic, meditative

---

5. Heidegger did not happen upon Hebel in the mid-1950s as he searched about for a symbol of originary German dialect. He had long been familiar with his work and had come to him, as he came to Hölderlin, from within the right-wing reception of native poets that flourished in Germany during the 1920s and 1930s. At the same conference of a "Badener Heimattag" that Heidegger first delivered his lecture "On the Essence of Truth" (1930), the Nazi poet Hermann Burte gave a presentation on "Alemannische Mundartdichtung bis zu Hebel." And, in 1937, the Nazi mayor of Freiburg published a volume of essays, *Alemannenland: Ein Buch von Volkstum und Sendung*, including an essay by Heidegger (Stuttgart: Engelhorns, 1937) on the problem of a German world mission and the preservation of the "autochthonous life" around Freiburg and its "landscape (11–12, 23, 10)." Four of the essays in Kerber's collection expressly connect Hebel to the theme of rootedness and autochthony, linking the Alemannic landscape and language "to the earth-and soil-bound race of peasants," "the dialect of Aryan peasants," and "the bloodlike commonality of German stock as well as its autochthonous racial character." This account of Hebel as a poet "deeply rooted in the Alemannic homeland" became an essential element in the National Socialist Hebel-reception of the 1930s. In a speech delivered at the *Hebelmähli* of 1933, Kerber would claim that out of his "deeply rooted love of the homeland . . . today Hebel too would support the National Socialist party." As Kerber put it, "the autochthonous men of the Markgräflerland speak and think in an Alemannic way and they are so intimately bound to their Johann Peter Hebel that they transmit this Alemannic dialect and racial character to their progeny" (NH: 280–281). This self-conscious attempt at what Kerber calls "die Gleichschaltung Hebels" (the bringing of Hebel into line with NS concepts) was part of a generational movement to overcome "the damage caused by liberal civilization and Jewish foreignness" that threatened "to tear German culture from the soil of its *völkisch* independence and to let the 'province' be devastated so that a new foreign spirit could be built on the asphalt of a metropolis." In his own essay from Kerber's *Alemannenland* collection, Heidegger too would focus on "the threat of thorough deracination" posed to German culture by the rootless forces within the West. Though Heidegger never mentions Hebel in his 1937 address, "Wege zur Aussprache," the other essays in the collection come together to form a kind of National Socialist celebration of autochthony in the Alemannic dialect, landscape, and character of Johann Peter Hebel.

thinking that might help to realize Hölderlin's vision of "dwelling poetically upon the earth" (PLT: 213–229/VA: 187–204). Throughout his Hebel lectures in the 1950s, Heidegger would keep returning to this theme of *Gelassenheit* as a way of preparing "the ground and soil of a futural autochthony" (GA 16: 526). In one speech on Hebel delivered at his own adopted village of Todtnauberg, he will forge a bond between his new ideal of autochthony and the old rural autochthony whose traces, he claims, can still be found in the speech patterns of rural Alemannic dialect with its poetic tones and rhythms. Renouncing the rootless language of the city and the academy, Heidegger will, in perfect idiomatic dialect, proclaim himself to be simply "e Ma us de Rütte" (GA 16: 641).[6] I think we need to ask, however, whether in this postwar Heideggerian discourse of a new autochthony there are traces of another form of the old autochthony of National Socialist blood and soil that animates the Rectorial Address, the Schlageter memorial speech, and the other political writings from the 1930s that have provided the main focus of this book. How are we to reconcile these two visions of Heidegger—the eco-poetic shepherd of being who calls us to a postmetaphysical form of meditative thinking *and* the Nazi rector who insists that "the Führer himself and he alone *is* the present and future German reality and its law"? (GA 16: 184). Can these two theatrical personae be traced back to a single author? Are the shepherd's cloak and the party member's insignia but different props that Heidegger employed at various stages of his public career? Or do they somehow represent variant ideals of a single vision? Does this curious and fateful joining/juxtaposition of *Gelassenheit* and *Selbstbehauptung*, of meditative calm and assertive control reveal perhaps something of Heidegger's own attempt to give expression to the agonal forces within being that he uncovered in Heraclitus and Nietzsche?

No matter how we read Heidegger—whether as rigorous phenomenologist, committed Nazi, Eckhartian shepherd, postmetaphysical prophet, or as a curious cross-pollination of these different historical flowerings— we will need to address these questions. As I read him, Heidegger never simply chose one identity, nor did he ever place his own thinking in the service of one ideal—whether political, institutional, historical, or metaphysical. I think it wrong to suggest that we can locate some singular thread of Heideggerian logic that unifies all of his writing—especially through and beyond those metaphysical markers indicated by the years "1933" and "1945." Nor would I claim that Heidegger ever embraced a singular, monotropic, homologous form of philosophical thinking that en-

6. In styling himself to be "a man from the Rütte," Heidegger reinforced his bond to the rural German peasant ideal of roots and soil. (The "Rütte" is the cluster of old farmhouses that constituted the center of Todtnauberg, just below Heidegger's cabin.)

dured through all of his various guises and personae. Heidegger read too widely over his life to become a monochromatic ideologue. From Luther, Aristotle, Schleiermacher, and Dilthey in the 1920s through Nietzsche, Jünger, and Hölderlin in the 1930s to Eckhart, Saint-Exupéry, and Lao Tsu in the 1940s–50s, Heidegger drew on a broad range of sources. Nevertheless, as I have tried to show, there is an enduring structure within Heidegger's work that can provide a meaningful historical context within and against which to read Heidegger's texts, a context provided by "roots" and "autochthony." This conviction (as Heidegger put it in a 1958 speech) that "there is no essential work of the spirit that does not have its roots in an originary form of autochthony" will help to shape Heidegger's path of questioning in critical and decisive ways (GA 16: 551). As I have tried to argue, this discourse concerning Heidegger's roots is not merely a curious or intriguing part of his cultural baggage; rather, it provides a way for Heidegger to confront the powerful tensions that he sees within German history and the history of modernity.

Autochthony functions within Heidegger's work as a poetic-philosophical myth of the originary—and *as* myth will never be subject to rigorous philosophical scrutiny or de-structuring. On the contrary, autochthony itself will provide a structure within which Heidegger's work of de-structuring (*Destruktion*) will take place. In the wake of the postwar trauma brought on by aerial bombing, the migration of civilians across national borders, the social and economic chaos of a state in the process of reconstructing itself, Heidegger will resurrect his old *mythos* of rootedness to address the new German situation. In so doing he will present it as an eco-poetic discourse on the dangers posed by modern technology, recruiting Hebel as a rustic voice of prophetic warning.

Between 1954 and 1960 in the Hebel lectures, this mythic thematics of autochthony will be deployed in such a carefully staged way that it will function *both* as an eco-poetic meditation on the plight of planetary civilization and as a geo-philosophical *re*configuration of Germany's metaphysical *Sonderweg*. In this sense, we need to see Heidegger as playing the role of both the shepherd of being and the philosophical director of the German *Volk*—but now aware that if he is to be heard he needs to renounce the mantle of *Führer*/rector for the more modest part of philosophical house-friend. To read Heidegger's essay "Hebel—Friend of the House" within this context is to understand that there are not "two" Heideggers (shepherd/*Führer*) who need to be reconciled. Rather, it is to see that both incarnations are roles that Heidegger plays upon the different political stages of German history.

In its 1957 staging, the thematics of autochthony will be presented as a rustic call for reconciling "the calculability of nature" and "the mystery of the world" (GA 13:146).The question remains, however, whether this myth of rootedness emerges as a response to the postwar crisis in Germany or whether it has deeper roots. Does Heidegger's song of the earth in praise of rootedness and autochthony (*Bodenständigkeit*) have any inner connection to Heidegger's earlier martial hymns from the NS years sung in praise of Germany's metaphysical-eschatological supremacy? Do the notes from the shepherd's flute and its pastoral roundelay need to be heard in consonance with the marching hymn of the *Horst Wessel Lied*? Throughout this book, I have tried to suggest that the two motifs of the pastoral and the martial belong together in Heidegger: not in opposition to, but rather in tension with, one another. That is, both need to be heard as musical-dramatic presentations performed at different times for different audiences, performances whose musical motifs merge with a metaphysics of the earth to offer competing, yet complementary, visions of a German future. Here Heidegger's martial and pastoral songs of the earth as German homeland can be read in and through the Heraclitean notion of strife or *eris*. Each stands in tension with the other in such a way that its singular force of contention emerges as a harmonic balance of mutual interpenetration and reciprocal appropriation.

Concretely, such a reading enables us to rethink Heidegger's own self-staged directions for reading his work and forces us back to the texts themselves in their specific historical contexts. If we follow this historical path of reading, against Heidegger's own authorial directions to forego context and concentrate solely on "die Sache des Denkens," then we are confronted by the persistence of the political throughout his life—even in those texts written after 1946 that self-consciously seek to efface all traces of politics from the historical record. By reading Heidegger both as author and producer/director of his texts, we might begin to see how powerfully the myth of autochthony comes to shape his work—both before and after the period 1933–1945.

Heidegger's rustic philosophy of the homeland and his martial ideology of struggle, valor, and self-assertion are not at odds. They come together to form a political metaphysics of the earth rooted in language, dialect, and poetic idiom. In this curious and fateful conjoining of Nietzsche's *Kampf* and Hebel's *Heimat,* of Heraclitus' *eris* and Eckhart's *Gelassenheit,* there emerges a Heideggerian discourse about roots that both brings together and sets asunder the counterposed realms of the martial and pastoral. In this *Auseinandersetzung* between the politics of National Socialism and the poetics of an Alemannic homeland there emerges a historical question-frame within which the questions of Heidegger's thinking will take shape in their different forms and incarnations.

If Heidegger still has anything to say to us, and I think he does, then it falls to us to work out in dialogue with his anti-democratic metaphysics of autochthonic supremacy a way of challenging his own mythic assumptions about the relation of philosophy and politics. By reclaiming the power of *Auseinandersetzung* in Heidegger's work, we might be able to set it into another question-frame than that provided by Heidegger himself. To put at issue not only the question of Heidegger's Nazism, but his whole reading of the history of philosophy, forces us back to the question of retrieving the power of the origin for the challenge of what is to come. Heidegger chose the Greeks, which is to say "his" Greeks, as the philosophical-poetic legacy that could engender a revolutionary *Aufbruch* for the German nation. In the process he would come to suppress, elide, banish, and expatriate those forces of the Asiatic, the Hebraic, the Roman, and the American that threatened the rootedness of the German *Volk*. But we are left with a different legacy: to take Heidegger at his word, which means to take *Auseinandersetzung* seriously by keeping it alive as the *Leitwort* for our own way of engaging his texts.

If in this way of reading we can contest his Germanocentric history of being and its commitment to autochthony, then perhaps we might be able to open up the homeland to settlement by those who have been displaced, uprooted, banished, and brought to destruction by the consanguineous myths of the old autochthony of blood and soil. In this contested reading of Heidegger's roots, the *topos* of being, the *da* of *Sein*, would no longer be demarcated by the boundaries of the Black Forest, the Bodensee, or the Swabian Alb, but would be open to resettlement even to those who have been exiled by the logic of autochthony and whose tragic visage haunts the history of the twentieth century. In this *topos* of being open to members of all tribes perhaps we could find a way of reclaiming the "greatness" of philosophy that Heidegger trumpeted in his Rectorial Address of 1933. Within such a space perhaps we could begin to hear the lesson from Plato's *Republic* where the ancient warrior Er, "a Pamphylian by race," teaches us to "always hold to the upper path and in every way practice justice with wisdom."[7] On the other side of that river traversed by the philosopher of justice, perhaps there we might be able to read Heidegger again, ever heeding the words of the poet,

> With promises it is fraught, and to me
> Seems threatening too, yet I will stay with it . . .
> —Hölderlin, "Germania."

7. "Pamphylian" is an adjective formed by the combination of the Greek terms *pan* + *phylum*, meaning "every" + "tribe"; hence Er is "Everyman," s/he who is a member of every race or tribe. Plato's *Republic*, trans. R. Sterling and W. Scott (New York: Norton, 1985), 304–311, Stephanus 614b–621d. For the poem by Hölderlin, see *Hyperion and Selected Poems*, ed. Eric Santner (New York: Continuum, 1990), 208–209.

Index

Index

Index

Europe: as cosmopolitan *Europa*, 130–32; crisis in, 167–68; cultural hegemony of, 169; defined against Asia, 172; Germany's role in, 121–25; and great politics, 159–67; and Greece, 167, 169–71, 173; Heidegger and, 135–36, 143–46; and identity, 172–75; and NS, 138
European man, 7–8
exclusion: and *Auseinandersetzung*, 257; and autochthony, 52–53, 211–12, 214; and biologism, 285; and community, 66; and German identity, 199–200; and Graeco-German affinity, 176–77, 200–208; in Greek myth, 196–200; Heidegger and, 201–3, 314, 335; metaphysics of, 202–3; and *pastorale militans*, 4–5; and *Seynsgeschichte*, 175–78
exile, 55

Fanon, Frantz, 178
Farias, Victor, 13
fatherland: death of soldier for, 57–63; Hölderlin and, 242–43; myth of, 51–52; and NS, 32; and *Volk*, 185, 230; and *Volksreligion*, 54–55
feminism, 282, 282 n.64
Ferry, Luc, 9
Fichte, Johann Gottlieb: and *Bodenständigkeit*, 131; on essence of human being, 147–48, 148 n.67; and foreign influence, 117; on German language, 55–56; on Germans as *Urvolk*, 72, 199, 200–201; and Graeco-German affinity, 116, 199–200; Heidegger and, 74, 85–86; NS and, 148 n.67; and science, 99
first beginning. *See arche*
flight of the gods, 329
Förster-Nietzsche, Elisabeth, 262–63, 262 n.25, 263 n.28, 315
fourfold, 329
France, 167; German conflicts with, 282; German conquest of, 304–5; German exclusion of, 117
Franco-Prussian War, 131, 259
Franz, Alfred, 310–11
freedom, 104, 131
free-floating (*freischwebende*) intelligence/speculation, 16, 34–35, 65–66
Freiburg: Allied air raid on, 326; De-Nazification Committee, 212, 253, 267–68, 323, 326; influence on Heidegger's philosophy, 166; Schlageter anniversary at, 62–63
Freiburg, University of, 57; Heidegger elected rector of, 82, 326
Freiburg National Socialism, 4, 4 n.4, 266, 266 n.33, 272, 300

Freikorps, 57
French Revolution, 230, 230 n.92
Fronterlebnis, 312
Frontgemeinschaft, 27 n.24, 59
Führer, 30; poet as, 241–42
Führerprinzip, 88, 158
future: as beginning, 193–94, 215; and German identity, 186; and *Volk*, 182–83. *See also* an/other beginning; *Heimkehr*

Gadamer, Hans-Georg, 43, 204 n.35
Gast, Peter, 263, 263 n.28
Geist (spirit), 97
Gelassenheit (releasement): and being, 51, 329; and *Bodenständigkeit*, 134–35, 332; and *Kehre*, 32, 321; and science, 285
Gemeinschaft (community): definition of, 66; vs. *Gesellschaft*, 27 n.24, 62; and Graeco-German affinity, 27; and language, 61–62; myth and, 47
geo-philosophy, critique of, 132–34
George, Stefan, 144
George Circle, 219–20, 230 n.92, 241, 260, 261
German Counter-Enlightenment, 49
"Germanic Hellenism," 121–22
German idealism, Heidegger and, 85–86
German language: and Graeco-German affinity, 202; as originary language, 55–56
Germany: Heidegger's idea of, 156–57; identity, 123–25; post-WWII democracy in, 328; secret, 205, 241–46, 302, 318; spatial/temporal centrality of, 137–43, 167, 184. *See also Sonderweg; Volk*
German Youth Movement, 30, 312; and *Gemeinschaft*, 27 n.24; Heidegger and, 107, 219, 280; lexicon of authenticity, 42–43
Gesellschaft (society): free-floating speculation of, 65–66; vs. *Gemeinschaft*, 27 n.24, 62
Ge-stell, Das, 327–28, 329
Gleichschaltung, 165, 274
Goethe, Johann Friedrich von, 116, 223
Göring, Hermann, 62–63, 307 n.99
Görres, Joseph, 49
Graeco-German affinity: and *arche*, 23, 243; and art, 295; and *Auseinandersetzung*, 234–35, 257; Baeumler and, 79, 117–21, 275–76; and *Bodenständigkeit*, 67–68, 97, 112–13, 251; and European identity, 173–75; and exclusion, 176–77, 200–208; and *Heimat*, 114–15, 116, 178–79; Hölderlin and, 56, 74, 112, 118, 199, 230–32, 237–41, 242–43;

Index

Heidegger, Martin (*continued*)
   tional Socialist State," 90; "Wege zur
   Aussprache," 251, 257; "What Are
   Poets For?," 321; "What Is Meta-
   physics?," 32, 37, 143; *Woodpaths*, 329.
   See also Being and Time; Hölderlin lec-
   tures; *Introduction to Metaphysics*; *Kehre*;
   Nietzsche lectures; "On the Essence of
   Truth" lectures; Parmenides lectures;
   Schlageter memorial speech; "Self-
   Assertion of the German University";
   Ursprungs-philosophie
"Heidegger Affair," 13
Heimat (homeland): concealed meaning
   of, 20, 42; earth as, 115; and exclusion,
   211; and Graeco-German affinity,
   114–15, 116, 178–79; and heroism,
   59–60; Hölderlin and, 236–37; and
   Kehre, 231–32, 233, 239–41, 328–29;
   and language, 55, 56–57; and myth,
   49–50, 156–57; and nationalism, 4;
   Nietzsche and, 303–4; and NS, 239; as
   political community, 8–9; and self-
   assertion, 334–35; and *Sonderweg*, 6
Heimkehr (homecoming): and Graeco-
   German affinity, 218–19; politics of,
   232–41; and *Volk*, 93
Hellenomania, 6; politics of, 208–13
Heller, Agnes, 186–87
Hellingrath, Norbert von: and Graeco-
   German affinity, 56–57; Heidegger
   and, 243–46, 310; and Hölderlin, 219,
   230; and Nietzsche, 145–46; and secret
   Germany, 123–24, 241–46, 318; and
   Sonderweg, 144
Hempel, Hans-Peter, 82
Heraclitus: and *Auseinandersetzung*, 256;
   Baeumler and, 275; and Graeco-Ger-
   man affinity, 185, 243; Heidegger and,
   17, 228; and *logos*, 309; Nietzsche and,
   224, 258, 278; and *physis*, 149, 225, 295;
   as primordial thinker, 215; and *Volk*,
   129–30; and Weimar classical philology, 221; and Western crisis, 113; and
   WWII, 306
Herder, J. G., 116
hermeneutical violence, of Baeumler,
   283
Herodotus, *Histories*, 52
heroic greatness, myth of, 107–11
heroism: and *Bodenständigkeit*, 43, 58; and
   German identity, 21; and *Heimat*,
   59–60; Nietzsche and, 31; and philosophy, 111, 203; rhetoric of, 30, 56–57;
   and sacrifice, 45
Hesiod, 258
Heyse, Hans: Nietzsche and, 26; and

Plato, 102, 102 n.34, 204, 204 n.36, 207,
   208–9; and university reform, 28–30
Hildebrandt, Kurt: Heidegger and, 213;
   and Hölderlin, 243; and Nietzsche,
   261; and Plato, 101 n.30, 102–3, 204,
   205–7, 205 n.41, 207 n.45; and Romanism, 314–15; and WWI, 6–7
historia abscondita, 290
historicism, 44
historicity, 17; and authenticity, 58–59; of
   Dasein, 18, 20; ontological understanding of, 19; and ontology, 23; and *Seynsgeschichte*, 191 n.12
history: of being, 194–95; and myth, 124,
   276; of truth, hidden, 290–91
Hitler, Adolf: *Friedensrede* of, 86; and German autonomy, 167; on Graeco-German affinity, 105; Heidegger and, 158,
   183–84, 269; and leadership, 88, 152;
   Mein Kampf, 105; and Nietzsche, 302–3;
   and revolution, 24, 77; rise to power,
   63
Hitlerism, 4
Hitler Youth, 62
Hoffmann, Ernst, 225–26
Hölderlin, Friedrich, 47; and *arche*,
   212–13; Baeumler and, 275; and confrontation with the "other," 20 n.14;
   and fatherland, 51–52, 185; and
   Graeco-German affinity, 56, 74, 112,
   118, 199; Heidegger and, 230–41,
   244–46, 279; and Hellenomania, 6;
   Hellingrath and, 241–46; and homecoming, 232–41; and ideas of 1789,
   230, 230 n.92, 244; and middle of
   being, 138–39, 139 n.58; and myth,
   124; and nature, 61; and NS, 121–22,
   145–46, 243; and Philhellenism,
   227–32; and "poetic dwelling," 155;
   and *Sonderweg*, 241, 245; translations
   by, 228, 237, 242–43; *Volksreligion* of,
   50, 63–68, 107; and will to power, 283
—works: "Death for the Fatherland," 61;
   "Germania," 61–62, 115, 138–39,
   139 n.58, 230, 335; "Der Ister," 232,
   235–36; "Migration," 243; "Oldest System-Program of German Idealism," 245
Hölderlin lectures: and exclusion, 176,
   211; and Graeco-German affinity, 174,
   230–32, 253; and homecoming, 232,
   234–41; and middle of being, 138–39;
   and myth of war, 56, 61; and violence,
   192–93 n.15; and *Volk*, 185
Hölderlin Renaissance, 219, 243
holocaust, 328
Holtorf, Herbert, 103, 204
homecoming. *See Heimkehr*

Index

Index

Wilamowitz-Moellendorf, Ulrich von, 101, 117–18, 205, 221

will to power: and art, 291–92; and Baeumler, 286; and Cartesian subjectivity, 272; Dionysian, 118; and eternal return, 287; and NS, 281–82, 308–9, 317; self-assertion as, 90–93, 299; and self-preservation, 91; and state, 283; and university, 27; and Versailles Treaty, 283

Winckelmann, Johann Joachim, 47, 51, 177, 199, 206, 223; Baeumler and, 276; and Philhellenism, 229

Wissenschaft (science): and *aletheia*, 284; crisis of, 100; as *philosophia*, 74, 94–99, 104; and university reform, 30–31, 77–78, 80; *völkische*, 73–74, 76, 95

worker, as soldier, 106

world domination, 188, 305, 307–8

worldview thinking, 16

World War I: and crisis, 28–29; cultural metaphysics of, 5–11; existential situation following, 21; generational consciousness of, 219–20; and geo-philoso-phy, 146; hardness/severity in, 9, 30, 36–37; and metaphysics of war, 61; and nihilism, 34, 282; and NS, 6–7, 7 n.9, 15–16 n.7, 128–29, 157; and *Sonderweg*, 122–25, 126–30, 128 n.38

World War II: and *Bodenständigkeit*, 317–25; and devastation, 319–20; and geo-philosophy, 146; and Graeco-German affinity, 186, 320–21; Heidegger and, 182–84, 272, 305–9, 301, 311–12; and Romanism, 316, 319; and *Sonderweg*, 306–8, 312–13, 312 n.106, 313–14, 321–23

Würzellosigkeit, 41 n.53

Yorck von Wartenburg, Paul, 17–18, 19–20, 191 n.12

Young, Julian, 32 n.42, 187 n.6

Zapata, Martha, 278

Zeller, Eduard, 101

Zemach, Stefan, 268

Zeno, 215, 221

Zimmermann, Michael, 136 n.52

LaVergne, TN USA
14 June 2010
186117LV00001B/158/P